Volume 2

The Story of
AMERICA

1865 to the Present

Volume 2
The Story of
AMERICA
1865 to the Present

JOHN A. GARRATY
Gouverneur Morris Professor of History
Columbia University

HOLT, RINEHART AND WINSTON, INC.
HARCOURT BRACE JOVANOVICH, INC.
Austin • Orlando • San Diego • Chicago • Dallas • Toronto

JOHN A. GARRATY is a distinguished historian and writer and the Gouverneur Morris Professor of History at Columbia University. His books include the widely adopted college textbook *The American Nation*, biographies of Henry Cabot Lodge and Woodrow Wilson, *The Great Depression*, and the popular *1,001 Things Everyone Should Know About American History*. He has held Guggenheim, Ford, and Social Science Research Council Fellowships. Professor Garraty is a former president of the Society of American Historians, editor of the *Dictionary of American Biography*, and coeditor of the *Encyclopedia of American Biography*.

PHILLIP BACON is Professor Emeritus of Geography and Anthropology at the University of Houston. He served on the faculties of Columbia University and the University of Washington and is former Dean of the Graduate School of Peabody College for Teachers at Vanderbilt University.

INSTRUCTIONAL REVIEWERS

ADVISORY COMMITTEES

Tim Beatty
History Teacher
Roehm Middle School
Berea, Ohio

Wayne Beddow
Social Studies Teacher
Hellgate High School
Missoula, Montana

Gloria Foster
History Teacher
Upland High School
Upland, California

Michael Gallagher
Social Studies Teacher
Mead Junior High School
Glenview, Illinois

David Vigilante
History Teacher
Gompers Secondary School
San Diego, California

Karen Tindel Wiggins
Director of Social Studies
Richardson Independent
  School District
Richardson, Texas

Jack Bovee
Social Studies Coordinator
Lee County Schools
Fort Myers, Florida

Arthur Cheatham
History Teacher
Roosevelt Middle School
Decatur, Illinois

Luis Cuevas
Adjunct Professor of History
Santa Fe Community College
Gainesville, Florida

William Curnow
History Teacher
Nolan Middle School
Detroit, Michigan

Dr. W. G. Freeman, Jr.
History Teacher
Montera Junior High School
Oakland, California

Kathleen Johnson
History Teacher
Area E Magnet School
Detroit, Michigan

Nelda Krohn
History Teacher
Oak Grove Middle School
Concord, California

Malcolm W. Moore, Jr.
Social Studies Teacher
Thomas Jefferson Middle School
Decatur, Illinois

Evelyn Nash
Social Studies Supervisor
Detroit Public Schools
Detroit, Michigan

Frank Taylor
Social Studies Supervisor
Fairfax County Schools
Annandale, Virginia

Mark Zink
Social Studies Teacher
Hampton Middle School
Detroit, Michigan

Cover: © B. Gelberg, 1989 *Sharpshooters*   *Chapter Opening Woodcuts:* Stefan Martin

Maps: R.R. Donnelley Company Cartographic Services

Printed in the United States of America

ISBN: 0-03-072899-1

7890 048 9876

Contents

Prologue
THE BEGINNINGS OF AMERICAN HISTORY
Beginnings to 1877

Unit One
A CHANGING AMERICA
1865–1900

Chapter 1
Reconstruction   52

Unit Four
A GLOBAL AMERICA
1940–1963

Unit Five
A MODERN AMERICA
1964 to the Present

Chapter 12
The Great Society   490

Chapter 13
The Vietnam Era   524

Chapter 14
Modern Times   552

REFERENCE SECTION

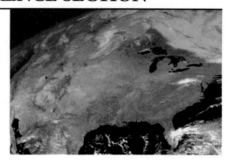

STRATEGIES FOR SUCCESS

FEATURES

LINKING HISTORY & GEOGRAPHY

PORTFOLIOS

INTERPRETING HISTORY

MAPS

CHARTS, GRAPHS, TABLES, & DIAGRAMS

To the Student

The Story of America tells our story because it is important in itself. It is a great epic and the unique tale of how hundreds of millions of people took possession of a vast continent, often at the expense of the original inhabitants. There are other reasons for telling our story. It may be read as a grand lesson that permits us to understand how past affects present. Our story is composed of many pasts that allow us to explain how our present experiment in democracy has gone on for more than 200 years. Thus we read history knowing full well that those who study the past can come to understand who we are and how far we've come and are sometimes able to caution us about our present course toward the future. But we also realize that historians have never been any better at telling the future than politicians, economists, or fortune tellers.

The Story of America was written especially for you, young Americans born in the last half of the 20th century. It provides the background to help you know about the people and values that make America great. It also presents the many controversies and challenges that have faced Americans from time to time throughout history. You can learn from their successes—and failures.

The author of *The Story of America* is ever mindful that chronology is the spine of history. Events are presented in the order in which they occurred. Time lines at the end of each chapter help you see and remember the chronology of important events.

The Story of America contains many original documents and lengthy excerpts from primary and secondary sources. These include eyewitness accounts, poems, song lyrics, diary entries, and excerpts from a variety of other sources. These materials can give you special insight into the thinking and attitudes of Americans. *The Story of America* also is filled with striking and memorable illustrations. These paintings, photographs, and other illustrations may indeed be worth a thousand words. Each captures a bit of the history of its time. The illustrations in *The Story of America* also show changing aspects of American life such as dress, art, and architecture.

An integral part of the story of America is the relation of people to the landscape. The beautifully detailed maps and special geography features in *The Story of America* illustrate this relationship and show its importance in the unfolding of our nation's story. The textbook also introduces you to the five themes of geography: location, place, relationships within places, movement, and regions. Charts, graphs, tables, and diagrams highlight the economic and sociological trends. Together, they portray a nation that has grown dramatically from such small beginnings.

When you have finished *The Story of America* you should understand the democratic values and ethical ideas that guide the American people and appreciate the civic responsibilities of all Americans to participate in American democracy. *The Story of America* will help you recognize the multicultural character of the American society and have empathy for the struggles of people to secure a place in society. With this information you will be able to take your place in society as an informed voter, more appreciative of the legacy that is the story of America.

HOW TO USE *The Story of America*

The Story of America contains a vast amount of information. It has many useful features to help you understand and use this information. Some features help you preview what you are about to read. Others help you read for that information or find additional information. Still other features help you review what you have read. Using the features of *The Story of America* wisely will help you become a better student of history.

Using the Textbook's Features

To get the most from *The Story of America,* here are some guidelines.

1. **Use the Table of Contents.** Make yourself familiar with the **Table of Contents** (pages v-xii). A quick skimming shows you how the book is organized and helps you anticipate what you will be reading. It shows that *The Story of America* is organized into five units, **A** and the units are further divided into a Prologue and 15 chapters. As its name implies, the Table of Contents shows the content of each chapter, the special features the textbook contains, and the page on which each unit, chapter, and feature can be found. To the right is a sample.

2. **Study the unit opening pages.** Each unit gives a preview of its content with a unit title, an illustration, an introduction, and a list of chapters that are included. Take time to study the **B** unit opening page. It contains clues to what you are about to read. For example, after studying the opening page of Unit One on page 51, what can you tell about the people and times covered in this unit?

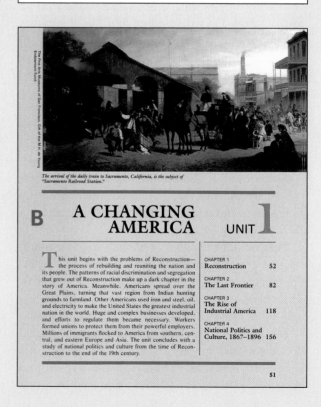

A Contents

The arrival of the daily train to Sacramento, California, is the subject of "Sacramento Railroad Station."

B **A CHANGING AMERICA** UNIT 1

This unit begins with the problems of Reconstruction—the process of rebuilding and reuniting the nation and its people. The patterns of racial discrimination and segregation that grew out of Reconstruction make up a dark chapter in the story of America. Meanwhile, Americans spread over the Great Plains, turning that vast region from Indian hunting grounds to farmland. Other Americans used iron and steel, oil, and electricity to make the United States the greatest industrial nation in the world. Huge and complex businesses developed, and efforts to regulate them became necessary. Workers formed unions to protect them from their powerful employers. Millions of immigrants flocked to America from southern, central, and eastern Europe and Asia. The unit concludes with a study of national politics and culture from the time of Reconstruction to the end of the 19th century.

51

CHAPTER 5

America in World Affairs, 1865–1912

C

ven those who thought manifest destiny a bold American notion might have been surprised by what happened after the Civil War. The parade of settlers marching "from sea to shining sea" stopped only to catch its breath before pressing on. Americans seemed to forget George Washington's warning to avoid foreign involvements. The country began to expand its influence in Latin America. Alaska and Hawaii were acquired. After the war with Spain, fought to free Cuba, the Philippines and Puerto Rico were taken by the United States. By the time Theodore Roosevelt became president at the turn of the century, America's influence in the Western Hemisphere was great. But how far could America stretch itself in world affairs?

Preview & Review

Use these questions to guide your reading. Answer the questions after completing Section 1. **Understanding Issues, Events, & Ideas.** Describe American expansion overseas, using the following words: isolationism, American expansionism, Midway Islands, imperialism, Alaskan Purchase, Seward's Folly, Hawaiian Islands, archipelago, McKinley Tariff, absolute monarch.
1. What was isolationism?
2. Why did the Japanese agree to open trade with the U.S.?
3. How did "Seward's Folly" turn out to be an immense bargain?
4. Who were the first Americans to reach Hawaii? Who followed?
Thinking Critically. 1. You are with Perry in Tokyo harbor. Describe your reactions. 2. You are a member of Congress. Would you vote for or against the the acquisition of Hawaii? Give reasons to justify your decision.

D

1. EXTENDING AMERICA'S INFLUENCE

Isolationism

For many Americans longtime suspicions of Europe had increased during the Civil War. Great Britain and France had sympathized with the Confederate government. British companies had built ships for the southerners. This had enabled the Confederacy to get around the United States blockade of southern ports. The *Alabama*, a British-built warship flying the Confederate flag, destroyed many American merchant ships during the rebellion. For a time Great Britain even considered entering the war on the side of the Confederacy.

While the United States was fighting its desperate struggle, France boldly sent an army into Mexico. The French then named a European prince, Maximilian of Austria, ás Emperor of Mexico. This was a direct challenge to the Monroe Doctrine, which had stated that no European colonies were to be established in the Americas.

Once the Civil War ended, the United States sent 50,000 soldiers to the Mexican border to aid the Mexican patriots who were fighting Maximilian and demand that France withdraw its army. The French pulled out. In June 1867 Mexican patriots led by Benito Juárez entered Mexico City. Maximilian was captured and put to death.

196   AMERICA IN WORLD AFFAIRS, 1865–1912

E

5. THE SEARCH FOR PEACE

Wilson's Plans for Peace

President Wilson had been preparing for making peace even before the United States entered the war. As we have seen, he wanted a peace without victory. Wilson believed the terms must not be so hard on the Central Powers as to cause them to begin planning another war to regain what was taken from them.

In January 1918, even before the end of the war, Wilson made a speech to Congress describing his plans for peace. "The world must be made safe for every peace-loving nation," he said. Unless all the nations are treated fairly, none can count on being treated fairly. In this respect "all the peoples of the world are in effect partners." The president then listed **Fourteen Points** that he said made up "the only possible program" for peace.

The first of Wilson's points promised that the peace treaty would

Preview & Review

Use these questions to guide your reading. Answer the questions after completing Section 5. **Understanding Issues, Events, & Ideas** Use the following words to describe the end of the Great War: Fourteen Points, self-determination, League of Nations, Big Four, reparations, Versailles Peace Treaty, sanction, mandate.
1. How did President Wilson describe to Congress his plans for peace?
2. What was to be the purpose of the League of Nations?
3. What were some outcomes of the Treaty of Versailles? Of what was President Wilson most proud?
Thinking Critically. Wilson felt that the 14th of his 14 Points was the most important. Of the points described in the textbook, which do you think is the most important? Why?

F

The National Gallery of Art

The flags of Great Britain, France, and the United States fly on Fifth Avenue. "Allies Day, May 1917" was painted by Childe Hassam in celebration of the alliance of these three nations.

The Search for Peace   305

---

3. **Study the Prologue.** The Prologue (pages 1–47) reviews America's story through 1865. It provides a brief description of the major events in our nation's history from its earliest explorations through the Civil War.

C

4. **Read the chapter introduction.** Every chapter of *The Story of America* begins with an introduction that provides an overview and states the main ideas of the chapter. When you read the introduction, begin forming questions you may have about the chapter's content.

C

5. **Use the section Preview & Review to guide your reading.** Every section of *The Story of America* begins with a **Preview & Review**. These contain key words and questions that can help guide your reading of the section. The questions are *the same ones* you use to review your mastery of the information in the section. The symbol 🔲 shows you when you have reached the end of the section. A note in the margin tells you to return to the Preview & Review to begin your review of the section. By carefully reading the Preview & Review *before* beginning the section you can identify important words or terms and major questions or ideas discussed in the section.

D

6. **Read the chapters and sections.** *The Story of America* has many features that make reading it easier. First, the headings and subheadings provide a kind of outline of the main ideas and important details.

E

Second, pay special attention to words printed in bold black type. These **boldfaced terms** call your attention to important history words. A definition follows most, right in that sentence or the next. You can also check a word's meaning in the glossary.

F

Third, study the illustrations and read the captions. Relate what you see to what you read. All of the pictures are chosen carefully to help you better understand what you are reading. One picture can be worth a thousand words.

A — STRATEGIES FOR SUCCESS

INTERPRETING EDITORIAL CARTOONS

Editorial cartoons are drawings that present points of view on particular issues. They are usually found in the editorial sections of newspapers and magazines and have been used throughout history to influence public opinion. Although some cartoons present a positive point of view, most are critical of a policy, situation, or person.

The two most important techniques cartoonists use to express their message are caricature and symbolism. A caricature is a drawing that exaggerates physical features. Symbolism is the use of one thing to represent another idea, feeling, or object. Common symbols for the United States, for example, are the bald eagle and Uncle Sam. Cartoons also use titles, labels, and captions to get their message across.

How to Interpret Editorial Cartoons
To interpret editorial cartoons, follow these steps.
1. **Identify the caricatures**. Note the people or objects being characterized and note what is exaggerated.
2. **Identify the symbols**. Determine the meaning of each of the symbols used.
3. **Read the title, labels, and caption**. Check the title, labels, and caption to help you understand the artist's message.
4. **Analyze the information**. Decide if the cartoonist's point of view is positive or negative. Determine what events or situation led to the cartoon.

Applying the Strategy
President Theodore Roosevelt was a favorite of editorial cartoonists. Study the cartoon of him at the top of the next column. Does the cartoonist use caricature? If so, what features are exaggerated? Is there symbolism? If so what symbols are used and what do they stand for? Does the cartoonist present a positive or negative point of view? How can you tell? In your own words, state the cartoonist's message. Now answer the same questions for the cartoon at the lower right.

For independent practice, see Practicing the Strategy on page 238.

NO MOLLY-CODDLING HERE
Both, The Granger Collection

Roosevelt and His Canal   235

B — THE LONE EAGLE

The most popular American hero of the 1920s was Charles A. Lindbergh. On May 20, 1927, Lindbergh took off from a muddy, rain-drenched airfield near New York City in a tiny, one-engine plane, the *Spirit of St. Louis*. He was headed for France. Alone, hour after hour, he guided his plane eastward across the Atlantic. His flew with a map in his lap and only some coffee and a few sandwiches to keep up his strength. Staying awake called for a tremendous feat of willpower. If he dozed off, even for a minute, the *Spirit of St. Louis* might crash into the sea. But Lindbergh did not doze

Culver Pictures

plane as 25,000 pairs of eyes strained toward it. At 10:24 the *Spirit of St. Louis* landed and lines of soldiers, ranks of policemen and stout steel fences went down before a mad rush as irresistible as the tides of the ocean.

Lindbergh returned home a grinning, modest hero. The idol of millions, he was given a tremendous ticker tape parade through New York City. The newspapers named him "The Lone Eagle." He was also known as "Lucky Lindy," but his success was due far more to courage and skill than to luck.

C — INTERPRETING HISTORY: Reconstruction

Reconstruction is one of the most controversial topics considered by historians. Lincoln hoped Reconstruction would "bind up the nation's wounds" caused by the Civil War. Lincoln based his plan on "malice toward none." But his plan was doomed to failure. As historian Eric Foner said, "What remains certain is that Reconstruction failed, and that for blacks its failure was a disaster whose magnitude cannot be obscured by the genuine accomplishments that did endure."

In the late 19th century white northerners and southerners concentrated on reconciling their differences. The historians of the period, the most influential being William A. Dunning of Columbia University, argued that the Radical Republicans had been cruel and vindictive people, eager for revenge. He also claimed that the freed blacks had proved to be incapable of self-government and that they had been taken advantage of by cynical carpetbaggers. The resulting "Black Republican" governments imposed high taxes on southerners and spent the money either wastefully or for their own direct benefit. Reconstruction became known as "the tragic era."

The first historian to challenge this view was W.E.B. DuBois. He claimed in *Black Reconstruction* (1935) that Reconstruction was an effort by both whites and blacks to create a "true democratic society." It failed because it did not go far enough,

explained DuBois: "One fact and one alone explains that attitude of writers toward Reconstruction, they cannot conceive of Negroes as men." DuBois described the achievements of the Reconstruction governments, such as the schools, railroads, and other public institutions that they built. Then in the 1960s, during the intense civil rights movement, historians began to further revise the traditional view. Kenneth Stampp, in *The Era of Reconstruction* (1965), insisted the Radicals were genuine reformers out to defend the rights of blacks and that most black legislators had been good public servants. Moreover, they had never dominated the state governments of the period. Reconstruction failed not because of what it did to southern whites but because it did not implement the reforms necessary to ensure African Amerians equal rights.

The most recent authority, Eric Foner, calls Reconstruction "America's Unfinished Revolution." The blacks took advantage of the new educational opportunities eagerly. They used their liberty to move from place to place and to relieve their wives and children of backbreaking labor. They changed the way southern crops, especially cotton, were grown. Their revolution was real, Foner writes, but unfinished in the sense that their full use of their freedom was denied them and even today has not been fully achieved.

58   RECONSTRUCTION

---

7. Study the special features. *The Story of America* has many features that enrich history and help you develop the tools of the historian. These features appear on tinted backgrounds.

A — On blue pages are **Strategies for Success**. These features appear in each chapter. They present additional information related to the specific chapter content and provide an opportunity for you to develop or sharpen your study skills. A Strategies Review in the Reference Section (pages 657-73) presents the strategies from Volume 1.

B — Most chapters also contain one or more brief features that highlight an important person, event, or idea. These features are easily identified by their three-column format and special heading. They are meant to give the reader a chance to pause and to consider their significance in our history.

C — A third feature, **Interpreting History,** teaches the historian's craft by discussing interpretations of events or ideas that have created historical controversy. Examples include the importance of the American Frontier, the motives of the progressives, and the political intrigue behind the Cold War.

Every chapter of *The Story of America* uses the words of historical figures whenever possible. Besides lengthy primary source quotations, marked with large red quotation marks,

D — you will often find a **Point of View** in the margin. This feature presents a statement about an event or person. Sometimes opposing opinions are presented as **Points of View.**

Another key feature is the map program. The maps illustrate physical, cultural, and historical information clearly and accurately. Almost every map contains relief shading showing major physical features, so you are constantly aware

E — of the interplay of history and geography. Several Strategies for Success will help you hone your map-reading skills. In addition, a special section titled **Maps: Portraying the Land** in the Reference Section provides a variety of information about maps and mapmaking.

The Story of America highlights the ethnic and cultural contributions of different groups to American culture. To help you visualize

F — some of the many contributions, you will find four pictorial essays, or portfolios, that contain the art and artifacts of some of the groups that have come to America. These four portfolios

D

Point of View

In his famous *Letter from a Birmingham Jail*, Dr. King described the impact of segregation on children.

❝ You suddenly find your tongue twisted and your speech stammering as you seek to explain to your six-year-old daughter why she can't go to the public amusement park that has just been advertised on television, and see tears welling up in her little eyes when she is told that Funtown is closed to colored children. . . . ❞
Martin Luther King, Jr., 1963

"Say I was a drum major for justice," said Martin Luther King, Jr., who knew, as did his followers, that an assassin would someday take his life. Try to listen to his famous speeches on records or tapes.

Martin Luther King, Jr.

The greatest leadership for blacks was provided by a Baptist minister, the Reverend Martin Luther King, Jr. After his success in leading the Montgomery bus boycott, King became a national figure. Everywhere he preached the idea of **nonviolent direct action,** as the best way to achieve racial equality. "Nonviolent resistance is not a method for cowards," he said. One must "accept blows from the opponent without striking back." Love, not hate or force, was the way to change people's minds.

The movement also used songs to tell its aim and hopes—songs of protest, adaptations of spirituals, and newly composed songs.

These expressed what King felt was fundamental to the movement's success: determination. The unofficial theme song of the movement was "We Shall Overcome," which was adapted from a version of an old spiritual by the staff at the Highland Folk School in Tennessee. It was sung everywhere the movement went. Here are the first three verses:

❝ We shall overcome, we shall overcome,
We shall overcome someday.
Oh, deep in my heart, I do believe,
We shall overcome someday.

We are not afraid, we are not afraid,
We are not afraid today.
Oh, deep in my heart, I do believe,
We shall overcome someday.

We are not alone, we are not alone,
We are not alone today.

516   THE GREAT SOCIETY

E

punished those who broke tribal laws, and protected the group against surprise attacks.

Within the circle of their band, warriors tried to prove their courage and daring on the battlefield. To touch an enemy or capture his weapon was proof of highest bravery, what the warriors called counting coup.

The Plains Indians, as we have seen, had become heavily dependent on the buffalo. After the European invasion of America they also captured and tamed wild horses. Spanish explorers had brought the first horses with them to America. Some of these animals escaped and ran wild. Eventually, large herds roamed parts of the West.

The Indians quickly became expert riders. On horseback they were better hunters and fighters. They could cover large distances swiftly and run down buffalo and other game. Horses became so

THE GREAT PLAINS

— Present-day state boundary
Sioux Name of Plains Indian tribe

ELEVATION
Feet	Meters
13,120	4,000
6,560	2,000
1,640	500
656	200
0	0
Below sea level	Below sea level

0   200   400 Mi.
0   200   400 Km.
Albers Equal-Area Projection

LEARNING FROM MAPS. *Many of the first European explorers of the Great Plains considered it a desert. Today, however, it is a region of rich agricultural production. Why did some of the first explorers consider it a desert? What has made it productive today?*

84   THE LAST FRONTIER

F

America's Indian Heritage

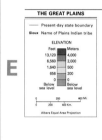

MAJOR CULTURAL REGIONS AND INDIAN TRIBES OF NORTH AMERICA, c. 1500
Albers Equal-Area Projection

0   250   500 Mi.
0   250   500 Km.

This map shows the geographic location of the major cultural groups into which American Indian tribes have been divided. It also shows some of the hundreds of tribes in each group. Of course many tribes moved about a great deal, so the locations shown are approximate.

This stone pipe found in Oklahoma shows a man playing chunky, a game popular everywhere in the region of the Mound Builders. Games lasted all day. Chunky was a bit like bowling, a bit like the javelin toss.

The Hopewell mounds yielded this mica serpent. Mica is a mineral silvery in color and so fine it is translucent—diffused light passes through.

12   PROLOGUE

F

America's Pacific Heritage

Since ships first sailed or land caravans carried off its treasure, westerners have been fascinated by the East. Marco Polo was bedazzled even though he came from Venice, a western jewel. The art of the Orient is the oldest in the world, but it was hidden behind the walls of Forbidden Cities. Emigrants from Asia were too poor to own eastern treasures such as we see on these pages, but traders like John Ellerton Lodge filled the holds of the ships *Kremlin* and *Magnet* with china, silk, ivory, spices, even fireworks that bloomed like chrysanthemums to bring Pacific culture to America.

This dragon comes from a Chinese embroidered chair of the 18th century. Eastern dragons seldom breathed fire and were seen as protectors.

Chinese porcelain has long been prized. The export ware above is an Orange platter in the "Fitzhugh" pattern.

Four children in holiday dress were photographed on the teeming streets of San Francisco's Chinatown before the earthquake of 1906.

America's Pacific Heritage   217

HOW TO USE *The Story of America*   **xvii**

A

LINKING HISTORY & GEOGRAPHY

FATAL ERROR: OIL ON WATER

Prince William Sound is an emerald jewel, one of Alaska's scenic wonders. It is a bay with 1,000 miles of shoreline. Its waters teem with fish. It is the playground of hundreds of thousands of sea otters, seals, sea lions, and whales. Sea birds and bald eagles nest along its rocky shores. Surrounding the sound are snow-capped peaks and enormous glaciers that send icebergs floating off into the crystal-clear water. This is how it had been for centuries. Then, a little after midnight, on March 24, 1989, a fatal error was made.

The Disaster Begins

1. What caused the *Exxon Valdez* to snag on the rocks in the sound?

Late Thursday night, March 23, the *Exxon Valdez,* a supertanker as long as three football fields, left the port of Valdez filled with crude oil. There was nothing unusual about the impending voyage. Since 1977 some 8,700 loaded tankers had made the trip out of Valdez with virtually no incidents. Visibility was 10 miles or more and the seas were calm that night. All electrical and mechanical systems aboard the ship were working perfectly.

The captain radioed the Coast Guard for permission to cross from the outbound lane to the inbound lane to avoid some small icebergs. It was a routine request. The Coast Guard gave permission. Within 10 minutes the huge ship had swung into the inbound lane. But instead of following the lane to the southwest, it headed due south. Fifteen minutes later it had completely crossed the inbound lane and had sailed into waters closed to oil tankers.

Half an hour later the *Exxon Valdez* passed close to Busby Island, far outside the well-established and clearly marked tanker lanes. Suddenly the unlicensed third mate commanding the ship realized that an error had been made. He frantically gave orders to turn sharply to the west to reenter the traffic lanes. Meanwhile, the captain was asleep in his cabin.

But the mate's orders came tou late. At four minutes after midnight the *Exxon Valdez* scraped the rocks of Bligh Reef. The enormous tanker crunched to a halt, balanced on a pinnacle of rock. From its ripped hull 10.1 million gallons of thick crude oil gushed into the pristine waters of Prince William Sound.

The Disaster Grows

2. Why did emergency plans fail?

In 1973, when Congress approved the Alaska pipeline, all of the oil companies involved made solemn promises in writing to do everything possible to protect Alaska's fragile environment. Yet on that tragic night, Alyeska Pipeline Service Company had no emergency crew on hand and little equipment ready for use. It did virtually nothing for three days. During those first few critical days the sound's waters were flat calm, there was almost no wind, and it was unseasonably warm and sunny. Conditions for clean-up were ideal. The spill spread to cover only a five-square mile area, and it was entirely manageable.

Then, 66 hours after the accident, rapidly rising winds and seas sent the main mass of oil racing southwestward. It surged forward at more than a mile per hour, churning the sound into a foamy mixture of oil and water.

By the second week the oil had sunk to depths of more than 90 feet, making the water hazardous even for bottom-feeding marine life. It had spread across more than 3,000 square miles of water. In the cold water, the surface of the spill had weathered into a heavy, tar-like substance. Under this coating was a 6- to 18-inch layer of oil with the consistency of peanut butter. The annual spring migration of salmon and herring was on a collision course with black, oily death.

Fourteen days after the ship hit the reef just 630,000 gallons out of 10.1 million gallons of oil had been picked up. The western beaches along the sound were covered with oozing, stinking tar. The poisoned bodies of otters and seabirds lay matted and almost unrecognizable in the gooey mess. Five weeks after the accident the spill covered an area the size of Massachusetts.

The Disaster's Effects

3. What human and environmental toll did the spill take?

The sound's fishing industry had been among Alaska's most productive. It had yielded about $100,000,000 annually. Now it was ruined.

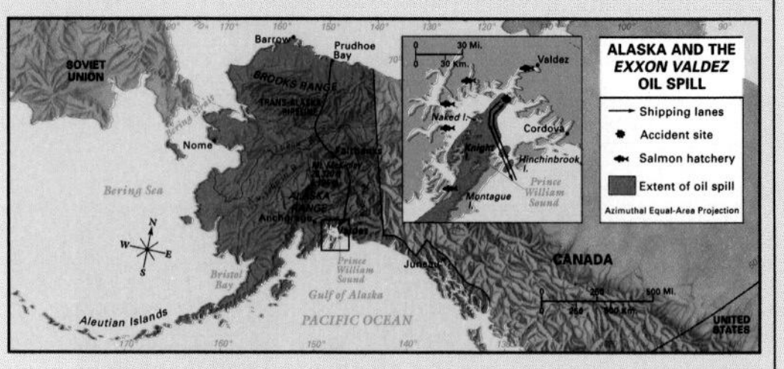

ALASKA AND THE *EXXON VALDEZ* OIL SPILL
Shipping lanes
Accident site
Salmon hatchery
Extent of oil spill
Azimuthal Equal-Area Projection
SOVIET UNION
Barrow
Prudhoe Bay
BROOKS RANGE
Nome
Bering Sea
Bering Strait
Anchorage
Valdez
Bristol Bay
Prince William Sound
Gulf of Alaska
PACIFIC OCEAN
Aleutian Islands
Juneau
CANADA
UNITED STATES
Naked I.
Cordova
Knight I.
Hinchinbrook I.
Montague I.
30 Mi.
30 Km.
500 Mi.

Despair tore at the hearts of the residents of tiny fishing villages. Their way of life was disappearing before their eyes. Not only were millions of fish dying, but there was danger that toxins in the oil might become embedded in the still-living fish, making them unfit to eat. The public would fear eating fish, shrimp, or crab from the sound. They knew it would be years before they could rebuild their industry, if ever.

Lessons to be Learned

4. What lessons can we learn from this disaster?

One of things that makes the situation difficult to analyze is that the issues are so loaded with emotion. Oil spills and dying animals make a powerful case against current methods of transporting dangerous materials.

But it should be remembered that for 12 years oil had flowed safely through the pipeline and had been safely transported out of Prince William Sound. Also for 12 years the oil industry had assured the public that through technological feats it could handle any emergency.

For 12 years few people worried. A large number of Alaskans make their living from the oil industry. The state's economy rests comfortably on the money received in taxes from the oil industry. Many schools, symphonies, and museums were handsomely financed by donations from large oil companies. Oil was good for Alaska!

Perhaps the most valuable long-term lesson to be learned is that alertness, when untested for too long, deteriorates into complacency. Human failing is the thing to attack, not oil exploration or oil transportation. The world needs oil.

History shows clearly that the oil-shipping industry is basically safe. There have been amazingly few spills considering the enormous volume of oil that has been transported around the world. But the industry seemed so safe that responsible people forgot that they are still required to run it properly. Environmental protection demands constant vigilance. Powerful incentives must keep that protection on task. Human errors must be made harder to repeat and too expensive and too dangerous to be tolerated.

APPLYING YOUR KNOWLEDGE

Your class will study environmental concerns in your local community. Each group will select or will be assigned a concern to research. The group will then create a display or presentation that informs others about the concern. Donate your display to the local library or perform your presentation for the city or county council.

584 MODERN TIMES Linking History & Geography 585

B

CHAPTER 1 REVIEW

Reconstruction — The Long Night

1865 — THE AFTERMATH OF WAR — 1875 — 1885 — 1895

1865 Lee surrenders to Grant ★ Lincoln assassinated ★ Reconstruction begins ★ Thirteenth Amendment
1866 Civil Rights Act
1867 Reconstruction Act passed ★
1868 Johnson impeached and acquitted ★ Fourteenth Amendment ★ Grant elected president
1870 Fifteenth Amendment ratified
1875 Civil Rights Act of 1875
1876 Presidential election disputed
1877 House elects Hayes ★ Compromise of 1877 ends Reconstruction ★ Long Night begins
1883 Civil Rights Cases decided
1890 Atlanta Compromise proposed
1896 *Plessy v. Ferguson*

Chapter Summary

Read the statements below. Choose one, and write a paragraph explaining its importance.

1. Andrew Johnson succeeded to office after the assassination of Lincoln but had trouble working with Congress, which impeached him.
2. Moderate congressmen wanted quick Reconstruction, while Radicals were less forgiving.
3. The Thirteenth Amendment abolished slavery.
4. Congress established the Freedman's Bureau to help newly freed slaves with schools, food, and medical needs.
5. The Fourteenth Amendment guaranteed equal protection of the laws to all Americans. The Fifteenth Amendment made it illegal to deny the right to vote based on race, color, or previous condition of servitude.
6. Organizations such as the Ku Klux Klan were formed to keep blacks in check.
7. The last federal troops were removed from the South under the Compromise of 1877, which made Hayes president.
8. White southerners used many methods to keep blacks as second-class citizens.

Reviewing Chronological Order

Number your paper 1-5. Then study the time line above and place the following events in the order in which they happened by writing the first next to 1, the second next to 2, and so on.

1. Reconstruction Act passed
2. *Plessy v. Ferguson*
3. Grant elected president
4. Atlanta Compromise proposed
5. Lincoln assassinated

Understanding Main Ideas

1. How did the three Civil War Amendments attack the Black Codes?
2. What were the provisions of the Reconstruction Act of 1867? Why did President Johnson veto it? How did Congress react to his veto?
3. How did the election of 1868 show Republicans the importance of the black vote?
4. What were the motives of some Carpetbaggers and Scalawags in the "Black Republican" governments of the South?
5. What situation was resolved by the Compromise of 1877? What were the terms of this agreement?

Thinking Critically

1. **Analyzing.** You are the one senator whose vote is needed to obtain the conviction of President Andrew Johnson on impeachment charges. Why would you vote against removing him from office?
2. **Determining Cause and Effect.** If you were a former slave living in the South in 1870, how would freedom change your life if you were a 58-year-old man? A 22-year-old woman? A 6-year-old boy?
3. **Interpreting.** Study the Thirteenth, Fourteenth, and Fifteenth Amendments in the Reference Section. Then rewrite the amendments in your own words.

Writing About History: Persuasive

You are a newspaper reporter in Washington D.C. Write an editorial on the impeachment trial of Johnson. Your editorial should include both a description of the trial and the reaction of participants. Conclude your editorial by trying to persuade your readers to support or oppose conviction. Use the information in Chapter 1 and in reference books to prepare your report.

Practicing the Strategy

Review the strategy on page 67.

Interpreting a Graph of Business Cycles. Study the two charts on page 70, then answer the following questions.

1. What kinds of agriculture are represented in the top chart?
2. What event occurred between 1860 and 1870 that badly damaged the South's agricultural production?
3. How many years passed before southern agricultural production recovered and surpassed the pre-war levels?
4. In the bottom chart there is a sudden jump in the percent of southern workers in manufacturing between 1880 and 1890. What does this suggest about the nature of manufacturing in the South during that time?

Using Primary Sources

For many years after the Civil War Frederick Douglass remained a leading African American spokesman. He continued to encourage blacks to struggle, now against the effects of Reconstruction and the Long Night. In this excerpt from John W. Blassingame's *Frederick Douglass: The Clarion Voice,* Douglass explained why active struggle was necessary. As you read the excerpt, imagine the conditions blacks were struggling against. Then answer the questions that follow it.

The whole history of the progress of human liberty shows that all concessions yet made to her august [mighty] claims have been born of earnest struggle. . . . If there is no struggle, there is no progress. Those who profess to favor freedom, and yet deprecate [say bad things about] agitation, are men who want crops without plowing up the ground, they want rain without thunder and lightning. They want the ocean without the awful roar of its many waters.

1. According to the excerpt, what had caused all progress in human liberty?
2. Do you agree that "If there is no struggle, there is no progress"? Use examples to support your point of view.
3. If you were a government leader during Reconstruction, what plan might you have suggested to help freed slaves begin a new life? Would your plan have been difficult to establish? Why or why not?

Linking History & Geography

Reconstruction meant more than just rebuilding southern governments. It also meant reconstructing land devastated by four years of war. To understand why this aspect of Reconstruction was so important to the South's recovery, answer the following questions.

1. A Virginia farmer in the Shenandoah Valley said soon after the war: "We had no cattle, hogs, sheep, or horses or anything else. The fences were all gone. . . . The barns were all burned; chimneys standing without houses; and houses standing without roofs or doors or windows." What are three things this farmer will have to do to make the farm productive again?
2. Destruction of southern railroads had been a prime Union military objective during the war. How had this isolated the South? What problems would such isolation cause?

Enriching Your Study of History

1. **Individual Project.** Imagine you are traveling through the South in 1867. Use your historical imagination to write five diary entries describing Reconstruction.
2. **Cooperative Project.** Members of your group will present a debate of the Atlanta Compromise. Half the group will argue for following Washington's suggestions. The other half will argue against the compromise. After you present your debate, the class will act as a convention and vote on the issue.

80 RECONSTRUCTION Chapter 1 Review 81

are titled: America's Indian Heritage, America's West African Heritage, America's Hispanic Heritage, and America's Pacific Heritage. The first contains unique works by American Indian artisans. The last three present beautiful and representative works of art from the native lands of their group's members.

Linking History & Geography features appear on beige pages. A six-page section before Unit One describes key elements of American geography, defines the five basic themes of geography with examples from American history, and discusses the development of the United States and important geographic concepts. In addition, two-page features that are part of the narrative appear in each unit. They highlight the importance of geography in the unfolding of America's history. Most contain beautifully detailed maps.

8. **Reviewing your study.** To check your understanding and to help you remember what you have learned, always take time to review. When you finish a section, return to the Preview & Review and answer the questions. Complete the **Chapter Review** when you finish your study of the chapter. Do the same for the **Unit Review.**

9. **Use the Reference Section.** *The Story of America* provides a **Reference Section.** When you need to refer to an important document, turn to **Documents in American History**, which begins on page 675. When you want to know the meaning of a boldfaced term, turn to the **Glossary,** which begins on page 716. Entries are listed alphabetically, with page references for pages in the text where the word appears in boldface type. When you need to know on which page something is mentioned, turn to the **Index,** which begins on page 734. Index entries are always in alphabetical order. Become familiar with the rest of the **Reference Section,** which contains an atlas and charts and graphs full of data about the story of America.

Studying Primary Sources

There are many sources of historical information. They include diaries, journals, and letters; memoirs and autobiographies; paintings and photographs; editorials and editorial cartoons. All of these are *primary sources.* They give firsthand eyewitness accounts of history.

Primary sources appear frequently in *The Story of America,* for they are the historian's most important tool. You should use primary sources, usually bracketed by large quotation marks, to gain an understanding of events only eyewitness accounts can provide.

How to Study Primary Sources

To study primary sources, follow these guidelines.

1. **Read the material carefully.** Look for main ideas and supporting details. Note what the writer or speaker has to say about the atmosphere or the mood of the people.
2. **Ask yourself questions.** Ask *who* or *what* is described. If sources conflict, and they often might, *who* is speaking and *what special insights do they have?* You may also want to ask *why* an action took place.
3. **Check for bias.** Be alert for words, phrases, or information that present a one-sided view of a person or situation when it seems evident that more than one point of view is possible.
4. **When possible, compare sources.** Study more than one primary source on a topic if available. By comparing what they have to say, you can get a much more complete picture than by using only one source.

Also, remember that historians use *secondary sources* as well as primary sources. These are descriptions or interpretations of events written after the events have occurred. History books such as *The Story of America,* biographies, encyclopedias, and other reference works are examples of secondary sources.

Developing Historical Imagination

When we read history, we tend to form opinions about events in the past. Sometimes these opinions can keep us from fully understanding history. To judge people and events of the past using today's standards can lead to a false picture of history. We need instead to develop our historical imagination.

To develop historical imagination, we need to put ourselves in the place of those who lived in the past. In that way we can better see why they thought and acted as they did. Remember that science, education, and all other fields of endeavor have advanced greatly in a relatively short time. So it is important to keep in mind what people in the past knew and *what they did not know.* Throughout *The Story of America* you will have the opportunity to use your historical imagination, to take yourself back to another time.

Writing About History

Writing is an important intellectual process. It helps us clarify our thoughts, learn information, and discover new ideas. *The Story of America* contains numerous writing opportunities. Although you may not always have time to use them all, the guidelines that follow can help you improve your writing. This is especially true of longer writing assignments.

How to Write More Effectively

To write more effectively, follow these guidelines.

1. **Prewrite.** Prewriting includes all the thinking and planning that you do before you write. Before you write, ask yourself these questions: Why am I writing? Who will read my writing? What will I write about? What will I say about the topic? How will I organize my ideas?
2. **Collect information.** Do research if necessary. You can write more effectively if you have many details to choose from.
3. **Write a first draft and evaluate it.** In your first draft, remember to use your prewriting plan as a guide. Write freely, but consider your purpose and audience.

    As you review and evaluate your first draft, note places where you need to add or clarify. It

may help to read your draft aloud or to exchange it with a partner.

4. **Revise and proofread your draft.** Add, cut, replace, and reorganize your draft as needed to say what you want to say. Then check for proper spelling, punctuation, and grammar.
5. **Write your final version.** Prepare a neat and clean final version. Remember that appearance is important. Although it does not affect the quality of your writing itself, it can affect the way your writing is perceived and understood.

Many writing opportunities in *The Story of America* ask you to create a specific type of writing —a diary entry, a letter, an advertisement, a poem, or a newspaper editorial. Most of these opportunities ask you to use your historical imagination—to write from the point of view of a person living then rather than now.

A diary is a personal log of your experiences. Each entry is dated and is a brief statement of what has happened and your reactions. Your diary entries should be the personal recollections of a person *at a particular time in history.*

You are probably familiar with writing letters. When you write a letter, be sure to indicate to whom you are writing and include in your letter the specific details called for in the assignment.

You also are probably familiar with advertisements. An effective advertisement captures the attention and highlights an important feature of the "product." When you develop an advertisement, make it memorable and to the point.

Writing a poem often can seem difficult. Remember, however, that poems do not have to rhyme. An example of such free verse is Carl Sandberg's "Chicago" on pages 249-50. Notice that although the lines do not rhyme, they are organized in a specific way. That is what makes it poetry. When you write a poem, let the words flow but keep them focused.

A newspaper editorial is a statement of opinion or point of view. It states a stand about an issue and provides the reasons for that stand. You might wish to read the editorial page of your local paper to see how the editorials are written there.

Using the guidelines listed in this section together with those developed in the Strategies for Success should help you write with confidence as you study *The Story of America.* Remember to have a plan and to use historical imagination when it is called for. Now, enjoy *The Story of America.*

LINKING HISTORY & GEOGRAPHY

A large part of America's story deals with the land. It is a magnificent and varied land with rich natural gifts. Over the years it has yielded these gifts to generations of Americans. Its geography has influenced their decisions and the nation's history. As you read, keep the following questions in mind.

1. Why is it important to consider geography as you study history?
2. How can America's location be viewed as both a blessing and a hindrance?
3. How have United States population patterns changed over the last century?
4. What are the four city zones?
5. How have attitudes toward using natural resources changed?
6. What are the five themes of geography?

THE HISTORY–GEOGRAPHY CONNECTION

To understand history it is usually important to know the **geography** of the places where historical events occurred. Geography, however, is more than a description of places. It is the study of the entire physical setting, including landforms and waterways, weather and climate, wildlife and natural vegetation, and also the cultural setting, the patterns of human activities and their impact on the **environment,** or natural surroundings.

These spatial aspects of history—those dealing with the place where an event happened—can be key to understanding why and how events unfolded as they did. Northern generals based their strategy during the Civil War on the geography of the Confederacy. They sealed off the ports on the long southern coastline with naval vessels. They tried to control the Mississippi River and the rivers that flow into it in order to prevent the movement of troops and supplies from Texas to the armies fighting in the East. And since Richmond, Virginia, the Confederate capital, was less than 100 miles from Union territory, its capture was a major objective from the start. If the capital had been in Alabama or Georgia, northern strategy would have been different. Seeing the geographic bases of strategy allows students to evaluate both the overall progress of the war and many of the key decisions made by both sides.

The physical landscape influences the decisions people make, but in many ways people also shape the landscape. Technological advances allow them to cultivate previously unused lands and to reclaim land from the sea. And historical events can themselves change geography. For example, the development of railroads and later of automobiles spurred population growth in previously inaccessible areas. Once transportation links were forged, cities such as Denver grew rapidly.

Many of the obstacles created by geography have been overcome in recent times. Irrigation projects have brought water to barren lands. Communications satellites beam messages across broad oceans and high mountains.

AMERICA'S PLACE IN THE WORLD

Geographers have divided the earth's large landmasses into seven **continents**—North America, South America, Europe, Africa, Asia, Australia, and Antarctica. North America stretches more than 4,500 miles (7,200 kilometers) from the tip of Panama to the icy Arctic Ocean. The United States shares the continent with Canada, Mexico, and the nations of Central America.

The Americas lie between two broad oceans: the Atlantic Ocean to the east and the Pacific Ocean to the west. Colonists viewed North America's size and location between two broad oceans as both a hardship and a blessing. It took a long time for supplies and communications to cross the vast distances. But the isolation afforded by the distance allowed the colonists to develop a way of life without interference, especially from the authorities "back home."

Today the size and location of the United States are viewed as more a blessing than a hindrance. Ports on the world's two largest oceans provide passageways for exports and imports. At the same time America's relative isolation has allowed its leaders to choose in which international conflicts and political situations to involve the United States and kept two devastating world wars at a distance. However, in the age of supersonic aircraft and missiles our former isolation has largely disappeared.

THE AMERICAN LAND

The United States is a varied and beautiful land of high mountains, vast plains, and great rivers. Several mountain ranges cut across the country from north to south, the older Appalachian Mountains

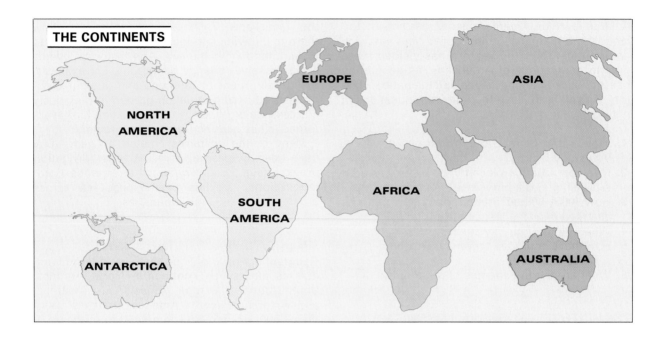

THE CONTINENTS

in the east, the rugged Rocky Mountains in the west. The newer Sierra Nevada and Cascade ranges soar skyward farther west. And the Coastal Ranges skirt the coast of the Pacific. Plains span much of the interior part of the United States between the Appalachian and Rocky Mountains.

The Mississippi River system drains the vast interior plain at the center of the United States. The Missouri, Ohio, Arkansas, Red, and many smaller rivers feed the Mississippi as it flows south to the Gulf of Mexico. In the east the Connecticut, Hudson, Delaware, Susquehanna, Potomac, James, and many smaller rivers empty into the Atlantic. The Colorado River, which drains the plateau between the Rockies and Sierra Nevada, has carved the Grand Canyon on its way to the Gulf of California. The Columbia River has also cut spectacular gorges as it flows to the Pacific.

The warm waters of the Gulf of Mexico are framed by a crescent-shaped coastline stretching from Florida to Texas. The country's dominant internal water feature is the Great Lakes. These lakes—the world's largest body of fresh water—were carved thousands of years ago by glaciers. Together with the St. Lawrence River, they provide a waterway for commerce that reaches from the Atlantic Ocean deep into the interior of the North American continent.

Geographers often identify—and historians constantly refer to—seven major physical regions of the United States—the Coastal Plains, Appalachian Highlands, Canadian Shield, Central Plains, Rocky Mountains, Intermountain Region, Pacific Coast, and the Hawaiian Islands. Dramatic physical features dominate each of these regions.

POPULATION PATTERNS

Population movements in America over the last 150 years have been just as varied as those of the early settlers, who came to America from every continent but Antarctica. In the late 1800s tens of thousands of European immigrants poured onto the plains, while other tens of thousands settled in cities such as New York, Chicago, and Milwaukee. Then in the first decades of the 20th century, large numbers of African Americans looking for job opportunities in industry moved from the rural South to places such as Detroit, Chicago, Cleveland, and Los Angeles.

For much of its history the American population grew rapidly. Today declining birth rates and limited immigration have resulted in somewhat slower growth. At the same time, while whites still make up a majority of the American people, the proportion of African Americans, Hispanics,

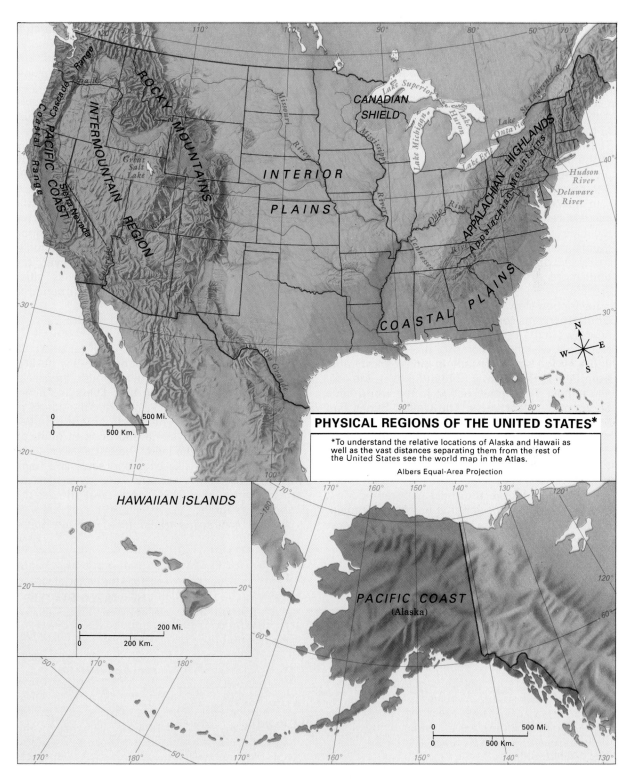

PHYSICAL REGIONS OF THE UNITED STATES*

*To understand the relative locations of Alaska and Hawaii as well as the vast distances separating them from the rest of the United States see the world map in the Atlas.

Albers Equal-Area Projection

ROCKY MOUNTAINS

Cascade Range

Coastal Pacific Range

PACIFIC COAST

Sierra Nevada

INTERMOUNTAIN REGION

Great Salt Lake

CANADIAN SHIELD

Lake Superior

Lake Michigan

Lake Huron

Lake Erie

Lake Ontario

St. Lawrence R.

INTERIOR PLAINS

Missouri River

Mississippi River

Ohio River

Tennessee River

APPALACHIAN HIGHLANDS

Appalachian Mountains

Hudson River

Delaware River

COASTAL PLAINS

Rio Grande

N
W E
S

HAWAIIAN ISLANDS

0   200 Mi.
0   200 Km.

PACIFIC COAST
(Alaska)

0   500 Mi.
0   500 Km.

0   500 Mi.
0   500 Km.

Asians, and other minorities in the population is increasing. Because of high birth rates and continued immigration, the two fastest-growing population groups today are the Hispanic and Asian Americans.

The United States has changed from a **rural** society in which most people lived in areas outside of towns and cities to an **urban,** city-centered one. The first census in 1790 revealed that 94 percent of the people lived in rural areas. Since then people have moved continuously and in ever-larger numbers from rural areas to urban ones.

In the late 1800s the "new" immigrants from eastern, central, and southern Europe flocked into the cities, as did Chinese and Japanese immigrants before they were excluded by law and treaty. According to the 1920 census, for the first time more Americans lived in urban than rural areas.

Restriction slowed immigration after World War I, but Americans continued to move to cities. Then new laws in the 1960s once again opened the door to people wishing to come to the United States, and they too settled mostly in cities. Immigrants from Puerto Rico, Cuba, Korea, Vietnam, Mexico, and almost every other nation in the world have done so in recent years. The United States had become so urbanized that by 1990 more than three quarters of the population lived in urban areas.

AMERICAN CITIES

American cities have a distinct geography. Most have four zones. The inner zone, or downtown, contains the business district and the oldest neighborhoods. This central business district is the economic core of the city. Next is a middle zone, an area of older homes, row houses, and small businesses. Highways crisscross this zone, giving it a crowded appearance.

Beyond the middle zone lie two others: the suburban zone and the outer zone. Suburbs are relatively new. Most were built after World War II, when improved public transportation and increased automobile ownership made living outside the city practical. Because they are some distance from the central business district, most suburbs have their own shopping centers, usually with multipurpose malls. The outer zone marks the transition from urban to rural land. The transition is not abrupt. Open fields and woodland gradually replace houses. In many places, however, the outer zone has virtually disappeared as cities sprawl together to form a continuous urban area called a **megalopolis.**

LAND USE

Americans have used the country's many **natural resources**—vegetation, wildlife, water, minerals, and soil—to build a strong and diversified economy. In so doing they have changed the nature of America's landscape. The Native Americans used only simple tools of stone and bone to hunt, till the soil, and clear the land. The European settlers added metal tools like axes and saws and hammers. Since then Americans have developed an amazing array of machines to harvest and use the nation's resources.

At first Americans transformed the landscape

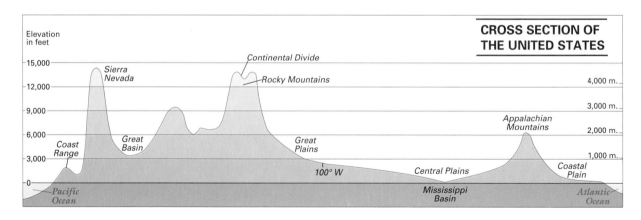

CROSS SECTION OF THE UNITED STATES

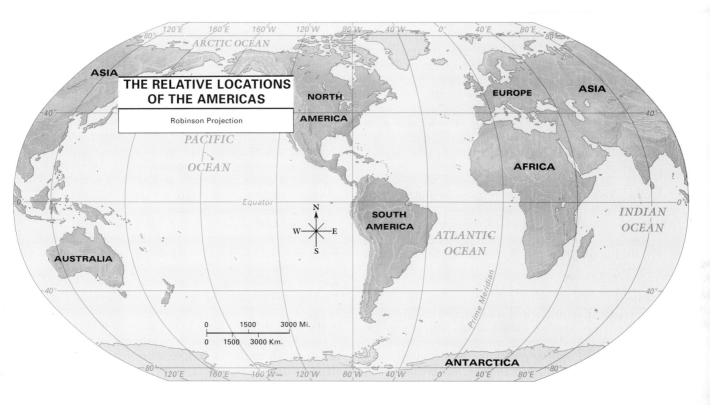

THE RELATIVE LOCATIONS OF THE AMERICAS

Robinson Projection

ARCTIC OCEAN

ASIA

NORTH AMERICA

EUROPE

ASIA

PACIFIC OCEAN

AFRICA

Equator

SOUTH AMERICA

INDIAN OCEAN

ATLANTIC OCEAN

Prime Meridian

AUSTRALIA

N
W E
S

0   1500   3000 Mi.
0   1500   3000 Km.

ANTARCTICA

with little concern for the future. But during the present century they have become aware that this was wasteful and dangerous. Conservationists, such as John Muir and Theodore Roosevelt, alerted the public to the threat to the country's natural beauty and resources. Scientists studying **ecology**—the interrelationships of organisms and their environments—have urged people to develop sensitive areas cautiously. The government has set aside large parcels of land as national parks and wilderness areas. And public and private **conservation** efforts—planned management of resources to prevent their depletion—began to protect the nation's natural gifts.

THE FIVE THEMES OF GEOGRAPHY

These topics deal with only a small part of the information geographers collect. They organize this information according to five themes: location, place, relationships within places, movement, and region. Categorizing the information in this way helps them to analyze facts and to see the relationships among them.

Absolute and Relative Location

Geographers describe location in two ways. The first is **absolute location**—exactly where on earth a place is. The second is **relative location**—where a place is in relation to other places.

Geographers have marked maps and globes with a grid of imaginary lines. These are the lines of **latitude** and **longitude**. Lines of latitude circle the earth parallel to the equator and are used to locate places north and south of the equator, which is marked as 0. Lines of longitude, or meridians, run from the North Pole to the South Pole, intersecting the lines of latitude at right angles. They are used to locate places east or west of the prime meridian, a meridian established by international agreement as 0. Both latitude and longitude are measured in degrees (°), and each degree is further divided into minutes (') and seconds (").

To describe the absolute location of a place, state its latitude first, then its longitude. For example, San Antonio is located at 29°25′30″N, 98°29′8″W. We read this as "twenty-nine degrees twenty-five minutes thirty seconds north, ninety-eight degrees twenty-nine minutes eight seconds

Linking History & Geography   **xxv**

west." To the north and slightly east is Dallas at 32°45'N, 96°45'W. To the east and slightly north is Houston at 29°45'N, 95°20'W. You may wish to review the Strategy for Success on page 659 to practice using latitude and longitude.

Geographers describe relative location in terms of distance and direction from a given point of reference. For example, you may live 3 miles west of your school. Or, Houston is 245 miles southeast of Dallas. You can determine almost any relative location by studying a map of an area.

The shifting location of the American West provides another example of relative location. Americans have usually applied the term "The West" to the frontier—the edge of settlement. The Linking History & Geography feature on page 270 explores the changing relative location of the American West.

Place

Every location on earth is unique. The features that make it unique are called **place** characteristics. Some of these are physical features—landforms, climate, and vegetation. Others are cultural characteristics—the roads, buildings, and farms placed on the land by humans.

Relationships Within Places

People adapt the environment to their needs. They clear and level sites for homes and till the soil in order to grow crops. They also adapt to the environment. American colonists learned to grow different crops and build types of homes different from those in the old country. Geographers classify information about such human-environment interactions under the theme of **relationships within places**.

Movement

The geographic theme of **movement** describes activities such as immigration to the United States, the movements of African Americans from the rural South to northern and western cities, and the shift of people from rural to urban areas. It also describes the movement of the ideas and information people carry with them.

Technology has had a great influence on movement, especially in the last 100 years. Inventions have reduced the obstacles created by geographic barriers. Telephones, radio and television, and computers flash ideas around the globe, while au-tomobiles and highway systems, airplanes, and other advances have sped the movements of people and goods.

Regions

Broad areas of the earth contain common characteristics. Geographers call these areas **regions**. They use cultural features such as language or economic activity to define cultural regions. The map on page 271 illustrates one example of United States cultural regions. Geographers use physical features such as landforms and climate to define physical regions. The map on page 109 shows United States climate regions.

Cultural and physical regions often overlap. Culturally, the Southwest includes the area on both sides of the U.S.–Mexico border, a region with a culture that includes Mexican, Native American, and Anglo features. The physical region of the Southwest includes the dry, mountainous lands of Arizona, New Mexico, and western Texas—generally the same as those in the cultural region.

People have been powerfully influenced by their ideas about regions. People who live along the Pacific Coast enjoy lands of great natural beauty. More than the people in any other region of the United States, they see themselves as the defenders of the environment. They have organized in support of state and federal laws protecting the environment, in their region and others too. Recognizing such regional thinking and attitudes will help you interpret actions and decisions.

As you read *The Story of America*, remember the themes of geography and other geographic factors. They will help you analyze our nation's development.

Geography Review

1. Why can knowing the geography of a place be important to understanding why and how historical events unfolded?
2. What are the advantages of America's location? What are the disadvantages?
3. Describe the major American population movements over the last 100 years.
4. Name the four city zones and describe each.
5. What efforts are being made to protect the natural beauty and resources of the United States?
6. Name and define each of the five themes of geography.

Portuguese carracks combined European square foresails with aftersails adapted from the Arabs.

The Beginnings of American History to 1865

T he vast Atlantic Ocean isolated the Americas from events elsewhere in the world until the late 1400s. Then Europeans pushed across the Atlantic Ocean to discover what were, to them, the new lands of North and South America. In this New World people from Europe, Africa, Asia, along with the original Americans, shaped a distinct way of life.

The ensuing 250 years were a time of growth—and conflict. By 1789 a new nation, the United States, had emerged. Not all groups in the United States enjoyed the benefits of independence and democracy outlined in the Declaration of Independence, but the nation struggled to resolve this serious inconsistency.

A spirit of compromise guided American leaders during its early years. But as differences among the regions grew, compromises were less successful, especially those concerning the institution of slavery. When attempts at compromise on this issue failed, a bitter civil war broke out. Four years of bloody fighting ensued before the Union was restored. At war's end the American people faced the difficult task of rebuilding the nation.

Use these questions to guide your reading. Answer the questions after completing Section 1.
Understanding Issues, Events, & Ideas. Use the following words to describe the development of America from earliest times to the colonial period: joint-stock companies, frontier, Great Awakening, assembly, mercantilism, duty, boycott.
1. List the three discoveries of America.
2. Why did English colonists come to America?
3. What was life like in colonial America?
4. How did the British govern the colonies?
Thinking Critically. Historical imagination is the ability to look at past events objectively, recognizing what people knew and did not know at a particular time. Using historical imagination, write a few paragraphs on how you think Native Americans felt when European settlers arrived in America.

The story of America began 30,000 years or more ago, when wanderers from Asia spread across North and South America. Much later European explorers crossed the Atlantic Ocean, and found what to them was a "New World." Settlers soon followed, and in time, they developed a new way of life—a distinctly American culture. Eventually these settlements along the Atlantic coast won their independence from their colonial ruler—England. They established a new nation, the United States of America. Throughout the first half of the 1800s, the United States expanded rapidly in both size and wealth. However, internal conflicts led in 1861 to a civil war that threatened the country's very existence. But the war ended with the Union intact, and Americans resumed their "rendezvous with destiny."

1. THE AMERICAN COLONIES

Three Discoveries of America

America's early history might be summed up in the word *discovery*. In fact, the region has been "discovered" three times. The first discovery came more than 30,000 years ago, during an Ice Age—a period when glaciers covered a good part of the earth's surface. These vast expanses of ice trapped so much water that the level of the Pacific Ocean dropped, exposing a "land bridge" between Asia and what is now Alaska. Scientists believe that people crossed from Asia to North America over this bridge in search of food. Then these people, who lived by herding or hunting, soon wandered southward through gaps in the ice cap. This pattern of migration continued for some 20,000 years until the great glaciers melted and the rising ocean waters swallowed the land bridge.

The wanderers gradually spread through all of North and South America. Experts believe that by the 1400s more than 50 million people inhabited the two Americas. They had developed many separate societies, each with its own values and customs.

These cultural differences stemmed from the ways the societies solved the problem of scarcity—how they used limited resources to fulfill their needs. Some hunted wild animals and gathered wild plants. Others learned to farm, cultivating the land and planting seeds. Farmers led more secure lives than hunters, because farming allowed them to settle in one place and build permanent homes. Over the centuries, these farming societies developed complex civilizations such as those of the Mayas, the Olmecs, the Aztecs, and the Incas in Central and South America. The hunters, in contrast, continued to roam from place to place.

The people of the Americas knew nothing of the world beyond the oceans, and the rest of the world was unaware of their existence.

Their first contact with the outside world—the second discovery of America—came around the year 1000, when the Vikings, a seafaring people from northern Europe, reached the region south of Labrador. After about 10 years, however, Viking visits ended. No other Europeans reached the American continents for almost 500 years.

In many ways, Europe was as sheltered and isolated as America during this period. But in 1095 the Roman Catholic church launched the first of a series of Crusades, religious wars aimed at driving the Moslems from the Holy Land of Palestine. Crusaders returned to Europe from the war with fine silk and cotton cloths, new fruits, such as dates and oranges, and spices like pepper, ginger, and nutmeg. These aroused the interest—and the taste buds—of the Europeans, and a brisk trade in these products soon developed.

Crusaders also brought back new ideas, for the Moslems had made major advances in mathematics, astronomy, medicine, and other sciences. This new knowledge spurred a Renaissance, "rebirth" of learning, in Europe. This thirst for knowledge triggered a great age of exploration.

The new spices, fabrics, and fruits that Europeans craved were brought from China and the East Indies to Palestine by Arab traders. Other merchants then transported these goods across the Mediterranean Sea to Venice, Naples, and Genoa. From there, Italian merchants carried them all over Europe. Middlemen profited each time the goods changed hands, and taxes and tolls along the way also added to their cost. People in western Europe realized that if they could find a sea route to China and the Indies, they could gain a share of the trade and reduce the prices of oriental products. Historian Barbara Tuchman described the dramatic changes this brought:

This oil portrait is believed to be an accurate likeness of Christopher Columbus, although none was painted during his lifetime. His face seems proud and strong willed. Why did Europeans such as Columbus seek a new route to the Far East?

66 Stimulated by commerce, a surge took place in art, technology, building, learning, explorations by land and sea, universities, cities, banking and credit, and every sphere that enriched life and widened horizons.[1] 99

The Portuguese, a seafaring people, set out to reach Asia by sailing south around Africa. Christopher Columbus, a captain from Genoa, Italy, believed he could reach Asia quicker by sailing westward. After persuading Ferdinand and Isabella, the king and queen of Spain, to finance the voyage, he set sail from Spain in August 1492. Two months later, he landed on what he thought was an island in the East Indies. He was actually in the Bahamas. When he reached Cuba, he thought he was on a peninsula of China.

Columbus returned to Spain with some local inhabitants, plant samples, and a few golden ornaments in 1493. Ferdinand and Isabella financed three other voyages by Columbus. He explored many Caribbean islands and the coast of Central America. Although he never accepted the fact, he had reached not Asia, but a New World.

[1]From *A Distant Mirror* by Barbara Tuchman

The Beginnings of American History   3

An Algonquin leader asked John Smith why the colonists used force with the Indians.

"Why will you take by force what you may have quietly by love? Why will you destroy us who supply you with food? What can you get by war? We can hide our provisions and run into the woods; then you will starve for wronging your friends. Why are you jealous of us? We are unarmed, and willing to give you what you ask, if you come in a friendly manner."

Powhatan, 1607

Vasco Núñez de Balboa, Ferdinand Magellan, and other explorers followed Columbus. They claimed the land for Spain, and soon settlers began building a huge empire. Some came simply for the adventure. Others hoped to find gold and silver, or to convert the native people to Christianity.

New Spain proved to be a treasure chest. Gold and silver from Mexico and South America poured into Spain's royal treasury.

English Colonies In America

The wealth of New Spain attracted other Europeans to the New World. In the 1500s and 1600s, English, French, Dutch, and Swedish colonists established settlements.

The first to claim territory for England was John Cabot, who explored the coast of Newfoundland in 1497. But the English made little effort to develop this claim until the late 1500s. In 1588 their navy destroyed an invading Spanish fleet, the Armada, off the coast of England and Ireland. This destroyed Spain's sea power.

Establishing a successful settlement in the world was dangerous and required a great deal of money. So English merchants interested in the New World joined together to form **joint-stock companies**—forerunners of today's corporations. One such company, the Virginia Company of London, received a charter from King James I in 1606 to settle in what is now Virginia. The next spring about 100 settlers landed on the banks of a river they named James after the king, and constructed a fortified settlement, which they named Jamestown.

Poorly equipped for survival in the wilderness and plagued by malaria-bearing mosquitoes and other diseases, the settlers made it through the first winter only with the help of Indians, who provided them with supplies and showed them how to cultivate the local food crop, maize. As Captain John Smith described the situation:

" There remained not past sixtie men, women and children, most miserable and poore creatures; and those were preserved for the most part, by roots, herbes, acornes, walnuts, berries, now and then a little fish . . . yea, even the very skinnes of our horses.[1]"

The cultivation of another local crop, tobacco, which could be exchanged in Europe for manufactured goods, proved to be the colony's economic salvation.

In 1619 a group of religious dissenters known as Pilgrims obtained a charter to settle in Virginia, where they hoped to practice their religion without interference. But bad weather blew their ship, the *Mayflower*, far to the north of Virginia. They decided to stay where they were, but they were outside the Virginia Company's

[1]From *The General Historie of Virginia* by Captain John Smith

territory, and thus not subject to the rules set down in the company's charter. Therefore they drew up a document stating that they would obey all the laws passed by the majority. This document, called the Mayflower Compact, was based on one of the fundamental principles of republican government—that government exists by the consent of the governed.

Life in this Plymouth Colony proved hard. Like the settlers of Jamestown, the Pilgrims survived their first winter only with the help of the Indians. Plymouth remained small and was soon absorbed by a much larger group of religious dissenters, the Puritans. The Puritans had tried to purify, or reform, the Church of England, but without success. By moving to America they hoped to build a perfect society based on their religious beliefs. It would be ''a city upon a hill'' that other Christians could turn to as a model. The Puritans set sail for Massachusetts in 1630. Well organized and adequately supplied, their settlement prospered from the start.

Though religious dissenters in England themselves, Puritans treated dissenters in their new home harshly. When two early settlers, Roger Williams and Anne Hutchinson, questioned many aspects of the Puritan faith, the government of the colony forced them to leave. Williams and Hutchinson, with their followers, founded what became

"Landing at Jamestown" was painted by John Gadsby Chapman in 1841. It depicts the arrival of the second group of Jamestown settlers.

The Beginnings of American History   5

Rhode Island, a colony where people of all religions could practice their faiths.

The desire for religious freedom also played a role in the founding of Maryland. In 1632 King Charles I gave Maryland, a land north of Virginia, to George Calvert, Lord Baltimore and a Roman Catholic. Calvert and his son, Cecilius, intended to create a place where fellow Catholics could worship freely. In time, however, Protestants outnumbered Catholics in the colony. In 1649 Maryland passed a Toleration Act, which granted freedom of worship to all Christians, but it was not always enforced.

In 1681 King Charles II gave William Penn the territory north of Maryland. Penn, a Quaker, allowed people of all backgrounds and religious faiths to live in this colony of Pennsylvania in the spirit of "brotherly love."

But economic opportunity played a major role in the founding of most English colonies. In 1663 Charles II gave a group of proprietors, or owners, the area between Virginia and Spanish Florida. These proprietors hoped to turn their colony, which they called Carolina, into a land of great estates worked by tenant farmers. They did not succeed, and in time the region was divided into two colonies, North Carolina and South Carolina. The founders of Georgia, the

Benjamin West, the most highly regarded artist of his day, went to Europe on the eve of the Revolution and never returned to America. He painted "Penn's Treaty with the Indians" around 1770. Do you think this painting gives an accurate picture of the meeting between Penn and the Indians? Explain.

last of the English colonies, provided a haven for English people who had been imprisoned for debt. Georgia also acted as a buffer between English territory and the Spanish in Florida.

The Native Americans who met the English settlers in North America were repaid for their help with hostility. Many died of contagious diseases, like measles and smallpox, contracted from the Europeans. Some colonists treated the Indians with respect and fairness, but the majority considered them inferior beings. As time passed the Indians were driven westward, their lands occupied by white "invaders."

Life in Colonial America

In America land was so plentiful that it was worth much less than in Europe. Labor, which made the land productive, was more valuable than in Europe; working people commanded high wages. It was relatively easy for workers to save enough to buy land. Those who were impatient to become landowners and who were willing to live under hard, dangerous conditions could move west to the edge of the settled area. They "squatted" on wild western land without paying for it. The edge of settled regions, constantly moving westward, was called the **frontier.**

The fact that so many colonists owned land affected the way the colonies were governed. It also influenced political attitudes. As in Europe, only people who owned land or other valuable property had the right to vote. But since land ownership was widespread, most white men could do so.

Compared to their status today, women had few rights in colonial times. Yet America did offer women advantages denied to most European women. Some women ran farms or plantations when their husbands were away or had died. Others managed newspapers, worked as lawyers and in other professions.

One word—*opportunity*—sums up the difference between life in America and Europe. Americans, regardless of their social status, could usually improve their way of life. Servants could become landowners.

Religion, of course, played an important role in everyday life. In the 1720s a religious movement known as the **Great Awakening** spread through the colonies. "Fire and brimstone" preachers like Jonathan Edwards and George Whitefield warned their congregations that merely going to church was no guarantee of salvation. Vividly describing the wrath of a just God, they cautioned "sinners" to repent immediately and change their ways. If not, they would burn in Hell forever.

Although the Great Awakening died down after several years, because of its come-one-come-all spirit, it was a force for both democracy and religious toleration. The strong emphasis on individual salvation emphasized the idea of social equality. All people, regardless of position or wealth, were equal before God. And as people experienced equality in their religious lives, they began to expect it in their political lives as well.

Although a distinctly American way of life developed in the colonies, divisions also began to appear. Westerners resented people in the long-settled east. They complained that the colonial governments, which were dominated by easterners, adopted policies that did little to protect frontier settlements from Indian attack. Resentment sometimes turned violent, as in the rebellion led by Nathaniel Bacon in Virginia in 1676.

Distinct societies, based on different social and economic systems, developed in the north and south. Especially in New England, poor soils and a short growing season made large-scale farming unprofitable. However, the forests of the region yielded lumber and naval stores—masts, tar, pitch—for sale to Britain. Fur traders found a ready market in England for the pelts of beaver, deer, and other animals that roamed New England's woodlands. And New Englanders caught fish in the Atlantic, dried and salted their catch, and sold it in Europe and the Indies. But the most important economic activities of the New Englanders were ship building and trade. New England merchants sailed the Atlantic, carrying goods between the colonies and Europe, Africa, and the Caribbean.

Agriculture was the major activity of the Southern colonies. The climate was good for growing cash crops—things for which a demand existed in Europe. Rice and indigo, a plant that produced a blue dye used by cloth manufacturers, were the cash crops of the Carolinas and Georgia. Tobacco was the export crop of Virginia and Maryland. Tobacco was so important in these colonies that it served as a kind of money.

Growers of tobacco, rice, and indigo did best with large plantations worked by gang labor. At first indentured servants, people who agreed to work for a certain time in return for their passage to America, provided the labor. But when their time had been served, they became planters on their own. Plantation owners soon began to look for a permanent source of labor. They found it on the West African coast—African slaves.

The first Africans were brought to the colony of Virginia in 1619. Some may have been treated as indentured servants, but by the end of the century, slavery was firmly established in the English colonies and throughout New Spain. European traders, assisted by local Africans, bought them from kings who had captured them in wars and sudden raids. The captives were taken in chains to the coast, held in slave pens until sold to the European traders. Then they were packed into the ships like animals for the dreadful "middle passage" across the Atlantic. Olaudah Equiano, a slave who eventually bought his freedom, described the dreaded "middle passage":

❝ We were all put below deck. The number of people was so great that each person barely had room to move. The stale air and the heat almost choked us. Everyone was dripping sweat, so that the air became unfit to breathe, from a variety of foul smells. . . . Many died. . . .[1] ❞

A British warship captured a Spanish slaveship on its way to the West Indies in the 18th century. A young English naval officer, Lt. Francis Meynell, went below and made this watercolor sketch on the spot. What part of a slave's journey does this picture depict?

Governing the American Colonies

As the colonies grew and prospered, the English worked out a system to govern them. At the head of each colony was a governor, appointed or approved by the king. Governors carried out orders from London. Councils, whose members were appointed, advised the governors. Legislative **assemblies** elected by the colonists were modeled on the House of Commons in Parliament. They enacted local laws and levied taxes to pay the cost of the system. Governors could veto or suspend laws passed by the assemblies. However, since the assemblies raised money, they could usually influence the governors' decisions. The first colonial legislature, the Virginia House of Burgesses, was established in 1619.

[1]From *The Interesting Narrative of the Life of Olaudah Equiano, or Gustavus Vassa, The African*, vol. 1, by Olaudah Equiano

The government in London regulated colonial trade closely. The object was to have the colonies provide the mother country with raw materials it could not produce and act as a market for English manufactured goods. To ensure that the colonies fulfilled their role, Parliament passed a series of Navigation Acts between 1651 and 1733. Tobacco, sugar, and other things the English needed could only be sent to England. Trade of all sorts had to involve English or colonial ships. This policy was called **mercantilism.** The Navigation Acts were relatively easy to evade because British authorities made little effort to enforce them. In general they caused little trouble.

Throughout the 1600s and 1700s England and France competed for power and influence in Europe and America. Four times actual war broke out between them. The last conflict, the French and Indian War, began in 1754 and lasted nine years. The British won that war, and France had to give up Canada and all claims to territory east of the Mississippi River.

The victory greatly extended Great Britain's American empire. But the fighting almost emptied the British treasury. Administration and protection of the newly gained territory further strained British finances. The British government therefore decided to make the colonies share this financial burden.

To raise the money, Parliament passed the Sugar Act of 1764. This law placed **duties,** or import taxes, on sugar, molasses, and several other products imported by the colonies. Although the Sugar Act resembled the old Navigation Acts, it was different in one important respect. The Navigation Acts were designed to control trade. Foreign molasses, for example, was taxed heavily to discourage importation, not to collect the tax. The purpose of the Sugar Act, however, was to raise money. The tax on foreign molasses was actually reduced. The colonists grumbled about the Sugar Act but did not refuse to obey it.

However, the next British effort to raise revenue, the Stamp Act of 1765, stirred a hornet's nest of complaint. This law taxed the use of all types of printed matter—newspapers, licenses, deeds, wills, and playing cards. This direct tax infuriated the colonists. Such taxes, they argued, could be imposed only by legislative bodies elected by the people. The colonists had not voted for the members of Parliament who passed the law. Taxation without representation, they said, was tyranny, a violation of their "rights as Englishmen."

Groups calling themselves "Sons of Liberty" attacked the homes and offices of the agents charged with selling the stamps and enforcing the Act. Merchants organized a **boycott.** They refused to buy any British goods until the Stamp Act was repealed. Realizing that this boycott was damaging British trade, Parliament repealed the act. However, Parliament also passed the Declaratory Act, which stated that it had the right to pass *any* law it desired regarding the colonies.

American Antiquarian Society

The British still needed to raise revenue, so in 1767 Parliament placed duties on tea, paper, and other products imported into the colonies. The colonists responded to these Townshend Acts with another boycott. The Massachusetts legislature sent a Circular Letter to the other colonial assemblies suggesting they take united action. The government then sent British troops to Boston. Tensions between these British "Redcoats" and the citizens of Boston mounted. In December 1770, a group of soldiers fired into a jeering crowd that was pelting them with snowballs and rocks. This Boston Massacre left five colonists dead.

Fortunately, cooler heads prevailed and further violence was avoided. But conflicts over the Sugar, Stamp, and Townshend acts had drawn colonists together. 🖱️

Paul Revere quickly published "The Boston Massacre" after the Redcoats fired in March 1770. Why might this engraving be considered a form of propaganda?

Return to the Preview & Review on page 2.

The Beginnings of American History   11

America's Indian Heritage

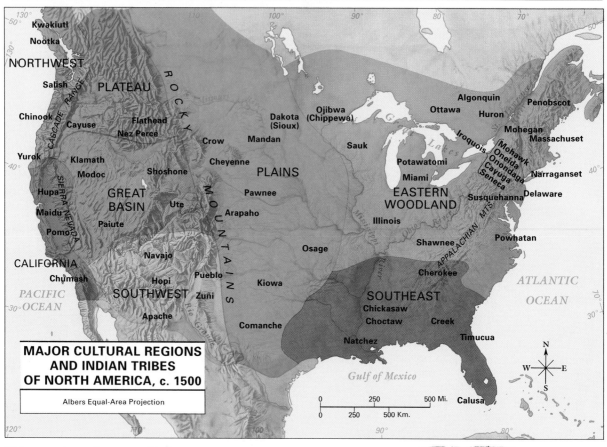

**MAJOR CULTURAL REGIONS
AND INDIAN TRIBES
OF NORTH AMERICA, c. 1500**

Albers Equal-Area Projection

This map shows the geographic location of the major cultural groups into which American Indian tribes have been divided. It also shows some of the hundreds of tribes in each group. Of course many tribes moved about a great deal, so the locations shown are approximate.

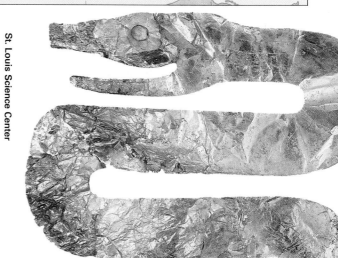

St. Louis Science Center

This stone pipe found in Oklahoma shows a man playing chunkey, a game popular everywhere in the region of the Mound Builders. Games lasted all day. Chunkey was a bit like bowling, a bit like the javelin toss.

Peabody Museum of Archaeology and Ethnology, Harvard University

The Hopewell mounds yielded this mica serpent. Mica is a mineral silvery in color and so fine it is translucent—diffused light passes through.

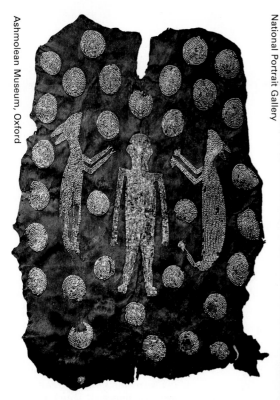

Powhatan's Mantle was worn by the great leader of the Algonquins, who lived on the Virginia tidewater—lands just inland from the ocean. It is the oldest example of American Indian art. The cloak is made of tanned buckskin and decorated with shells.

Pocahontas, daughter of the great Powhatan, is seen here in a 1616 painting. She married John Rolfe of Jamestown and was taken to England. In 1617 she died of smallpox.

This painted fish bowl was made by the Mimbres, a Mogollon people of southern New Mexico. The Mogollon were among the first people of the Southwest to make pottery. They are best remembered for their black-on-white ware.

A fragment of a woven basket was found at Hogup Cave near the Great Salt Lake in Utah. The baskets were so tightly woven that they could hold water into which hot stones were lowered to boil stews.

The Beginnings of American History   13

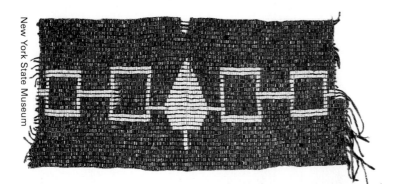

The Hiawatha Belt shows the unity of the five Iroquois tribes. The squares are connected to a central tree, or heart. The beads from which the belt is fashioned were probably brought to America by Europeans.

The mask of painted wood below depicts the moon. It was carved by the Haida, a people of the Queen Charlotte Islands, which are west of British Columbia.

The men of the Hopi spun cotton yarn on a spindle. Weaving was also primarily man's work.

The wooden deer mask was made by inhabitants of Key Marco, off Florida's swampy coast.

A thunderbird—the mythical creator of the storms that rolled over the Great Plains—swoops out of the sky, hurling lightning flashes on this Pawnee ceremonial drum.

14   PROLOGUE

Those who knew the old ways wove this Navajo blanket.

The great photographer of the American West was Edward Sheriff Curtis. He took "A Pigean Dandy" (above) showing traditional Indian dress and hairstyle. More recently Norman New Rider, a Pawnee Indian, was expelled from school for refusing to cut his braided hair. The Supreme Court held that his hairstyle had no direct link to long-standing tradition or religious identity.

George Catlin was one of America's greatest painters of western Indian life. His 1832 portrait of Black Rock shows Catlin's attention to detail. The chief of the Two Kettle tribe of the Blackfoot Nation wears a split-horn ermine cap with a trail of eagle feathers, the mark of the bravest of leaders.

The Beginnings of American History 15

Use these questions to guide your reading. Answer the questions after completing Section 2.
Understanding Issues, Events, & Ideas. Use the following words to describe the creation of the United States: democracy, constitution, legislature, executive, judiciary, emancipation, Articles of Confederation, federalism, checks and balances, impeachment, amendment, Bill of Rights, Alien and Sedition Acts.
1. Why did the colonies go to war with Britain?
2. What forms did the new state governments take?
3. What economic and foreign policies did George Washington follow as president?
Thinking Critically. 1. If you could advise British leaders to change their attitudes in order to avoid conflict with the colonies, what actions would you suggest they take? 2. Imagine that you are a supporter of strong central government for the United States at the Constitutional Convention. What arguments would you use to sway others to your side?

2. THE AMERICAN NATION

The Revolutionary War

Parliament repealed all the Townshend duties except the one on tea. But trouble flared again in 1773, when a group of Bostonians disguised as Indians dumped about £15,000 worth of tea in Boston Harbor to protest the tax. This "Boston Tea Party" caused the British to pass the Coercive Acts, designed to make the people of Boston pay for the tea. The colonists called these measures the Intolerable Acts.

Representatives of the colonies met in New York in September 1774. This First Continental Congress organized another boycott of trade with Britain. Colonists in Massachusetts and elsewhere formed militia companies of citizen soldiers called Minute Men. Patrick Henry, a member of the Virginia House of Burgesses, said:

" Gentlemen may cry peace, peace. But there is no peace. The war is actually begun! . . . Is life so dear, or peace so sweet, as to be purchased at the price of chains and slavery? Forbid it, Almighty God! I know not what course others may take; but as for me, give me liberty or give me death![1] "

In April 1775 British troops clashed with militiamen at Lexington and Concord, west of Boston. Many colonists still hoped to avoid further bloodshed. The Second Continental Congress called for a peaceful settlement. But the British reply was blunt: the colonists were rebels. They must submit or face the consequences.

The colonists then took the final step. On July 4, 1776, the Continental Congress declared the colonies independent, a new nation—the United States of America.

Thomas Jefferson of Virginia was the principal author of the Declaration of Independence. Echoing the ideas of Enlightenment philosophers like John Locke, he claimed that all men are created equal and are endowed by their Creator with certain "unalienable rights," rights that cannot be taken away. These include the right to "life, liberty, and the pursuit of happiness." Jefferson went on to explain that people form governments to protect these natural rights. Governments exist only with the consent of the governed. Any government that abuses the rights of the people may be replaced by the people with another.

The Declaration said only that "all men" were created equal; no mention was made of rights for slaves. But to condemn the Declaration for these omissions is to judge it by modern standards. Given typical 18th-century values, it was a compelling argument for

[1]From *Sketches of the Life and Character of Patrick Henry*, 3d ed., edited by William Wirt

democracy—the idea that everyone has a right to equal opportunity and that governments exist only with the consent of the people.

Having declared independence, the Continental Congress organized the Continental Army and appointed George Washington to command it. Washington faced a daunting task. The British army was much larger and better trained and equipped than Washington's. But the Americans were fighting on and for their own soil. And they had a cause—independence!

The Continental Army lost more battles than it won, especially early in the war. At times it seemed that only Washington's determination and character kept the troops together. But the Americans won battles when it mattered. In 1781, American troops, along with French naval and land forces—France had entered the war in 1778—trapped the British army at Yorktown, Virginia. After a brief siege, the British army surrendered.

Great Britain then gave up the war, and recognized American independence. The Treaty of Paris of 1783 set the boundaries of the new nation roughly at Florida in the south, the Mississippi River in the west, and the Great Lakes in the north.

Creating the United States

Changing a colony into a state involved replacing the old royal charter with a **constitution,** a written description of the state's system of government. The state constitutions were pretty much alike. The governments consisted of three branches: an elected **legislature**; an **executive,** to carry out the law and run everyday operations; and a **judiciary,** or system of courts. Most also included a bill of rights, describing the liberties that the people could not be deprived of. Americans wanted to make sure that the state governments had only limited powers.

Most state constitutions limited the right to vote to adult white males who owned some property. Even so, voting was far more widespread than in any European nation. Once functioning, many northern legislatures passed laws providing for the gradual freeing, or **emancipation,** of slaves.

The government of the new United States was also outlined in a constitution, the **Articles of Confederation,** adopted in 1781. The Articles stressed the powers of the separate states and pointed out that the United States was to be only a "firm league of friendship"—a kind of alliance. Congress could declare war, make peace, deal with foreign governments, and settle disputes between the states. It also could decide how territory west of the Appalachian Mountains was settled. The Land Ordinances of 1785 and 1787, which established the method for selling land and admitting new states into the Union, were the most important accomplishments of Congress under the Articles.

Washington carried this miniature of his "dear Patsy" throughout the Revolutionary War. It was painted by Charles Willson Peale in about 1776. Below, Washington stands in 1782 with his horse Nelson. John Trumbull painted this picture in 1790.

The Beginnings of American History   17

"The Declaration of Independence" was painted by John Trumbull in 1786. Thomas Jefferson and Benjamin Franklin are near the center of the painting.

Point of View

An English writer whose books take us backward *and* forward in time made this observation about the American Revolution.

❝From the point of view of human history, the way in which the Thirteen States became independent is of far less importance than the fact that they did become independent. And with the establishment of their independence came a new sort of community into the world. It was like something coming out of an egg. . . . It had no dukes, princes, counts, nor any sort of title-bearers claiming to ascendancy or respect as a right. Even its unity was as yet a mere unity for defence and freedom. It was in these respects such a clean start in political organization as the world had not seen before. . . .❞

From *The Outline of History,*
H. G. Wells, 1920

But Congress had to ask the states for the money it needed to run the government and to pay the country's debts. And it could not regulate trade between the states and with foreign countries. The weaknesses of the Articles led some to suggest that they needed revising. A meeting of delegates from the states was convened at Philadelphia in 1787. This Constitutional Convention quickly decided to draft a completely new, much stronger constitution. But the delegates did not want the new government to swallow up the states. In addition to the powers already exercised under the Articles, the delegates gave the national government the power to regulate trade, impose taxes, and coin money. Of course the state consitutions were not changed in any important way. This system of shared powers is known as **federalism.**

The basic organization of the national government resembled that of the states. The executive branch was headed by the president. The legislative branch, the Congress, was made up of a Senate and a House of Representatives. The judiciary was headed by a Supreme Court. A system of **checks and balances** divided power among these branches, ensuring that no one branch would dominate the government. For example, the president appointed Supreme Court justices and cabinet ministers, but the Senate could reject such appointments. The president could veto bills passed by Congress, but a two-thirds majority in both houses of Congress could override a veto. Judges served for life "during good Behavior," but Congress, through a process called **impeachment,** could bring to trial and remove judges and other government officials, including even the president, if they committed "high crimes and misdemeanors."

The "Great Compromise" in the Constitution balanced the interests of the small and large states. Representation in the House of Representatives was based on population. But each state would have two representatives in the Senate.

The Constitution required that the new government would go into effect when nine states had ratified it. Opinions on the Constitution differed sharply. Supporters, called Federalists, felt that the strong central government the Constitution provided was essential. Those in opposition, the Antifederalists, believed that the new system would undermine the independence of the states and the rights of the people.

In the debates over ratification, it became clear that changes, or **amendments,** to the Constitution protecting the rights of the states and of individuals were necessary. The promise to add these made ratification easier in key states. By June 1788 the necessary nine states had voted to ratify.

Governing the United States

Elections were held to choose congressmen and a president. Washington, of course, was elected to that office. The new Congress then drafted the promised amendments, which were also ratified by the states. These amendments, known as the **Bill of Rights,** guaranteed the people freedom of speech, assembly, and religion, and such basic rights as trial by jury. The amendment process showed that the writers of the Constitution, while wanting to create a government that would guide the nation, also were mindful that society might change in the future.

President Washington's secretary of the treasury, Alexander Hamilton, promptly set about paying off the debts the country had built up during the Revolution. He also proposed to assume, or take over, the debts of the separate states. His method of retiring the debts—gradually raising taxes—met with much criticism but did reestablish the country's credit.

To further strengthen the economy, Hamilton proposed to create a national bank. This Bank of the United States, he argued, would be a safe place to store the government's money and provide financial services to private business. But was such a bank authorized by the Constitution? Secretary of State Thomas Jefferson argued that because the Constitution did not say specifically that the government had the power to create a bank, it could not do so. Hamilton, however, argued that since a bank would help in carrying out powers directly granted in the Constitution, the government could found a bank. Washington supported Hamilton's argument, and the bank was established by Congress.

When revolution erupted in France in 1789, most Americans greeted the news with pleasure. But by 1793 the French Revolution

John Adams, elected president in 1796, was painted by John Singleton Copley. In contrast to Washington, Adams was short and stocky.

Return to the Preview & Review on page 16.

had become more radical, and most of the nations of Europe had joined in a war against France. Since the American treaty of alliance with France was still in effect, the question of the United States' obligations to France had to be answered. President Washington issued a neutrality proclamation stating that America would be "friendly and impartial" to both sides in the war. In 1794 the United States and Great Britain signed a treaty, negotiated by John Jay, settling differences dating back to the Revolution. Jay's Treaty was unpopular in the United States, but Washington preferred peace to another war with Great Britain.

The president restated his belief in neutrality in his Farewell Address published in 1796. He warned them to avoid "passionate attachments" to foreign countries and to "steer clear of permanent alliances."

Washington also urged Americans to avoid extreme political partisanship, but his advice was largely ignored. Two political parties had already developed. The Federalist party, led by Alexander Hamilton, stood for a strong central government, the development of industry, and sound government finance. The Democratic-Republican party, led by Thomas Jefferson and James Madison, favored a less-active government and a nation composed primarily of farmers.

In 1796 Washington's vice president, John Adams, was elected president. Since under the Constitution the person with the second-largest number of electoral votes was to be vice president, Thomas Jefferson, the Democratic-Republican candidate for president, became the new vice president!

The war in Europe caused sharp divisions among Americans. In choosing neutrality and peace rather than going to war against France, Adams angered many Federalists. Then the Federalist majority in Congress passed the **Alien and Sedition Acts.** These laws reduced the rights of foreigners in the United States and made it a crime to "write, print, utter, or publish" statements critical of the government. This attack on the First Amendment contributed to the defeat of the Federalists in the election of 1800. 🖅

3. A GROWING AMERICA

Preview & Review

Use these questions to guide your reading. Answer the questions after completing Section 3.
Understanding Issues, Events, & Ideas. Use the following words to describe the growth of America in the first 40 years of the 1800s: *Marbury v. Madison,* Monroe Doctrine, protective tariff, Industrial Revolution, urbanization.
1. What were Thomas Jefferson's major accomplishments as president?
2. What were the causes and outcome of the War of 1812?
3. What did the American government do to protect manufacturers from foreign competition?
Thinking Critically. What do you think was the most important technological development in America's first industrial revolution? Give reasons for your answer.

The Age of Jefferson

In the election of 1800 the two candidates of the Democratic-Republicans, Thomas Jefferson and Aaron Burr, received the same number of electoral votes. Which one was to be president had to be decided by the House of Representatives. Alexander Hamilton used his influence to persuade Federalists to vote for Jefferson, whom he preferred to Burr.

Because of the development of political parties, the existing presidential election system did not work. As a result, the Twelfth Amendment, requiring electors to vote separately for president and vice president, was adopted.

When Jefferson took office in 1801, many Federalists expected trouble. They viewed Jefferson as an extreme radical. Jefferson, however, calmed their fears in his inaugural speech. "We are all Republicans!" he announced, "We are all Federalists!" He also made it clear, however, that he thought the states should enjoy wide powers and the authority of the central government should be limited. But as it turned out, many of the actions Jefferson took as president served to strengthen the federal government.

One of the first actions of Jefferson's presidency helped to establish the power of the Supreme Court. In his last evening in office John Adams signed commissions appointing many new federal judges. However, some of the commissions for these "midnight justices" were not delivered before Jefferson took office, and Jefferson refused to have them delivered. One of Adams' appointees, William Marbury, sued to have his commission given to him. In the case of *Marbury v. Madison* (1803), Chief Justice John Marshall ruled against Marbury, on the ground that the law of Congress authorizing the suit was unconstitutional. By declaring a law unconstitutional, Marshall asserted the Supreme Court's authority to decide on the meaning of the Constitution.

One of Jefferson's most important accomplishments was the purchase of Louisiana, the vast region between the Mississippi River and the Rocky Mountains. What he really wanted was only the city of New Orleans—a vital port for western farmers. When France, which owned Louisiana, barred Americans from using the port, Jefferson decided to try to buy New Orleans. When he did, Napoleon Bonaparte was in need of money to finance his war with Great Britain. The French leader offered the Americans not merely New Orleans but the whole of Louisiana for $15 million—only $5 million more than Jefferson had been prepared to pay for New Orleans alone. The Senate approved the resulting treaty in December 1803. Some 800,000 square miles (2,072,000 square kilometers) of territory was added to the United States. In 1804 Jefferson sent Meriwether Lewis

The Metropolitan Museum of Art

Thomas Jefferson wanted to keep government as small as possible. This fine miniature portrait is by John Trumbull. Later Jefferson stopped wearing powdered wigs.

and William Clark to explore the new land and gather information about the Indians and the plant and animal life of the region.

In dealing with foreign nations, Jefferson tried to follow the path of neutrality established by Washington and Adams. But war between France and Britain made this policy difficult. The British navy seized dozens of American merchant ships, claiming that they were trading with France. But what most angered Americans was the British practice of impressment, the boarding of American ships and seizing of anyone thought to be British for service on their warships.

In an effort to stop British violations of neutral rights, Congress passed the Embargo Act of 1807, which prohibited all exports from the United States. Jefferson reasoned that if there were no American ships on the seas, there would be no cargoes seized and no seamen impressed. However, the embargo proved costly. Thousands of American sailors and longshoremen were thrown out of work. In 1809 Congress repealed the Embargo Act. American resentment of British policy increased.

War and Peace, 1812-1823

Other events leading toward war occurred on the frontier. When settlement reached the Ohio Valley, progress was stopped by Indian tribes headed by Tecumseh, a Shawnee chief. Tecumseh believed that God, the ''Great Spirit,'' had given the land to Indians to *use* but not to own. Therefore, the Indians had no right to sell it to the whites. Tecumseh said:

" White people are never satisfied. . . . They have driven us from the great salt water, forced us over the mountains. . . . We are determined to go no farther."

But in November 1811 militiamen commanded by General William Henry Harrison defeated the Indians at Tippecanoe Creek, in western Indiana. Harrison was convinced that the British had been encouraging Indians to attack settlers, and members of Congress who favored war, called War Hawks, demanded action. Reluctantly, President Madison asked Congress for a declaration of war. In June 1812 the United States and Britain were again involved in armed conflict.

In the first year of the war, the tiny American navy had remarkable success against the much larger British fleet. But an American attempt to invade Canada was thrown back. In 1814, British victories over Napoleon in Europe freed thousands of soldiers for the American campaign. The British sea raiders overran Washington, setting most of the city ablaze. But when they attacked Baltimore, they were stopped. The sight of a tattered American flag flying defiantly over Fort McHenry in Baltimore Harbor inspired Francis Scott Key to write ''The Star-Spangled Banner''—later to become the national anthem.

Typical of the battles of the War of 1812, bombs really did burst in air. Flags told of victory and loss. This is the bombardment of Fort McHenry, which Francis Scott Key made so memorable.

In 1815 the British launched another attack, this time against New Orleans. But American troops commanded by General Andrew Jackson defeated them. Even before Jackson's victory, American and British diplomats in Holland had negotiated a peace treaty. No territory changed hands. The Treaty of Ghent simply restored peace.

During the presidency of James Monroe (1817-1825), the United States signed more treaties with Great Britain. These fixed the American-Canadian border at the 49th parallel north latitude and put the Oregon Territory under their joint control. In the Transcontinental Treaty of 1819, Spain gave Florida to the United States, and the two nations extended the southern boundary of the United States to the Pacific Ocean.

By 1822 most of the Spanish colonies in the Americas had revolted and become independent. This turn of events pleased Great Britain and the United States, who hoped to profit from trade with the newly independent nations. The British therefore suggested that they and the Americans issue a joint statement warning other nations not to try to restore Spanish control in Latin America. President Monroe, at the suggestion of Secretary of State John Quincy Adams, decided instead to make his own statement of policy. In his 1823 State of the Union message, he announced that the independent nations of the Americas were "henceforth not to be considered as subjects for further colonization by any European powers."

Most European leaders paid little attention to this **Monroe Doctrine.** However, Monroe's warning to Europe to keep hands off the Western Hemisphere became a basis for future American foreign policy.

Building America, 1790-1840

The British had always discouraged manufacturing in the colonies. They wanted them to buy British-made manufactured goods. After independence, Americans remained dependent on foreign-made manufactures, but they gradually realized that profits could be made by producing such articles themselves. However, this new industry was threatened by British companies dumping low-priced goods on the American market. To protect the American producers, in 1816 the government put heavy import duties—called **protective tariffs**—on foreign-made goods. In the same year, Congress created a new Bank of the United States, replacing the first, which had gone out of business in 1811.

The American manufacturing plants were small and relatively inefficient. In Great Britain by this time the burden of manufacturing had been shifted from human labor to power-driven machinery. This **Industrial Revolution** first took place in the making of cotton thread and, later, of cloth as well. By about 1800 British mechanized mills, or factories, were exporting thread and cloth all over the world.

The British tried to keep other nations from copying their revolutionary methods. However, Samuel Slater, a British mechanic, memorized designs of the cotton-spinning machinery. Then he immigrated to the United States. He went into partnership with Moses Brown, a Rhode Island merchant, and built a cotton factory. The factory produced thread, which workers wove into cloth in their homes. Next, in 1814, Francis Cabot Lowell, a Boston merchant, constructed a factory that produced cotton cloth by machine in Waltham, Massachusetts.

Industrial development spurred **urbanization**—the growth of towns and cities. The population of New York, the country's leading commercial center and largest city, grew from 125,000 to about 250,000 during the 1830s. Boston and Philadelphia had populations in excess of 60,000 by 1840. Much of this growth resulted from European immigration.

Life for these newcomers was far from easy. Immigrants often lived in crowded buildings, called tenements, that had no running water, and only outside toilets. Garbage littered the unpaved streets. Unsanitary conditions encouraged the spread of contagious diseases in the crowded tenement slums. But despite these problems, the cities were a vibrant and important part of American life. Their theaters, libraries, newspapers, cafes, and taverns became centers of excitement, thought, and adventure for people from all regions and all walks of life.

The growth of manufacturing and of larger cities depended on the development of efficient transportation systems to move food and raw materials to the producers and to ship their goods all over the country. By 1800 a system of turnpikes—privately owned roads on

which users paid tolls—linked most of the eastern cities. But the National Road, begun in 1811, which eventually reached Vandalia, Illinois, was the only route into the central United States built by the federal government in this period.

In the West, people had to depend on waterways for transportation. The rivers of the area flow into the Mississippi, so goods could be transported to New Orleans from anywhere. Steamboats made transportation on the larger rivers much more efficient. In 1807 Robert Fulton proved that such craft were practical. By 1840, more than 500 steamboats were operating on the Mississippi River alone.

No continuous waterway connected West and East. Engineers overcame this problem by digging the Erie Canal. This canal stretched 363 miles (580 kilometers) from Buffalo on Lake Erie to Albany, New York, on the Hudson River. This engineering achievement, which took eight years to build, provided an all-water route from New York City to the Great Lakes. Traffic on the Erie Canal was so heavy that tolls quickly paid for the canal's construction. The success of the Erie Canal led to a canal-building boom. By 1840, 3,300 miles (5,280 kilometers) of canals had been built. Still more significant was the development of steam engines for railroads. In 1830, only about 17 miles (21 kilometers) of railroad track existed. Within 10 years, 3,000 miles (4,828 kilometers) had been added, mostly in the Northeast. By 1850 the railroads had replaced canals as the most important form of transportation in the nation. 📧

With the crack of a whip the driver of this stagecoach urges his horses westward. The wheels of the stagecoach sink into the muddy road, which is marked by the stumps of the trees probably felled to build the bridge at right. Whenever the horses galloped around a curve such as this, there was always the chance the overland travelers would "be stumped"—or stopped by stumps that broke the coach's wheels. How were America's first roads a good example of private enterprise in action?

Return to the Preview & Review on page 21.

The Beginnings of American History 25

America's Hispanic Heritage

"Princess Margarita after Velázquez" was painted by Fernando Botero of Colombia in 1978. His figures with large heads satirize the Spanish nobility and their displays of wealth.

The "Maids of Honor" shows Princess Margarita surrounded by her friends and dwarf. Velázquez himself stands to the left, holding a brush. The mirror at the back reflects the smiling king and queen.

More than 300 years pass before our eyes when we see these two paintings of the same little Spanish princess. The first is by Diego Rodriquez de Silva y Velázquez. In 1656 he painted *Las Meñinas* ("Maids of Honor") in the court of Philip IV of Spain. The second portrait of Princess Margarita was painted in our time by Fernando Botero of Colombia. His painting, like the others on these pages, shows our Hispanic heritage. Botero is modern and at the same time pays homage to the American Indians whose art and architecture flourished long before the painted sails of Columbus' ships hoved into view.

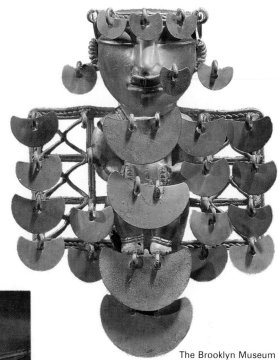

From Colombia comes this Quimbáya gilded pendant fashioned in 500–1000 A.D. The medallions cover the likeness of a woman whose face we see but whose torso is demurely covered.

New Orleans—a Spanish frontier city—seems an appropriate home for "Archangel with a Gun," painted on cotton in the 17th century by a Peruvian disciple in the circle of an artist known as the Master of Calamarcha. The artist contrasts finery typical of Europe with an essential tool of the frontier–the rifle.

The Beginnings of American History   27

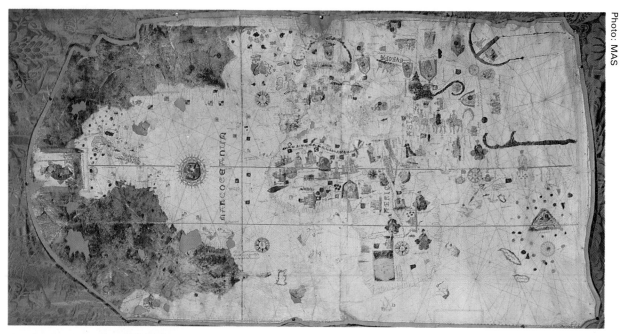

From Juan de la Cosa, a Spaniard, we have this world map published in 1500. It shows for the first time the islands and coasts of the Americas.

A TAHVALLPA INGA XIIII. Y vltimo Edvenc ido Hijo de Mama Chachapoya Reyna de Quito aclamado por Rey del Cuzco Fue vencido y prezo el desdichado Monarca del Conquistador D.ⁿ Francisco Pizarro, y despues degollado en Cajamarca, Hallase que fue Bautizado y se llamo Donjuan ATAHUALLPA. El año de 1533.

A Spanish-trained Indian artist made this Peruvian miniature of "Atahualpa, Last King of the Incas."

The first great native-born Puerto Rican painter was José Campeche. His "Dama a Caballo" ("Lady on Horseback") shows how strong the Spanish influence was in 1785.

28   PROLOGUE

Amelia Pelaez del Casal is a Cuban painter who studied for a time in Europe. There she was influenced by the Cubist style of Pablo Picasso of Spain and Georges Braque of France. To these influences she brought the vivid colors of her Caribbean homeland, as seen in "Fishes," on the right, painted in 1943.

One of Mexico's greatest artists was Diego Rivera, best known for his murals. "Women Washing Clothes in a River among Zopilotes" was painted in 1928.

Miguel Martinez, a contemporary Hispanic American who lives in Taos, New Mexico, is the artist of this contemporary painting entitled "Taos Mesa."

The Beginnings of American History   29

4. A WESTERING AMERICA

Use these questions to guide your reading. Answer the questions after completing Section 4.
Understanding Issues, Events, & Ideas. Use the following words to describe westward expansion, the development of sectionalism, and the growth of reform movements between 1820 and 1850: sectional conflicts, popular vote, spoils system, states' rights, manifest destiny, Missouri Compromise, Compromise of 1850, popular sovereignty, abolitionist, temperance, prohibition, ideal community.

1. What three major issues faced Andrew Jackson during his presidency? How were these issues resolved?
2. What did manifest destiny mean to Americans in the mid-1800s?
3. What was life like for slaves in the South?
4. What major reform groups developed during the mid-1800s?

Thinking Critically. 1. Do you agree or disagree with the Jacksonians' view that the "common sense of the common man" was the only requirement necessary for working in government? Why? **2.** Write a script for an argument about slavery between a southern plantation owner and a northern abolitionist. **3.** If you were a reformer in the mid-1800s, what aspect of society would you try to reform? Why?

The Age of Jackson

Shortly after James Monroe became president, "an Era of Good Feelings" began. On the surface, this was true. The country was at peace, prosperous, and growing. When Monroe ran for reelection in 1820, no one opposed him.

Yet beneath the surface, **sectional conflicts** based on regional economic and social differences were developing. By the end of Monroe's second term, these conflicts had produced three geographical areas: the Northeast, the South, and the West.

The people of each region had distinct political and economic viewpoints. Leaders emerged who represented these sectional interests. Four of them, all Democratic-Republicans, ran for president in 1824—John Quincy Adams from the Northeast, William Crawford from the South, and Andrew Jackson and Henry Clay from the West. Jackson won in the electoral college, but he did not get a majority. The House of Representatives had to decide who would be president. Clay, who had the fewest votes, was thereby eliminated. He threw his support to Adams, who was then elected. When he took office, Adams appointed Clay secretary of state. The Jacksonians then accused him of having made a "corrupt bargain" with Clay.

Four years later Jackson was elected, the first westerner to occupy the White House. His election symbolized the growth of democracy in America. During the 1820s, many states dropped property requirements for voting. And more and more presidential electors were chosen by **popular vote**—that is, by the people—rather than by state legislatures. Political parties became more democratic. Elected delegates at nominating conventions chose the parties' presidential and vice presidential candidates.

Jackson's time in office is sometimes called the era of the common man. Jacksonians believed that ordinary people could handle most government jobs without special training. Jackson discharged many government workers and replaced them with his own supporters. This practice became known as the **spoils system.**

Jackson was personally popular, but his election did not end sectional conflicts. The tariff question proved particularly troublesome. The Northeast favored high tariffs on imported manufactured goods to protect its industries. The South, which had few industries, opposed high tariffs because they tended to push up prices. John C. Calhoun of South Carolina, Jackson's vice president, argued that protective tariffs were unconstitutional. He insisted that a state could "nullify" federal laws they considered unconstitutional.

In 1832, South Carolina put Calhoun's theory into practice by nullifying the tariff. Jackson, however, denied that nullification was legal. If South Carolina refused to obey the tariff, he said, he would bring the army into the state to enforce it. Calhoun and Henry Clay worked out a "compromise" tariff that gradually lowered duties. When Congress passed this bill, South Carolina repealed its ordinance of nullification. The crisis ended, but the issue of **states' rights** versus the power of the federal government remained unsettled.

Jackson had been willing to compromise on the tariff. But on the issue of the Second Bank of the United States he was more stubborn. He distrusted all banks because he thought their practice of issuing more paper money than the gold and silver in their vaults was immoral. When Congress rechartered the Bank in 1832, Jackson vetoed it. Jackson's veto was popular, and he was easily reelected.

Jackson then determined to destroy the Bank. He withdrew all government money deposited in it, and put the money in "pet" state banks. But these banks used it to back huge amounts of paper money. Soon so much money was in circulation that prices soared. An inflationary spiral resulted that ended in a collapse of the economy in the Panic of 1837.

The third great issue of Jackson's presidency was the fate of the southern Indians. When Jackson took office, several southern tribes, including the Cherokee of Georgia, controlled large parts of the South. The Cherokee had adopted many white values. Many became farmers. They developed a written language, and in 1828 drew up a constitution. They claimed to be a kind of nation within the nation. The state of Georgia did not recognize the Cherokee Nation. In the case of *Worcester v. Georgia,* the Supreme Court declared that

In this political cartoon called "Office Hunters for the Year 1834," Jackson is a devilish puppet master pulling the strings attached to a crowd of political office seekers. What is the cartoonist's view of those who seek to ride their candidate's coattails for political gain? Do you agree?

Georgia had no jurisdiction over Cherokee land, but with Jackson's encouragement, Georgia ignored the ruling.

Nevertheless, in 1835, the Cherokee and other southern tribes were forced to move beyond the Mississippi River to land in the Oklahoma Territory.

Manifest Destiny

During the 1840s, as the country expanded westward many Americans believed the United States would soon reach the Pacific and eventually dominate all of North America. A journalist, John L. O'Sullivan, voiced this attitude in 1845. It was America's "**manifest destiny**' to occupy and to possess the whole of the Continent," he claimed.

In 1821, when Mexico became independent of Spain, it controlled all of what is now the states of Texas, New Mexico, Arizona, California, Nevada, Utah, and parts of Colorado and Wyoming. At that time, about 250,000 Indians and 50,000 Mexicans lived in this region. Encouraged at first by the Mexican government, people from the United States poured into Texas. By 1830 20,000 of them, many slaveholders, had settled there.

Most had little loyalty to the Mexican government. Few troubled to learn Spanish. Most viewed Texas as their country and themselves more Texans than citizens of Mexico. When the Mexican government abolished slavery and tried to end immigration into Texas, they revolted.

In March 1836 President Antonio López de Santa Anna of Mexico marched north and attacked the rebels. He trapped one group at the Alamo, in San Antonio, killing the entire force. A similar rout occurred at Goliad a few days later. But the Texans, commanded by Sam Houston, won a decisive victory at San Jacinto in April 1836, and Texas became independent.

While the Texans were winning their independence, people in the East were catching "Oregon Fever." Wagon trains carrying as many as a thousand people followed the Oregon Trail over the Rockies. The trip was hazardous and seemingly endless. The travelers averaged about 20 miles (32 kilometers) a day. As one pioneer wrote in 1852:

> **❝** That this journey is tiresome no one will doubt, that it is perilous, the deaths of many will testify . . . and often as I passed the freshly made graves, I have glanced at the side boards of the wagon, not knowing how soon it might serve as a coffin for some one of us.[1] **❞**

But the opportunities in Oregon made the voyage worth the risk.

[1] From "Diaries and Reminiscences of Women on the Oregon Trail: A Study in Consciousness," an unpublished essay by Amy Kesselman

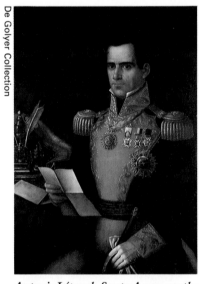

Antonio López de Santa Anna was the general who called himself the Napoleon of the West. In 1836 he led the Mexican army's siege of the Alamo. Why did Santa Anna feel he was right in leading the Mexican army into Texas? Do you think he was right?

After his election in 1844, President James K. Polk moved to bring the Republic of Texas and all of Oregon Territory into the Union. The Lone Star Republic became the Lone Star *state* in 1845. Although Polk wanted the whole of Oregon Territory, which was controlled jointly with Great Britain, in 1846 a compromise was reached. Oregon was divided by extending the boundary between Canada and the United States to the Pacific.

Mexico did not recognize the annexation of Texas by the United States, and when American troops clashed with Mexican soldiers north of the Rio Grande, Polk persuaded Congress to declare war. By summer American troops had seized much of northern Mexico, including part of California. By February 1847 San Francisco, Los Angeles, and San Diego were in American hands. In September 1847, another army led by General Winfield Scott captured the Mexican capital, Mexico City.

In the Treaty of Guadalupe Hidalgo, which ended the war, Mexico surrendered its vast northwestern territories to the United States. All told the nation had added another 2 million square miles (5 million square kilometers) to its territory.

The people who lived in the Southwest, mostly Indians and Mexicans, were very different from the Anglo Americans. Easterners who settled there were deeply influenced by the way the Mexicans and Indians lived. Today, life in the Southwest is a blend of Indian, Mexican, and Anglo cultures.

Thousands of Americans were on the move west. Most dramatic was the flood of people to California. A few days before the Treaty of Guadalupe Hidalgo was signed, gold was discovered in California. The Gold Rush was on. In 1849, more than 80,000 people flocked to California in search of fortune.

The rapid growth of California meant that it would soon become a state. The **Missouri Compromise** of 1820 admitted Missouri as a slave state. It made the rest of the Louisiana Purchase free territory north of 36°30′, but slave territory south of that line. If extended, the line would cut right through California. Many Californians wanted to enter as a free state, hoping thereby to prevent African Americans—slave or free—from entering the state. But this would break the balance of 15 slave states and 15 free states.

The issue was settled by the **Compromise of 1850,** drafted by Henry Clay. The compromise allowed California to enter the Union as a free state. The rest of the Southwest was divided into two territories where the issue of slavery would be determined by **popular sovereignty.** That is, the settlers in the territories would make that decision themselves.

The compromise prompted a famous Senate debate, but eventually it was adopted. Most Americans assumed that it would settle the issue of the spread of slavery once and for all. But, in fact, the settlement lasted only a few years.

Sam Houston commanded the Texas army. He sits astride his horse in this oil painting by Steven Seymour Thomas. Why did Houston grant Santa Anna his freedom in 1836?

The Beginnings of American History   33

Slavery and Abolition

The variety of cotton that grew well in the South was difficult to separate from the seeds. It took a skilled worker a day to remove the seeds from a single pound of this cotton. It was therefore not profitable for a farmer to grow it. But in 1793 Eli Whitney invented a simple machine—called a cotton gin—that enabled a worker to remove the seeds from fifty pounds of cotton a day. The production of cotton soared. In just eight years the output increased tenfold.

Growing cotton was a year-round activity. Seeds were planted in the early spring. The growing plants had to be weeded frequently during the summer. The harvest ran from late September to the end of the year. Large scale cotton farmers depended on slaves to do this work. As the price of cotton rose, so did the price of slaves and their importance in the southern economy.

A slave's day began early. Sunup to sundown was spent in the cotton fields or at other tasks around the plantation, always under the intimidating eye of an overseer. As a former slave described:

      " The hands are required to be in the cotton field as soon as it is light in the morning, and, with the exception of ten or fifteen minutes, which are given to them at noon to swallow their allowance of cold bacon, they are not permitted to be a moment idle till it is too dark to see, and when the moon is full, they often times labor until the middle of the night.[1]**"**

[1]From *Twelve Years a Slave* by Solomon Northrup

Culver Pictures

This is one half of a stereopticon slide, once very popular, that would show a three-dimensional image of these slaves picking cotton. Imagine viewing the slide in the comfort of your northern home in 1850. How might your future life be different from the lives of these children held as slaves?

Most planters took adequate care of their slaves because they were valuable. But some were harsh and cruel, using the whip to punish even the smallest infraction of the rules. All slaveholders looked upon their slaves as property to be bought, sold, and used as they saw fit. Slaves had no rights. Yet they maintained a distinct African American culture based on spiritual values and family relationships. Novelist Ralph Ellison has called their success in accomplishing this "one of the great triumphs of the human spirit."

Many slaves found ways to resist their masters quietly. Others rose in rebellion. These slaves had little chance of success and when captured were quickly killed by the whites. The rebels Gabriel Prosser, Denmark Vesey, Nat Turner, and their followers, for example, were all executed.

A number of whites who thought slavery wrong, but who considered blacks inferior beings, proposed freeing the slaves and then returning them to Africa. In 1817 the American Colonization Society acquired land on the west coast of Africa and enabled several thousand slaves to settle there. The area became the nation of Liberia.

More radical **abolitionists**, both black and white, demanded the immediate end of slavery. These people insisted that slavery was a barbaric practice against the laws of God. William Lloyd Garrison, the publisher of the antislavery newspaper, *The Liberator,* Sarah and Angelina Grimke, Quakers from South Carolina, and African Americans such as Frederick Douglass, Sojourner Truth, and Harriet Tubman were important abolitionists.

But in the 1850s there were very few white abolitionists. Many people of the North had come to realize that slavery was an inhuman institution. But they believed there was no legal way to force the southern states to abolish it. For the federal government to do so, every legal authority agreed, would be unconstitutional.

Reform and Romanticism

Some of the most persistent abolitionists were women, who themselves were not entirely free. Discrimination based on sex was the case everywhere in the nation. In 1848 Elizabeth Cady Stanton and Lucretia Mott organized a Women's Rights Convention at Seneca Falls, New York. The delegates to the convention issued a statement that was closely modeled on the Declaration of Independence.

While women made only limited gains, the drive for free, public, government-financed schooling for white children succeeded. In 1800 few communities in the United States maintained free schools. Reformers argued that democracy would not work unless everyone could read and write, and that public schools would train children to be patriotic, hardworking, and law-abiding citizens. By the 1850s communities all over the country had established public elementary

Elizabeth Cady Stanton, above, and Lucretia Coffin Mott, below, organized and led the Women's Rights Convention at Seneca Falls, New York.

The Beginnings of American History   35

Horace Mann was a great leader in the efforts to improve public education. How did he use the Age of Reform to build on Massachusetts' tradition for education?

Return to the Preview & Review on page 30.

schools. By 1860 about 90 percent of white adults could read and write. The public school system of Massachusetts, developed by Horace Mann, became the model for other states.

Many reformers sought to help handicapped people. Samuel Gridley Howe, a Boston doctor, founded a school for the blind. Dorothea Dix, another Massachusetts reformer, tried to improve the treatment of the mentally ill. Insanity was a disease, she insisted. She convinced many state legislatures to build asylums for the care of the mentally ill. Dix also tried to reform America's prisons.

Reformers also wanted to change the way juvenile delinquents were treated. As one put it, the system of keeping them in adult prisons turned ''little Devils'' into ''great ones.'' Other reformers viewed delinquent children as victims rather than criminals.

The crusade against drunkenness, another reform movement, began with a call for **temperance**—drinking in moderation. This soon turned into a demand for the **prohibition,** outlawing, of the manufacture and sale of all alcoholic beverages.

The religious revival known as the Second Great Awakening influenced many reformers of this period. The leading preacher of this revival, Charles Grandison Finney, stressed the duty of people to take the ''right ground . . . on all subjects of practical morality.'' Moral and social reform became the central interest of many church groups. Finney and others challenged the notion ''that Christians can remain neutral and keep still, and yet enjoy the . . . blessing of God.'' Some religious reformers thought the best way to improve society was by creating **ideal communities**—places where people could develop and practice one or another special way of life. These groups included the Shakers, Amana in Iowa, and Oneida in New York.

A group of New Englanders calling themselves transcendentalists believed that people could transcend, or go beyond, reason if they had faith in themselves. The transcendentalists celebrated basic human goodness, individualism, and self-reliance.

Transcendentalists like Ralph Waldo Emerson and Henry David Thoreau were part of the Romantic movement. Romantics valued feeling and instinct more than reason and logic. They saw nature as a beautiful, if mysterious, teacher.

Edgar Allan Poe—master of the detective story and horror tale—was probably the most original of the Romantic writers. The novelists Nathaniel Hawthorne and Herman Melville explored the darker side of life, focusing on the struggle between good and evil. In contrast, Walt Whitman—among the greatest of American poets—emphasized the positive aspects of life.

A number of New Englanders other than the transcendentalists contributed to the literature of the mid-1800s. Henry Wadsworth Longfellow gained fame for such long narrative poems as *The Song of Hiawatha*. Other poets of this ''flowering of New England'' were Emily Dickinson and John Greenleaf Whittier.

America's West African Heritage

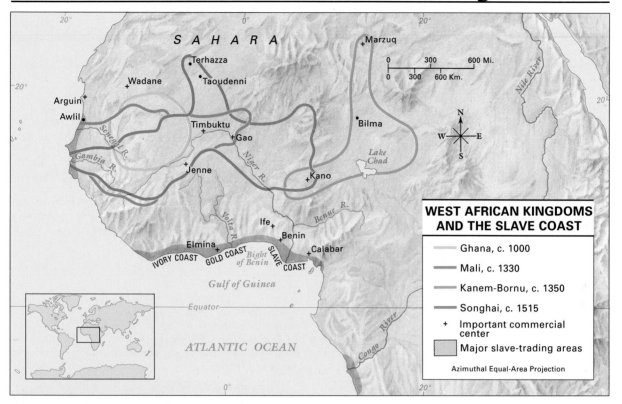

WEST AFRICAN KINGDOMS
AND THE SLAVE COAST

Ghana, c. 1000
Mali, c. 1330
Kanem-Bornu, c. 1350
Songhai, c. 1515
+ Important commercial center
Major slave-trading areas

Azimuthal Equal-Area Projection

For more than a thousand years great civilizations rose and fell in West Africa south of the Sahara. Why these kingdoms came to be—the will of a powerful ruler, a favorable place to trade—and why so little of their grand architecture remains—is as much a mystery to us as why Egypt and Rome declined and fell, or, closer to home, what fate befell the Mayan civilization.

Our African heritage is not that of a "dark continent" but rather that of the place where civilizations developed and culture advanced. Consider Egypt, one of the world's greatest civilizations. Consider Ghana, Mali, and Songhai, in the Western Sudan. Each of these kingdoms had an elaborate court life with artisans organized into guilds before Europe's Renaissance.

Other West African kingdoms—Asante, Dahomey, the Yoruba, and Benin—flourished in the forest lands farther south toward the West African Coast. Trade was important to their economies, and travelers to Africa wrote descriptions of the regal courts, especially in Benin, where magnificent bronzes were cast. Only with the permission of the king could artisans cast brass.

In eastern Africa later kingdoms—Zimbabwe and Mwanamutapa—grew powerful. Recent research shows that slaves preserved many aspects of their culture. However, because slaves were forbidden to speak their own tongues and produce their own art, much of our African heritage was lost. But their voices still speak to us of Africa's past in the art we look at here.

West Africa was the site of several great trading kingdoms. For centuries they traded mostly with Arab merchants who traveled in camel caravans. When Europeans began to explore the coast in the early 1500s, many turned to coastal trade. They soon discovered that captured Africans, sold as slaves, were a valuable commodity.

The Brooklyn Museum

A hornblower from Benin summons us to our study of Western African culture. This figure was cast in brass in the 17th century.

37

Below is the figure of a king of the Asante culture in Ghana. He was carved from wood in the 19th century and wields the symbol of his authority.

Metropolitan Museum of Art

Royalty's pride is evident in this dark bronze altarpiece displayed in Benin City in Nigeria. To this day the Nigerian king wears a cap and choker similar to that in this 16th-century work.

Metropolitan Museum of Art

Again from the 19th century, this beaded stool, surely fit for a ruler, comes from the Cameroons. It may have been fashioned by workers from Benin or Yoruba.

Metropolitan Museum of Art

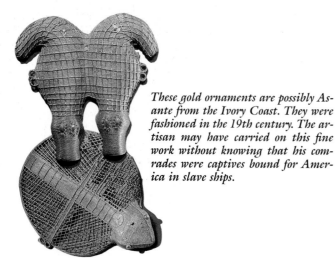

These gold ornaments are possibly Asante from the Ivory Coast. They were fashioned in the 19th century. The artisan may have carried on this fine work without knowing that his comrades were captives bound for America in slave ships.

Metropolitan Museum of Art

Asante kings drank their palm wine from this 19th-century calabash vessel decorated with gold.

© Lee Boltin

Earlier than its sister civilizations, Egypt produced this 12th-dynasty head of a sphinx made of polished stone in about 1900 B.C.

What grace there is in this wooden antelope head! It would have been attached to a cap made of basketry for ceremonies commemorating tyi wara, who taught humans the secret of agriculture. The head comes from the Bambara culture of Mali.

An ivory spoon in the figure of a man was made in Sierra Leone (in the style of Portuguese explorers) in the 16th century.

The Beginnings of American History   39

Photo by Don Renner, Courtesy of Folklorica

This woman's wrapper woven from costly threads was made by the Asante people of Ghana in the early part of this century.

The unidentified maker of this child with a bucket may have recalled traditional African figures. But the carving was made in 1860 in New York.

These dolls, probably made between 1880–1900, consist of fabric, leather, ceramics, and metal. They may recall earlier dolls held secretly in slumber by slave children.

Romare Bearden used his African American heritage for inspiration to make this 1970 collage, SHE-BA. The artist has clothed the woman in a contemporary fashion but he also recalls the famous Queen of Sheba.

Wadsworth Atheneum, Hartford

Colonial Williamsburg

40   PROLOGUE

5. A DIVIDED AMERICA

Causes of the Civil War

Politicians had expected the Compromise of 1850 to put the issue of slavery to rest. Instead, it made the situation worse. The **Fugitive Slave Act**, which made it a crime to assist an escaping slave and required people in the North to help slaveholders recapture runaways, caused great resentment.

Harriet Beecher Stowe's novel *Uncle Tom's Cabin* (1852), turned many northerners into abolitionists. The book tells the story of Tom, a devoutly religious slave who quietly accepts his bondage. Tom's goodness stands in stark contrast to the evil actions of the overseer, Simon Legree, who eventually has Tom whipped to death. Southerners condemned the book as propaganda. But its portrayal of slaves as human beings with deep feelings and emotions personalized the issue of slavery for northerners.

In 1854 the issue of slavery in the territories rose again when Senator Stephen A. Douglas of Illinois introduced a bill creating the territories of Kansas and Nebraska. Slavery was forbidden in both by the Missouri Compromise, but Douglas's bill substituted the principle of popular sovereignty. The settlers were to be allowed to decide

Preview & Review

Use these questions to guide your reading. Answer the questions after completing Section 5.
Understanding Issues, Events, & Ideas. Use the following words to describe the causes and course of the Civil War: Fugitive Slave Act, free soiler, *Dred Scott v. Sandford,* secession, border state, total war.
1. How did the split between the North and the South develop during the 1850s?
2. What were the major turning points of the Civil War? How did they change the war's course?
Thinking Critically. **1.** Imagine that as a justice on the Supreme Court in 1857, you disagree with Chief Justice Taney in *Dred Scott v. Sandford.* List your reasons for disagreeing with his ruling. **2.** Do you think President Lincoln issued the Emancipation Proclamation for moral reasons, political reasons, or both? Explain your answer.

The Brooklyn Museum

Eastman Johnson painted "A Ride for Liberty—the Fugitive Slave" in about 1862. Johnson was a famous genre *painter—that is, his frequent subject was everyday life. But this is no everyday event for the family riding fearfully north to freedom.*

whether or not to permit slavery. Antislavery northerners were determined that slavery should not gain a foothold in Kansas. Hundreds of **free soilers** rushed to settle there in order to vote against slavery. Proslavery forces in Missouri, however, crossed the border into the territory in large numbers, merely to vote. Then they returned to their homes. In the 1855 election for the territorial legislature, proslavery forces easily won a majority, largely because 5,000 of these "Border Ruffians" from Missouri voted illegally. The new legislature passed laws allowing slavery, but free soil Kansans set up their own government. Fighting broke out. Kansas territory became known as "Bleeding Kansas."

The Kansas-Nebraska Act resulted in major changes in the Whig and Democratic parties. Douglas was a Democrat. The passage of his bill caused that party to lose thousands of supporters in the North, but it made the party the leading party in the South. The Whig party lost heavily there.

Two new political organizations emerged. They attracted unhappy Whigs and northern Democrats. People alarmed by the ever-growing influx of immigrants joined the Native American party, or Know-Nothings. Other northerners joined the Republican party. The Republican platform was simple: Free Soil and Free Men. Keep slavery out of the territories.

In 1857 a new crisis erupted. A slave in Missouri, Dred Scott, had sued for his freedom because his owner had taken him to Illinois and then to Wisconsin territory, where the Missouri Compromise had prohibited slavery. The case of **Dred Scott v. Sandford** eventually worked its way to the Supreme Court. The Court declared that Scott, being a black man, was not a citizen and therefore could not sue in a federal court. It added that the Missouri Compromise was unconstitutional. Because of the Fifth Amendment of the Constitution, which stated that citizens could not be deprived of their property without due process of law, Congress could not prohibit slavery in any federal territory.

The Dred Scott case roused a storm of protest in the North. The Court had used the Bill of Rights to keep people in chains! Douglas's policy of leaving the question of slavery in the territories to the settlers was illegal. Douglas was furious because this argument weakened his position in Illinois, where he was running for reelection to the Senate in 1858.

His opponent for the Senate seat was the Republican Abraham Lincoln. During the campaign Douglas and Lincoln held seven debates in different parts of Illinois. They attracted huge crowds and much newspaper coverage all over the country. Their most important exchange came in the debate at Freeport. Lincoln asked Douglas how, after the Dred Scott decision, people could exclude slavery before a territory became a state. Douglas's answer, known as the Freeport Doctrine, was that it did not matter what the Supreme Court

Although little is known about Dred Scott, we do have this portrait made in 1858. It was painted from a photograph of Scott taken earlier.

said. Slavery could not exist in a territory if the territorial legislature did not pass laws enforcing it. This argument won him reelection in Illinois, but it ruined any hope he had of gaining southern support for the l860 Democratic presidential nomination.

Then in October l859, an abolitionist zealot, John Brown, led an attack on the federal armory at Harpers Ferry, Virginia. His aim was to seize the weapons there, arm the local slaves, and lead them in a rebellion to overthrow the peculiar institution. Troops quickly trapped the rebels. Many were killed. Brown was captured, quickly tried, found guilty of treason, and hanged. But many northerners considered Brown a martyr who had died in the cause of freedom.

The presidential election of 1860 showed how deep the rift between North and South had become. The Democratic party split in two, a southern faction nominating the incumbent vice president, John Breckinridge. Northern Democrats nominated Stephen A. Douglas. The Republicans chose Abraham Lincoln, whose debates with Douglas in the Illinois senatorial race had won him national recognition. The Constitutional Union party, which tried to ignore the controversial issues plaguing the country, chose John Bell, a senator from Tennessee. In the election Lincoln carried the North and West, Breckinridge the South, Douglas and Bell the border states. And although Lincoln got less than half the popular vote, he won a majority in the electoral college.

Many southerners feared that with a Republican in the White House, slavery would soon come under attack. Within days of Lincoln's election, the legislature of South Carolina called a special convention to consider **secession,** or leaving the Union. Southerners based their right to leave the Union on the fact that the original 13 states had existed before they joined the United States. Since each state had freely joined, surely each was free to leave the Union if it so desired. In late December South Carolina issued a declaration dissolving "the Union now hitherto existing between South Carolina and the other states." Alabama, Florida, Georgia, Louisiana, Mississippi, and Texas soon followed. These states then created the Confederate States of America, with Jefferson Davis as president.

The Civil War

While the southern states were making the decision on secession, politicians in Washington, D.C., frantically looked for solutions to the crisis. They offered several, all based on a constitutional amendment to protect slavery in the South, but none succeeded.

Lincoln tried to calm southerners' fears in his inaugural address. He said:

      66 I have no purpose, directly or indirectly, to interfere with the institution of slavery in the states where it exists. I believe I have no lawful right to do so. . . We are not

The "Little Giant," Stephen A. Douglas, was the Henry Clay of this generation. He was able to put the needs of the nation above self-interest.

The Beginnings of American History   43

The "Rail Splitter," Abraham Lincoln, is beardless in this early photograph.

enemies, but friends. We must not be enemies. Though passion may have strained, it must not break, our bonds of affection.[1]

Lincoln did not threaten to stop secession by sending troops into the South, as Jackson had. But he believed that the Union must be preserved. When he sent supplies by ship to soldiers holding Fort Sumter in the harbor of Charleston, South Carolina, the Confederates bombarded the fort, forcing its surrender. Lincoln then declared the seceded states to be in rebellion. The Civil War had begun.

Arkansas, North Carolina, Tennessee, and Virginia then seceded, but the **border states**, Delaware, Kentucky, Maryland, and Missouri, where slavery existed, remained in the Union. The North thus had an overwhelming edge in wealth and population. It had 90 percent of the nation's factories and a much better transportation system. But the southerners were defending their own homes. The North would have to invade the South to force it back into the Union. In addition, southerners expected the backing of the European nations whose textile mills desperately needed "King Cotton."

In both the North and the South thousands of young men rushed to volunteer for the fight. The two armies reflected Lincoln's vivid phrase, "a house divided against itself." Colonel Robert E. Lee of Virginia, Lincoln's first choice to be commander of the Union army, refused to fight against his own state and was soon put in charge of the Confederate army. Friends (even brothers) fought on opposite sides in battles as bloody as any the world had ever seen.

The first major battle came in July 1861 at Bull Run Creek, southwest of Washington, D.C. Northern civilians, some carrying picnic lunches, came out to watch the battle. The northern forces broke through the enemy lines at first, but the Confederates stopped them and drove them back in disorder toward Washington.

No quick victory was possible for either side. The Confederates felt that if they fought a defensive war and could draw the war out, the people of the North would tire of the fight and ask for peace. Union strategists knew they had to attack. Their three-part strategy was aimed at squeezing the life out of the Confederacy. The Union navy would blockade southern ports, cutting off supplies from abroad. A western army would seize control of the Mississippi, thus splitting the Confederacy in two. And another army would strike directly at the Confederate capital, Richmond, Virginia.

Life in both sections changed dramatically as the war dragged on. As casualties increased, both sides instituted conscription, the drafting of men for military service. The draft laws favored the rich, however, because they allowed draftees to hire substitutes or to pay a fee exempting them from service. Poor people complained that the conflict was "a rich man's war and a poor man's fight."

[1]From "First Inaugural Address" by Abraham Lincoln

This is ever the price of war. Here lie Confederate soldiers who have fallen in front of Dunker Church at Antietam in September 1862.

With so many men in the military, many women took their places on farms and in offices and factories. Government offices depended on female clerks. Both northern and southern women also became nurses, following the lead of Clara Barton. The North, which already had an efficient industrial system, was able to function at full output. But the South had to build foundries and factories from scratch. It lagged far behind the North in war production. Both sides suffered from inflation. Prices in the North nearly doubled, but in the South they soared by over 9,000 percent! The Union blockade slowly choked off foreign trade with the Confederacy. Eventually the South suffered severe shortages, even of basic necessities.

During the early years, the fortunes of war favored the South. Lee and the other confederate generals repeatedly outmaneuvered Union leaders, inflicting defeat after defeat on them. But when Lee tried to invade the North, the Union won an important victory at Sharpsburg, Maryland, on Antietam Creek (September 1862). Both sides suffered heavy losses at Antietam, but Antietam was a turning point in the war. The cost of the war in blood and money was changing the way many northerners felt about slavery. Lincoln had decided to try to free the slaves as a way to weaken the Confederacy. However, he needed to link such an announcement to a military victory. Antietam gave him the victory he needed to act.

The Emancipation Proclamation stated that after January 1, 1863, "all persons held as slaves within any States . . . in rebellion against the United States shall be . . . forever free."

However, the crucial turning point of the war came in July 1863. Lee had again invaded the North, hoping that a decisive victory on

The Beginnings of American History   45

Ulysses S. Grant posed for this picture during the Battle of the Wilderness in 1864. What strategy devised by Grant brought the war to an end?

northern soil would cause the United States to give up the struggle. On July 1 some of his soldiers accidentally ran into Union troops in Gettysburg, Pennsylvania. Swiftly the two armies converged. After fierce fighting, Union forces held the ground, and the Confederates had to retreat to the South. Shortly thereafter Lincoln went to Gettysburg to dedicate a cemetery for the Union dead. His Gettysburg Address was a noble expression of the purpose of the Civil War and of the ideals of American democracy:

> **❝** Four score and seven years ago our fathers brought forth on this continent a new nation, conceived in liberty, and dedicated to the proposition that all men are created equal.
>
> Now we are engaged in a great civil war, testing whether that nation, or any nation so conceived and so dedicated, can long endure. We are met on a great battlefield of that war. We have come to dedicate a portion of that field as a final resting place for those who here gave their lives that that nation might live. It is altogether fitting and proper that we should do this.
>
> But, in a larger sense, we cannot dedicate—we cannot consecrate—we cannot hallow—this ground. The brave men, living and dead, who struggled here, have consecrated it far above our poor power to add or detract. The world will little note nor long remember what we say here, but it can never forget what they did here. It is for us, the living, rather, to be dedicated here to the unfinished work for which they who fought here have thus far so nobly advanced. It is rather for us to be here dedicated to the great task remaining before us—that from these honored dead we take increased devotion to that cause for which they gave the last full measure of devotion; that we here highly resolve that these dead shall not have died in vain; that this nation, under God, shall have a new birth of freedom; and that government of the people, by the people, for the people, shall not perish from the earth. **❞**

At the same time that Union troops were defeating the Confederates at Gettysburg, a western army was gaining control of the Mississippi River. In April 1862 a fleet commanded by Admiral David Farragut had captured New Orleans. Now the troops of General Ulysses S. Grant put the Confederate stronghold of Vicksburg, Mississippi, under siege. On July 4, 1863, Vicksburg surrendered. Texas and Arkansas were cut off from the rest of the Confederacy.

In March 1864 Lincoln gave Grant command of all the Union forces. Grant then devised a strategy that ended the war. He would lead the Army of the Potomac against Lee, seeking a showdown in northern Virginia. Another army, under General William Tecumseh Sherman, would drive into Georgia and attack Atlanta. Sherman

captured Atlanta in September 1864 and burned the city to the ground. He then marched through Georgia to Savannah on the Atlantic Coast. On this march his troops left a path of destruction 60 miles (96 kilometers) wide. This was carrying out what is now called **total war,** the destroying of civilian as well as military resources in order to break the enemy's will to fight. Sherman's troops entered Savannah in December. They then turned north, destroying large parts of the Carolinas with the same cold-blooded efficiency.

During the spring of 1864 Grant made slow headway in his offensive against Richmond. Lee repeatedly foiled Grant's maneuvers, inflicting heavy casualties. In one month, the Union army lost more than 55,000 men. But the Confederates took heavy losses too. Backed by the almost unlimited resources of the North, Grant continued to advance. But Lee was running out of equipment and men. By summer, Grant had put the city of Petersburg, a few miles south of Richmond, under siege.

In early April 1865 Lee had to abandon Petersburg. Grant's troops cut off his retreat and on April 8 Lee had to surrender. The following day, he met with Grant at Appomattox Court House and signed the terms of surrender. The war was over. It had cost more than 600,000 lives. The North had become an industrial giant. The South had been devastated: it would need to be rebuilt, and the sectional wounds that had caused the war would have to be healed. Lincoln closed his second inaugural address with these hopeful words:

66 With malice toward none, with charity for all, with firmness in the right as God gives us to see the right, let us strive on to finish the work we are in, to bind up the nation's wounds, to care for him who shall have borne the battle and for his widow and his orphan, to do all which may achieve and cherish a just and lasting peace among ourselves and with all nations."99

It remained to be seen if the rest of the nation would adopt Lincoln's forgiving approach.

Above, "Summer" shows Robert E. Lee on Traveller with his generals at his side in 1863.

Point of View

Despite his use of total war to bring the South to its knees, Sherman despised war.

66 It is only those who have neither fired a shot nor heard the shrieks and groans of the wounded who cry aloud for more blood, more vengeance, more desolation. War is hell. 99

William Tecumseh Sherman, 1865

Return to the Preview & Review on page 41.

PROLOGUE REVIEW

| 25,000 B.C. | 1475 | | 1575 | |

25,000 B.C.
Great
Migration
begins

1492
Columbus
sails to
America

1565
St. Augustine
founded

1607
Jamestown
founded

1619
First Africans
brought to colonies

Prologue Summary
Read the statements below. Choose one, and write a paragraph explaining its importance.
1. America was discovered at least three times—by Asian wanderers, by the Vikings, and by Columbus.
2. Early Native American cultures were strongly influenced by the environment and developed many unique life styles.
3. Objections to British colonial policies led to the development of the independence movement in America.
4. The major task after the Revolutionary War was establishing government—at the state and national levels. The Articles of Confederation proved inadequate to the task, prompting the writing of the U.S. Constitution.
5. The Louisiana Purchase in 1803 and the Transcontinental Treaty of 1819 more than doubled the area of the United States.
6. Disagreements between the United States and Britain continued, pushing the two countries into another war in 1812.
7. The Industrial Revolution, European immigration, and the Transportation Revolution caused rapid change in the early 1800s.
8. Andrew Jackson's election as president reflected a trend of growing democracy.
9. Between 1820 and 1850 an attitude of manifest destiny swept the country, and large numbers of people moved westward.
10. The failure of various compromises on the slavery issue caused increased sectional conflict that resulted in the outbreak of the Civil War, which the North eventually won.

Reviewing Chronological Order
Number your paper 1-5. Then study the time lines throughout the Prologue and place the following events in the order in which they happened by writing the first next to 1, the second next to 2, and so on.

1. Emancipation Proclamation
2. Jamestown founded
3. Boston Massacre
4. Nullification Crisis
5. United States Constitution ratified

Understanding Main Ideas
1. How did changes in Europe lead to the exploration and colonization of the Americas?
2. What steps did the framers of the Constitution take to make sure no one branch of government gained too much power?
3. What regional differences had developed in the United States by the 1820s?
4. In your own words, explain what manifest destiny meant to Americans in the mid-1800s.
5. Why did the Union win the Civil War?

Thinking Critically
1. **Synthesizing.** Imagine that you are a member of Virginia's ratifying convention. You are reluctant to ratify the Constitution while it has no Bill of Rights. Give reasons for this stand. What might convince you to accept the Constitution without a Bill of Rights?
2. **Evaluating.** You are a slave attempting to persuade your fellow slaves to revolt against your cruel master. What would you say to convince them?
3. **Drawing Conclusions.** Some historians suggest that the failure of politicians caused the Civil War. What do you think these historians mean by this? Do you agree or disagree? Give reasons for your answer.

Writing About History: Expressive
Imagine you are a newspaper editor in the early 1860s. Write an editorial predicting what the nation will face in the aftermath of the Civil War. Include what you think should be solutions to the major problems facing the country.

1675	1775	1875

1740
Great Awakening

1750
Enlightenment
in America

1763
England wins
French and Indian
War

1770
Boston
Massacre

1775
Lexington
and Concord

1776
Declaration of
Independence

1781
War ends in
colonial victory

1788
United States
of America
established

1791
Bill of Rights
adopted

1803
Louisiana
Purchase

1812
War with
Britain

1823
Monroe
Doctrine

1836
Republic of
Texas proclaimed

1848
Seneca Falls
Convention

1849
California
Gold Rush

1860
Lincoln elected
president

1861
Civil War
begins

1865
Civil War
ends

★
Reconstruction
begins

Using Primary Sources

After a visit to the United States, French writer and politician Alexis de Tocqueville wrote *Democracy in America,* an analysis of the American political and social system in the early 1800s. As you read the following excerpt, ask yourself why de Tocqueville found the workings of American democracy so fascinating. Then answer the questions below.

Democratic government makes the idea of political rights spread to all citizens, just as the division of property puts the general idea of property rights within reach of all. That, in my view, is one of its greatest advantages.

I'm not saying that it is an easy matter to teach all people to make use of political rights; I only say that when that can happen, the results are important. . . .

In America the people were given political rights at a time when it was difficult for them to misuse them because the citizens were few and their ways of life simple. As they have grown more powerful, the Americans have not greatly increased the powers of democracy. Rather they have extended their democracy by increasing the number of people who have political rights. . . .

1. According to de Tocqueville, what is one of democracy's greatest advantages?
2. Why do you think de Tocqueville was so fascinated with democracy in America?
3. British leader Sir Winston Churchill once said that democracy was the worst form of government ever invented, except for all the rest. Do you think that de Tocqueville would agree with Churchill's assessment? Give reasons for your answer.

Linking History & Geography

Because of the great distance to Canada, slaves on the Underground Railroad faced many hardships. Below are a number of Underground Railroad routes. Refer to a map of the United States for help in creating a map that shows each route. For each route, indicate the number of miles (and kilometers) from the first "station" to the Canadian border. Then on the map indicate with special symbols the hardships escaped slaves might encounter on these routes.

1. Charleston (South Carolina), Philadelphia, New York City, Albany, Canada.
2. Evansville (Indiana), Indianapolis, Toledo, Detroit, Canada.
3. Norfolk (Virginia), Boston, Montpelier, Canada.

Enriching Your Study of History

1. **Individual Project.** Complete *one* of the following projects: draw an eye-catching poster with an attention-getting slogan to attract European settlers to one of the early American colonies; construct a model or large-scale drawing of either a southern plantation or a northern textile mill; *or* draw a map of one of the ideal communities set up in the United States in the mid-1800s. Display your finished project for the class.
2. **Cooperative Project.** Working with other members of the class, create a map of the United States using place names that illustrate the many different cultures that have contributed to life in the United States. Display the map on the bulletin board.

The Beginnings of American History   49

The arrival of the daily train to Sacramento, California, is the subject of "Sacramento Railroad Station."

A CHANGING AMERICA

UNIT 1

This unit begins with the problems of Reconstruction—the process of rebuilding and reuniting the nation and its people. The patterns of racial discrimination and segregation that grew out of Reconstruction make up a dark chapter in the story of America. Meanwhile, Americans spread over the Great Plains, turning that vast region from Indian hunting grounds to farmland. Other Americans used iron and steel, oil, and electricity to make the United States the greatest industrial nation in the world. Huge and complex businesses developed, and efforts to regulate them became necessary. Workers formed unions to protect them from their powerful employers. Millions of immigrants flocked to America from southern, central, and eastern Europe and Asia. The unit concludes with a study of national politics and culture from the time of Reconstruction to the end of the 19th century.

Reconstruction

When the Civil War was ended and the slaves were set free, the problem of racial prejudice in the United States was not solved. When the slaves were freed, few thought of returning to Africa. In many cases America had been home for their families for 200 years. Yet African Americans still did not enjoy full citizenship during Reconstruction. Instead, they were now systematically excluded in the clearest form of prejudice, based on race. So-called "Jim Crow laws" and "Black Codes" passed after the Civil War greatly restricted the movement of former slaves. Amendments to the Constitution attempted to do away with race or skin color as a condition of voting, but "separate but equal" facilities, then permitted by the Supreme Court, effectively segregated black people from white. What long night of injustice and terror lay ahead?

Library of Congress

The assassin who tore Abraham Lincoln from a nation finally at peace also took the president from his son Tad. A photographer from Brady Studio made this nice study of father and son.

1. RADICALS AND MODERATES

Lincoln is Assassinated

On the evening of April 9, 1865, President Lincoln received a telegram from General Grant: ''GENERAL LEE SURRENDERED THE ARMY OF NORTHERN VIRGINIA THIS MORNING.'' Next day the whole country had the news. Bells rang out, bands played, flags and banners flew everywhere in the North. A crowd gathered outside the White House. ''Tad'' Lincoln, the president's 12-year-old son, appeared at the window happily waving a captured Confederate flag. Everyone cheered.

Unfortunately, this happy national mood did not last. On the evening of April 14 Abraham and Mary Todd Lincoln were attending a play at Ford's Theater in Washington. Suddenly a shot rang out. John Wilkes Booth, a little-known actor who sympathized with the South, had slipped into the president's box and fired a bullet into his head. A popular writer described the assassination with these words:

> Booth kept his eye to the gimlet hole. The head in front of him barely moved. The universe seemed to pause for breath. Then Trenchard [a character on stage] said:' 'Don't know the manners of good society, eh?' Booth did not wait to hear the rest of the line. The derringer was now in his hand. He turned the knob. The door swung inward. Lincoln, facing diagonally away toward the left, was four feet from him. Booth moved along the wall. . . .
>
> The derringer was behind the President's head between the left ear and the spine. Booth squeezed the trigger and there was a sound as though someone had blown up and broken a heavy paper bag. It came in the midst of laughter, so that some people heard it, and some did not. The President did not move. His head inclined toward his chest and he stopped rocking. . . .
>
> A chrysanthemum of blue smoke hung in Box 7. Booth, with no maniacal [crazy] gleam, no frenzy, looked at the people who looked at him and said, 'Sic semper tyrannis! [Thus always to tyrants!] . . . Revenge for the South!'[1]

The next day the president died.

Booth escaped from the theater in the confusion and fled to Virginia. He was hunted down and trapped in a barn. The barn was set on fire, but Booth was killed by a bullet. Whether he was shot by someone else or killed himself is not clear.

The people of the North were shocked and grief-stricken. The Confederacy had surrendered, but the nation was still badly divided.

[1]From *The Day Lincoln Was Shot* by Jim Bishop

Use these questions to guide your reading. Answer the questions after completing Section 1.
Understanding Issues, Events, & Ideas. Describe the political problems after the Civil War, using the following words: assassination, Moderates, amnesty, Radicals, watershed, freedmen, Thirteenth Amendment, Black Codes, Reconstruction, Freedman's Bureau, veto, Civil Rights Act, override.
1. What did the Moderate Republicans think should be done to the South after the Civil War? What did the Radical Republicans think?
2. Why was the Thirteenth Amendment passed? What was the purpose of the Black Codes?
3. Why did Congress pass the Civil Rights Act?
Thinking Critically. Write a newspaper obituary for Abraham Lincoln. Include what you consider to be his greatest accomplishment.

Lincoln lay for nine hours in a boarding house near Ford's Theater before he expired from his assassin's bullet. Alexander Hay Ritchie made this etching.

Few people realized the tremendous task of binding the nation's wounds that lay ahead. But now the leader who had guided them through the war was gone. Walt Whitman wrote a memorial to the dead president:

     " O Captain! my Captain! our fearful trip is done,
       The ship has weathered every rack, the prize we sought
         is won,
       The port is near, the bells I hear; the people all
         exulting.
       While follow eyes the steady keel, the vessel grim and
         daring;
        But O heart! heart! heart!
         O the bleeding drops of red,
           Where on the deck my Captain lies,
            Fallen cold and dead.[1] **"**

The president's death left a terrible void at such a critical time. No one knew it yet, but another great struggle—this one over control of the defeated South—would extend the bitterness of the war for several more years.

President Andrew Johnson

Much now depended on Andrew Johnson, who became president after the **assassination** of President Lincoln. Before the Civil War Johnson had served in both houses of Congress and as governor of Tennessee. The Republicans had picked him to run for vice president in 1864, even though he was a Democrat. He was one of the few

[1]From "O Captain! my Captain!" by Walt Whitman

pro-Union politicians who came from a Confederate state. His home state of Tennessee was not even a member of the Union when he became president!

All through his career Johnson had been a champion of the small farmer. He favored laws to improve public education and provide free farms, or homesteads, for families who would settle on the public lands. He was always critical of great wealth. This helps explain his hatred of the southern planters he called "traitorous aristocrats."

Most Republican politicians expected Johnson to make a fine president. Moderate Republicans believed that "malice toward none" was the best policy and hoped he would extend it to the South. They hoped, as Lincoln had put it in his moving speech at his second inauguration, "to bind up the nation's wounds" quickly.

Johnson pleased the **Moderates** by issuing an **amnesty,** or pardon, to most former Confederates. Those who would take an oath of loyalty to the United States would regain full citizenship. The states of the former Confederacy could hold elections and send representatives and senators to Congress.

On the other hand, Republicans who were determined to protect the rights of the newly freed slaves, called **Radicals,** expected Johnson to act on his well-known dislike of the southern planter class and force the planters to accept the new ways. Congressman Thaddeus Stevens of Pennsylvania was one of the Radical leaders. He demanded that the United States seize the property of the large slaveholders and give it to the ex-slaves. There would be plenty of "rebel land," he said, to give a 40-acre farm (16 hectares) to every adult male ex-slave in the South. His plan was never put into effect.

The Aftermath of War

The American Revolution had been a **watershed,** or turning point in history, bringing great political changes. The new nation forged out of that revolution was unique, a government based on the consent of the governed. The Civil War also was a watershed. The secession of the southern states had challenged the very existence of the nation. From the ashes of war a dramatically different society emerged. The Civil War, historian Bruce Catton pointed out, destroyed "the old bases on which society stood. . . . The Civil War was a beginning, rather than an end, simply because it ended forever one of the things on which American society had been built." All Americans had to face the moral and legal questions of slavery. Had the war to end slavery in the United States succeeded? What would now happen to the former slaves?

War's end freed more than 4 million Americans from slavery. But their social and economic positions in the reconstructed nation were still undefined. The war also demolished the life style white southerners had enjoyed before the war. Plantations could no longer rely on slaves for labor, and the war had virtually destroyed the wealth of many planters. The structure of southern society had been disrupted. Was it fair that a few planters had controlled so much of the southern wealth and power? Everyone in the South, rich and poor, now found themselves in a world almost as new as that encountered by the first colonists.

Who in the South gained from the changes? Certainly the slaves gained their freedom. But their world had been torn apart too. They now faced social and economic conditions totally unlike any they had ever known. All were eager to test the limits of their new freedom. Poor whites also gained something. Although they now had to compete with the freed slaves for jobs and status, many hoped to obtain farmlands from the shattered plantations. This gave them hope for a better future.

Northerners' views of southern society changed too. At first many wanted to punish the "rebels." Later, myths about a land of prosperous plantations, fatherly masters, and contented slaves began to emerge. Such a South became the setting for many books and plays published in the years after the war. But the southerners, black and white, knew that these tales were of a South that had never existed.

Finally, the war cost the nation more than 600,000 lives. It caused enormous property losses, especially in the Confederacy. The total war just ended had ravaged farms, railroads, and factories throughout the South. How long would it take to rebuild what the war had destroyed and at what cost?

The Black Codes

The Radicals were also concerned about the way former slaves, called **freedmen**, were being treated in the South. By the end of 1865 all the southern state governments set up under Johnson's amnesty plan had ratified the new **Thirteenth Amendment** to the Constitution, which officially abolished slavery. But white people formed the majority in most parts of the South. They were powerful and well organized. Southern blacks could not protect their new rights without northern help. The new southern governments did not allow black people to vote. Their legislatures swiftly passed regulations called **Black Codes** designed to keep blacks in a condition of semi-slavery.

These codes barred blacks from any kind of work except farming and household service. Some states forced blacks to sign labor contracts with landowners at the beginning of each year. If they left their work, they received no pay. If they refused to sign, they were arrested and charged with being tramps. The "sentence" was to work for one of the landowners for the year.

These Black Codes alarmed most northerners. The results of the new southern elections alarmed them even more. Southern voters,

The Granger Collection

all of them white, chose as leaders many of the same people who had led them during the rebellion. Several Confederate generals were elected to Congress. The Georgia legislature picked Alexander H. Stephens, vice president of the Confederacy, to represent the state in the United States Senate. Stephens had recently been paroled from prison after being charged with treason for his role in the Confederacy.

The newly elected representatives were members of the Democratic party. Admitting them was too much even for Moderate Republicans to accept. Both houses of Congress voted not to admit the new southern representatives. Johnson's plan for **Reconstruction—** bringing southern states back into the Union—was rejected.

Life for many freed slaves did not seem to improve after the Civil War. Such is the plight of these Virginia farmers in about 1900. The butchered hogs had to be lowered into scalding water until their bristles could be scrubbed off. What must have been the joys of freedom? What the sorrows?

Johnson and the Republicans

The Republicans in Congress then began to reconstruct the South according to their own ideas. Before the end of the war Congress had created a **Freedman's Bureau** run by the army to care for refugees. Early in 1866 a new bill was passed increasing the power of the Bureau to protect southern blacks.

President Johnson decided to **veto,** or refuse to approve, this Freedmen's Bureau Bill. He claimed that he approved of the purpose of the bill. He was eager, he said, "to secure for the freedmen . . . their freedom and property and their entire independence." But he argued that it was unconstitutional to apply military law to civilians in peacetime.

Congress therefore attacked the Black Codes by passing a **Civil Rights Act.** This law made blacks citizens of the United States. It

Radicals and Moderates 57

INTERPRETING HISTORY: Reconstruction

Reconstruction is one of the most controversial topics considered by historians. Lincoln hoped Reconstruction would "bind up the nation's wounds" caused by the Civil War. Lincoln based his plan on "malice toward none." But his plan was doomed to failure. As historian Eric Foner said, "What remains certain is that Reconstruction failed, and that for blacks its failure was a disaster whose magnitude cannot be obscured by the genuine accomplishments that did endure."

In the late 19th century white northerners and southerners concentrated on reconciling their differences. The historians of the period, the most influential being William A. Dunning of Columbia University, argued that the Radical Republicans had been cruel and vindictive people, eager for revenge. He also claimed that the freed blacks had proved to be incapable of self-government and that they had been taken advantage of by cynical carpetbaggers. The resulting "Black Republican" governments imposed high taxes on southerners and spent the money either wastefully or for their own direct benefit. Reconstruction became known as "the tragic era."

The first historian to challenge this view was W.E.B. DuBois. He claimed in *Black Reconstruction* (1935) that Reconstruction was an effort by both whites and blacks to create a "true democratic society." It failed because it did not go far enough, explained DuBois: "One fact and one alone explains that attitude of writers toward Reconstruction, they cannot conceive of Negroes as men." DuBois described the achievements of the Reconstruction governments, such as the schools, railroads, and other public institutions that they built. Then in the 1960s, during the intense civil rights movement, historians began to further revise the traditional view. Kenneth Stampp, in *The Era of Reconstruction* (1965), insisted the Radicals were genuine reformers out to defend the rights of blacks and that most black legislators had been good public servants. Moreover, they had never dominated the state governments of the period. Reconstruction failed not because of what it did to southern whites but because it did not implement the reforms necessary to ensure African Americans equal rights.

The most recent authority, Eric Foner, calls Reconstruction "America's Unfinished Revolution." Blacks took advantage of the new educational opportunities eagerly. They used their liberty to move from place to place to escape from backbreaking labor and find new opportunities. They changed the way southern crops, especially cotton, were grown. Their revolution was real, Foner writes, but unfinished in the sense that their full use of their freedom was denied them and even today has not been fully achieved.

was necessary to state this specifically because the Dred Scott decision had declared that even free blacks were not American citizens. The bill also forbade the southern states from restricting the rights of freedmen by special laws like the Black Codes.

President Johnson vetoed this bill too. It was a mistake to make blacks citizens, he now insisted. They needed to go through a period of "probation" before receiving this "prize." It was unconstitutional to give blacks "safeguards which go infinitely beyond any that the . . . Government has ever provided for the white race," he said.

As this veto made clear, Johnson's dislike of southern planters did not keep him from being prejudiced against blacks. Great wealth in the hands of a few plantation owners was what he really hated, not slavery. He had once said that he wished every white family in America could have one slave "to take the drudgery" out of life!

In April 1866 both houses of Congress again passed the Civil Rights Act. They obtained the two-thirds majority necessary to **override** the president's veto. This was the first veto of an important law ever to be overridden. Thus the Civil Rights Act became law a year after the war ended. 📧

Return to the Preview & Review on page 53.

2. THE CIVIL WAR AMENDMENTS

The Reconstruction Acts

Next, Congress passed and sent to the states for ratification what became the **Fourteenth Amendment** to the Constitution. In many ways this measure was even more important than the Thirteenth Amendment. The Republicans in Congress drafted it in order to put the terms of the Civil Rights Act directly into the Constitution.

"All persons born or naturalized in the United States," the amendment said, "are citizens of the United States *and of the State wherein they reside.*" This made blacks citizens no matter where in the nation they lived. Then the amendment struck down the Black Codes. "No State shall . . . abridge the privileges and immunities of citizens of the United States; nor shall any State deprive any person of life, liberty, or property, without due process of law."

The Fourteenth Amendment guaranteed equal protection of the laws to all Americans. It did not make racial **segregation,** or separation, illegal. It did not even tell states to allow blacks to vote. It did provide blacks with equal access to the courts, and it forbade laws that applied only to backs but not whites. Nevertheless, most white southerners objected to it strongly. Since the southern states refused to ratify the amendment, it was impossible to get the approval of three fourths of the states, which was necessary to make it part of

Use these questions to guide your reading. Answer the questions after completing Section 2.
Understanding Issues, Events, & Ideas. Using the following words, explain how the rights of African Americans were affected after the Civil War: Fourteenth Amendment, segregation, Reconstruction Act, impeachment, Tenure of Office Act, Fifteenth Amendment, Civil War Amendments.

1. Why was the Fourteenth Amendment passed?
2. How did Republicans use the Reconstruction Act to force southerners to give blacks the right to vote?
3. Why did the Republican leaders of Congress want to remove President Johnson from office?
4. How would northern blacks have influenced the election of 1868 if they had been allowed to vote?

Thinking Critically. 1. How would you view the Fourteenth Amendment if you were a conservative white southerner? A Radical Republican? An ex-slave in the South? 2. Which of the Civil War Amendments do you think is the most important? Why?

The Granger Collection

"The First Vote" is the title of this drawing. Discuss whether or not elections such as these counted—or whether the votes were even tallied.

59

Andrew Johnson's course toward the South was watched with special interest by Ulysses S. Grant.

"But for the assassination of Mr. Lincoln, I believe the great majority of the Northern people, and the soldiers unanimously, would have been in favor of a speedy reconstruction on terms that would be least humiliating to the people who rebelled against their government. . . ."

From *Personal Memoirs,*
Ulysses S. Grant, 1885

White House Historical Association

Although cartoonists often poked fun at him, there was a kindliness about Lincoln that his photographers captured. Andrew Johnson, shown here in his presidential portrait, lacked this trait. Was it his manner or his policies that riled his critics, according to what you've read?

the Constitution. These amendments became the legal basis of the Civil Rights movement of the 1960s.

President Johnson made his conflict with the Republicans an issue in the Congressional elections of November 1866. He campaigned back and forth across the country, arguing for his own approach. He failed to change many minds. Indeed, most historians believe that Johnson's angry speeches probably lost more votes for his policies than they gained. The Republicans easily maintained their large majorities in both houses of Congress.

After the failure of the southern states to ratify the Fourteenth Amendment, Congress passed the **Reconstruction Act** of March 1867. This stern measure divided what it called "the rebel states" into five military districts. "Sufficient military force" to "protect all persons in their rights" was stationed in each district. To end army rule, each former state would have to draw up a new constitution that guaranteed blacks the right to vote. The state would also have to ratify the Fourteenth Amendment.

In other words, Congress ordered a military occupation of the South. Lincoln's hope that the nation could bind up its wounds in harmony had come to nothing.

White southerners hated military rule, but they hated the idea of racial equality even more. They still refused to ratify the Fourteenth Amendment. A second, and a third, and finally a fourth Reconstruction Act were passed by Congress. Each put more pressure on "the rebel states." At last, in June 1868, southern governments in which blacks participated began to be formed. These governments ratified the amendment. The final state to complete the process was Georgia, in July 1870, more than five years after the end of the Civil War.

President Johnson Is Impeached

Radical Republicans blamed President Johnson for much of the stubborn resistance of white southerners to the Reconstruction Acts. He had urged the states not to accept the Fourteenth Amendment. He had vetoed each of the Reconstruction bills, even though their repassage by large majorities was certain. In February 1868 angry Congressional leaders decided to try to remove the president from office by impeaching him.

The Constitution provides that the House of Representatives, by majority vote, can bring charges against a president. This is called **impeachment.** The charges are judged by the Senate, with the chief justice of the United States presiding over the trial. A two-thirds majority vote is required for conviction and removal from office.

The Radicals brought 11 charges against the president. Most of them were totally without merit. The most serious accusation was that he had violated the **Tenure of Office Act** of 1867 by dismissing Edwin M. Stanton, the secretary of war. This law prohibited the

president from *discharging* appointed officials without the consent of Congress.

Johnson believed that the Tenure of Office Act was unconstitutional. The Constitution states only that Senate approval is necessary for the *appointment* of high officials. In the past no one had challenged the right of a president to remove an appointee without consulting the Senate.

Johnson dismissed Stanton deliberately to bring the issue before the Supreme Court, where it could properly be decided. Impeaching the president was clearly not justified by the facts. Indeed, his term was almost over. But many members of Congress believed that Reconstruction would never be successful unless Johnson were removed from office.

The Senate sits as a court to judge whether or not Andrew Johnson will be convicted in his impeachment trial in 1868. Below is a ticket to the Senate chamber. What is the difference between impeachment and conviction?

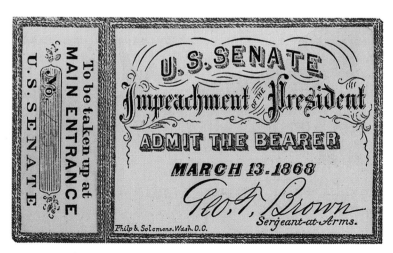

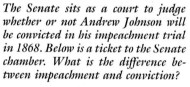

U. S. SENATE
Impeachment of the President
ADMIT THE BEARER
MARCH 13·1868
Geo. T. Brown
Sergeant-at-Arms.

To be taken up at MAIN ENTRANCE
No.
U. S. SENATE
U. S. SENATE
Philp & Solomons. Wash. D.C.

The Civil War Amendments 61

The president was spared conviction by a single vote. On each charge the Senate failed to obtain a two-thirds majority by only one vote.

Andrew Johnson remained in office until March 1869. He was a poor president. All his life he had been a valuable public servant when he was battling for reform, a lone "outsider" stubbornly attacking "the Establishment." When fate made him the head of that Establishment, he proved unable to adjust. He could not work well with other people. He made a dreadful mess of his time in the White House.

Yet Johnson was not an evil man. His Reconstruction policies seem wrong to us today, but he did not deserve to be accused of committing crimes against the nation. His problem was his inability to think of blacks as equal members of society.

The Election of 1868

A majority of the white people of his generation shared Andrew Johnson's low opinion of the character and intelligence of blacks. As we have seen, most northern states did not allow blacks to vote. However, the results of the presidential election of 1868 led to a dramatic change in this situation.

Blacks in the southern states *had* voted in that election. Federal troops stationed there under the Reconstruction Act prevented whites from keeping blacks from the polls. Eager to exercise their civic duty for the first time, many voted, and they naturally cast their ballots overwhelmingly for the Republican party.

The Republican presidential candidate, General Grant, won an easy victory in the electoral college, 214 votes to 80 for the Democratic candidate, Horatio Seymour. But in many northern states the popular vote was extremely close.

Republican politicians also felt that guaranteeing the right to vote for blacks was necessary. Maybe in future elections they could make an important difference. They reasoned that blacks could not have much power in the North. Blacks made up only about one percent of the population in that section. Why not allow them to vote? Certainly blacks would vote solidly Republican. Perhaps the hated Democrats could be kept out of power forever.

Early in 1869 the overwhelmingly Republican Congress drafted still another Constitutional amendment: "The right of citizens of the United States to vote shall not be denied . . . on account of race, color, or previous condition of servitude." Within about a year this **Fifteenth Amendment** was ratified by the states. With the Thirteenth and Fourteenth Amendments, it is one of the **Civil War Amendments** which later formed the basis of the civil rights movement of the 1960s. 🖵

Ulysses S. Grant posed for this portrait as president. After leaving the White House, poor and suffering from cancer, Grant wrote his Personal Memoirs, *which became a national best seller. Was Grant as good a president as he was a general?*

Return to the Preview & Review on page 59.

3. FREEDOM AFTER SLAVERY

The Privileges of Freedom

The Civil War Amendments did bring certain freedoms to black Americans. Freedom meant first of all the right to decide what to do with one's own time, from minute to minute and day to day. It meant lifting a terrible weight off the *minds* of nearly 4 million former slaves. It meant freedom to move about.

With freedom from slavery, most blacks had to work less hard. Now they could put down their hoes and stretch their tired muscles for a few minutes without fear of a blow or a harsh word. Parents did not send the youngest children into the fields as their former owners would have done. Old people labored less and rested more. Mothers devoted more time to their homes and children, less to planting, hoeing, and harvesting.

The former slaves also organized religious congregations. Their number and growth surprised whites who had not realized the extent to which Christian beliefs had won the hearts of the slaves. Northern black congregations sent ministers to the South to assist these new organizations.

Another use that blacks made of freedom was to seek education. Very few slaves could read and write. There had been no schools for slave children, and indeed it was against the law in most southern states even to teach a slave to read.

The preacher comes to call, making the children watchful and shy. All here are former slaves. In what ways did freedom change their lives?

Preview & Review

Use these questions to guide your reading. Answer the questions after completing Section 3.
Understanding Issues, Events, & Ideas. What was the significance during Reconstruction of the following words: ''Black Republican,'' Carpetbagger, Scalawag, sharecropping, lien, crop-lien system, world market.
1. What were some of the privileges of freedom for blacks?
2. What were some reasons Carpetbaggers and Scalawags sought public office?
3. Why was it difficult for freedmen to begin farming under the Homestead Act of 1862?
4. What were the unfortunate side effects of the crop-lien system?
Thinking Critically. 1. Imagine that you are a former slave who is now attending school. In your diary, tell why you think education is important for all blacks.
2. Compare and contrast black politicians with white politicians of the Reconstruction period.

Corcoran Gallery of Art

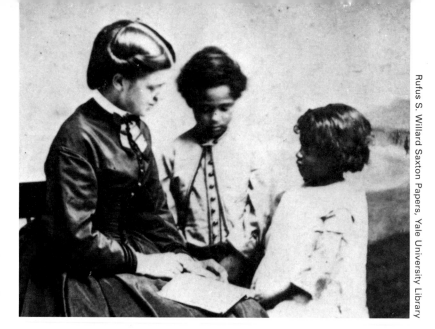

In one of the Freedman's Bureau schools eager pupils gather around their teacher, who no doubt came down from the North as a volunteer. What lie told by prejudiced whites did these schools put to rest?

The Freedmen's Bureau began to oversee schools in the South as soon as the war ended. Many religious and private groups from the North also contributed time, money, and teachers. Nearly every northern denomination founded schools and colleges to educate the most talented among the former slaves. Among the outstanding colleges for blacks started at this time were Howard University, Hampton Institute, and Fisk University.

Blacks responded eagerly to this opportunity for schooling. In South Carolina, for example, a school for blacks was set up in Charleston as soon as the Union army captured the city. By 1867 there were about 20,000 blacks attending school in that state. All over the South elderly ex-slaves could be seen learning their ABC's alongside their grandchildren.

At first most white southerners sneered at the very idea of educating the freedmen. Remember that there had not even been state-supported public schools for whites in the prewar South. But many came to admit that blacks could learn as well as whites. Most blacks who were educated became useful citizens. Thus all but the most prejudiced whites changed their minds. These whites continued, however, to oppose teaching black and white children in the same schools.

Blacks in Government

While the United States army occupied the South, blacks voted and held office in all the states of the former Confederacy. Nothing made white southerners more bitter and resentful than to be "ruled" by the very people they had totally dominated for so long.

"Rule" is not, however, the proper word to describe the role of blacks in southern politics during Reconstruction. Twenty two had served in Congress and a handful were elected to high state office during the period. Blacks held many local offices, but they seldom controlled any branch of a local government. The only state legislature that ever had a black majority was South Carolina's between 1868 and 1877.

Most of the members of the **"Black Republican"** governments, as their opponents called them, were whites. Those who came from the northern states were called **Carpetbaggers** because travelers of the period usually carried their belongings in soft-sided bags made of carpeting. The name implied that these "invaders" had no stake in the South but to get rich. Southern white Republicans were referred to scornfully by their Democratic neighbors as **Scalawags**—good-for-nothing rascals.

Carpetbaggers and Scalawags came from all walks of life—military personnel, planters, businessmen, and speculators. Some genuinely wanted to help blacks achieve political influence. Others intended to win power for themselves by controlling black votes. Some were plain thieves. Black politicians in the South also varied widely in ability and devotion to duty. There were fewer Carpetbaggers than Scalawags and blacks in Reconstruction governments. But their undoubted loyalty to the Union and connections in Washington gave them great influence.

During the 1870s white people who objected to blacks holding office emphasized the numerous examples of black corruption and incompetence that came to light. A northern observer, James S. Pike, reported that the 1873 session of the South Carolina legislature was marked by total confusion. "No one is allowed to talk five minutes without interruption," Pike complained. There was "endless chatter" and much "gush and babble." Pike said of one speaker:

> **"** He did not know what he was going to say when he got up . . . and he did not know what he had said when he sat down. **"**

A black politician in Arkansas collected $9,000 for repairing a bridge that had cost the state only $500 to build in the first place. The black-controlled South Carolina legislature spent $16,000 a year on paper and other supplies. The average spent on these materials before the war was $400. The black South Carolina senators had a kind of private club in the capitol building where fine food and wines and the most expensive cigars were always available. Many black legislators routinely accepted money in exchange for their votes on important issues.

Such things did indeed happen. What white critics failed to mention was that many white politicians were just as corrupt and inefficient. In fact most of the corruption during this time can be traced to whites. One commentator watched the disorderly behavior of members of the United States House of Representatives at about this time. He said that trying to make a speech in the House was like

WHAT YOU GIVE TO ONE CLASS YOU MUST GIVE TO ALL.

WHAT YOU DENY TO ONE CLASS YOU SHALL DENY TO ALL.

HON. R. B. ELLIOTT'S Speech, Page 4

Robert B. Elliott of South Carolina addresses his fellow state legislators on civil rights in 1874. What influence do you suppose this well-educated African American had in the state legislature?

trying to speak to a crowd in a passing trolley while standing on the curb of a busy city street.

As for corruption, the main difference between white and black thieves was that the white ones made off with most of the money. After studying the actions of black and white officials during Reconstruction, the historian Joel Williamson concludes that "the most gigantic steals" were engineered by white politicians like "Honest John" Patterson, a Carpetbagger who systematically bribed South Carolina legislators to vote for a bill worth nearly $2 million to a railroad Patterson controlled.

However, the southern state governments also accomplished a great deal of good during these years. They raised taxes in order to improve public education, which had been badly neglected before 1860. They also spent large sums on roads, bridges, railroads, and public buildings damaged during the war. They also expanded public support for medical care and orphans. They began to rebuild the southern economy. And in many cases they established civil rights laws.

STRATEGIES FOR SUCCESS

INTERPRETING A GRAPH OF BUSINESS CYCLES

As you have learned, the United States has a free enterprise economy. This means that businesses are privately owned and operated with little interference by the government. American business is directly affected by the needs and wants of consumers—or the *market*. Prosperity goes in cycles. Events that influence consumers cause the economy to expand or recede. Graphs throughout *The Story of America* illustrate these cycles.

How to Read a Graph of Business Cycles

To read a graph of business cycles, follow these guidelines.

1. **Read the title.** The title identifies the time period illustrated by the graph.
2. **Check the key.** The key explains what the colors and special symbols on the graph mean.
3. **Study the trends.** The graph shows the ups and downs of the business cycle. Periods of expansion rise above the trend line (which may also be called the base line). Periods of recession, or slowdowns, dip below the trend line.
4. **Note the labels.** Historical events that strongly influence economic cycles help explain the reasons for the surge or sag of the economy.

5. **Compare the fluctuations.** The highs and lows differ in intensity and duration (length of time). Compare them to understand the business situation at that time in American history.

Applying the Strategy

Study the graph below. The title, "Business Cycles, 1840–1870" tells you that it illustrates the ups and downs of business from just before the Civil War to immediately after it. Note that the graph shows a period of general expansion, or business growth, from 1840 to 1857. What events helped spur this growth? What happened in 1857 to slow the growth? The Civil War strongly affected American business. Secession caused a recession. Why would this happen? Business recovered to expand during the war as businesses began producing for the war. You can see a brief primary recession immediately after the war as war production ended. Soon however, the economy began to grow again as businesses replaced what was lost in war. What do you think the business cycle from 1870 to 1900 would show?

For independent practice, see Practicing the Strategy on page 81.

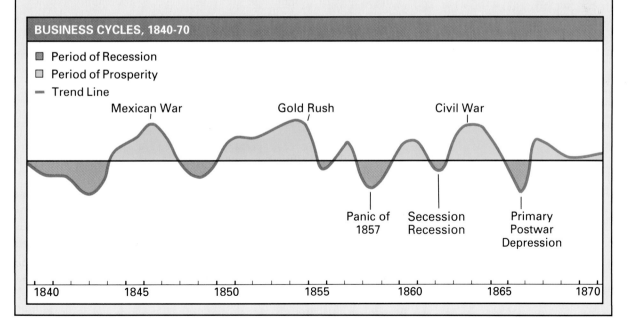

BUSINESS CYCLES, 1840-70

- ▢ Period of Recession
- ▢ Period of Prosperity
- ▬ Trend Line

Mexican War · Gold Rush · Civil War

Panic of 1857 · Secession Recession · Primary Postwar Depression

1840 · 1845 · 1850 · 1855 · 1860 · 1865 · 1870

In her diary the mistress of Mulberry Plantation wrote in Sherman's wake.

"Nothing but tall blackened chimneys to show that any man has ever trod this road before. This is Sherman's track. It is hard not to curse him. I wept incessantly at first. The roses of the garden are already hiding the ruins. My husband said Nature is a wonderful renovator. He tried to say something else and then I shut my eyes and made a vow that if we were a crushed people, crushed by weight, I would never be a slave."

Mary Boykin Chesnut, May 2, 1865

The Ravaged Land

Economic ruin and social chaos swept the South. Wherever armies had clashed, houses and barns were shattered or burned, crops ruined, and livestock taken or killed. After the war seed to plant new crops and horses or mules to plow the land were scarce. Even labor was scarce. A quarter of a million southern soldiers had died and many former slaves did not want to work for their former masters.

Many southern industries also were badly damaged, and loans to rebuild or restart them were unavailable. Rubble littered cities that had stood in the path of invading armies.

Southerners set about working their land as best they could. Many whites felt relieved that slavery had ended. But they wondered what lay ahead. Some feared vengeance from former slaves. Others could not adjust to dealing with a free labor force. They had always been members of a group that viewed itself as superior and that thinking continued. In the late spring of 1865, however, both groups knew that unless food crops were planted, there would be nothing to eat in the winter, and unless cash crops were raised, there would be no money to buy seed for next year's crop.

Sharecropping

Nearly all the slaves had been farm workers and nearly all continued to work on the land after they became free. The efforts of Radicals like Thaddeus Stevens to carve up the large plantations and give each black family "forty acres and a mule" never attracted much support among northern whites. In theory, a freedman could get a 160-acre farm (64 hectares) under the Homestead Act of 1862. Only a handful of blacks were able to do so. They lacked the tools, seed money, and the means of getting to the distant frontier. The price of land was only a small part of the cost of starting a farm. As one congressman reported from Georgia in 1866:

" The blacks own absolutely nothing but their bodies; their former masters own everything, . . . If a black man draws even a bucket of water from a well, he must first get permission of a white man. . . . If he asks for work to earn his living, he must ask it of a white man."

Most of the former slaves therefore continued to cultivate land owned by whites. At first they worked for cash wages. But the South was poor after the war. Most landowners were very short of cash. So a new system called **sharecropping** was worked out.

Sharecropping means sharing the crop. Under this system the landowner provided the laborers with houses, tools, seeds, and other supplies. The sharecroppers provided the skill and muscle needed to

grow the crops. When the harvest was gathered, it was shared, half to two thirds for the landowner, the rest for the sharecropper.

This system allowed black workers to be free of the close daily control they had endured under slavery. Each black family had its own cabin and tilled its own land as a separate unit. Sharecroppers could at least hope that by working hard and saving they might some-day have enough money to buy a farm of their own. Then they would be truly free. For this reason most blacks much preferred sharecrop-ping to working for wages.

A long time passed before many sharecroppers owned their farms. Partly this was because most whites tried to keep blacks from obtaining land of their own. The landowners wanted to make sure they had enough workers for their own farms. And they wanted to keep all the blacks dependent upon them.

Some landowners cheated the sharecroppers when the harvest was divided. Local storekeepers also cheated them. Share-croppers had to buy supplies on credit. They ran up bills at the general store during the growing season. When the crop was sold in the autumn, they used the money to pay off this debt. Frequently the merchant added items to the bill the farmers had never purchased. Blacks who objected were threatened with the loss of credit in the future, or with violence. During Reconstruction, with blacks on local

Winslow Homer painted the cotton pickers whose toils sometimes stained the cotton red with blood. In the en-graving below a slave is shown with his sack of cotton. Has freedom made this work easier?

Freedom After Slavery　69

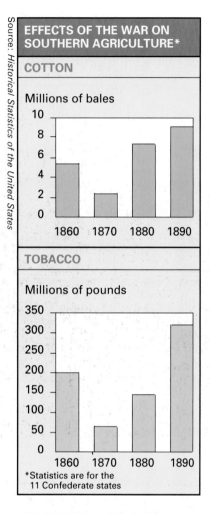

Source: Historical Statistics of the United States

EFFECTS OF THE WAR ON SOUTHERN AGRICULTURE*

COTTON

Millions of bales

TOBACCO

Millions of pounds

*Statistics are for the 11 Confederate states

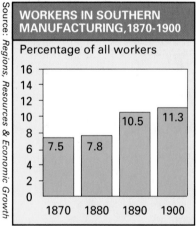

Source: Regions, Resources & Economic Growth

WORKERS IN SOUTHERN MANUFACTURING, 1870-1900

Percentage of all workers

7.5 7.8 10.5 11.3

1870 1880 1890 1900

LEARNING FROM GRAPHS.
What generalization about the southern economy can you draw from these graphs?

juries, there was some hope for justice. After the end of Reconstruction, with blacks once again barred from juries, the local courts were not likely to give justice to blacks who sued any white person.

Even when dealing with honest landowners and merchants, it was hard to make much more than a bare living as a sharecropper. Prices were high in the stores because the storekeepers also had to borrow to get the goods they sold. They paid high interest rates because money was so scarce in the South. They had to charge high prices to cover that expense. So it was lack of money more than cheating by whites or racial prejudice that kept black sharecroppers from getting farms of their own. White sharecroppers hardly fared better.

The whole system seemed strangely similar to slavery. Blacks were again tied to the land they worked, with little hope of leaving. It gave them, however, the power to control their own day-to-day activities. No longer must they work in gangs, carrying out the orders of a master or overseer. Some sharecroppers, by a combination of good luck and hard work, earned enough to buy land and become truly independent farmers.

The Crop-Lien System

The shortage of money made everyone dependent on bankers and other people with funds to invest. These investors wanted to be sure that the loans they made in the spring were repaid in the fall after the crops had been harvested. They demanded that the landowners pledge the future crop as security for the loan. This meant that they had a claim on the crop, called a **lien,** before it was even planted. If the borrower failed to pay when the loan fell due, the lender could take possession of the crop.

This **crop-lien system** was fair enough on the surface. However, it had an unfortunate side effect. The lenders insisted that the borrowers grow one of the South's major cash crops, such as cotton or tobacco. These were products for which there was a **world market.** They could be converted into cash anywhere and at any time. If the price was low, they could be safely stored until market conditions improved.

The landowners and sharecroppers of the South would have been better off if they could have grown many different things—vegetables and fruits as well as cotton and the other cash crops. By concentrating on one crop, they exhausted the fertility of the soil more rapidly than if they had grown a variety of crops or had alternated crops from year to year. In addition, if they had a larger-than-normal harvest, the price of the cash crop fell steeply because supply was greater than demand.

Everyone was caught up in the system. The bankers put pressure

Brown Brothers

on the landowners and storekeepers. They, in turn, forced the sharecroppers to plant what the bankers wanted. The tendency is to blame the bankers. The charge is that they were greedy and short-sighted. But the bankers really had little choice. It would have been extremely risky, for example, to lend a farmer money to grow tomatoes, for they had to be sold locally when they were ripe or they would rot and become worthless within a few days.

So most southern black people stayed poor. The South itself stayed poor. It took about 20 years for the region to get production back to where it had been when the Civil War broke out. As we shall see, during those years the rest of the country was increasing its output at a rapid rate.

Yet for black southerners the Reconstruction era was a time of genuine progress. Any change from slavery had to be an improvement. They had power over many aspects of their life for the first time. Gradually their standard of living improved. They had more to eat, better clothes, and more comfortable houses. When they supplied these things for themselves by their own labor, they were better off than when they got only what their owners chose to give them. ⬛

Sharecroppers stand in front of their cabin, the cotton growing right up to the back porch. What do you suppose the man in the buggy has come for?

Return to the Preview & Review on page 63.

Freedom After Slavery 71

Preview & Review

Use these questions to guide your reading. Answer the questions after completing Section 4.
Understanding Issues, Events, & Ideas. Describe how white southerners resisted Reconstruction, using the following words: Ku Klux Klan, Amnesty Act of 1872, Compromise of 1877.
1. Why was the outcome of the 1876 presidential election in doubt? How was the president finally selected?
2. Why did another Civil War threaten the nation in 1877?
3. What were the terms of the Compromise of 1877?
Thinking Critically. **1.** You are a black living in the South. Write a letter to the editor of your local newspaper, explaining why you have decided not to vote in the presidential election of 1876. **2.** Write a magazine article describing the events that led to the Compromise of 1877.

Resistance to Reconstruction

It is safe to say that the great majority of white southerners strongly resisted the changes forced upon them during Reconstruction, sometimes openly, sometimes in the dead of night. The Black Codes were one attempt to keep blacks in a lowly status. In 1866 the whites also began to form secret organizations to hold blacks down by terror.

The most important of these organizations was the **Ku Klux Klan.** Klan members were determined to keep blacks from voting and thus influencing political events. Klansmen tried to frighten blacks by galloping through the night dressed in white robes, hoods, and masks. They claimed to be the ghosts of Confederate soldiers. They burned crosses on the hillsides, a hint of the terrible tortures that awaited blacks who tried to vote. When blacks refused to be frightened, the Klan often carried out its threats. Hundreds of black southerners were beaten, other hundreds actually murdered by the Klan.

The federal government managed to check the Klan by about 1871. It sent troops to areas where violence had broken out. Many Klan leaders were arrested. Gradually, more white southerners joined in efforts to keep blacks from voting. They joined the Democratic

Blacks attempting to vote are halted by the sharp-featured election judge who keeps his gun at the ready. The man at the door holds a "Republican ticket," but it will not be used in this election. The Republican ticket won in no southern elections. What chance of voting do you think the freedman believed he had?

party. In 1874 groups in Mississippi began an organized effort, its aim printed prominently in several newspapers, "Carry the election peacefully if we can, forcibly if we must." They formed military companies and marched about in broad daylight. They gave merciless beatings to those blacks they found "uppity" or rebellious. Many blacks fought back against this kind of violence. In some areas small-scale but bloody battles broke out between armed bands of whites and blacks.

The Election of 1876

Since blacks were in the minority in the South and had fewer weapons than whites, they lost most battles when they clashed. Northern whites, meanwhile, began to lose interest in controlling the South by means of the army. They became satisfied that southern whites did not actually intend to reenslave blacks. They began to put the South's problems out of their minds. Gradually the number of troops stationed in the southern states was reduced. Many blacks then chose not to risk voting and exercising their other rights.

In state after state during the 1870s Conservative parties, made up entirely of whites, took over the government from the Republicans. These parties resisted the changes proposed for the South. Many of the members of the parties were former Confederate officials and soldiers. They had been barred from holding office by Section 3 of the Fourteenth Amendment, but the **Amnesty Act of 1872** ended the disability for all but the highest Confederate officials. Former Confederates flocked to the Conservative parties and ran in almost every southern election.

The Republican party was further hurt by the failure of President Grant to live up to expectations as president. The military hero was honest and a true democrat, but he was a poor chief executive. He became the innocent victim of scandals and corruption in his administration. Although he was reelected in 1872 by 800,000 votes more than the Democratic party nominee, Horace Greeley, his party grew weaker. By 1876 the Republicans controlled only three southern states—Louisiana, Florida, and South Carolina. They rejoined their former Confederate partners after the election of 1876. In South Carolina, the last state to be reclaimed politically, the Red Shirts, a band patterned after similar groups in Mississippi, secured the election of a former planter and Confederate general, Wade Hampton.

The presidential election of 1876 pitted Governor Samuel J. Tilden of New York, the Democrat, against Governor Rutherford B. Hayes of Ohio, the Republican. Tilden won in his home state, New York, in neighboring New Jersey and Connecticut, in Indiana, and in all the southern states. This gave him a substantial majority of the electoral vote, 203 to 165. In the popular vote he won by 250,000 votes—4.28 million to 4.03 million.

National Portrait Gallery

Switched votes by three southern states kept the story of America from telling of the presidency of Samuel J. Tilden. Tilden won the popular election but it was Rutherford B. Hayes who became president in 1877. Tilden is above, Hayes below.

White House Historical Association

But when Republican leaders added up the votes on election night, they discovered that switching the electoral votes of the three southern states they still controlled would give the majority to Hayes, 185 to 184! Republican officials in these three states swiftly threw out enough Democratic ballots to change the result. Then they forwarded to Washington "official" results showing Hayes the winner.

Of course the Democrats protested loudly. They filed another set of "official" results that showed Tilden the winner in the three disputed states.

For weeks no one knew who the next president would be. The Constitution did not provide a clear method for solving the problem. According to the Constitution the votes had to be counted. But by whom? Certainly not the Republican-controlled Senate or the Democratic-controlled House of Representatives. Instead, Congress appointed a special commission to settle the issue. It was made up of ten members of Congress—five Democrats and five Republicans, and five members of the Supreme Court. The Supreme Court justices were supposed to be nonpolitical, but three were Republicans, the other two Democrats.

The commission held an investigation and heard evidence from both sides. It soon became clear that both parties had behaved in a completely corrupt manner in the three states in dispute. More Democrats had almost certainly voted than Republicans. But large numbers of blacks who would surely have voted Republican had been kept away from the polls by force and threats.

The Compromise of 1877

When the commissioners finally voted, they split 8 to 7 on each of the disputed states. Every Republican voted for Hayes, every Democrat for Tilden. Obviously they had not paid much attention to the evidence. The Democrats felt cheated. Many were ready to fight to make Tilden president. For a time another Civil War seemed about to break out.

In this crisis the leaders of the two parties worked out what is known as the **Compromise of 1877.** Hayes agreed to recall all the remaining federal troops stationed in the South. He promised to appoint a conservative southerner to his Cabinet. He said also that he supported a proposal sponsored by southerners to build a railroad from Texas to southern California.

In exchange the Democrats promised to guarantee blacks their own rights and not to use their power in the southern states to prevent blacks from voting. After all these details had been settled in a series of informal, behind-the-scenes discussions, the Democrats agreed to go along with the electoral commission's decision. On March 4, 1877, Hayes was inaugurated as president in an orderly, entirely peaceful ceremony.

Return to the Preview & Review on page 72.

5. THE LONG NIGHT BEGINS

Second-Class Citizens

After the Compromise of 1877 the white citizens of the North turned their backs on the black citizens of the South. Gradually the southern states broke their promise to treat blacks fairly. Step by step they deprived them of the right to vote and reduced them to second-class citizens. Thus began the **Long Night** of racial segregation.

The first step was to pass **poll tax** laws. A poll tax is a charge made for voting. It can be avoided simply by not going to the polls. For poor people, paying a poll tax was a great sacrifice. Many preferred to spend what little money they had in other ways. In most southern states the tax *accumulated* when not paid. That is, a person who skipped one election would have to pay double if he wished to vote at the next year's local election. A person who voted only in presidential elections would pay four times the regular tax.

Another technique for keeping blacks from the polls was to require a **literacy test** for voting. People who could not read could not vote. And those blacks who could read were usually asked to read a difficult, technical legal passage of some kind. Poll taxes and literacy tests did not violate the Fifteenth Amendment because they were not directly based on "race, color, or previous condition of servitude."

These measures prevented many poor white people from voting too. But when they wanted to, the authorities could find ways of allowing whites to vote anyway. One method was to permit people who could not read to vote if they could "understand" and explain a passage that an election official read to them. A white person might be asked to explain a clause in the state constitution that said: "The term of the governor shall be four years." A black person who sought to qualify would then be asked to explain a more complicated passage. And whatever the black said, he would be told his explanation was incorrect and that he had not "understood."

Another technique was the so-called **grandfather clause.** Grandfather clauses provided that literacy tests and poll taxes did not apply to persons who had been able to vote before 1867, or to their children and later descendants. Of course most whites came under this heading, but no blacks did at all. By about 1900 only a handful of black citizens were voting in the southern states. Not until 1915, in *Guinn v. U.S.*, did the Supreme Court rule that grandfather clauses were unconstitutional.

The Court and Segregation

When blacks ceased to have an influence on elections, elected officials stopped paying much attention to their needs and desires. The segregation of blacks and whites in public places became widespread.

Preview & Review

Use these questions to guide your reading. Answer the questions after completing Section 5.
Understanding Issues, Events, & Ideas. Using the following words, discuss the segregation of black Americans: Long Night, poll tax, literacy test, grandfather clause, Civil Rights Act of 1875, Jim Crow law, Civil Rights Cases, *Plessy v. Ferguson,* separate but equal, buffalo soldiers, Tuskegee Institute, Atlanta Compromise, accommodation.
1. Why did southern whites want to keep blacks from voting?
2. What was the result of the Civil Rights Cases decided by the Supreme Court in 1883?
3. What was the importance of the decision in *Plessy v. Ferguson?*
4. What happened to blacks in the 1890s who protested against injustice?
Thinking Critically. 1. You have just read of the Court's ruling on *Plessy v. Ferguson.* Write a letter to your state representative, protesting the ruling. **2.** Imagine that you are a black person in the South in 1895. Do you agree or disagree with Booker T. Washington's Atlanta Compromise? Why or why not?

Frederick Douglass had this to say about the plight of blacks in the South after the Civil War.

<< No man can be truly free whose liberty is dependent upon the thought, feeling, and actions of others, and who has himself no means in his hands for guarding, protecting, defending, and maintaining that liberty. >>
Frederick Douglass, 1882

There had always been a good deal of segregation in the North and South alike. In part it had been based on economics. Poor people could not afford to eat in the same restaurants as rich people, for example, and most blacks were poor. On the other hand, in the decades before the Civil War blacks and whites had often met together informally. This happened perhaps even more in the South than in the North.

After the destruction of the Confederacy, Congress had ruled out segregation in the South. The **Civil Rights Act of 1875** provided specifically that "citizens of every race and color" were entitled to "the full and equal enjoyment" of restaurants, hotels, trains, and all "places of public amusement."

But after 1877 whites began to ignore this law. In part they were more eager now for segregation because blacks were now unquestionably free. Separation had seemed less important to whites when blacks were clearly in lowly positions and under white "command." The typical southern white did not object to sitting next to a black on a streetcar if the black was a nursemaid caring for a white child. The same woman entering the car alone would cause the white to bristle if she tried to occupy the next seat. It became the common practice throughout the South to separate the races in schools, hospitals, orphanages, and other public and private institutions. But this practice was not the law.

That began to change in 1881, when Tennessee passed the first **Jim Crow law.** This law required blacks to ride in separate railroad cars. Florida in 1887 and Texas in 1889 passed similar laws. The name was taken from the black-faced white actors in 19th-century song and dance acts. In time Jim Crow laws extended separation of the races to all places where it had become practice—and beyond.

When blacks began to be turned away from public places like theaters in cities all over the country, some went to court to seek their constitutional rights. In one case, W. H. R. Agee protested against being denied a room in a hotel in Jefferson City, Missouri. In another, Sallie J. Robinson sued because she was forced to ride in a second-class railroad car while traveling from Tennessee to Virginia, even though she had a first-class ticket.

These and other suits, known as the **Civil Rights Cases,** were decided by the Supreme Court in 1883. The majority of the justices ruled that the Civil Rights Act was unconstitutional. It was therefore not illegal for private businesses to practice racial segregation. The guarantees of the Fourteenth Amendment were protections against actions by state governments, not by private persons.

After this, segregation became more and more the rule, especially in the South. Then, in 1896, the Supreme Court heard the case of ***Plessy v. Ferguson.*** Homer Adolf Plessy, a light-skinned Louisiana black man, was arrested for sitting in a railroad car reserved by Louisiana law for whites. His attorneys argued that the law under

which he was arrested was unconstitutional. Judge John H. Ferguson ruled against Plessy on the grounds that the railroad provided separate but equally good cars for blacks, as required by law. The Supreme Court upheld this reasoning.

The Court's decision permitted other "separate but equal" facilities. Thus segregation was legal, even in public schools, provided the schools for black children were equal to those for whites. The majority ruling stated in part:

> " We consider the underlying fallacy [faulty reasoning] of the plaintiff's argument to consist in the assumption that the enforced separation of the two races stamps the colored race with a badge of inferiority. If this be so, it is not by reason of anything found in the act, but solely because the colored race chooses to put that construction upon it. . . . The argument also assumes that social prejudices may be overcome by legislation, and that equal rights cannot be secured to the negro except by an enforced commingling [mixing] of the two races. We cannot accept this proposition. . . . If the civil and political rights of both races be equal one cannot be inferior to the other civilly or politically. If one race is inferior to the other socially, the Constitution of the United States cannot put them upon the same plane.[1] "

[1]From *Plessy v. Ferguson*, 163 U.S. 537, 1896.

"Kept In." One sorrowful little girl remains after school, perhaps until she finishes her lessons. Her loneliness is a reminder of the physical barriers of segregation. Where else besides schools was segregation practiced?

The Long Night Begins 77

Justice John Marshall Harlan came from a family that once kept slaves in Kentucky. But he believed that segregation was in violation of the Constitution. What did he mean by "Our Constitution is color-blind"?

One justice, John Marshall Harlan, born in Kentucky, a slave state, objected to this **separate-but-equal** argument. Harlan's family had owned slaves. But the experiences of Reconstruction had caused him to change his mind about race questions. In his dissent he said:

❝ The white race deems itself to be the dominant race in this country. And so it is, in prestige, in achievements, in education, in wealth and power. . . . But in view of the Constitution in the eye of the law, there is in this country no superior, dominant, ruling class of citizens. There is no caste here. Our Constitution is color-blind, and neither knows nor tolerates classes among citizens. In respect of civil rights, all citizens are equal before the law. The humblest is the peer of the most powerful. The law regards man as man, and takes no account of his surroundings or of his color when his civil rights as guaranteed by the supreme law of the land are involved.[1] ❞

But in 1896 Harlan's was the minority view both of the Court and among white citizens in all parts of the country.

Efforts to prevent segregation practically ended as a result of these court decisions. Blacks could not stay at hotels used by white travelers. Theaters herded them into separate sections, usually high in the balcony. Blacks had to ride in the rear sections of streetcars. They could not enter "white" parks or swim at "white" public beaches. Even cemeteries were segregated.

The schools, parks, and other facilities open to blacks were almost never as good as those open to whites. The separate-but-equal rule was ignored everywhere. In 1876 South Carolina spent the same amount on the education of each child, black or white. By 1895, when school segregation was complete in South Carolina, the state was spending three times more on each white child.

The Atlanta Compromise

It is easy to imagine how depressed and angry American blacks must have been in the 1890s. Segregation was only the visible surface of the way they were mistreated. In almost any conflict between a black person and a white, the white had every advantage. Blacks were punished more severely when they were convicted of crimes. Many kinds of jobs were entirely closed to blacks. When they did the same work as whites, they received lower pay. If they refused to act humbly and politely to whites, they were insulted or even beaten. If they wanted to adjust to white ideas of how they ought to act, they had to behave like children or clowns.

African Americans even faced discrimination in the armed

[1]From the Dissent of Mr. Justice John Marshall Harlan, *Plessy v. Ferguson*, 163 U.S. 537, 1896.

forces. In 1866, Congress approved several black regiments. Between 1869 and 1890, these regiments, notably the Ninth and Tenth Cavalries, were assigned to fight Indians and protect settlers in the West. Although they too risked their lives, the black soldiers, nicknamed **"buffalo soldiers"** by the Indians, were strictly segregated. Often, if any buffalo soldiers were granted leave to visit a town, local settlers would refuse to serve them in stores, restaurants, or hotels.

Some blacks protested violently against all this injustice. Those who did were dealt with still more violently by the white majority. Lynchings, the killing without trial of supposed criminals by mobs, became ever more frequent.

Faced with these handicaps, many black Americans adopted the strategy proposed by Booker T. Washington, the founder of a trade school for blacks in Alabama, **Tuskegee Institute.** Washington had been born a slave. He obtained an education by working as a janitor at the school he attended. His experiences convinced him that a person of lowly origins could rise in the world by a combination of hard work and a willingness to go along with the wishes and prejudices of powerful people. He had seen firsthand what happened to black people, especially in the South, who openly fought the prejudices of whites.

Washington was expert at obtaining the support of well-to-do whites who wanted to help blacks without actually treating them as equals. His school prospered. He was already well known when, in a speech at Atlanta, Georgia, in 1895, he proposed what became known as the **Atlanta Compromise.**

Blacks should accept the separate-but-equal principle, Washington said. They should learn skilled trades so that they could earn more money and thus improve their lives. And there was nothing shameful about working with one's hands. "There is as much dignity in tilling a field," he said, "as in writing a poem." Furthermore, it would be "the extremest folly" for blacks to demand truly equal treatment from whites. The way to rise in the world was to accept the system and try to get ahead with it.

Washington asked whites only to be fair. Help blacks who went along with segregation, he argued, by making sure that what was separate was really equal.

Most important white southern leaders claimed to be delighted with the Atlanta Compromise. In fact they made very little effort to change the attitude and behavior of average white citizens.

Today Washington seems to have buckled under with the Atlanta Compromise. Yet the failure of Reconstruction had awakened old fears and suspicions about blacks. Once again blacks had to move with caution. Historical imagination helps us see the Atlanta Compromise as a desperate effort to hold on to a few gains. For black people who had to live through those postwar years, going along, **accommodation,** was not cowardice but survival. 🖂

Booker T. Washington founded Tuskegee Institute. What reason did he give for starting his famous school?

This classroom scene at Tuskegee Institute was photographed in about 1900. What forms of segregation does this classroom reveal?

Return to the Preview & Review on page 75.

The Long Night Begins 79

CHAPTER 1 REVIEW

1865	THE AFTERMATH OF WAR	1875	

1865
Lee surrenders to Grant
★
Lincoln assassinated
★
Reconstruction begins
★
Thirteenth Amendment
1866
Civil Rights Act

1867
Reconstruction Act passed
★
1868
Johnson impeached and acquitted
★
Fourteenth Amendment
★
Grant elected president

1870
Fifteenth Amendment ratified

1875
Civil Rights Act of 1875
1876
Presidential election disputed

1877
House elects Hayes
★
Compromise of 1877 ends Reconstruction
★
Long Night begins

Chapter Summary

Read the statements below. Choose one, and write a paragraph explaining its importance.

1. Andrew Johnson succeeded to office after the assassination of Lincoln but had trouble working with Congress, which impeached him.
2. Moderate congressmen wanted quick Reconstruction, while Radicals were less forgiving.
3. The Thirteenth Amendment abolished slavery.
4. Congress established the Freedman's Bureau to help newly freed slaves with schools, food, and medical needs.
5. The Fourteenth Amendment guaranteed equal protection of the laws to all Americans. The Fifteenth Amendment made it illegal to deny the right to vote based on race, color, or previous condition of servitude.
6. Organizations such as the Ku Klux Klan were formed to keep blacks in check.
7. The last federal troops were removed from the South under the Compromise of 1877, which made Hayes president.
8. White southerners used many methods to keep blacks as second-class citizens.

Reviewing Chronological Order

Number your paper 1-5. Then study the time line above and place the following events in the order in which they happened by writing the first next to 1, the second next to 2, and so on.
1. Reconstruction Act passed
2. *Plessy v. Ferguson*
3. Grant elected president
4. Atlanta Compromise proposed
5. Lincoln assassinated

Understanding Main Ideas

1. How did the three Civil War Amendments attack the Black Codes?
2. What were the provisions of the Reconstruction Act of 1867? Why did President Johnson veto it? How did Congress react to his veto?
3. How did the election of 1868 show Republicans the importance of the black vote?
4. What were the motives of some Carpetbaggers and Scalawags in the "Black Republican" governments of the South?
5. What situation was resolved by the Compromise of 1877? What were the terms of this agreement?

Thinking Critically

1. **Analyzing.** You are the one senator whose vote is needed to obtain the conviction of President Andrew Johnson on impeachment charges. Why would you vote against removing him from office?
2. **Determining Cause and Effect.** If you were a former slave living in the South in 1870, how would freedom change your life if you were a 58-year-old man? A 22-year-old woman? A 6-year-old boy?
3. **Interpreting.** Study the Thirteenth, Fourteenth, and Fifteenth Amendments in the Reference Section. Then rewrite the amendments in your own words.

Writing About History: Persuasive

You are a newspaper reporter in Washington D.C. Write an editorial on the impeachment trial of Johnson. Your editorial should include both a description of the trial and the reaction of participants. Conclude your editorial by trying to persuade your readers to support or oppose conviction. Use the information in Chapter 1 and in reference books to prepare your report.

1883
Civil Rights Cases decided

1895
Atlanta
Compromise
proposed

1896
Plessy v. Ferguson

Practicing the Strategy
Review the strategy on page 67.
Interpreting a Graph of Business Cycles.
Study the two charts on page 70, then answer the following questions.

1. What kinds of agriculture are represented in the top chart?
2. What event occurred between 1860 and 1870 that badly damaged the South's agricultural production?
3. How many years passed before southern agricultural production recovered and surpassed the pre-war levels?
4. In the bottom chart there is a sudden jump in the percent of southern workers in manufacturing between 1880 and 1890. What does this suggest about the nature of manufacturing in the South during that time?

Using Primary Sources
For many years after the Civil War Frederick Douglass remained a leading African American spokesman. He continued to encourage blacks to struggle, now against the effects of Reconstruction and the Long Night. In this excerpt from John W. Blasingame's *Frederick Douglass: The Clarion Voice,* Douglass explained why active struggle was necessary. As you read the excerpt, imagine the conditions blacks were struggling against. Then answer the questions that follow it.

> *The whole history of the progress of human liberty shows that all concessions yet made to her august [mighty] claims have been born of earnest struggle. . . . If there is no struggle, there is no progress. Those who profess to favor freedom, and yet deprecate [say bad things about] agitation, are men who want crops without plowing up the ground, they want rain without thunder and lightning. They want the ocean without the awful roar of its many waters.*

1. According to the excerpt, what had caused all progress in human liberty?

2. Do you agree that "If there is no struggle, there is no progress"? Use examples to support your point of view.
3. If you were a government leader during Reconstruction, what plan might you have suggested to help freed slaves begin a new life? Would your plan have been difficult to establish? Why or why not?

Linking History & Geography
Reconstruction meant more than just rebuilding southern governments. It also meant reconstructing land devastated by four years of war. To understand why this aspect of Reconstruction was so important to the South's recovery, answer the following questions.

1. A Virginia farmer in the Shenandoah Valley said soon after the war: "We had no cattle, hogs, sheep, or horses or anything else. The fences were all gone. . . . The barns were all burned; chimneys standing without houses; and houses standing without roofs or doors or windows." What are three things this farmer will have to do to make the farm productive again?
2. Destruction of southern railroads had been a prime Union military objective during the war. How had this isolated the South? What problems would such isolation cause?

Enriching Your Study of History
1. **Individual Project.** Imagine you are traveling through the South in 1867. Use your historical imagination to write five diary entries describing Reconstruction.
2. **Cooperative Project.** Members of your group will present a debate of the Atlanta Compromise. Half the group will argue for following Washington's suggestions. The other half will argue against the compromise. After you present your debate, the class will act as a convention and vote on the issue.

Chapter 1 Review   81

The Last Frontier

The history of the Plains Indians shows that truth is often stranger and more interesting than fiction. A favorite subject of American books and movies is the "Winning of the West," or the plunder of the prairie and the end of the American Indian way of life, depending on your point of view. For about a hundred years, from around 1780 to 1880, the Plains Indians lived in the midst of an immense grassland, feeding upon the numberless buffalo and moving freely on their fleet ponies. Yet much of their culture was a direct result of the Indians' adopting such elements of European civilization as horses, guns, and metal tools. And in the end the European lust for land, the diseases spread by the conquerors and settlers, and the deadly efficiency of America's mechanical genius ended the Plains civilization. With the discovery of vast gold, silver, and copper deposits on the Indian lands—and the buffalo's grazing lands taken by the ranchers of the cattle kingdom—could there be much hope for the first Americans and their independent way of life?

The Great Plains is strewn with skulls in Albert Bierstadt's 1889 oil painting, "The Last of the Buffalo."

Corcoran Gallery of Art

1. THE BATTLE FOR THE PLAINS

The Great Plains

The vast region we call the **Great Plains** extends from western Texas north to the Dakotas and on into Canada. Endless acres of grassland roll westward from the Mississippi, gradually rising until they reach the towering ranges of the Rocky Mountains. Explorers and hunters once described this region and the mountains beyond as the **"Great American Desert,"** although it was *no* desert. Before the 1850s the Spanish settlers in the Southwest and the Mormons in Utah had made the only permanent settlements in this huge area with its few lonely travelers.

The land of the Great Plains is mostly level. There are few trees. Winter blizzards roar unchecked out of the Arctic. Temperatures fall far below freezing. In summer the thermometer can soar halfway to the boiling point.

Until well after the Civil War, farming on the plains seemed impossible. There was too little rain to raise crops and no wood to build houses or fences. Most people thought the desert was home only for the donkey-eared jackrabbit, the prairie dog, the antelope, the wolflike coyote, and the great, shaggy buffalo. The buffalo in particular seemed the lords of the Great Plains, by their numbers alone. About 12 million of them grazed on the seemingly arid prairie there at the time the Civil War ended.

The Plains Indians

Long before the European settlement of America, people lived on the Great Plains. In the 19th century there were 31 Plains tribes. The **Apache** and **Comanche** lived in Texas and eastern New Mexico. The **Pawnee** occupied western Nebraska, the **Sioux** the Dakotas. The **Cheyenne** and **Arapaho** were the principal tribes of the central plains. In 1850 these tribes contained about 175,000 people. Although they spoke many different languages, all could communicate with one another. They had developed a complex and efficient sign language.

The Plains Indians differed from tribe to tribe. Most were nomads, but some established villages where they grew corn during the warm months. Some tribes were divided into bands. The Cheyenne, for example, consisted of ten bands with names like the Aorta Band, the Hairy Band, the Scabby Band, and the Dogmen Band. Although each band was a separate community, bands joined together for religious ceremonies and to fight other tribes or the European invaders. Their chiefs and councils of elders acted mostly as judges. Their decisions were enforced by small groups of warriors called soldier bands. The soldier bands settled disputes between band members,

Use these questions to guide your reading. Answer the questions after completing Section 1.
Understanding Issues, Events, & Ideas. Using the following words, trace the history of the Plains Indians: Great Plains; "Great American Desert"; Apache; Comanche; Pawnee; Sioux; Cheyenne; Arapaho; concentration; Pacific Railway Act; right of way; Promontory, Utah; transcontinental railroad; Mexican American.
1. Why did farming on the Great Plains seem impossible?
2. What was the purpose of the system of concentration?
3. How did Congress encourage the building of a transcontinental railroad?
4. Why were settlers in the Southwest able to gain much of the land held for many years by Mexican Americans?

Thinking Critically. 1. Imagine that you are a member of the Dogmen Band. Describe a typical day in your life. 2. It is 1865. You are a Chinese worker on the Central Pacific railroad line. Write a letter to your family in China, describing your job.

punished those who broke tribal laws, and protected the group against surprise attacks.

Within the circle of their band, warriors tried to prove their courage and daring on the battlefield. To touch an enemy or capture his weapon was proof of highest bravery, what the warriors called counting coup.

The Plains Indians, as we have seen, had become heavily dependent on the buffalo. After the European invasion of America they also captured and tamed wild horses. Spanish explorers had brought the first horses with them to America. Some of these animals escaped and ran wild. Eventually, large herds roamed parts of the West.

The Indians quickly became expert riders. On horseback they were better hunters and fighters. They could cover large distances swiftly and run down buffalo and other game. Horses became so

THE GREAT PLAINS

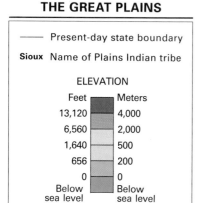

—— Present-day state boundary

Sioux Name of Plains Indian tribe

ELEVATION

Feet	Meters
13,120	4,000
6,560	2,000
1,640	500
656	200
0	0
Below sea level	Below sea level

0   200   400 Mi.
0   200   400 Km.

Albers Equal-Area Projection

LEARNING FROM MAPS. *Many of the first European explorers of the Great Plains considered it a desert. Today, however, it is a region of rich agricultural production. Why did some of the first explorers consider it a desert? What has made it productive today?*

84   THE LAST FRONTIER

Colorado Historical Society

important to the Plains Indians that many tribes went to war against their neighbors for them. Many counted their wealth in horses. Some paid their debts with horses.

Indians wore many kinds of clothing. In some tribes the men wore breechcloths and long leggings which went from hip to ankle. During the winter they wore buffalo robes. Women might wear sleeveless dresses made of deerskin. In desert regions Indians wore moccasins with double leather soles for protection against the heat or the hard ground.

The typical Plains warrior carried a bow about three feet long (nearly one meter). It was usually made of bone or ash wood. His arrows had points made of bone, flint, or metal. Some warriors were armed with long, stone-tipped lances and carried round shields made of buffalo hide. These buffalo-hide shields were smoked and hardened with glue made from buffalo hooves. They were so tough that bullets striking them at an angle would not go through.

In battle an Indian warrior could fire off half a dozen arrows from his stubby, powerful bow while an enemy was cramming a single bullet into his muzzle-loading rifle. Galloping on horseback at full speed, a warrior could shoot arrows so fast that the next would be in the air before the first found its target. These arrows struck with great force. At short range an Indian could sink the entire shaft of an arrow into the body of a buffalo.

The simplicity of the lives of Plains Indians is seen in S. C. Stobie's "Indian Camp." From your other reading and observations, how much can you find in this camp that is already familiar to you—in lodging, family roles, child care, food preparation, and so on?

The Battle for the Plains 85

Fort Laramie, shown in this water-color sketch by Alfred Jacob Miller, was a fur-trading post built in 1834. The army bought it in 1849 to protect travelers on the Oregon Trail. How does this picture add to the description of Indian life begun on page 83.

Removing the Plains Indians

The Plains Indians rarely came into conflict with settlers before the 1850s. They usually traded in peace with hunters. The pioneers who crossed the plains on their way to Oregon did everything they could to avoid the Indians.

In the early 1850s settlers began moving into Kansas and Nebraska. After the Mexican War, promoters planned to build railroads to the Pacific through the newly won territory. They demanded that the government remove the Plains Indians from this territory.

In 1851 agents of the United States called a meeting of the principal Plains tribes at Fort Laramie, in what is now Wyoming. The agents persuaded the Indians to sign the Fort Laramie Treaty. The Indians agreed to stay within limited areas and not to attack whites passing through them. The government promised them money and presents. The United States also agreed to serve as a mediator in disputes between tribes.

This new system was called **concentration.** Once a tribe had agreed to live in a particular region, it could be forced to give up its holdings without arousing the others.

As soon as Senator Stephen A. Douglas pushed the Kansas-Nebraska Act through Congress, settlers and storekeepers came pouring into lands that had been reserved for the Indians. The Indians were pushed into even smaller areas. By 1860 there were very few Native Americans left in eastern Kansas and Nebraska.

Railroads in the West

In 1862 Congress passed the **Pacific Railway Act.** This law granted a charter to the Union Pacific Railroad Company to build a line westward from Nebraska. Another company, the Central Pacific Railway of California, was authorized to build a connecting line eastward from the Pacific.

The government granted each company the **right of way**—the thin strip of land on which the tracks were actually laid. In addition it gave them large amounts of land for every mile of track built. This land could be sold and the money used for construction. Or it could be held in reserve and sold later when the land became more valuable. The government also lent the companies large amounts of money at low interest. Private fortunes were to be had here.

The Central Pacific employed thousands of Chinese immigrants to lay its tracks. Most of the Union Pacific workers came from Ireland. Construction got under way in 1865.

Building the railroad was tremendously difficult. The Central Pacific had to cross the snow-capped Sierra Nevada range. Omaha, Nebraska, where the Union Pacific began, had not yet been connected to eastern railroads. Thousands of tons of rails, crossties, and

While Chinese railroad workers watch, the Central Pacific train enters a snow shed in the Sierra Nevada. Snow sheds kept tracks clear and gave some protection to the wooden cars in the event of an avalanche. Why is it so appropriate that the workers pictured are Chinese Americans?

other supplies had to be shipped up the Missouri River by boat or hauled across Iowa by wagon.

The two companies competed with each other in order to get the lion's share of the land and money authorized by the Pacific Railway Act. Charles Crocker, manager of the Central Pacific's construction crews, drove his men mercilessly. During one winter they dug tunnels through 40-foot (12-meter) snowdrifts high in the Sierras in order to lay tracks on the frozen ground.

The two lines met on May 10, 1869, at **Promontory,** Utah. The Union Pacific had built 1,086 miles of track (1,738 kilometers), the Central Pacific 689 miles (1,102 kilometers). There was a great celebration. Leland Stanford of the Central Pacific was given the honor of hammering home the last spike connecting the two rails. The spike was of gold, the hammer of silver.

Soon other **transcontinental railroads** were built. These included the Atchison, Topeka & Santa Fe and the Southern Pacific in the Southwest and the Northern Pacific, which ran south of the Canadian border. The transcontinentals connected with the eastern railroads at Chicago, St. Louis, and New Orleans. Once they were completed, a traveler could go from the Atlantic Coast to San Francisco and other Pacific Coast cities in a week's time. The swiftest clipper ship had taken three months to make the journey from New York to San Francisco.

This painting shows "East and West Shaking Hands" in the 1869 meeting of the Union Pacific and Central Pacific at Promontory, Utah. Why was this a day to celebrate with champagne?

Union Pacific Railroad

Larry Sheerin

Theodore Gentilz, whose paintings capture much of our Spanish heritage, called this scene "Selling of the Cardinals on the Plaza." Research the layout of a typical Spanish settlement with its plaza, church, and workshops.

Settling the Southwest

During these same years settlers poured into the Southwest—western Texas, New Mexico, Arizona, and southern California—to look for gold, raise cattle, and claim land. When they arrived, they found the land occupied by Mexican Americans. These people were the descendants of the Mexicans who were living there when the region became part of the United States after the Mexican War. Rather than learn Spanish, most settlers looked down on the Mexican Americans. The newcomers treated the old settlers like foreigners.

This was unjust. Many Mexican Americans had lived on their land long before it became United States territory. The land-hungry settlers discovered that most of the land was not registered. Often they simply claimed the occupied land or bought it from the territorial government. By the 1880s Mexican Americans owned but one fourth of the land they had owned in 1848. They were denied their civil rights and faced discrimination and segregation until the 1960s.

Return to the Preview & Review on page 83.

The Battle for the Plains 89

Use these questions to guide your reading. Answer the questions after you complete Section 2.
Understanding Issues, Events, & Ideas. Use the following words to explain the tragedies of the Indian Wars: Fifty-Niners, Chivington Massacre, Washita, Bozeman Trail, ambush, Battle of the Little Bighorn, Nez Perce, Wounded Knee, Dawes Severalty Act.
1. Why did the Sioux try to stop prospectors from using the Bozeman Trail?
2. How did Helen Hunt Jackson and Sarah Winnemucca help Indians?
3. How did the Dawes Act show lack of understanding of Indian ways of life?
Thinking Critically. 1. Write a newspaper obituary for Chief Joseph. 2. Write a diary entry about Wounded Knee from the point of view of either an Indian or a member of the 7th Cavalry.

Red Cloud, the Oglala Sioux chief, and his great-grandaughter Burning Heart were painted by Henry Cross. From your reading or a cooperative research project, what statements can you make to describe the family life of the Plains Indians?

Thomas Gilcrease Institute, Tulsa

2. INDIAN WARS

"Pikes Peak or Bust"

The transcontinental railroads brought many more settlers into the West. Wherever they went, fighting with the Indians followed. Even before the Civil War there was trouble in the Pikes Peak area of Colorado, where gold was discovered. By 1859 a seemingly endless stream of wagons was rolling across the plains. Many had the slogan "Pikes Peak or Bust!" lettered on their canvas covers. The attraction of the West remained the same: a new start for discontented Americans, mostly easterners.

About 100,000 of these **Fifty-Niners** elbowed their way onto Cheyenne and Arapaho land. The Indians fiercely resisted this invasion. Between 1861 and 1864 they rode several times into battle against army units. Then, in November 1864, Colonel John M. Chivington attacked a peaceful Cheyenne encampment at Sand Creek without warning. The Cheyenne, under Chief Black Kettle, tried to surrender by first raising an American flag and then a white flag of truce.

Chivington ignored these flags. "Kill and scalp all, big and little," he ordered. His soldiers scalped the men, ripped open the bodies of the women, and clubbed the little children to death with their gun butts.

During this **Chivington Massacre** about 450 Cheyenne were killed. The Cheyenne answered with equally bloody attacks on undefended white settlements. In 1868 the Cheyenne and Arapaho were attacked in a similar way at **Washita,** in present-day Oklahoma. They were forced to settle on reservations, one in the Black Hills of Dakota, the other in Oklahoma.

Meanwhile, the Pikes Peak boom had become a bust. Little gold was found. About half the miners returned to their homes. This time the signs on their wagons read "Busted, By Gosh!"

Yet if Colorado had proved a bust, many prospectors still believed that gold could be found elsewhere. New prospectors crossed the Great Plains and spread through the mountains in the 1860s. Many followed a route pioneered by John M. Bozeman, a prospector from Georgia. This **Bozeman Trail** ran from Fort Laramie in Wyoming north to Montana. It cut through the rolling foothills of the Big Horn Mountains, the hunting grounds of the western Sioux.

The Sioux pitched their teepees beneath the sheltering mountains. There they hunted the plentiful game—deer, buffalo, elk, antelope, and bear. The Sioux chief, Red Cloud, protested strongly when prospectors and settlers began to use the new Bozeman Trail. He warned that the Sioux would fight to save their hunting grounds.

In 1865 Red Cloud's warriors made repeated attacks on white parties. The United States army responded by building forts along

Library of Congress

the trail. In December 1866 an army supply caravan approaching one of the forts was attacked. When a small troop of soldiers commanded by Captain W. J. Fetterman appeared, Red Cloud's warriors quickly dashed off into the wilderness. Captain Fetterman foolishly followed them. He blundered into a trap, or **ambush.** Fetterman and all 82 of his soldiers were killed. A few months later John Bozeman himself was killed crossing the Yellowstone River on the very trail he had marked.

At this point prospectors stopped crossing the Sioux country. A new treaty was signed in 1868. The Sioux agreed to live on a reservation in the Dakota Territory west of the Missouri River.

Custer's Last Stand

Still the fighting went on. Between 1869 and 1875 over 200 clashes between Indians and army units took place. In 1876 the territory of the Sioux was again invaded, this time by the construction crews of the Northern Pacific Railroad and by prospectors looking for gold in the Black Hills. War broke out.

This astonishingly beautiful photograph of a Sioux camp was taken in 1891 near Pine Ridge, South Dakota. Make an estimate of the size of the encampment.

Above is "Custer's Last Stand," the situation already hopeless for his cavalry troops. How is the artist's view similar to the real battle described on these pages?

This is one of many portraits we have of George Armstrong Custer, with his flowing yellow hair and moustaches. Do you agree with critics who found him a vain man searching for glory?

At this time Lieutenant Colonel George Armstrong Custer made his famous last stand in the **Battle of the Little Bighorn** in southern Montana. George Custer looked more like an actor than a soldier. He had long, flowing yellow hair. He wore buckskin trousers, red-topped boots, and a broad-brimmed hat. He was a good soldier, a graduate of the United States Military Academy at West Point. During the Civil War he fought at Bull Run and Gettysburg, and he accepted a Confederate flag of truce on the battlefield near Appomattox. But he sometimes deliberately led his men into dangerous situations in hopes of winning what he called ''glory.''

On June 25, 1876, Custer led a cavalry troop of 264 men toward what he believed to be a small Sioux camp. Instead, at the Little Bighorn River, his tiny force stumbled upon between 2,500 and 4,000 Sioux, commanded by Crazy Horse and Rain-in-the-Face.

Sitting Bull helped prepare for battle. He had become chief of his band nine years earlier. He was a solid, muscular man, 42 years old in 1876. He had a slightly hooked nose and piercing black eyes. Deep lines marked his weather-beaten brow. His dark hair hung in two heavy braids in front of his shoulders.

Sitting Bull was the most important Sioux chief and a shaman, or

INTERPRETING HISTORY: The American Frontier

During the late 19th century millions of Americans headed westward into vast frontier lands. As each area along the frontier became "settled," the next wave of pioneers pushed the frontier farther west. What role did the frontier play in the development of America and the American character? Was it merely a safety valve for an ever-increasing population? Or did Greeley write "Go west, young man!" because America was a land of unlimited opportunity?

Frederick Jackson Turner is the historian most closely linked to theories about the American frontier. In 1893 Turner published his theories in "The Significance of the Frontier on American History." In it he claimed that the seemingly inexhaustible frontier, more than the country's European heritage, shaped America. He wrote that frontier life spurred the development of independence and rugged individualism. He even suggested that the growth of democracy in America could be directly traced to the frontier experience. Simply put, he felt that the most important values and characteristics of the American spirit—courage, determination, democracy, independence, and others—grew out of people's trials on the frontier. Many generations of Americans experienced frontier life as they moved westward, and they drew on their experiences as they continually refined American values. This national experience officially came to an end, according to Turner, with the 1890 census. Maps in that census no longer carried a frontier line showing where population was less than two persons per square mile. "Now four centuries from the discovery of America, at the end of a hundred years of life under the Constitution, the frontier is gone, and with its going, has closed the first period of American history," wrote Turner.

Historians have since debated the validity of Turner's "frontier thesis." Professor Robert E. Riegal accused Turner of placing too much emphasis on the impact of the physical environment on the American people. He and many other historians attacked Turner's idea that the frontier was the "seedbed of democracy." He carefully traced America's democratic ideals to their roots in European life. He added, "Turner's feeling that each new frontiersman shed his old customs, started anew and became a real American appears to have been more a hope than a fact. Several historians have demonstrated very clearly the extent to which national characteristics were retained in western settlement."

The noted historian Ray Allen Billington disagreed with many of Turner's conclusions. But he agreed that the frontier indeed endowed its inhabitants with "characteristics and institutions that distinguished them from other nations." In other words, the frontier made Americans uniquely American.

Historians studying American society continue to argue to what degree the frontier shaped American life.

---

priest. Sitting Bull was a fiercely proud and independent man. He resisted all efforts to get his people to give up their lands or ancient customs. He would never sign a treaty with the whites, no matter how favorable the terms might seem. More than most Indians, Sitting Bull firmly believed that no compromise with the whites was possible.

These views made Sitting Bull famous and extremely popular with many Plains tribes. "I hate all the white people," he once explained. "You are all thieves and liars. You have taken away our land and made us outcasts."

At the Little Big Horn, the Sioux warriors surrounded Custer's little force. Racing round and round on their ponies, they poured a deadly fire upon the troops. Desperately the soldiers dismounted and tried to use their horses as shields. Their situation was hopeless. A hail of bullets and arrows poured upon them from every direction. One bullet struck Custer in the temple, another in the chest. Within half an hour the entire company was wiped out.

Sitting Bull's portrait is by Henry Cross.

Chief Joseph was the subject for Cyrenius Hall in 1878, just after the chief's flight for Canada. Although his nose is not pierced, he wore many ornaments. What decorations can you find in this portrait?

Point of View

Plains Indians were divided and conquered by disease as well as by soldiers.

"How many Indians from the Missouri tribes died of smallpox within the next few years can hardly be estimated. Possibly one hundred thousand. Some who recovered from the plague committed suicide after seeing their faces in a mirror. Vacant lodges stood on every hilltop. Starving people wandered aimlessly back and forth. 'No sound but the raven's croak or the wolf's howl breaks the solemn stillness. . . ."

From *Son of the Morning Star,*
Evan S. Connell, 1984

Chief Joseph

The search for gold also drew miners to Indian lands in the mountains of western Idaho. The whites called the Indians of this region the **Nez Perce,** or "pierced nose," although they did not wear ornaments in their noses. They were a peace-loving people. They claimed that no member of their tribe had ever killed a white. When Lewis and Clarke traveled through Nez Perce lands on their expedition to the Pacific Coast, the explorers had been treated as honored guests.

The Nez Perce chief was a man the whites called Joseph. His real name was Hinmaton-Yalaktit, which means "Thunder coming out of the water and over the land." Like Tecumseh, the great Shawnee leader, Joseph believed that Indians had no right to sell the land they lived on. Joseph had promised his father that he would not surrender the lands to white settlers. It was his father's dying wish. Joseph was one of the greatest Indian spokesmen. Oratory was a fine art among the Nez Perce. Much of the power and prestige of the chiefs depended on their ability to speak. Perhaps when you read his words you can understand why he fought so hard.

"My father sent for me. I saw he was dying. I took his hand in mine. He said: 'My son, my body is returning to my mother earth, and my spirit is going very soon to see the Great Spirit Chief. When I am gone, think of your country. You are the chief of these people. They look to you to guide them. Always remember that your father never sold his country. You must stop your ears whenever you are asked to sign a treaty selling your home. A few years more, and white men will be all around you. They have eyes on this land. My son, never forget my dying words. This country holds your father's body. Never sell the bones of your father and your mother.' I pressed my father's hand and told him I would protect his grave with my life. My father smiled and passed away to the spirit-land.

I buried him in that beautiful valley of winding waters. I love that land more than all the rest of the world. A man who would not love his father's grave is worse than a wild animal.[1]"

Now the government insisted that Joseph make way for the whites and move his band to the Lapwai Reservation in Idaho. Joseph had only 55 men of fighting age. He decided to yield. He selected land on the reservation in May 1877. Then the government gave him only one month to move his people to the reservation.

While on the march to Idaho, a few angry Nez Perce killed some white settlers. Troops were sent to capture them. Chief Joseph and the other chiefs decided to take their people to Montana and

[1]From *Touch the Earth: A Self-Portrait of Indian Existence* by T.C. McLuhan

THE BUFFALO VANISHES

What finally put an end to Indian independence was the killing off of the buffalo. Thousands had been slaughtered to feed the gangs of laborers who built the western railroads. In one 18-month period the scout William Cody shot some 4,000 buffalo for the Kansas Pacific Railroad construction camps. This won him the nickname Buffalo Bill.

Once the railroads were built, shooting buffalo became a popular sport for tourists and hunters from the East. Bored rail passengers sometimes opened their windows to blast away at the grazing buffalo.

In 1871 a Pennsylvania tanner discovered that buffalo hides could be made into useful leather. Hides that were once worthless now brought $1 to $3 each. Buffalo hunting then became a profitable business. Between 1872 and 1874, 9 million buffalo were killed. By 1900 there were fewer than 50 buffalo left in the entire United States! The buffalo had been nearly sacred to many Indian tribes. It gave them food, clothing, and shelter. Without it, the Indians were powerless to resist the advance of the whites.

Wyoming and later into Canada instead of Idaho. For months the band slipped away from thousands of pursuing troops in the rugged country along the border between Oregon and Montana. In September 1877 they reached the Bear Paw Mountains, only 30 miles (48 kilometers) from Canada.

Joseph thought they were safe at last. He stopped to rest. Many of his people were starving. Children were dying. This is when army cavalry units suddenly attacked. Joseph and his warriors held out for four days. Finally they surrendered.

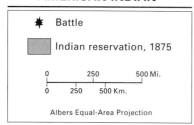

★ Battle

▨ Indian reservation, 1875

0   250   500 Mi.

0   250   500 Km.

Albers Equal-Area Projection

LEARNING FROM MAPS. *As settlers moved westward they pushed the Indians off much of the land they once held. In what states and territories were the largest reservations in 1875? Why do you think they were located in those places?*

Joseph's speech upon surrender is one of the most famous and admired of all such speeches. He hoped his words would carry a message to the warriors who were still fighting. He told his captors:

❝ I am tired of fighting. Our chiefs are killed. Looking Glass is dead. It is the young men who say yes or no. He who led the young men is dead. It is cold and we have no blankets. The little chidren are freezing to death. My people, some of them have run away to the hills and have no blankets, no food; no one knows where they are—perhaps freezing to death. I want to have time to look for my children and see how many I can find. Maybe I shall find them among the dead. Hear me my chiefs. I am tired; my heart is sick and sad. From where the sun now stands, I will fight no more forever.[1] ❞

Wetatonmi, widow of Ollokot, Joseph's brother, spoke of leaving the tribe's lands the night of Joseph's surrender. Imagine the sadness of being torn from your home as the Indians were. Wetatonmi said:

❝ It was lonesome, the leaving. Husband dead, friends buried or held prisoners. I felt that I was leaving all that I had but

[1]From *Touch the Earth: A Self-Portrait of Indian Existence* by T.C. McLuhan

did not cry. You know how you feel when you lose kindred [family] and friends through sickness—death. You do not care if you die. With us it was worse. Strong men, well women and little children killed and buried. They had not done wrong to be so killed. We had only asked to be left in our own homes, the homes of our ancestors. Our going was with heavy hearts, broken spirits. . . . All lost, we walked silently into the wintry night.[1] 99

Joseph's band was settled on a barren reservation in Oklahoma. Far from the mountains of Idaho, this land was "the malarial bottom of the Indian Territory." Joseph, however, was sent to a reservation in Washington state. There he lived in exile, separated from his people and removed from the land he loved. When he died in 1904, the official cause of his death was listed as a broken heart.

The Ghost Dance

The final bloody battle in this chapter of the story of America was fought on the northern plains. In 1889 a religious revival swept through the Indian tribes. Chiefs and medicine men called their people to what whites called the "Ghost Dance." The celebration was based on the vision that an Indian leader would come to drive the whites from Indian lands and the buffalo would again roam the plains.

The Ghost Dance was not a call to war but a celebration of treasured Indian ways of life. Settlers and miners were alarmed at the energy and the mystery of the celebration. They demanded the army put an end to it.

The end came at **Wounded Knee** in South Dakota in December 1890. The 7th Calvary arrested a band of Sioux men, women, and children who were traveling in search of food and shelter as winter came. Suddenly a shot rang out. Without warning the troops opened fire with rifles and Hotchkiss guns, a type of small cannon. They poured a deadly hail of lead into the Indian band, killing 90 men and 200 women and children. The massacre ended armed Indian resistance to white demands.

The End of Indian Independence

All of the wars between the Indians and the army were hard fought. Yet many of the soldiers sympathized with their enemies. They understood why the Indians were fighting. Even Colonel John Gibbon, who discovered the bodies of Custer's men after the Battle of the Little Bighorn, blamed the wars on the settlers. Another officer said, "If I had been a red man . . . I should have fought as bitterly."

The way the government treated Indians shocked a great many

[1]From *Touch the Earth: A Self-Portrait of Indian Existence* by T.C. McLuhan

Head held in his hand, the Hunkpapa Sioux chief Sitting Bull squints at the camera in this 1882 photograph. Here at Standing Rock reservation in the Dakota Territory the chief is living in exile. On his left is Catherine Weldon, a Boston widow and admirer. Sitting Bull offered to make her his wife, but she declined. What clues in the photograph tell you that Sitting Bull's wars have all been waged?

Helen Hunt Jackson's novel Ramona *told the plight of the Indian people when the frontier closed. How did many Americans react to the government's treatment of the Indians?*

Return to the Preview & Review on page 90.

Americans. They were particularly upset when the government broke treaties it had made with the tribes. In *A Century of Dishonor*, published in 1881, Helen Hunt Jackson showed how the government broke promises to Indians. In her novel *Ramona* she tried to do for the Indians what Harriet Beecher Stowe's *Uncle Tom's Cabin* had done for the slaves.

Another fighter for Indian rights was Sarah Winnemucca, the daughter of a Paiute chief. Winnemucca wrote a book and gave lectures describing how unjustly the Indians had been treated. She demanded that the United States return much of the land it had taken from her people.

Congress finally responded by passing the **Dawes Severalty Act** of 1887. This law broke up reservation lands into individual family units. Each family got 160 acres (64 hectares). To protect the owners against speculators, they were not allowed to sell the property for 25 years. Only then did they have full rights to the land. And only then were they allowed to become citizens of the United States.

The Dawes Act was supposed to protect and help the Indians. However, it was written entirely from a white point of view. It ignored the Indians' culture and traditions. Its aim was to turn them into farmers, which would destroy their tribal organizations. It was well meant, but it simply showed once again that most white Americans had little understanding of or sympathy for the plight of the Indians. In this sense it was typical of most of the laws that Congress passed affecting the lives of the original Americans. 🔲

3. MINING THE WEST

The Comstock Lode

The Dawes Act spoke of encouraging the Indians to adopt "the habits of civilized life." The lawmakers apparently wanted them to copy the life styles of their white neighbors. How "civilized" those life styles were is another question!

The miners of the West offered one model. They carried their "civilization" into the mountains of Colorado, Nevada, Arizona, Idaho, Montana, and Wyoming. In each case they struck the region like a tornado.

The first important strikes after the California discovery of gold in 1848 came in Nevada in 1859. The center of this activity was Gold Canyon, a sagebrush-covered ravine on the southern slope of Mt. Davidson. At first the miners panned for gold in the gravel beds of streams. When their yields began to decline, the prospectors moved farther up the mountainside. Among these miners was Henry Comstock, known to his friends as "Old Pancake." His partner, James Fennimore, was called "Old Virginia." They began digging at the head of Gold Canyon on a small rise called Gold Hill. Another pair, Peter O'Riley and Patrick McLaughlin, started digging at Six Mile Canyon, a ravine on the northern slope of Mt. Davidson.

O'Riley and McLaughlin soon came upon a dark, heavy soil sprinkled with gold. Just as they were shouting news of their discovery, Henry Comstock came riding by. Jumping from his horse, he made a quick examination of the find. "You have struck it, boys!" he announced.

Then the old prospector bluffed his way into a partnership. "Look here," he said, "this spring was Old Man Caldwell's. You know that. . . . Well, Manny Penrod and I bought this claim last winter, and we sold a tenth interest to Old Virginia the other day. You two fellows must let us in on equal shares."

At first O'Riley and McLaughlin said no. Then they were afraid they might lose everything, so they said yes.

The partners went to work at once. They found very little gold. Instead they struck large deposits of heavy, bluish sand and blue-gray quartz. Not knowing what that "blasted blue stuff" was, they simply piled it beside the mine. Another miner, however, gathered up a sack of the blue quartz and had it tested, or **assayed.** The assayers' reports went beyond anyone's wildest dreams. The "blue stuff" was rich in silver and gold. The partners had hit upon what was known as a **bonanza**—a large find of extremely rich ore.

News of the discovery caused 15,000 people to swarm into the region in the next few months. Henry Comstock gained everlasting fame by giving the find his name. The enormous **Comstock Lode** ran along the eastern face of Mt. Davidson. It crossed the heads of Gold

Preview & Review

Use these questions to guide your reading. Answer the questions after completing Section 3.
Understanding Issues, Events, & Ideas. Describe mining discoveries in the West, using the following words: assayed, bonanza, Comstock Lode, Virginia City, boom town, vigilance committee, vigilante.
1. Where was the Comstock Lode struck?
2. What was life in a mining camp like? How was life in these camps similar to life in California mining camps in 1849?
3. How did vigilantes keep the law?
Thinking Critically. The author says that the Dawes Act encouraged the Indians to "adopt 'the habits of civilized life.' . . . How 'civilized' those life styles were is another question!" Suppose you are a Native American who has been displaced under the Dawes Act. What is your opinion of your neighbors, the miners? Explain your answer.

Culver Pictures

"Old Pancake"

Mining the West   99

Montana Historical Society

"Main Street will run north and south in a direct line through that cow," said the planners of Anaconda in 1887.

In Montana and Arizona the mining riches were in copper, not gold and silver. In the late 1870s Marcus Daly bought a small silver mine in Butte, Montana, for $30,000. For some reason this silver mine was named Anaconda. An anaconda is a large snake like a boa constrictor. Perhaps the silver ore ran in a curved, snakelike vein.

To finance the Anaconda, Daly turned to George Hearst, a millionaire California developer who had already invested in many western mines. Daly began operations in 1880.

The silver of Anaconda soon gave out. Beneath it, however, Daly found a rich vein of copper.

Hearst supplied the huge sums needed to mine and smelt this copper. By the late 1880s the Anaconda Copper Corporation had become the greatest producer of copper in the world. Eventually, Daly and his associates took over $2 billion worth of copper out of the "richest hill in the world."

and Six Mile Canyons and dipped underneath the crowded mining camps.

Most of the gold and silver the prospectors sought was buried deep in veins of hard quartz rock. Heavy machinery was needed to dig it out. Huge steam-powered drills, tested in California, chiseled away massive chunks of earth. Newly developed steam shovels moved the chunks to waiting wagons, which carried them to smelters. Huge rock crushers and smelters, some like giant blast furnaces, separated the ore from the rock. By 1872 a railway wound through the mining communities, bringing coal to the smelters. But mine owners soon realized that large smelters, located in Golden or Denver, were more efficient. So the railroad hauled raw ore—rich with silver, copper, lead, and gold—to these plants. Tunneling operations called for experienced mining engineers. Powerful pumps were needed to remove groundwater that seeped in as the shafts grew deeper. Prospectors like Comstock, O'Riley, and McLaughlin did not have the skill or the money such operations required. Comstock eventually sold his share of the mine for a mere $10,000.

Nevada Historical Society

"Old Virginia"

The real "bonanza kings" were John W. Mackay, James G. Fair, James C. Flood, and William S. O'Brien. All were of Irish ancestry. All had been born poor. All had come to California during the Gold Rush. In 1868-69 these four men formed a partnership. They used the profits of one strike to buy up other mines. Eventually they took precious metals worth over $150 million from the rich Nevada lode.

Mining Camp Life

Whenever a strike was made, mining camps seemed to sprout out of the surrounding hillsides like flowers after a desert rain. The camps were ramshackle towns of tents and noisy saloons. The most famous was **Virginia City,** Nevada. It was given its name by Henry Comstock's partner, "Old Virginia." While on a spree, "Old Virginia" tripped and fell, smashing his bottle of whiskey. Rising to his knees he shouted drunkenly, "I baptize this town Virginia Town."

Virginia City was a typical **boom town,** so crowded that a horse and wagon could take half an hour to cross the main street. The life of miners, shopkeepers, and others in these mining towns was sometimes as difficult as life on the open range. In these towns it was difficult to keep the peace. Smooth-talking gamblers, gunslingers, and other outlaws sidled alongside claim jumpers, shifty types who specialized in seizing ore deposits that had been staked out by others. Some camps were taken over by these outlaws, who ruled the terror-filled citizens at gunpoint. Such communities provided rich material for American writers. Mark Twain in *Roughing It* and Bret Harte in "The Luck of Roaring Camp" told of life in California mining camps. Charles Farrar Browne wrote this somewhat fictionalized account of a Nevada silver-mining town:

66 Shooting isn't as popular in Nevada as it once was. A few years since [ago] they used to have a dead man for breakfast every morning. A reformed desperado [bandit] told me that he supposed he had killed enough to stock a grave-yard. 'A feeling of remorse,' he said, 'sometimes comes over me! But I'm an altered man now. I hain't killed a man for over two weeks! What'll you poison yourself with?' he added, dealing a resonant [noisy] blow to the bar.[1] 99

Compare Browne's description to the following remembrances of some Virginia City residents. Which seems to be closer to the image of the "Old West" you have?

66 The men who worked in the mines . . . were [a] happy-go-lucky set of fellows, fond of good living, and not particularly interested in religious affairs. . . .

As regarded deportment [behavior], everyone was a law unto himself. . . . Most of the men employed in the

[1]From *Artemus Ward: His Travels* by Charles Farrar Browne

mines were unmarried and enjoyed none of the refining, humanizing influences of home life. They boarded at a restaurant, slept in a lodging-house, and, as a general rule, spent their leisure time on the street or at the gambling-tables.

During the flush times [when there was plenty of money] as many as twenty-five faro games [a gambling game in which players bet on cards drawn from a box] were in full blast night and day. When sporting men . . . sat down of an evening to a friendly game of poker it was no uncommon occurrence for five or six thousand dollars to change hands in a single sitting. Some idea of the amount of money in circulation may be inferred from the fact that every working-man's wages amounted to at least 120 dollars per month.

From what has already been written there is no desire to convey the impression that a low standard of morality was the rule in the Comstock mining district. Men quarreled at times and firearms were discharged [fired] with but slight provocation [cause]. Nevertheless they all had an acute instinct of right and wrong, a high sense of honor, and a chivalrous feeling of respect for the gentler sex. . . .

One of the most prominent traits of character as regarded the miners was their generous response to any worthy object. If a man of family lost his life in the mines thousands of dollars would be contributed to those dependent on him. Each miner contributed regularly one or two days' wages for benevolent causes [those for the public good]. . . .[1] 〞

[1]From *The Mining Frontier: Contemporary Accounts from the American West in the Nineteenth Century,* edited by Marvin Lewis

When conditions in a mining camp got too bad, the respectable residents took action. They formed **vigilance committees** to watch over their towns. Sometimes they even drew up formal constitutions. The members of these committees were called **vigilantes.**

Vigilantes hunted down troublemakers and tried them before judges and juries made up of the same men who had captured them. The usual punishment for the guilty was death by hanging. In one six-week period Montana vigilantes hanged 22 outlaws.

Of course vigilante trials were not legal. And sometimes vigilantes used their power to punish or control blacks and other minorities for no reason other than racial prejudice.

Once a town was properly governed, more and more settlers moved in. Some opened stores. Others turned to farming. Lawyers, ministers, teachers, and doctors moved in. The people built schools and churches, started newspapers and opened hospitals. They built roads to other communities. They put down solid roots. 📑

Return to the Preview & Review on page 99.

4. THE END OF THE OPEN RANGE

The Cattle Kingdom

While the miners were searching the mountains for gold and silver, other pioneers were seeking their own fortunes on the grasslands of the High Plains. The land that formed the **cattle kingdom** stretched from Texas into Canada and from the Rockies to eastern Kansas. This area made up nearly one quarter of the entire United States.

Spanish explorers had brought the first European cattle into Mexico in the early 1500s. Over the years their cattle had grown to enormous herds. Many ran wild. New breeds developed. These great herds spread northward as far as Texas.

By 1860 about 5 million wild cattle were grazing in Texas. These were the famous **Texas longhorns,** so named because their horns had a spread of as much as seven feet (over two meters). After the Civil War, cattle that were worth from $3 to $5 a head in Texas could be sold for $30 to $50 a head in the cities of the eastern United States. The problem was how to get them there. Joseph G. McCoy, an Illinois meat dealer, thought he knew the answer. He could make a fortune, he believed, if he could establish a convenient meeting place for eastern buyers and Texas cattle ranchers.

McCoy chose **Abilene,** Kansas, as this meeting place. There he put up a hotel for the cowhands and dealers and built barns, pens, and loading chutes for the cattle. He persuaded officials of the Kansas Pacific Railroad to ship cattle to **Chicago,** the meat-packing center of the United States, at special low rates.

To get Texas longhorns to Abilene and other **cattle towns** meant herding them slowly northward over the plains. This **long drive** was a two-month journey. On the first drive Texans herded 35,000 longhorns over the **Chisholm Trail** to Abilene. During the next 20 years about 6 million head of cattle were driven north over the open grasslands crossed by trails such as the Goodnight-Loving, Western, and Shawnee.

Open-Range Ranching

The key to the success of the long drive was the grass and water along the trail northward from Texas. Cattle ranchers discovered that prairie grass made an excellent food for their cattle. Then they discovered that the tough, rangy longhorns got along very well in the harsh winters of the northern plains. Soon millions of cattle were grazing on land belonging to the government. Ranchers could fatten their herds on this **open range** of lush grass without paying a cent for it. The cattle roamed freely across the unfenced plains.

Of course the cattle also needed water. It was a very dry region, almost a desert. Water rights, or **range rights,** along a stream meant

Use these questions to guide your reading. Answer the questions after completing Section 4.
Understanding Issues, Events, & Ideas. Describe the work on a cattle drive, using the following words: cattle kingdom, Texas longhorns, Abilene, Chicago, cattle towns, long drive, Chisholm Trail, open range, range rights, cattle baron, round up, brand, *vaquero,* Dodge City, boot hill, range war, sod house, drought, dry farming, bread basket of America.
1. How did Joseph G. McCoy plan to ship Texas longhorns to eastern cities?
2. Why was the open range so important to cattle ranchers?
3. What caused range wars?
4. What was the importance of the windmill, barbed wire, the steel plow, and the twine binder?
Thinking Critically. 1. You are a magazine reporter in 1875. Compose an article titled "A Day in the Life of a Cowhand." 2. It is the late 1800s. You can be a rancher, a cowhand, or a farmer. Which occupation will you choose? Give reasons for your decision.

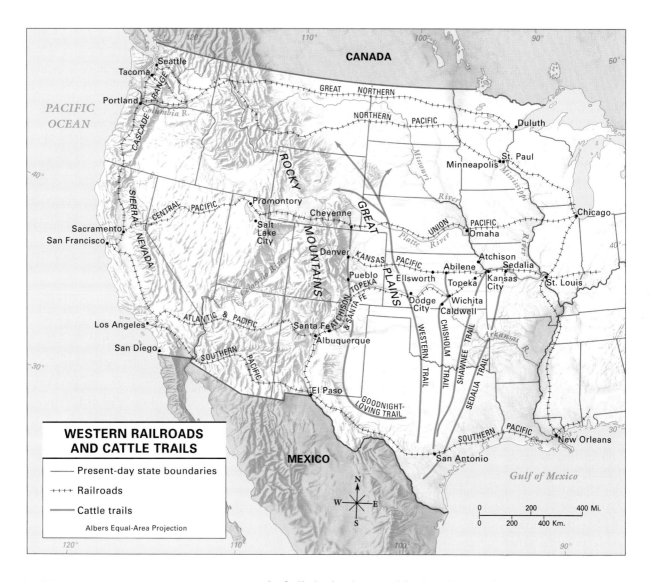

WESTERN RAILROADS AND CATTLE TRAILS

——— Present-day state boundaries

+++++ Railroads

——— Cattle trails

Albers Equal-Area Projection

LEARNING FROM MAPS. *Extension of the railroads across the nation meant many economic changes. One of the most important was the development of the cattle industry in Texas. Cattle were driven along established trails to railroad depots. How far was a long drive from the southern end of the Sedalia Trail to Sedalia? How long was the Chisholm Trail?*

control of all the land around it. Ranchers quickly bought up all the land around their water supply. By owning a few acres along a small river, a rancher could control thousands of acres of surrounding grasslands without actually owning it.

One Colorado **cattle baron,** John F. Iliff, had the use of an area the size of Connecticut and Rhode Island. Yet he owned only about 15,500 acres (6,200 hectares). His land consisted of 105 small parcels on which there was running water.

To secure adequate range rights, a number of ranchers would band together into an association. They would buy up all the land along the banks of a stream or claim it under the Homestead Act. Only *their* cattle would be allowed on this private property. Only *their* cattle could drink from the stream. Although the rest of the range was public property, no other rancher for miles around could graze cattle without water.

Under this system the cattle belonging to the ranchers who owned the banks of the stream became thoroughly mixed. Each spring and fall, cowhands would **round up** all the animals to a central place. The cowhands would fan out across the range, each riding up a canyon or hill. Each would return driving all the cattle in the area before him.

Next the cowhands sorted each rancher's cattle from the rest by checking every animal's marking, called a **brand.** The brand mark was a scar made by pressing a red-hot branding iron onto the animal's hide. Each rancher's brand had a distinct shape, so it was easy to determine who owned which cattle. Those that were ready for market were penned up and shipped off by rail. The rest were turned loose, free to roam the range again until the next roundup.

Of course, newborn calves had not been branded. But calves always trailed close beside their mothers, so it was easy to tell whose property they were. They were branded and sent bawling back to their mothers.

The Cowhand

That colorful figure, the cowhand, was the master of the drive and the roundup. Indians and Mexican Americans were the first cowhands. These *vaqueros* invented almost all the tools of the cowhand's trade, from his broad-brimmed felt hat, his cotton bandana, and his

Charles Marion Russell painted "Jerked Down." These cowhands rope a steer while scrambling to get free of its sharp hooves and horns. How does a great painter like Russell tell an entire story with his brushes and oil paints?

The End of the Open Range   105

The Anschutz Collection

Above are "California Vaqueros" by James Walker. How did Mexican Americans influence the life of every cowhand?

rope lariat to his special western saddle. The word *rodeo* is the Spanish word for "roundup."

A cowhand's life was a hard one. The men worked sunup to sundown and received lower wages than most factory workers. Their legs became bowed from long days in the saddle. They developed permanent squints from peering into the glaring sunlight of the treeless plains. Their faces were lined and leathery, their hands calloused from constantly handling coarse ropes.

Not all cowhands were the strong, silent types portrayed in the movies by white actors. Many came from poor families or from groups outside the mainstream. About one third of the men who worked cattle on the open range were either Mexican Americans or African Americans.

Every item of the cowhand's clothes and equipment served a necessary function. The wide brim of his "ten-gallon hat" could be turned down to shade his eyes or drain off rainfall. His bandana could be tied over his nose and mouth to keep out the dust raised by the pounding hooves of countless cattle. The bandana also served as a towel, a napkin, a bandage, and a handkerchief. Cowhands sometimes wore leather trousers, called chaps, over regular overalls. Chaps were fastened to a broad belt buckled at the back. They protected a rider's legs from injury if he fell from his horse or when he had to ride through cactus, sagebrush, or other thorny plants.

The cowhand's western saddle had a sturdy horn, or pommel, for help in roping powerful steers and horses. These western saddles were heavy but comfortable. A weary cowhand could doze in the saddle while he rode. At night his saddle became a pillow and his saddlecloth a blanket when he stretched out beside the campfire and settled down to sleep. Around the campfire cowboys sang—to relax themselves and the herd. Their songs, such as "Home on the Range," have become a rich part of American music.

To the riders, the trail cook was the most important member of the team! Cowhands drank potfuls of thick, strong coffee to stay awake on the trail. They ate mostly stews, kidney beans, biscuits, and corn bread.

E. C. Abbott wrote of the cowhand's life from firsthand experience. Although his descriptions are generalizations, they provide a vivid picture of the American cowhand.

> " In person cowboys were mostly medium-sized men, as a heavy man was hard on horses, quick and wiry, and as a rule very good-natured. . . . They were intensely loyal to the outfit they were working for and would fight to the death for it. They would follow their wagon boss through hell and never complain. I have seen them ride into camp after two days and nights on herd, lay down on their saddle blankets in the rain, and sleep like dead men, then get up laughing and joking about some good time they had had in . . . Dodge City. Living that kind of life, they were bound to be wild and brave.[1] "

The time spent on the job made for a lonely life. This explains why cowhands were famous for letting off steam when they reached cattle towns such as **Dodge City,** Kansas, the "Cowboy's Capital." Many cowhands were heavy drinkers and gamblers when they came to town. Sometimes there were brawls and gunfights, but the violence and disorder have been exaggerated. Life in the West was much calmer than it is usually pictured in movies. Nevertheless, many cattle towns did have **boot hills**—cemeteries for those who "died with their boots on."

The End of the Open Range

The cowhand rode tall on the open range. In the 1880s, however, the days of the open range were ending. By 1884 there were more than 4.5 million head of cattle roaming free on the Great Plains. The range was becoming overstocked. Good grazing land was scarce. In the foothills of the Rockies sheepherders squared off against local cattle

[1]From *We Pointed Them North: Recollections of a Cowpuncher* by E. C. Abbott ("Teddy Blue") and Helena Huntington Smith.

A cattleman gave this testimony on pasturing his livestock on the open range.

> **I have two miles of running water. That accounts for my ranch being where it is. The next water from me in one direction is 23 miles; now no man can have a ranch between these two places. I have control of the grass, the same as though I owned it.**
> **Testimony Before Public Laws Commision, c. 1880s**

ranchers. Cattle ranchers believed that sheep cropped the grass right down to the roots so that cattle could no longer find it. Many **range wars** broke out between cattle ranchers and sheep ranchers for control of the grasslands.

Farmers also competed with ranchers for land. The cattle trampled their crops. The farmers feared the free-roaming herds would infect their cattle with a dread disease called "Texas fever."

Then came two terrible winters. In 1885-86 and in 1886-87 blizzards howled across the plains. Theodore Roosevelt, then a "gentleman rancher" in Dakota Territory, wrote:

> Furious gales blow down from the north, driving before them the clouds of blinding snow-dust, wrapping the mantle of death around every unsheltered being. . . .

When the spring came in 1887, ranchers discovered that the storms had wiped out a large percentage of their herds.

The boom times were over. Cattle ranchers could no longer count on the free grass of the plains. They had to fence in their herds and feed them hay and fodder in the winter. Cattle ranchers became cattle feeders, their work, like mining, less risky but also less adventurous. This change was important, especially to farmers on the Great Plains. Demand for corn, grains, and hay soared, as did the prices paid for them. Now economics urged Americans to find ways to farm the hard, dry soil of the plains.

Farming on the Great Plains

The soil of the Great Plains was fertile, but farming there proved to be very difficult. Still, settlers came by the thousands to claim their 160 acres under the Homestead Act or to buy land from the railroads. Some were the sons and daughters of farmers in states like Illinois and Iowa and Arkansas. Others were emigrants from Norway, Sweden, and a dozen other lands. O. E. Rölvaag wrote of several Norwegian families and the land they settled. Imagine the plains they saw as he describes them:

> Bright, clear sky over a plain so wide that the rim of the heavens cut down on it around the horizon. . . . Bright, clear sky, to-day, to-morrow, and for all time to come.
>
> . . . And sun! And still more sun! It sets the heavens afire every morning; it grew with the day to a quivering golden light—then softened into all the shades of red and purple as evening fell. . . . Pure colour everywhere. A gust of wind, sweeping across the plain, threw into life waves of yellow and blue and green. Now and then a dead black wave would race across the scene . . . a cloud's gliding shadow . . . now and then. . . .

STRATEGIES FOR SUCCESS

READING A CLIMATE MAP

Like election maps, climate maps are special-purpose maps. They show the climate of an area. *Climate* is the average daily weather conditions over a long period of time. Climate often influences human activity and decision making.

There are 13 major climate types. *Tropical wet* areas are hot and rainy all year. *Tropical wet-and-dry* areas are hot, with most rain falling in the summer. *Desert* regions receive little or no rain, while *semiarid* areas receive between 10 and 20 inches (25 and 50 centimeters) of rain a year. *Mediterranean* areas are mild and dry in the winter and hot and dry in the summer. *West coast marine* climates have cool summers and abundant rain all year. *Humid subtropical* areas have mild winters, hot and rainy summers. Regions with *continental* climates vary. All have severely cold winters, but some have cool summers while others have scorching ones. *Polar* climates—boreal, subarctic, and ice cap—are very cold. *Mountain* climates vary depending on elevation.

How to Read a Climate Map

To read a climate map, follow these guidelines.
1. **Study the key.** The key explains what the colors and special symbols on the map mean. Generally different colors will indicate different climatic regions.
2. **Note the map's patterns.** Climatic regions often follow a predictable pattern.
3. **Use the information.** The information on the climate map can help you form hypotheses and draw conclusions about economic activities and life styles in each climate area.

Applying the Strategy

Study the climate map of the United States below. Note that there are nine major climate regions in the United States. What generalization can you make about climate and human activity after studying the map?

For independent practice, see Practicing the Strategy on page 117.

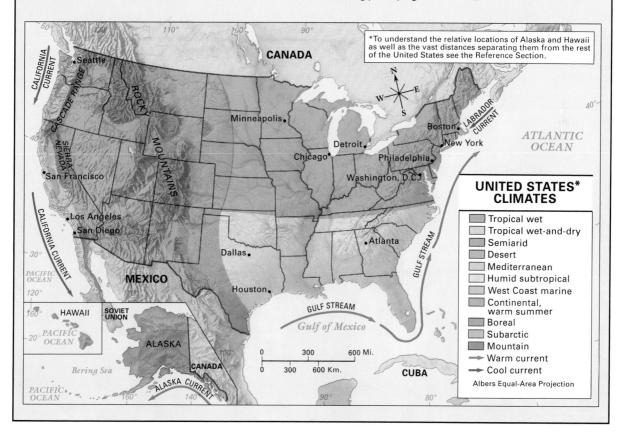

It was late afternoon. A small caravan was pushing its way through the tall grass. The track that it left behind was like the wake of a boat—except that instead of widening out astern it closed in again.

'Tish-ah!' said the grass. . . . 'Tish-ah, tish-ah!' . . . Never had it said anything else—never would it say anything else. It bent resiliently under the trampling feet; it did not break, but it complained aloud every time—for nothing like this had ever happened to it before. . . . 'Tish-ah, tish-ah!' it cried, and rose up in surprise to look at this rough, hard thing that had crushed it to the ground so rudely, and then moved on. . . .

This was the caravan of Pers Hansa, who with his family and all his earthly possessions was moving west from Fillmore County, Minnesota, to Dakota Territory. There he intended to take up land and build himself a home; he was going to do something remarkable out there, which should become known far and wide. No lack of opportunity in that country, he had been told![1] 〟

On the treeless plains the pioneers built their first homes out of the earth itself. The thick roots of the wild grasses made it possible to cut sod into bricklike chunks. Only the roofs of these **sod houses** were made of wood. Sod houses were smoky and damp, but they provided shelter until the railroads reached the frontier. Then lumber could be brought in at reasonable rates.

[1]From *Giants in the Earth* by O.E. Rölvaag

This sod house is typical of those built in the land where wood was scarce. Use historical imagination to ask what the boy will do next.

Fencing was a more difficult problem. Farmers had to protect their crops. But nothing they used stood up to the pounding of the cattle and other farm animals. The problem was solved by Joseph Glidden, who invented barbed wire in 1873. Barbed-wire fences soon crisscrossed the open range.

In the East farmers got water from bubbling springs or from wells. They hauled ground water to the surface in buckets or pumped it up easily by hand. But on the Great Plains water flowed deep beneath the surface. Farmers needed powerful pumps to get it. Fortunately, the winds of the plains blew steadily enough to turn windmills. These powered the pumps that drew up the water.

The biggest problem facing the farmers of frontier Nebraska, Kansas, and the Dakotas was the lack of rainfall. In some years there was plenty of rain to grow wheat and other grain crops. But often there were dry years, even **droughts,** when almost no rain fell. Well water could be used to irrigate a small plot or a vegetable garden, but it was not enough for any large-scale farming.

Hardy W. Campbell, a Nebraska farmer, developed a technique called **dry farming** that made it possible to raise certain crops when as little as 15 or 20 inches (37 to 50 centimeters) of rain fell a year. Campbell plowed the land deeply and repeatedly until the soil was almost as absorbent as blotting paper. The idea was to make sure that all the rain that did fall was absorbed directly into the soil where the roots of the plants could use it. Campbell also planted special varieties of wheat that did not need as much water as other types. Using dry-farming methods, farmers could raise crops in drought years.

Despite such advances farming the plains remained tremendously hard work. Willa Cather captured this in her widely read *My Ántonia*. In this excerpt Jim Burden, the narrator, tells of a visit with his friend Ántonia Shimerda, the only daughter of immigrant parents from Czechoslovakia. Remember as you read that Ántonia's day is fairly typical.

The windmill above might have pumped water for the thirsty pony.

❝ The Shimerdas were in their new log house by then. The neighbors had helped them to build it in March. It stood directly in front of their old cave, which they used as a cellar. The family were now fairly equipped to begin their struggle with the soil. They had four comfortable rooms to live in, a new windmill—bought on credit—a chicken-house and poultry. Mrs. Shimerda had paid grandfather ten dollars for a milk cow, and was to give him fifteen more as soon as they harvested their first crop. . . .

When the sun was dropping low, Ántonia came up the big south draw with her team. How much older she had grown in eight months! She had come to us a child, and now she was a tall, strong young girl, although her fifteenth

Willa Cather, a Nebraskan, wrote her novels set in the Midwest after she herself moved to New York City. Her novels include O Pioneers!, One of Ours, A Lost Lady, *and* Death Comes for the Archbishop—*her masterpiece, set in colonial New Mexico.*

birthday had just slipped by. I ran out and met her as she brought her horses up to the windmill to water them. She wore the boots her father had so thoughtfully taken off before he shot himself, and his old fur cap. Her outgrown cotton dress switched about her calves, over the boot-tops. She kept her sleeves rolled up all day, and her arms and throat were burned as brown as a sailor's. Her neck came up strongly out of her shoulders, like the bole [trunk] of a tree out of the turf. One sees that draught-horse neck among the peasant women in all old countries.

She greeted me gaily, and began at once to tell me how much ploughing she had done that day. Ambrosch, she said, was on the north quarter, breaking sod with the oxen.

'Jim, you ask Jake how much he ploughed to-day. I don't want that Jake get more done in one day than me. I want we have very much corn this fall.'

While the horses drew in the water, and nosed each other, and then drank again, Ántonia sat down on the windmill and rested her head on her hand.

'You see the big prairie fire from your place last night? I hope your grandpa ain't lose no [hay] stacks?'

'No, we didn't. I came to ask you something, Tony. Grandmother wants to know if you can't go to the term of school that begins next week over at the sod school-house. She says there's a good teacher, and you'd learn a lot.'

Ántonia stood up, lifting and dropping her shoulders as if they were stiff. 'I ain't got time to learn. I can work like mans now. My mother can't say no more how Ambrosch do all and nobody to help him. I can work as much as him. School is all right for little boys. I help make this land one good farm.'

She clucked to her team and started for the barn. I walked beside her, feeling vexed. Was she going to grow up boastful like her mother, I wondered? Before we reached the stable, I felt something tense in her silence, and glancing up I saw that she was crying. She turned her face from me and looked off at the red streak of dying light, over the dark prairie.

I climbed up into the loft and threw down the hay for her, while she unharnessed her team. We walked slowly back toward the house. Ambrosch had come in from the north quarter, and was watering his oxen at the tank.

Ántonia took my hand. 'Sometime you will tell me all those nice things you learn at the school, won't you, Jimmy?' she asked with a sudden rush of feeling in her voice. 'My father, he went much to school. He know a great deal; how to make the fine cloth like what you not got here.

National Archives

He play horn and violin, and he read so many books that the priests in Bohemie [Bohemia, a district now in southern Germany] come to talk to him. You won't forget my father, Jim?'

'No,' I said, 'I will never forget him.' . . .'[1]

[1]From *My Ántonia* by Willa Cather.

This farmer was photographed while turning the soil of the prairie. The picture is titled "Mares of Percheron," which is the type of work horse pulling the harrow. What time of year do you suppose this photograph was taken? Explain your answer.

The gigantic "bonanza farms" of the Red River Valley of North Dakota and Minnesota were the most spectacular farms on the plains. These farms spread over thousands of acres. One big wheat farm in Dakota Territory was managed by Oliver Dalrymple. He ran the farm like a factory. Everything possible was mechanized. When the wheat was ripe, he used 155 binders and 26 steam threshers to harvest it. In 1877 Dalrymple's workers harvested 75,000 bushels of wheat.

Farms of this type were unusual. Still, by the 1880s the average plains farmer was using a great deal of machinery. In 1868 James Oliver of Indiana began manufacturing a cast iron plow. This plow could easily slice through the tough sod of the plains. In the 1870s John Appleby invented a twine binder. This machine gathered up bundles of wheat and bound them with twine or string automatically. Soon an acre of wheat that had taken 60 hours to harvest by hand could be harvested in only 3 hours by machine.

By the 1890s the land west of the Mississippi Valley was no longer thought of as a desert. It had become the **breadbasket of America** and the greatest wheat-producing region in the world. By 1890 about 5 million people were living on the Great Plains. There was still unsettled land, but there was no longer a frontier separating settlement from wilderness. The march westward that had begun in Virginia in 1607 had overrun the continent.

Return to the Preview & Review on page 103.

The End of the Open Range 113

LINKING HISTORY & GEOGRAPHY

GOLD! GOLD! GOLD!

Prospectors differed from typical pioneers. They dreamed not of fertile valleys and rich farmlands. They sought steep mountainsides where roaring streams covered beds of ore, deserts where shifting sand hid precious metal, or highlands where jagged rock outcroppings protected great veins of mineral wealth.

Prospecting in California

1. What were the chief methods of mining used by prospectors and miners?

Gold! The word was magic. Like a magnet it attracted hopeful prospectors from all over the world to California in 1849. These Forty-Niners used simple devices—usually a pan or sluice box—to wash the ore to separate the particles of gold.

Once the easily obtained surface gold was gone, however, more sophisticated mining methods were necessary. Gold still remained but it was often locked in hard rock called quartz and was typically found deep beneath the earth's surface. To extract this gold, shafts had to be dug to reach the beds of ore. Crushing mills then separated the unyielding ore from the quartz. But shafts and crushing mills were too expensive for most miners. As a result, eastern bankers furnished the money to develop California's mining industry. Individual prospectors had to look elsewhere if they were to realize their dream of striking it rich on their own.

Searching the West

2. What attracted miners to Colorado?

Throughout the late 1850s and 1860s prospectors scoured the West, ranging from the Pacific to the Rockies. Every likely stream was panned and every promising outcropping of rock was examined in their quest to find pay dirt. Whenever a strike was made, a horde of hopeful miners swarmed in. A handful quickly became rich. Most were lucky if they found enough gold to pay their expenses.

Then in 1858 a number of important discoveries were made, all the way from British Columbia to Colorado. The Colorado strike was the most exciting. Rumors of gold in the region had persisted for years. These rumors were kept alive by the tales of an occasional trapper who would emerge from the mountains with a leather pouch filled with gold nuggets and of Indians who were said to fire bullets made of yellow metal. Add these rumors to the very real presence of water available from the many mountain streams and Colorado had all of the makings of a prospector's paradise.

The site of the original Colorado discovery was on the Cherry Creek near its junction with the Platte River—the very site of Denver, a dozen miles east of the Rockies. A number of small strikes were made during the summer of 1858 and news of each discovery was carried in newspapers throughout the country. By the spring of 1859 more than 100,000 hopeful prospectors flocked to what was known as Pikes Peak Country.

Most of Colorado's gold seekers came from California rather than from the settled lands of the Mississippi Valley. They had learned the basic elements of mining in California, and they attacked the Colorado gold fields with the same techniques. But by 1865 the day of the lone prospector in Colorado had ended, as it had 10 years earlier in California.

The Colorado Mining Industry

3. How did mining develop in Colorado?

Although Pikes Peak gold turned out to be a disappointment to most individual miners, mining continued to grow in Colorado. Large mining companies soon arrived, sinking deep mine shafts and feeding hungry milling machinery. Boom towns such as Central City and Blackhawk were squeezed into narrow ravines. Buildings appeared to be glued to steep slopes and jammed into gulch bottoms. Diggings and test pits were as thick as anthills.

As the miners burrowed deeper and deeper in their search for gold, new mining, milling, and smelting techniques were developed. A railroad wound its way to the communities by 1872, bringing coal to fuel the smelters. But people soon realized smelting was done more efficiently in Golden or Denver, nearer both coal and labor. So the railroad carried heavy machinery into the mining communities and the raw ore—rich with silver, copper, and lead as well as precious gold—out. By 1880 the population of the Central City-Blackhawk area had soared to 10,000. The area became known around the

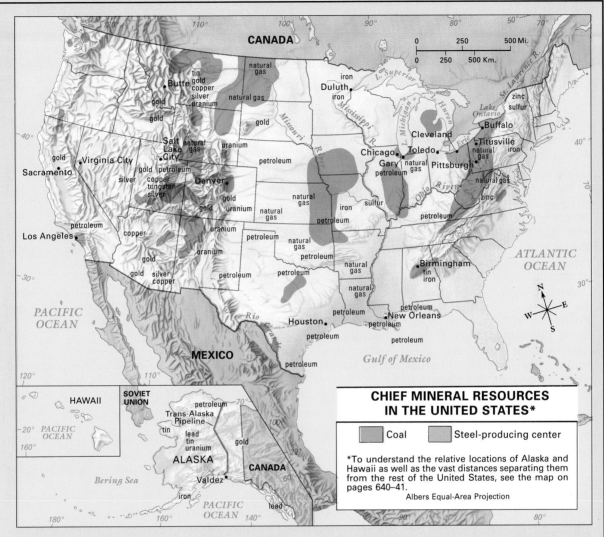

CHIEF MINERAL RESOURCES IN THE UNITED STATES*

Coal   Steel-producing center

*To understand the relative locations of Alaska and Hawaii as well as the vast distances separating them from the rest of the United States, see the map on pages 640–41.

Albers Equal-Area Projection

world as the richest square mile on earth. The future of Colorado gold mining seemed assured.

The Decline of Mining

4. Why did the large-scale mining industry in Colorado decline?

The ultimate decline of the mining industry would have been difficult to foresee during its heyday of the 1870s and 1880s. But decline did come. Mining costs continued to rise as shafts got deeper. The quality of the ore lessened. Problems with ground water became very real. It seeped into the mines as miners penetrated below the water table. Costs of pumping were enormous. Ventilation also became increasingly complex and costly as the shafts angled deeper

and deeper. Finally, the market value of the minerals, with the exception of gold, began a downward slide. In time, copper, lead, and silver could be mined far more inexpensively in other parts of the country.

Applying Your Knowledge

Your class will create an exhibition of America's mineral wealth. Each group will select or be assigned a mineral to display in the exhibition. The display should include a description (or sketch) of the mineral (and a sample if available), a list of its uses, and a map of the locations of major deposits. Your class may wish to set up the exhibition in an appropriate place in the school or community.

CHAPTER 2 REVIEW

1845			1860		

1848 Treaty of Guadalupe Hildago

1849 California Gold Rush

1851 Treaty of Fort Laramie

1859 Fifty-Niners surge to Colorado

1860 Cattle kingdom established on Plains

1862 Pacific Railway Act

1864 Chivington Massacre

Chapter Summary
Read the statements below. Choose one, and write a paragraph explaining its importance.
1. Before the 1850s only Indians, Mexicans, and a few Mormons lived on the Great Plains. Until then it was considered a desert.
2. Plains Indians developed unique ways of life, even adapting European items such as the horse and metal tools to their life styles.
3. As settlers and railroads sought land on the Plains the Indians were removed to reservations. This process led to brief but bitter battles between the Indians and government troops. Settlers also seized land from Mexican Americans living in the Southwest.
4. Rich ore deposits west of the Plains brought a flurry of prospectors who built ramshackle mining camps.
5. The grasslands of the High Plains soon became the cattle kingdom. Thousands of cattle grazed on the open range and were then shipped to Chicago.
6. The open range closed as technical improvements made it possible to farm the Great Plains. Chief among these was dry farming, barbed wire, the steel plow, and the twine binder.

Reviewing Chronological Order
Number your paper 1–5. Then study the time line above and place the following events in the order in which they happened by writing the first next to 1, the second next to 2, and so on.
1. Treaty of Fort Laramie
2. Dawes Act
3. Wounded Knee
4. Transcontinental Railroad completed
5. Cattle kingdom established

Understanding Main Ideas
1. How was the system called concentration used to remove the Plains Indians?

2. How did the government encourage the building of transcontinental railroads?
3. Describe life in a typical mining town.
4. Describe the life of a cowhand. What were some inventions of the *vaqueros* used by cowhands?
5. What ended the open range? Why?
6. Describe the inventions and farming techniques that helped turn the Great American Desert into the breadbasket of America.

Thinking Critically
1. **Analyzing.** Putting yourself in the place of a Plains Indian of the early 1800s, make a list of the animals that are important to your tribe. Alongside the name of each animal, list the uses you make of it.
2. **Synthesizing.** Imagine that you are Leland Stanford writing your autobiography in June 1869. Describe your company's part in building America's first transcontinental railroad. Then tell of the important role other such railroads will play in the nation's future.
3. **Problem Solving.** You are a member of a vigilance committee in a rowdy boom town. You have called a meeting with other vigilantes to make plans for bringing law and order to your town. To prepare for your opening remarks at the meeting, outline the problems facing you. Then outline two or three ideas for how to solve these problems.

Writing About History: Classificatory
Use historical imagination to place yourself in one of the mining boom towns of the 1860s or as a cowhand on a long drive. Write a letter home to your family in the East telling about your life in the West. Describe the good and bad aspects of your life and the place where you live. Use the information in Chapter 2 and in reference books to prepare your letter.

68
st iron plow developed

69
anscontinental
ilroad completed

1874
Barbed
wire
patented

1876
Battle of the Little Bighorn

1877
Chief Joseph surrenders

1881
Sitting Bull surrenders

★
A Century of Dishonor

1887
Dawes Act

★
Blizzards end open range

1890
Wounded Knee

Practicing the Strategy
Review the strategy on page 109.
Reading a Settlement Map. Study the settlement map in the Reference Section and answer the following questions.
1. Into what three states of the Ohio Valley had settlement spread by 1790?
2. Large parts of Wyoming, Montana, western Texas, and several other states were not fully settled until after 1880. Why?
3. Oklahoma was not considered settled until much later than most of its neighbors. What fact in Oklahoma's history explains this?
4. Compare the settlement map to the population distribution map below it. How are the patterns similar? How would you explain this similarity?

Using Primary Sources
The winter of 1884–85 was one of the most disastrous in America's cattle-ranching history. As you read the following excerpt from J. Frank Dobie's *The Longhorns,* think about how people and animals struggled to survive on the Great Plains. Then answer the questions that follow.

> *When a terrible blizzard struck in late December, cattle from southwestern Kansas and No Man's Land [a geographic area in northern Oklahoma] went with it. The grass lay under a pavement of sleet and ice. The plains afforded no harbor or shelter. As endless strings of cattle going with the wind crowded up to the first drift fence, the leaders stopped, stiffened and went down, to be trampled on by followers until piles of dead made overpasses. In places the posts were shoved over and cattle struggling through cut themselves to pieces on the barbed wire. . . . After the storm the fence lines were marked by tens of thousands of frozen bodies. In the spring cattle from the upper ranges were found five hundred miles south in Texas.*

1. How do you think cowboys might have described "No Man's Land?"

2. Although the drift fences presented problems for trail drivers during a blizzard, what purpose does the reading suggest the fences served?
3. How do you think the harsh winters during the mid-1880s affected the cattle industry economically? Use evidence from the excerpt to support your opinion.

Linking History & Geography
As you read in this chapter, water is an especially valuable resource on the Great Plains. In 1820 Major Stephen Long led an army expedition through the region. Noting the dry, treeless plain, he labeled it the "Great American Desert." Except for reservoirs, there are no lakes on the Great Plains. Rivers are generally fewer and shallower than back east. On the eastern plains, precipitation—rain and snow together—averages 25 inches (64 centimeters) or more; on the western plains it is as little as 10 inches (25 centimeters). How did this lack of water affect the settlement of the Great Plains?

Enriching Your Study of History
1. **Individual Project.** A *diorama* is an exhibit of lifelike figures in natural settings in the foreground with a painting in the background. Make a diorama of an Indian camp on the Great American Desert, of a mining boom town, or of a farm on the Great Plains in the 1880s.
2. **Cooperative Project.** Your class will prepare a special section for a newspaper. Each group will use historical imagination to be newspaper reporters assigned to cover the Battle of Little Bighorn. Some of you will write biographical sketches of the key figures. Others will create illustrations, and still others will prepare a relief map of the battle site, showing the topography.

Chapter 2 Review   **117**

The Rise of Industrial America

B etween 1860 and 1900 the United States went through one of the most dramatic periods of change in its entire history. In 1860 about 80 percent of the nation's 31 million inhabitants lived on farms. About 1.5 million, less than 5 percent, worked in factories. By the 1890s about 5 million Americans worked in factories. America's manufactured products were worth almost as much as the manufactured goods of Great Britain, France, and Germany combined. By the end of the century the new industrial growth was visible nearly everywhere. Railroads crossed and recrossed the continent. Small towns had been changed as if by magic into great cities. In 1900 about 40 percent of America's 76 million people lived in towns and cities. The steel, oil, and electrical industries, tiny in 1865, had become giants. Imagine how the United States would have seemed in 1900 to a person who had been out of the country since the Civil War!

An appropriate symbol for America in the 19th century is the ironworks at Pittsburgh. What can you say about the forms of transportation in this engraving? How would environmentalists today appraise this scene?

The Granger Collection

1. THE POWER OF THE RAILS

The Railroad Network

Americans were fascinated by railroads. Poets celebrated the "pant and roar" of the locomotives, so powerful as to shake the ground, and the elaborate decorations painted on their sides. They even praised the "dense and murky" clouds that belched from the locomotives' smokestacks. To all sorts of people railroads symbolized the boundless energy of the nation. In 1879 the great American poet Walt Whitman traveled by rail west from Philadelphia to the Rocky Mountains and back. He then wrote this prose poem in tribute to railroads:

> 66 What a fierce weird pleasure to lie in my berth at night in the luxurious palace-car, drawn by the mighty Baldwin [a make of locomotive]—embodying, and filling me, too, full of the swiftest motion, and most resistless strength! It is late, perhaps midnight or after—distances join'd like magic—as we speed through Harrisburg, Columbus, Indianapolis. The element of danger adds zest to it all. On we go, rumbling and flashing, with our loud whinnies thrown out from time to time, or trumpetblasts, into the darkness. Passing the homes of men, the farms, barns, cattle—the silent villages. And the car itself, the sleeper, with curtains drawn and lights turn'd down—in the berths the slumberers, many of the women and children—as on, on, on, we fly like lightning through the night—how strangely sound and sweet we sleep! . . .[1] 99

When the Civil War began, there were only 30,000 miles (48,000 kilometers) of railroad track in the United States. Most railroads were very short, averaging only about 100 miles (160 kilometers). They had been built to serve local needs. Few direct lines connected distant cities. Passengers and freight traveling between New York and Chicago, for example, had to be transferred from one line to another 17 times! The trip took at least 50 hours.

The main task of the postwar generation was to connect these lines into one network. "Commodore" Cornelius Vanderbilt was a pioneer in this work. Vanderbilt could barely read and write, but he was aggressive and hard-nosed. He had made a fortune in shipping, but when river traffic fell during the Civil War, he invested in railroads. By 1869 he had control of the New York Central Railroad, which ran between Buffalo and Albany, and two other lines that connected the Central with New York City.

[1] From *The Collected Prose* (1891–1892) by Walt Whitman

Use these questions to guide your reading. Answer the questions after completing Section 1.
Understanding Issues, Events, & Ideas. Using the following words, describe the economic changes in the United States after 1870: railroad baron, corporation, stock certificate, stockholder, board of directors, limited liability, partnership, Bessemer converter, Mesabi Range, smelt, division of labor, mass production, oil refining, "Drake's Folly," wildcatter, "black gold."
1. How did railroads stimulate the national economy?
2. Why did the railroad boom lead business leaders to set up corporations?
3. What effect on the production of steel did the Bessemer converter have?
4. What created the demand for kerosene? How did the discovery of oil lead to a boom?
Thinking Critically. 1. The year is 1870. You have just seen a passing locomotive for the first time. Write a brief description of your impressions. **2.** Which do you think was the most important scientific achievement in the 1800s: mass production of steel or the process of oil refining? Give reasons for your decision.

The Power of the Rails   119

Travelers to ancient Greece saw the bronze Colossus of Rhodes, over 100 feet (30.5 meters) high. It was one of the seven wonders of the ancient world. Ships were said to have sailed between its legs, but in truth the Colossus stood on a hillside. "The Colossus of Roads" by Joseph Keppler makes Cornelius Vanderbilt a modern colossus with his empire of railroads. Explain how a man barely able to read and write amassed a fortune of 100 million dollars.

In 1870 Vanderbilt bought the Lake Shore and Michigan Southern Railroads. His growing New York Central system then extended 965 miles (1,544 kilometers) from New York to Chicago by way of Cleveland and Toledo. Passengers could travel between New York and Chicago in less than 24 hours without leaving their seats. When Vanderbilt died in 1877, he left a railroad system of over 4,500 miles (7,200 kilometers) serving a vast region. He left a personal fortune of $100 million.

In much the same way J. Edgar Thomson, head of the Pennsylvania Railroad, built up direct routes from Philadelphia to St. Louis and Chicago by way of Pittsburgh. In 1871 the Pennsylvania Railroad extended its tracks to New York City. Other lines were extended by wealthy developers such as Jay Gould, Jim Fisk, and James J. Hill.

Besides combining railroads to make through connections, the **railroad barons,** as the men who financed and profited from railroads were called, built many new lines. By 1900 the United States had about 200,000 miles (320,000 kilometers) of railroad track. This was more than were in all the nations of Europe combined.

In addition to speeding the movement of goods and passengers, the railroads supplied thousands of jobs for laborers, train crews, repair workers, and clerks. By 1891 the Pennsylvania Railroad alone employed over 110,000 workers. The largest United States government employer, the post office, had only 95,000 on its payroll in 1891.

Railroads stimulated the national economy in countless ways. They were great users of wood, copper, and steel. They made it possible to move bulky products like coal and iron ore cheaply over long distances. This made such products available at reasonable prices in regions where they had formerly been very expensive. Railroads enabled farmers in California to sell their fruits and vegetables in New York. Flour milled in Minneapolis could be purchased in Boston. Wherever railroads went, new towns sprang up almost overnight, and older towns grew to be big cities.

LEARNING FROM TABLES. *This table illustrates the growth of railroads between 1870 and 1900. Why was the extension of the railroad network essential to the development of the American economy?*

RAILROADS, 1870-1900			
Year	Miles of Track	Capital Invested (Millions)	Total Income (Millions)
1870	52,922	$ 2,476	NA
1880	93,262	$ 5,402	$ 503
1890	166,703	$10,122	$1,092
1900	193,346	$12,814	$2,013
NA= Not Available			

Source: *Historical Statistics of the United States*

The Corporation

Railroads were very expensive to build and operate. The sums needed to build even a small one were far larger than the amount John C. Calhoun had to raise to buy his South Carolina plantation, more than John Ellerton Lodge had invested in his fleet of merchant ships, greater than Francis Cabot Lowell and the Boston Associates needed when they built their first textile mill.

One person or family or even a group of partners rarely had enough money to construct and operate a railroad. Railroad developers had to raise money from other investors. To do this, they set up their businesses as **corporations.**

When a corporation is formed, the organizers sell shares called **stock certificates.** People who buy shares are called **stockholders.** These stockholders own the corporation, which is usually run by a **board of directors.** Stockholders can sell their shares to anyone for whatever price they can get. If the business is doing poorly, the value of the shares will fall.

For the organizers of big businesses the chief advantage of the corporation is that it brings together the money of many investors. For the investors the chief advantage is **limited liability.** This means that the individual investors risk only the money they have paid for their stocks. In a **partnership,** on the other hand, all the partners are responsible for the debts of the firm. For example, a partner who had invested only $100 could be held responsible for a $5,000 debt of a partnership. The same person investing $100 in the stock of a corporation could lose only that $100, no matter how much money the corporation owed.

Changing Iron into Steel

The railroad industry could not have grown as large as it did without steel. The first rails were made of iron. But iron rails were not strong enough to support heavy trains running at high speeds. Railroad executives wanted to replace them with steel rails because steel was 10 or 15 times stronger and lasted 20 times longer. Before the 1870s, however, steel was too expensive to be widely used. It was made by a slow and expensive process of heating, stirring, and reheating iron ore.

Then an English inventor, Henry Bessemer, discovered that directing a blast of air at melted iron in a furnace would burn out the impurities that made the iron brittle. As the air shot through the furnace, the bubbling metal would erupt in showers of sparks. When the fire cooled, the metal had been changed, or *converted,* to steel. The **Bessemer converter** made possible the mass production of steel. Now three to five tons of iron could be changed into steel in a matter of minutes.

"Forging the Shaft: A Welding Heat" was painted in 1877 by John F. Weir. It captures the glow of molten metal that filled American steel mills in the 19th century. Use your historical imagination to describe the sensations you would have felt working in front of a blast furnace.

Just when the demand for more and more steel developed, prospectors discovered huge new deposits of iron ore in the **Mesabi Range,** a 120-mile-long region (192 kilometers) in Minnesota near Lake Superior. The Mesabi deposits were so near the surface that they could be mined with steam shovels.

Barges and steamers carried the iron ore through Lake Superior to depots on the southern shores of Lake Michigan and Lake Erie. With dizzying speed Gary, Indiana, and Toledo, Youngstown, and Cleveland, Ohio, became major steel-manufacturing centers. Pittsburgh was the greatest steel city of all. The large coal fields near Pittsburgh supplied cheap fuel to **smelt** the ore—that is, to melt it down to remove impurities.

Steel was the basic building material of the industrial age. After steel rails came steel bridges. Next came steel skeletons for tall buildings. Nails, wire, and other everyday objects were also made of steel. Production skyrocketed from 77,000 tons in 1870 to over 11 million tons in 1900.

Andrew Carnegie was by far the most important producer of steel. Born in 1835 in Scotland, he came to the United States at age 12 and settled with his parents in Allegheny, now a part of Pittsburgh. At 14 he was working 12 hours a day as a bobbin boy in a cotton mill for $1.20 a week. He studied hard and at 16 had progressed to a telegraph clerk earning $4.00 a week—a fair salary in those days. At 17 Carnegie became the private secretary to the president of the Pennsylvania Railroad.

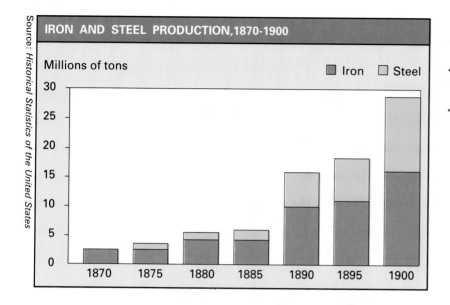

Source: *Historical Statistics of the United States*

IRON AND STEEL PRODUCTION, 1870-1900

Millions of tons

■ Iron □ Steel

30
25
20
15
10
5
0

1870 1875 1880 1885 1890 1895 1900

LEARNING FROM GRAPHS.
Note the rapid increase in the production of iron and steel shown on this graph. Iron and steel, like railroad and communication networks, were necessary for modern industrial growth. Why?

Carnegie then invested in an oil well and began to make money in the new oil industry. But he soon turned to the steel industry. He frankly admitted he knew nothing about making steel when he started. Early in his career as an ironmaster, he visited a plant in England where the Bessemer process was being used. This new process made large quantities of steel cheaply. Now Carnegie became convinced that the day of cheap steel had arrived. He rushed home and built the largest Bessemer plant in America. He did so in the midst of the worst depression in the history of the United States. Labor and materials were cheap. Thus Carnegie got a large, up-to-date steel mill at a bargain price.

But Carnegie's true success was as a promoter and seller. He captured the largest share of the railroad business—the nation's largest steel users—with several shrewd deals. He also knew how to gather specialists and manage them. He was a relentless boss. By 1900 Andrew Carnegie, who came to America as a poor immigrant boy, was the second richest man in the world. In 1901 he sold his steel property for nearly $500 million!

Mass Production

The rapidly growing production of steel formed the foundations of an industrial system that would eventually make the United States the most productive country in the world. Besides rails, bridges, and steel-framed buildings, steel went into heavy machines, factories, and mills. Businesses expanded and factories grew larger. Owners and managers developed more efficient production methods.

You have read about Eli Whitney's development of interchangeable parts. This led to a **division of labor.** A shoemaker no longer made an entire shoe. Instead, in large shoe factories one worker

Brown Brothers

Andrew Carnegie came to America from Scotland and began work in the factories as a bobbin boy. How did this hard-working immigrant make his fortune?

The Power of the Rails   123

might run a machine that cut only heels. Another might run a machine that cut out the soles, and so forth. All the parts were then brought together at a central place and assembled by still other workers into a shoe. Vast quantities of shoes could be made quickly in this way. Most American industries soon adopted division of labor. It made possible the **mass production** of large quantities of products of every kind.

"Black Gold"

An important new industry, **oil refining,** grew after the Civil War. Crude oil, or petroleum—a dark, thick ooze from the earth—had been known for hundreds of years. But little use had ever been made of it. In the 1850s Samuel M. Kier, a manufacturer in western Pennsylvania, began collecting the oil from local seepages and refining it into kerosene. Refining, like smelting, is a process of removing impurities from a raw material.

Kerosene was used to light lamps. It was a cheap substitute for whale oil, which was becoming harder to get and therefore more expensive. Soon there was a large demand for kerosene. People began to search for new supplies of petroleum.

The first oil well was drilled by E. L. Drake, a retired railroad conductor. In 1859 he began drilling in Titusville, Pennsylvania. The whole venture seemed so impractical and foolish that onlookers called it **"Drake's Folly."** But when he had drilled down about 70 feet (21 meters), Drake struck oil. His well began to yield 20 barrels of crude oil a day.

News of Drake's success brought oil prospectors to the scene. By the early 1860s these **wildcatters** were drilling for **"black gold"** all over western Pennsylvania. The boom rivaled the California gold rush of 1848 in its excitement and Wild West atmosphere. And it brought far more wealth to the prospectors than any gold rush.

At first oil was shipped to refineries in barrels. The barrel was replaced first by railroad tank cars and then by oil pipelines. Crude oil could be refined into many products. For some years kerosene continued to be the principal one. It was sold in grocery stores and door-to-door. In the 1880s refiners learned how to make other petroleum products such as waxes and lubricating oils for new industrial machines. The discovery of these oils and the invention by Elijah McCoy, the son of runaway slaves, of a lubricating cup that fed the oil to parts of a machine while it was operating were important industrial breakthroughs.

Not until the 1890s was petroleum used to make gasoline or heating oil. The development then of the internal combustion engine, which burned gasoline or diesel fuel, finally turned oil into one of the nation's major sources of power. By the turn of the century modern factories were turning to oil as their source of energy. 🖱

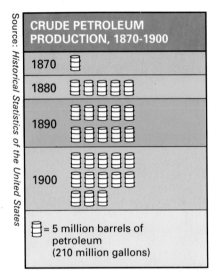

CRUDE PETROLEUM PRODUCTION, 1870-1900

1870	🛢
1880	🛢🛢🛢🛢🛢
1890	🛢🛢🛢🛢🛢 🛢🛢🛢🛢🛢
1900	🛢🛢🛢🛢🛢 🛢🛢🛢🛢🛢 🛢🛢🛢

🛢 = 5 million barrels of petroleum (210 million gallons)

LEARNING FROM CHARTS. *Petroleum production boomed during the second half of the 19th century, as you can see from this chart. What were its main uses in American industry?*

Return to the Preview & Review on page 119.

2. THE COMMUNICATIONS REVOLUTION

The Telegraph and Telephone

Rapid, cheap communication over long distances is an essential part of modern industrial society. The **communications revolution** began in 1837 when Samuel F. B. Morse invented the **telegraph** to send electronic signals over wire. By 1861 telegraph lines connected all parts of the country. One line stretched all the way across the still-unsettled Great Plains to the Pacific Coast.

The telegraph made it possible for people to communicate over great distances in seconds. It took much of the guesswork out of business. Managers could know when supplies would arrive, where demand was greatest for their products, and what prices were being charged across the country.

In 1866 the Western Union Telegraph Company obtained control of the national telegraph network. The same year Cyrus W. Field succeeded in laying the first successful telegraph cable across the Atlantic Ocean to Europe. Not long after that, a telegraph network gave the United States almost instant communication with countries all over the world.

Next came the **telephone**. The telephone was invented in 1876 by Alexander Graham Bell, a teacher of the deaf in Boston. Work

Preview & Review

Use these questions to guide your reading. Answer the questions after completing Section 2.

Understanding Issues, Events, & Ideas. Using the following words, summarize how inventions in the late 1800s changed the nation: communications revolution, telegraph, telephone, quadruplex telegraph, phonograph, electric light, suspension bridge, skyscraper, department store, chain store.

1. How did the communications revolution affect business?
2. How did Samuel F. B. Morse contribute to the communications revolution? How did Alexander Graham Bell contribute?
3. What did Thomas Edison say was the secret of his success as the great inventor of the era?
4. How did new marketing techniques help business grow?

Thinking Critically. It is 1880. Write and send a telegram to your family, telling them what you think is the most important invention of the late 1800s.

Cyrus Field, above, made the world a little smaller with his Atlantic cable. Mathew Brady was his photographer. Left is Alexander Graham Bell placing the first public telephone call in 1876. Imagine out loud what he might have said.

with the deaf had led to the study of *acoustics*, the science of sound. His telephone turned sound waves into an electrical current. The current passed through a long wire and was then changed back into sound in a distant receiver.

Bell first demonstrated the telephone in 1876. When he offered Western Union the right to use his invention, the telegraph company turned him down. President William Orton of Western Union called the telephone an "electrical toy."

Fortunately, other people realized the telephone's usefulness. By 1880, 85 towns and cities had telephone systems. Five years later, more than 100 telephone companies were combined to create the American Telephone and Telegraph Company. Telephone wires soon wove spidery webs across the skies of America.

A web of wires—electric and telephone—crisscrosses Broadway in New York City. Perhaps no scene better illustrates the coming of the electrical age than this 1880s lithograph. But the wires came tumbling down when the wet snows fell during the Blizzard of 1888. Where are most electric and telephone lines in most cities today?

New York Historical Society

The Wizard of Menlo Park

In the same year that Bell invented the telephone, Thomas Alva Edison established the nation's first industrial research laboratory, at Menlo Park, New Jersey. Edison was the greatest inventor of the age. He was an inspired tinkerer and a hard worker, not a great thinker. "Sticking to it is the genius," he once said. He had only four years of off-and-on schooling.

Edison's first major invention, the **quadruplex telegraph,** was a machine that could send four messages over one wire at the same time. At Menlo Park he made several improvements on Bell's telephone. He invented the **phonograph** in 1877. But the **electric light** was his most important invention.

Using electricity to make light was not a new idea. In 1867 the boulevards of Paris were illuminated with arc lights. Arc lights, in which an electric discharge passed continuously between electrodes, were noisy and smoky. They could only be used outdoors. Edison was able to design a small light for indoors. His basic idea was to pass electricity through a fine wire inside an airless glass globe. The electricity heated the wire white hot, causing it to glow brightly. The wire could not burn up because there was no oxygen in the globe.

Edison spent two years experimenting with different filaments,

At five o'clock in the morning of June 16, 1888, Thomas Edison first heard his recorded voice reciting "Mary Had a Little Lamb." He perfected his "talking machine," while going without sleep for 72 hours. What did Edison say made him successful?

A biographer of Thomas Edison writes about what great expectations the public had for the inventor.

> **On April 1 the *New York Daily Graphic* bannered: "Edison Invents a Machine that will Feed the Human Race—manufacturing Biscuits, Meat, Vegetables, and Wine out of Air, Water, and Common Earth." It was, of course, an April Fool's story, but other newspapers around the country picked it up and ran it straight. Nothing seemed impossible for a man who could make a machine that talked. . . .**
>
> From *A Streak of Luck,* Robert Conot, 1979

or wires, that would glow for long periods without breaking. In December 1879 he found one. Soon "the Wizard of Menlo Park" was setting up city lighting companies and power stations to generate electricity and selling light bulbs by the millions. In 1900 only about 2 percent of America's manufacturing plants were powered by electricity. But soon it would join oil as the most important sources of energy for industry.

More American Inventiveness

The telegraph, the underwater cable, the telephone, and the discoveries of Thomas Edison were landmarks in the history of communications. But other important inventions and developments also reshaped American life. Engineers and architects tackled the most difficult problems. **Suspension bridges,** their roadways held by heavy cables, crossed broad bays and rivers. **Skyscrapers** poked their steel fingers into the sky. New machines for making cheap paper from wood pulp for printing newspapers, books, and magazines contributed to more effective communications. The typewriter, developed in the 1860s, and adding machine, invented in the 1870s, both soon became essential tools of American business. George Eastman's roll film and "Kodak" camera provided new forms of recreation as well as new techniques for industry and research.

Inventors of all races were caught up in the creative spirit. An African American inventor, Granville T. Woods, developed the automatic air brake for trains and was called "the greatest electrician in the world." Lewis Howard Latimer, who worked with both Bell and Edison, was the only African American member of the famous Edison Pioneers. That famous group of inventors issued a statement of their high regard upon his death in 1928.

> **It was Mr. Latimer who executed the drawings and assisted in the preparing the application for the telephone patents of Alexander Graham Bell. In 1880 he entered the employ of Hiram S. Maxim, Electrician of the United States Electric Lighting Co., then located at Bridgeport, Connecticut. It was while working in this employ that Mr. Latimer successfully produced a method of making carbon filaments for the Maxim electric incandescent lamp, which he patented. His keen perception of the possibilities of the electric light and kindred [related] industries resulted in his being the author of several other inventions. . . . Broadmindedness, versatility in the accomplishment of things intellectual and cultural, a linguist, a devoted husband and father, all were characteristic of him, and his genial presence will be missed from our gatherings.[1]**

[1] From "Statement of the Edison Pioneers," December 11, 1928

Surely most Americans have shopped in the five- and ten-cent stores that spread across the country at the turn of the century. Pictured at left is the first Woolworth's store, opened in 1879.

New Ways of Selling Products

Businesses came up with creative new ways to market their products. Just as factories and businesses grew bigger, so did stores. The small general store became less important. New types of stores arose to handle the ever-growing number of products.

The specialty store carried a single line of goods—hardware, clothing, groceries, shoes, and so forth. The **department store** combined many specialty stores under one roof. John C. Wanamaker opened the first department store in the United States in Philadelphia. Marshall Field opened another in Chicago in 1881. Soon others opened in larger cities.

Chain stores—stores with branches in many cities—also began to appear. The Great Atlantic and Pacific Tea Company (A & P) stores and Woolworth's were the first chain stores. Like department stores, they bought large quantities of goods at lower prices and passed the savings on to shoppers. And since women were both the major customers and commonly were paid less than men, managers gladly hired women as clerks.

Specialty stores, department stores, and chain stores were part of cities. In 1872, Aaron Montgomery Ward started a mail-order business aimed at the rural market. A few years later the Sears, Roebuck mail-order company started business. Customers received catalogs picturing goods for sale. They placed orders and paid for goods by mail; their goods were shipped to them by mail or railway express. Catalogs from the two companies became prized possessions in rural areas, helping bring the outside world to isolated parts of America.

Professional advertising also began to appear in the 1880s. It introduced new products and helped create large national markets for the streams of new manufactured products becoming available almost weekly. 📧

Return to the Preview & Review on page 125.

3. REGULATION OF BIG BUSINESS

Use these questions to guide your reading. Answer the questions after completing Section 3.

Understanding Issues, Events, & Ideas. Defend government regulation of big business, using the following words: entrepreneur, fixed cost, overhead, rebate, monopoly, pool, Standard Oil Company, trust, Interstate Commerce Act, regulatory agency, antitrust movement, interstate commerce, Sherman Antitrust Act, free enterprise.

1. In what ways were new American business leaders pioneers?
2. What practice did railroads use to reduce competition?
3. How did Rockefeller accomplish his objective of combining the country's oil refineries?
4. Why were the Interstate Commerce Act and Sherman Antitrust Act ineffective?

Thinking Critically. You are a farmer in a small "one-railroad town" in 1887. Write a letter to the Interstate Commerce Commission, complaining of the problems you are having and suggest ways that you think these problems can be solved.

American Business Pioneers

The people who presided over new worlds of throbbing machines, noisy factories, and crowded cities were business leaders and financiers called **entrepreneurs.** They invested their money in new businesses. Although they varied greatly in personalities, abilities, and business methods, they were all pioneers. Some were rough, some were refined. All were eager to seize the seemingly unlimited opportunities of the new industrial world emerging around them. Some were fabulously successful. Others, the small-business owners, never gained a huge fortune or power. But all of them—big-business leaders and small-business owners alike—shared the American ideal of self-reliant individualism. The men as well as the women of this group such as Nettie Fowler McCormick in farm machinery, Lydia Pinkham in patent medicine, and Kate Gleason in machine tools became the most influential people in America.

What motivated these people to take the risks of investing their money in business? See if you can feel his excitement as Andrew Carnegie describes receiving his first dividend:

> ❝ Adams Express stock then paid monthly dividends of one per cent, and the first check for five dollars arrived. I can see it now, and I well remember the signature of 'J.C. Babcock, Cashier'. . . .
>
> The next day being Sunday, we boys—myself and my ever-constant companions took our usual Sunday afternoon stroll in the country, and sitting down in the woods, I showed them this check, saying, 'Eureka! We have found it.'
>
> Here was something new to all of us, for none of us had ever received anything except from toil. A return from capital was something strange and new.
>
> How money could make money, how, without any attention from me, this mysterious golden visitor should come, led to much speculation upon the art of the young fellows, and I was for the first time called a 'capitalist.'
>
> You see, I was beginning to serve my apprenticeship as a business man in a very satisfactory manner.[1] ❞

Many of America's business leaders—Vanderbilt, Rockefeller, and others—told the same story: poor boy works hard and gets rich. Horatio Alger, Jr. made this "rags to riches" theme the most popular reading of the day. Alger, the son of a Massachusetts minister, had been the chaplain of a shelter for orphaned youth in New York City.

[1]From *The American Society* by Kenneth S. Lynn

He wrote over 130 books for boys, each preaching the rewards of hard work and good fortune. In his most famous, *Ragged Dick and Mark, the Match Boy*, he wrote:

> 'I hope, my lad [said Mr. Whitney], you will prosper and rise in the world. You know in this free country poverty in early life is no bar to a man's advancement. I haven't risen very high myself,' he added, with a smile, 'but have met with moderate success in life; yet there was a time when I was as poor as you.'
>
> 'Were you, sir?' asked Dick, eagerly.
>
> 'Yes, my boy, I have known the time when I have been obliged to go without my dinner because I didn't have enough money to pay for it.'
>
> 'How did you get up in the world?' asked Dick, anxiously.
>
> . . .
>
> 'A taste for reading and study. During my leisure hours I improved myself by study, and acquired a large part of the knowledge which I now possess. Indeed, it was one of my books that first put me on the track of the invention, which I afterwards made. So you see, my lad, that my studious habits paid me in money, as well as in another way.
>
> 'I'm awful ignorant,' said Dick, soberly [seriously].
>
> 'But you are young, and, I judge, a smart boy. If you try to learn, you can, and if you ever expect to do anything in the world, you must know something of books.'
>
> 'I will,' said Dick, resolutely [determined]. 'I ain't always goin' to black boots for a livin'.'
>
> 'All labor is respectable, my lad, and you have no cause to be ashamed of any honest business; yet when you can get something to do that promises better for your future prospects, I advise you to do so. Till then earn your living in the way you are accustomed to, avoid extravagance, and save up a little money if you can.'[1]

The new American hero was the successful entrepreneur. One minister even crossed the country telling people that "acres of diamonds" lay at their feet. He said, "It is your duty to get rich" and assured Americans that "Money is power, and you ought to be reasonably ambitious to have it." He preached his "gospel of wealth" over 6,000 times. The people heard his message.

The American economy began to shift into high gear. Fine transportation and communication networks had been completed. New sources of energy were developed and used to run the new machines of industry. Business leaders and investors created bigger businesses,

[1]From *Ragged Dick and Mark, the Match Boy* by Horatio Alger, Jr.

This political cartoon is titled "A Tournament of Today—A Set To Between Labor and Monopoly." Which side represents monopoly? Which labor?

One observer of Industrial America called the period the "Great Barbecue." Everyone seemed to be rushing to get a share of the national inheritance. People were like hungry picnickers crowding around the roasting pit at one of the popular political outings of the time.

Yet one should not take too dark a view of Industrial America. At this time, perhaps more than any other, the American people showed their greatest vigor, imagination, and confidence in themselves and in the future of their country.

For some, especially the new arrivals from Eastern Europe and those crowded into teeming cities, this was an age of "survival of the fittest." This notion is sometimes called Social Darwinism, the argument that if left to themselves without government regulations or other restrictions, the most efficient would survive in every field— farming, commerce, industry. When a Yale student asked his professor, "Don't you believe in any government aid to industries?," the response was, "No! It's root, hog, or die."

A sugar baron added to the barnyard metaphor. "Let the buyer beware; that covers the whole business. You cannot wetnurse people from the time they are born until the time they die. They have to wade in and get stuck, and that is the way men are educated."

Fortunately few practical people held such extreme views. Yet the notion of Social Darwinism was sometimes used to excuse child labor, unregulated working conditions, and hands-off policies of government toward big business.

and developed new methods of producing, distributing, and selling their products and services. Everywhere it seemed that creative Americans were improving ways of doing things. Businesses, both agricultural and industrial, sprang up throughout the land, each playing its part in the ever-expanding, interlocking economic system.

Competition Among the Railroads

The railroad industry had extremely heavy **fixed costs.** Track and stations had to be maintained. Cars had to be cleaned and painted. It cost almost as much to run an empty train as one crowded with passengers or freight. These fixed costs, or **overhead,** were the same whether business was good or bad.

To attract more business, railroads often used what was called "cutthroat competition"—using any means to shoulder aside rival companies. Railroads often reduced rates. Between February and July 1869 the cost of sending 100 pounds (45 kilograms) of wheat from Chicago to New York fell from $1.80 to 25 cents.

Railroads also gave large shippers illegal kickbacks called **rebates.** In return for their business they would give these shippers lower rates than those charged their smaller competitors. In this way railroad competition was a force leading to **monopoly** in other fields. Monopoly is the total control of a product, service, or trade in a region.

Sometimes railroads tried to make up for low, competitive rates by charging high rates for shipping goods from places where no other railroad existed. It often cost more to ship a product from a small "one-railroad town" a short distance from the market than from a large city much farther away. This "long haul" versus "short haul" pricing also led to monopoly because it favored producers in large cities where railroads competed for traffic.

Railroads tried to reduce competition by making agreements called **pools.** Those who joined the pool agreed to divide up available business and charge a common price for shipments. Pools rarely worked very long. Whenever business fell off, the railroads could not resist the temptation to cut rates. There was no way to enforce pooling agreements when individual companies broke them.

John D. Rockefeller

Most industries were eager to keep business steady and to avoid costly struggles for customers. A new way of doing this was developed in the oil industry by John D. Rockefeller. The method helped Rockefeller become the richest man in the United States, possibly in the entire world.

Rockefeller was born in Richford, New York, in 1839. After

John D. Rockefeller's portrait makes us recall the lines of Edward Arlington Robinson: "He was a gentleman from sole to crown, / Clean-favored, and imperially slim." Do you think a man can be deeply religious and at the same time a deadly competitor, as was said of Rockefeller?

making a modest fortune in the wholesale food business in Cleveland, he decided to go into the oil business. He bought his first refinery in 1865. In 1870 he organized the **Standard Oil Company.** Soon he expanded from refining into drilling for oil and selling kerosene and other oil-based products to consumers. By the late 1870s Rockefeller controlled 90 percent of the oil business in the United States.

Rockefeller was a deeply religious person. Even before he became wealthy, he made large contributions to charity. But he was a deadly competitor. He forced railroads to give him rebates on his huge oil shipments. He sold below cost in particular communities to steal business from local refiners. Then he gave the refiners a choice: sell out to Standard Oil or face bankruptcy. He hired spies and paid bribes to informers to tell secrets about other refiners' activities.

Rockefeller was also an excellent businessman. His plants were so efficient that he could undersell competitors and still make sizable profits. He detested waste. He kept close track of every detail of Standard Oil's complicated affairs.

Rockefeller wanted to buy all the refineries in the country and combine them. Then the industry could develop without petty business squabbles. He always gave competitors a chance to join Standard Oil. Only if they refused did he destroy them.

The man who designed Rockefeller's supercompany was Samuel C. T. Dodd. Dodd's creation was called a **trust**—a legal agreement under which several companies group together to regulate production and eliminate competition. To do this, stockholders of the separate oil companies turned their stock over to a group of directors called trustees. By controlling the stock of all the companies in the supercompany, the trustees could control the industry.

The Antitrust Movement

The trust idea soon spread to other businesses. By 1900 almost every branch of manufacturing was dominated by a small number of large producers. The size and power of these trusts alarmed many Americans. They were afraid that the trusts would destroy small companies and cheat consumers by charging high prices once competition had been eliminated. In the following excerpt from his article, one journalist warned Americans of what he called "the dangers of the age of combination:"

        6 6 On the theory of 'too much of everything' our industries, from railroads to workingmen, are being organized to prevent milk, nails, lumber, freights, labor, soothing syrup, and all these other things from becoming too cheap. The majority have never yet been able to buy enough of anything. The minority have too much of everything to sell. Seeds of social trouble germinate fast in such conditions. Society is

letting these combinations become institutions without compelling them to adjust their charges to the cost of production, which used to be the universal rule of price. . . . The change from competition to combination is nothing less than one of those revolutions which march through history with giant strides. . . .[1]"

Rockefeller, the leader most responsible for business combinations, often defended the practice. His defense was simple. He was in business to make money, and combinations were more profitable. He told a government commission:

" *Question*. What are . . . the chief advantages [of] industrial combinations?

Answer. It is too late to argue about the advantages of industrial combinations. They are a necessity. And if Americans are to have the privilege of extending their business in all the states of the Union, and into foreign countries as well, they are a necessity on a large scale, and require the agency of more than one corporation. Their chief advantages are:

(1) Command of necessary capital.
(2) Extension of limits of business.
(3) Increase in the number of people interested in business.
(4) Economy in business.
(5) Improvements and economies which are derived from knowledge of many interested persons of wide experience.
(6) Power to give the public improved products at less prices and still make a profit for stockholders.
(7) Permanent work and good wages for laborers. . . .

I speak from experience. . . . Our first combination was a partnership and afterwards a corporation in Ohio. That was sufficient for a local refining business. But dependent solely upon local business we should have failed years ago. We were forced to extend our markets and to seek for export trade.

We soon discovered as the business grew that the primary method of transporting oil in barrels could not last. . . . Hence we . . . adopted the pipe-line system, and found capital for pipe-line construction. . . . To perfect the pipe-line system required fifty millions in capital. This could not be obtained or maintained without industrial combination. . . .

[1]From "Lords of Industry," by Henry D. Lloyd in *North American Review*, CXXXVIII (June 1884)

Every step taken was necessary in the business if it was to be properly developed, and only through successive steps and by such an industrial combination is America to-day enabled to utilize the bounty which its land pours forth, and to furnish the world with the best and cheapest light ever known.[1]*"*

The demand for government regulation of the economy increased steadily. The first target was the railroad industry. In 1887 Congress passed the **Interstate Commerce Act.** This law stated that railroad rates must be "reasonable and just." Rates must be made public and could not be changed without public notice. Pools, rebates, and other unfair practices were declared unlawful. To oversee the affairs of railroads and to hear complaints from shippers, the law created the Interstate Commerce Commission (ICC), a board of experts. This was the first of the many **regulatory agencies**—government commissions charged with protecting the public interest—that came to control so many aspects of American life.

The ICC had to overcome many difficulties. The Interstate Commerce Act was vague. How was it possible to decide what a "reasonable and just" freight rate was? The Commission did not have a large enough staff to handle the more than 1,000 complaints it received in its first few months of operation. Nor did the Commission have the power to enforce its decisions. It could only sue violating railroads in court. Of the 16 cases it brought to trial between 1887 and 1905, it won only 1.

The Interstate Commerce Act was supposed to *regulate* competition—that is, to make certain that railroads did not cheat the public. It did not attempt to *control* the size of any railroad company. The way of dealing with the monopoly problem was to break up large businesses into smaller businesses which would compete with one another. This approach was called the **antitrust movement.**

In the late 1880s several states tried to restore competition by passing laws prohibiting trusts. These laws were difficult to enforce because industrial combinations usually did business in more than one state. Under the Constitution only the federal government could regulate such **interstate commerce.**

Then, in 1890, Congress passed the **Sherman Antitrust Act.** This law banned combinations "in the form of trust or otherwise" that restricted interstate trade or commerce. Anyone "who shall monopolize, or attempt to monopolize" such commerce could be fined or sent to jail for up to a year. This law was also difficult to enforce. It did not define "restraint of trade" or monopoly. Every attempt the government made to break up a trust resulted in a lawsuit.

[1]From "Report of the United States Industrial Commission, I," December 30, 1899 in *Government and the American Economy, 1870-Present* by Thomas G. Manning and David M. Potter

The Granger Collection

The courts usually sided with the business combinations. The first important Supreme Court case involving the Sherman Act was *U.S. v. E. C. Knight Co.* (1895). It involved an attempt to break up the American Sugar Refining Company. This trust had obtained control of about 90 percent of the sugar refining of the country by buying up four competing companies. The Court ruled that this combination was not illegal because it did not restrain trade. Since the trust refined its sugar in one state, interstate commerce was not involved. How it could dispose of all its sugar without selling it in many different states, the Court did not say.

The Interstate Commerce Act and the Sherman Antitrust Act had little effect on big business at this time. Most judges still put great stress on the right of individuals to run their affairs more or less as they pleased. Nevertheless, these two laws were extremely important. Both are still in effect and have been greatly strengthened over time. They established the practice of the federal government attempting to control the way American companies do business. After 1890 totally **free enterprise** was diminished in the United States. Free enterprise is the private operation of business with no government interference. The Industrial Revolution had made the power of business so great that some public control over business practices came to be increasingly accepted. 🖰

When Congress began to debate the Sherman Antitrust Act, Joseph Keppler drew this carton for Puck, *a popular humor magazine. Titled "Bosses of the Senate," the cartoon shows bloated trusts symbolized by bulging money bags entering the Senate through a door marked "Monopolists." The "People's Entrance" at the left is padlocked shut. What opinion of the Senate does this artist leave us with?*

Return to the Preview & Review on page 130.

Regulation of Big Business 137

Preview & Review

Use these questions to guide your reading. Answer the questions after completing Section 4.

Understanding Issues, Events, & Ideas. Explain how industrial growth affected American workers in the 1800s. Use the following words: specialization, Knights of Labor, strike, Haymarket bombing, American Federation of Labor, bread and butter issue, collective bargaining, Homestead Strike, lockout, yellow-dog contract, blacklist.

1. Why was the Knights of Labor organized? How was it changed under the leadership of Terence Powderly?
2. Who were the members of the American Federation of Labor?
3. What caused the Homestead Strike? How did Henry Frick respond? What was the outcome?

Thinking Critically. Imagine that you are a worker in a large factory in 1900. Describe your typical day at work, and explain how the increased use of machines has affected your job.

4. WORKERS AND WORK

Specialization

Post–Civil War industrial changes also greatly affected the men and women who worked in the factories of the United States. Division of labor changed the way things were made. Factory jobs became steadily more specialized. More and more workers tended machines. Usually they performed one task over and over, hundreds of times each day. In a steel plant, for example, some laborers shoveled coke and ore. Others loaded furnaces. Still others moved the finished steel. No single worker could make steel alone. This division of labor was called **specialization.**

Machines greatly increased the amount a worker could produce. This tended to raise wages and lower prices. Machines brought more goods within the reach of the average family. But they made work less interesting because it took little skill to operate most machines.

Manufacturing corporations grew larger and larger. In 1850 Cyrus McCormick's reaper manufacturing plant in Chicago employed 150 workers. By 1900 it had 4,000.

Such large factories had to be run like armies. The boards of directors were the generals. They set policy and appointed the people who carried it out. Next in the chain of command were the plant superintendents. Like the colonels of regiments, they were responsible for actually running the operation. They issued instructions to the foremen of the various departments, who were like army sergeants. The foremen in turn issued orders to the men and women who did the actual work.

LABOR FORCE BY SEX AND AGE*, 1870-1900					
YEAR	**TOTAL LABOR FORCE**	**SEX**		**AGE**	
		Male	**Female**	**10-15 Years**	**16 and Older**
1870	12,925	11,008	1,917	765	12,160
1880	17,392	14,745	2,647	1,118	16,274
1890	23,318	19,313	4,006	1,504	21,814
1900	27,640	22,641	4,999	4,064**	23,576†

* in thousands of workers
** 16 to 19 Years
† 20 and Older

Source: *Historical Statistics of the United States*

LEARNING FROM TABLES. *One of the most important needs of American business and industry was a large labor force. This chart contains data about those workers. In what ways did the labor force change between 1870 and 1900?*

Factory workers by the hundreds use lathes and presses to create their product. What do you suppose the belts connecting the machines to pulleys are for? What hazards do you see in this workplace?

These workers were expected to follow orders as obediently as army privates. In a Rochester, New York, carriage factory each worker had a number. To get a drink of water, a worker had to get the foreman's permission. To make sure that the rule was followed, the water faucets were locked up. In a Massachusetts tannery, guards patrolled the shop and reported any worker who talked during the workday. These were extreme examples. Workers hated all such rules. Many did not meekly submit to them. Instead, they sought ways to get around overly strict regulations.

Conditions in the clothing industries often were among the worst. In cities like New York and Chicago much of the work was done in "sweatshops," with the labor done mostly by women and children. Imagine the lives of those who toiled in the shop described in this excerpt.

❝ The *sweat-shop* is a place where, separate from the tailor-shop or clothing-warehouse, a "sweater" (middleman) assembles journeymen tailors and needle-women to work under his supervision. He takes a cheap room outside the dear [expensive] and crowded business center, and within the neighborhood where the work-people live. Thus is rent saved to the employer, and time and travel to the employed. The men can do work more hours than was possible under the centralized system [in a factory], and their wives and children can help. . . . For this service, at the prices paid, they cannot earn more than twenty-five to forty cents a day, and the work is largely done by Italian, Polish, and Bohemian women and girls. . . .

Girls, hand-sewers, earn nothing for the first month, then as unskilled workers they get $1 to $1.50 a week, $3 a week, and (as skilled workers) $6 a week. . . .

The 'sweat-shop' day is ten hours; but many take work home to get in overtime; and occasionally the shops themselves are kept open for extra work, from which the hardest and ablest workers sometimes make $14 to $16 a week. . . . The average weekly living expenses of a man and wife, with two children . . . are as follows: Rent (three or four small rooms), $2; food, fuel, and light, $4; clothing, $2; and beer and spirits, $1. . . .

A city ordinance enacts that rooms provided for workmen shall contain space equal to five hundred cubic feet of air for each person employed; but in the average 'sweat-shop' only about a tenth of that quantity is found. In one such place there were fifteen men and women in one room, which contained also a pile of mattresses on which some of the men sleep at night. The closets [toilets] are disgraceful. In an adjoining room were piles of clothing, made and unmade, on the same table with the food of the family. Two dirty children were playing about the floor. . . .[1]"

Unionization

In part because large corporations had so much power over their labor force, more workers began to join unions after the Civil War. This was especially true of skilled workers. In 1869 the **Knights of Labor** was founded in Philadelphia by Uriah Stephens, a tailor. At first it was a secret organization, with an elaborate ritual. Soon it expanded and began to work openly to organize workers into a "great brotherhood." By 1879 the Knights claimed to have 9,000 members. In that year Terence V. Powderly, a Pennsylvania machinist and one-time mayor of Scranton, Pennsylvania, became its head.

Under Powderly the Knights admitted women, African Americans, immigrants, and unskilled workers. This was a radical step. Most unions would not accept these workers. But Isaac Myers, the leading African American labor leader of the time, told the group: "American citizenship for the black man is a complete failure if he is proscribed [barred] from the workshops of the country." After his speech a majority of the delegates voted to admit all workers to the union. The Knights advocated the eight-hour workday and strict regulation of trusts. They hoped to avoid **strikes,** the refusal of laborers to work until their demands are met. Cooperation between

[1]From "Among the Poor of Chicago" by Joseph Kirkland in *The Poor in the Great Cities*

Collection, Lee Baxandall, Laurie Pratt Winfrey, Inc.

owners, workers, and consumers should be possible, Powderly insisted.

Powderly was a good speechmaker but a very poor administrator. He had little patience with anyone who disagreed with him. He tried to supervise every detail of the union's business.

In the 1880s local leaders of the Knights organized and won several important strikes against railroads. Membership soared. By 1886, 700,000 workers belonged to the organization. This was more than the central leadership could manage. Local units called strikes, which failed. Workers became discouraged and dropped out of the union.

Then the Knights were blamed, quite unfairly, for a terrible bombing incident in Haymarket Square in Chicago in 1886. When the police tried to break up a meeting called by radicals during a strike, someone threw a bomb that killed seven policemen. Public opinion turned against unions after the **Haymarket bombing.** Thousands of workers dropped out of the Knights of Labor as a result.

In 1881, long before the Knights of Labor began to decline, representatives of a number of craft unions founded the Federation of Organized Trades and Labor Unions of the United States and Canada. In 1886 this group changed its name to the **American Federation of Labor** (AFL).

The AFL was led by Samuel Gompers, a cigar maker. Unlike the Knights, the AFL was made up exclusively of skilled workers, organized by particular crafts such as printers, bricklayers, and plumbers. The AFL concentrated on **bread and butter issues**—higher

Angry workers bring their grievances to the top-hatted factory owner in "The Strike" by Robert Koehler. Use historical imagination to tell what argument is making tempers flare.

He may look like a sheriff sent to break up a strike, but this is the great Samuel Gompers, head of the AFL. The photograph was taken during a drive to organize West Virginia coal miners. Report on accounts of strikes in today's newspapers.

AFL/CIO George Meany Memorial Archives

Workers and Work 141

wages, shorter hours, better working conditions. The way to obtain these benefits, Gompers and other leaders of the AFL insisted, was **collective bargaining** with employers. In collective bargaining union officials, representing the workers, negotiate with management about wages, working conditions, and other aspects of employment. If negotiation fails, workers may strike to support union demands.

The Homestead Strike

One of the most violent strikes in American history involved an AFL union, the Amalgamated Association of Iron and Steel Workers. In the early 1890s the Amalgamated was the most powerful union in the country. It had 24,000 dues-paying members. Some worked at the Carnegie steel plant in Homestead, Pennsylvania. In 1892, when the company reduced wages because of a slump in its business, the union called a strike.

Carnegie was in Scotland when the **Homestead Strike** began. The company was being run by one of his partners, Henry Clay Frick. Frick was a tough executive and a bitter opponent of unions. He decided to resist the strike and to try to destroy the Amalgamated with a **lockout**. With Carnegie's approval he closed the mill. He then announced that he would hire strikebreakers—nonunion workers— and reopen the Homestead mill. To protect the new workers, he hired private police from the Pinkerton Detective Agency, a company known to specialize in strikebreaking.

The Pinkerton Agency sent 300 armed men—Pinkertons—to Homestead. They approached the plant on barges on the Monongahela River in the dead of night. The strikers had been warned of their coming. They met them at the docks with gunfire and dynamite. A small-scale war broke out. When it ended, seven Pinkertons and nine strikers were dead. The governor of Pennsylvania then sent 8,000 National Guard troops to Homestead to keep the peace. The strike went on for more than four months. Finally the union gave up the struggle. The workers went back to the plant on Frick's terms.

Frick won the contest, but public opinion turned against him. Then a Russian immigrant, Alexander Berkman, attacked Frick in his Homestead office. To protest the use of Pinkertons, Berkman shot Frick three times in the neck and shoulder. He then stabbed him once in the leg and after that tried to chew a percussion capsule, an explosive device, which guards pried from his mouth. Frick survived, Berkman went to prison, and the public's attitude softened.

Employers looked for ways to keep their workers from forming or joining unions. Some used **yellow-dog contracts,** a written agreement not to join a union. An employee who broke the contract was fired. Others used **blacklists.** These were lists of workers who were members of unions and therefore undesirable employees. Blacklisted workers often found it impossible to get jobs. 🗐

Return to the Preview & Review on page 138.

142   THE RISE OF INDUSTRIAL AMERICA

5. THE GROWTH OF CITIES

Preview & Review

Use these questions to guide your reading. Answer the questions after completing Section 5.
Understanding Issues, Events, & Ideas. Use the following words to describe how American cities changed between 1860 and 1900: Gilded Age, Statue of Liberty, ethnic neighborhood, New Immigration, literacy test, Chinese Exclusion Act, settlement house, Hull House, cable car, electric trolley, Brooklyn Bridge.
1. How did the immigrants coming to the United States after the 1880s differ from those who had come earlier?
2. How were Chinese immigrants treated? Mexican immigrants?
3. What problems were faced by cities during their rapid growth? What were some solutions?
Thinking Critically. In 1890 you arrive in New York City from Poland. Write a letter to your cousin back home, describing your new life in the United States.

The New Immigration

About three quarters of the workers in the Carnegie steel mills had been born in Europe. Like most immigrants, including Carnegie himself, they had come to America to find work. To millions of poor people in other parts of the world, industrial expansion had made the United States seem like the pot of gold at the end of the rainbow. Mark Twain used a similar metaphor when he called this era the **Gilded Age.** The surface was dazzling, but only base metal lay below.

It was as though the country were an enormous magnet drawing people into it from every direction. Between 1860 and 1900 about 14 million immigrants arrived. Most settled in large cities. In 1880, 87 percent of the residents of Chicago were either immigrants or the children of immigrants. The situation was similar in New York, San Francisco, Milwaukee, Cleveland, Boston, and most other cities.

Before the 1880s most immigrants had come from western and northern Europe, especially from England, Ireland, Germany, and the Scandinavian countries. We have already noted that established Americans frequently resented the newcomers of this ''Old Immigration.'' However, people from western Europe had certain advantages that helped them to adjust in their new homeland. British and Irish immigrants spoke English. Many German immigrants were well educated and skilled in one or another useful trade. Scandinavians were experienced farmers and often came with enough money to buy land in the West. Except for the Irish and some of the Germans, most of these immigrants were Protestants, as were most Americans.

In the 1880s the trend of immigration changed. Thousands of Italians, Poles, Hungarians, Greeks, and Russians flocked in. Many were Roman Catholics, a few were Greek Catholics, or Eastern Orthodox Christians, and many of the Poles and Russians were Jewish. These people believed in the golden dream of opportunity. America was the ''golden door.'' One Jewish girl living in Russia, 13 years old at the time, waited for her father already in America to send for the family. When the letter arrived, she wrote:

> 66 So at last I was going to America! Really, really going, at last! The boundaries burst. The arch of heaven soared. A million suns shone out for every star. The winds rushed in from outer space, roaring in my ears, 'America! America!'[1] 99

After 1886 the immigrants' first sight of America was often the **Statue of Liberty.** At the base of the statue were the words written by the poet Emma Lazarus:

[1]From *The Promised Land* by Mary Antin

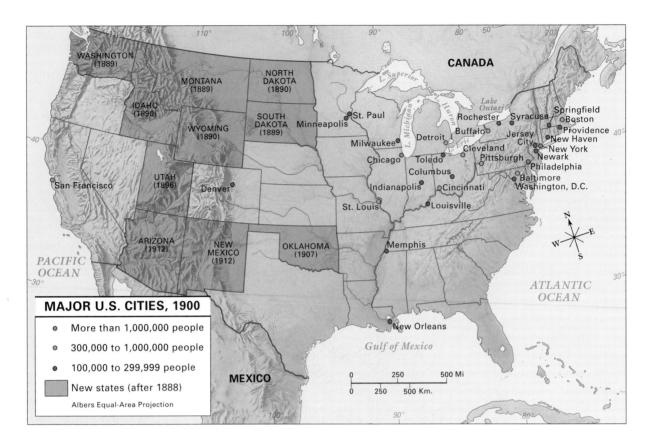

MAJOR U.S. CITIES, 1900

- ● More than 1,000,000 people
- ● 300,000 to 1,000,000 people
- ● 100,000 to 299,999 people
- New states (after 1888)

Albers Equal-Area Projection

LEARNING FROM MAPS. *The second half of the 19th century saw the growth of many of America's largest cities. Still, even by 1900 few of the largest cities are west of the Mississippi River. Why do you think this is true?*

❝ Give me your tired, your poor,
Your huddled masses yearning to breathe free,
The wretched refuse of your teeming shore,
Send these the homeless, tempest-tossed, to me:
I lift my lamp beside the golden door. . . . ❞

But although America was a vast improvement in most cases, it had a hard time living up to the dream of most immigrants. Anzia Yezierska wrote:

❝ Between the buildings that loomed like mountains, we struggled with our bundles. . . . Up Broadway, under the bridge, and through the swarming streets of the ghetto [a segregated neighborhood], we followed Gedalyeh Mindel [a friend].

I looked about the narrow streets of squeezed-in stores and houses, ragged clothes, dirty bedding oozing out of the windows, ashcans and garbage cans cluttering the sidewalks. A vague sadness pressed down on my heart—the first doubt of America.[1] ❞

Most immigrants were indeed poor. They had little or no education and no special skills. They knew no English. Their habits and

[1]From *Hungry Hearts* by Anzia Yezierska

Museum of the City of New York

The colossal Statue of Liberty raises the torch of freedom in New York Harbor. It was first known as "Liberty Enlightening the World." Here we see the dedication of the magnificent gift from France. The sculptor, F. A. Bartholdi, wished to pay tribute to the alliance of France with the American colonies during the Revolution. What does the statue symbolize today?

cultures were very different from those of native-born Americans. The majority were Roman or Greek Orthodox Catholics or Jews.

Many of these immigrants came from areas where money was seldom used. People there exchanged food for cloth, a cow for a wagon, and so on. It was difficult for such people to adjust to life in a large industrial city. Most took the lowest-paid jobs. Whole families toiled to earn enough to survive.

The immigrants from each country or district tended to cluster together in the same city neighborhood. In 1890 a New York reporter wrote that a map of the city showing where different nationalities lived would have "more stripes than the skin of a zebra, and more colors than any rainbow." These **ethnic neighborhoods** were like cities within cities. They offered people newly arrived in the strange new world of America a chance to hold on to a few fragments of the world they had left. There the immigrants could find familiar foods,

Simply making the journey to America did not ensure immigrants that they would quickly become Americans. First, immigrants had to be examined. To conduct the examinations, the Immigration and Naturalization Service set up stations on both coasts. In New York Harbor, tiny Ellis Island was the first place in America that immigrants crossing the Atlantic landed. With military precision, immigrants lined up for physical examinations. The sick were sent back to their native lands. Inspectors then questioned those who passed the physical examination. Those who had a prison record, no money, or no sponsor in the United States were refused entry. Between 1892 and 1943, 16 million immigrants passed through Ellis Island, which became the "island of tears" as almost 20 percent were turned away.

Angel Island in San Francisco Harbor was where immigrants who crossed the Pacific were processed. Because the Chinese Exclusion Act sharply limited Asian immigration, this station served only about 50,000 immigrants between 1910 and 1940.

The Chinese Exclusion Act stated that Chinese immigrants would be granted residency if their father had been born in the United States or if they were merchants, members of merchant families, tourists, teachers, or students. But to gain entry, the Chinese had to prove their claims. Until 1906 immigration officials had little difficulty verifying those claims. In that year, however, the tragic San Francisco earthquake destroyed all citizenship records in the city. Officials then had to take immigrants' word.

Soon, a thriving, if unusual, trade sprang up in China. For a price, people could buy information about someone already living in the United States. The buyers then studied the information carefully so that they could pose as the son or daughter of the Chinese American. Upon arriving at Angel Island, inspectors would grill the immigrant. If officials were satisfied with the answers, the immigrant was admitted. But often the examinations would take days, weeks, or even months. During the entire time, the immigrant was detained on the island, where conditions were unsanitary and food was often foul. Poems scratched on the wall of the barracks at Angel Island express the immigrants' frustration:

> "I intended to come to America to earn a living.
> The Western styled buildings are lofty; but I have not the luck to live in them.
> How was anyone to know my dwelling place would be a prison?[1]"

Eventually fully 30 percent of the Chinese applicants were sent home.

Neither Angel nor Ellis islands serve as immigration stations today. Both are museums that remind all who visit them of the pain and joy of the immigrant experience.

[1]From *Island: Poetry and History of Chinese Immigrants on Angel Island, 1910-1940* by Him Mark Lai, Genny Lim, and Judy Yung

Angel Island, 1908-22

people who spoke their language, churches and clubs based on old-country models.

Many native-born Americans resented this **New Immigration.** They insisted that the newcomers were harder to assimilate, or "Americanize" than earlier generations. Workers were disturbed by the new immigrants' willingness to work long hours for low wages. American Protestants believed the mass immigration would weaken their political and social clout. A new nativist organization, the American Protective Association, blamed the hard times of the 1890s on immigration. Nativists charged that the new immigrants were physically and mentally inferior. They were dangerous radicals, the nativists said, who wanted to destroy American democratic institutions.

Museum of the City of New York

"The Battery, New York" was painted about 1855 by Samuel B. Waugh. This detail shows a shipful of immigrants arriving in New York. Immigrants were processed at Castle Garden, at the left in the background. Why did some Americans resent the new immigration?

One poet expressed these fears in this excerpt.

> " Wide open and unguarded stand our gates,
> And through them presses a wild motley throng—
> Men from the Volga and the Tartar steppes [Russia],
> Featureless figures from the Hwang Ho [China],
> Malayan, Scythian [Greek], Teuton [German], Celt [Irish],
>   and Slav,
> Flying the Old World's poverty and scorn;
> These bringing with them unknown gods and rites,
> Those, tiger passions, here to stretch their claws,
> In street and alley what strange tongues are loud. . . .[1] "

In the 1890s the Immigration Restriction League called for a law preventing anyone who could not read and write some language from entering the country. The League knew that such a **literacy test** would keep out many immigrants from southern and eastern Europe. In that part of the world many regions did not have public school systems.

Congress passed a literacy test bill in 1897, but President Grover Cleveland vetoed it. He insisted that America should continue to be a place of refuge for the world's poor and persecuted. Many

[1] From "Unguarded Gates" by Thomas Bailey Aldrich in *The Works of Thomas Bailey Aldrich, Poems, vol. II*

STRATEGIES FOR SUCCESS

READING A TABLE

Tables, like charts, are ways visually to organize statistics. (Review the strategy on page 674.) Tables are most often used to show the changes in numbers over time. In a table, statistics are usually listed side-by-side in columns for easy reference. Effectively using a statistical table can tell you a great deal about a particular topic.

How to Read a Statistical Table

To read a statistical table, follow these guidelines.

1. **Note the title.** As in all graphics, the title of a table will tell you the subject for which statistics are given. Remember that all the numbers are related in some way to the subject of the table. Part of the skill of reading a table is understanding how all its parts are related. (As with charts, be sure to read any footnotes or other special notes.)
2. **Read the headings.** Quickly skimming the headings will show you how the data is organized and into what categories it has been divided.
3. **Study the information.** Read across each row. Note the statistical trends.
4. **Apply critical thinking skills.** Compare the numbers. Ask questions about the trends. Form hypotheses, make inferences, and draw conclusions.

Applying the Strategy

Study the statistical table above. It provides population statistics for major United States cities for three years—1860, 1880, and 1900. Note that these are at 20-year intervals. Why do you think that is so? The equal intervals give you a clearer picture of the rate of growth than random years

GROWTH OF MAJOR U.S. CITIES, 1860–1900			
City	1860	1880	1900
New York City	1,174,800	1,912,000	3,437,000
Philadelphia	565,500	847,000	1,294,000
Boston	177,800	363,000	561,000
Baltimore	212,400	332,000	509,000
Cincinnati	161,000	255,000	326,000
St. Louis	160,800	350,000	575,000
Chicago	109,300	503,000	1,698,000

might. As you read across each row you can see how the population of a given city changed. New York City grew from 1,174,800 to 3,437,000 during that time period. Reading down the columns allows you to compare the statistics among the cities. In 1880 847,000 people lived in Philadelphia while 255,000 lived in Cincinnati. Based on what you have read in *The Story of America,* what is one reason why Philadelphia was larger than Cincinnati in 1880? Can you think of other reasons? Studying the chart as a whole gives you the opportunity to note trends and ask questions. What generalizations can you state about the growth of United States cities in the second half of the 19th century based on the seven cities in this table? Note that all the cities more than doubled in population between 1860 and 1900. Which ones grew the fastest? Note that Chicago grew much faster than Baltimore. Why do you think that happened? What other trends do you notice? Which ones can you explain from your reading of *The Story of America* and other books on American history?

For independent practice, see Practicing the Strategy on page 154.

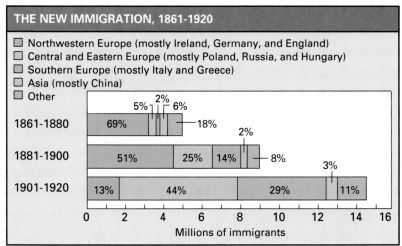

THE NEW IMMIGRATION, 1861-1920

☐ Northwestern Europe (mostly Ireland, Germany, and England)
☐ Central and Eastern Europe (mostly Poland, Russia, and Hungary)
☐ Southern Europe (mostly Italy and Greece)
☐ Asia (mostly China)
☐ Other

1861-1880: 69%, 5%, 2%, 6%, 18%
1881-1900: 51%, 25%, 14%, 2%, 8%
1901-1920: 13%, 44%, 29%, 3%, 11%

Millions of immigrants: 0, 2, 4, 6, 8, 10, 12, 14, 16

Source: *Historical Statistics of the United States*

LEARNING FROM GRAPHS. *Immigrants to America between 1861 and 1920 had different points of origin from those that came earlier. Where were most of the earlier immigrants from? Where were most of the "new immigrants" from? Also note that the origins of immigrants between 1861 and 1920 shifted. What shift took place?*

employers opposed any check on immigration for less humane reasons. They knew that unlimited immigration would assure them a steady force of low-paid but hard-working laborers.

Congress *did* exclude one type of immigrant during this period—the Chinese. By 1880 there were about 75,000 Chinese immigrants in California. They were extremely hard-working people. Most were Buddhists, a religion little understood in America. Because of language and cultural differences, the Chinese tended even more than most immigrants to stick together. They seemed unwilling to try American ways. Older residents feared and resented them. When a depression swept the country, California workers worried that Chinese workers would steal their jobs at lower wages. In 1882 Congress responded to the demands of Californians by passing the **Chinese Exclusion Act.** It prohibited Chinese workers from entering the United States for a period of ten years. Later the ban was extended. It was not lifted until 1965.

By 1900 about 100,000 Mexicans, most Roman Catholics, had emigrated to the United States, and the number was growing quickly. Increasingly they provided the labor force that developed the southwestern part of the nation. Unlike most other immigrants, these newcomers seldom settled in large cities. Many had to move continually from place to place. They encountered many social, economic, and political handicaps. Yet Mexican American communities survived and even thrived, strengthened by their family ties and close-knit community life. Some Mexican Americans found jobs as laborers building the railroads. When the lines were completed, they became section hands—men whose job it was to maintain the railroad right-of-way and repair damaged tracks and ties. Many families had to live in railroad boxcars. Other Mexican immigrants worked as cowhands on cattle ranches. Still others became farm laborers. Like so many immigrants, most were poorly paid and often badly treated.

The Growth of Cities   149

"Not everyone was equally poor. When an immigrant family could occupy a two- or three-room apartment without several boarders, they were considered lucky. Boarders were a natural institution, particularly in the early years when most immigrants came without their families. But even the privilege of being a boarder was not enjoyed by every greenhorn.

There were various categories of boarders. A star boarder slept on a folding bed. But I knew a printer who every night unscrewed a door, put it on two chairs; he couldn't pay as much as the one who had the bed."

From *The World of Our Fathers,*
Irving Howe, 1976

Problems of City Life

American agriculture was expanding with American industry. But machinery was reducing the need for human labor on farms. Cyrus McCormick's reapers and other new farm machines were displacing thousands of farmhands who had previously plowed, planted, hoed, and harvested the nation's crops. For every city dweller who took up the plow between 1860 and 1900, 20 farmers moved to the city.

The growth of cities after the Civil War was both rapid and widespread. In 1860 places like Denver, Memphis, and Seattle were no more than small towns. By 1900 they were major urban centers. In that same year there were 50 cities of over 100,000 people.

The largest cities were centers of both manufacturing and commerce, and they did not depend on any one activity for their prosperity. Some smaller cities specialized in making a particular product. Dayton, Ohio, manufactured cash registers. Minneapolis, Minnesota, became a flour-milling center.

People moved to cities far more rapidly than housing and other facilities could be built to care for their needs. City land values soared. A New York City lot selling for $80 in the early 1840s sold for $8,000 in 1880. Because of the high cost of property, builders put up tenement apartments on plots only 25 feet (about 8 meters) wide. They were crowded so closely together that light and moving air were blocked out.

A five- or six-story tenement usually had four apartments on each floor. Front apartments contained four rooms, rear apartments three. Many of the rooms had no windows. In most cases two families had to share a single toilet located in a dark and narrow hallway. Dark, musty, garbage-cluttered "air shafts" separated one tenement building from the next. One resident described the air shaft of his tenement to the New York State Tenement House Commission in 1900:

"The Secretary: How long have you lived in tenement houses?

Mr. Moscowitz: Seventeen years. . . .

The Secretary: What have you to say about the air shaft; do you think it is a good thing?

Mr. Moscowitz: I think it is decidedly a bad thing. I must confirm the statements made by other witnesses that the air shaft is a breeder of disease, and especially that there can be no fresh air in any building with an air shaft, from my experience, because of the refuse [garbage] thrown down the air shaft, the stench is so vile and the air is so foul that the occupants do not employ the windows as a means of getting air. . . .

The Secretary: Are there any other objections to the air shaft?

Mr. Moscowitz: It destroys privacy.

The Secretary: How does it do that?

Mr. Moscowitz: I know where I lived in a house where there was a family opposite, the windows which are usually diagonal, I heard everything, especially loud noises, and when the windows are not covered one sees into the house. . . .[1] 99

Police and fire protection remained inadequate in most cities. Garbage collection was haphazard at best. City water was often impure. Sewers were smelly and often clogged. Disease could spread quickly under these conditions. In one crowded Chicago neighborhood three out of every five babies born in 1900 died before they were three years old. Jacob Riis, who wrote *How the Other Half Lives*, the most famous book on the tenements, described similar conditions in New York City:

66 There are tenements everywhere. Suppose we look into one on Cherry Street. Be a little careful, please! The hall is dark and you might fall over the children pitching pennies back there. Not that it would hurt them. Kicks and punches are their daily diet. They have little else. . . .

Here is a door. Listen! that short hacking cough, that tiny helpless cry—what do they mean? They mean that the soiled bow of white you saw on the door downstairs [when someone died, a bow was hung on the door—black for an adult, white for a child] will have another story to tell—oh, a sadly familiar story—before the day ends. The child is dying of measles. With half a chance it might have lived. But it had none. That dark bedroom killed it. . . .[2] 99

Of course, many people worked hard trying to solve the cities' problems and improve urban living conditions. Boards of health made studies and established standards for sewage and garbage disposal. Elaborate systems of pipes and reservoirs brought pure water from distant lakes and rivers. Social and religious workers established community centers called **settlement houses** in poor neighborhoods. Settlement houses had something for everyone—day nurseries for little children, gymnasiums and social activities for young and old, English classes for immigrants.

The most famous of the settlement houses was **Hull House** in Chicago, founded in 1889 by Jane Addams. Many of the settlement

University of Illinois Library

Jane Addams as a young woman was photographed in about 1890. She founded Hull House in Chicago with Ellen Gates Starr. In 1931 Addams was awarded the Nobel Peace Prize. In your own words describe life for a poor person before and after settlement houses.

[1]From "Testimony of a Tenant" by Dr. Henry Moscowitz in *The Tenement House Problem*, edited by Robert W. DeForest and Lawrence Veiller

[2]From *How the Other Half Lives* by Jacob Riis

The Growth of Cities   151

workers were young women who had graduated from college. They lived in the settlement houses and tried to become part of the community. They believed that they could grow personally by involving themselves in local political and social affairs. At the same time they were helping local people.

As cities grew larger, transportation became a problem. In 1865 most large cities had streetcars drawn by horses. Horses were slow and needed a great deal of care. In 1873 Andrew S. Hallidie installed **cable cars** on the steep hills of San Francisco, which horses could not climb. Hallidie used a long wire cable attached to a stationary steam engine to pull the cars.

Then, in the late 1880s, Frank J. Sprague designed the first electrified street railway in America. In 1887 he opened a 12-mile line (about 19 kilometers) in Richmond, Virginia. By 1890, 51 American cities had **electric trolley** systems.

As time passed, hundreds of bridges, paved roads, parks, and grand public buildings improved the appearance of cities and the

The Brooklyn Bridge is a fitting symbol of the rise of industrial America. The bridge opened in 1883 with fireworks and a water parade.

quality of city life. The most famous symbol of the modern city was the **Brooklyn Bridge** in New York City. The Brooklyn Bridge took 13 years to build. It was designed by John A. Roebling and built by his son Washington. Washington Roebling was disabled during the construction and unable to walk about. He supervised the project from a nearby apartment, keeping track of progress with binoculars and a telescope. The bridge is now more than 100 years old and heavily

Culver Pictures

Watching from his window is the son of the designer of the Brooklyn Bridge, Washington Roebling, who was disabled for life by working in the compressed air caissons—water tight chambers used in construction work under water.

traveled by commuters moving between Brooklyn and Manhattan. New Yorkers remain fiercely proud of their bridge.

Thus arose industrial America. In 1865 most people lived much the same way as their parents and grandparents had. The lives of the people of 1900 were far different—closer to what we know today. 🖹

Return to the Preview & Review on page 143.

CHAPTER 3 REVIEW

1860	THE RISE OF INDUSTRIAL AMERICA

1861
Telegraph wires span nation

1865
Civil War ends

1866
Field lays transatlantic cable

1869
Knights of Labor founded

★
Vanderbilt begins railroad empire

1870
Standard Oil Company

1876
Bell demonstrates telephone

Chapter Summary

Read the statements below. Choose one, and write a paragraph explaining its importance.
1. Soon after the Civil War railroads and a communications network linked the nation.
2. The expense of developing railroads led to the new business arrangement of the corporation.
3. The growth of the steel industry paralleled the growth of railroads. At the same time, the oil industry began to develop.
4. Eventually the government banned business practices that harmed the public.
5. Workers fought to improve their conditions, eventually turning to unionization.
6. Immigrants from new regions—southern and eastern Europe, China, and Mexico—provided many of the workers for the industrial surge.
7. Most of the new immigrants crowded into ethnic neighborhoods in the growing cities.

Reviewing Chronological Order

Number your paper 1–5. Then study the time line above and place the following events in the order in which they happened by writing the first next to 1, the second next to 2, and so on.
1. Chinese Exclusion Act
2. Sherman Antitrust Act
3. Homestead Strike
4. Knights of Labor founded
5. Standard Oil Company

Understanding Main Ideas

1. What were some of the major changes in the United States in the years between the Civil War and 1900?
2. How did the railroads and the steel industry help each other grow?
3. What is a monopoly? How did railroad competition lead to monopoly in other fields?
4. What were some problems faced by growing cities between 1860 and 1900? What were some attempts to improve city life?

Thinking Critically

1. **Analyzing.** Suppose you have $500 to invest. Your choices are: a corporation with shares whose value has risen slowly but steadily for six years, or a partnership that stands a 50-percent chance of doubling your money in two years. In which business would you invest? Why?
2. **Judging.** You are a Supreme Court judge in 1895. The case before you involves a salt manufacturing trust in Louisiana. It has purchased five competing companies in its own state and three competing companies in the adjacent state of Texas. Would you rule that this trust violated the law? If so, which law or laws, and how? If not, why not?
3. **Evaluating.** If you were a member of Congress in the late 1800s, would you have voted for the literacy test bill? The Chinese Exclusion Act? Why or why not?

Writing About History: Expressive

Write a story on the following idea: An ordinary citizen who lived in 1800 returns for a look at America in 1900. What are the reactions of this traveler from the time of Jefferson's "nation of farmers" to the sprawling cities and industries of 1900? Which changes impress your time traveler, and which might be upsetting? Use the information in Chapter 3 and in other reference books to prepare your story.

Practicing the Strategy

Review the strategy on page 148.
Reading a Table. Study the table on page 138, then answer the following questions.
1. What is the interval between the years in this table? What information is contained in the headings?

1882
Chinese Exclusion Act

1886
Haymarket
Square bombing

1889
Hull House
founded

1892 Homestead Strike

★
American
Federation of Labor

1890
Sherman Antitrust Act

1887
Interstate Commerce Act

2. Between 1870 and 1900, what was the rate of increase of the male workers as compared to the female workers?
3. Which 10-year interval saw the greatest increase in the total number of workers?
4. In 1900, the table shows a new age group: 16–19. What changes may have resulted in this new age group for workers?

Using Primary Sources

In the late 1800s people began arriving in America from eastern Europe. The following excerpt is from an essay that was submitted in a competition organized by the Committee for Immigrants in America. The essay appeared in a journal called *Immigrants in America Review*. As you read the excerpt from "What America Means to a Russian Jewess," think about an immigrant's point of view of "Americanization."

America means for an Immigrant a fairy promised land that came out true, a land that gives all they need for their work, a land which gives them human rights, a land that gives morality through her churches and education through her free schools and libraries. The longer I live in America the more I think of the question of Americanising the immigrants. At first I thought that there is not such a question as that, for the children of immigrants naturally are Americans and good Americans. America is a land made up of foreigners and the virtues of American life is the best Americaniser. The first generation of American immigrants can't be Americanized much for they were raised in different ways the mode of living is different. And yet how much it is when they love America and are such patriots.

1. According to the excerpt, what has America given the new immigrants?

2. The author thinks that "the virtues of American life is the best Americaniser." What do you think the author means by this statement?
3. What might the use of grammar and spelling tell you about the author of the article?
4. Think about recent immigrants to the United States. Do you think that "Americanization" is necessary? Why or why not?

Linking History & Geography

Immigration has been an important aspect of the development of the United States. To understand immigration, reread "The New Immigration" on pages 143–49 and on an outline map of the world, color the countries from which most of these new immigrants came. Then find out the countries of origin of the immigrants that came to America between 1820 and 1850. Mark in a different color the countries from which these earlier immigrants came.

Enriching Your Study of History

1. **Individual Project**. Complete *one* of the following projects. Using historical imagination, place yourself in a telegraph office in Homestead, Pennsylvania, in 1892. Prepare a telegraph message that reports on the clash of strikers and Pinkertons. Include the views of both sides in the Homestead strike. *Or* using historical imagination, place yourself in the year 1890. A few months ago, on your twenty-first birthday, you moved from your parents' farm to find work in the city. Write a letter to the folks at home telling them about city life.

2. **Cooperative Project**. Your class will prepare a multimedia presentation on the railroad network that was built after the Civil War. Various groups will use pictures, stories, and songs to show the development and effects of railroads.

Chapter 3 Review 155

National Politics and Culture, 1867–1896

The Civil War and the rapid expansion of the economy that followed it had important effects on American government and politics. So did the great social changes, especially the flood of new immigrants and the shift of population from the farms to the cities. New issues arose as conditions changed. Older political questions had to be reconsidered too. The Democratic and Republican parties had to deal with difficult and confusing social, economic, and human rights issues. By and large, they failed to find clear solutions. Their efforts are worth studying closely if we are to understand how industrialization, the rise of cities, and the new immigration affected American politics and culture.

The Democratic donkey and the Republican elephant were popularized by the great political cartoonist Thomas Nast, who also gave us the plump bearded image of Santa Claus. Do you think the elephant and donkey are good symbols of the parties they represent?

Culver Pictures

The Granger Collection

1. POLITICS AFTER THE WAR

Republican North and Democratic South

From a political point of view the Civil War did not end in 1865. Nor did it end in 1877 when the North gave up trying to control the South by force. Indeed, the war affected American politics for more than a century.

In the 1850s the controversy over slavery in the territories led most white southerners to become Democrats. When the war ended, most stayed Democrats. After southern whites regained control of their local governments in the 1870s, they voted Democratic in national elections almost to a man. With southern blacks not permitted to vote, the Republican party had no chance at all in any southern state. People spoke of the **Solid South**. Every state that had seceded from the Union cast its electoral votes for the Democratic candidate in every presidential election from 1880 until 1928.

The Republican party had become the leading party in the North and West by 1860. It remained so throughout the decades after the Civil War. Memories of the war stirred up strong emotions and had a great influence on how people voted. Tens of thousands saw the Republicans as the saviors of the Union, the Democrats as the disloyal dividers of the United States. These views held long after slavery had been done away with and the idea of secession abandoned by even its most extreme southern supporters.

After the war Congress had dozens of important issues to decide. Few of these issues had any connection with the geographical division that separated Democrats from Republicans. Yet Republican politicians constantly made emotional appeals to voters by reminding them that the Democrats were "ex-rebels."

This tactic was called "waving the bloody shirt." It got the name in 1866. During a speech in Congress, Benjamin Franklin Butler of Massachusetts displayed the blood-stained shirt of a carpetbagger official who had been beaten by a mob in Mississippi. The incident, according to Butler, proved that the South was still disloyal and must not be trusted.

Here is a famous example of the bloody shirt oratory of the period:

> **66** Every man that tried to destroy this nation was a Democrat.
> . . . Soldiers, every scar you have on your heroic bodies
> was given you by a Democrat.**99**

Waving the bloody shirt helped keep northerners voting Republican. Yet Republicans never dominated the northern states as completely as the Democrats controlled the South. New England and most states west of the Mississippi River were Republican strongholds. So were Pennsylvania, Wisconsin, and Michigan. But New

Preview & Review

Use these questions to guide your reading. Answer the questions after completing Section 1.
Understanding Issues, Events, & Ideas. **1.** Create a word web about politics after the Civil War, using these words: Solid South, close state, native son, political machine, Tammany Hall, boss, franchise, kickback, sitting on the fence. **2.** Briefly describe the domestic issues such as the tariff, money crisis, and government jobs, using these words: monetary policy, greenback, hard money, deflation, inflation, civil service reform, merit system, patronage, Pendleton Act, Civil Service Commission.
1. What was "waving the bloody shirt"? How did it influence elections?
2. How did the political machines in northern cities attract the votes of recent immigrants?
3. Why were political parties afraid to take a stand on controversial issues?
4. How were farmers hurt by deflation after the Civil War?
Thinking Critically. **1.** If you were a member of Congress in 1875, would you have voted for or against protective tariffs? Give reasons for your decisions. **2.** The year is 1882. Write a newspaper editorial explaining the need for civil service reform.

"Fitzgerald found the bluff and genial Keany in his usual position, behind his desk in the back room of the red brick grocery store. . . . Into this low-ceilinged room which served as his headquarters, thousands of men and women had entered over the years in search of assistance. By Keany's word, a man's son could be liberated from prison, a widow provided with food, an aspiring peddler issued a permit and a destitute father given a coffin to bury his infant child. . . . [There] Fitzgerald reported all summer long in order to help the boss dispense the hundred and one favors regularly awarded in the course of a day, favors which spread the boss's influence, like a huge spider, over the entire district. . . ."

From *The Fitzgeralds and the Kennedys*, 1987

York, New Jersey, and Connecticut were a cluster of states where Democrats could sometimes win. Ohio, Indiana, and Illinois made another group where elections were usually very close.

In nearly every presidential election after the Civil War, the party that won the majority of the electoral votes of the "close" northern states won the presidency. For this reason both parties usually chose presidential and vice presidential candidates from these **close states.** These candidates were called **native sons.** Their names on the ballot could increase the chances of carrying the candidates' home states and perhaps winning the election.

Every president from Rutherford B. Hayes, elected in 1876, to William Howard Taft, elected in 1908, came from either Ohio, Indiana, or New York. Of the 27 men who were nominated for president or vice president by the Democrats and Republicans between 1876 and 1908, 19 came from these three states. Not a single southerner was nominated by the major parties for either office during the period. This shows how the Civil War continued to affect politics.

Ordinary people paid a great deal of attention to politics. A much larger proportion of eligible voters actually voted than has been true in recent times. Did they do so because the campaigns were so intense and colorful? Or were the campaigns intense and colorful because the people were so interested in politics? Unfortunately, these are questions almost impossible for historians to answer!

The Poor and Political Machines

One reason why elections were close in northern industrial states like New York and Ohio was that large numbers of recent immigrants lived in them. These immigrants, as we have noted, tended to settle in the cities. They were "outsiders," poor and without much influence. Most people with wealth and social position looked down upon them. And in the northern states the wealthy and socially prominent were nearly all Republicans.

This explains why most immigrants in the cities joined the Democratic party. Their position was somewhat like that of blacks in the southern states. Each group supported the minority party of its part of the country. Northern immigrants voted Democratic, southern blacks Republican. Northern blacks, on the other hand, while definitely not part of the majority, supported the Republican party. They were mindful that the Republican party had abolished slavery.

In most northern cities local politicians took advantage of the immigrants' preference for the Democratic party to build up **political machines.** These organizations nominated candidates for local office and turned out large numbers of loyal voters on election day. One such machine was **Tammany Hall,** run by New York City Democrats. Of course, these descriptions of which groups voted for which party and which party controlled political machines are generalizations.

Culver Pictures

The leaders of the machines, called **bosses,** provided many benefits to poor city dwellers. Well-to-do residents and most political reformers disliked the machines. The bosses used shady and even clearly illegal methods to win votes. But they certainly helped new people, especially immigrants, to make the adjustment to city life. They helped immigrants find jobs. When neighborhood workers were ill or out of work, the bosses would supply their families with food and small sums of money. The machines ran community picnics on holidays. They helped local youngsters who got in trouble with the law.

In return for their help the bosses expected the people to vote for the machine's candidates. By controlling elections, the bosses could reward their friends or line their own pockets. For example, companies that wanted to operate streetcar lines or sell gas or electricity for lighting homes or businesses needed city permits called **franchises.** Bosses often demanded bribes before they would have these franchises issued by the local officials they controlled. They also made deals with contractors who put up public buildings or did other work for the city. The bosses agreed to pay needlessly high prices for the work in return for large **kickbacks,** the illegal return to them of part of the payment made to contractors.

Politics for profit seemed to be the method of operation. This made politics and politicians the target of many reformers. Lincoln

"New York's New Solar System" was drawn by Joseph Keppler in 1898. Here Richard Croker, the head of the Tammany machine, is the sun. Around him revolve lesser corrupt politicians. What do you think is Keppler's point?

The Granger Collection

Thomas Nast first drew a Tammany tiger in 1871. When this cartoon appeared in Harper's *magazine, the city bosses threatened to cancel all orders of Harper Brothers' textbooks. "The Tammany Tiger" upset Boss Tweed, who controlled Tammany Hall and who had said, "as long as I count the votes, what are you going to do about it?" Nast asked the same question in the cartoon's subtitle, "What Are You Going to Do About It?" On what Roman practice is this cartoon based?*

Steffens, the leading reformer of political corruption, wrote:

" There is hardly a government office from United States Senator down to alderman in any part of the country to which some business leader has not been elected. Yet politics remains corrupt and government pretty bad. Business leaders have failed in politics as they have in good citizenship. Why?

Because politics is business. . . . The commercial spirit is the spirit of profit, not patriotism; of credit, not honor; of individual gain, not national prosperity; of trade, not principle. . . .

We cheat our government and we let our leaders rob it. We let them persuade and bribe our power away from us. True, they pass strict laws for us, but we let them pass bad laws too, giving away public property in exchange. Our good, and often impossible, laws we allow to be used for oppression and blackmail. And what can we say? We break our own laws and rob our own government—the woman at the tax office, the lyncher with his rope, and the captain of industry with his bribe and his rebate. The spirit of graft and of lawlessness is the American spirit.

We Americans have failed. We may be selfish and influenced by gain. . . . [But] there is pride in the character of American citizenship. This pride may be a power in the land. So this record of shame and yet of self-respect, disgraceful confession, yet a declaration of honor, is dedicated, in all good faith, to the accused—to all the citizens of all the cities in the United States.[1]"

The machines did both good and harm in their day. Not all of them were associated with the Democratic party. The powerful Philadelphia machine, for example, was a Republican organization. So were many of the machines in middle-sized cities. But most of the big-city machines were run by the Democrats. They were very useful to the national Democratic party in presidential elections in close states like New York.

Sitting on the Fence

Extremely important social and economic problems were being discussed and settled after the Civil War. There were problems caused by industrial expansion and technological change. Other problems resulted from the growth of cities. Still other problems related to racial questions and to immigration. Logically, the parties should have fought their campaigns on these issues.

They rarely did so. Each was afraid that a strong stand on any controversial question would cost votes. It seemed politically safer to make vague statements that everyone could accept, even if no one entirely agreed with them. This was called **sitting on the fence.**

Still, the issues remained, and politicians had to deal with them in one way or another. For example, the need to regulate railroads and other big businesses resulted in the Interstate Commerce Act and the Sherman Antitrust Act. The Indian lands of the West were seized and divided up. During these years Congress and the presidents struggled with high protective tariffs on imported manufactured goods. They tried to solve what was known as "the money question." And they attempted to reform the way government employees were hired and fired.

The Tariff Issue

When the United States first began to develop manufacturing about the time of the War of 1812, a strong case could be made for tariffs which heavily taxed foreign manufactured goods. American "infant industries" needed protection in order to compete with larger, more efficient producers in Europe.

After the Civil War the need for protection was much less clear. America was rapidly becoming the greatest manufacturing nation in the world. Its factories were efficient. The costs of doing business were lower than in many foreign countries. Manufacturers did not, however, want to give up the extra profits that the protective tariffs made possible.

[1]From *The Shame of the Cities* by Lincoln Steffens

This cartoon captured the plight of the American farmer. Its title tells all: "The Tariff Cow—the Farmer Feeds Her—the Monopolist Gets the Milk." Hasn't the artist highlighted the difference between the farmer and the rich man? Whose side is the artist on?

High tariffs raised the prices that farmers and other consumers had to pay for manufactured goods. Many, therefore, were opposed to the policy of protection. A number of tariff laws were passed by Congress between 1865 and 1900. Democrats and Republicans devoted much time to arguing about tariff policy. Neither party took a clear stand on the question. The rates of various imported products were raised and lowered, then lowered and raised, then raised again. No firm decision was ever made about whether protective tariffs were good for the nation as a whole.

The Democrats tended to be for lowering the tariff, the Republicans for keeping it high. But so many members of Congress from each party voted the other way that it is impossible to say that the tariff was a clear-cut party issue.

The Money Question

From the days of Andrew Jackson to the Civil War, the United States had followed a **monetary policy** that was conservative and cautious. All paper money in circulation could be exchanged for gold or silver coins at a bank. Yet during the Civil War, as we have seen, the government could not raise enough money by taxing and borrowing to pay all its expenses. It had to print $492 million in paper money called **greenbacks,** which could not be exchanged for coin. The back sides of these bills were printed in green ink. Paper money printed in yellow ink, popularly called **hard money,** could be exchanged for gold.

The question after the war was what should be done about the greenbacks? Most people believed either that they should be able to exchange greenbacks for gold or silver or that greenbacks should be withdrawn from circulation entirely.

People who had bought government bonds during the war had paid for them with greenback dollars, which were worth much less than gold or silver coins of the same face value. If these purchasers were paid back in gold when the bonds fell due, they would make very large profits. If the greenbacks were withdrawn by the government, the amount of money in circulation would decline. This would cause **deflation.** Prices of all goods would fall. Every dollar would buy more. Once again, those with money on hand would make large gains. But those people who had borrowed greenbacks would have to repay their loans with more valuable money. They would lose.

Farmers in particular tended to be hurt by deflation after the Civil War. During the war they had borrowed money to buy more land and machinery. They had paid high prices because scarcity had caused **inflation** during the war. If the price level fell, the money they paid out to cancel their debts would be more valuable than the money they had borrowed. If wheat sold for $1.50 a bushel when the money was borrowed and for only 50 cents a bushel when it had to be repaid, the farmer would have to produce three times as much wheat to pay off the debt.

Beginning in 1866, the government gradually withdrew greenbacks from circulation. This was called "retiring the greenbacks." The fewer greenbacks in public hands, the less people would fear that the government would print more and cause inflation. As the secretary of the treasury explained, the purpose of retiring the greenbacks was to end uncertainty about the money supply and encourage people to be "industrious, economical [and] honest."

However, reducing the money supply alarmed many business leaders. Early in 1868 Congress decided not to allow any further retirement of greenbacks. The argument continued until 1879 when the remaining greenbacks were made convertible into gold. Thereafter, greenbacks were the same as other American bank notes.

Peter Cooper was the candidate of the National Greenback party in 1876. He received 81,000 votes for president. He was the builder of the Tom Thumb *and Cooper Union, where working folks could get an education. His party supported currency inflation. Explain the difference between inflation and deflation.*

Civil Service Reform

As the United States grew larger, the number of people who worked for the government increased rapidly. There were about 27,000 postmasters in 1869 and over 75,000 in 1900. In the same period the treasury department payroll grew from about 4,000 persons to over 24,000. In the 1830s the entire government had employed fewer than 24,000 people.

Much of the work done by the government became increasingly technical. This meant that federal workers needed more skills and experience to perform their jobs efficiently. The new department of agriculture, created in the 1860s, employed chemists and biologists in large numbers. Even so-called routine jobs required people with

The good ship **Democracy** *tosses in stormy seas while its captain, Grover Cleveland, cuts away at mutineers who promote a silver purchase bill. On deck is the Tammany tiger gorging itself. The message of this cartoon from an 1894* Harper's Weekly *is that reforms in civil service and tariffs are about to be "deep sixed," or tossed overboard to drown. Explain how the cartoonist shows this.*

specialized skills. The introduction of the typewriter in the 1880s, for example, affected the training needed to become a government secretary or clerk.

These developments made the spoils system and the Jacksonians' idea of rotation in office badly out-of-date. The dismissal of large numbers of government workers each time a new president took office caused much confusion and waste. The president and other officials had to spend weeks deciding who of the tens of thousands of employees was to be kept, who fired, and who hired.

At the same time it became difficult to recruit properly trained people for government service. Men and women of ability did not want to give up good jobs to work for a government department. They knew that they might be fired after the next election no matter how well they had done their work.

After the Civil War many thoughtful people began to urge **civil service reform.** Most government jobs below the level of policy makers like cabinet members and their assistants should be taken out of politics, the reformers said. Applicants should have to take tests, and those with the best scores should be selected without regard for which political party they supported. Once appointed, civil service workers should be discharged only if they failed to perform their duties properly. This was known as the **merit system.**

President Rutherford B. Hayes was a leading advocate of reform. In his inaugural address in 1877 he stated his support:

“ I ask the attention of the public to the paramount [most important] necessity of reform in our civil service—a reform not merely as to certain abuses and practices of so-called official patronage which have come to have the sanction of usage in several Departments of Government, but a change in the system of appointment itself; a reform that shall be thorough, radical, and complete; a return to the principles and practices of the founders of the Government. They neither expected nor desired from public officers any partisan [favoring one political party] service. They meant that the officer should owe their whole service to the Government and the people. They meant that the officer should be secure in his tenure as long as his personal character remained untarnished and the performance of his duties satisfactory. They held that appointments for office were not to be made nor expected as rewards for partisan services. . . .[1]"

[1]From *Inaugural Addresses of the Presidents of the United States*

The problem with civil service reform was that the political parties depended upon the spoils system for rewarding the organizers who ran political campaigns. Presidents and state governors used their powers of appointment, called **patronage,** to persuade legislators to support their programs. They would promise to give government jobs to friends and supporters of the legislators in exchange for the legislators' votes on key issues.

Civil service reform was not an issue that a particular party favored. When the Republicans were in office, the Democrats called for reform. When the Democrats won elections, the Republicans became civil service reformers. The party that controlled the government tended to resist reform. Its leaders needed the jobs to reward their supporters. Nevertheless, the need for government efficiency could not be ignored much longer.

Then came the tragic assassination of President James A. Garfield. Shortly after he took office in 1881, Garfield was shot in a Washington railroad station by Charles Guiteau, a Republican who had been trying without success to get a job in the state department. Chester A. Arthur succeeded to the presidency. A great public cry went up for taking government jobs out of politics. Finally, in 1883, Congress passed the **Pendleton Act,** which created a **Civil Service Commission.** Its charge was to make up and administer examinations for applicants seeking certain government jobs. Those with the best scores on the tests were to get the appointments. The Pendleton Act also outlawed the practice of making government employees contribute to political campaign funds.

At first only 15,000 jobs were classified, or placed under civil service rules, by the 1883 law. But the number of posts covered was steadily increased over the years. By 1900 about half of all federal employees were under the civil service system. ⬚

James Garfield, above, was assassinated in 1881 and Chester A. Arthur, bottom, succeeded him.

Return to the Preview & Review on page 157.

2. THE AGE OF REALISM

Use these questions to guide your reading. Answer the questions after completing Section 2.
Understanding Issues, Events, & Ideas. In your own words, explain the historical importance of the Age of Realism.
1. What was the source of inspiration for American realists?
2. How would working as a newspaper reporter serve as good training for a realist?
3. What subjects did realistic painters illustrate?
Thinking Critically. Write a character description of a boss of a political machine, a cowhand, or a factory worker as if you were a realist writer.

Changes in American Literature

American literature was still dominated by the romantics after the Civil War. Poe, Hawthorne, Melville, and the New England poets Longfellow, Whittier, and Holmes still held sway. As today, many of the most popular offerings were by women. Susan Warner's *The Wide, Wide World* (1850) was the sad tale of a meek and pious little girl who cried "more readily and steadily than any other tormented child." "Tears on almost every page" could have been her advertising slogan.

But the great changes of industrial America—the cities teeming, the family farmland no longer worked by its children—brought about a new style of writing, known as Realism. Novelists treated such problems as slum life, labor unrest, and political corruption. They created three-dimensional characters and wrote about persons of every walk of life. The period came to be known as the **Age of Realism.** Dialect and slang helped capture the flavor of local types. A good example is Joel Chandler Harris, whose "Uncle Remus" stories reproduced the dialect of the black people of Georgia so faithfully that some critics today think the stories make fun of the southern traditions they relate.

Mark Twain

Mark Twain papers, The Bancroft Library

Here we see Samuel Clemens as a printer's apprentice. How might the newspaper office have provided a good training for the future Mark Twain?

The outstanding figure of western literature, the first great American realist, was Samuel Clemens, who wrote under the name Mark Twain. Clemens was born in 1835 and grew up in Hannibal, Missouri, on the banks of the Mississippi. He worked for a time as a riverboat pilot and in 1861 went west to Nevada to look for gold. Soon he began publishing humorous stories about the local life. In 1865, while working in California, Twain wrote "The Celebrated Jumping Frog of Calaveras County," a story that made him famous. He then toured Europe and the Holy Land and published *Innocents Abroad*.

In Mark Twain we find all the zest and enthusiasm of the Gilded Age—and its materialism, as well. Twain pursued the almighty dollar with his pen and lost a fortune in foolish business ventures. He wrote tirelessly about America and Europe and created some of America's most famous characters. From *The Gilded Age* there was eyewash salesman Colonel Beriah Sellers and his "Infallible Imperial Oriental Optic Liniment." From the classic *Huckleberry Finn* (1864), came the slave Jim, loyal, patient, yet above all a man. When Huck takes advantage of Jim, the slave turns from him coldly and says: "Dat trick duh is *trash;* and trash is what people is dat puts dirt on de head er ey fren's en makes 'em ashamed." And, of course, there is

Huck Finn himself on a raft with Jim floating down the Mississippi River. Through Huck's voice, Twain describes the closeness of Huck and Jim and the beauty of the river.

> ❝ It was kind of solemn, drifting down the big, still river, laying on our backs looking up at the stars, and we didn't ever feel like talking loud, and it warn't often that we laughed—only a little kind of a low chuckle. We had mighty good weather as a general thing, and nothing ever happened to us at all—that night, nor the next, nor the next.

This is the frontispiece of the original 1876 edition of Tom Sawyer. *From your reading could you produce a similar illustration for the front of* Huckleberry Finn?

From *The Adventures of Tom Sawyer,* 1876.

Every night we passed towns, some of them away up on black hillsides, nothing but just a shiny bed of lights; not a house could you see. The fifth night we passed St. Louis, and it was like the whole world lit up. In St. Petersburg they used to say there was twenty or thirty thousand people in St. Louis, but I never believed it till I see that wonderful spread of lights at two o'clock that still night. There warn't a sound there; everybody was asleep. **"**

Twain's other works include *Tom Sawyer* (1876), *Life on the Mississippi* (1883), and *A Connecticut Yankee in King Arthur's Court* (1889). "The truth is," he once wrote, "my books are mainly autobiographies." A story, he said, "must be written with the blood out of a man's heart." His works catch the spirit of the Age of Realism more than those of any other writer.

William Dean Howells

Mark Twain's long-time friend William Dean Howells of Ohio, born in 1837, was self-educated. He learned the printer's trade, then became a newspaper reporter. In 1860 he wrote a campaign biography of Abraham Lincoln. After the Civil War he became editor of the *Atlantic Monthly* and then, in 1886, of *Harper's*. Both these magazines are still published today.

Howells wrote many novels, one of which, *The Rise of Silas Lapham* (1885) dealt with the ethics of business in a competitive society. But Howells' greatest impact on American literature was as a critic. He encouraged important young novelists such as Stephen Crane, Frank Norris, and Theodore Dreiser. Like Twain and Howells, many novelists of the Age of Realism began as reporters, a job which provided an excellent training for any realist. They wrote about the most primitive emotions—fear, lust, hate, and greed. Crane's best-known work is *The Red Badge of Courage* (1895), which captures the pains and horrors of a young soldier in the Civil War. You can almost feel the youth's fear as those around him flee the battle:

" He slowly lifted his rifle and catching a glimpse of the thick-spread field he blazed at a cantering cluster [trotting group of enemy]. He stopped then and began to peer as best he could through the smoke. He caught changing views of the ground covered with men who were all running like pursued imps and yelling.

To the youth it was an onslaught of redoubtable [fearful] dragons. He became like a man who had lost his legs at the approach of the red and green monster. He waited in a sort

[1]From *The Adventures of Huckleberry Finn* by Mark Twain

of horrified, listening attitude. He seemed to shut his eyes and wait to be gobbled.

A man near him who up to this time was working feverishly at his rifle suddenly stopped and ran with howls. A lad whose face had borne an expression of exalted courage, the majesty of he who dares to give his life, at an instant, smitten abject [struck down with degrading fear]. He blanched [turned white] like one who has come to the edge of a cliff at midnight and is suddenly made aware. There was a revelation. He, too, threw down his gun and fled. There was no shame in his face. He ran like a rabbit.[1] **99**

Norris' *McTeague*, published in 1899, is the story of a brutal, dull-witted dentist and his miserable wife Trina, the winner of $5,000 in a lottery. Dreiser's *An American Tragedy* (1925) is the account of a young man's seduction by the apparent wealth and beauty of a social circle to which he does not belong.

Clockwise from top left are Frank Norris, Theodore Dreiser, Stephen Crane, and William Dean Howells. How did these "realists" portray America?

Realism in Art

American painters after the Civil War also treated more "realistic" subjects. The most prominent realist was Thomas Eakins. He mastered human anatomy and painted graphic illustrations of surgical operations. He experimented with early motion pictures to capture the attitudes of humans and animals in motion. Like his friend Walt Whitman, whose portrait is one of his greatest achievements, Eakins gloried in the ordinary.

Realism was also characteristic of the work of Winslow Homer, a Boston-born painter best known for his watercolors. He worked during the Civil War as a reporter for *Harper's Weekly,* and he

[1]From *The Red Badge of Courage* by Stephen Crane

The Age of Realism 169

Thomas Eakins, "Max Schmitt in a Single Scull," 1871.

Winslow Homer, "The Croquet Game."

James McNeill Whistler, "Arrangement in Gray and Black."

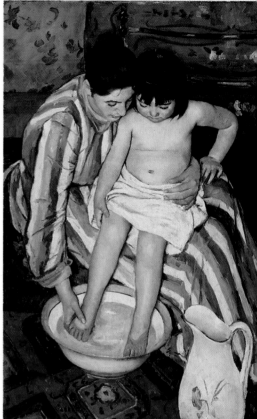

Mary Cassatt, "The Bath."

continued to create illustrations for some years thereafter. He roamed America, painting scenes of southern life, Adirondack camps, and magnificent seascapes.

At least two of America's great painters of the era abandoned their country for Paris. James A. McNeill Whistler left the United States when he was 21. His best-known painting, *Arrangement in Gray and Black* ("Whistler's Mother"), is one of the most famous canvases ever painted by an American. It hangs in the Orsay Museum in Paris.

A second expatriate artist was Mary Cassatt. (An expatriate is one who rejects and leaves the country of his—or her—birth.) The daughter of a wealthy Pittsburgh banker, she went to Paris as a tourist and remained, caught up in the Impressionist movement. Her studies of women, particularly mothers and daughters, hang in the finest museums in the world, including several fine paintings in the Art Institute in Chicago.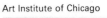

Return to the Preview & Review on page 166.

The Age of Realism   171

Use these questions to guide your reading. Answer the questions after completing Section 3.
Understanding Issues, Events, & Ideas. Describe the issues faced by farmers in the late 1800s, using the following words: third party, mandate, National Grange, Crime of 1873, Bland-Allison Act, Sherman Silver Purchase Act, free coinage, Farmers Alliance, co-op, People's party, Populist party.

1. Why did the presidents elected after the Civil War have little influence? Why was Congress inefficient?
2. How were Granger Laws supposed to help farmers?
3. Why did farmers favor coining silver money? What did the ratio of 16 to 1 mean in coinage?
4. How did the Populists differ from Republicans and Democrats in the election of 1892?
5. Why were Hispanic communities often able to thrive despite economic troubles and discrimination?

Thinking Critically. **1.** Write an article for the business section of an 1890 newspaper, explaining how the coinage of silver will change the economy. **2.** Compose a note to a friend, explaining why you will or will not vote for the Populist candidate in the 1892 election. Give reasons to justify your decision.

3. POPULISM

Political "Musical Chairs"

Since neither Democrats nor Republicans took firm stands on the real issues, there were few real differences between them. This helps explain why elections were usually close.

In 1880 James A. Garfield got 48.3 percent of the popular vote for president. He defeated the Democrat, Winfield Scott Hancock, by only 7,000 votes out of nearly 9.2 million cast. Four years later, Grover Cleveland, a Democrat, won with 48.5 percent of the popular vote. His margin over Republican James G. Blaine was 4.87 million to 4.85 million.

In 1888 Cleveland was defeated by Benjamin Harrison. Although President Cleveland got more popular votes, Harrison had a majority of the electoral vote, 233 to 168. In the next presidential election Cleveland defeated Harrison and returned to the White House. Yet he got only 46 percent of the popular vote to Harrison's 43 percent.

In all of these elections no one got a majority of the popular vote because third-party candidates were in the field. A **third party** is a political party competing with the two major parties. Third-party candidates *did* stand for "real issues." There were Greenback party candidates running in 1880 and 1884, for example. They demanded that more rather than fewer greenbacks be put in circulation. Other candidates ran on platforms calling for prohibition of liquor.

The presidents were elected by such narrow margins that they had relatively little influence while in office. They could not claim to have a **mandate**—the backing of a solid majority of the people—when they presented their programs to Congress.

Ewing Galloway National Portrait Gallery

Presidents Grover Cleveland, left, and Benjamin Harrison played political leapfrog with the White House. Explain how. Harrison's portrait is by the distinguished photographer Eastman Johnson, c. 1889.

The Granger Collection

"His grandfather's hat was too big for his head," sang the opponents of Benjamin Harrison when he became president. A bust of William Henry Harrison, the presidential grandfather, is above the door. Joseph Keppler drew this caricature. What seems to be his opinion of the man who was elected president in 1888?

In Congress the Democrats had a majority of the House of Representatives from 1874 to 1880 and from 1882 to 1888. But they had a majority of the Senate for only two years during this entire period. Turnover among representatives was extremely rapid. Often more than half the members of the House were in their first terms. Without experienced members, Congress was inefficient. With narrow, shifting majorities, controversial measures seldom were passed.

Populism 173

Hard Times for the Farmer

The times were particularly frustrating for farmers. Falling agricultural prices hurt them badly. So did the protective tariffs which raised the prices of the manufactured goods they purchased. But neither party was willing to work for laws that would bring much relief. The farmers found themselves left behind in American society's pursuit of wealth and status. Between 1860 and 1891 the number of farms rose from 2 million to 4.5 million. But farmers lacked the political clout of industry. So some farmers turned elsewhere in their agonizing search for help.

"I Pay for All" says the legend below this sturdy Granger. Rural scenes in this 1873 poster include the Biblical Ruth and Boaz, lower right; a harvest dance, lower left; and the Grange in session, upper right. Study the picture to find other scenes of agrarian life.

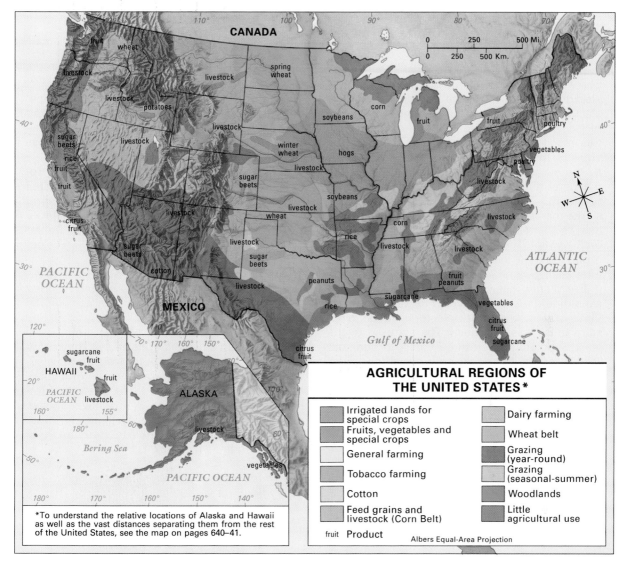

AGRICULTURAL REGIONS OF THE UNITED STATES *

Irrigated lands for special crops	Dairy farming
Fruits, vegetables and special crops	Wheat belt
General farming	Grazing (year-round)
Tobacco farming	Grazing (seasonal-summer)
Cotton	Woodlands
Feed grains and livestock (Corn Belt)	Little agricultural use

fruit Product

Albers Equal-Area Projection

*To understand the relative locations of Alaska and Hawaii as well as the vast distances separating them from the rest of the United States, see the map on pages 640–41.

In the 1870s many farmers joined the **National Grange.** The Grange was originally a kind of social club. It soon became a political organization as well. Many branches sprang up, especially in New York, Pennsylvania, Ohio, and the Middle West.

Granger leaders believed that railroad freight charges were too high. Because railroads had a monopoly on moving bulky goods to distant markets, Granger leaders demanded government regulation of rates. Their efforts led to the passage of Granger laws in many states. These measures set the rates that railroads and grain warehouses could collect so farmers would not be overcharged.

This raised the question of whether businesses like railroads could be regulated "in the public interest." Yes, ruled the Supreme Court in the case of *Munn v. Illinois* (1877). Granger laws were constitutional. Businesses like railroads that provided broad public services could not be considered completely private.

LEARNING FROM MAPS. *The United States has long been noted for its agricultural abundance. Note the wide variety and the productiveness of such a large percentage of the land. Compare this map to the one on page 109 and state a generalization about agriculture and climate in the United States.*

STRATEGIES FOR SUCCESS

INTERPRETING ELECTION RESULTS

Every four years the people of the United States elect a president. Or more correctly they elect electors who choose the president. This group of electors is called the *electoral college*. Election results are given for both *popular votes*—votes by the people—and *electoral votes*—votes by the electoral college. It is the electoral votes that determine which of the candidates becomes president.

The members of the electoral college are faceless and, in two thirds of the states, nameless on the ballot. They never assemble as a national group but meet instead in their respective states after each general election to cast their votes.

Every state has one electoral vote for each senator and representative. Thus, the more populous states have more electoral votes. What state today has the most? The states with the least population have three votes. In addition, the District of Columbia now has three votes. Today there are a total of 538 electoral votes. In order to be elected, a candidate must receive a simple majority, or 270, of those 538 votes.

The electoral system has often been criticized for its *unit rule*. That is, in each state the winner takes all. A candidate who receives one more vote than the closest rival gets all the state's electoral votes. Why do you think such a result would be controversial?

How to Interpret Election Results

To interpret election results, follow these steps.
1. **Check the figures.** Note both popular and electoral vote totals. In some elections the result of the popular vote is extremely close but the electoral vote is not.
2. **Note the trends.** See which states and regions voted for which candidate. Candidates have learned to effectively use the electoral system to their benefit. They spend a majority of their campaign time and money in the states with the largest populations—and electoral votes.
3. **Study the results.** Consider what factors influenced the election's outcome and resulted in the voting figures.

Applying the Strategy

Study the map and pie graphs below. They show the electoral and popular vote totals for the election of 1888. The map shows the electoral votes held by each state. Which three states had the largest totals? The close states have always played an important part in deciding elections. Which candidate won the close states of New York and Indiana in 1888?

For independent practice, see Practicing the Strategy on pages 192–93.

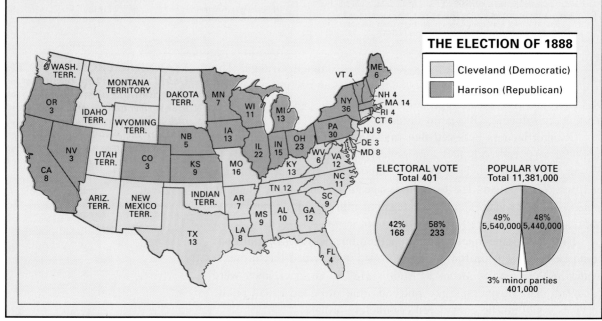

THE ELECTION OF 1888
Cleveland (Democratic)
Harrison (Republican)

ELECTORAL VOTE
Total 401
42% 168
58% 233

POPULAR VOTE
Total 11,381,000
49% 5,540,000
48% 5,440,000
3% minor parties 401,000

Other farmers, especially Mexican Americans, African Americans, and new immigrants, had nowhere to turn. As in other occupations, they faced prejudice and discrimination. They were not welcomed in many of the local granges, and they had even less political influence than established farmers.

Yet though life was shockingly hard for these people, in many places their communities thrived. In the West and Southwest close-knit Mexican American communities developed. The following passage from Jovita Gonzalez's book, *Among My People,* discusses what life was like in such a community in the state of Texas. See if you can get a feeling for life in the Southwest by reading Gonzalez's words:

" In August, down towards the Rio Grande, the rays of the sun beat vertically upon the sandy stretches of land, from which all tender vegetation has been scorched, and the white, naked land glares back at the sun; the only palpitating [moving] things discoverable between the two poles of heat are heat devils. The rattlesnakes are as deeply holed up and as quiet as in midwinter. In the thickets of brush the roadrunners, rusty lizards, mockingbirds, and all other living things pant. Whirlwinds dance across the stretches of prairie interspersed between the thickets of thorn. At six o'clock it is hotter than at midday. Seven o'clock, and then the sun, a ball of orange-pink, descends below the horizon at one stride. The change is magical. A soft cooling breeze, the pulmotor [breathing apparatus] of the Border lands, springs up from the south.

Down in the *cañada* [brook between mountains], which runs by the ranch, doves coo. Out beyond, cattle are grazing and calves are frisking. In the cottonwood tree growing beside the dirt "tank" near the ranch house the redbird sings. Children shout and play. From the corrals come the voices of vaqueros [cowboys] singing and jesting. Blended with the bleatings of goats and sheep are the whistles and hisses of the *pastor* (shepherd). The locusts complete the chorus of evening noises. Darkness subdues them; then, as the moon rises, an uncounted mob of mongrel curs [mixed-breed dogs] set up a howling and barking at it that coyotes out beyond mock.

It was on a night like this that the ranch folk gathered at the Big House to shell corn. All came: Tío Julianito, the *pastor,* with his brood of sunburned half-starved children ever eager for food; Alejo the fiddler, Juanito the idiot, called the Innocent, because the Lord was keeping his mind in heaven; Pedro the hunter, who had seen the world and spoke English; the vaqueros; and, on rare occasions, Tío

Esteban, the mail carrier. Even the women came, for on such occasions supper was served.

A big canvas was spread outside, in front of the kitchen. In the center of this canvas, ears of corn were piled in pyramids for the shellers, who sat about in a circle and with their bare hands shelled the grains off the cobs.

It was then, under the moonlit sky, that we heard stories of witches, buried treasures, and ghosts. . . . Then the *pastor* told of how he had seen spirits in the shape of balls of fire floating through the air. They were souls doing penance for their past sins. As a relief to our fright, Don [a title of respect] Francisco suggested the Tío Julianito do one of his original dances to the tune of Alejo's fiddle. A place was cleared on the canvas, and that started the evening's merriment. . . .[1] **99**

The Silver Issue

Lower freight and storage charges did not help farmers as much as the Grangers had hoped. Costs were not reduced much. So farmers tried instead to raise the prices of their produce. The best way to push up prices seemed to be by causing inflation. Farmers looked for a way to put more money in circulation so their prices would rise. One way was by coining silver money.

Throughout the period before the Civil War both gold and silver had been minted into coins and used to back bank notes. But in 1873 Congress had voted to stop coining silver. That seemed a terrible mistake to those who favored inflation.

Many new silver mines had been discovered. If miners could bring their silver to the United States mint for coining, more money would be created. With more money in circulation, prices would rise. Yet silver was a relatively scarce metal. The amount that could be mined would place a limit on the amount of new money that could be put into circulation. This would prevent "runaway" inflation, which might result if there was no limit on how much paper money could be printed.

Farmers and silver miners joined to make a powerful political force. People began to refer to the law that had discontinued the coining of silver as the **Crime of 1873.** They demanded that the government once again coin all the silver brought to the mint.

The result of their pressure was a political compromise. In 1878 Congress passed a bill sponsored by Representative Richard Bland of Missouri and Senator William B. Allison of Iowa. Bland was a Democrat who believed sincerely in coining both gold and silver.

[1]From *Among My People* by Jovita Gonzalez

A silverite runs away with the Democratic donkey pursued by a sound money Democrat. Which side of the pursuit does this 1896 cartoon seem to favor? The sign can help you answer.

Allison, a Republican, was a shrewd political manipulator. (It was said of Allison that he would make no more noise walking across the Senate floor in wooden shoes than a fly made walking on the ceiling.)

The **Bland-Allison Act** ordered the secretary of the treasury to purchase and coin between $2 and $4 million in silver each month. In 1890 another coinage law, the **Sherman Silver Purchase Act,** increased the amount of silver bought to 4.5 million ounces a month. This came to about the total being mined at that time.

The price of silver was usually expressed by comparing it to the price of gold. In 1873, when the mint had stopped coining silver, an ounce of gold was worth about 16 times as much as an ounce of silver. By 1890, when the Sherman Silver Purchase Act was passed, an ounce of gold was worth 20 times as much. This was because the

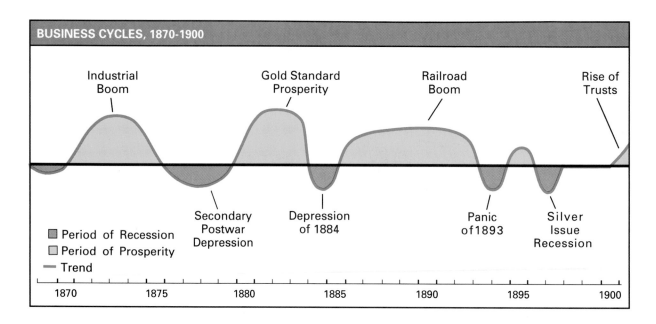

BUSINESS CYCLES, 1870-1900

Industrial Boom

Gold Standard Prosperity

Railroad Boom

Rise of Trusts

Secondary Postwar Depression

Depression of 1884

Panic of 1893

Silver Issue Recession

■ Period of Recession
■ Period of Prosperity
— Trend

1870   1875   1880   1885   1890   1895   1900

LEARNING FROM GRAPHS. *As you can see, the United States economy had extended ups and downs between 1870 and 1900. Why might there have been little change in the economy between 1898 and 1900?*

price of silver was falling steeply at the same time as the supply was increasing from new mines in the West.

Farmers and others who favored inflation wanted as much silver coined as possible in order to increase the money supply. If the United States would coin all the world's silver, the price of other products would rise because more money would be in circulation. Those who favored inflation therefore urged **free coinage**—that is, a law requiring the mint to turn all the silver offered it into silver dollars.

The silver miners were more interested in driving up the price of their silver than in what was done with it. They wanted the United States to exchange an ounce of gold for 16 ounces of silver. Thus, farmers and silver miners combined their interests. They demanded free coinage of silver at a ratio of 16 to 1 with gold.

The Populist Party

While the demand for free silver was developing, farmers were looking for other ways out of their hard times. First in Texas, and then elsewhere in the South, a new movement was spreading. It was the **Farmers Alliance.**

Like the earlier National Grange, the Alliance began as a social organization. In many areas local Alliance clubs formed cooperatives, or **co-ops,** to sell their crops at better prices. These co-ops set a single price for produce and purchased goods wholesale to save money for their members. By 1890 the Alliance movement had spread northward into Kansas, Nebraska, and the Dakotas.

Like the Grange, the Alliance became an important political

force. Its leaders campaigned against high railroad freight rates and high interest rates charged by banks for mortgages and other loans. Alliance members began to run for local offices, promising if elected to help farmers.

An angry rural editor wrote in 1890:

“ There are three great crops raised in Nebraska. One is a crop of corn, one is a crop of freight rates, and one is a crop of interest. One is produced by farmers who by sweat and toil farm the land. The other two are produced by men who sit in their offices and behind their bank counters and farm the farmers.”

In 1890 several southern states elected governors backed by the Alliance. More than 45 "Alliancemen" were elected to Congress. Alliance officials were encouraged by these results. They decided to establish a new political party and run a candidate for president in 1892. To broaden their appeal, they persuaded representatives of labor unions to join with them. They named their new organization the **People's party,** but it is usually referred to as the **Populist party.**

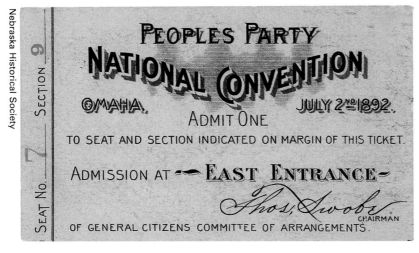

In July 1892 the first Populist nominating convention met in Omaha, Nebraska. The delegates adopted a platform that called for a long list of specific reforms. One was government ownership of railroads and of the telegraph and telephone network. Another was a federal income tax. Still another was a program of government loans to farmers who would store their crops in government warehouses as security for the loans.

To win the support of industrial workers, the Populist platform called for the eight-hour workday and for restrictions on immigration. It also demanded the "free and unlimited coinage of silver and gold at . . . 16 to 1."

The Populists chose James Baird Weaver of Iowa as their candidate for president in 1892. He had fought bravely for the Union in

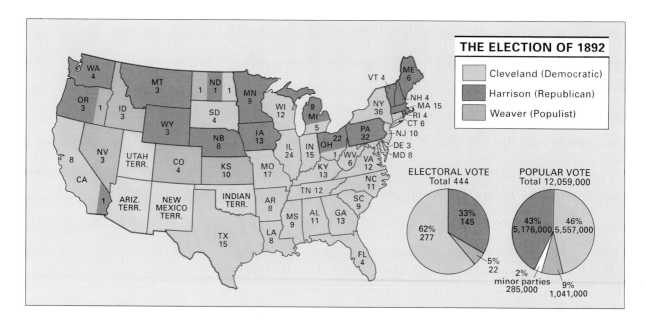

THE ELECTION OF 1892

	Cleveland (Democratic)
	Harrison (Republican)
	Weaver (Populist)

ELECTORAL VOTE
Total 444

62% 277
33% 145
5% 22

POPULAR VOTE
Total 12,059,000

43% 5,176,000
46% 5,557,000
2% minor parties 285,000
9% 1,041,000

LEARNING FROM MAPS. *Compare the results of the election of 1892 shown on this map with the results of the 1888 election shown on the map on page 176. What major differences do you see? What major similarities?*

HBJ Collection

James B. Weaver was the nominee of the People's party at its convention in Omaha in 1892. How did the party balance its ticket?

Return to the Preview & Review on page 172.

the Civil War, rising from lieutenant to brigadier general. Their candidate for vice president was James G. Field of Virginia, a former general in the Confederate army.

The Populists created "a multi-sectional institution of reform," according to historian Lawrence Goodwyn. But they were not revolutionaries. They felt betrayed by what we today call "the establishment." They did not share the national passion for free enterprise, and they felt their problems were created by clever and selfish interests who used the American system to their advantage. As one Populist writer stated it:

❝ The farmer has been the victim of a gigantic scheme of plunder. Never has such a vast combination of brains and money forced people into labor for the benefit of a few. . . .[1]❞

[1]From *The Farmer's Side: His Troubles and Their Remedy* by William A. Peffer

The Populists took clear stands on controversial issues, seeking voters who agreed with their ideas. Democratic and Republican leaders continued to duck controversial questions. In the South the Populists tried to unite black and white farmers. There were many blacks in the Alliance movement in the southern states, although their groups were segregated from the whites.

The 1892 presidential election was an exciting one. General Weaver got over a million votes, a large number for a third-party candidate. The Populist party won many local contests. On balance, however, the results disappointed the Populists. They lost many votes in the South because large numbers of their white supporters refused to vote for candidates who appealed openly for black support.

4. UNEMPLOYMENT AND UNREST

Preview & Review

Use these questions to guide your reading. Answer the questions after completing Section 4.
Understanding Issues, Events, & Ideas. Using the following words, describe the key instances of labor unrest during the Depression of 1893: gold standard, Coxey's Army, Pullman Strike.
1. Why did President Cleveland want the nation to return to the gold standard?
2. How would Coxey's plan have put people to work and caused prices to rise?
3. Why did many people turn against President Cleveland after the Pullman Strike?
Thinking Critically. Which amendment in the Bill of Rights might Jacob Coxey have used to protest his arrest in March 1894? Why? Restate the amendment in your own words.

The Depression of 1893

Shortly after the presidential election, which Grover Cleveland won, the country entered into the worst period of hard times in its history. Business activity slowed down. Unemployment increased. By the end of 1893 more than a hundred railroads had gone bankrupt. People hoarded money, withdrawing their savings in gold from the banks.

As usual the depression hurt African Americans, Hispanics, and recent immigrants worst of all. Many were the first to be laid off. Others barely scraped out a living. Farmers now could not sell their produce at decent prices. One historian wrote of "the absolute destitute condition of the colored people of the South." It was as bad if not worse elsewhere.

The long period of deflation that began in the 1870s was an important cause of this depression. Farmers and wage earners blamed the depression on "the money shortage." They felt that the Sherman Silver Purchase Act had not gone far enough. They demanded that the government coin even more silver.

President Cleveland believed the business decline was caused by the uncertainty people had about the safety of their money. The government should stop coining silver, he insisted, and go back to the single **gold standard.** This meant that only gold would be used to back the currency. In October 1893 he persuaded Congress to repeal the Sherman Silver Purchase Act.

This action angered those who favored coining silver as well as gold. It split the Democratic party. And it did not end the depression. During 1894 and 1895, economic conditions got worse rather than better.

Other people blamed the depression on the government's failure to regulate big business. Unsafe working conditions, child labor, low wages, and unfair pricing policies had gone on for most of the century. Government on all levels had ignored these and other effects of industrialization. "The wheel of progress is to be run over the whole human race and smash us all," one journalist predicted sadly.

Coxey's Army

As the depression dragged on, large numbers of unemployed men took to wandering about the countryside. These people were called tramps. Some thought them dangerous troublemakers, perhaps even revolutionaries who wanted to overthrow the government. In truth, they only wanted work.

Small groups of unemployed workers began making protest marches to seek government relief. This increased fear of the "tramp

The Granger Collection

Jacob Coxey seems a timid, mild sort in this 1894 photograph. But appearances can be deceiving. You know him as the leader of Coxey's Army. How successful was he?

problem.'' The most important of these marches was headed by Jacob Coxey, who was himself a prosperous business leader.

Coxey's Army marched from Massillon, Ohio, to Washington, attracting an enormous amount of attention. One observer claimed that for every two marchers there was at least one newspaper reporter tagging along to describe the happenings.

Coxey's Army set out in March 1894 and reached Washington in May. There were only a few hundred marchers, most of them obviously harmless people. But when Coxey tried to present a petition to Congress, he was arrested for trespassing on the grounds of the Capitol. The police then broke up Coxey's followers and sent the marchers straggling home. Their march came to nothing.

What makes Coxey's Army important historically is the plan that Coxey worked out for dealing with the depression. The federal government should spend $500 million improving rural roads, he said. It should also lend money to state and local governments for other public works projects. The work itself should be done by the unemployed. Anyone without a job should be put to work.

Coxey further proposed that both the $500 million spent by the federal government and the money lent to local governments should simply be printed by the treasury. Like the Civil War greenbacks, this money would not be backed by gold or silver. This inflation of the money supply would cause prices to rise. That would help farmers and debtors of all sorts. Coxey's program seemed radical and impractical in 1894. Forty years later it appeared a perfectly reasonable way to deal with deflation and unemployment in a depression.

The Pullman Strike

Since he was president when the depression struck, Cleveland was blamed for the hard times. Emergency soup kitchens were set up to feed the long lines of hungry people who could not find work. Critics unfairly called them ''Cleveland Cafes.'' But Cleveland did little to help the jobless or to stimulate the lagging economy.

More people turned against Cleveland when a great strike broke out in May 1894, shortly after the arrest of Jacob Coxey. The strike had begun in the factory of the Pullman Palace Car Company in Illinois, which manufactured and operated sleeping and dining cars for the railroads. After the strike had gone on for several weeks, engineers, conductors, and other workers of the American Railway Union, in sympathy with the strikers, voted not to handle trains to which Pullman cars were attached. This paralyzed the railroads in and around Chicago. It threatened to disrupt the nation's already depressed economy.

A federal judge ordered the railroad workers back to work. When they refused, President Cleveland sent troops into Chicago to make sure that the United States mail was not held up. The union was

The Granger Collection

willing to operate mail trains. However, railroad officials insisted on attaching Pullman cars to these trains. The **Pullman Strike** continued.

Rioting broke out when blue-coated soldiers entered the Chicago rail yards. The violence turned public opinion against the union. Its president, Eugene Victor Debs, was arrested and thrown in jail. The strike collapsed.

Conservatives praised Cleveland's defense of "law and order." But thousands of union members were alarmed by his use of the army to break a strike. The governor of Illinois, John Peter Altgeld, had bitterly objected to the use of federal troops in his state. Altgeld claimed that Chicago police and state militia units could preserve order. He accused Cleveland of being a strikebreaker. Altgeld's opposition weakened Cleveland politically since Altgeld, like Cleveland, was a Democrat. 🖎

Illinois national guardsmen are firing on striking Pullman Company workers in this artist's sketch. Their fortress is the equipment brought in to get the train back on track. Describe this scene from both points of view—that of the guardsmen and that of the strikers.

Return to the Preview & Review on page 183.

Unemployment and Unrest   185

Use these questions to guide your reading. Answer the questions after completing Section 5.
Understanding Issues, Events, & Ideas. Give a brief eyewitness account of William Jennings Bryan's Cross of Gold speech.
1. What stand did the Republicans take on the money issue in their platform of 1896?
2. How did the Republican campaign of 1896 differ from the Democratic campaign?
3. How did McKinley's victory in 1896 mark the end of the post-Civil War era?
Thinking Critically. From the point of view of either a Republican or a free-silver Democrat, write a brief campaign pamphlet about the money issue for the election of 1896.

The Bettmann Archive

In a wicker rocker on his front porch William McKinley waits for visitors during his presidential campaign in 1896.

5. GOLD VERSUS SILVER

The Democrats Choose Silver

As the election of 1896 drew near, the Democrats had to make a difficult decision. President Cleveland was extremely unpopular. Rightly or wrongly, he was being blamed for the continuing depression. Furthermore, the public knew he was totally opposed to measures that would stimulate the economy by raising prices, especially the coining of silver.

In the southern states where the Democrats were in control, the Populist party was making large gains by calling for the free coinage of silver. Southern farmers were hard hit by the depression. If the Democrats again chose Cleveland, who defended the gold standard, they seemed sure to be defeated in the national election. They might even lose the South to the Populists.

The 1896 election was one which gave the Democrats a chance to hold the presidency and to take Republican seats in Congress. This was because the Republican party convention in June 1896 had nominated Congressman William McKinley of Ohio as its candidate for president. McKinley would be running on a platform that declared squarely for the gold standard. "We are . . . opposed to the free coinage of silver," the platform stated.

Many normally Republican farmers in the Middle West and nearly all the miners in the Rocky Mountain states were in favor of free silver. The Republican platform made them furious. States like Nebraska and Colorado, traditionally Republican, might go Democratic if that party would come out for free silver.

The Democratic convention met in St. Louis in July. Before picking a candidate, the delegates had to adopt a platform. The key issue to be decided was the money question. A formal debate took place. Three speakers defended the gold standard. Three others spoke in favor of the free coinage of silver.

The final debater was William Jennings Bryan, a young ex-congressman from Nebraska. Bryan was not a particularly thoughtful person, but he had a deep faith in democracy. He believed that legislators should represent the ideas of the people who elected them. As early as 1892 he said, "The people of Nebraska are for free silver, and [therefore] I am for free silver. I will look up the arguments later."

Bryan had served two terms in Congress. But few people outside Nebraska had ever heard of him. He was only 36, barely a year older than the minimum age set by the Constitution for becoming president. Nevertheless, he decided that he had a good chance of getting the 1896 presidential nomination.

Bryan's speech on the silver question was his great opportunity to attract attention. He succeeded brilliantly. Bryan was one of the

The labels in the cartoon read: "CROWN of THORNS USED BY BRYAN IN CAMPAIGN SPEECHES."; "USED IN BRYAN'S CHICAGO SPEECH CROSS of GOLD"; "SPEECH PREACHED FROM THE BIBLE"; "SPEECH TAKEN FROM THE BIBLE"; "ANARCHY"; "BIBLE". Signed "HAMILTON."

William Jennings Bryan's "Cross of Gold" speech inspired this caricature. He is seen here as a despoiler of the Bible, but Bryan was actually a very religious person who based courtroom arguments on the Bible. In what other ways does this cartoonist criticize Bryan?

greatest political orators in American history. He did not make any new economic arguments for free silver. Instead, like a skillful musician, he played upon the emotions of the delegates. His voice rang through the hall like a mighty organ in a great cathedral. As he approached the climax of his appeal, almost every sentence brought forth a burst of applause.

He likened those who favored coining silver to the Crusaders who had freed Jerusalem from the Moslems. He praised western farmers as "hardy pioneers who have braved the dangers of the wilderness" and "made the desert bloom." The country could exist without the cities, Bryan said, but without the nation's farms, "grass will grow in the streets of every city in the country." He concluded by likening the silver forces to Jesus Christ, saying to the defenders of the gold standard:

> You shall not press down upon the brow of labor this crown of thorns, you shall not crucify mankind upon a cross of gold.

Gold Versus Silver 187

After cheering this **Cross of Gold speech,** the Democratic convention adopted a platform calling for "the free and unlimited coinage of both silver and gold at the . . . ratio of 16 to 1." The next day the delegates nominated the "Nebraska Cyclone," William Jennings Bryan, for president.

The Election of 1896

The presidential campaign of 1896 roused people throughout the nation. When it was over, many Republicans and Democrats had changed sides.

Nearly all business people and manufacturers supported McKinley. Like most other wealthy citizens, these people felt that the issue of silver inflation versus the gold standard and "sound money" was more important than party loyalty. They believed that if Bryan were elected, their businesses would collapse and their wealth would vanish.

Beyond question these people were wrong. There was nothing magical about the gold standard, and Bryan was no threat to their wealth. But they misunderstood the situation. They saw the campaign as a crusade. They thought that McKinley was a great patriotic hero, almost a Washington or a Lincoln, who would save the nation in an hour of terrible danger.

Free silverites have unhitched their wagon from the Democratic donkey as they roll out of control. This is the view of C. J. Taylor, who made this lithograph in 1896. Bryan has his arms stubbornly folded while Governor Altgeld of Illinois waves a firebrand. Explain why the red banner says "Repudiation."

The Granger Collection

McKinley ran what was called a front-porch campaign for the presidency. He stayed home in Canton, Ohio, partly to be near his wife, Ida, who had epilepsy. Groups from all over the country came to hear his views.

These visits were carefully planned. Each delegation was greeted at the railroad station by the "Canton Home Guards" mounted on horses. The visitors then marched to McKinley's modest house. The town took on the appearance of one long Fourth of July celebration. The streets were lined with flags and banners. Pictures of McKinley were everywhere. Stands along the route sold hot dogs, lemonade, and souvenirs.

When a delegation reached McKinley's house, the candidate came out to meet them, usually with his wife and mother at his

Ida McKinley

White House Historical Association

side. He called their leaders by name and seemed to show keen interest in their problems. A member of the delegation would make a speech while McKinley listened to him "like a child looking at Santa Claus."

McKinley's responses showed how well he knew his audience. To a group of Civil War veterans he might speak about pensions. To manufacturers or factory workers he might stress the importance of the protective tariff. Always he pictured himself as a patriot defending America and the gold standard against the dangerous free-silver Democrats. "Patriotism," he would say, "is above party and National honor is dearer than party name. The currency and credit of the government are good, and must be kept good forever."

Newspaper reporters covered each of these visits. They wrote articles describing the crowds. They quoted the remarks of the candidate in detail. In this way McKinley reached voters all over the country without stepping off the front porch of his house.

Actually, McKinley was a rather ordinary person. He was hard working, forward looking, and politically shrewd. But he was not especially intelligent, imaginative, or creative. His greatest advantage in the election was the solid support of his business backers.

The Republican campaign was organized by Marcus Alonzo Hanna, an Ohio industrialist. Mark Hanna and his assistants raised enormous amounts of money for the contest. Some of the contributions came from wealthy individuals, many of whom were normally Democrats. But most of the money came from large corporations. As one bank president explained, "We have never before contributed a cent to politics, but the present crisis we believe to be as important as the [Civil] war." It was not then illegal for corporations to give money to political candidates.

Hanna used this money very cleverly. Republican speakers spread across the country. At one point 250 Republican orators were campaigning in 27 states. Pamphlets explaining the Republican program were printed and 250 million distributed. Over 15 million pamphlets on the money question were handed out in two weeks.

Committees were set up to win the support of all kinds of special groups. One committee tried to influence German American voters,

Gold Versus Silver 189

another those of African descent, and so on. There was even a committee assigned to campaign among bicycle riders, for bicycling was an especially popular sport in the 1890s.

The Democrats had very little campaign money, in part because so many wealthy Democrats were supporting the Republican candidate. The party organization was also weak. In many of the industrial states Democratic politicians would not support free silver. These "Gold Democrats" formed a National Democratic party and nominated Senator John M. Palmer of Illinois for president.

The Democrats did have one very valuable asset—Bryan himself. His magnetic personality and his brilliance as a speaker made him a great campaigner. He traveled constantly, speaking all over the nation. Sometimes he addressed huge crowds in city auditoriums. Sometimes he spoke to only a handful of listeners at rural railroad stations from the back platform of his train. All told, he made over 600 speeches between August and election day in November.

Most important newspapers supported McKinley. Their reporters frequently misquoted Bryan in order to make him appear foolish or radical. *The New York Times* even suggested that he might well be insane. But the papers did report Bryan's speeches in detail. In this election voters could readily learn where both candidates stood on all the issues of the day.

The election caused major shifts in voting patterns. After much debate the Populists nominated Bryan instead of running a candidate of their own. The effect was to end the Populist movement. Yet if the Populist party had run someone else, the free-silver vote would have been split. Then McKinley would have been certain to win the election.

Populist strongholds in the South and West went solidly for Bryan in November. So did the mountain states, where silver mining was important. But thousands of formerly Democratic industrial workers voted Republican. City people did not find Bryan as attractive as did farmers and residents of small towns. McKinley was popular with workers, despite his close connections with big business. He convinced workers that free silver would be bad for the economy. And he argued that a high tariff would protect their jobs by keeping out goods made by low-paid foreign laborers.

Boston, New York City, Baltimore, Chicago, and many other cities that had gone Democratic in the presidential election of 1892 voted Republican in 1896. Chicago, for example, had given Grover Cleveland a majority of over 35,000 in 1892. In 1896 McKinley carried the city by more than 56,000 votes.

The Election Ends an Era

The election was a solid Republican triumph. The electoral vote was 271 for McKinley, 176 for Bryan. Looked at one way, McKinley won

Courtesy, Museum of Fine Arts, Boston, Gift of Miss Maude E. Appleton

simply because his party spent more money and was better organized than the Democrats. He carried all the crucial close states of the Northeast by relatively small margins. If Bryan had won in New York, Ohio, Indiana, and Illinois, he would have been president.

In a larger sense, however, McKinley's victory marked the end of the post-Civil War era. Within a year or two, new gold discoveries and improved methods of refining gold ore ended the money shortage. Free silver was no longer an issue. But the changes in voting patterns caused by the Depression of 1893 and the free-silver fight continued long after those problems were settled.

The farm states voted for Bryan, the industrial states for Mc-Kinley. But the election was not a victory for industry nor a defeat for American farmers. Agriculture remained important. As Bryan had said in his Cross of Gold speech, the cities and their industries could not prosper unless farmers were prosperous too.

The election marked the birth of the modern industrial age. To most people of that day, Bryan seemed to be pressing for change, McKinley defending the old, established order. In fact, McKinley was far more forward looking than Bryan. His view of the future was much closer to what the reality of the 20th century would be. 🖅

The century ends with the glow of lamplight on Boston Common. Childe Hassam painted this twilight scene in the early 1900s. But what lies ahead in the story of America? How do you imagine this scene will appear in 1920? 1960? 2000?

Return to the Preview & Review on page 186.

Gold Versus Silver 191

CHAPTER 4 REVIEW

1866
Tammany Hall

1870
National
Grange
movement

1872
Eakin's
The Agnew Clinic

1873
Coining of silver
discontinued

1876
Tom Sawyer

1877
Hayes elected
president

★
Reconstruction ends

★
Munn v. Illinois

1878
Bland-Allison Act

Chapter Summary

Read the statements below. Choose one, and write a paragraph explaining its importance.

1. The United States remained politically divided after the Civil War into the Republican North and Democratic South.
2. Political machines controlled many local elections. These machines helped the poor and immigrants, and then counted on their votes.
3. Tariffs, the money question, and civil service reform posed important issues for Americans after the Civil War.
4. American writers and artists turned to a movement called Realism after the Civil War.
5. Presidential elections during the last half of the 19th century were very close. This happened because few candidates took a real stand on the issues.
6. After the war, times were hard for American farmers. They created the Grange and the Farmers Alliance to help them deal with their problems.
7. Farmers and consumers wanted free coinage of silver. Many wealthy people wanted to remain on the gold standard.
8. The Depression of 1893 led to severe unemployment and unrest such as Coxey's Army and the Pullman Strike.
9. McKinley's defeat of Bryan in 1896 ended the post-Civil War era.

Reviewing Chronological Order

Number your paper 1–5. Then study the time line above and place the following events in the order in which they happened by writing the first next to 1, the second next to 2, and so on.

1. Pendleton Act
2. Cross of Gold speech
3. National Grange formed
4. Coxey's Army marches to Washington
5. Garfield assassinated

Understanding Main Ideas

1. Why did the Democrats and Republicans nominate so many national candidates from close states after the Civil War?
2. What reforms were made in civil service after Congress acted in 1883?
3. What was the money question? How were greenbacks a part of it?
4. Which groups supported the Populist party? What was its platform in 1892?
5. Which groups supported the Republicans in 1896? Which supported the Democrats? Why did the Republicans win?

Thinking Critically

1. **Evaluating.** Suppose you are a political reformer in 1898. You will publish a pamphlet exposing the corruption of your local political machine. Write the introduction to the pamphlet, explaining various wrongs that the machine has committed in your community.
2. **Analyzing.** Although the Populist party lost the election of 1892, several reforms listed in the party's platform were later put into effect. Of these reforms, which do you think was the most important? Why?
3. **Synthesizing.** It is 1896. Write a letter to a friend, giving your eyewitness account of either (a) a meeting of the local Grange discussing farmers' concerns or (b) a Congressional debate on the pros and cons of civil service reform.

Writing About History: Persuasive

Use historical imagination to write a letter to a friend describing what you saw and heard at the Democratic convention in July 1896 when Bryan delivered his "Cross of Gold" speech. Then try to persuade your friend to vote for or against Bryan. Use the information in Chapter 4 and in reference books to prepare your letter.

Practicing the Strategy

Review the strategy on page 176.

30
rfield
cted
sident

81
rfield
sassinated

1882
Homer paints
Harvest Moon

1883
Pendleton
Act passed

1884
Cleveland elected president

1888
Harrison
elected
president

1890
Sherman
Silver
Purchase Act
★
Farmers
Alliance
formed

1892
Populist party
enters national
election
★
Cleveland again
elected
president

1893
Depression
sweeps nation
and world

1894
Coxey's Army
marches
on Washington
★
Pullman Strike

1895
*Red Badge
of Courage*

1896
Bryan's Cross
of Gold speech
★
McKinley
elected
president
★
Post-Civil War
era ends

Interpreting Election Results. Compare the election maps on pages 176 and 182, then answer the following questions.

1. In which part of the country were the Democrats strongest in 1888? In 1892?
2. In which part were the Republicans strongest in 1888? In 1892?
3. In which part of the country were the Populists strongest?
4. How would you explain the geographic location of each party's strength?
5. How can you tell that the unit rule was in effect in 1888 but not in 1892?

Using Primary Sources

The following excerpt from Richard Hofstadter's book *The Age of Reform* examines the controversy that arose from the Populist movement. As you read the excerpt, note differences in the two points of view presented. Then answer the questions that follow.

> *On the one hand the failure of the revolt has been described . . . as the final defeat of the American farmer. John Hicks, in his history of the movement, speaks of the Populists as having begun "the last phase of a song and perhaps a losing struggle—the struggle to save agricultural America from the devouring jaws of industrial America," while another historian calls Populism "the last united stand of the country's agricultural interest . . . the final attempt made by the farmers of the land to beat back an industrial civilization whose forces had all but vanquished them already."*

1. According to the excerpt, how did the perspectives of the two historians differ?
2. Which of the views presented by the two historians reveals bias against industrial America? Quote from the reading to support your answer.
3. How might American farmers today agree or disagree with the views of Populism presented in the excerpt? Support your answer with specific examples.

Linking History & Geography

Agricultural land use is in part determined by a number of natural factors. Topography, rainfall, length of growing season, and other variables influence what is produced in an area. Study the maps on pages 84, 109, and 175 and answer these questions.

1. Why is the Great Plains topography well suited to growing grain?
2. What factors limit the agricultural use of land in Alaska? Wyoming?
3. What natural features help make the Central Valley of California so productive?

Enriching Your Study of History

1. **Individual Project** In your library and other American history books find examples of the cartoons of Thomas Nast. It was Nast who created the symbols of the Tammany Hall tiger, the Republican elephant, and the Democratic donkey. Study a copy of a Nast cartoon from this era and explain his use of one of these symbols. You also may wish to draw your own cartoon to express your view of a key point in the chapter.
2. **Cooperative Project** Presidential campaigns after the Civil War were hard fought and much discussed. Yet time seems to drop a veil over the occupants of the White House during this period, to say nothing of the candidates they defeated. Various members of your group will research and report on each of the following campaigns:
   1868 Grant v. Seymour
   1872 Grant v. Greeley
   1876 Hayes v. Tilden
   1880 Garfield v. Hancock
   1884 Cleveland v. Blaine, Butler
   1888 Harrison v. Cleveland
   1892 Cleveland v. Harrison, Weaver

Chapter 4 Review 193

UNIT ONE REVIEW

Summing Up and Predicting
Read the summary of the main ideas in Unit One below. Choose one statement, then write a paragraph predicting its outcome or future effect.
1. Although the Civil War Amendments—the 13th, 14th, and 15th—guaranteed civil rights to blacks, white southerners found ways to continue to deny those rights.
2. The end of Reconstruction by the Compromise of 1877 and the Supreme Court's *Plessy* decision led to the start of a Long Night of racial segregation.
3. The tremendous growth of America brought it to the last frontier—the Great Plains—where settlers eventually displaced the Plains Indians.
4. Completion of railroad and communications networks prepared the nation for the rise of industry.
5. American industry became so large that new business organizations, such as corporations and trusts, were developed.
6. Workers turned to unionization to make their demands for improved conditions heard.
7. The "New Immigration" brought people from southern and eastern Europe to American cities and factories.
8. After the Civil War political machines controlled many of the nation's cities.

Connecting Ideas
1. In 1877 Congress ended the military reconstruction of the South. Eighty years later President Eisenhower ordered federal troops to Little Rock, Arkansas, to enforce a Supreme Court ruling on integration. Cite the articles, sections, and paragraphs of the Constitution that give Congress and the president the power to send troops into an area.
2. What problems might immigrants to the United States today face? How are these problems like those faced by immigrants in the late 1800s? How are they different?
3. Does the author's description of what happened to the Indians in the late 1800s differ from what you have seen in movies and on television? Why or why not?

Practicing Critical Thinking
1. **Drawing Conclusions.** It is the late 1800s. How has the Homestead Act changed your life if you are a Plains Indian? A railroad baron? A farmer? A cattle baron?

2. **Synthesizing.** You know that cartoonist Thomas Nast created the elephant to represent the Republican party and the donkey to represent the Democratic party. Create two new symbols for these political parties and explain why you chose these symbols.
3. **Evaluating.** Of W.E.B. DuBois, Thomas Edison, Alexander Graham Bell, Henry Bessemer, Jane Addams, John D. Rockefeller, and Cornelius Vanderbilt, who do you think made the greatest contribution to the world? Why?

Exploring History Together
1. Have your group use the library or other American histories to report on the life of each of the following figures in industrial America:

   Cornelius Vanderbilt Thomas A. Edison
   Andrew Carnegie Samuel Gompers
   John D. Rockefeller Jane Addams

2. The two great artists of the West were Frederic Remington and Charles Marion Russell. Members of your group will report on these popular artists and show reproductions of their works. Then make one or more poster-size drawings of the cowhands of the Old West.
3. Your group will make a scale model of an Indian village or a sod house that might have stood on the Great Plains. Design a roof that will lift off so you can show how the inside of the house might have been furnished.

Reading in Depth
Durham, Philip and Everett L. Jones. *The Adventures of the Negro Cowboys.* New York: Dodd Mead. Contains stories about the most famous African American cowboys.

Hansen, Joyce. *Out of This Place.* Houston: Walker. Describes the challenges faced by ex-slaves during the Civil War and Reconstruction.

Harvey, Brett. *Cassie's Journey: Going West in the 1860s.* New York: Holiday House. Describes the dangers and struggles of Cassie and her family as they migrate westward to California.

Hoexter, Corinne. *From Canton to California: The Epic of Chinese Immigration.* New York: Four Winds Press. Portrays the immigration of Chinese to California and their reception there.

Wolfson, Evelyn. *From Abenaki to Zuñi: A Dictionary of Native American Tribes.* Includes discussions of tribal customs, foods, clothing, and means of travel.

Ships of the U.S. Fleet, a symbol of what a mighty power America had become by the turn of the century, enter San Francisco's Golden Gate.

AN EXPANDING AMERICA

UNIT 2

s America's economy grew, so did the need to secure new foreign markets for its products. Before the Civil War the notion of manifest destiny had filled the heads of westward-moving pioneers. After the war the urge to expand became even greater. Victory in the Spanish-American War gave America colonies in many parts of the world. Still, most Americans remained distrustful of entangling involvements with other nations, particularly European. Within the nation a new mood developed near the turn of the century. A progressive spirit led many Americans to seek solutions to the problems brought about by becoming an industrial nation so fast. This unit deals with the careers of the two giants of the progressive movement: Theodore Roosevelt and Woodrow Wilson.

America in World Affairs, 1865–1912

Even those who thought manifest destiny a bold American notion might have been surprised by what happened after the Civil War. The parade of settlers marching "from sea to shining sea" stopped only to catch its breath before pressing on. Americans seemed to forget George Washington's warning to avoid foreign involvements. The country began to expand its influence in Latin America. Alaska and Hawaii were acquired. After the war with Spain, fought to free Cuba, the Philippines and Puerto Rico were taken by the United States. By the time Theodore Roosevelt became president at the turn of the century, America's influence in the Western Hemisphere was great. But how far could America stretch itself in world affairs?

Preview & Review

Use these questions to guide your reading. Answer the questions after completing Section 1.
Understanding Issues, Events, & Ideas. Describe American expansion overseas, using the following words: isolationism, American expansionism, Midway Islands, imperialism, Alaskan Purchase, Seward's Folly, Hawaiian Islands, archipelago, McKinley Tariff, absolute monarch.
1. What was isolationism?
2. Why did the Japanese agree to open trade with the U.S.?
3. How did "Seward's Folly" turn out to be an immense bargain?
4. Who were the first Americans to reach Hawaii? Who followed?
Thinking Critically. 1. You are with Perry in Tokyo harbor. Describe your reactions. 2. You are a member of Congress. Would you vote for or against the the acquisition of Hawaii? Give reasons to justify your decision.

1. EXTENDING AMERICA'S INFLUENCE

Isolationism

For many Americans longtime suspicions of Europe had increased during the Civil War. Great Britain and France had sympathized with the Confederate government. British companies had built ships for the southerners. This had enabled the Confederacy to get around the United States blockade of southern ports. The *Alabama*, a British-built warship flying the Confederate flag, destroyed many American merchant ships during the rebellion. For a time Great Britain even considered entering the war on the side of the Confederacy.

While the United States was fighting its desperate struggle, France boldly sent an army into Mexico. The French then named a European prince, Maximilian of Austria, as Emperor of Mexico. This was a direct challenge to the Monroe Doctrine, which had stated that no European colonies were to be established in the Americas.

Once the Civil War ended, the United States sent 50,000 soldiers to the Mexican border to aid the Mexican patriots who were fighting Maximilian and demand that France withdraw its army. The French pulled out. In June 1867 Mexican patriots led by Benito Juárez entered Mexico City. Maximilian was captured and put to death.

These events demonstrated that European powers were eager to take advantage of any weakness of the United States. Americans wanted nothing from Europe except the right to buy and sell goods. They considered European governments undemocratic. They also believed that European diplomats were tricky and untrustworthy. To get involved with a European diplomat meant the risk of becoming involved in the wars and rivalries of Europe. Better, believed the average American, to have as little as possible to do with Europe.

This was the popular view. American political leaders never took such an extreme position. But the policy of American relations with the European powers was **isolationism.** The United States should keep pretty much to itself, as Washington had cautioned in his Farewell Address. It should not meddle in European affairs. And it should not permit Europeans to meddle in American affairs. This latter point had been most strongly stated in the Monroe Doctrine.

Americans who were isolationists were taking no serious risks. As the nation grew in wealth and numbers, the possibility that any European country might attack it rapidly disappeared.

The Closing of the Frontier

Manifest destiny had carried the American people more than three thousand miles across the North American continent. They had conquered all obstacles as they spread from "sea to shining sea," from the Atlantic to the Pacific. But by the late 19th century the frontiers of the continent had virtually disappeared. The lands of the Great Plains and the Southwest were filling with people and within two decades—by 1912—all would become states. Only Alaska in the frigid north still represented an American frontier.

What did the closing of the frontier mean to America? To what would that boundless energy that had fueled manifest destiny be

Benito Juárez was the high-minded leader of the Mexican people when France attempted to make the nation its colony.

Culver Pictures

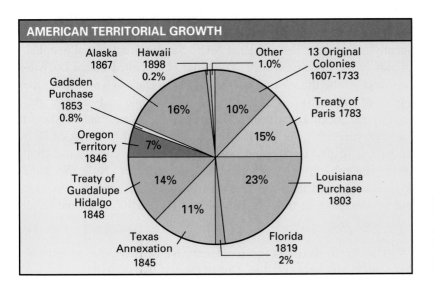

AMERICAN TERRITORIAL GROWTH

Alaska 1867
Hawaii 1898 0.2%
Other 1.0%
13 Original Colonies 1607-1733
Gadsden Purchase 1853 0.8%
Oregon Territory 1846
Treaty of Paris 1783
16%
10%
15%
7%
Treaty of Guadalupe Hidalgo 1848
14%
23%
Louisiana Purchase 1803
11%
Texas Annexation 1845
Florida 1819 2%

LEARNING FROM GRAPHS. *This chart shows how the United States has added to its territory throughout its history. During which century did the country add the most territory?*

Extending America's Influence 197

turned? Certainly there were problems and challenges to be solved within the United States. Yet manifest destiny was something else, a part of the adventurous restlessness that was so much a part of the American character. Had the first period of American history ended with the closing of the frontier, as Frederick Jackson Turner claimed? Or would Americans turn their restless spirits elsewhere and continue to expand the nation's boundaries?

Expansionism

Americans never adopted an isolationist attitude toward the rest of the world. Many people believed that the same manifest destiny that had brought the Great West into the Union would eventually bring all of North and South America under the control of the Stars and Stripes—and the islands of the Pacific Ocean as well. This attitude was known as **American expansionism.**

Remember that the Monroe Doctrine had stated that no more *European* colonies should be established in the Americas. It said nothing about the United States extending its control in the Western Hemisphere.

In the years after the Civil War Americans began to extend their influence in Latin America and in the Pacific Ocean. In August 1867 the United States navy occupied the **Midway Islands,** located about 1,000 miles (1,600 kilometers) northwest of Hawaii. Most Americans then gave not another thought to these uninhabited flyspecks on the map of the vast Pacific until a great American-Japanese naval battle was fought there in World War II.

What convinced Americans to look beyond their boundaries? Writers such as Josiah Strong, a Congregational minister, claimed America had an ''Anglo-Saxon'' mission to expand overseas. These writers based their views on two ideas. The first was the concept of an Anglo-Saxon ''race,'' which to Americans meant the people of Great Britain and their descendants. This concept of race is scientifically inaccurate. The so-called Anglo Saxons are a mix of peoples, all part of the Caucasoid race. The other idea, called Social Darwinism, applied the theories of scientist Charles Darwin—especially the theory of the ''survival of the fittest''—to people and nations. According to Social Darwinism, the energetic, strong, and fit should rule everyone else. As you have read, people had used Social Darwinism to justify unsafe and unsanitary working conditions, child labor, and other types of exploitation of workers. Now the same argument claimed that the American people—the energetic, strong, and fit—should rule the other peoples of the earth, or at least teach them what was ''right.'' As Strong stated it:

“ The Anglo-Saxon is the representative of two great ideas, which are closely related. One of them is that of civil liberty.

Nearly all the civil liberty in the world is enjoyed by Anglo-Saxons. . . . The other great idea represented by the Anglo-Saxon is that of pure, spiritual Christianity. It follows, then, that Anglo-Saxons, as the great representatives of these two ideas, have a special relationship to the world's future. They are divinely commissioned to be, in a sense, their brother's keeper. . . .[1] **"**

America was not the only expansionist country. Many European nations were involved in what is called **imperialism**—the domination by one country of the political, economic, and cultural affairs of another. Countries did this for a number of reasons. Industrial nations established colonies or "spheres of influence" so that they could control raw materials needed for their factories. Colonies also provided markets for their manufactured products, and they increased national pride by making people feel big and powerful. But many imperialists had humanitarian goals as well. Missionaries wanted to spread Christianity in regions where other religions flourished. Many people thought that it was their moral duty to bring "civilization" to parts of the world that they considered "backward."

In the late 1800s European imperialists expanded their influence rapidly. They carved up Africa until only the nations of Liberia and Ethiopia remained independent. They also dominated much of Asia.

Establishing colonies and spheres of influence had both benefits and costs for the people being controlled. The Europeans built roads and railroads as well as cities. The Europeans also introduced medicines and sanitary improvements that saved many lives. But development often reduced the amount of land available for cultivation and disrupted the local economy. And of course imperialism was fundamentally undemocratic. The local people lost control of their own fate. It often changed the very fabric of their society, much as the societies of Native Americans had been disrupted by Americans in earlier times.

The Opening of Japan

The first example of the American mood of global expansion took place in Japan. For centuries Japan had kept itself isolated from the rest of the world. Except for Chinese and Dutch traders, Japan did not permit any foreigners to enter the country. Then, quite suddenly, their peaceful harbor was invaded.

On July 8, 1853, a crowd of astonished Japanese watched a fleet of ships move into Tokyo harbor. These ships were steam powered; they belched black smoke from their funnels. The "black dragons," as the Japanese called them, were the coal-powered steamships of the American navy.

[1]From *Our Country: Its Possible Future and Its Present Crisis* by Josiah Strong

In the opening lyric for *Pacific Overtures,* a musical based on the opening of Japan, a reciter sings:

**"In the middle of the world we float
In the middle of the sea.
The realities remain remote
In the middle of the sea.
Kings are burning somewhere.
Wheels are turning somewhere,
Trains are being run,
Wars are being won,
Things are being done
Somewhere out there, not here.
Here we paint screens. . . ."**
from *Pacific Overtures,*
Music and lyrics by
Stephen Sondheim, 1975

Commodore Matthew Perry commanded the American fleet. President Millard Fillmore had sent him to ask the Japanese emperor to open several Japanese ports to American trade. Perhaps frightened by American technology and naval power, the Japanese signed a treaty of friendship with the United States.

The Purchase of Alaska

Americans also knew little to nothing about Alaska, then called Russian America, until William H. Seward, secretary of state, purchased it from Russia in March 1867. Russian explorers, fur trappers, and merchants had been in the area since the 1790s. But Alaska had never brought them the riches they sought. The Russian government decided to sell the vast land. The United States seemed the logical customer. Seward jumped at the opportunity to add more territory to the United States. He agreed to a purchase price of $7.2 million.

News of this **Alaskan Purchase** surprised everyone in America. Congress knew little about the negotiations until the treaty was presented to it, along with the bill for $7.2 million.

To win support, Seward launched a nationwide campaign. Alaska was worth far more than $7.2 million, he claimed. Its fish, furs, and lumber were very valuable. By controlling it, America would increase its influence in the North Pacific. These arguments convinced the senators to accept the treaty by a vote of 37 to 2.

The House of Representatives, however, hesitated to provide the $7.2 million. Seward again ran through his arguments about the virtues of this land in the frozen North. The Russian minister to the

**ALASKA AND
THE UNITED STATES**

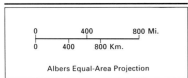

Albers Equal-Area Projection

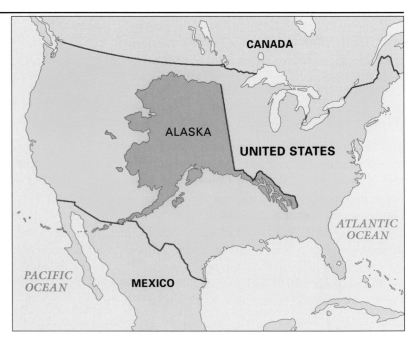

LEARNING FROM MAPS. *Alaska's size is truly amazing. It is by far the largest state. This map compares the size of Alaska to that of the continental United States. In your own words, state how they compare in size.*

United States, Baron Edouard de Stoeckl, wined, dined, and probably bribed a number of House members. Stoeckl later claimed that he had spent almost $200,000 getting the House to appropriate the money.

Many Americans thought buying Alaska was a mistake. They called the territory **"Seward's Folly,"** "Frigidia," and "President Andrew Johnson's Polar Bear Garden." One joke said that in Alaska a cow would give ice cream instead of milk. But most people were pleased. What a bargain Seward made! For about two cents an acre he obtained nearly 600,000 square miles (1,560,000 square kilometers) of land, a region twice the size of the state of Texas. The land contained immense resources of lumber, gold, copper, and other metals. A gold rush in the 1890s brought thousands of eager Americans to Alaska and led to the development of Seattle as a major Pacific port. More recently, rich deposits of oil and natural gas have been discovered there.

Hawaii

After the Civil War Americans also became interested in the **Hawaiian Islands.** This **archipelago,** or island group, is located in the Pacific about 2,000 miles (3,200 kilometers) southwest of San Francisco.

The first Americans to reach these beautiful, sunny islands were New England whalers and traders. Beginning in the late 1700s, they stopped there for rest and fresh supplies on their lonely voyages. These sailors were followed by missionaries who came to Hawaii hoping to convert the inhabitants to Christianity.

The foreign missionary movement, long important to both Catholics and Protestants, offered many Americans their first glimpse of the world beyond American shores. These Americans felt that the spread of Christianity around the world must precede the spread of democracy and social justice. The Hawaiian missionaries, besides spreading the gospel, settled down, built houses, and raised crops. In the 1840s and 1850s their children and grandchildren were beginning to cultivate sugar.

By the time of the American Civil War, the missionary families dominated the Islands' economy and government. Sugar was the Hawaiians' most important export. They sold most of it in the United States.

The Hawaiians were ruled by a king who made all the decisions and owned all the land. But in 1840 King Kamehameha III issued a constitution modeled after the United States Constitution. This was not surprising since many of Kamehameha's advisers were Americans. In 1875 the two countries signed a treaty which allowed Hawaiian sugar to enter the United States without payment of a tariff. In exchange the Hawaiian government agreed not to give territory or special privileges in the islands to any other nation.

HAWAII

Refer to the map on pages 640–41 for relative location to the United States.

Albers Equal-Area Projection

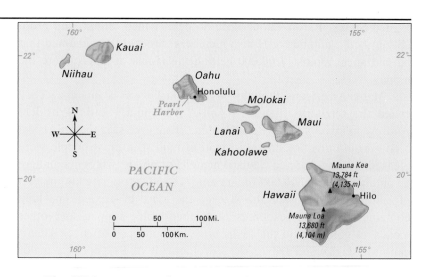

LEARNING FROM MAPS. *The Hawaiian Islands lie like a string of pearls in the Pacific Ocean. What are the three largest islands?*

The Bishop Museum

Queen Liliuokalani took the throne in 1891. She wrote the popular song "Aloha O" or "Farewell to Thee." Read these pages and Queen Liliuokalani's letter on page 239 to decide whom she might wish to bid farewell.

The 1875 treaty greatly encouraged sugar production. The missionary families formed corporations and imported thousands of low-paid Chinese and Japanese immigrants to work on the plantations. Most of these laborers signed long-term contracts similar to the ones that indentured servants had signed with Virginia tobacco planters 250 years earlier.

Between 1875 and 1890 the amount of Hawaiian sugar shipped to the United States jumped from 18 million to 160 million pounds (about 8 million to 72 million kilograms). But the Hawaiian sugar boom came to a sudden end when Congress passed the **McKinley Tariff** of 1890, a law that took away the special advantage of the Hawaiians. Their sugar now had to compete with sugar grown in the United States and also with sugar produced in Cuba and other countries. Prices fell, and the economy of the Hawaiian Islands suffered a serious depression.

Along with Hawaii's economic crisis came a political crisis. In 1890 the government changed hands. The new ruler was Queen Liliuokalani. She was intelligent and fiercely patriotic. She resented the influence of American planters and merchants in her country. Her attitude was expressed in the slogan "Hawaii for the Hawaiians."

Queen Liliuokalani was determined to break the power of the foreign-dominated Hawaiian legislature. In January 1893 she proclaimed a new constitution making her an **absolute monarch**—a ruler who holds all power.

The Americans responded by organizing a revolution. John L. Stevens, the American minister to Hawaii, supported the rebels. He ordered 150 marines ashore from an American warship in Honolulu harbor. They did not have to fire a shot to persuade Liliuokalani and the Hawaiians not to resist. The revolutionaries promptly raised the American flag.

Stevens announced that Hawaii was now under the protection of the United States. A delegation hurried off to Washington to

The Hawaiian Island of Oahu seems a paradise in this 1821 watercolor. The ship lying at anchor in the foreground flies the U.S. flag. What do you predict the U. S. presence will mean to Oahu and the rest of the Hawaiian Islands?

negotiate a treaty of annexation to bring Hawaii under American control. In February 1893 President Benjamin Harrison sent this treaty to the Senate for approval. But Harrison's term was about to end. President-elect Cleveland asked the Senate not to vote on the treaty until he had a chance to consider it. The Senate therefore postponed action.

After taking office, Cleveland withdrew the treaty. He sent a special commission headed by James H. Blount of Georgia to investigate conditions in the islands. Blount reported that the Hawaiian people did not want to be annexed to the United States.

After reading Blount's report, Cleveland decided to scrap the treaty. He called Stevens back to Washington and sent a new representative to the islands. This new United States minister met with the president of the revolutionary government, Sanford B. Dole, and urged him to resign. Cleveland wanted to return control of the islands to Queen Liliuokalani, who by this time was popularly known in America as ''Queen Lil.''

Dole (whose pineapples would soon be well-known in the United States) refused to resign. If the United States did not want Hawaii, the revolutionaries would remain independent. On July 4, 1894, they proclaimed Hawaii a republic. 🖳

Sanford B. Dole was born in Hawaii to American missionaries. He was president of the government that overthrew the queen. He later became first governor of the Territory of Hawaii. What hint can you find in the last paragraph on this page that pineapples as well as politics may have been behind Dole's motives?

Return to the Preview & Review on page 196.

Extending America's Influence   203

Use these questions to guide your reading. Answer the questions after completing Section 2.
Understanding Issues, Events, & Ideas. Use the following words to explain American attempts to police the Western Hemisphere: Pan-American Conference, Chilean Crisis, arbitration, Venezuela Boundary Dispute.
1. Why did Secretary of State Blaine want to bring the nations of the Western Hemisphere together?
2. Why did President Cleveland want to arbitrate the Venezuela Boundary Dispute?
3. What was the United States' notice to Europe and Latin America in the Venezuela Boundary Dispute?
Thinking Critically. Americans in the 1800s enjoyed "twisting the British lion's tail." Name a country or foreign group that recently has done the same thing to the United States. Why do you think they did it?

2. AMERICA AND ITS SOUTHERN NEIGHBORS

Pan-Americanism

American interest in the nations of Latin America also increased after the Civil War. Again American missionaries led the way. These countries sold large quantities of coffee, bananas, fertilizer, and many other products to the United States. But they bought most of their manufactured goods in Europe. In the 1890s James G. Blaine, who was secretary of state under Presidents Garfield and Harrison, set out to develop closer trade ties with Latin America. His strategy was simple but one-sided.

Blaine wanted all the nations of the Western Hemisphere to see themselves as belonging to a group with common interests. In his opinion the United States would obviously dominate such a group. This was one reason why many Latin American nations hesitated to cooperate with Blaine. In 1889 Blaine invited the Latin American countries to send representatives to Washington for a meeting. After a whirlwind tour of 41 cities, these representatives assembled for the first **Pan-American Conference.**

The conference did not accomplish much. The delegates rejected Blaine's suggestion that they lower their tariffs on American goods. Still, it was the first time the nations of North and South America had come together. They began to sense that the common interests of the Western Hemisphere were in many ways different from those of other nations.

The Chilean Crisis

Any goodwill that the Pan-American Conference generated suffered a setback in the **Chilean Crisis** of 1891-92. During a civil war in Chile between a faction supporting its president and one backing its congress, the United States supported the presidential side. Unfortunately for the United States, the other side won the war. The Chileans called people from the United States *Yanquis.* Anti-*Yanqui* feeling was now high.

In this heated atmosphere some sailors from the U.S.S. *Baltimore,* on shore leave in the city of Valparaiso, got in a fight outside the True Blue Saloon. Apparently the fight started when a local civilian spat in the face of one of the sailors. A mob attacked the sailors, and the Valparaiso police did nothing to stop the fighting. Two sailors were killed and 16 injured.

President Harrison threatened to break diplomatic relations unless the Chilean government apologized. A war scare resulted. Fortunately, the Chilean government did apologize. It also paid $75,000 in damages to the injured sailors and to the families of the dead.

The Venezuela Boundary Dispute

In 1895 the United States again flexed its muscles in South America. For decades Great Britain and Venezuela had haggled over the boundary line separating Venezuela and British Guiana, a small British colony on the north coast of South America. Venezuela had tried to settle the dispute in the past, but Great Britain had always refused to permit an outside judge to draw the boundary. Tensions increased in the 1880s when one of the largest gold nuggets ever found—509 ounces (14,252 grams)—was discovered in the territory both countries claimed.

President Grover Cleveland was afraid that if the British took any more territory in the Western Hemisphere, other European powers might follow. Then the economic and political interests of the United States in Latin America would be injured. He was determined to make Great Britain agree to settle the argument of who owned the territory by **arbitration**—that is, to allow a neutral judge to decide. President Cleveland ordered Richard Olney, his secretary of state, to send a stern message to the British government.

Olney's note of July 20, 1895, was extremely strong and quite insulting in tone. Cleveland described it as a "20-inch gun." The United States, said Olney, was the supreme power in the hemisphere. The Monroe Doctrine prohibited further European expansion in the Western Hemisphere. The United States would intervene in disputes between European and Latin American nations to make certain that the Monroe Doctrine was not violated.

Despite the harsh tone of Olney's message, the British prime minister, Lord Salisbury, dismissed it as a bluff. He thought Cleveland was playing the political game called "twisting the British lion's tail." The game's goal was to try to anger Great Britain. Any statement threatening Great Britain was sure to be popular with Americans of Irish origin. Most Irish Americans hated the British because they refused to give Ireland its independence. Instead of answering the note promptly, Salisbury delayed nearly four months.

When he did reply, Salisbury rejected Olney's argument that the Monroe Doctrine applied to the boundary dispute. Britain's dispute with Venezuela, he said politely but firmly, was no business of the United States.

This response made Cleveland "mad clean through." The Monroe Doctrine *did* apply to the situation. The United States would "resist by every means in its power" any British seizure of Venezuelan territory. The president asked Congress for money to finance a United States commission that would investigate the dispute. If the British refused to accept its findings, the United States would use force.

Nearly all people seemed to approve of Cleveland's tough stand. Venezuelans were delighted. When the news reached the capital of

The Granger Collection

President Grover Cleveland twists the tail of an outraged British lion while his supporters look on. Judging from the president's supporters, had the old feelings against England cooled over a hundred years?

Venezuela, Caracas, a cheering crowd of at least 200,000 people gathered at the home of the United States representative.

For a brief time war between the United States and Great Britain seemed possible. But neither government wanted war. Cleveland was mainly interested in reminding the world of the Monroe Doctrine. Great Britain had too many other diplomatic problems to be willing to fight over what they considered a relatively unimportant piece of land in South America.

As soon as he realized that the situation had become dangerous, Lord Salisbury agreed to let an impartial commission decide where to place the boundary. In 1899 this commission gave Britain nearly all the land in question.

On the surface the United States seemed to be defending a small Latin American nation against a great European power in what came to be known as the **Venezuela Boundary Dispute.** In fact, it was putting both Europe and Latin America on notice that the United States was the most important nation in the Western Hemisphere. Throughout the crisis Cleveland ignored Venezuela. Its minister in Washington was never once consulted. 🖻

Return to the Preview & Review on page 204.

3. THE SPANISH-AMERICAN WAR

Preview & Review

Cuba and Spain

Early in 1895, shortly before Secretary Olney fired his "20-inch gun" over the Venezuela boundary, real gunfire broke out in Cuba. The Spanish had called their colony in Cuba the "Ever-Faithful Isle." Cuba was one of Spain's few colonies in America that had not revolted in the early 1800s. It was Spain's last important possession in the Americas.

In 1868 there had been a revolution in Cuba which lasted for ten years. It had failed, but now, in 1895, Cuban patriots again took up arms. Independence was their objective. The rebels engaged in the surprise attacks of **guerrilla warfare.** They burned sugar cane fields, blocked railroads, and ambushed small parties of Spanish soldiers. By the end of 1896 they controlled most of rural Cuba.

The Cuban patriots were led by José Martí, a poet, statesman, and essayist. Martí was a tireless critic of Spanish rule in Cuba. His poems, articles, and speeches were carried in many American newspapers. They helped focus America's attention on the brutality taking place in Cuba. When fighting broke out, Martí returned to Cuba. He was killed in the fighting a few days after his arrival. Martí became a national hero. Although he died three years before Cuban independence, he is often credited with doing more than any other individual to win his Cuba's freedom. An excerpt from one of Martí's patriotic poems is followed by the English translation.

> "   **Dos patrias**
> Dos patrias tengo yo: Cuba y la noche.
> ¿O son una las dos? No bien retira
> su majestad el Sol, con largos velos
> un clavel en la mano, silenciosa
> Cuba cual viuda triste me aparece.
> ¡Yo sé cuál es ese clavel sangriento
> que en la mano le tiembla! Está vacío
> mi pecho, destrozado está y vació
> en donde estaba el corazón. Ya es hora
> de empezar a morir. La noche es buena
> para decir adiós. La luz estorba
> y la palabra humana. El universo
> habla mejor que el hombre.
>   Cual bandera
> que invita a batallar, la llama roja
> de la vela flamea. Las ventanas
> abro, ya estrecho en mí. Muda, rompiendo
> las hojas del clavel, como una nube
> que enturbia el cielo, Cuba, viuda, pasa. . . . "

Use these questions to guide your reading. Answer the questions after completing Section 3.
Understanding Issues, Events, & Ideas. Discuss the Spanish-American War, using the following words: guerrilla warfare, *reconcentrado, junta,* yellow journalism, Teller Amendment, ultimatum, Spanish-American War, Manila Bay, Rough Riders, expeditionary force, Santiago, El Caney, San Juan Hill, Puerto Rico.
1. Why had the Spanish called Cuba their "Ever-Faithful Isle"?
2. Why did General Weyler place farm people in concentration camps?
3. Why was the *Maine* sent to Cuba? How did the explosion of the *Maine* bring the United States and Spain to the brink of war?
4. How did President McKinley try to prevent war with Spain? In general, what was the attitude of Congress?
Thinking Critically.   1. If you were an ambassador to Cuba in the 1890s, would you have urged the United States to go to war? Explain your reasoning.   **2.** Yellow journalists wrote very persuasive articles that influenced many people. Imagine that you are a journalist. Select a current issue about which you feel strongly and write a persuasive article about it.

José Martí

The Granger Collection

The Granger Collection

The inspiration for this 1898 cartoon is the old saying, "Out of the frying pan and into the fire." The young woman who represents Cuba is caught between "Spanish Misrule" (the pan) and the flame of "Anarchy" burning on the isle of Cuba. Explain the artist's caption: "The Duty of the Hour—To Save Her Not Only from Spain, but from a Worse Fate."

" Two Motherlands

I have two homelands: Cuba and the night.
Or are they both one? No sooner has the sun
withdrawn its grandeur than Cuba appears
beside me in silence, a mournful widow
who clasps a carnation to funeral robes.
I know the bloody carnation
that trembles in her hand. My breast
is now hollow, the niche that once held my heart
is empty and shattered. Now is the hour
to start dying. Night is a good time
for bidding farewell. Human words and the light
only stand in our way. The universe
speaks more clearly than man.
                              Like a banner
that calls us to battle, the flame of the candle
is burning red. My body no longer contains me,
I open the window. In silence, as she crushes
the carnation's petals, like a cloud
that darkens the sky, Cuba, the widow, passes. . . .[1] **"**

[1]Both versions from "Two Motherlands" by José Martí in *The Canary Whose Eye Is So Black,* edited and translated by Cheli Duran

In an effort to regain control of the countryside, the Spanish Governor-General, Valeriano Weyler, began herding farm people into what were called *reconcentrados*—concentration camps. He penned up about 500,000 Cubans in these camps. Weyler did this for two reasons. First, Cubans in the camps could not supply the rebels with food. Second, anyone outside the camps could be considered an enemy of Spain and arrested or shot on the spot.

Conditions inside the concentration camps were unspeakably bad. About 200,000 Cubans died in the camps, victims of disease and malnutrition.

Most people in the United States sympathized with the Cubans' wish to be independent. They were horrified by the stories of Spanish cruelty. Cuban revolutionaries fanned these fires. They established committees called *juntas* in the United States to raise money, spread propaganda, and recruit volunteers.

Explosion in Havana

Both President Cleveland and President McKinley had tried to persuade Spain to give the Cuban people more say about their government. They failed to make much impression. Tension increased. Then, in January 1898, President McKinley sent a battleship, the U.S.S. *Maine,* to Cuba. There had been riots in Havana, the capital city. McKinley sent the *Maine* to protect American citizens there against possible attack.

On February 15, while the *Maine* lay at anchor in Havana harbor, a tremendous explosion rocked the ship. Of the 350 men aboard, 266 were killed. The *Maine* quickly sank.

To this day no one knows for sure what happened. Many Americans jumped to the conclusion that the Spanish had sunk the ship with a mine, a kind of underwater bomb. The navy conducted an investigation. It concluded that the *Maine* had indeed been destroyed by a mine. Another American investigation in 1911 also judged that an explosion from outside destroyed the ship.

The Spanish government claimed the disaster was caused by an explosion inside the *Maine*. This is certainly possible. A short circuit in the ship's wiring might have caused the *Maine*'s ammunition to explode, for example. It is difficult to imagine that the Spanish would have blown up the ship. The last thing Spain wanted was a war with the United States.

Emotions were inflamed on all sides. The Spanish government, or some individual officer, may indeed have been responsible. Or it is possible that the Cuban rebels did the job, knowing that Spain would be blamed.

In any case, a demand for war against Spain swept the United States. In New York City a man in a Broadway bar raised his glass and proclaimed, "Remember the *Maine!*" This became a battle cry

Point of View

A selected list of speeches delivered in 1898 by graduating high school seniors in Black River Falls, Wisconsin.

"Girls:
A Woman's Sphere
Home Training
Our Duty to Unfortunates
A Modern Reformer
Boys:
Individual Independence
Is the Cuban Capable of Self-Government?
The Stars and Stripes
Spain's Colonial System
Should the United States Extend Its Territory?
War and Its Effects on the Nation."
From *Wisconsin Death Trip,*
Michael Lesy, 1973

The Granger Collection

In strong detail this 1898 lithograph shows the explosion of the Maine *in Havana Harbor. What are two theories that might explain such a terrible explosion?*

similar to "Remember the Alamo!" during the Texas Revolution of the 1830s.

As tension mounted, the publisher of the New York *Journal*, William Randolph Hearst, had sent the artist Frederic Remington to Cuba to draw pictures of the Cuban Revolution. When Remington complained that there was no revolution and asked to come home, Hearst telegraphed:

> " PLEASE REMAIN. YOU FURNISH THE PICTURES AND I'LL FURNISH THE WAR. "

War Is Declared

President McKinley wanted to avoid war. He told a friend:

> " I have been through one war. I have seen the dead piled up, and I do not want to see another. "

McKinley did not let the sinking of the *Maine* cause a break with Spain. But he also wanted to stop the bloodletting in Cuba. He believed the Spanish must do away with the concentration camps and negotiate a truce with the Cubans. He also felt that more self-government should be granted Cuba.

Spain was at last willing to do this. However, the rebels demanded total independence. The Spanish government did not dare to give in completely. The Spanish people were proud and patriotic. Any government that "gave away" Cuba would surely be overthrown. Perhaps the king himself would be deposed. These unsettling thoughts made Spain stand firmly against Cuban independence.

Still, some peaceful solution might have been found if all sides had been patient. McKinley knew that Spain was earnestly exploring several possible compromises. He had also been promised that in time all his demands would be met. But he finally made up his mind that Spain would never give up Cuba voluntarily.

On April 11, 1898, the president told Congress that he had "exhausted every effort" to end the "intolerable" situation in Cuba. He asked Congress to give him the power to secure in Cuba "a stable government, capable of . . . insuring peace."

Congress had been thundering for war for weeks. By huge majorities it passed a joint resolution stating that the people of Cuba "are, and of right ought to be, free and independent." If the Spanish did not withdraw "at once" from the island, the president should use "the entire land and naval forces of the United States" to drive them out. Then Congress protected itself against being accused of going to war for selfish reasons. Its members approved a resolution

This elaborate 1898 cartoon shows President McKinley in a plumed hat, like Shakespeare's Hamlet, who also was unable to make up his mind. McKinley has several choices: heed the pleas of Uncle Sam to protect Cuba and close down the reconcentrados, or revenge the watery ghosts who have risen from the Maine by going to war or compensating the victims' families. How did he decide? What had Congress already decided?

The Spanish-American War 211

proposed by Senator Henry M. Teller of Colorado. This **Teller Amendment** stated that the United States had no intention of taking Cuba for itself or trying to control its government.

McKinley gave the Spanish government three days to accept his terms or face war. Unwilling to yield to McKinley's **ultimatum**—do this or face the consequences—the Spanish broke relations with the United States.

The Battle of Manila Bay

The first important battle of the **Spanish-American War** was fought not in Cuba but rather in the Far East on the Spanish-held Philippine Islands. The United States had a naval squadron stationed in Hong Kong, China, under the command of Commodore George Dewey. When war was declared, Dewey's ships sailed for instant action. He had been ordered weeks earlier to prepare for battle by Theodore Roosevelt, the assistant secretary of the navy.

Dewey steamed swiftly from Hong Kong across the China Sea to Manila, capital of the Philippines. His fleet entered **Manila Bay** on the night of April 30. Early the next morning, he gave the captain of his flagship, the cruiser *Olympia,* the famous command "You may fire when ready, Gridley." The American fleet far outgunned the

A great cheer rises from the crowds who have come to see the 10th Pennsylvania Volunteers set sail for Manila. What signs of patriotism are apparent in this lithograph?

YELLOW JOURNALISM

In the 1890s two popular New York newspapers, the *Journal,* owned by William Randolph Hearst, and the *World,* owned by Joseph Pulitzer, were competing bitterly for readers. Both played up crime and scandals to increase sales. This type of writing was called yellow journalism because the *World* printed a comic strip called "The Yellow Kid."

Both the *World* and the *Journal* supported the Cuban revolution. General Weyler's policy of *reconcentrado* provided the raw material for many of their stories about Spanish brutality. The actual conditions in Cuba were bad enough. But Hearst and Pulitzer made the camps seem even more shocking. Their exaggerated and untrue stories were topped by screaming headlines and accompanied by spine-chilling drawings and ugly cartoons.

This one-sided picture of the revolution no doubt influenced the United States' decision to go to war with Spain. How much influence the newspapers had is not an easy question to answer. It had some effect on many people. What is more clear is that Hearst and Pulitzer favored war partly for selfish reasons. They knew it would produce exciting news that would help them sell more papers.

Spanish warships guarding Manila. By noon the Spanish fleet had been smashed. Not one American sailor was killed. It was a marvelous triumph.

Dewey's victory made him an instant hero in the United States. Many people named babies after him. A chewing gum manufacturer came out with a gum named "Dewey's Chewies." However, until troops arrived from America, Dewey did not have enough men to occupy Manila or conquer any other part of the Philippine archipelago. So he set up a blockade of Manila harbor. When reinforcements reached him in August, he captured the city.

Moving an Army to Cuba

The war in Cuba did not begin so quickly. McKinley called for volunteers and received an enthusiastic response. In two months 200,000 recruits enlisted. Theodore Roosevelt, for example, promptly resigned as assistant secretary of the navy. Although he was nearly 40, he announced that he would organize a regiment and go off to fight in Cuba. He was commissioned a lieutenant colonel in the First Volunteer Cavalry.

Roosevelt led people as easily as the fabled Pied Piper of Hamelin. He came from a wealthy New York family of Dutch origin. He had been a sickly child with poor eyesight, but he had enormous determination. He built up his scrawny body and became a skillful boxer. He loved hunting, hiking, and horseback riding. He also loved

The Spanish-American War 213

Remington Art Museum

Frederic Remington painted this masterful "Charge of the Rough Riders Up San Juan Hill" in 1898. The scene is as Remington saw it, for he was a war correspondent in Cuba. Roosevelt leads the charge on horseback. You and your classmates might take turns describing Roosevelt's Rough Riders, about whom you have just read.

politics and scholarship. While still in college, he wrote an excellent history of the naval side of the War of 1812.

Roosevelt had served in the New York state legislature. He had been police commissioner of New York City. And he had run a cattle ranch on the open range of the Dakota Territory until the terrible winter of 1885-86 wiped out his herds.

Roosevelt's call for volunteers brought forth no fewer than 23,000 applicants. The colorful colonel chose a remarkable collection of soldiers from this mass. He enlisted several hundred cowboys, many of whom he had known in his ranching days, and 20 American Indians. Several well-known athletes and some police who had worked for him in New York City also joined up. The chaplain of the regiment was a former football player. The outfit became known to the public as the **Rough Riders.**

With men like Roosevelt recruiting, the army soon had more volunteers than it could efficiently organize in so short a time. Dozens of new units were shipped off to Tampa, Florida, where the invasion force was to be trained and supplied. That city became a near madhouse.

All the railroad lines around Tampa were clogged by long lines of unopened freight cars jammed with guns and ammunition, uniforms, and food. The trainees sweated in heavy blue woolen uniforms while the temperature climbed into the humid 90s. Lightweight summer uniforms for the **expeditionary force** did not arrive at Tampa until after the soldiers had sailed off for Cuba. Tropical fevers and other diseases raged through camp. Spoiled foods caused outbreaks of diarrhea and more serious illnesses. The longer the army remained at Tampa, the worse conditions became. Roosevelt raged:

" No words could describe . . . the confusion and lack of system and the general mismanagement of the situation here. "

The Capture of Santiago

Although Cuba was only 90 miles (144 kilometers) from Florida, the slow-moving transport ships that would carry the army there could not put to sea until the Spanish fleet in the Atlantic had been located. That fleet could raise havoc with the transports.

The Spanish commander, Admiral Pascual Cervera, had tried to avoid the American navy by putting into the harbor of **Santiago,** a city on the southern coast of Cuba. In late May an American squadron discovered his fleet there and blockaded the entrance to the harbor. It was then safe for the army transports to set out.

In mid-June 17,000 men boarded ship in Tampa. There was incredible confusion. Many lost contact with their units. Fearful of being left behind, dozens simply climbed aboard whatever ship they could find. At last the expedition managed to set sail.

Library of Congress

Colonel Roosevelt and some of his Rough Riders posed for this picture atop San Juan Hill shortly after taking the strategic point. Compare and contrast this photograph with the painting on the opposite page.

215

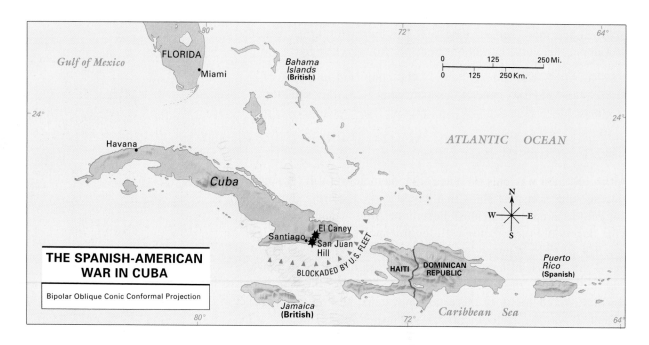

THE SPANISH-AMERICAN WAR IN CUBA

Bipolar Oblique Conic Conformal Projection

LEARNING FROM MAPS. *Most of the Spanish-American War in the Caribbean was fought on Cuba. Where were the important battles?*

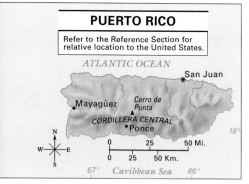

PUERTO RICO

Refer to the Reference Section for relative location to the United States.

LEARNING FROM MAPS. *Puerto Rico, the only American commonwealth, lies in the Caribbean. Mountains slope from the center to sandy beaches along the sea. Puerto Ricans are American citizens. Why did the United States value control of Puerto Rico in the early 1900s?*

Return to the Preview & Review on page 207.

American strategy called for an attack on Santiago. The army, commanded by General William R. Shafter, landed at Daiquiri, a town to the east of Santiago. Once ashore, it began its advance, assisted throughout the war by the Cuban rebel army. The Spanish put up a stiff resistance.

Major battles were fought at **El Caney** and **San Juan Hill.** At El Caney a member of the Second Massachusetts regiment complained:

❝ [The Spaniards] are hidden behind rocks, in weeds and in underbrush, and we just simply can't locate them. They are shooting our men all to pieces.❞

The Rough Riders and African American soldiers of the Ninth and Tenth Cavalries took San Juan Hill by storm on July 1. In this battle Colonel Roosevelt seemed to have no care for his own safety. He galloped back and forth along the line, urging his men forward. Luckily, Roosevelt was not hit. Many of his men were not so fortunate. Most were firing bullets charged with black powder. Each time they fired, a puff of smoke marked their location for Spanish gunners on top of the hill.

After the capture of San Juan Hill the American artillery could be moved within range of Santiago harbor. Admiral Cervera's fleet had to put to sea. When it did, the powerful American fleet swiftly blasted it. Every one of the Spanish vessels was lost. Only one American sailor was killed in this one-sided fight.

On July 16 the Spanish army commander surrendered Santiago. A few days later another American force completed the occupation of the Spanish island of **Puerto Rico,** about 500 miles (800 kilometers) east of Cuba. The Spanish-American War was over.

America's Pacific Heritage

Since ships first sailed or land caravans carried off its treasure, westerners have been fascinated by the East. Marco Polo was bedazzled even though he came from Venice, a western jewel. The art of the Orient is the oldest in the world, but it was hidden behind the walls of Forbidden Cities. Emigrants from Asia were too poor to own eastern treasures such as we see on these pages, but traders like John Ellerton Lodge filled the holds of the ships the *Kremlin* and *Magnet* with china, silk, ivory, spices, even fireworks that bloomed like chrysanthemums to bring Pacific culture to America.

This dragon comes from a Chinese embroidered chair of the 18th century. Eastern dragons seldom breathed fire and were seen as protectors.

Chinese porcelain has long been prized. The export ware above is an Orange platter in the "Fitzhugh" pattern.

Four children in holiday dress were photographed on the teeming streets of San Francisco's Chinatown before the earthquake of 1906.

"Four black dragons spitting fire" is how Japanese artists described Commodore Perry's ships landing at Yokohama.

A gilded bronze Buddha from 10th-century Thailand reminds us that Buddhism has nearly 245 million followers in the East.

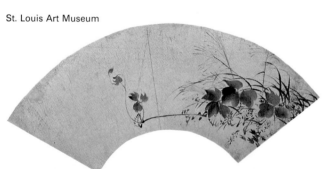

Autumn leaves and grasses were painted c. 1850 for this Japanese fan by Shibata Zeshiu.

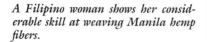

A Filipino woman shows her considerable skill at weaving Manila hemp fibers.

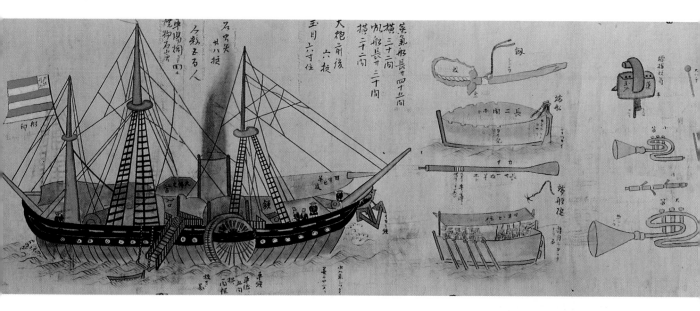

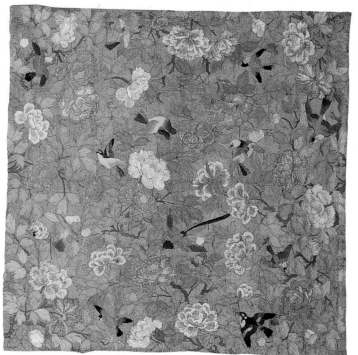

Birds and flowers are the subjects of this 18th-century silk embroidery from Korea.

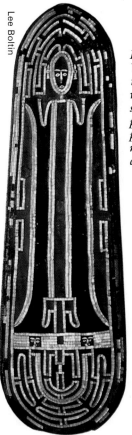

Little known before World War II, the tiny Solomon Islands were home to artisans who created the prized mother-of-pearl inlay for this mid-19th-century ceremonial shield.

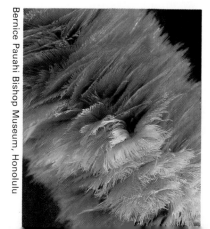

Leis made from the feathers of birds have adorned the nobility of Hawaii even before the rule of Kamehameha III or his successor, Queen Liliuokalani.

America's Pacific Heritage   219

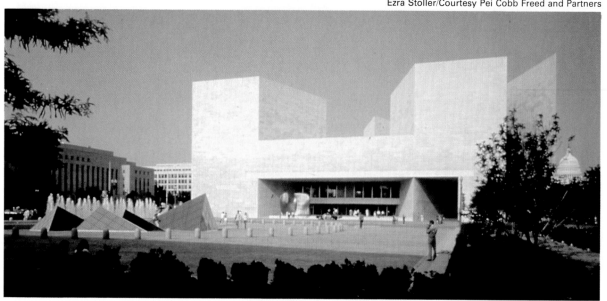

Isamu Noguchi, one of the greatest sculptors of the 20th century, was born in Los Angeles but taken to Japan when he was two. He called this sleek sculpture piece "California Scenario." It was completed in 1982 and covers 1.6 acres in Costa Mesa, California.

The Isamu Noguchi Garden Museum, Long Island City, N.Y.

In the shadow of the nation's capitol is the east building of the National Gallery of Art. I. M. Pei, a Chinese American, designed this streamlined structure. Other works by Pei and his partners include the John F. Kennedy Library in Boston and the glass pyramid that is now the entrance to the Louvre museum in Paris.

Ezra Stoller/Courtesy Pei Cobb Freed and Partners

4. AMERICA EXPANDS FURTHER

Preview & Review

The Treaty of Paris

On July 30 President McKinley sent the Spanish government his peace terms. Spain must leave Cuba. It must give Puerto Rico and an island in the Pacific midway between Hawaii and the Philippines to the United States. American troops would continue to hold the city of Manila until the future of the Philippine Islands could be settled at a peace conference.

These demands were far greater than the original aim of winning independence for Cuba. The excitement of military victory caused McKinley and many other Americans to forget why they had first gone to war.

There was little the Spaniards could do. They accepted McKinley's preliminary terms. Representatives of the two nations then met in Paris in the autumn of 1898. There they framed a formal treaty of peace.

McKinley appointed five American peace commissioners. Three of these were United States senators. The president put the senators on the commission because he expected them to influence their fellow senators. Under the Constitution the treaty would be submitted to the Senate for its approval.

The Spanish commissioners agreed to give up Cuba and to turn Puerto Rico and the island of **Guam** in the Pacific over to the United States. The Americans, acting on McKinley's order, also demanded possession of the Philippines. The Spaniards objected strongly. The United States had not conquered the islands, they argued. Even Manila had not been captured until after the preliminary terms of peace had been agreed to. McKinley said this of his decision to annex the Philippines:

> **"** I walked the floor of the White House night after night until midnight, and I am not ashamed to tell you . . . that I went down on my knees and prayed Almighty God for light and guidance more than one night. And one night late it came to me this way—I don't know what it was, but it came . . . that there was nothing left for us to do but to take them all, and to educate the Filipinos, and uplift them and civilize and Christianize them, and by God's grace do the very best we could by them, as our fellow-men for whom Christ died. And then I went to bed, and went to sleep, and slept soundly. . . .[1] **"**

The Spaniards had to give in. To make it easier for them, the Americans agreed to pay $20 million for the islands. This Treaty of

[1]From *In the Days of McKinley* by Margaret Leech

Use these questions to guide your reading. Answer the questions after completing Section 4.
Understanding Issues, Events, & Ideas. Use the following words to first explain America's expansion and then the opposition to it: Guam, anti-imperialist, anarchist, sphere of influence, Open Door Note, Boxer Rebellion, Second Open Door Note.
1. What peace terms did President McKinley demand of the Spanish? Why had he increased his demands?
2. What did the U.S. gain by its victory in the war?
3. How would ruling the Philippines make the United States an imperialist nation? What position did anti-imperialists take on annexing the Philippines?
4. What two principles were stated by the Open Door Notes?
Thinking Critically. 1. Often public sentiment can influence political decisions. The Filipinos and the Boxers opposed American involvement in their countries. Why did America get involved anyway? Do you agree with the American decision? Explain. **2.** Imagine that you are William Jennings Bryan in 1901, and you are writing your memoirs. Explain your reasons for supporting the Treaty of Paris of 1898.

Paris was signed on December 10, 1898, only ten months after the war was declared.

At relatively little cost in money and lives, the United States had accomplished its objective of freeing Cuba. It had also won itself an empire. No wonder that McKinley's secretary of state, John Hay, called the conflict "a splendid little war." Of course, it was splendid only if one put aside the fact that the United States had defeated a country that was much smaller and poorer than itself. Nor was it splendid for the brave soldiers who died or were injured or for their families.

The Fight Against the Treaty

Many people in the United States opposed the treaty with Spain. They insisted that imperialism was un-American. Taking Puerto Rico was bad enough, but it was one small island. It might be needed for national defense in case of another war. However, ruling the Philippine Islands without the consent of the Filipinos would make the United States an imperialist nation like Britain, France, Germany, and other European countries that owned colonies in Africa and Asia.

The Filipinos certainly would not consent to American rule. They wanted their independence. After his victory at Manila Bay, Commodore Dewey had returned the exiled leader of the Filipino patriots, Emilio Aguinaldo, on an American warship. Dewey encouraged Aguinaldo to resume his fight against the Spanish. Aguinaldo did so. He assumed that the United States was there to help liberate his country from Spanish rule, just as it had promised to free Cuba.

The **anti-imperialists,** as they were called, included many important Americans. Among the best-known were Andrew Carnegie, the steel manufacturer; Samuel Gompers, the labor leader; Jane Addams, the social worker; and Mark Twain, the author of *Tom Sawyer, Huckleberry Finn,* and many other novels. The anti-imperialists in the Senate were led by George F. Hoar of Massachusetts. Hoar argued:

> 66 [The United States was] trampling . . . on our own great Charter, which recognizes alike the liberty and the dignity of individual manhood. 99

Many anti-imperialists were not opposed to expansion. Senator Hoar, for example, voted for the annexation of Hawaii, which was finally approved during the Spanish-American War. Andrew Carnegie always favored adding Canada to the United States. But they all believed that it was morally wrong to annex the Filipinos without their consent.

Emilio Aguinaldo was the popular Filipino patriot who the U.S. returned from exile to fight the Spanish. Later he opposed the U.S. occupation of his country and fought for Filipino freedom.

Few issues have erupted into such a national debate as the fate of the Philippines. The issue bitterly divided the American people. Like slavery, most of the arguments, pro and con, centered on right and wrong. Still, the success of the United States in the Spanish-American War led some Americans to dream of a colonial empire. One enthusiastic supporter stated his position in a Senate campaign speech in 1898. Note how close his argument is to that of Josiah Strong on pages 198–99.

> 66 It is a noble land God has given us—a land that can feed and clothe the world; a land set like a guard between the two oceans of the globe. It is a mighty people that God has planted on this soil. It is a people descended from the most masterful blood of history and constantly strengthened by the strong working folk of all the earth. It is a people imperial by virtue of their power, by right of their institutions, by authority of their heaven-directed purposes. . . .
>
> Shall the American people continue their restless march toward the commercial supremacy of the world? Shall free institutions extend their blessed reign until the empire of our principles is established over the hearts of all humanity?
>
> We have no mission to perform, no duty to discharge to our fellow humans? Has the Almighty Father given us gifts and marked us with His favor, only to rot in our own selfishness? . . .
>
> We cannot escape our world duties. We must carry out the purpose of a fate that has driven us to be greater than our small intentions. We cannot retreat from any soil where Providence has placed our flag. It is up to us to save that soil for liberty and civilization. For liberty and civilization and God's purpose fulfilled, the flag must from now on be the symbol of all mankind.[1] 99

In 1899 Rudyard Kipling, a British writer, penned a poem called "The White Man's Burden." On quick reading, the poem seems to state the expansionist attitude well. It immediately became a popular defense of American expansion. But Kipling meant the poem to be a satire and is actually critical of America's determination to civilize childlike and untamed captive people. Can you see the satire in this first stanza of Kipling's seven-stanza poem?

> 66 Take up the White Man's burden—
>   Send forth the best ye breed—
> Go bind your sons to exile
>   To serve your captives' need;

---

[1] From *Modern Eloquence*, vol. 10, by Albert J. Beveridge, edited by Ashley H. Thorndike

To wait in heavy harness,
  On fluttered folk and wild—
Your new-caught sullen peoples,
  Half-devil and half-child.[1] **"**

The anti-imperialists even started a national organization, the American Anti-Imperialist League in 1899. Carl Schurz, a former senator from Missouri and secretary of the interior in President Hayes' cabinet, was its spokesman. Schurz stated the league's view:

" We hold that the policy known as imperialism is hostile to liberty and tends toward militarism, an evil from which it has been our glory to be free. We regret that it has become necessary in the land of Washington and Lincoln to reaffirm that all men, of whatever race or color, are entitled to life, liberty, and the pursuit of happiness. We maintain that governments derive their just powers from the consent of the governed. We insist that the subjugation of any people is 'criminal aggression' and open disloyalty to the distinctive principles of our government. . . .

We earnestly condemn the policy of the present national administration [McKinley's presidency] in the Philippines. It seeks to extinguish the spirit of 1776 in those islands. We deplore [hate] the sacrifice of our soldiers and sailors, whose bravery deserves admiration even in an unjust war. We denounce the slaughter of Filipinos as a needless horror. . . .

We hold with Abraham Lincoln, that 'no man is good enough to govern another man without the other's consent. When the white man governs himself, that is self-government, but when he governs himself and also governs another man, that is more than self-government—that is despotism [rule by an absolute authority].' 'Our reliance is in the love of liberty which God has planted in us. Our defense is in the spirit which prizes liberty as the heritage of all men in all lands. Those who deny freedom to others deserve it not for themselves, and under a just God cannot long retain it.'[2] **"**

Albert J. Beveridge, now a senator, led the imperialists in Congress. He responded to the Anti-Imperialist League statement:

" The opposition tells us that we ought not to govern a people without their consent. I answer, the rule of liberty that all just government derives its authority from the consent of the governed, applies only to those who are capable of self-

---

[1]From "The White Man's Burden" by Rudyard Kipling
[2]From "The Policy of Imperialism" by Carl Schurz in *A History of the American People*, vol. 2, by Stephan Thernstrom

The Granger Collection

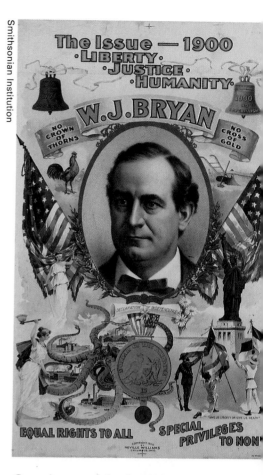

Campaign posters for the 1900 presidential election show the Republican "ticket" of McKinley and Roosevelt on the left and William Jennings Bryan, the Democratic nominee above. Which patriotic symbols can you find in these posters?

government. We govern the Indians without their consent; we govern our Territories without their consent; we govern our children without their consent. I answer, would not the natives of the Philippines prefer the just, humane, civilizing government of the Republic to the savage, bloody rule of pillage [ruthless plunder] and extortion [forcible theft] from which we have rescued them? Do not the blazing fires of joy and the ringing bells of gladness in Puerto Rico prove the welcome of our flag? And . . . do we owe no duty to the world? Shall we turn these peoples back to the reeking hands from which we have taken them? . . .[1] **99**

The anti-imperialists needed the votes of only one more than one third of the Senate to defeat the treaty. They seemed likely to succeed. Many Democratic senators would vote against the treaty to embarrass President McKinley and the Republican party.

But the McKinley administration received unexpected help from William Jennings Bryan. Although Bryan was against taking the Philippines, he believed that the Senate should consent to the treaty in order to bring an official end to the war.

Bryan planned to run for president again in 1900. He would make imperialism an issue in the campaign. He was convinced that a majority of the people were opposed to annexing the Philippines. After winning the election, he intended to grant the Filipinos their independence.

Bryan persuaded enough Democratic senators to vote for the

[1]From "The March of the Flag" by Albert J. Beveridge in *A History of the American People*, vol. 2, by Stephan Thernstrom

treaty to get it through. The vote was 57 to 27, only one vote more than the two thirds necessary. Senator Henry Cabot Lodge of Massachusetts, a leading supporter of the treaty, described the Senate debate this way:

❝ [It was] the closest, most bitter, and most exciting struggle I have ever known.❞

Fighting in the Philippines

William Jennings Bryan's strategy backfired. He was nominated again for president in 1900, and he did make the Philippines a prominent issue in the campaign. But McKinley, running for reelection, defeated him easily. The electoral vote was 292 to 155.

The Republican ticket had been strengthened by the nomination of the popular Rough Rider Theodore Roosevelt for vice president. After returning from Cuba in triumph, Roosevelt had been elected governor of New York. He had intended to run for reelection as

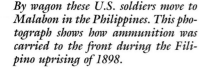

By wagon these U.S. soldiers move to Malabon in the Philippines. This photograph shows how ammunition was carried to the front during the Filipino uprising of 1898.

Library of Congress

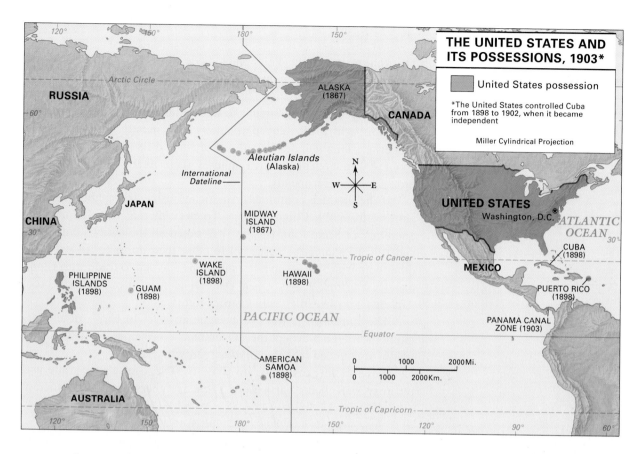

THE UNITED STATES AND ITS POSSESSIONS, 1903*

◼ United States possession

*The United States controlled Cuba from 1898 to 1902, when it became independent

Miller Cylindrical Projection

RUSSIA

ALASKA (1867)

CANADA

Arctic Circle

Aleutian Islands (Alaska)

International Dateline

JAPAN

CHINA

UNITED STATES

Washington, D.C.

ATLANTIC OCEAN

MIDWAY ISLAND (1867)

Tropic of Cancer

MEXICO

CUBA (1898)

WAKE ISLAND (1898)

HAWAII (1898)

PUERTO RICO (1898)

PHILIPPINE ISLANDS (1898)

GUAM (1898)

PACIFIC OCEAN

PANAMA CANAL ZONE (1903)

Equator

AMERICAN SAMOA (1898)

0   1000   2000 Mi.

0   1000   2000 Km.

AUSTRALIA

Tropic of Capricorn

governor in 1900. However, in November 1899 McKinley's vice president, Garret A. Hobart, had died. Roosevelt was persuaded to accept the Republican vice presidential nomination.

Then, less than a year after the election, President McKinley was shot and killed by an anarchist named Leon Czolgosz. An **anarchist** is one who believes that all government should be done away with. Theodore Roosevelt had been a mere assistant secretary of the navy two and one-half years earlier. Now he was president of the United States! This was the third time in the young nation's history that an assassin's bullet thrust the vice president to the seat of power in the White House.

There was still another unforeseen result of the Treaty of Paris. Even before the Senate voted for the treaty, the Filipino leader Emilio Aguinaldo had organized a revolution against American rule. Bloody jungle fighting broke out.

Peace was not restored until 1902. By that time more than 4,000 Americans and tens of thousands of Filipinos had been killed, a great many more wounded.

The United States continued to have great influence in many regions. Often it acted in ways that the local people resented. But opposition to imperialism was growing. Most Americans quickly lost their taste for owning colonies in distant parts of the world.

LEARNING FROM MAPS. *This map shows the extent of United States territory in 1903. How far is it from Washington, D.C., to the Philippines? To American Samoa? How could this distance create problems?*

The Open Door Notes

The annexation of the Philippines made the United States a power in the Far East. For many years Great Britain, France, Germany, and other European nations had been seizing **spheres of influence** in China. This meant they forced the weak Chinese government to grant them the right to develop particular areas, mostly around Chinese seaports. China's undeveloped resources and its huge population of about 400 million made such spheres seem likely to bring in large profits for the Europeans.

If the practice continued, American businesses might be cut off entirely from the China market. To prevent that from happening, Secretary of State John Hay in 1899 asked all the nations with such spheres of influence to agree not to close their doors to traders from other countries. All businesses should be allowed to trade with China on equal terms. Hay's **Open Door Note** was intended to protect America's trade rather than China's rights.

The European powers sent vague answers to Hay's note. Certainly they did not accept the "Open Door" principle. However, Hay boldly announced that they *had* agreed with him.

None of this exchange involved the Chinese, whose trade and territory were being carved up. Then, members of a secret society

Hubert Vos, *Portrait of H.I.M. The Empress Dowager of China, Tz'u-hsi, 1905-1906*, (detail), oil on canvas, 54 1/2 x 36", The Fogg Art Museum, Harvard University, Cambridge, Massachusetts, Bequest of Grenville L. Winthrop, 1943.162.

Tz'u-Hsi was the dowager empress of China who encouraged the Boxer Rebellion. This detail comes from her portrait.

228

Library of Congress

of Chinese nationalists known as the "Righteous, Harmonious Fists," or Boxers, launched an attack on foreigners in Peking, the capital, and in other parts of China.

Armed with swords and spears, the Boxers destroyed foreign property and killed missionaries and business people. Frightened foreigners fled for protection to the buildings which housed their governments' representatives in Peking. They remained there for weeks, virtual prisoners cut off from the outside world.

The western nations quickly organized an international army to put down this **Boxer Rebellion** of 1900. A force of 20,000, including 2,500 Americans, was rushed to the area. They rescued the trapped foreign civilians and crushed the Boxers.

Meanwhile, Hay feared that the European powers would use the Boxer Rebellion as an excuse to expand their spheres of influence. He sent off a **Second Open Door Note.** This one stated that the United States opposed any further carving up of China by foreign nations. The Open Door thus included two principles: equal trade rights for all in China and a guarantee of independence for China.

None of the European nations officially accepted these principles. In practice, however, Hay got what he wanted. American business interests were able to trade freely in the spheres and throughout the sprawling Chinese Empire.

An international army of Americans, British, French, Germans, Russians, and Japanese storm their own embassies to free their diplomats trapped inside by the Boxer Rebellion in China.

Return to the Preview & Review on page 221.

5. ROOSEVELT AND HIS CANAL

Preview & Review

Use these questions to guide your reading. Answer the questions after completing Section 5.
Understanding Issues, Events, & Ideas. Describe American efforts to build the Panama Canal, using the following words: Clayton-Bulwer Treaty, Hay-Pauncefote Treaty, isthmus, canal zone, Republic of Panama, Hay-Bunau-Varilla Treaty, lock, Roosevelt Corollary, dollar diplomacy, gunboat diplomacy, big stick diplomacy.

1. Why did the U.S. feel a canal was needed?
2. What were the arguments for and against building a canal across Panama? Across Nicaragua?
3. Why did Bunau-Varilla's "revolution" in Panama succeed?
4. Why did dollar diplomacy replace gunboat diplomacy?

Thinking Critically. 1. Imagine that you are Dr. Walter Reed, just returned from Cuba. Explain how you wiped out yellow fever in Cuba and the influence of your work on Major Gorgas. **2.** If you had been a Cuban tobacco farmer in 1910, how would Taft's dollar diplomacy change your way of life? How would you view this change? Why?

The Panama Canal

The United States needed to link the Atlantic and Pacific Oceans. The Spanish-American War and the expansion of the United States into the Pacific made it obvious that a canal across Central America would be extremely valuable.

During the war the new American battleship *Oregon* had to steam 12,000 miles (19,200 kilometers) from the West Coast around South America in order to help destroy Admiral Cervera's fleet at Santiago. It took the *Oregon* 68 days, traveling at top speed. A canal would have reduced the *Oregon*'s voyage to 4,000 miles (6,400 kilometers) or one third the distance.

The United States government was eager to build a canal. The first step was to get rid of the **Clayton-Bulwer Treaty** of 1850 with Great Britain. That agreement stated that any such canal would be controlled by *both* nations.

The treaty had made sense in 1850 when the United States had barely reached the Pacific. It did not make sense in 1900. Therefore, in 1901, Secretary Hay negotiated a new agreement with the British. This **Hay-Pauncefote Treaty** gave the United States the right to build and control a canal by itself. In return the United States promised that all nations would be allowed to use the canal on equal terms.

There were two possible canal routes across Central America. One roughly followed the path the explorer Balboa had taken across the Isthmus of Panama when he discovered the Pacific in 1513. An **isthmus** is a narrow neck of land connecting two landmasses. This route was short, but it passed through mountainous country covered by dense tropical jungles. The other was in the Republic of Nicaragua. There the land was more level, and part of the route could make use of Lake Nicaragua, which was 50 miles (80 kilometers) wide. The total distance was much longer, but Nicaragua was closer to the United States.

A private French company had obtained the right to build a canal across Panama, which was then part of the Republic of Colombia. This company had spent a fortune but made little progress. Thousands of its laborers had died of yellow fever and malaria. The company was now bankrupt. There was no chance that it would ever be able to complete a canal. In an effort to regain some of its losses, the company offered to sell its right to build a canal to the United States for $40 million.

A representative of the bankrupt company, Philippe Bunau-Varilla, worked to persuade Congress to take over the canal project. His campaign succeeded. By 1903 President Roosevelt had made up his mind to build the canal in Panama. Congress went along with this decision.

To persuade Congress to choose Panama over Nicaragua for the new canal, Philippe Bunau-Varilla depended heavily on 90 one-centavo stamps. Bunau-Varilla was the representative of the bankrupt French company that had begun the canal.

Bunau-Varilla had mailed out 13,000 copies of a pamphlet, *Panama or Nicaragua?* One of his arguments against a Nicaraguan canal was that there were volcanoes there. No matter that nearly all had long been inactive. He wrote, "What have the Nicaraguans chosen to characterize their country . . . on their postage stamps? Volcanoes!"

The Senate was about to begin debate on the canal site. Far from Washington (and from Nicaragua) rumblings began coming from Mount Pele, a long-dormant volcano on the island of Martinique. On May 8, 1902, the entire mountain exploded,

killing nearly 30,000 people in two minutes. "What an unexpected turn of the wheel of fortune," wrote Bunau-Varilla. He thought again of the Nicaraguan stamp.

Bunau-Varilla went to every stamp dealer in Washington until he had 90 of the one-centavo Nicaraguan stamps. Each showed a puffing locomotive in the foreground and an erupting volcano in the background. Bunau-Varilla pasted the stamps on sheets of paper. He mailed one to each of the 90 United States senators with the neatly typed caption: "An official witness of the volcanic activity on the isthmus of Nicaragua."

The Panama "Revolution"

Next, Secretary of State Hay and the Colombian representative in Washington negotiated a treaty in which Colombia leased a **canal zone** across Panama to the United States. Colombia was to receive $10 million and a rent of $250,000 a year. The United States Senate promptly consented to this treaty.

But the Colombian senate rejected it. The reason was simple. The Colombians wanted more money. The bankrupt French company was being offered four times as much for its rights in Colombia. And Colombia had granted those rights in the first place.

When Colombia rejected the treaty, Bunau-Varilla organized a revolution in Panama. There had been many such uprisings against Colombia there in the past. All had been easily put down. But this time the rebels had the support of the United States. Their "revolution" therefore succeeded.

The small rebel army was made up of railroad workers and members of the Panama City fire department. But when Colombian troops, sent by sea, landed at the port of Colón, they were met by the powerful U.S.S. *Nashville*. The Colombians were forced to return to their home port.

Thus was born the **Republic of Panama**. Only three days later, on November 6, 1903, the United States government officially recognized Panama. On November 18, in Washington, Secretary Hay signed a canal treaty with a representative of the new nation. This

Point of View

Just how massive a project was the Panama Canal is revealed in this study.

"To build the Great Pyramid or the Wall of China or the cathedrals of France, blocks of stone were set one on top of the other in the age-old fashion. But the walls of the Panama locks were poured from overhead, bucket by bucket, into gigantic forms. . . . "
From *The Path Between the Seas,*
David McCullough, 1977

Death took a holiday in the fever-ridden swamps of Panama when William Gorgas, above, drained the swamps to eliminate yellow fever. Below him is Colonel George Goethals of the Army Engineers who led the canal builders.

representative was none other than Philippe Bunau-Varilla. The **Hay-Bunau-Varilla Treaty** granted the United States a ten-mile-wide Canal Zone (16 kilometers). The financial arrangements were the same ones that Colombia had turned down.

Building the Canal

Before work on the Panama Canal could begin, malaria and yellow fever had to be stamped out. Carlos Juan Finlay, a Cuban doctor trained in Philadelphia, had first suggested that yellow fever was spread by a certain kind of mosquito. The United States sent a delegation headed by Doctor Walter Reed to Cuba to find a way to wipe out the disease. Reed studied Finlay's experiments and agreed with his findings. The United States army under the direction of Major William Gorgas then proceeded to eliminate yellow fever in Cuba. Gorgas was now sent to Panama to rid the area of the mosquitoes which carried the disease. He drained the swamps and ponds where the mosquitoes laid their eggs.

Now the actual construction could begin. Colonel George Goethals of the Army Engineers had charge of the project. The level of the canal had to be raised as high as 85 feet (over 25 meters) above the sea. Water-filled chambers called **locks** would raise and lower ships from one level to another.

For ten years, from 1904 to 1914, a small army of workers drilled and blasted, dug and dredged. They had to cut a 9-mile-long channel (over 14 kilometers) through mountains of solid rock. In this

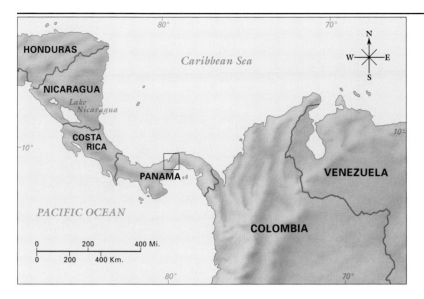

PANAMA AND THE CANAL ZONE

Modified Azimuthal Equal-Area Projection

excerpt a writer captured the problems of cutting through a particularly stubborn spot near the middle of the canal.

❝ Culebra Cut! Here the barrier of the continental divide resisted to the utmost the attacks of the canal army; here disturbed and outraged Nature conspired with gross mountain mass to make the defense stronger and stronger; here the mountain must be moved. . . .

Grim, now, but still confident, the attackers fought on. The mountain was defeated.

Now stretches a man-made canyon across the backbone of the continent; now lies a channel for ships through the barrier; now is found what Columbus sought in vain—the gate through the West to the East. Men call it the Culebra Cut. [It was later renamed the Gaillard Cut.]

Nine miles long, it has an average depth of 120 feet (37 meters). At places its sides tower nearly 500 feet (152 meters) above the channel bottom, which is nowhere narrower than 300 feet (91 meters).

It is the greatest single trophy of the triumph of man over the terrestrial arrangement of the world. . . . It is majestic. It is awful. It is the Canal. . . .

No one had the remotest idea of the actual difficulties that would beset the canal builders; no one dreamed of the avalanches of material that would slide into the cut. . . . No less than 26 slides and breaks were encountered in the construction of the Culebra cut.

To remove the 105,000,000 cubic yards of earth from the backbone of America required about 6,000,000 pounds of high-grade dynamite each year to break up the material, so

LEARNING FROM MAPS. *Completion of the Panama Canal meant a new route to the West Coast. How had ships traveled before the canal? American control of the canal also involved the United States more deeply in Latin American affairs. What are the advantages for the United States of that involvement? What are the disadvantages?*

Roosevelt and His Canal   233

Culver Pictures

The Cut of Las Cascadas, shown above, and the Gaillard Cut were two of the engineering wonders that made it possible to complete the Panama Canal in just ten years. Do you think such a project could be completed so quickly today? Why or why not?

that it might be successfully attacked by the steam shovel. . . . So carefully was the dynamite handled that during a period of three years, in which time some 19,000,000 pounds were exploded in Culebra Cut, only eight men were killed. . . .

Today Culebra Mountain bows its lofty head to the genius of the American engineer and to the courage of the canal army. . . . Through it now extends a ribbon of water broad enough to permit the largest vessels afloat to pass one another under their own power and deep enough to carry a ship with a draft [depth in the water] beyond anything in the minds of naval constructors today. . . . It is the mightiest deed the hand of man has done.[1] **99**

The channel was named the Gaillard Cut after Colonel David Gaillard, the engineer in charge of this part of the project.

The canal was finally finished in 1914. It was a truly magnificent

[1]From "The Culebra Cut" by Frederic Haskin

STRATEGIES FOR SUCCESS

INTERPRETING EDITORIAL CARTOONS

Editorial cartoons are drawings that present points of view on particular issues. They are usually found in the editorial sections of newspapers and magazines and have been used throughout history to influence public opinion. Although some cartoons present a positive point of view, most are critical of a policy, situation, or person.

The two most important techniques cartoonists use to express their message are caricature and symbolism. A caricature is a drawing that exaggerates physical features. Symbolism is the use of one thing to represent another idea, feeling, or object. Common symbols for the United States, for example, are the bald eagle and Uncle Sam. Cartoons also use titles, labels, and captions to get their message across.

How to Interpret Editorial Cartoons

To interpret editorial cartoons, follow these steps.

1. **Identify the caricatures.** Note the people or objects being characterized and note what is exaggerated.
2. **Identify the symbols.** Determine the meaning of each of the symbols used.
3. **Read the title, labels, and caption.** Check the title, labels, and caption to help you understand the artist's message.
4. **Analyze the information.** Decide if the cartoonist's point of view is positive or negative. Determine what events or situation led to the cartoon.

Applying the Strategy

President Theodore Roosevelt was a favorite of editorial cartoonists. Study the cartoon of him at the top of the next column. Does the cartoonist use caricature? If so, what features are exaggerated? Is there symbolism? If so what symbols are used and what do they stand for? Does the cartoonist present a positive or negative point of view? How can you tell? In your own words, state the cartoonist's message. Now answer the same questions for the cartoon at the lower right.

For independent practice, see Practicing the Strategy on page 238.

NO MOLLY-CODDLING HERE

Both, The Granger Collection

achievement. President Roosevelt took full credit for the project and for its swift completion:

 " I am interested in the Panama Canal because I started it. If I had followed traditional conservative methods . . . debate would have been going on yet. But I took the Canal Zone and let Congress debate, and while the debate goes on the canal does also. "

Roosevelt blamed Colombia for the revolution in Panama. He once told a friend that trying to make a deal with that country was like trying to nail jelly to a wall. Yet many Americans at that time and many more in later years felt that Roosevelt's behavior had been entirely wrong. In 1921, after Roosevelt was dead, Congress gave Colombia $25 million to make up for the loss of Panama. And in 1978 a new treaty provided that at the end of this century the Canal Zone itself would be turned back to Panama.

This powerful portrait of Theodore Roosevelt was painted by John Singer Sargent. Portraits of all former presidents and first ladies hang in the White House and are well worth the tour of the president's house. Your member of Congress can get you tickets in advance.

The Roosevelt Corollary

President Roosevelt was eager to prevent any European country from interfering in the affairs of the small nations of the Caribbean. These countries were all poor, and most of them were badly governed. Their governments frequently borrowed money from European banks and investors and did not repay them when the loans fell due. Sometimes, European governments sent in troops to force them to pay.

Before he became president, Roosevelt did not object. After he became president, he had second thoughts. Any European interference in the affairs of Latin American nations violated the Monroe Doctrine, he decided.

Debts, however, must be paid. If a nation in the Western Hemisphere did not pay its debts, the United States must make it do so. That way justice could be done to the lenders, but there would be no European interference in the hemisphere. This policy became known as the **Roosevelt Corollary** to the Monroe Doctrine. *Corollary* means "what naturally follows from."

Roosevelt always said that he applied the Corollary with the greatest reluctance. When he sent marines into the Dominican Republic in 1905, he insisted that he had no more desire to make that nation a colony of the United States than a snake would have to swallow a porcupine backwards. Many Americans always protested the use of force in such situations.

After William Howard Taft became president in 1909, it seemed shrewder to try to control the nations of the region indirectly. By investing money in countries like Cuba, Nicaragua, and the Dominican Republic, more stable economies would result. Then the governments of these countries would also be more stable. This policy

The Granger Collection

The American eagle stretches all the way to the Philippines in the 1904 cartoon by Joseph Keppler. He called it, "His 126th Birthday—'Gee, But This Is An Awful Stretch.'" Do you agree, particularly when you use historical imagination to put yourself back to the beginning of this century?

came to be known as **dollar diplomacy** to distinguish it from the **gunboat diplomacy** of the Roosevelt Corollary. Because Roosevelt felt that the U.S. should carry a "big stick," or the threat of force, in its foreign policy, people also referred to gunboat diplomacy as **big stick diplomacy.**

The difficulty with dollar diplomacy was that, without meaning to, it often injured the people of the countries involved. An American company might purchase a number of small tobacco farms in Cuba. Then it might convert the land into a vast sugar plantation. The plantation would be more efficient. Its crops could be sold for larger amounts of money. But the Cubans who had been independent tobacco farmers now became hired plantation laborers. They were forced to change their entire way of life.

At this time people were just beginning to realize how heavy-handed the United States had become in the Western Hemisphere. Most people still assumed that the Latin American nations shared the values of the United States. Later they would understand that they were seriously mistaken.

Return to the Preview & Review on page 230.

Roosevelt and His Canal   237

CHAPTER 5 REVIEW

1867
U.S. occupies the Midway Islands

★
Alaskan Purchase

1875
U.S. and Hawaii sign sugar treaty

Chapter Summary
Read the statements below. Choose one, and write a paragraph explaining its importance.
1. Manifest destiny led many Americans to look beyond the nation's borders, especially across the Pacific and into the Caribbean.
2. Spanish rule in Cuba had become increasingly harsh. When the fight for Cuban independence finally erupted, the United States backed the rebels, leading to the Spanish-American War.
3. Spanish and American forces fought in the Philippines and in the Caribbean.
4. As a result of the U.S. victory in the Spanish-American War, the country gained Puerto Rico, Guam, and the Philippines.
5. Despite strong anti-imperialist opposition, the U.S. continued to expand. The Open Door Notes secured American trading rights in China and the Panama "Revolution" cleared the way for the American-controlled Panama Canal.
6. The Roosevelt Corollary to the Monroe Doctrine further warned against foreign interference in the Western Hemisphere. Dollar diplomacy soon replaced the gunboat diplomacy of the Corollary as America sought to help its neighbors pay their foreign debts.

Reviewing Chronological Order
Number your paper 1–5. Then study the time line above and place the following events in the order in which they happened by writing the first next to 1, the second next to 2, and so on.
1. Open Door Notes
2. U.S.S. *Maine* explodes
3. Alaskan Purchase
4. Panama Canal completed
5. Chilean Crisis erupts

Understanding Main Ideas
1. What events during the Civil War caused Americans to be suspicious of Europe?
2. What was the purpose of the Pan-American Conference? How was its goodwill set back by the Chilean Crisis?
3. What did John Hay call for in the Open Door Notes?
4. Explain the steps the U.S. took to build and control the Panama Canal.
5. What was the Roosevelt Corollary? Why did the president issue this policy?

Thinking Critically
1. **Synthesizing.** Suppose you are an American farmer or business owner in the 1890s. Would you have favored an American policy of isolation or expansion? Why?
2. **Evaluating.** Was the United States justified in going to war against Spain in 1898? Explain your reasoning. Would the same circumstances cause the United States to go to war today? Why or why not?
3. **Distinguishing Fact from Opinion.** Reread the quotation by Josiah Strong in Section 1. Rewrite the quotation in your own words and tell whether Strong is stating a fact or giving his opinion.

Writing About History: Expressive
Imagine you are in Alaska in 1890, Manila Bay with Dewey, San Juan Hill with Roosevelt, or in Panama during the building of the Panama Canal. Use your historical imagination to write a letter describing what is happening. Use the information in Chapter 5 to help you develop your letter.

Practicing the Strategy
Review the strategy on page 235.
Interpreting Editorial Cartoons. Study the cartoon at the bottom of page 257 and answer the following questions.
1. What symbols are used by the cartoonist? What caricatures?
2. Why do you think the cartoonist chose those symbols? Why did the cartoonist caricature those particular features?
3. What is the message of the cartoon?

1891
Chilean
Crisis
erupts

~~ican~~
~~erence~~

~~ıley~~

1893
American
revolt in
Hawaii

1894
Republic
of Hawaii
declared

1895
Cuban
Revolution
begins
★
Venezuela
Boundary
Dispute

1898
U.S.S.
Maine
explodes
in Havana
★
U.S.
declares
war on
Spain
★
Treaty
of Paris
ends war

1899
Open Door Notes

1900
Boxer
Rebellion
★
McKinley
reelected
president

1901
McKinley assassinated
★
Roosevelt becomes president
★
Fighting in the Philippines

1903
Republic of Panama

1904
Roosevelt Corollary
proclaimed
★
Building of Panama
Canal begins

1909
Dollar diplomacy begins
★
Taft becomes president

1914
Panama
Canal
completed

Using Primary Sources

One of the most eloquent voices raised in opposition to American expansion was that of Queen Liliuokalani of Hawaii. Read the following excerpt from *Hawaii's History By Hawaii's Queen* to understand her argument. Then answer the questions below.

> *Perhaps there is a kind of right, depending on the precedents of all ages, and known as the "Right of Conquest," under which robbers and marauders may establish themselves in possession of whatsoever they are strong enough to ravish for their fellows. I will not pretend to decide how far civilization and Christian enlightenment have outlawed it. But we have known for many years that our Island monarchy has relied upon the protection always extended to us by the policy and the assured friendship of the great American republic.*
>
> *Oh, honest Americans, . . . hear me for my downtrodden people! Their form of government is as dear to them as yours is precious to you. Quite as warmly as you love your country, so they love theirs. With all your goodly possessions, covering territory so immense that there yet remain parts unexplored . . . do not covet the little vineyard of Naboth's [Hawaii], so far from your shores.*

1. According to Queen Liliuokalani, what is the "Right of Conquest"? Do you think a country should be allowed to take what it is strong enough to control? Why or why not?
2. In the second paragraph of the excerpt, the Hawaiian queen appeals directly to "honest Americans." What argument does she use? Do you agree or disagree with her? Why?

Linking History & Geography

Building the Panama Canal was a great engineering feat. Panama is a land of rugged mountains and dense jungles. To help understand the difficulty of building the canal and how the canal works, make a model of the Isthmus of Panama, using clay or plaster of paris. Show the route of the Panama Canal and label the locks. Use the model to explain the stages by which a ship passes through the canal.

Enriching Your Study of History

1. **Individual Project.** Choose one of the nations of Latin America and present a short report in class on its historical and present-day relationships with the U.S. Choose from among these countries:

Argentina	Guatemala
Bolivia	Haiti
Brazil	Honduras
Chile	Mexico
Colombia	Nicaragua
Costa Rica	Panama
Cuba	Paraguay
Dominican Republic	Peru
Ecuador	Uruguay
El Salvador	Venezuela

2. **Cooperative Project.** Less than 20 years after the Spanish-American War the American flag flew over many new lands. To illustrate the extent of the expansion, different groups in your class will research the following information: the lands that came into U.S. possession between 1865 and 1918, how America gained control of these lands, and the present political status of each. Then your class will create a three-column chart illustrating this information.

Chapter 5 Review   239

Reformers and the Progressive Movement

Hopeful and expectant at the turn of the century, these strollers in New York's Central Park were painted about 1905 by William Glackens. His art is impressionistic. Rather than try to paint a photographic likeness, impressionists seized upon a detail of light or shadow that played on their subjects. What parts of this scene would you say are more impressionistic than realistic?

Around the turn of the century a new mood spread through the nation. People seemed to be full of hope about the future. This mood lasted for about 15 years in the early 1900s and was known as the Progressive Era. It was a time when large numbers of people were working to improve society. These reformers were called progressives. They were trying to make progress. They hoped to make a better world. This belief in progress was part of the American character. Thomas Jefferson and nearly every westward-moving pioneer had shared it. During the Progressive Era the feeling was especially strong. People consciously spoke of themselves and the times as "progressive." Some progressives belonged to the Republican party, some to the Democratic. Theodore Roosevelt, one of the two great presidents of the era, was a Republican. The other, Woodrow Wilson, was a Democrat. Progressivism was a point of view about society and politics, not a political organization.

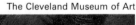

The Cleveland Museum of Art

1. THE PROGRESSIVE IDEA

The Turn of the Century

What causes shifts of public feeling such as the **Progressive Movement** is a mystery. There were several reasons, but no one can say exactly how they were related to one another.

People looked forward because they were beginning the 20th century. They sensed they were at the beginning of new and probably better times. The return of prosperity after the long depression of the 1890s changed their mood. The easy victory in the Spanish-American War increased their self-confidence. They seemed likely to accomplish whatever they set out to do. These **progressives** felt stronger and more important because the war had added new territory to the nation in many parts of the world. When Senator Albert J. Beveridge of Indiana made a speech describing "the march of the flag" in the Caribbean and Pacific, he was cheered to the rafters.

Many Americans looked back on the time after the Civil War as good years. Tremendous technological changes had advanced life. The telephone, the camera, and other scientific breakthroughs had a positive effect on people's lives. So did changes in the educational system. Individual schools had been consolidated into district systems. A manager, usually the superintendent, oversaw its operations and consulted with professional educators. Curriculum changed with the times. Less attention was paid to "the classics," to Latin and Greek. More was spent on mathematics, science, and the mechanical arts. High school enrollments soared. No longer was high school the reserve of the wealthy few. More and more families were making enough money to allow their children to attend.

Problems of Growth

Yet the same Americans who were so confident and hopeful were aware that conditions in the country were far from perfect. Many serious problems remained unsolved. Speaking broadly, these problems were produced by the Industrial Revolution.

In the great cities of the United States lived both the richest and poorest people in the country. The mansions of millionaire manufacturers stood only a few blocks from ugly, unhealthy districts that housed the poor families who labored in their factories. Few Americans objected to the Carnegies and Rockefellers and Morgans being so wealthy. But sometimes the rich seemed too powerful, the poor too weak. What power the poor did have was in the control of the big-city political machines, which used their votes to steal from the rich and the middle class.

The continued growth of great corporations and trusts was

Preview & Review

Use these questions to guide your reading. Answer the questions after completing Section 1.
Understanding Issues, Events, & Ideas. Explain the goals of the reforms in the late 1800s and early 1900s, using the following words: Progressive Movement, progressives, Social Gospel.
1. What changes were there in the national mood at the turn of the century?
2. How did the world's first billion-dollar corporation come into being?
3. How did the progressives differ from reformers of the past?
4. What was the role of the government as progressives saw it?
Thinking Critically. Why do you think the national mood of America changed around 1900? What might cause a change today?

AVERAGE RETAIL PRICE OF SELECTED ITEMS, 1905*	
Item	Price
Beef (per pound)	$0.10
Butter (per pound)	$0.19
Bacon (per pound)	$0.11
Eggs (per dozen)	$0.13
Oranges (per dozen)	$0.20
Ice cream cone	$0.10
Men's suit	$9.50
Ladies' shoes (per pair)	$1.65
*in Omaha, Nebraska	

LEARNING FROM TABLES. *Compare the 1905 prices for the listed items with their prices today. How would you explain the differences?*

John Sloan, who painted "Women's Work" in 1911, is another American impressionist. He and his contemporaries painted common scenes from everyday life rather than fancy formal pictures. Critics called their group the "Ashcan School" but today these paintings give us valuable views of life at the turn of the century. Compare this painting with the one on page 240. In what ways is this painting impressionistic?

The Cleveland Museum of Art

another cause of concern. The revival of the economy increased business profits. This encouraged businesses to expand their operations. Big companies bought out small ones. In the year 1899 alone, over 1,000 firms were swallowed up.

The largest corporations were merging with each other to form giant monopolies. In 1901 the banker J. P. Morgan bought Andrew Carnegie's huge steel company. He then combined it with corporations that made finished steel products like pipe and wire and rails. He called the result the United States Steel Corporation.

U.S. Steel became the world's first billion-dollar corporation. Because it was so large and powerful, many people considered such a supercompany dangerous no matter what the policies of its owners and managers.

Many people asked how, in America, these problems could have grown so large. Working conditions in factories and living conditions in parts of most cities were unsafe and unsanitary. The nation's wealth seemed to belong to a few very rich people. Why didn't governments—national, state, and local—do something? Why did they instead seem to pass many laws that favored "big business"?

As you have read, Social Darwinism was the excuse most often given for the hands-off approach of governments. Charles Darwin had used certain theories to explain the development of animals. One, survival of the fittest, became a theory of social change as well. The most energetic and aggressive people would rise to the top of society and take control. And that is just what was happening. Business leaders were transforming America into an economic and industrial power. Government should do everything it could to help. Often that meant looking the other way!

It was just that attitude the progressive set out to combat. Social Darwinism was based on incorrect assumptions, they said. Perhaps survival of the fittest did apply to animals and plants in the wild. But Americans lived in a society, not the wilderness. And further, the United States was a democracy. And a democracy, as the abolitionist Theodore Parker had written and Abraham Lincoln had paraphrased in his *Gettysburg Address*, "is government of the people, by the people, for the people." American government should work for *all* Americans, not just the fit. Many progressive reformers realized that changing American attitudes toward industrial growth and progress would be as hard as tackling the problems caused by it.

Many kinds of people called themselves progressives. One type consisted of city dwellers concerned about political corruption, crime, and public health problems. Another group consisted of the owners and managers of small businesses. Many of these business leaders felt squeezed between the rising demands of organized labor and the power of the railroads and the monopolistic corporations with which they had to compete. Settlement house workers such as Jane Addams became reformers after observing the squalid conditions that recent immigrants encountered. The settlement houses did what they could to improve conditions for these slum dwellers. But they came to believe that many more efforts were needed if any real improvement was to be made. So too did the growing number of women who joined women's organizations founded to help the poor.

Urban religious leaders such as Walter Rauschenbusch and Washington Gladden also became progressives. These clergymen developed a new theory to combat Social Darwinism. Known as the **Social Gospel,** this theory maintained that it was a person's moral obligation to help those who were less fortunate. In other words, it was immoral for wealthy people to sit by idly when thousands of

Point of View

A fictional family feels the sting of society in this brief excerpt from the novel *Ragtime.*

"One Sunday, in a wild impractical mood, they spent twelve cents for three fares on the streetcar and rode uptown. They walked on Madison Avenue and Fifth Avenue and looked at the mansions. Their owners called them palaces. They had all been designed by Stanford White. Tateh [the father] was a socialist. He looked at the palaces and his heart was outraged. The family walked quickly. The police in their tall helmets looked at them. On these empty sidewalks in this part of the city the police did not like to see immigrants. Tateh explained that this was because an immigrant some years before had shot the steel millionaire Henry Frick in Pittsburgh. . . ."
E. L. Doctorow, 1975

Americans were desperately poor. Those who preached the Social Gospel observed firsthand the horrible conditions of the tenements. Many used the Social Gospel to fight against the materialism that they saw in their wealthy parishioners. In general, these progressives believed in moderate change rather than a radical restructuring of society.

The Progressive Mood

The concerns of the reformers did not suddenly come in with the 20th century. The problems of the Industrial Revolution existed long before 1900. Reformers had been fighting political bosses and machine politics for years. Efforts had been made to improve conditions in the slums. Many state laws had been passed to protect workers. The federal government had tried to check the growth of monopolies by the Sherman Antitrust Act. It had regulated the great railroad corporations through the Interstate Commerce Act. In the 1890s the Populists had vigorously attacked the evils they saw in the industrial age.

What was different about progressives was their new mood. They were happy, cheerful reformers. Most Populists had seen themselves as underdogs being taken advantage of by powerful bankers and railroad tycoons. Progressives attacked bankers and tycoons of all sorts. But they did so more to protect others than to help themselves. Good times made it possible for people to be more generous. Progressives wanted to share their prosperity with people less fortunate than themselves.

Like Thomas Jefferson, the progressives believed that if the people knew the truth, they would do what was right. Like Alexander Hamilton, they believed that the government should act forcefully to increase the national wealth and to improve the standard of living.

This is how the typical progressive reasoned. First of all, most ordinary people are basically decent and public spirited. When they realize what needs to be done to improve society, they will do it. Informing the people is the first step toward reform.

Next, the political system must be thoroughly democratic. If the wishes of the people are to be carried out, the government must respond to public opinion. Government officials must be both honest and efficient. It must be easy to remove dishonest or lazy officials and replace them with good public servants.

Then, with the will of the people behind it, the government should take action. It should check and control greedy special interests seeking selfish benefits at the expense of the people. It should try to improve the condition of weaker members of society—children, old people, the poor. And as one progressive put it:

Return to the Preview & Review on page 241.

66 That would change all of us—not alone our neighbors, not alone the grafters [dishonest people], but you and me. 99

2. REFORMERS

The Muckrakers

Progressives depended heavily on newspapers and magazines to get their messages to the people. They placed more stress on describing what was wrong with society than on offering specific plans for reform. They assumed that once the people knew what was wrong, they would do something to correct the problem.

A small army of writers and researchers was soon engaged in what later came to be called investigative journalism. These writers dug into public records. They talked to politicians and business people, to city clerks and police officers, to factory workers and recent immigrants. Then they published their results in hard-hitting articles and books. They were specific. They named names. They demanded that "something be done." Improvements in printing and better ways of reproducing photographs added greatly to the effectiveness of their writing.

Theodore Roosevelt, not intending to praise the authors who exposed the evils of the time, called them **muckrakers.** They were raking up muck, or dirt, in order to make people aware of it. Muckrakers exposed the corrupt activities of political bosses. They described the terrible living conditions of the slums. They showed children laboring in factories and sweatshops. They wrote about the sale of impure foods and drugs. There were even articles describing secret payments of money to college football players and other evils resulting from an "overemphasis" on college sports.

Among the best-known of the muckrakers were Lincoln Steffens, Ida Tarbell, and Upton Sinclair. Steffens specialized in exposing

Preview & Review

Use these questions to guide your reading. Answer the questions after completing Section 2. **Understanding Issues, Events, & Ideas.** Evaluate the success of some of the reformers, using the following words: muckrakers, Golden Rule, Wisconsin Idea, direct primary, primary election, lobbyist, initiative, referendum, recall, Seventeenth Amendment, municipal socialism, socialist, free enterprise, Triangle Fire, minimum wage, Brandeis brief.

1. How did the Wisconsin Idea give voters more voice in selecting their candidates for public office?
2. Why did reformers believe states should make laws to protect workers?
3. What is the importance of the decision in *Muller v. Oregon?*

Thinking Critically. Imagine that you are a muckraker. What problem would you publicize? Why? How would you propose solving the problem or at least improving conditions?

Both, Brown Brothers

Lincoln Steffens and Ida Tarbell were two of the leading muckrakers of the early 1900s. Steffens examined city governments. Tarbell wrote a landmark study of Standard Oil.

Reformers   245

HISTORY OF STANDARD OIL BY Ida M. Tarbell

Mc.CLURE'S MAGAZINE

NOVEMBER

PUBLISHED MONTHLY BY THE S. S. McCLURE CO., 141-155 E. 25th ST., NEW YORK CITY
20 Norfolk St., Strand, London, W.C., Eng. Copyright, 1902, by The S. S. McClure Co. Entered at N.Y. Post-Office as Second-Class Matter

The November 1902 issue of Mc-Clure's magazine contains stronger stuff than its cover would indicate. Inside is an installment of Ida Tarbell's History of Standard Oil.

Culver Pictures

corrupt city governments. In *McClure's* magazine, which was the most important muckraking periodical, he reported on conditions in St. Louis, Minneapolis, Cincinnati, and other "boss-ridden" cities. In 1904 Steffens published these articles in a book, *The Shame of the Cities*. He also wrote about corruption in state governments. But Steffens was not a mere scandal seeker. When he discovered well-run cities and honest officials, he praised them highly.

Ida Tarbell was one of the leading journalists of her day. She was also an important historian. Before she turned to muckraking, she wrote biographies of the French Emperor Napoleon as well as

Abraham Lincoln. But she specialized in business investigations. Her detailed study of the methods used by John D. Rockefeller's Standard Oil Company was published in 19 installments in *McClure's*. She claimed Rockefeller "employed force and fraud to obtain his end."

Sinclair, along with Frank Norris and Jack London, were primarily novelists. Sinclair's sensational novel *The Jungle* exposed the disgustingly unsanitary conditions in meat-packing plants. Norris' *The Octopus* described the railroads' control over the economic life of farmers. London's stories, such as *The War of the Class, The Iron Heel,* and *Revolution,* warned of a workers' uprising that could wipe out private capitalism.

Few muckrakers called attention to the plight of black Americans. The most important work was *Following the Color Line* by Ray Stannard Baker. In this series of magazine articles Baker reported on segregation and racial discrimination in America.

Some reformers used the camera to tell their story. As you have read, Jacob Riis made a study of life in the tenements of New York City. His photographs and essays captured the terrible conditions of the slums and tenements. Scenes of cramped conditions, dilapidated buildings, and filth shocked middle-class Americans who had never seen the slums. In *How the Other Half Lives,* Riis wrote:

Ray Stannard Baker, whose photograph appears above, was one of the few muckrakers concerned with the plight of African Americans.

“ Go into any of the 'respectable' tenement neighborhoods . . . where live the great body of hard-working Irish and German immigrants and their descendants, who accept naturally the conditions of tenement life, because for them there is nothing else in New York. . . .

With the first hot nights in June police dispatches, that record the killing of men and women by rolling off roofs and windows-sills while asleep, announce that the time of greatest suffering among the poor is at hand. It is the hot weather, when life indoors is well-nigh [nearly] unbearable with cooking, sleeping, and working, all crowded into the small rooms together, that the tenement expands, reckless of all restraint. . . . In the stifling July nights, when the big barracks [buildings] are like fiery furnaces, their very walls giving out absorbed heat, men and women lie in restless, sweltering rows, panting for air and sleep. Then every truck on the street, every crowded fire-escape, becomes a bedroom, infinitely preferable to any the house affords. A cooling shower [rain] on such a night is hailed as a heaven-sent blessing in a hundred thousand homes.

Life in the tenements in July and August spells death to an army of little ones whom the doctor's skill is powerless to save. When the white badge of mourning [a white ribbon] flutters from every second door, sleepless mothers walk the streets in the gray of the early dawn, trying to stir a cooling

Both, Museum of the City of New York

Jacob Riis documented the slums of the cities with his camera, not his pen. Two of his most famous scenes are "Baxter Street Alley—Rag Picker's Row" (left) and "Street Arabs in Night Quarters, Mulberry Street" (right). Describe in your own words what you think is happening in each photograph.

breeze to fan the brow of the sick baby. There is no sadder sight than this patient devotion striving against fearfully hopeless odds. Fifty 'summer doctors,' especially trained to this work, are sent into the tenements by the Board of Health, with free advice and medicine for the poor. Devoted women follow their track with care and nursing for the sick. . . . but despite all efforts the grave-diggers in Calvary [a city cemetery] work over-time, and little coffins are stacked mountains high in the deck of the Charity Commissioners' boat that makes its semi-weekly trips to the city cemetery. . . .[1]"

Riis also documented crowded and dangerous working conditions in tenement sweatshops (see pages 150–151). Because of his active interest in helping the poor and the immigrants in the slums, Riis was called by many "the most useful citizen of New York."

[1]From *How the Other Half Lives* by Jacob Riis

248   REFORMERS AND THE PROGRESSIVE MOVEMENT

Reforming City Governments

The struggle to rid cities of corrupt political bosses and their powerful machines was almost endless because more large cities were developing as the nation grew larger and more industrialized. By 1910 there were 50 American cities with populations of more than 100,000.

Among the notable reformer mayors of the Progressive Era was Samuel M. Jones. Jones was a poor farm boy who made a fortune drilling for oil. Then he sold out to Standard Oil and became a manufacturer of oil-drilling equipment in Toledo, Ohio.

During the depression of the 1890s Jones was shocked by the condition of the unemployed men who came to his plant looking for jobs. He set out to apply the **Golden Rule** in his factory: "Do unto others as you would have them do unto you." He raised wages. He reduced the workday to eight hours. He sold lunches to workers at cost. He created a park, gave picnics for his employees, and invited them to his home.

In 1897 "Golden Rule" Jones was elected mayor of Toledo. He held this office until his death in 1904. His election was a victory for honest government. He stressed political independence rather than party loyalty. He established the eight-hour day for many city workers. He built playgrounds and a city golf course. He provided kindergartens for young children.

Another progressive mayor, also from Ohio, was Tom L. Johnson of Cleveland. Johnson was less idealistic than Jones, but he got even more done. He forced the local streetcar company to lower its fares. He reduced taxes by cutting out wasteful city agencies and running others more efficiently. He improved the Cleveland parks. And he reformed the city prisons. After his investigation of Cleveland, Lincoln Steffens called Johnson "the best mayor of the best-governed city in the United States."

Other cities where important reform movements were organized by progressives included Philadelphia, Chicago, and Los Angeles. In San Francisco the corrupt machine of Boss Abraham Ruef was defeated by reformers led by Fremont Older, editor of the San Francisco *Bulletin,* and Rudolph Spreckles, a wealthy sugar manufacturer. In St. Louis a lawyer, Joseph W. Folk, headed the reformers.

Despite their problems, America's cities were a wonder. They were places of energy, industry, of progress. Most Americans were proud of their cities. Carl Sandburg's poem is an example.

"   **Chicago**

Hog Butcher for the World,
Tool Maker, Stacker of Wheat,
Player with Railroads and the Nation's Freight Handler;
Stormy, husky, brawling,
City of the Big Shoulders:

Point of View

Again from *Ragtime,* compare this fictional account with Riis' description.

"This was early in the month of June and by the end of the month a serious heat wave had begun to kill infants all over the slums. The tenements glowed like furnaces and the tenants had no water to drink. . . . Families slept on stoops and in doorways. Horses collapsed and died in the streets. The Department of Sanitation sent drays around the city to drag away horses that had died. But it was not an efficient service. Horses exploded in the heat."
E. L. Doctorow, 1975

They tell me you are wicked and I believe them, for I
have seen your painted women under the gas lamps
luring the farm boys.
And they tell me you are crooked and I answer: Yes, it is
true I have seen the gunman kill and go free to kill
again.
And they tell me you are brutal and my reply is: On the
faces of the women and children I have seen the marks
of wanton hunger.
And having answered so I turn once more to those who
sneer at this my city, and I give them back the sneer
and say to them:
Come and show me another city with lifted head singing
so proud to be alive and coarse and strong and cunning.
Flinging magnetic curses amid the toil of piling job on job,
here is a tall bold slugger set vivid against the little soft
cities;
Fierce as a dog with tongue lapping for action, cunning as
a savage pitted against the wilderness,
 Bareheaded,
 Shoveling,
 Wrecking,
 Planning,
 Building, breaking, rebuilding.
Under the smoke, dust all over his mouth, laughing with
white teeth,
Under the terrible burden of destiny laughing as a young
man laughs,
Laughing even as an ignorant fighter laughs who has
never lost a battle,
Bragging and laughing that under his wrist is a pulse, and
under his ribs the heart of the people,
 Laughing!
Laughing the stormy, husky, brawling laughter of Youth,
half-naked, sweating, proud to be Hog Butcher, Tool
Maker, Stacker of Wheat, Player with Railroads and
Freight Handler of the Nation.[1] **99**

Reforming State Governments

Progressives also tried to make state governments more responsive
to the wishes of the people. The most ''progressive'' state by far was
Wisconsin. The leading Wisconsin progressive was Robert M. La
Follette, who was elected governor of the state in 1900.

 La Follette's program was known as the **Wisconsin Idea.** To give

[1]"Chicago" by Carl Sandburg

Robert M. La Follette was the pro-
gressive governor and later senator
from Wisconsin. His strongest adviser
was his wife, Belle Case La Follette,
who studied law and worked for wom-
en's suffrage.

voters more control over who ran for public office, he persuaded the legislature to pass a **direct primary** law. Instead of being chosen by politicians, candidates had to campaign for party nominations in **primary elections.** The people, not the politicians, could then select the candidates who would compete in the final election.

While La Follette was governor, the Wisconsin legislature also passed a law limiting the amount of money candidates for office could spend. Another law restricted the activities of **lobbyists**—those who urge legislatures to pass laws favorable to special interests.

La Follette had great faith in the good judgment of the people. If they were "thoroughly informed," he said, they would always do what was right. La Follette also realized that state government had to perform many tasks which called for special technical knowledge that ordinary citizens did not have.

La Follette believed that complicated matters such as the regulating of railroads and banks and the setting of tax rates should *not* be decided by popular vote. Appointed commissions of experts ought to handle these tasks. This idea was not original with La Follette. There were state boards of education and railroad commissions in nearly every state long before 1900. But the spread of such organizations in the Progressive Era was rapid.

The Wisconsin Idea was copied in other states. Many passed direct primary laws. Some allowed ordinary citizens to sign petitions which would force the legislature to vote on particular bills. Others authorized the initiative, the referendum, and the recall. The **initiative** enables voters to initiate, or propose, laws when the state legislatures have not done so. Under the **referendum** a particular proposal could be placed on the ballot to be decided by the yes or no votes of the people at a regular election. The **recall** allowed voters to remove an elected official before the official's term expired.

Many states responded to the demands of women that they be allowed to vote. By 1915 two thirds of the states permitted women to vote in certain elections, such as for members of school boards. About a dozen states had given women full voting rights by that date.

The National American Women's Suffrage Association led this fight. The president of the association from 1900 to 1904 was Carrie Lane Chapman Catt. She was intelligent and better informed about public issues than the average man. But she could not vote. She had become active in the fight for women's rights in her home state of Iowa in the 1880s and later in the national suffrage movement.

One further progressive effort to give the people more control over elected officials was the **Seventeenth Amendment** to the Constitution, which was ratified in 1913. Article I of the Constitution had provided that United States senators should be elected by members of the state legislatures. Sometimes, such as in the contest in Illinois between Abraham Lincoln and Stephen A. Douglas in 1858, the voters were able to make their wishes clear before the legislators

Point of View

In *Richard Milhous Nixon,* his biographer sees a darker side of reform.

66Intended as tools of popular participation in government, the new and exploitable levers of petition politics allowed well-financed special interest groups and other disciplined factions—those with the price of a public relations firm, the quarter-a-signature for petitions, the budget for advertising—to seize the legislative agenda or punish a foe.99
    Roger Morris, 1990

National Portrait Gallery, detail

Carrie Lane Chapman Catt was painted in 1927 by Mary Foote. Remembered as the founder of the League of Women Voters, Carrie Lane was once the superintendent of schools in Mason City, Iowa.

To call attention to their cause, these women hiked from New York City to Washington, D.C. in 1913.

acted. Often they were not. The Seventeenth Amendment changed the system. Thereafter, senators were to be "elected by the people" of the state.

Social and Economic Reforms

Progressives were making state and local governments more democratic. At the same time they were insisting that these governments do something about the social and economic problems of the times. Many city governments responded by taking over waterworks that had been privately owned. Some extended this policy, sometimes called **municipal socialism,** to the public ownership of streetcar lines and to gas and electric companies.

Not many progressives were **socialists.** Socialists favored government ownership of all the means of production. Most progressives believed in the free enterprise system—that is, the right of a business to take its own course without government controls. Its success or failure lay in how fit it was to survive, argued the Social Darwinists, whom we discussed earlier. But many progressives made an exception for local public utilities. To have more than one privately owned gas company or to set up competing streetcar lines would have been inefficient. Believers in municipal socialism thought the best way to

INTERPRETING HISTORY: The Progressives

At one time or another we have all wondered what makes people do what they do. Historians ask the same question—and sometimes arrive at far different answers. For example, historians differ about what motivated the reformers of the Progressive Movement of 1900–1915.

In *The Age of Reform* (1955) Richard Hofstadter described the leaders of the Progressive Movement. Many were middle-class professionals, such as attorneys, teachers, ministers, and business people. Most were financially comfortable, and some were quite wealthy. But by the turn of the century these people were beginning to feel they were losing their place as society's leaders and decision makers to powerful corporations and newly-rich millionaires.

According to Hofstadter, these reformers did not want to lose influence in their communities. They believed that they knew best what was good for all Americans. So they supported laws that benefited themselves—laws that limited the power of big corporations, cleaned up political corruption at the state and local level, and made all government more responsive to public opinion.

Historian Gabriel Kolko found a different motive for the progressives' actions. In *The Triumph of Conservatism* (1963) Kolko insisted that the progressives were conservatives, not reformers. They did not pass laws that reduced the influence of giant corporations and monopolies. Rather, the laws favored by many progressives were actually less economically dangerous than the cutthroat competition of rival companies. Kolko claims that because the progressives were really conservatives working to preserve the status quo, they missed a unique opportunity to restructure the American economy and society so that all classes would benefit equally.

Professor David P. Thelen offers yet another interpretation. He believed that the progressives presented many types and classes of Americans. In his article "Social Tensions and the Origins of Progressivism" (1969) he points to the impact that the depression of 1893 had on Americans. He argued that the social problems tackled by progressives had been under attack for at least a decade. The depression forced Americans from different walks of life to confront "the failures of industrialism" because these failures threatened their financial security. The result was the broad-based, popular movement for reform that we call the Progressive Era.

Historians develop their own interpretations. Sometimes they agree. More often they disagree, as these historians disagree about what motivated the progressives. One of the most interesting aspects of studying history is that there is often no final answer.

---

protect the public against being overcharged was to have the people, through their local governments, own all public utilities.

The progressives continued the efforts to improve the health and housing of poor city dwellers begun by earlier reformers. In New York City, for example, an improved tenement house law was passed in 1901. Better plumbing and ventilation had to be installed in all new tenements. Older buildings had to be remodeled to meet the new standards. During the Progressive Era more than 40 other cities passed similar tenement house laws.

Conditions in factories also attracted much attention, especially after the terrible tragedy known as the **Triangle Fire.** In 1911 a fire in the Triangle Shirtwaist Company factory on the upper floors of a building in New York City caused the deaths of more than 140 women. After this disaster New York state passed 35 new factory inspection laws. Other states also passed stronger laws to improve the safety of factories. Many began to require manufacturers to insure their workers against accidents.

Reformers   253

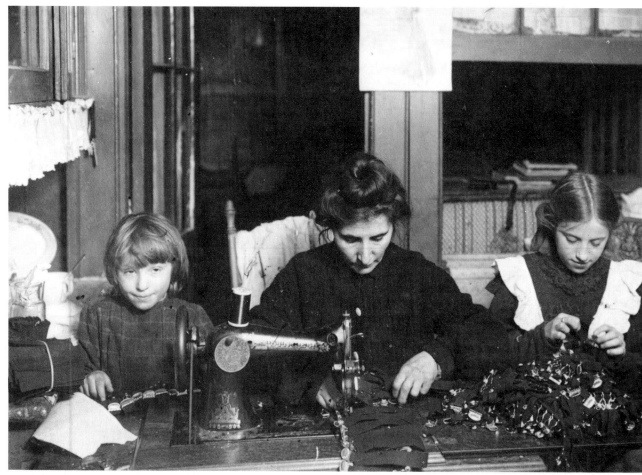

Children who worked at home were safer than those who worked in factories, but the work was repetitive and tedious. And after such long days at the sewing machines, what could they know of the world beyond their tenement dwellings?

Urged on by progressives, most states outlawed the employment of young children in factories. They realized that child labor disrupted schooling, thereby blocking a way out of poverty and condemning those children to a life of often backbreaking and disheartening work. Many states also limited the hours that women and older children could work. Most people agreed that states had the power to regulate child labor. But many employers and workers claimed that laws regulating where or how long adults could work took away the right of individuals to decide such matters for themselves.

The Fourteenth Amendment, these people argued, says a state may not "deprive any person of life, liberty, or property." Laws that say women cannot work more than ten hours a day, or that coal miners cannot work more than eight hours a day, violate this amendment, they claimed. These employers and workers ignored the fact that the Fourteenth Amendment had been added to the Constitution to protect the civil rights of blacks in the southern states after the Civil War.

254   REFORMERS AND THE PROGRESSIVE MOVEMENT

Those favoring reforms argued back by stressing the power of the state to protect the public. Despite the Fourteenth Amendment, criminals can be jailed or fined. Such actions must deprive them of liberty and property in order to protect the public against crime. By the same reasoning, laws that prevent people from working long hours or under unhealthy conditions protect their families and society in general, not only the workers themselves. Reformers even insisted that the state had the right to make laws setting a **minimum wage.** They argued that if workers did not earn a certain minimum wage, their families would suffer. Crime and disease and a general loss of energy would result. This would injure the entire society.

Reformers in the Courts

Both state and federal courts tried to resolve the conflict between the Fourteenth Amendment and the need for state governments to look after the common good. In the case of *Lochner v. New York* (1905) the Supreme Court decided that a New York law limiting bakers to a ten-hour workday was unconstitutional. Such laws were "meddlesome interference with the rights of the individual," the Court ruled. Bakers could work as long as they liked.

Three years later, however, the Supreme Court took the opposite position. This time the case involved an Oregon law that limited women laundry workers to a ten-hour workday. The Court decided that this law was a proper use of a state's power. Many women laundry workers are also mothers, the Court noted. If working too long injured their health, the health of any children they might have would suffer. Therefore, said the Court, "the well-being of the race" would be threatened.

This case, known as *Muller v. Oregon* (1908), is particularly important. For the first time the Supreme Court paid attention to economic and social evidence, not only to legal arguments. A lawyer for Oregon, Louis D. Brandeis, presented a detailed brief, or argument, showing that long hours of work in fact injured the health of women and thus the public health.

The research on which this **Brandeis brief** was based was done by two remarkable women, Florence Kelley and Josephine Goldmark. Kelley and Goldmark were officials of the National Consumers' League. They were deeply interested in many progressive reforms. The material they collected for Brandeis had a direct influence on the justices. More important, it changed the way future cases of this type were argued and decided.

Muller v. Oregon did not end the controversy about the power of a state to protect its weaker members. But by the end of the Progressive Era, many state laws had been passed to help workers and poor people. 🖺

Louis D. Brandeis was called "the people's attorney" after he persuaded the Supreme Court that limited work hours for women was reasonable. In 1916 he himself became a member of the Court.

Return to the Preview & Review on page 245.

Use these questions to guide your reading. Answer the questions after completing Section 3.
Understanding Issues, Events, & Ideas. Use the following words to describe Theodore Roosevelt's actions as a progressive: trust buster, restraint of trade, Northern Securities Case, Hepburn Act, Pure Food and Drug Act, conservation.
1. Why did some progressives want to break up supercompanies? Why did others believe corporations should be allowed to combine?
2. Why is Roosevelt described as an activist president?
3. Why was President Taft expected to carry on Roosevelt's policies?
Thinking Critically. 1. Do you think large corporations today are becoming too powerful? Why or why not? **2.** You are J.P. Morgan. Write a memo to your employees at the Northern Securities Company, explaining why your company is being broken up and giving your view of Roosevelt.

3. GOVERNMENT VERSUS BIG BUSINESS

Progressives and Big Business

The "trust problem" of the 1880s and 1890s continued to be a matter of great concern in the early 1900s. Most progressives looked with some alarm at large corporations—the supercompanies. They argued that supercompanies like U.S. Steel had too much power over important industries. Some sort of government check or control on these large corporations was necessary. But progressives did not agree as to how these giants should be regulated.

Some progressives favored using the Sherman Antitrust Act to break up large combinations into smaller competing businesses. Others argued that big businesses were more efficient than small ones. Competition between them would be dangerous and wasteful. Corporations in the same field should be allowed to combine or to cooperate with one another, these progressives believed. But the government should supervise and regulate their activities. They should not be allowed to use their great size and power to hold down small producers or take advantage of the consuming public.

Roosevelt and the Trusts

During Theodore Roosevelt's first term as president, he developed a reputation for being a **trust buster.** He charged a railroad combination, the Northern Securities Company, with violating the Sherman Antitrust Act.

The Northern Securities Company controlled three railroads—the Great Northern Railroad, which ran from St. Paul, Minnesota, to the West Coast; the Northern Pacific Railroad, another transcontinental line; and the Chicago, Burlington, and Quincy Railroad. These three lines carried most of the rail traffic between Chicago and the Pacific Northwest.

The Northern Securities Company was owned by J. P. Morgan and two railroad tycoons, E. H. Harriman and James J. Hill. Harriman also controlled the Union Pacific and Southern Pacific lines. Roosevelt charged that the Northern Securities Company was so powerful a combination that it caused **restraint of trade** and that it should be broken up.

The **Northern Securities Case** was decided by the Supreme Court in 1904. The Court agreed with Roosevelt. It ordered the combination dissolved. Roosevelt then brought antitrust suits against the meat-packers trust, the tobacco trust, and the Standard Oil trust.

But President Roosevelt did not want to break up all large combinations. There were, he insisted, "good" trusts and "bad" trusts.

(He tended to see things as all bad or all good.) Only the bad ones must be destroyed. Good trusts should be allowed to exist. But they must operate under rules laid down by the government.

In 1903 Roosevelt established a Bureau of Corporations. The bureau was to conduct investigations and issue reports indicating whether or not large corporations were being run properly. When "wrongdoing" was discovered, the bureau should call the evil to the attention of a corporation's executives. If they did not correct their errors voluntarily, their corporations could be broken up under the Sherman Act.

During his second term President Roosevelt became completely convinced that federal regulation was the only practical solution to the problems caused by the growth of big business combinations. In 1906 he persuaded Congress to increase the powers of the Interstate Commerce Commission. Under this law, the **Hepburn Act,** the Commission could inspect the business records of railroad companies to see how much money they were making. It also could fix the maximum rates the railroad lines could charge for moving freight and passengers.

At Roosevelt's urging, Congress also passed the **Pure Food and Drug Act** of 1906 as well as a meat inspection law. Roosevelt had read Sinclair's *The Jungle* and was revolted by its revelations. The Pure Food and Drug Act provided for federal control of the quality of most foods and drugs and for the supervision of slaughterhouses.

Roosevelt and the Presidency

In addition to expanding the government's regulation of businesses, Roosevelt strengthened the powers of the office of the president. His own personality had much to do with this. He was an activist by nature. He had to grit his powerful teeth to control himself whenever

These three titans of industry were owners of the Northern Securities Company. They are, from left to right, J. Pierpont Morgan, Edward Henry Harriman, and James Jerome Hill. The photographer of J. P. Morgan was Edward Steichen, who became an artist of the camera lens.

"Uncle Sam Unmasked" perfectly captures the power of President Roosevelt.

Government Versus Big Business   257

Culver Pictures

Theodore Roosevelt was an extremely popular president. People responded eagerly to his colorful personality. They admired his tremendous energy and his vivid imagination. There was a youthful, almost childlike quality to him. An English friend said of him: "You must always remember that the president is about six." Yet no one could doubt that he was also tough, brave, and public spirited.

"TR" was the first president to be affectionately referred to by his initials. He loved to make visitors go on long hikes with him in the woods around Washington, especially those who were overweight and unused to exercise. He invited the heavyweight champion of the world to the White House so that he could box with him.

Ordinary citizens read about events like these with glee. Newspaper reporters could count on Roosevelt to say something interesting or do something that was newsworthy almost every day. He made their work easy. They liked him and tended to write favorable stories about him.

Another Englishman said of Theodore Roosevelt: "Do you know the two most wonderful things I have seen in your country? Niagara Falls and the President of the United States, both great wonders of nature!" Some observers came to agree with the cartoon on page 257, "Uncle Sam Unmasked."

Point of View

Theodore Roosevelt's biographer explains what a peaceful presidency the Rough Rider had.

> ❝Yet the extraordinary truth about this most pugnacious of Presidents is that his two terms in that office have been completely tranquil. . . . At the same time he has managed, without so much as firing one American pistol, to elevate his country to the giddy heights of world power.❞
>
> From *The Rise of Theodore Roosevelt*, Edmund Morris, 1979

Congress or the courts or some state governor was dealing with an important problem.

Life in a large industrial country like the United States had become so complicated that Roosevelt believed decision making had to be centralized. The president was the logical person to make the decisions. Large elected legislatures like Congress were inefficient, he claimed. They could not "meet the new and complex needs of the times."

As early as 1902 Roosevelt involved himself in a national coal strike by forcing mine owners and miners into arbitration. Today presidents routinely bring pressure to bear on employers and workers when strikes threaten to disrupt the economy. But it had never been dealt with as Roosevelt did. He threatened to take over the mines unless the owners agreed to a settlement. Then he appointed a special commission to work out the terms to end the dispute.

Because he was a great nature lover, Roosevelt was particularly interested in **conservation** of the nation's natural resources. He used his power as president very effectively in this area. He did not object to allowing lumber companies to cut down trees on government lands. But he believed in scientific forestry. Bypassing Congress, he placed large forest areas in federal reserves by executive order. Reserved land could not be claimed or purchased by special interests. But it could be leased to lumber companies. Their cutting, however, was strictly controlled by government experts.

Roosevelt applied the same principle to resources such as coal, waterpower, and grazing lands. He did a great deal to focus public attention on the importance of conserving natural resources and protecting the natural environment. In this respect he was a typical progressive. He assumed that when the people were informed, they would bring pressure on their representatives to do the right thing.

William Howard Taft

Roosevelt's views about federal regulation of business and about presidential power eventually caused a split in the Republican party. They also divided the Progressive Movement.

When he completed his second term as president, Roosevelt did not run again. Instead he used his influence to get the Republican nomination for his close friend William Howard Taft. Taft was easily elected, defeating William Jennings Bryan, who was running for president for the third and last time.

Taft was from Cincinnati, where he had been a federal judge. After the Spanish-American War he had moved from the court of appeals to the post of governor general of the Philippine Islands. In 1904 Roosevelt had appointed him secretary of war.

By the time he became president, Taft weighed over 300 pounds. He was good natured. He had an excellent sense of humor. When he laughed, his belly shook like the well-known bowlful of jelly. But Taft was not a success as president, and his great weight was partly to blame.

Taft found it hard to get all his work done. Because he was so overweight, he needed much rest and relaxation. Further, he was a poor politician. Theodore Roosevelt had often been able to keep both sides happy by taking a middle position on controversial questions. When Taft took a middle position, he usually made both sides angry with him.

Taft tried to continue the policies of the Roosevelt administration. He supported a new law to further increase the powers of the Interstate Commerce Commission. He added more forest lands to the national reserves. He also continued Roosevelt's policy of attacking "bad" trusts under the Sherman Act.

Taft allowed conservative Republicans to influence his policies in many ways. He bungled a well-meant attempt to get Congress to lower the tariffs on manufactured goods. There was a nasty fight within his administration over conservation policy between Secretary of the Interior Richard A. Ballinger and Gifford Pinchot, the chief forester of the department. The controversy was over Alaskan coal lands. Taft sided with Ballinger and dismissed Pinchot. He was probably correct in doing so. But Pinchot then persuaded ex-president Roosevelt that Ballinger and the president were not true friends of conservation. 🖅

William Howard Taft, like the other presidents of the United States, had his portrait painted while he was in the White House.

Return to the Preview & Review on page 256.

Government Versus Big Business 259

Preview & Review

Use these questions to guide your reading. Answer the questions after completing Section 4. **Understanding Issues, Events, & Ideas.** Explain how President Wilson's program continued the spirit of reform, using the following words: Progressive party, Bull Moose party, New Nationalism, welfare state, New Freedom, Underwood Tariff, income tax, Sixteenth Amendment, Federal Reserve Act, Federal Reserve Board, Clayton Antitrust Act, Federal Trade Commission.

1. Why did ex-president Roosevelt form the Progressive party? What did Roosevelt mean by the New Nationalism?
2. How did Woodrow Wilson's New Freedom differ from Roosevelt's New Nationalism?
3. Why did Wilson win the presidency so easily?

Thinking Critically. Of the legislative acts passed under Wilson's New Freedom, which do you think is the most important? Why?

The Progressive Party

Roosevelt did not want to interfere with Taft's handling of the presidency. Nor did he want to second-guess him. As soon as Taft was inaugurated, Roosevelt went off to hunt big game in Africa. But when he returned to the United States in 1910, he quickly came into conflict with Taft. He soon decided that Taft was not really a progressive. Taft was not using the powers of his office forcefully, the way Roosevelt had. Roosevelt decided that Taft was a weak leader.

In particular Roosevelt objected to the president's antitrust policy. When Taft ordered an antitrust suit against the U.S. Steel Corporation, Roosevelt was furious. In his opinion U.S. Steel was a "good" trust. Its officers had cooperated faithfully with the Bureau of Corporations.

By 1911 all sorts of Republican leaders, conservatives as well as progressives, were telling Roosevelt that Taft was so unpopular that he could not be reelected in 1912. They urged Roosevelt to seek the nomination. Roosevelt finally agreed. He entered and won nearly all the Republican primaries.

However, there were far fewer presidential primaries in 1912 than there are today. In most states party professionals chose the convention delegates, and Taft got nearly all of them. When the Republican convention met in June, the Taft delegates were in the majority. The president was renominated on the first ballot.

Roosevelt was now ready for a fight. Republican progressives urged him to make the run for president. He agreed to form a new **Progressive party** and seek the presidency under its banner. Large numbers of religious people, who had embraced the idea of democratic change in politics, supported the new party. They rallied to "Onward Christian Soldier," a favorite Protestant hymn.

In his enthusiasm for the coming battle for the White House, Roosevelt announced that he felt "as strong as a bull moose." Cartoonists promptly began to use a moose as the symbol for the Progressive party to go along with the Republican elephant and the Democratic donkey. Soon people were referring to the party as the **Bull Moose party.**

Roosevelt's 1912 platform was ahead of its time. Corporations should be brought "under complete federal control," he said. Presidential candidates should be chosen by the people in primary elections, not by machine politicians at conventions. He also came out for a law to insure workers who were injured on the job, to assure a minimum wage for women, and to end child labor. He supported a Constitutional amendment giving women the right to vote.

Roosevelt called his program the **New Nationalism.** By nationalism he meant a stronger and more active national government. He

was thinking of something similar to what we today call the **welfare state.** The government should be prepared to do "whatever . . . the public welfare may require," he said.

The Election of 1912

Roosevelt hoped to attract Democratic as well as Republican voters to the Progressive party. But since he had been a lifelong Republican, the new party was sure to draw most of its support from Republicans. This presented Democrats with a golden opportunity. With Republican voters split between Taft and Roosevelt, the Democrats' chances of winning the election were excellent. All they needed to nail down the victory was an attractive presidential candidate.

"Come Moosie," shows the Bull Moose of Roosevelt's third party. Why are both the Democrats and the Republicans eager that the bull moose eat their oats?

A Progressive Victory   **261**

Woodrow Wilson studied law and opened a law office in Atlanta. But he soon returned to college to study history and political science. How did the subjects Wilson studied help prepare him for public office?

The struggle for the nomination at the Democratic convention was hard fought. The person who won it was Woodrow Wilson, the governor of New Jersey.

Wilson was a newcomer to politics. He had been born in Virginia in 1856. After graduating from Princeton College and studying law, he studied political science and became a professor. Most of his teaching was done at Princeton, where he was very popular. In 1902 he had been elected president of Princeton. As president he introduced several important reforms in education. He hired more teachers and encouraged closer contacts between professors and students. He also added a large number of courses to the curriculum.

In 1910, however, Wilson resigned as president of Princeton to run for governor of New Jersey on the Democratic ticket. He was elected. He immediately proposed a number of progressive reforms. More important, he displayed remarkable political skill in getting the state legislature to enact his proposals into law. This success explains how he defeated the other Democratic presidential hopefuls in 1912.

The Democratic program was in the progressive tradition. Wilson called it the **New Freedom.** The *objectives* of the New Freedom were quite similar to those of the New Nationalism. The *methods* proposed were quite different.

Wilson did not believe in close government regulation of big business. Instead he wished to rely on antitrust laws to break up monopolies. Unlike Roosevelt, who thought that competition was wasteful, Wilson thought competition made business more efficient. The federal government should pass laws defining fair competition, Wilson believed. Any company or individuals who broke those laws should be severely punished.

Wilson also disliked Roosevelt's New Nationalism because he thought it would make government too big and let it interfere too much in the affairs of citizens. He opposed federal laws that told large corporations how to manage their affairs. He also opposed laws that gave special privileges to labor unions or farmers or women or any other group.

In a way, Wilson wanted the federal government to act like the referee in a football game. The government should enforce the rules of the game strictly but evenhandedly. It should keep a sharp eye on the players and penalize any team that broke the rules. But it should not try to call the plays or choose sides.

A Victory for Reform

Wilson easily won the election of 1912. He received 435 electoral votes to Roosevelt's 88 and Taft's 8. However, he got less than 42 percent of the popular vote. Slightly over half the voters cast their ballots for either Roosevelt or Taft. In other words, Wilson was elected because of the breakup of the Republican party.

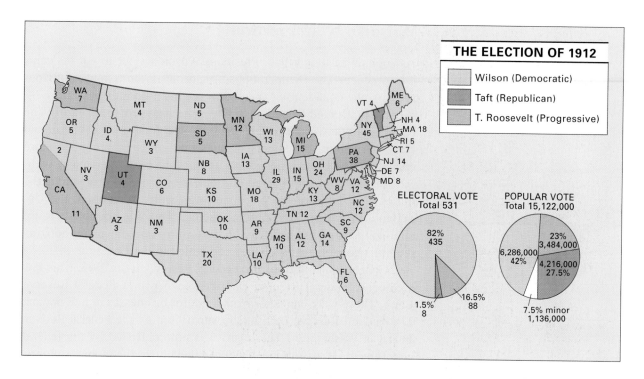

THE ELECTION OF 1912

Wilson (Democratic)
Taft (Republican)
T. Roosevelt (Progressive)

WA 7
OR 5
ID 4
MT 4
ND 5
MN 12
WI 13
MI 15
VT 4
ME 6
NH 4
MA 18
NY 45
RI 5
CT 7
WY 3
SD 5
IA 13
OH 24
PA 38
NJ 14
DE 7
MD 8
NV 3
UT 4
NB 8
IL 29
IN 15
WV 8
VA 12
CA 11
CO 6
KS 10
MO 18
KY 13
NC 12
AZ 3
NM 3
OK 10
AR 9
TN 12
SC 9
TX 20
LA 10
MS 10
AL 12
GA 14
FL 6
2

ELECTORAL VOTE
Total 531

82%
435

1.5%
8

16.5%
88

POPULAR VOTE
Total 15,122,000

23%
3,484,000

6,286,000
42%

4,216,000
27.5%

7.5% minor
1,136,000

Nevertheless, the election was an overwhelming victory for progressivism and reform. Together, Wilson and Roosevelt received almost 70 percent of the popular vote. In addition almost 900,000 voters, about 6 percent of the total, cast their ballots for the Socialist party. The Socialists were demanding government ownership of railroads, banks, and "all large-scale industries."

The Socialist presidential candidate was Eugene V. Debs, the leader of the railroad workers who had been jailed for his role in the Pullman strike in 1894. While in prison, Debs had done a good deal of reading about government and politics. He became a socialist. He had run for president on the Socialist ticket in 1904 and in 1908, each time receiving about 400,000 votes. In 1912 his vote more than doubled. Clearly the American people were in a reform-minded mood.

Was the election a victory for Wilson's New Freedom philosophy? The answer to this question is unclear. The argument between Wilson and Roosevelt was the same one that Jefferson had with Hamilton in the 1790s about the role of the federal government. On the one hand, the large Socialist vote suggests increased support for the Hamilton (and Roosevelt) "big government" position. On the other hand, both Taft and Wilson believed, as Jefferson had, in competition rather than government regulations. Both promised to enforce the antitrust law strictly. When the Taft and Wilson votes are combined, they come to about 70 percent of the total.

Probably most citizens did not have a firm opinion about how reform should be accomplished. Most were voting for "a reformer" but not for a particular program.

LEARNING FROM MAPS. *Roosevelt's nomination by the Progressive party may have cost the Republicans the election of 1912. Roosevelt captured several states outright. How did the unit rule of the electoral college make the split of the Republican party that much more damaging?*

Wilson's New Freedom

As soon as he took office, President Wilson set out to put his ideas into practice. The Democrats had majorities in both houses of Congress, so he confidently expected to see his proposals passed.

He first urged Congress to lower the high protective tariff. The resulting **Underwood Tariff** of 1913 allowed food products, iron and steel, agricultural machinery—things that could be produced more cheaply in the United States than abroad—to enter the country without any tariff at all. For goods that needed some protection, the duties were lowered but not done away with. In addition, the Underwood Act provided for an **income tax.** This was possible because another progressive reform, the **Sixteenth Amendment** authorizing federal income taxes, had just been added to the Constitution.

Congress also passed the **Federal Reserve Act** in 1913. This law created 12 Federal Reserve Districts, each with a Federal Reserve Bank. These were banks for banks, not for businesses or individuals. The Federal Reserve Banks were supervised by the **Federal Reserve Board** in Washington. The board was not controlled by the federal government. It was an independent regulator of the money supply.

All national banks were members of the Federal Reserve system. All state banks that met certain requirements could also join. In times of depression when weak banks were on the brink of failing, Federal Reserve Banks could transfer money to prevent losses. The Federal Reserve system also made it possible to put more money into circulation to stimulate the economy or take some out to slow it down.

In practice the Federal Reserve system did not work quite so smoothly. It was not always easy to know whether to stimulate the economy or slow it down. Still, the Federal Reserve was a great improvement over the old national banking system established during the Civil War. It is still in operation today.

Then, in 1914, Congress passed the **Clayton Antitrust Act.** This law made it illegal for directors of one corporation to be directors of other corporations in the same field. It provided that the officers and managers of a company that violated the antitrust laws could be held personally responsible for the violations. It also stated that labor unions were *not* to be considered "combinations . . . in restraint of trade under the antitrust laws."

In 1914 Congress also created the **Federal Trade Commission.** This Commission conducted investigations of large corporations. If it found them acting unfairly toward competitors or the public, it issued "cease and desist orders," making them stop.

The Federal Trade Commission was closer in spirit to Theodore Roosevelt's New Nationalism than to the New Freedom. So was the Federal Reserve system. Wilson was not a rigid believer in old-style competition. Like Roosevelt, he was willing to use more than one technique in order to check the power of big business.

Return to the Preview & Review on page 260.

5. LIMITS OF PROGRESSIVISM

Restrictions on Immigration

By the end of 1914 the Progressive Movement had accomplished many political, social, and economic reforms. But the progressives had prejudices and blind spots that limited their achievements. Most were not very sympathetic to immigrants during a time of heavy immigration. Some years at the height of the progressive period, more than 1 million newcomers settled in the United States. In 1907 Americans demanded that the government stem the tide of Japanese immigration. In 1907 the United States and Japan reached what is known as the **Gentlemen's Agreement.** Japan promised not to allow unskilled workers to come to the United States.

Progressives who were alarmed about corruption in politics blamed the recent immigrants. These people cast a large proportion of the votes that kept corrupt bosses in power. Social workers and many others who were trying to help the poor thought that too many immigrants were crowding into the slums. They argued that the famous American **melting pot** could not absorb so many people so quickly. They were afraid that the character of American life would be undermined unless immigration was somehow limited.

Even Uncle Sam seems disturbed by the horde of new arrivals—"Anarchists in Chicago" and "Socialists in New York."

Use these questions to guide your reading. Answer the questions after completing Section 5.
Understanding Issues, Events, & Ideas. Explain the limits of progressivism, using these words: Gentlemen's Agreement, melting pot, Niagara Movement, National Association for the Advancement of Colored People, Great War.
1. Why were progressives not sympathetic to immigrants? What was the attitude of most progressives toward blacks? Why?
2. How did Booker T. Washington continue to work for black people? How did William E. B. Du Bois work for blacks?
3. What event slowed the pace of progressive reform?
Thinking Critically. Suppose you are a speaker at the Niagara Falls meeting of 1905. What demands would you make? How would you expect the government to meet those demands?

The Granger Collection

STRATEGIES FOR SUCCESS

COMPOSING PARAGRAPHS

You will often be asked to write a description or explanation. To do so effectively, you must organize your thoughts into paragraphs. A paragraph consists of several sentences that state a main idea and add an explanation or supporting details. For the paragraph to communicate your message, these sentences should be presented in a logical sequence.

How to Write a Paragraph

To write a paragraph, follow these guidelines.

1. **State a main idea.** Develop a clear statement of the main point you want your readers to understand.
2. **Support your main idea.** Include sentences that add detail or interest. These sentences should explain, support, or expand the main idea of the paragraph.
3. **Explain key terms.** Define or explain any special words you use in the paragraph. This can be done best in a separate sentence within the paragraph.
4. **Connect the sentences.** Make sure that your paragraph has a beginning and an end. Also make sure that all the information is tied logically together.

Applying the Strategy

Read the paragraph in the next column. The main idea is stated in the first sentence: *Progressives who were alarmed about corruption in politics blamed recent immigrants.* This main idea is supported by the sentence: *These people cast a large proportion of the votes that kept corrupt bosses in power.* The other sentences in the paragraph expand on the situation faced by immigrants: *Social workers and many others who were trying to help the poor thought that too many immigrants were crowding into the slums. They argued that the famous American melting pot could not absorb so many people so quickly. They were afraid that the character of American life would be undermined unless immigration was somehow limited.* How would you restate the main idea of the paragraph?

Progressives who were alarmed about corruption in politics blamed the recent immigrants. These people cast a large proportion of the votes that kept corrupt bosses in power. Social workers and many others who were trying to help the poor thought that too many immigrants were crowding into the slums. They argued that the famous American melting pot could not absorb so many people so quickly. They were afraid that the character of American life would be undermined unless immigration was somehow limited.

Culver Pictures

For independent practice, see Practicing the Strategy on page 272.

Equality in the Progressive Era

The most glaring weakness of the progressive reformers was their attitude toward racial problems. The Progressive Era was probably the low point in the history of racial relations after the Civil War.

A few progressives believed in racial equality. But most believed that blacks were entitled at best to second-class citizenship. The most common attitude was that of the Alabama progressive who said that blacks were meant "to be protected by Government, rather than to be the directors of Government." Most felt the same way about American Indians.

Most progressives claimed to want to help blacks. But they had little understanding of the effects of racial discrimination on black people. Theodore Roosevelt once invited Booker T. Washington to have a meal with him at the White House. When newspapers reported that the president had eaten with a black man, Roosevelt was flooded with complaints. Instead of defending his invitation, Roosevelt practically apologized for it. Washington had just happened to be there on public business at mealtime. Roosevelt never invited another black person to dine at the White House.

Still, the early 20th century marked a turning point in the history of racial relations. Booker T. Washington remained an important figure. He raised a great deal of money for black schools. He worked cleverly behind the scenes to get political jobs for blacks and to fight racial discrimination cases in the courts. However, he was no longer the only significant black public figure. Younger leaders were beginning to reject his whole approach to the racial problem.

William E. B. Du Bois was the most important of the new black leaders. Du Bois grew up in Massachusetts and proved to be a brilliant and hardworking student. He won scholarships, first to Fisk, a college for African Americans, and then to Harvard, where in 1895 he was awarded a Ph.D. in history.

Du Bois was proud of being black. "Beauty is black," he said. He urged people to be proud of their African origins and culture. He set out to make other blacks realize that they must speak out for their rights. If they did not, they would actually be inferior, he warned. The trouble with Booker T. Washington is that he "apologizes for injustice," Du Bois wrote in 1903. Blacks will never get their "reasonable rights" unless they stop "voluntarily throwing them away," Du Bois said. He continued:

> " While it is a great truth to say that the Negro must strive and strive mightily to help himself, it is equally true that unless his striving be not simply seconded, but rather aroused and encouraged, by the initiative action of the richer and wiser environing group [whites and wealthy African Americans], he cannot hope for success.

Booker T. Washington remained a powerful leader of African Americans as a younger generation joined the struggle for equality.

In his failure to realize and impress this last point, Mr. Washington is especially to be criticized. His doctrine has tended to make the whites, North and South, shift the burden of the problem to the Negro's shoulders and stand aside as critical and rather pessimistic spectators; when in fact the burden belongs to the nation, and the hands of none of us are clean if we bend not our energies to righting these great wrongs.[1] 🙶

In 1905, at a meeting at Niagara Falls, Canada, Du Bois and a few other black leaders began the **Niagara Movement.** They demanded equality of economic and educational opportunities for blacks, an end to racial segregation, and protection of the right to vote. And they closed with this:

🙶 *Duties:* And while we are demanding, and ought to demand, and will continue to demand the rights enumerated [listed] above, God forbid that we should ever forget to urge corresponding duties upon our people:

The duty to vote.
The duty to respect the rights of others.
The duty to work.
The duty to obey the laws.
The duty to be clean and orderly.
The duty to send our children to school.
The duty to respect ourselves, even as we respect others.

This statement, complaint, and prayer we submit to the American people, and Almighty God.[2] 🙶

This portrait of Du Bois was made in 1925. What did Du Bois mean by "beauty is black?"

Then in 1909, Du Bois joined with seven white liberals to form the **National Association for the Advancement of Colored People (NAACP).** Du Bois became editor of the NAACP journal, *The Crisis.*

The NAACP's chief purpose in its early years was to try to put an end to lynching. Lynching was a terrible American problem. Ku Klux Klan mobs had killed many blacks during the Reconstruction period, and western vigilantes had hanged large numbers of gunslingers, horse thieves, and outlaws.

During the 1880s and 1890s about 150 to 200 persons a year were lynched. Many were white. Of 638 persons lynched between 1882 and 1886, 411 were whites. Throughout the Progressive Era about 100 persons were lynched each year in the United States. More than 90 percent of the victims were black. Lynching became a means of controlling and frightening blacks. The NAACP crusade to end lynching followed the effort of African American journalist Ida B. Wells, who started her campaign against lynchings in 1901. She studied the

[1]From *The Souls of Black Folk* by W.E.B. Du Bois
[2]From *The Niagara Movement Declaration of Principles* in *Afro-American History: Primary Sources,* edited by Thomas R. Frazier

Johnson Publications

Leaders of the Niagara Movement posed for this photograph in front of a studio backdrop after their meeting in 1905. W.E.B. Du Bois is second from right in the second row.

records of hundreds of lynchings and found that most of the victims were killed for "no offense, unknown offense, offenses not criminal, misdemeanors, and crimes not capital."

The NAACP did not succeed in reducing the number of black lynchings, which remained high until well into the 1920s. Yet the organization grew rapidly both in members and in influence. By the end of the Progressive Era more and more blacks were speaking out strongly for their rights.

The Great War

After 1914 the pace of progressive reform slowed. President Wilson announced that the major goals of the New Freedom had been reached. Former president Roosevelt turned his attention to other matters.

This does not mean that the national mood that we call progressivism came to an end. Such movements rarely stop suddenly. Indeed, the basic beliefs of the progressives still influence American life. But in 1914 what was soon to be called the **Great War** broke out in Europe. After 1914 that war turned the thoughts of Americans from local problems to international ones. 🖅

Return to the Preview & Review on page 265.

LINKING HISTORY & GEOGRAPHY

IDENTIFYING GEOGRAPHIC REGIONS

In the vocabulary of geographers the word *region* is very important. It is used to describe parts of the earth that share certain specific features. These features may be physical, such as climate, soil, or vegetation. They may be cultural, such as language, economic activity, or cultural heritage. Or, the region may represent a combination of both. Whatever the qualities used to identify the region, it is the commonality of features that make an area a region. Understanding how regions are identified is an important geographic skill.

The American West

1. What are some of the common images of the American West?

One of the regions of the United States that Americans today are most familiar with is the one that is labeled "The West." The very word *west* conjures up an entire collection of images in the minds of Americans. These images usually include both physical features—mountains, deserts, bright blue skies, buffalo, cattle, and cactuses—and cultural features—Indians, hearty cowboys, villainous outlaws, long barbed-wire fences, waving fields of wheat, and gold mines.

You should note, however, that all these images of the geographic region we call the West are comparatively recent. Most are scarcely more than a century old. What, then, was "the West" to the first explorers and settlers who arrived on the shores of North America in the 1500s and 1600s?

The Importance of Point of View

2. Why has the geographic label "West" referred to so many different regions during America's history?

As the brave European explorers and settlers first turned their eyes toward the New World, even the Atlantic Ocean was the West to them. When they stepped off their ships on the eastern seaboard, the West must have been just a short distance inland or the not-so-distant horizon.

The West, then, like all regions, is really a mental function. A region is what and where we *think* it is, and its boundaries are the boundaries we place upon it. What makes up a region depends greatly on our point of view. As a result, through the centuries there have been many "Wests" in the minds of the American people.

The First American West

3. Where was the first area of America labeled "the West"?

The first of the Wests that colonists spoke about and labeled on maps was the territory just beyond the Appalachian Mountains. Settlers quickly filled the lands between the Atlantic and the Appalachians, looking across the mountainous spine to the frontier—the West. Rugged terrain, hostile Indians and French colonists, and British laws kept many from crossing the mountains until after the Revolutionary War. As soon as the war was over, settlers began pouring across the Appalachians, and Congress set about organizing these "western territories." In 1785 and 1787 laws established what they called the Northwest Territory.

A New "West"

4. What new area became the West?

As the westward movement of American people continued, the concept of the West moved with them. People pushed beyond the Northwest Territory and in time this first American west became known as "The Old Northwest." And for good reason. By the late 1830s and early 1840s another Northwest—the Oregon Territory—was being settled. This "new" Northwest, named for its geographic location, was soon labeled "The Pacific Northwest."

Actually the term "Old Northwest" never really did occupy a prominent place in the minds of its inhabitants or other Americans. More frequently another regional label was used—"The Middle West," or more simply stated, "The Midwest." As pioneers settled the lands west of the Mississippi, the "Old West" just beyond the Appalachians was now between the East and the frontier. Such labels demonstrate an important geographic concept: it is people, not the compass or the map, that create regional labels.

This concept is illustrated quite simply. What if the United States had been settled by explorers landing along the West Coast. What regional titles would have been applied to the land between the coasts? Would the region that we now call the Middle West have been called the Middle East? (If so, that would make the Rocky Mountain states the Near East!) All this shows that regional labels reflect a particular point of view.

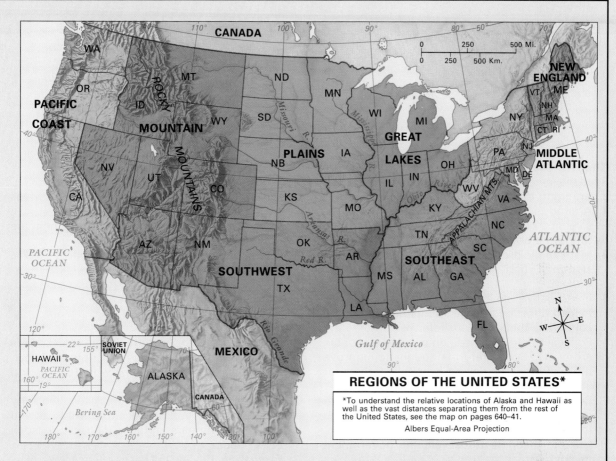

The map shows Regions of the United States with labels including CANADA, WA, OR, ID, MT, ND, MN, WI, MI, NY, NEW ENGLAND (VT, ME, NH, MA, CT, RI), PACIFIC COAST, ROCKY MOUNTAIN, WY, SD, NB, IA, GREAT LAKES, OH, PA, NJ, MIDDLE ATLANTIC, NV, UT, CO, KS, MO, IL, IN, WV, MD, DE, VA, CA, AZ, NM, OK, AR, KY, TN, NC, SC, SOUTHEAST, ATLANTIC OCEAN, SOUTHWEST, TX, MS, AL, GA, LA, FL, PACIFIC OCEAN, Gulf of Mexico, MEXICO, HAWAII, SOVIET UNION, ALASKA, CANADA, Bering Sea, Rio Grande, Missouri R., Mississippi R., Ohio River, Arkansas R., Red R., APPALACHIAN MTS., ROCKY MOUNTAINS

REGIONS OF THE UNITED STATES*

*To understand the relative locations of Alaska and Hawaii as well as the vast distances separating them from the rest of the United States, see the map on pages 640–41.

Albers Equal-Area Projection

The Concept of Regions

5. Why do regional labels depend on your point of view?

In the late 1840s and 1850s prospectors and entrepreneurs flocked to California, Colorado, and Nevada, adding still another "West" to the map of the United States! How could the same geographic term be applied to so many different areas? Because, like all regions, labeling depends on point of view. What was the West to colonists arriving along the East Coast was now *back East* to California miners!

So the term "the West"—confusing in its many uses—was applied to different areas as Americans settled the land. "The West" was a point just beyond the frontier. Americans soon learned that compass direction alone did not determine the limits and labels of regions. Instead, point of view, changing as the nation grew, became the most important element in labeling regions in America.

Regions of the United States Today

6. Into what regions do geographers divide the United States today?

Geographers use a variety of criteria to divide the United States into regions today. For that reason, not all regional divisions are identical. The map illustrates one of the most common regional divisions of the nation. What common features do you think were the basis for each of these regions?

Applying Your Knowledge

Your class will create a regional map of the United States that differs from the one on this page. After a class discussion identifies the new criteria for grouping the states, groups will recommend regional groupings. A volunteer from each group should then explain the group's reasoning. The class will then reach a consensus and create a map illustrating the new regional groupings.

CHAPTER 6 REVIEW

1890
Sherman Antitrust Act

1900
La Follette elected in Wisconsin

1901
Morgan forms U.S. Stee[l]

Chapter Summary
Read the statements below. Choose one, and write a paragraph explaining its importance.
1. Around the turn of the century a new progressive mood swept the country. Reformers hoped to make a better world.
2. Many of the problems attacked by progressives stemmed from rapid industrial and urban growth.
3. Investigative journalists called muckrakers helped publicize political, industrial, and social conditions that called for reforms.
4. Political reforms focused on city and state governments. Social reforms sought to improve the welfare of the people, particularly the poor and workers.
5. Reformers in government tackled the problem of big business. Many supercompanies had formed trusts and had eliminated competition. Led by Theodore Roosevelt, the government began to break the trusts.
6. Although Taft continued many of Roosevelt's reform programs, he was not as effective. With the Republican party split between Taft and Roosevelt, the Democrats won the election of 1912.
7. President Wilson's New Freedom continued the progressive direction in government.
8. Although the progressive spirit continued in America, the Great War in Europe ended the Progressive Era.

Reviewing Chronological Order
Number your paper 1–5. Then study the time line above and place the following events in the order in which they happened by writing the first next to 1, the second next to 2, and so on.
1. Morgan forms U.S. Steel
2. La Follette elected In Wisconsin
3. *The Shame of the Cities*
4. Progressive, Bull Moose, party formed
5. Pure Food and Drug Act

Understanding Main Ideas
1. What was the Progressive Movement?
2. What national problems did the progressives hope to solve?
3. How and why did Roosevelt strengthen the powers of the presidency?
4. How was the result of the election of 1912 a victory for reform?
5. What were the views of most progressives toward immigrants and blacks?

Thinking Critically
1. **Relating Past to Present**. If the muckrakers were investigating problems in American society today, what do you think would be the top five problems on their list?
2. **Synthesizing**. You are a progressive in the early 1900s. How do you propose to make local and state governments more responsive to society's needs?
3. **Evaluating**. Review the cases of *Lochner v. New York* and *Muller v. Oregon*. Do you think a feminist in 1908 would have supported the Court's decision regarding working women? Why or why not?

Writing About History: Persuasive
The progressive spirit continues in America. Newspapers and news magazines often carry articles about problems similar to those tackled by the progressives at the turn of the century. Choose a current issue that calls for reform. Write a letter to your representative in Congress stating your views and persuading him or her to side with you.

Practicing the Strategy
Review the strategy on page 266.
Composing Paragraphs. Reread Section 1 of this chapter on pages 240–44. Then write a paragraph of at least six sentences restating the main idea and supporting it.

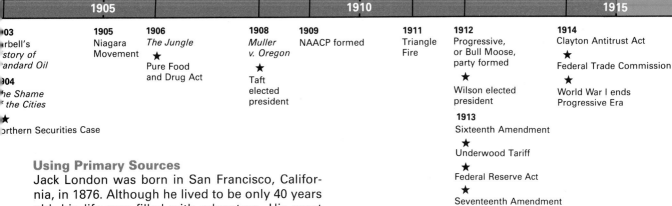

1903
rbell's
story of
andard Oil

1904
he Shame
f the Cities
★
orthern Securities Case

1905
Niagara
Movement

1906
The Jungle
★
Pure Food
and Drug Act

1908
*Muller
v. Oregon*
★
Taft
elected
president

1909
NAACP formed

1911
Triangle
Fire

1912
Progressive,
or Bull Moose,
party formed
★
Wilson elected
president

1913
Sixteenth Amendment
★
Underwood Tariff
★
Federal Reserve Act
★
Seventeenth Amendment

1914
Clayton Antitrust Act
★
Federal Trade Commission
★
World War I ends
Progressive Era

Using Primary Sources

Jack London was born in San Francisco, California, in 1876. Although he lived to be only 40 years old, his life was filled with adventure. His most popular novels, *The Call of the Wild* and *White Fang,* were set in the Klondike, which is part of Yukon Territory in northwestern Canada. There London spent time as a gold prospector. But on April 17, 1906, Jack London was in San Francisco. The following excerpt is from an article he wrote for a local newspaper. As you read, think about the effects of natural disasters on the people they strike.

> *On Wednesday morning at a quarter past five came the earthquake. A minute later the flames were leaping upward. In a dozen different quarters south of Market Street, in the working-class ghetto, and in the factories, fires started. There was no opposing the flames. There was no organization, no communication. All the cunning adjustments of a twentieth-century city had been smashed by the earthquake. The streets were humped into ridges and depressions and piled with debris of fallen walls. The steel rails were twisted into perpendicular and horizontal angles. The telephone and telegraph systems were disrupted. And the great water mains had burst. All the shrewd contrivances and safeguards of man had been thrown out of gear by thirty seconds' twitching of the earth crust.*

1. From London's account, what seems to be the biggest problem faced by the city?
2. What effect will the damage caused by the earthquake have on the people who live in San Francisco?
3. What does the last sentence suggest about people and nature?

Linking History & Geography

Many people were horrified at the abuse the natural environment had taken. They became determined to conserve natural resources and protect the environment. To understand the situation the progressives found so shocking, answer these questions.

1. What effect had the booming Industrial Revolution on America's natural resources?
2. How was urbanization affecting the natural landscape of America?
3. Many business owners and builders claimed that resources were a God-given gift to the people who owned the land. The government countered by saying such gifts belonged to all Americans—especially future generations. To use them up or to destroy the natural setting was not fair to others. Which argument do you support? Explain your reasoning.

Enriching Your Study of History

1. **Individual Project.** Read further in your library and other American history books into the life of Theodore Roosevelt. Report on one of the following topics, or on a topic of your own:
Roosevelt the Young Naturalist
Roosevelt the Rancher
Roosevelt the Rough Rider
Roosevelt the Trust Buster
Roosevelt the Conservationist
Roosevelt the Family Man
2. **Cooperative Project.** Groups in your class will collect examples of contemporary journalism and classify them as objective or biased reporting. Your group will find stories in magazines and newspapers, then exchange them with the collections of another group. Compare your classifications, and reach a consensus.

Chapter 6 Review   273

UNIT TWO REVIEW

Summing Up and Predicting

Read the summary of the main ideas in Unit Two. Choose one statement, then write a paragraph predicting its outcome or future effect.
1. In the late 1800s the United States began to acquire territories overseas.
2. For partly humanitarian and partly imperialistic reasons, the United States became involved in the Spanish-American War.
3. The United States secured trading rights in Japan and China, and built the Panama Canal, and issued the Roosevelt Corollary to the Monroe Doctrine.
4. As the progressive mood swept America around 1900, reformers attacked problems in industry, cities, politics, and society.
5. Muckrakers were journalists who called attention to areas needing reform.
6. Theodore Roosevelt was an active reformer, leading the way as a trustbuster.
7. Taft and Wilson followed in Roosevelt's footsteps as reformers.

Connecting Ideas

1. As you have learned, Filipinos and others who came under American control in the late 1800s protested that control. Why do you think they did not want the United States to take control? What were some benefits for those areas controlled by the U.S.?
2. What reforms begun by the progressives at the turn of the century are continuing today?
3. Scandals and corruption in government have been widely publicized in recent years, as they were in the early 1900s. Do you think there will always be corruption in government? Why or why not?

Practicing Critical Thinking

1. **Evaluating.** In 1977 the United States and Panama signed a treaty returning control of the canal zone to Panama in the year 2000. What are the risks of turning the canal zone over to Panama? Do you agree with this action? Explain your reasoning.
2. **Synthesizing.** You are a turn-of-the-century progressive who has been transported by a time machine into the 1990s. How would you solve the problem of homelessness in America?

3. **Drawing Conclusions.** Do you agree with Roosevelt, who thought competition in business was wasteful, or with Wilson, who thought it made business more efficient? Why?

Exploring History Together

1. Working in groups, your class will assemble a notebook on the key people who helped build the Panama Canal. Include brief biographies of Theodore Roosevelt, Philippe Bunau-Varilla, Carlos Juan Finlay, Walter Reed, William Gorgas, George Goethals, David Galliard, and William Howard Taft. Donate your notebook to the school library.
2. You know that a spirit of reform swept the United States at the turn of the 20th century. Now another century approaches. Imagine you are filled with the spirit of the progressive movement. Write a letter to a classmate, telling why you are so optimistic, or pessimistic, about the events at the turn of the 21st century. Have your classmate respond, agreeing or disagreeing with you. Your teacher may post all pairs of letters in the classroom so that you can compare yours with others.

Reading in Depth

Antin, Mary. *The Promised Land.* Boston: Houghton Mifflin. Tells the story of a young immigrant's experiences.

Brau, M.M. *Island in the Crossroads: The History of Puerto Rico.* New York: Doubleday. Describes the importance of Puerto Rico's location.

Castor, Henry. *Teddy Roosevelt and the Rough Riders.* New York: Random House. Presents the exciting story of Americans in combat.

Cook, Fred J. *The Muckrakers: Crusading Journalists Who Changed America.* New York: Doubleday. Provides an inside look at investigative reporting in the progressive era.

Gluck, Sherna, ed. *From Parlor to Prison: Five American Suffragists Talk About Their Lives.* New York: Random House. Contains vignettes on the crusade for women's right to vote.

Reynolds, Robert L. and Douglas MacArthur, 2nd. *Commodore Perry in Japan.* New York: American Heritage. Describes Perry's landing and the events surrounding the opening of Japan.

John Steuart Curry painted "Tornado over Kansas" in 1929.

A TROUBLED AMERICA

UNIT **3**

When the Great War broke out in Europe in 1914 few people understood what hard times lay ahead. But between 1914 and 1917 America was drawn into the largest war yet fought in history. Germany was defeated but Wilson's hopes of "peace without victory" and making the world "safe for democracy" were shattered by the Senate's refusal to ratify the peace treaty. Next came the Roaring Twenties and prosperity for the United States that lasted until the devastating crash of the stock market in 1929. Then the United States entered the Great Depression, the longest in its history. Franklin Roosevelt's New Deal helped relieve some of the suffering, but economic recovery came only when the United States found itself on the eve of another world war.

The Great World War

The Great War began in Europe in 1914. It had been simmering since the late 19th century. Germany, France, Great Britain, Russia, and Austria-Hungary continually quarreled. Holding colonies in Africa and spheres of influence in China caused frequent disputes. While some European countries were expanding their influence abroad, others like Austria-Hungary and Germany had become unified nations, forged together in war by "blood and steel." The Slavic people—Poles, Czechs, Slovaks, Serbo-Croatians, and Bulgarians—resented being ruled by German-speaking Austria-Hungary. Complicated alliances prevented outright war for a time, but in 1914 the Allies (Great Britain, France, Russia, Serbia, and Belgium) began fighting against the Central Powers (Germany and Austria). How long could the United States resist entering what was becoming the largest war yet fought on the planet?

UPI/Bettmann Newsphotos

In the streets of Sarajevo, sabers flash moments after an assassin's bullets sparked the Great War. In this rare photograph the assassin of the Austro-Hungarian archduke and duchess is dragged from the street. He was a student still in high school and a member of the terrorist Black Hand. Four years later the assassin—Gavrilo Princip—died in prison of tuberculosis. Explain why this assassination had such wide consequences.

1. THE SPARK IS LIT

War in Europe

The **Great War,** which later generations came to call World War I, broke out following the assassination of an Austro-Hungarian prince, Archduke Ferdinand, and his wife, Sophia, in the city of Sarajevo in what is now Yugoslavia. The killer was a member of the Black Hand, a terrorist organization in the part of Yugoslavia that was then the nation of Serbia. Serbians wanted the Austro-Hungarians out of their country. Austria declared war on Serbia. What had led to this explosive situation?

At first there seemed no reason why these murders would lead to a long and terrible war. However, several pressures were at work in Europe under the surface. The most important was **nationalism,** the feeling of pride and loyalty that people have for their country or for a shared language or customs. Nationalism helped unite Germany and brought many Slavic people closer together. However, some national groups such as the Serbians were ruled by other nations. Increasingly these people called for independence.

Another powerful force was **imperialism.** Some European nations had built great colonial empires in Asia and Africa. Others, such as Germany and Italy, envied these empires and wanted to build their own. Their attempts to do this brought them into conflict with the established imperialist nations.

Empires brought power and prestige. So did military might. By 1900 the kaiser—the king of Germany—had built Germany's army into Europe's largest and best equipped. The other nations of Europe also began to strengthen their forces. Before long a dangerous arms race was under way.

To further increase their power, European nations had signed a complicated network of treaties. Two powerful groups called **alliances** had been created. European leaders claimed these alliances maintained a **balance of power.** That is, they kept the two groups of nations at nearly equal strength. These leaders hoped that a balance of power would preserve the fragile peace.

But alliances proved to be a grave danger. When a member of one alliance was threatened, the other members were pledged to support it. Austria and Serbia belonged to rival alliances. Austria held Serbia responsible for the assassinations. Quickly allies on both sides became involved, and their conflict resulted in a war that spread throughout Europe.

Germany and Austria were the principal members of one alliance. They were known as the **Central Powers** because they dominated the middle of Europe. Later they were joined in the war by Bulgaria and Turkey. Opposing them were a number of nations known as the **Allies.** Great Britain, France, and Russia were the

Preview & Review

Use these questions to guide your reading. Answer the questions after completing Section 1.
Understanding Issues, Events, & Ideas Using the following words, describe the events that led to war in Europe: Great War, nationalism, imperialism, alliance, balance of power, Central Powers, Allies.

Use the following words to explain how most Americans felt about going to war: arbitration treaty, peace movement, neutrality.

Describe Wilson's foreign policy in Mexico, using the following words: Mexican Revolution, military dictatorship, ABC Powers, mediate.
1. What did signers of arbitration treaties agree to do?
2. What did President Wilson believe should be the role of the United States in foreign affairs?
3. Why did the United States become involved in the Mexican Revolution?
Thinking Critically. Imagine that it is 1910, and you are a Mexican refugee who has crossed the Mexican border into New Mexico. Write a diary entry explaining why you decided to leave Mexico and what hopes you have for the future.

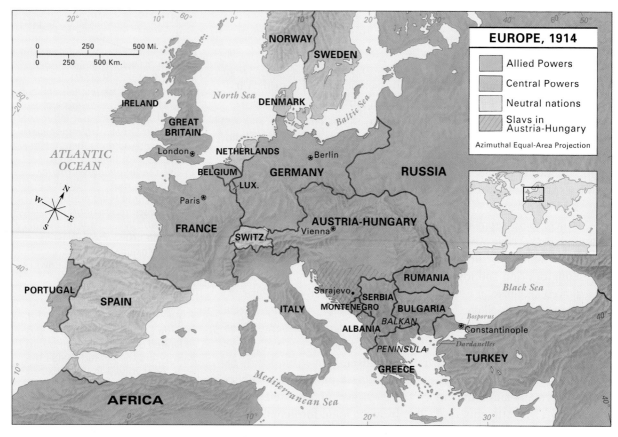

EUROPE, 1914

- Allied Powers
- Central Powers
- Neutral nations
- Slavs in Austria-Hungary

Azimuthal Equal-Area Projection

LEARNING FROM MAPS. *By 1914 Austria-Hungary had been unified into a huge country occupying central Europe. Many ethnic groups had been brought under its control. The struggles of these groups, seeking independence and the chance to form a nation of their own, helped cause the Great War. What countries made up the Central Powers? Why were they called that?*

leading members of this alliance. The United States was most concerned by the fighting between Great Britain and Germany.

American Neutrality

News of the outbreak of war caught Americans by surprise. There had not been a major war in Europe since the defeat of Napoleon at the battle of Waterloo in 1815. Prosperity and progress had encouraged people to hope that the nations of the world had become too "civilized" to resort to warfare to settle their disagreements.

Under Presidents Taft and Wilson the United States had negotiated **arbitration treaties** with a number of nations. The signers agreed in advance to discuss any differences during a "cooling off" period to last about a year. Only if a solution could not be found would they consider going to war.

In America the search for worldwide peace went even further. Both religious and secular groups became deeply involved in a **peace movement**. The Carnegie Endowment for International Peace, drawing upon funds provided by Andrew Carnegie's millions, mounted a campaign to promote peaceful solutions to international problems. William Jennings Bryan, Wilson's secretary of state, used both rational and religious arguments to further the quest for peace.

This American attitude helps explain why President McKinley

hesitated to ask Congress to declare war on Spain in 1898. Wars were to be fought only for a noble purpose and only after every reasonable effort had been made to negotiate a settlement.

Nearly all Americans felt the United States should not become involved in the war in Europe. Many persons of German or Austrian origin hoped that the Central Powers would win. So did large numbers of Irish Americans, who were anti-British because Great Britain still refused to grant Ireland its independence. People whose ancestors had come from the Allied nations tended to favor that side in the war. But for the vast majority of Americans the obvious policy for the United States was **neutrality.** Europe was far away. Its rivalries had always been viewed by Americans with distrust.

President Wilson expressed the general attitude clearly on August 18, 1914. Every American ought to "act and speak in the true spirit of neutrality," he said. This meant behaving with "impartiality and fairness and friendliness" to all the nations at war.

Wilson's Foreign Policy

As president of the United States, Woodrow Wilson had the chief responsibility for deciding the country's foreign policy. He had run for president, however, on the domestic issues of the Progressive Era. Foreign questions had not played much part in the 1912 campaign. Before 1912 Wilson had never been especially concerned with foreign affairs. Nevertheless, he had very strong opinions about what was morally correct in foreign affairs.

This is how Wilson reasoned: The United States did not need any more territory. It had no enemies. It did not want to injure any foreign country. Indeed, Wilson thought, being rich and powerful, the United States had a duty to help less fortunate nations, particularly its neighbors in Central and South America. America's destiny was not to control other countries but to encourage the spread of democratic ideas. After all, he felt no other country knew as much about democracy as the United States. The brief period of American imperialism had been a bad mistake, the president insisted.

Wilson thought the United States should help other nations and try to make life better for their people. His trouble was that he was convinced that he knew what was best for the rest of the world. He often tried to impose his ideas on people who did not agree with him.

Wilson did not seem to understand that nations with different cultures and traditions often saw things differently than he did. Even nations which sought the same goals as Wilson sometimes resented his efforts to assist them. Perhaps because he had been a teacher for so many years, the president had a tendency to lecture to the officials of other nations. His manner, rather than his actual words, created the impression that Wilson thought he knew better than foreign leaders what was best for their countries.

Victoriano Huerta became military dictator of Mexico in 1913. President Wilson said he headed a "government of butchers."

Revolution in Mexico

Even before the war in Europe began, Wilson had to deal with an important foreign problem. This was the **Mexican Revolution.** This upheaval, which began in 1910, was against the dictator Porfirio Díaz who had ruled Mexico for many years and allowed foreign companies to exploit his country's resources. It was of concern to Wilson because United States investments in Mexico were threatened by the troubles. Also, many Mexican refugees from the fighting were crossing the border into Texas, New Mexico, Arizona, and California against U.S. wishes.

Before Wilson became president, the revolution had been led by Francisco Madero, a progressive-type reformer who had forced Díaz to resign and leave Mexico. Madero became president but early in 1913 was murdered by General Victoriano Huerta. Huerta set up a **military dictatorship** with all powers of government held by the generals. Wilson called this "a government of butchers." He refused to recognize Huerta as the legitimate leader of the Mexicans.

Many Mexicans agreed with Wilson. A new revolt broke out, led by Venustiano Carranza. Wilson was urged on by United States companies whose Mexican properties were in danger. He asked Huerta to order free elections and promise not to be a candidate himself. If he agreed, the United States would try to persuade the Carranza forces to stop fighting.

Wilson meant well. But even supporters of Carranza resented Wilson's interference. Mexico's problems were none of his business, insisted both sides. If we agreed to United States interference, said an official of the Huerta government, "all the future elections for president [of Mexico] would be submitted to the veto of any president of the United States."

Then, in April 1914, some American sailors on shore leave in Tampico, Mexico, were arrested. They were soon released, but by this time Wilson was so angry at Huerta that he used the incident to try to overthrow him. He sent a naval force to occupy the city of Veracruz.

Wilson did not intend to start a war. He expected his "show of force" would cause the downfall of Huerta. But 19 United States sailors and 126 Mexicans were killed before Veracruz was captured. Again, Carranza joined with his enemy Huerta in speaking out against the interference of the United States in Mexican affairs.

Fortunately, the ambassadors of the **ABC Powers**—Argentina, Brazil, and Chile—offered to **mediate** the dispute—that is, to act as neutral go-betweens to find a peaceful settlement. Wilson eagerly accepted their offer. The crisis ended. By summer Carranza had forced Huerta from power. The United States then withdrew its naval force from Veracruz.

Yet Wilson's troubles in Mexico were far from over. No sooner

To some Mexicans Pancho Villa and Emiliano Zapata were Robin Hood and Little John. To others they were bandits. In this photograph of the only meeting of the two leaders, they have taken over the presidential palace in Mexico City in 1914. Villa is seated at the center, and Zapata is to his left. Do these men seem at ease in the palace of the president?

1931, Fresco, 7'9 ¾" × 6'2", Collection, The Museum of Modern Art, New York. Abby Aldrich Rockefeller Fund.

"¡Viva Zapata!" shouted supporters of Mexico's great fighter for land reform. The muralist Diego Rivera called his fresco of Zapata and his white horse "Agrarian Leader Zapata." With the slogan on his lips, "land and liberty," Zapata led an army of Indians in seizing plantations and villages. His movement called zapatismo had as its single purpose the breaking up of the large estates of the rich into small farms for the poor. How does this mural show that Rivera saw Zapata as a man of the people?

Return to the Preview & Review on page 277.

had Carranza defeated Huerta than one of his own generals, Francisco "Pancho" Villa, rebelled against him. Wilson supported Villa. He had resented Carranza's independence and refusal to follow United States advice. Villa seemed to be sincerely interested in improving the lives of poor Mexicans. Wilson also thought Villa could be more easily influenced by the United States.

Supporting Pancho Villa was probably the president's worst mistake. Villa was little better than a bandit, while Carranza was genuinely interested in improving the condition of the people of Mexico. From a practical point of view, Carranza had the stronger forces. His troops soon drove the Villistas, Villa's followers, into the mountains of northern Mexico.

At last, in October 1915, Wilson realized that the best policy for the United States was to keep hands off Mexico and let the people of that nation decide for themselves how they were to be governed. He then officially recognized the Carranza government.

This decision angered Pancho Villa. In January 1916 the Villistas stopped a train in northern Mexico and killed 17 citizens of the United States on board in cold blood. Then in March Villa and his men crossed the border and attacked the town of Columbus, New Mexico. They killed 17 more United States citizens and set the town on fire.

Wilson ordered troops under General John J. Pershing to capture Villa. This meant invading Mexico. Pershing was an experienced soldier. He had served during the Indian fighting of the 1880s, in Cuba during the Spanish-American War, and in the Philippine Islands. He earned the nickname "Black Jack" while commanding the 10th Cavalry regiment, which was made up entirely of black enlisted men. One of his first decisions when he was ordered to hunt down Villa was to include part of the 10th Cavalry in his expedition.

Pershing's men pursued Villa vigorously, but they could not catch him on his home ground. As had happened when Veracruz was occupied in 1914, United States interference angered Carranza. Wilson called off the invasion, which accomplished nothing.

2. WAR ON LAND AND SEA

Preview & Review

Use these questions to guide your reading. Answer the questions after completing Section 2.
Understanding Issues, Events, & Ideas Describe the Great War, using the following terms: Eastern Front, Western Front, Battle of the Marne, no man's land, trench warfare, stalemate, U-boat, *Lusitania,* Sussex pledge.

1. What was the war on the Western Front like?
2. How did the U-boats break the rules of the high seas?
3. Why was Wilson unwilling to cut off trade with Great Britain?

Thinking Critically. Imagine that you are an American who has just learned about the torpedoing of the *Lusitania*. Write a letter to the editor of your local newspaper, describing your reaction and explaining what you think President Wilson should do about it.

The War on the Western Front

As early as 1915 the Great World War had become the bloodiest conflict ever fought. On the **Eastern Front** Russian troops clashed with Austrian and German armies in a series of seesaw battles. There was also fighting in Turkey and Serbia. In Africa and on the islands of the Pacific, Allied troops clashed with German colonial forces. In May 1915 Italy entered the war on the side of the Allies and attacked Austria-Hungary from the south.

The greatest interest of the United States at this time was in the fighting on the so-called **Western Front** in Europe—Belgium and France—and on the high seas. When the war began, the Germans marched into Belgium on their way to invade France. No matter that they had promised by treaty in 1870 to respect the neutrality of tiny Belgium in the event of war with France.

The Belgians resisted bravely, but they could not stop the invaders. By September 1914 the German armies had swept across Belgium and were within 20 miles (32 kilometers) of Paris. There, in the **Battle of the Marne,** they were checked by French and British troops.

The two armies then dug trenches to protect themselves from bullets and artillery shells. They put up mazes of barbed wire in front of their positions. Lines of these trenches ran all the way across

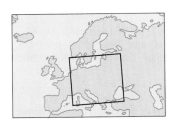

LEARNING FROM MAPS. *Russia invaded the Central Powers in 1914 in keeping with their alliance with Serbia. However, the Central Powers had soon pushed far into Russia. What ended the Russian war effort?*

Culver Pictures

northern France from the sea to Switzerland. Between the opposing trenches lay a narrow **no man's land.**

This was **trench warfare.** Soldiers ate and slept in the gravelike damp. First one side, then the other would try to break through at some point along the line. The artillery would begin the attack by firing exploding shells at the enemy trenches for hours. Soldiers would then climb from their trenches and rush "over the top" with fixed bayonets at the enemy line. The defender's artillery would rain shells upon them while sharpshooters and machine gunners from the trenches riddled the attackers with a hail of bullets. These attacks resembled the British attack at Breed's Hill in the first weeks of the American Revolution. But millions, not hundreds, of soldiers were involved. And their weapons were far more deadly.

The armies had reached a **stalemate**—neither side could win a decisive victory despite repeated attacks and counterattacks which cost hundreds of thousands of lives. No man's land came to look like the surface of the moon. No tree or house stood there. Scarcely a blade of grass could be found, so heavy was the bombardment. The surface, like the moon, was pockmarked by tens of thousands of craters where artillery shells had exploded.

The war on the Western Front was unlike any other war in

In the words of historian Barbara Tuchman, the soldiers who fought in these miserable trenches could do little more than "exchange one wet-bottomed trench for another." How was this kind of warfare like the early British attacks at Breed's Hill in the American Revolution? How was it far different?

Barbara Tuchman wrote of the visions of a better world after the Great War.

"Men could not sustain a war of such magnitude and pain without hope— . . . Like the shimmering vision of Paris that kept Kluck's° soldiers on their feet, the image of a better world glimmered beyond the shell-pitted wastes and leafless stumps that had once been green fields and waving poplars. Nothing less could give dignity or sense to the monstrous offensives in which thousands and hundreds of thousands were killed to gain ten yards and exchange one wet-bottomed trench for another. When every autumn people said it could not last through the winter, and when every spring there was still no end in sight, only the hope that out of it all some good would accrue to mankind kept men and nations fighting." From *The Guns of August*, 1962

°Kluck was a German general.

history. The battle between the Union and Confederate armies around the city of Petersburg, Virginia, in the last stages of the Civil War comes closest to it. That battle lasted only a few months. The terrible struggle on the Western Front went on for years.

The War on the Atlantic

On the Atlantic Ocean a new kind of struggle developed in 1914-15. The British navy was far stronger than Germany's. It attempted to blockade all northern European ports in order to keep Germany from obtaining supplies from the United States and other neutral nations. The Germans, in turn, tried to keep supplies from the British by using swift submarines, which they called "Undersea ships" or **U-boats.**

All the major navies had submarines by 1914. Both Great Britain and the United States had more in operation at that time than Germany. Submarines were small, relatively slow vessels. Most naval authorities did not consider them important weapons. However, the German navy did not have enough surface ships to operate in the Atlantic against the Allied fleets. U-boats were the only naval weapon the Germans could use.

Like privateers during the American Revolution and the War of 1812, U-boats roamed the seas looking for unarmed merchant vessels to attack. When they sighted powerful enemy warships, they slipped away beneath the surface. These tactics worked so well that the Germans ordered that more U-boats be constructed as quickly as possible.

Both the British blockade and the German submarine campaign hurt American business interests. Both of these activities on the high seas also violated the rights of neutral nations according to international law. British warships stopped American ships and forced them to put into Allied ports for inspection. Goods headed for Germany were seized. The British even tried to limit the amount of goods shipped to neutral countries like Norway and Sweden. Otherwise, they claimed, those nations could import more American products than they needed for themselves and ship the surplus to the Central Powers.

The Germans refused to follow the international rules for stopping merchant ships in wartime. These rules provided that ships could be stopped and their cargoes examined. Enemy vessels and neutrals carrying war materials to enemy ports could be taken as prizes or sunk. Before destroying a merchant ship, the attacker was supposed to take the crew prisoner or give it time to get clear of the vessel in lifeboats.

It was extremely dangerous for submarines to obey these rules. If a submarine surfaced and ordered a merchant ship to stop, the merchant ship might turn suddenly and ram the submarine before it

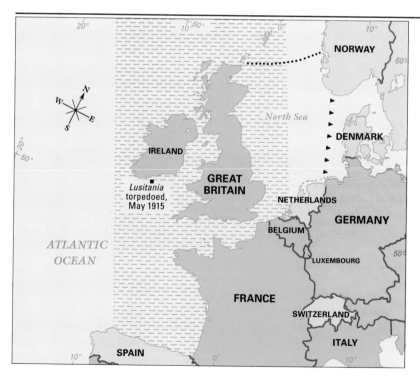

Hearts skipping a beat, the passengers on this Spanish steamer see the sleek German submarine surface from its prowls of the North Sea and ask to inspect their ship. Imagine such a close encounter at sea and describe it in your own words.

THE GREAT WAR IN THE ATLANTIC

LEARNING FROM MAPS. *What was the purpose of each of the war strategies shown on this map?*

War on Land and Sea   **285**

could react. Some merchant ships carried concealed cannon. A single cannon shell could send a submarine to the bottom in seconds. If an enemy warship should appear on the horizon while part of a U-boat's crew was examining the cargo of a merchant ship, the U-boat would almost certainly be blown out of the water before it could call back its men and submerge.

Therefore the U-boats attacked their targets from below the surface, firing torpedoes packed with TNT—a powerful explosive—without warning. Many sailors and passengers lost their lives when their ships went down.

Wilson on Neutral Rights

President Wilson protested strongly against both British and German violations of the international rules. If he had threatened to cut off trade with Great Britain as Jefferson had done in 1807, the British would undoubtedly have obeyed the rules. They could not fight the war without supplies from America. But Wilson was unwilling to go that far, in large part because the profitable trade with the Allies was extremely important to the United States.

Wilson took a much stronger stand against Germany. When U-boats began to sink ships without warning, he announced in February 1915 that Germany would be held to strict accountability for any American property destroyed or lives lost. In the language of diplomacy the phrase "strict accountability" was a polite way of saying, "If you don't do what we ask, we will probably declare war."

The danger of war over submarine attacks became suddenly critical on May 7, 1915, when the German *U-20* torpedoed the British liner *Lusitania* without warning. Technically this sinking could be defended. The *Lusitania* had deck guns. It was carrying a cargo of guns and ammunition. Its captain was guilty at least of carelessness, for a slow-moving submarine should never have been able to get close enough to a swift ocean liner to hit it with a torpedo.

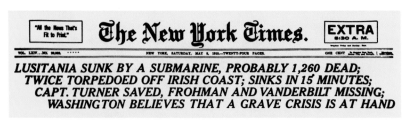

Brown Brothers

The *Lusitania* was crowded with civilian passengers. About 1,200 of them, including 128 American citizens, lost their lives in the sinking. The American public was shocked and furious. If Wilson had called for a declaration of war, Congress would probably have acted promptly. Instead, Wilson demanded only that the Germans

TORPEDO WARFARE

Brown Brothers

Aiming a torpedo accurately from a German U-boat was very difficult. Torpedoes were launched from tubes in the bow of the submarine. The submarine captain's vision was limited because he had to view the target through a periscope. He had to point the entire submarine in the direction he wanted to aim the torpedo.

The captain aimed ahead of his target the way a hunter "leads" a flying duck. He had to estimate the speed of the target and compare it to the speed of the torpedo, which traveled at about 30 miles (48 kilometers) an hour. Nowadays such calculations can be made accurately by computers. In 1915 such equipment was not available. Once fired, the torpedo traveled a fairly straight line. Its direction could not be changed by the captain, although waves and currents might cause it to veer off course.

The Lusitania had a top speed of about 25 miles (40 kilometers) per hour. If it had simply changed direction every few minutes, traveling in a zigzag course, it would have been practically impossible for the slow-moving U-20 to get close enough to aim a torpedo. If by great luck he did get within range, the captain, Lieutenant Walter Schwieger, would not have known where to aim a torpedo if the Lusitania were zigzagging. Between the time the torpedo was fired and the time its course intersected with the Lusitania's, the liner would have changed direction. Obviously, Captain William T. Turner assumed the Lusitania was in no danger and took no evasive action.

apologize, pay damages, and promise not to attack passenger ships in the future. Long negotiations followed. In March 1916, after another passenger vessel, the *Sussex,* was torpedoed with the loss of 80 lives, Germany finally gave in. It promised not to sink any more passenger or merchant ships without warning. This promise is known as the **Sussex pledge.** 🗐

Return to the Preview & Review on page 282.

Use these questions to guide your reading. Answer the questions after completing Section 3.

Understanding Issues, Events, & Ideas Describe the importance of the following words: peace without victory, Zimmermann Note.

1. Which groups of people opposed Woodrow Wilson's reelection? Why did each group oppose his reelection?
2. Why did the Zimmermann Note alarm many Americans?
3. What did President Wilson mean by his statement, "The world must be made safe for democracy"?

Thinking Critically. If you had been able to vote in the presidential election of 1916, would you have voted for the reelection of Woodrow Wilson or not? Give reasons to justify your decision.

3. AMERICA ENTERS THE WAR

The Election of 1916

By late 1916 some Americans, including ex-president Theodore Roosevelt, were arguing that the United States should enter the war on the side of the Allies. A larger number believed that the United States should at least prepare for war by building up the armed forces. Still, a majority of the people wanted to remain neutral. They appreciated Wilson's patient attempts to avoid involvement and his efforts to persuade the warring nations to make peace.

The depth of their feelings came out during the 1916 presidential campaign. One Democratic slogan, "He kept us out of war," proved to have enormous appeal. Wilson was not particularly popular in 1916. Many progressives who had voted for him in 1912 felt that he had not done enough for reform. African Americans considered him a racist, for he had actually increased the amount of segregation in government offices in Washington. Women found him reluctant to support their drive to obtain the right to vote. Yet the Progressive party, led by Theodore Roosevelt, had decided not to run a separate candidate in 1916. Instead the Progressives nominated the Republican candidate, Charles Evans Hughes, a justice of the Supreme Court.

Wilson tried to hold his progressive supporters in 1916 by backing a bill making child labor illegal and another making it easier for farmers to obtain low-interest loans. He approved a strong workman's compensation law. He appointed the liberal lawyer, Louis D.

This Wilson campaign van has at least one version of his popular slogan, "He kept us out of war." What else did Wilson do for the American people, according to the posters on the van?

Brandeis, famous for the "Brandeis brief" in the *Muller v. Oregon* case, to a vacancy on the Supreme Court. Many liberals applauded the choice of Brandeis, who was Jewish. But large numbers of Americans were prejudiced against Jews and probably voted against Wilson because he appointed Brandeis.

The presidential election was very close. Wilson got 277 electoral votes to Hughes' 254. Nearly everyone agreed that the president's success in keeping out of the Great War saved him from defeat.

Wilson was too intelligent to take comfort from this fact. He knew that if the Germans ever decided to sink merchant ships again without warning, America could not stay neutral.

America Seeks Peace Without Victory

Wilson's fear of being forced into the war led him to make a strong effort to end it by negotiation. On January 22, 1917, he made a moving speech calling for **peace without victory.** If either side tried to profit from the war by taking land or money from the other, Wilson said, the only result would be hatred that would cause more wars. All the nations, including the United States, must try to make a peace based on "justice throughout the world."

Unfortunately, neither the Allies nor the Central Powers would settle for peace without victory. The cost in lives and money had been so great after two and one-half years of war that neither side could face the idea that all that expense had been wasted. At the very least each intended to make the other pay the entire monetary cost of the war. The German government already had secretly decided to resume submarine attacks on shipping without warning.

The Germans realized that unleashing their sharklike U-boats would probably cause the United States to declare war. Nevertheless, they expected that "ruthless submarine warfare" would keep food and munitions from reaching Great Britain. Then the British would have to surrender. The war would be over before the United States could raise and train an army and get its soldiers across the Atlantic to France.

Less than two weeks after Wilson's "peace without victory" speech, an American merchant ship was sunk by a U-boat. Wilson then broke diplomatic relations with Germany. He ordered the German ambassador out of the United States and recalled his own ambassador from Germany.

Late in February the president learned that German Foreign Relations Secretary Arthur Zimmermann was trying to make an alliance with Mexico. Zimmermann had sent a telegram to the German ambassador in Mexico with the following instructions:

❝ We intend to begin unrestricted submarine warfare on the first of February. We shall endeavor in spite of this to keep the United States neutral. In the event of not succeeding,

All eyes are upon the president as Wilson asks Congress to declare war on Germany. "The world," he said, "must be made safe for democracy."

we make Mexico a proposal of alliance on the following basis: Make war together, make peace together, generous financial support, and an understanding on our part that Mexico is to reconquer the lost territory of Texas, New Mexico, and Arizona. . . .

Inform the President [of Mexico] of the above most secretly as soon as the outbreak of war with the United States is certain. . . .[1] **99**

[1]From *The Zimmermann Telegram* by Barbara Tuchman

In the event of war with the United States, Germany wanted an alliance with Mexico. Americans would then send some troops to the Mexican border rather than sending them all to Europe. In return, Germany would help Mexico "reconquer" the "lost territory" of Texas, New Mexico, and Arizona. Nothing officially came from this **Zimmermann Note.** Yet when it was made public, it caused many Americans to call for war against Germany.

In February and March the number of merchant ships sunk by U-boats increased steadily. The *Housatonic,* the *Laconia,* the *Algonquin* were all torpedoed and sunk. Against this grim background the president took the oath of office for his second term. Almost a month later, on April 2, 1917, Wilson asked Congress to declare war. The reason, he said, was to make a just peace possible. "The world," he added in a famous sentence, "must be made safe for democracy."

Wilson did not mean by this that the purpose of the war was to make all nations democracies. Rather he meant that the world must be made a place where democracies could exist and flourish. He believed that if the United States did not help to bring the conflict to an early end, the losses and hatreds would be so great that no democratic government could survive. 🖅

Return to the Preview & Review on page 288.

4. THE WAR AT HOME AND ABROAD

Organizing Wartime America

Building an army and supplying it in a hurry was a huge task. Many changes had to be made in the way goods were manufactured and businesses run. The antitrust laws were suspended. In wartime Wilson agreed with Theodore Roosevelt's argument that large-scale organizations supervised by the government were more efficient than small competing firms. Because so many goods had to be moved, it became necessary to place all the nation's railroads under government management. Wilson appointed William G. McAdoo, the secretary of the treasury, to run the entire system.

The president also set up a **War Industries Board** to oversee the production and distribution of manufactured goods. The head of this board was Bernard Baruch, a millionaire stockbroker. Baruch was active in Democratic party politics at a time when most wealthy stockbrokers were Republicans. A friend and adviser of Wilson, he was a natural choice to head the War Industries Board. In this post he performed brilliantly.

Baruch's idea was to organize American industry as though it were one big factory. He decided what was to be made and where the raw materials were to come from. He controlled the distribution of scarce commodities and in some cases even set the price at which they were to be sold. His job was made easier because most producers were eager to cooperate with the War Industries Board. Profit and patriotism were pushing them in the same direction.

Both, Culver Pictures

Baruch's board had to supply both American needs and much of the war supplies, called **matériel,** and food for the Allied nations. Great Britain, in particular, depended on American wheat, meat, and other products for its survival. Wilson appointed Herbert Hoover as United States Food Administrator. It was Hoover's job to make sure

Preview & Review

Use these questions to guide your reading. Answer the questions after completing Section 4.
Understanding Issues, Events, & Ideas Explain the efforts of wartime America, using the following words: War Industries Board, matériel, American Expeditionary Force, Selective Service Act, propaganda, Industrial Workers of the World, Wobblies, Espionage Act, Sedition Act, Communist Revolution. Then describe the Great War overseas using these words: tanks, poison gas, dogfights, aces, machine guns, Verdun, Château-Thierry, Saint-Mihiel salient, Battle of the Argonne Forest, Hindenburg Line, armistice.

1. What were Herbert Hoover's main goals as United States Food Administrator?
2. How did the war affect African Americans? Women? Mexican Americans?
3. How did the war end?

Thinking Critically. 1. Do you think that the Espionage and Sedition Acts violated First Amendment rights? Why or why not? **2.** Imagine that you are an American soldier in Verdun in 1917. Write a letter home, explaining how the development of new weapons has changed the fighting in the Great War.

Preparing to fight a war 3,000 miles away are William G. McAdoo, left, who managed the nation's railroads, and Bernard Baruch, right, who organized American industry as if it were one big factory.

The War at Home and Abroad   291

Herbert Hoover, another of Wilson's advisers for the war on the homefront, is shown at right inspecting a shipment of supplies to Europe. Hoover campaigned to persuade Americans to eat less. What catchy slogans did he use?

that enough foodstuffs were produced and that they were distributed fairly.

Hoover had been head of the Commission for the Relief of Belgium early in the war. As Food Administrator he set out both to increase production and to reduce domestic consumption. At the same time it was important to keep prices from skyrocketing.

Hoover had little trouble increasing production. It was in the farmers' interest to grow more because the demand for their crops was increasing. For example, they raised 619 million bushels (218 million hectoliters) of wheat in 1917 and 904 million bushels (318 million hectoliters) in 1918.

Getting Americans to consume less was more difficult. Hoover organized a vast campaign to convince the public of the need for conservation. Catchy slogans carried his message. "Food will win the war" was the best known. Others included "When in doubt, eat potatoes," which was designed to save wheat, and "If you have a sweet tooth, pull it," to reduce sugar consumption.

Hoover also organized "Meatless Tuesdays" when no one was supposed to eat meat and "Wheatless Wednesdays" too. He even started a campaign to get every American family to raise a pig. Pigs could live on scraps and garbage and eventually be turned into bacon and pork chops. Hoover's rules could not be enforced. His technique was to depend on (and praise) voluntary cooperation. He made it clear that patriotic citizens were *expected* to obey the rules. The results were excellent.

Any African American could be drafted under the Selective Service System, but he could not fight side by side with his white colleagues. Blacks who were not drafted began a great migration to the North, where they found jobs in war plants.

Labor in Wartime

Organizing the human resources of the nation was also complicated. During the war the United States Employment Service directed almost 4 million people to new jobs. When war was declared, thousands of young men volunteered for military service. To raise the huge **American Expeditionary Force** (AEF) that was to fight in Europe, however, it was necessary to pass a draft law, the **Selective Service Act** of 1917.

For those men who were not drafted, and for women workers, the war brought many benefits. Wages rose. Unskilled workers got opportunities to move to better jobs. Union membership rose from about 3 million to over 4 million in a year.

It was important to prevent strikes from slowing down the production of vital goods. In December 1917 a National War Labor Conference Board was set up to try to settle disputes between workers and their employers. This board also tried to make sure that workers were not fired for trying to organize unions.

The American Federation of Labor grew to about 3 million members in 1918. AFL unions cooperated with the Conference Board in most cases. Samuel Gompers, president of the AFL, served as a presidential adviser. Gompers never promised that union members would not strike during the war. But he went along with the government's request that workers agree to arbitrate conflicts with their employers whenever possible.

The need for laborers especially helped African Americans, women, and other groups that had been discriminated against in the job market in the past. Thousands of descendents of slaves had already migrated from the South to northern cities before the war began. Half a million more followed between 1914 and 1919. Most of these newcomers earned far more in war plants than they could make raising cotton or tobacco in the South.

The Selective Service System drafted people of all races, although soldiers were still segregated in the armed forces. African

What message for readers of this book is found in the navy's recruiting poster?

American soldiers were better treated and were given more opportunities than 20 years earlier during the Spanish-American War. About a thousand became officers. Emmett J. Scott of Tuskegee Institute was appointed an assistant to the secretary of war.

Of course, this did not amount to equal treatment. Yet while some African Americans protested, the strong-minded William E. B. Du Bois did not. "Fight for your rights but . . . have sense enough to know when you are getting what you are fighting for," Du Bois urged.

Women were not drafted under the Selective Service Act, although many served as army nurses and as volunteer workers overseas. Many others did volunteer work in hospitals and for such organizations as the Red Cross. Women from all walks of life, the wealthy of New York's Fifth Avenue and the poor immigrants from Grand Street, worked side by side preparing bandages for hospitals and first-aid stations. Most knew that it was only the war that threw such different people together. One American poet described her wartime experience.

> **❝** I sat beside her, rolling bandages.
> I peeped. "Fifth Avenue" her clothes were saying.
> It's "Grand Street," I know well, my shirtwaist° says,
> And shoes, and hat, but then, she did not hear,
> Or she pretended not, for we were laying
> Our coats aside, as we were so near,
> She saw my pin like hers.
> And when girls are
> Wearing a pin these days that has a star°°,
> They smile out at each other. We did that,
> And then she didn't seem to see my hat.
>
> I sat beside her, handling gauze and lint,
> And thought of Jim. She thought of someone too;
> Under the smile there was a little glint
> In her eyelashes, that was how I knew.
> I wasn't crying—but I haven't any
> Pride in it; we've a better chance than they
> To take blows standing, for we've had so many.
> We two sat, fingers busy, all that day. . . .
> We're sisters while the danger lasts, it's true;
> But rich and poor's equality must cease
> (For women especially), of course, in peace.[1] **❞**

Thousands of women also found jobs in factories and offices they could not have hoped to get before the war. "This is a woman's age!" the leader of the National Women's Trade Union League

°a type of dress
°°Women wore star-shaped pins to show they had loved ones in the war.
[1]From "Fifth Avenue and Grand Street" by Mary Carolyn Davies

Culver Pictures

The Salvation Army brought its good works to France, where kitchens were set up to feed the hungry soldiers.

announced in 1917. "Women are coming into the labor [movement] on equal terms with men." This was an exaggeration. Yet women workers did make important gains. Recognizing how necessary women were to the war effort, the Wilson administration established a Women's Bureau in the department of labor.

Mexican Americans also benefited from the labor shortage in the United States. Beginning in 1911, thousands had crossed the border

National Archives

Women would have been thought incapable of lifting and weighing these steel cables until the shortage of men during the Great War made them do so. Of course they had been capable of factory work all along, and many did very well. What chance had these women for employment when the soldiers returned from the war?

295

Octaviano Larrazolo was one of the thousands of Mexican Americans who came north for wartime jobs. Larrazolo became governor of New Mexico and later represented New Mexico in the U.S. Senate.

to escape the disorder resulting from the Mexican Revolution. Even more came after the Great War began. Some settled in northern cities, attracted by jobs in war plants. The jobs were unskilled and low paid, but these workers could earn much more than they could in farming. By the end of the war there were communities of Mexican-born families in St. Louis, Chicago, Detroit, and several other northern cities. Many also served with distinction in the armed forces.

However, most Mexicans settled in the Southwest. Most found work in the cotton fields of Texas and Arizona or on farms in Colorado and California. But some became railroad laborers, construction workers, and miners. Established Mexican American leaders worked hard to involve the new immigrants in American life. When New Mexico and Arizona became states in 1912, many Mexican Americans were able to vote in a United States election for the first time. In 1916 Ezekial Cabeza de Baca was elected governor of New Mexico, the first Hispanic American governor. He died one month later and was succeeded by Octaviano Larrazolo, who in 1928 became the first Hispanic American elected to the Senate.

Propaganda and the Great War

From the beginning most Americans enthusiastically supported America's involvement in the war. But Wilson realized that other Americans opposed that involvement. So the government attempted to gain the cooperation of all Americans in the war effort. A week after war was declared, Wilson created the Committee on Public Information, headed by George Creel. The CPI used **propaganda** to influence people's opinions about the war. For example, it circulated millions of leaflets praising America's official war aims and criticizing the German government.

These releases portrayed the Germans as bloodthirsty Huns, willing to do anything to conquer the world. They even hinted that there were German spies in every office, factory, labor union, and university. And perhaps more important, they implied that any disagreement with the American war effort was unpatriotic.

Using propaganda also sold war bonds to raise money to pay for the war, convinced young men to join the armed forces, and even helped convert some doubters. Churches and religious groups, colleges and groups of their students, women's organizations, and civic groups joined in the government's efforts to ''sell the war to the American people.''

The Treatment of Protesters

The government's propaganda campaign failed to convince everyone of the rightness of United States actions. Despite the urgings of union leaders like Samuel Gompers, some workers were unwilling to go along with the government's labor policies. Radicals in the labor movement had founded a new organization, the **Industrial Workers of the World** (IWW), in 1905. According to the IWW, "the working class and the employing class have nothing in common." Workers should organize, "take possession of the earth and the machinery of production, and abolish the wage system."

One of the founders of the IWW was William D. Haywood. "Big Bill" Haywood had gone to work as a miner in Colorado at the age of 15. In 1896 he joined the Western Federation of Miners. A few years later he became a socialist. In 1904 he led a violent strike of miners in Cripple Creek, Colorado. The next year he was accused of planning the assassination of the governor of Idaho. He was successfully defended by the famous attorney Clarence Darrow. When the Great War broke out, Haywood was secretary-treasurer of the IWW, whose members were known as **Wobblies,** probably because of the way some mispronounced its initials.

Workers should stick together, Haywood said in 1915. They could

Culver Pictures

Big Bill Haywood was a radical founder of the IWW. He headed a violent strike of miners in Cripple Creek, Colorado. When war came, his members, known as Wobblies, were raided and sometimes arrested. Why did the government think it was proper to do so?

> 66 stop every wheel in the United States . . . and sweep off your capitalists and state legislatures and politicians into the sea. 99

In 1917 the IWW staged strikes in the lumber and copper-mining industries. The reaction of the government was swift. Federal agents raided IWW headquarters looking for evidence that the Wobblies were trying to slow war production. Over a hundred members, including Haywood, were arrested.

The Wobblies were revolutionaries. Their arrest when they deliberately interfered with the war effort was perfectly proper. But the times made people fearful and uncertain. This led the government to violate the civil rights of many radicals who did nothing but speak or write unpopular words. In 1917 Congress passed the **Espionage Act.** This law made it a crime to aid enemy nations or to interfere with the recruiting of soldiers. It also allowed the Postmaster General to censor mail. The next year a much stronger law, the **Sedition Act,** was passed. This law even cracked down on expressions of opinion. Heavy fines and prison sentences of up to 20 years could be imposed on persons who spoke or wrote anything critical of the government, the army or navy, or even the uniforms worn by soldiers and sailors.

One national political party—the Socialist party of America— also opposed the war, the only political party to do so. Surprisingly, the Socialists' stance helped them at the polls. Many non-Socialists voted for Socialist candidates as a way to express their disagreement with America's involvement in the war.

The government moved quickly to end this antiwar movement. In New York seven Socialists were expelled from the state legislature simply because they opposed the war. Victor Berger, a Socialist representative from Wisconsin, was denied his seat in the House.

The War at Home and Abroad 297

Even more notable was the arrest of Eugene V. Debs, leader of the Socialist party. Debs was jailed following a speech opposing the draft. At his trial in 1918 Debs spoke forcefully against the government's suppression of opinions it disagreed with. But Wilson and other government officials made it clear they would not tolerate opposition on the war issue.

An unreasoning hatred of anything German swept the country. Persons with German names were likely to be insulted by strangers. Schools stopped teaching the German language. Libraries took books by long-dead German authors off the shelves. German-born immigrants who had not become United States citizens were forced to register so that they could be watched closely.

The nation seemed to be in constant fear that radicals and spies would cause the country to lose the war. This was especially true after November 1917, when the **Communist Revolution** occurred in Russia. Americans were suspicious of the communists, and feared they would try to spread their revolution. The Russian communist government soon made peace with Germany. That enabled the Germans to transfer troops from the Eastern Front to France just when large numbers of American soldiers were going into battle and convinced Americans that the communists were against them.

A sensible limit on freedom of speech in wartime was finally set by the Supreme Court in *Schenck v. United States* (1919), a case that questioned the constitutionality of the Espionage Act. The decision, written by Justice Oliver Wendell Holmes, Jr., one of the greatest of American legal thinkers, upheld the law.

The right of free speech is not an unlimited right, Holmes declared. No one has the right, for example, of "falsely shouting 'Fire!' in a theater and causing a panic." If there is "a clear and present danger" that something said or written might hurt the war effort, the government may take action. The Supreme Court did not hand down this decision until after the war was over. Before it did so, local, state, and national officials frequently punished persons whose words had no effect on the war effort at all.

Weapons of the Great War

After nearly four years of war, many new weapons had been developed. The fighting in Europe became more and more mechanized. The British and French were the first to use **tanks**—armored, truck-like vehicles that ran on treads rather than wheels. The first tanks were slow, clumsy, and unreliable. They were used to protect advancing troops rather than to attack enemy forces directly.

Another new weapon was **poison gas.** The Germans used gas first, but the Allies soon copied them. Gas was a horrible weapon, choking and blinding its victims. It was not very effective, however. If the wind shifted, it might blow back on those who released it.

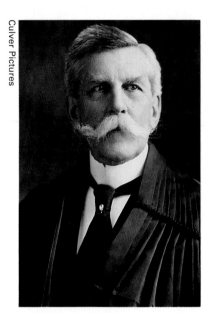

Culver Pictures

Oliver Wendell Holmes was known as the Great Dissenter for his carefully reasoned minority opinions as a justice of the Supreme Court. What did he say about the right of free speech?

For all the brave chargers and white-eyed stallions who carried their men into battle, for all who shielded their riders or burst their lungs in a last heroic charge, let us not be too impressed by the British tank that rolls through this devastated French village. The Great War was the last in which cavalry units on horseback were used but the first to use poison gas—a horrible weapon that choked and blinded its victims. Do you think chemical warfare should be banned from the planet?

The War at Home and Abroad   299

Captain Edward V. Rickenbacker was America's most famous flying ace. Below, Norman Rockwell, a popular artist of several decades, pictures soldiers around the campfire for the songsheet of George M. Cohan's "Over There." The tune inspired all kinds of people to sing, "The Yanks are coming, the Yanks are coming."

Your Song—My Song—Our Boys' Song

OVER THERE

PHOTO © 1918
LIFE PUB. CO

WORDS AND MUSIC BY
GEORGE M. COHAN

POPULAR
LEO. FEIST INC. NEW YORK
HERMAN DAREWSKI MUSIC PUBLISHING CO LONDON ENG.

Airplanes were used increasingly as time passed. There were some bombing planes but none powerful enough to carry heavy loads of bombs for great distances. Mostly planes were used to locate enemy positions and signal artillery units where their shells were hitting so they could aim more effectively.

Yet control of the air was important. There were many exciting air battles called **dogfights** between Allied and German pilots. In this huge war of faceless fighters, pilots were individual heroes. Those who shot down five or more enemy planes were known as **aces.** Rene Fonck, a French ace, shot down 75 enemy planes. Edward Mannock, an Englishman, bagged 73. The most famous German ace, Baron Manfred von Richthofen, claimed 80 kills. Captain "Eddie" Rickenbacker was the leading American ace. He shot down 26 German planes.

But the deadliest weapons remained the artillery and **machine guns.** By 1917 each side had tens of thousands of cannon ranged behind the lines. To prepare for one offensive, the French fired 6 million shells into an area only 20 miles long (32 kilometers). The number of machine guns increased even more rapidly. Before the war American regiments were equipped with four machine guns. By the end of the war each regiment had 336.

Yet all these death-dealing weapons did not give either side enough advantage to end the long struggle quickly. Throughout the summer of 1918 the fighting continued with few movements in either direction. Day by day the number of Americans in the trenches increased from about 27,000 in early June to 500,000 by the end of August.

"Over There"

President Wilson put General Pershing in command of the American Expeditionary Force. The first units of the AEF reached Paris on Independence Day 1917 and took up positions on the front near **Verdun** in October. The AEF went into action in France just in the nick of time. In March 1918 the Germans launched a tremendous attack at the section of the Western Front nearest Paris. With the help of thousands of veterans transferred to France after the Russians left the war, the Germans advanced as far as **Château-Thierry,** a town on the Marne River northeast of Paris. There, in late May, American units were thrown into battle to reinforce French troops. The German advance was stopped.

The Americans who arrived at the front were shocked at the conditions. Soldiers spent weeks in muddy, rat-filled trenches. They faced steady artillery bombardment and the threat of poison gas attacks. One American soldier wrote home describing what it was like in an American artillery unit.

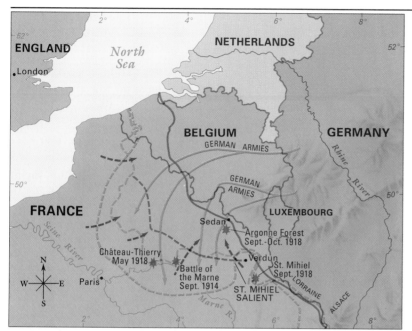

Source: Encyclopedia Britannica

THE WESTERN FRONT

- - - - Farthest German advance, Sept. 1914
- - - - German advance, Summer 1918
- - - - Hindenburg Line
- - ▶ Allied advance, Fall 1918
—— Armistice Line, Nov. 11, 1918
✳ Allied Victories

0   50   100 Mi.
0   50   100 Km.

Lambert Conformal Conic Projection

LEARNING FROM MAPS. *After marching through Belgium and deep into France, the German advance on the Western Front ground to a halt. When American troops arrived in late 1917 the tide of war turned in favor of the Allies. How close to Paris did the German armies push?*

CASUALTIES IN THE GREAT WAR		
Country	**Number of Casualties**	
	Dead*	**Wounded**
Allies		
Russia	1,700,000	4,950,000
France	1,357,800	4,266,000
Britain	908,371	2,090,212
Italy	650,000	947,000
United States	126,000	234,300
Rumania	335,706	120,000
Serbia	45,000	133,148
Belgium	13,716	44,686
Others	15,522	45,658
Total	**5,152,115**	**12,831,004**
Central Powers		
Germany	1,773,700	4,216,058
Austria-Hungary	1,200,000	3,620,000
Turkey	325,000	400,000
Bulgaria	87,500	152,390
Total	**3,386,200**	**8,388,448**
Total	**8,538,315**	**21,219,452**

*Estimated deaths from all causes

LEARNING FROM TABLES. *As this table of casualties in the Great War shows, the war had tremendous effects on the European population. Although American troops did not enter the war until the last year, American casualty totals are quite high. Why do you think this is so?*

The War at Home and Abroad   301

Somewhere in France
July 8, 1918

My Dear Folks:

I believe I told you in another letter that because of the fine record we have made since we have been at the front, we have been chosen as "shock troops." Well, we sure are being shocked!

Try and picture the very worst thunderstorm you have ever heard. Then multiply it by about 10,000 and you will get some idea of the battle that has been and still is raging along this front and in which we are taking a very active part!

The battle started shortly after midnight a few days ago and had been raging ever since. It started with a very heavy bombardment all along the front, as the country here is very flat, you can see for a long way. I can tell you that it is some sight at night to see the blinding flashes of the guns all along the line. Even far off on the horizon you can see the pink glow flare up and die down and flare up and die down again—very much like a city burning in the distance. The roar and crash of the guns just seems to tear the air to pieces, and explosions shake the ground. To add to the confusion you have the whine and shriek of the shells, some coming and some going! . . .

Allied troops enter a devastated French village near Verdun, site of one of the major battles on the Western Front. At Verdun there were nearly 750,000 casualties. By the end of the war many villages and towns in northwestern France had been virtually destroyed.

Of course every so often the Germans send over poison gas. We have to be constantly on the alert for it and wear our gas clothes most of the time, and carry our gas masks all the time!

We all have cotton in our ears. Still, the noise of the guns has made us temporarily deaf. We have not taken off our clothes or gone to bed since the battle started. When it slows up a little we just lie down on the ground, right by the guns, and get what little rest and sleep we can. Our meals are brought to us, as we may not leave the position long enough to go and get them! . . .

This kind of warfare means a great many killed and wounded. But I prefer it, as it is the only way to end the war—just kill off all the Germans!

I have given you details and described disagreeable things, but I just wanted you to know what war is and what it means for us and for everyone!

But I think it's great sport and certainly am glad I'm here and taking part in this—one of the greatest battles the world has ever known.

Love,
E.J. Canright
Medical Artillery
149th Field Artillery
A.E.F.
A.P.O. No. 715[1]

The Rock of the Marne, *by Mal Thompson, illustrates warfare along the Marne River on the Western Front. Here soldiers from the 30th and 38th U.S. Infantry Regiment line a trench near Mezy, France, in July 1918 as German shells explode around them. U.S. troops such as these reinforced Allied defenses and then led the surge that turned the tide of war against the Central Powers.*

[1]From "Some War-Time Letters" by Eldon J. Canright in the *Wisconsin Magazine of History,* V: 192—195 (1921—1922)

The worldwide influenza epidemic killed 20 million people, more than twice the number who died in the Great War.

Point of View

In his autobiography Charles Lindbergh recalls the end of the Great War.

"I was attending a farm auction sale when the first announcement was made, on November 11, 1918. Word came by telephone. The auctioneer broke off his chant to tell us. Time was allowed for celebration before the sale continued. Men cheered, slapped each other on the back, and then, with nothing else to do, they simply stood about.**"**

Charles A. Lindbergh, 1976

Return to the Preview & Review on page 291.

Finally the long stalemate began to break. In mid-September American and French forces pushed the Germans back from a wedge-shaped section of the front known as the **Saint-Mihiel salient.** Next came the long, desperate **Battle of the Argonne Forest.** The Argonne lay northwest of Saint-Mihiel. It was a rocky, hilly region crisscrossed by streams and blasted by constant shelling. Between September 26 and mid-October the Americans struggled through this hellish wilderness. German artillery rained high explosives upon them from the hills on their right flank.

Beyond the Argonne the Allies advanced against the **Hindenburg Line.** The line was actually three rows of trenches several miles apart. It bristled with machine gun nests and was guarded by mile after mile of rusty tangles of barbed wire. By this time over a million Americans were in combat. Another million had landed in France and more were arriving steadily.

On November 7 American units finally broke through the Hindenburg Line. They then advanced more swiftly toward Sedan, a city near the Belgian border. All along the front, French and British armies were also driving the Germans back, rapidly gaining ground. On November 11, 1918, the Germans gave up the hopeless fight. They signed an **armistice,** or truce, that was actually a surrender.

Some 126,000 Americans died during the Great War. Another 230,000 were wounded. About half the deaths were caused by disease, many by Spanish influenza. This world-wide epidemic, which struck after the war, killed 20 million people. America's war losses were much smaller than those of any of the other major nations. Still, during the last few months Americans bore their full share of the fighting and suffered their full share of the casualties.

5. THE SEARCH FOR PEACE

Wilson's Plans for Peace

President Wilson had been preparing for making peace even before the United States entered the war. As we have seen, he wanted a peace without victory. Wilson believed the terms must not be so hard on the Central Powers as to cause them to begin planning another war to regain what was taken from them.

In January 1918, even before the end of the war, Wilson made a speech to Congress describing his plans for peace. "The world must be made safe for every peace-loving nation," he said. Unless all the nations are treated fairly, none can count on being treated fairly. In this respect "all the peoples of the world are in effect partners." The president then listed **Fourteen Points** that he said made up "the only possible program" for peace.

The first of Wilson's points promised that the peace treaty would

Use these questions to guide your reading. Answer the questions after completing Section 5.
Understanding Issues, Events, & Ideas Use the following words to describe the end of the Great War: Fourteen Points, self-determination, League of Nations, Big Four, reparations, Versailles Peace Treaty, sanction, mandate.
1. How did President Wilson describe to Congress his plans for peace?
2. What was to be the purpose of the League of Nations?
3. What were some outcomes of the Treaty of Versailles? Of what was President Wilson most proud?

Thinking Critically. Wilson felt that the 14th of his 14 Points was the most important. Of the points described in the textbook, which do you think is the most important? Why?

The National Gallery of Art

The flags of Great Britain, France, and the United States fly on Fifth Avenue. "Allies Day, May 1917" was painted by Childe Hassam in celebration of the alliance of these three nations.

The Search for Peace   305

not contain secret clauses. "Diplomacy shall proceed . . . in the public view." Another point called for freedom of the seas "in peace and in war." Restrictions like the ones the Germans and the Allies had imposed on neutral shipping must not be permitted. But this point, like urging disarmament and calling for the lowering of protective tariffs "so far as possible," was more hopeful than practical.

A more important point dealt with the future of colonies. In settling "all colonial claims," the interests of those who lived in the colonies must be taken into account, not merely the interests of the ruling powers.

Most of Wilson's other points concerned redrawing the boundaries of European nations. Belgium should get back all the territory occupied by Germany during the war. France should regain the province of Alsace-Lorraine on its eastern border. This region had been lost to Germany in an earlier war.

Elsewhere the boundaries should follow "lines of allegiance and nationality." Areas where the inhabitants thought of themselves as Italians should be part of Italy, Poles part of Poland, and so on. This became known as the right of **self-determination.** All peoples should be able to determine for themselves what nation they belonged to.

The 14th point was to Wilson the most important. It called for the creation of an "association of nations." The purpose of this international organization would be to guarantee the independence and the territory "of great and small nations alike." This **League of Nations,** as it was soon named, was to be a kind of international congress that would settle disputes between nations. When necessary, the League would use force against any nation that defied its rulings.

The "just peace" that Wilson was proposing appealed powerfully to millions of people all over the world. It helped to shorten the Great War by encouraging the Germans to surrender when their armies began to suffer defeats in the autumn of 1918.

After the signing of the armistice on November 11, 1918, Wilson became a world hero. Millions of people believed that his idealism, backed by the wealth and power of the United States, would bring about basic changes in international relations. A new era of peace and prosperity seemed about to begin.

The Versailles Peace Conference

In January 1919 representatives of the victorious Allies gathered at the Palace of Versailles, outside Paris, to write a formal treaty of peace. President Wilson headed the American delegation himself. No earlier president had ever left the nation while in office or personally negotiated a treaty. The chief British representative was Prime Minister David Lloyd George. The French premier, Georges Clemenceau, and the Italian prime minister, Vittorio Orlando, completed the

STRATEGIES FOR SUCCESS

ANALYZING BOUNDARY CHANGES

Some national boundaries seem to change with amazing regularity while others remain the same for centuries. Recognizing why boundary changes take place will help you understand important events in history.

Boundary changes are usually the outcome of war or purchase, and are usually contained in the terms of a treaty. For example, as you have learned, the United States acquired vast western lands as a result of the Treaty of Guadalupe Hidalgo at the end of the Mexican War. Other treaties are agreements of sale.

How to Analyze Boundary Changes

Before learning the steps for analyzing boundary changes, review Comparing Maps on page 673. Then to analyze boundary changes, follow these steps.

1. **Compare maps illustrating the changes.** Note where the differences in the boundaries are.
2. **Determine why the boundary changed.** Check if the change resulted from a war or a land purchase. If the change was an outcome of war, find out who won and why the boundary change was part of the treaty terms.

3. **Analyze the change.** Draw conclusions and form hypotheses about the new boundaries. Determine if the new boundaries solve a previous problem or create a new one. Consider how people in the area of the change feel about the change.

Applying the Strategy

The Treaty of Versailles, drawn up in 1919, ended the Great War. That treaty contained sweeping boundary changes in Europe. Compare the map below to the one on page 278. Note that some nations no longer exist—Serbia and Montenegro. Why? Several new countries now appear on the map. What are they? The delegates to the peace conference used such considerations as nationalism and self-determination to guide their redrawing of the map of Europe. Do you foresee any problems with creating new countries as the treaty did? Give some examples.

For independent practice, see Practicing the Strategy on pages 310–11.

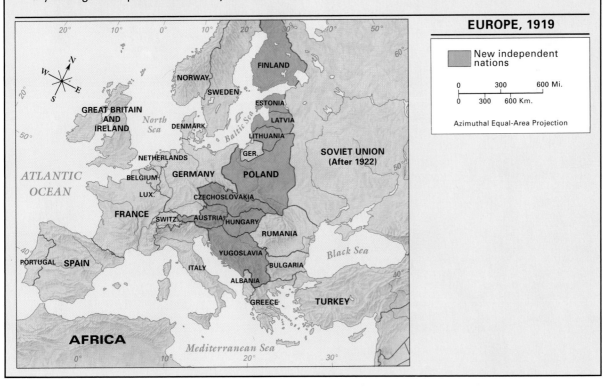

EUROPE, 1919

New independent nations

0   300   600 Mi.
0   300   600 Km.

Azimuthal Equal-Area Projection

Council of Four, popularly called the **Big Four.** Working under them were many hundreds of lawyers, mapmakers, economists, historians, military leaders, and all sorts of other experts.

Wilson had a difficult time persuading the other leaders to accept his idea of peace without victory. Clemenceau wanted to make Germany pay the entire cost of the war. France especially had been bled white. Most of the fighting had taken place on French soil. The northern part of the country was a vast no man's land. And almost 1.4 million French soldiers had been killed out of the country's total population of only about 40 million, including women, children, and elderly people.

Lloyd George and Orlando also put the interests of their own nations first. Wilson was forced to agree to a clause in the treaty stating that Germany alone had caused the war. He even accepted a clause making Germany pay ''for all damage done to the civilian population of the Allies and their property.''

This sum, called **reparations,** was so enormous that the Allies were not able to decide an actual amount. They made the Germans sign ''a blank check'' agreeing to pay whatever the victors finally demanded. The amount eventually named was $33 billion. This was far more than the Germans could possibly pay, whether or not they

The "Big Four" of the Great War are, left to right: Vittorio Orlando of Italy, David Lloyd George of Great Britain, Georges Clemenceau of France, and Woodrow Wilson of the United States.

Culver Pictures

were entirely responsible for the war. This was certainly not the peace without victory Wilson had promised.

Even if the Big Four had wanted to do so, putting all the 14 Points into practice would have been impossible. Self-determination was an excellent idea, but in many parts of Europe people of different nationalities were mixed together. There were villages of Germans living in Polish areas, Slavs in the midst of Italians or Hungarians.

Many agreements already in existence conflicted with the idea of self-determination. The victorious nations had made promises in order to win the war that violated this and other of Wilson's points. Britain and France had promised Italy parts of Austria-Hungary. The British had agreed to back an Arab nation in the Middle East and also to support a homeland for the Jews in the same region.

Yet, on balance, the final **Versailles Peace Treaty** did come close to the goal Wilson had aimed at in his 14 Points speech. Poland and Czechoslovakia became new states based on the principle of self-determination. The new map of Europe probably came closer to putting all the people of that continent under the flag of their choice than had ever been done before.

The treaty included what Wilson considered his most important point of all. This was the Covenant, or constitution, of the League of Nations.

The League consisted of a General Assembly of representatives of 42 Allied and neutral nations and a Council controlled by the Big Four and Japan. All League members were required to protect one another's territories against attack. All disputes between members were to be submitted to arbitration. Nations which did not obey League decisions could be punished by **sanctions.** These could take the form of a ban on trade with the offending country or even military force.

Furthermore, the former German colonies in Africa and the Far East and the parts of the Middle East that were taken from Turkey were made **mandates,** or dependencies, of the League as a whole. They were to be managed by individual Allied nations. Great Britain, France, and Japan held most of them. The entire League was made responsible for seeing that the interests of the local inhabitants were properly protected.

The League of Nations was Woodrow Wilson's proudest accomplishment. He believed that its founding marked the beginning of an era of permanent world peace. He knew that the Versailles Treaty was not the true "peace without victory" he had sought. Yet he was absolutely certain that the League would be able to deal with the problems the treaty had created. He believed that the entire arrangement made at Versailles depended on the acceptance and support of the League by all the powers. This was the message he brought when he returned to the United States from France. In July 1919 he submitted the treaty to the Senate. 🖅

Return to the Preview & Review on page 305.

The Search for Peace   309

CHAPTER 7 REVIEW

1910
Mexican Revolution

1914
American tro
capture Vera
★
Great War sta
★
First Battle o
the Marne

Chapter Summary
Read the statements below. Choose one, and write a paragraph explaining its importance.
1. A variety of factors caused Europe to erupt into war in 1914. The conflict grew into the largest war in history.
2. The United States peace movement tried to end war, and most Americans felt the country should remain neutral.
3. Wilson's foreign policy was unsuccessful in dealing with the Mexican Revolution.
4. After a swift advance into France, German troops were battled to a stalemate. Trench warfare across a no man's land yielded no winner.
5. German U-boats eventually led the U.S. to declare war on the Central Powers in 1917.
6. At home the war effort led to special industrial and food programs. Women and minorities found increased job opportunities.
7. Modern weapons made the Great War especially deadly.
8. The Treaty of Versailles that ended the war was not the peace without victory Wilson felt was so essential to future peace.

Reviewing Chronological Order
Number your paper 1-5. Then study the time line above and place the following events in the order in which they happened by writing the first next to 1, the second next to 2, and so on.
1. Wilson reelected president
2. Great War starts
3. Battle of the Argonne Forest
4. Battle of the Marne
5. *Lusitania* sunk

Understanding Main Ideas
1. Why was the Mexican Revolution of concern to the United States? Why was Wilson's interference resented?
2. Describe trench warfare on the Western Front.

3. Give at least three reasons why the U.S. declared war on Germany in 1917.
4. How did Americans at home contribute to the war effort?
5. What was Wilson's Fourteen-Points plan? Why did he consider the League of Nations his most important point?

Thinking Critically
1. **Problem Solving.** Suppose that you were a close friend of President Woodrow Wilson. What personal advice would you give to help him deal more effectively with leaders of foreign nations? Explain your answer.
2. **Evaluating.** Do you think that President Wilson was justified in asking Congress to declare war in order to make the world safe for democracy? Why or why not?
3. **Synthesizing.** If you had been a patriotic American in 1917, believing Hoover's slogan, "Food will win the war," what would you have done to conserve food supplies?
4. **Drawing Conclusions.** You are to help the Allies negotiate the Versailles Peace Treaty. Do you think Germany should be held totally responsible for the cost of the Great War? Explain.

Writing About History: Informative
Imagine you and your classmates are war reporters. Each of you will phone in a report on one of the following events: an aerial dogfight, trench warfare, the spotting of a U-boat. The "general editor" who receives the calls will write reports from the descriptions given over the phone. Use the information in Chapter 7 to help you develop your report. Reporters should hand in their "notes" and the general editor should submit their groups' reports.

Practicing the Strategy
Review the strategy on page 307.

Wilson's Presidency

15	THE GREAT WAR	1920

| **15** Ison announces trict accountability" | **1916** American troops pursue Villa ★ Sussex pledge ★ Wilson reelected president | **1917** Germans resume submarine warfare ★ U.S declares war ★ A.E.F. arrives in Europe | **1918** Wilson issues 14 Points ★ Battle of Argonne Forest ★ Armistice ends fighting | **1919** Versailles Peace Treaty League of Nations established |
| sitania sunk | | | | |

Analyzing Boundary Changes. Compare the map on page 307 with the map of Europe in the Reference Section, and answer these questions.

1. What three countries north of Poland appear on the map of Europe in 1919 but are not on the map of Europe in the Reference Section? What do you think happened to them?
2. How have the boundaries of each of the following countries changed since 1919: Finland, Germany, Poland, and Rumania?
3. How have the name and boundary of Great Britain and Ireland changed? Why do you think the name and boundary changed?

Using Primary Sources

On April 2, 1917 President Wilson made a formal request to Congress for a declaration of war. As you read the last paragraph of Wilson's message, note how he appeals to the emotions of the American people.

> . . . we shall fight for the things which we have always carried nearest our hearts—for democracy, for the right of those who submit to authority to have a voice in their own governments, for the rights and liberties of small nations, for a universal dominion of right by such a concert of free peoples as shall bring peace and safety to all nations and make the world itself at last free. To such a task we can dedicate our lives and our fortunes, everything that we are and everything that we have, with the pride of those who know that the day has come when America is privileged to spend her blood and her might for the principles that gave her birth and happiness and the peace which she has treasured. God helping her, she can do no other.

1. Why do you think President Wilson says that "America is privileged to spend her blood"?
2. After reading this excerpt, what inference can you make about what President Wilson thought was important for the world?

3. President Wilson was famous for his speaking ability. In your opinion, what is the most moving phrase or sentence in this excerpt? Why?

Linking History & Geography

New weapons and tactics used in the Great War changed the geography of warfare. Many geographic barriers no longer offered protection. Distances no longer seemed so great. To understand how advances in technology helped shape the Great War, answer the following questions.

1. What weapon enabled Germany to break through British naval defenses?
2. How did airplanes help overcome certain geographic barriers? How did tanks? How did new, more powerful guns lead to trench warfare and vast spaces of no man's land?
3. How have advances in the technology of war almost completely eliminated geography as a factor of war?

Enriching Your Study of History

1. **Individual Project.** Create a series of posters (at least 3) to promote the war on the home front. You might develop posters for recruiting, for the war effort in the U.S., or for the Food Administrator (such as "Food will win the war" or the campaign for "Meatless Tuesdays"). Display your posters for the class.
2. **Cooperative Project.** Your group will use its historical imagination to present to the class a White House meeting between President Wilson and his advisers. The president is considering U.S. involvement in the Great War. One of your group will portray Wilson, and others will speak for each of the following positions: (a) remaining neutral, (b) protesting strongly to Great Britain and Germany for violations of international shipping rules, (c) holding Germany "strictly accountable" for attacks on American ships, and (d) declaring war on Germany.

Chapter 7 Review   311

The Twenties

When President Wilson returned to the United States with the Versailles Treaty, almost everyone believed the Senate would ratify it. Certainly everyone wanted the war to be officially over. And the idea of an organization like the League of Nations seemed a good one. A large majority of Americans probably favored the League, although few understood it entirely or were happy with its every detail. Now came the task of winning over the American Senate. But a difficult time lay ahead for the president.

Preview & Review

Use these questions to guide your reading. Answer the questions after completing Section 1.
Understanding Issues, Events, & Ideas. Explain Wilson's political troubles, using the following words: mild reservationists, strong reservationists, Lodge Reservations, Irreconcilables, Nineteenth Amendment.
1. What problem did the 1918 Congressional elections create for President Wilson?
2. How did Wilson's health influence the political situation in the United States?
3. Why was the voter turnout so large in 1920?
Thinking Critically. If you were a member of the Senate in 1919, would you have been a mild reservationist, a strong reservationist, or an Irreconcilable? Describe the factors you considered as you made your decision.

1. THE TRAGEDY OF WOODROW WILSON

Republican Opponents

The Democrats had lost political power in the United States during the war. The Republicans gained in the Northeast by claiming that the heavy wartime income tax unfairly punished industrial areas. They gained in the Midwest and West, where farmers were angry over farm policies that seemed favorable to southern farmers. They also gained in urban areas, where laborers were unhappy with Democratic support of prohibition. As a result, in the 1918 Congressional elections the Republicans won majorities in both the House and the Senate. Wilson now needed the support of a large number of Republican senators to get the two-thirds majority necessary to ratify the Versailles Treaty.

Wilson had expected the Democrats would continue to control the Senate. He had campaigned for Democrats so that his peace policies would be carried out smoothly. After the election he made matters worse for himself by not including any Republican senators on the peace commission.

Why he did not is a mystery. Perhaps the president assumed the peace treaty would be so popular that senators would not dare vote against it. "The Senate must take its medicine," he said privately.

Wilson seemed to not realize that some parts of any complicated document like the Versailles Treaty were sure to displease many different people. When its details became known, various special interest groups demanded many changes in the treaty. But Wilson refused to agree to any changes whatsoever.

The most important criticism involved the League of Nations. The United States would be only one among many members. Suppose the League voted to use force against a nation. Was it not up to Congress to say when American troops were sent into battle? Old suspicions of tricky European diplomats now began to reappear. Senator William Borah, a leading foe of America's joining the League, stated the problem this way in a speech to the Senate:

“ What is the result of this Treaty of Versailles? We are in the middle of all of the affairs of Europe. We have entangled ourselves with all European concerns. We have joined in alliance with all the European nations which have thus far joined the League, and all nations which may be admitted to the League. We are sitting there dabbling in their affairs and meddling in their concerns. In other words—and this comes to the question which is fundamental to me—we have surrendered, once and for all, the great policy of 'no entangling alliances' upon which the strength of this Republic has been based for 150 years.[1] ”

The Senate Debate

In the Senate debate nearly all the Democrats supported the League without question. Many Republican senators also favored joining the League. Some of these, known as **mild reservationists,** were willing to vote for the treaty if a few minor changes were made. They had reservations about the League, but their reservations would not block American membership.

Other Republicans were willing to vote for the treaty—and the League—only if more important changes were made. These **strong reservationists** were led by Senator Henry Cabot Lodge of Massachusetts. He introduced what were called the **Lodge Reservations** to the treaty. The most important of these stated that American armed forces could not be sent into action by the League of Nations until Congress gave its approval.

If Wilson had been willing to accept the Lodge Reservations, the Versailles Treaty would have been ratified easily. Only a small group of senators, known as the **Irreconcilables,** refused to vote for it on any terms. The president could probably have gotten the two-thirds vote by making some small concessions to the mild reservationists alone. Yet he refused to budge. It had to be all or nothing.

[1]From *American Problems: A Selection of Speeches and Prophecies by William E. Borah,* edited by Horace Green

Henry Cabot Lodge was the leading foe of President Wilson even before the fight over the treaty. Another of Lodge's Democratic enemies, Boston's legendary mayor John Fitzgerald, never forgot his first view of the Lodge wealth. The Lodge family cook invited him to peek into the Beacon Street mansion. "That playroom was the most extraordinary sight," Fitzgerald later recalled, "filled with the most elaborate wooden toys you could ever imagine." Lodge's portrait is by John Singer Sargent.

The Tragedy of Woodrow Wilson   313

Partially paralyzed by the stroke he suffered in 1919, Woodrow Wilson is helped by a servant as he leaves his home in 1923. He has just made an Armistice Day broadcast.

A White House Invalid

For Wilson the basic issue of the treaty ratification was the idea of a truly international government. He argued that the United States must join the League on the same terms as all the other nations. His position was *reasonable* but not *realistic*. America had too long seen itself as "different" from the countries of Europe.

Americans were being asked to enter into the kind of "entangling alliances" that Jefferson had warned against in his first inaugural address in 1801. It was true that the United States had become an international power. But people needed to adjust gradually to modern conditions. "All or nothing" was not the way to educate them.

If the president had been in good health, he would probably not have taken such a rigid stand. But he was in very poor health. While in Paris, he had suffered a mild stroke—the breaking of a blood vessel in his brain. It had not been recognized as a stroke at the time by his doctor. The attack seriously affected Wilson's judgment.

Still Wilson took the debate to the American people. He went on a whirlwind tour of the United States, making 37 speeches in 29 cities in early September. At the beginning of the tour he stated what he felt was at the heart of the matter:

      I wonder if some of the opponents of the League of Nations have forgotten the promises we made before we went to the peace table. We had taken men from every household, and we told mothers and fathers and sisters and wives and sweethearts that we were taking those men to fight a war to end all wars. If we do not end wars, we are unfaithful to the loving hearts who suffered in this war.

      That is what the League of Nations is for—to end this war justly, and then to serve notice on other governments which might consider trying to do the same things that Germany attempted. The League of Nations is the only thing that can prevent another dreadful catastrophe and fulfill our promises. . . .

      Now, look at what else is in the treaty. It is unique in the history of humankind, because the heart of it is the protection of weak nations. . . . If there is no League of Nations, the military point of view will win out in every instance, and peace will not last. . . .

      If I were to state what seems to me to be the central idea of this treaty, it would be this: Nations do not consist of their governments but of their people. That is a simple idea. It seems to us in America to go without saying. But, my fellow citizens, it was never the leading idea in any other international congress made up of the representatives of governments. They were always thinking of national policy, of national advantage, of the rivalries of trade, of the

STRATEGIES FOR SUCCESS

COMPARING POINTS OF VIEW

Historical interpretations of an important event, person, or situation often vary widely. This is because people bring to their interpretations different points of view. One way you can better understand history is to compare historical points of view.

How to Compare Points of View

To compare points of view, follow these steps.

1. **Note the sources.** Find out about each author or speaker.
2. **Compare the main ideas expressed.** Note the similarities and differences. Some points will be quite similar. Others will be opposites.
3. **Compare supporting details.** Consider the amount of support and its logic as you make your comparison.
4. **Do research.** Find out as much as you can about the situation.
5. **Use your thinking skills.** Use your critical thinking skills to understand why people have different views of the event, person, or situation. Decide which point of view you think is most reliable, based on your study of the situation.

Applying the Strategy

As you have read, a lengthy debate over ratification of the Treaty of Versailles raged in the Senate in 1919. The main area of contention was the provision requiring the United States to join the League of Nations. President Woodrow Wilson fought long and hard in support of the United States joining the League. He thought that the League of Nations was "the only thing that can prevent another dreadful catastrophe" such as the Great World War. He also claimed that "the only country in the world that is trusted at this moment is the United States. The peoples of the world are waiting to see whether their trust is justified or not."

On the other hand, many Americans, including several influential members of Congress, opposed United States membership. Senator William E. Borah felt that joining the League would involve the United States in Europe's complex affairs and would mean "we have surrendered, once and for all, the great policy of 'no entangling alliances' upon which the strength of this Republic has been based for 150 years."

Now read and compare these other excerpts taken from the debate over American membership in the League.

Excerpt A

Our isolation ended twenty years ago. . . . There can be no question of our ceasing to be a world power. The only question is whether we refuse the leadership that is offered."

President Woodrow Wilson

Excerpt B

I object in the strongest possible way to having the United States agree, directly or indirectly, to be controlled by a League which may at any time . . . be drawn in to deal with internal conflicts in other countries. . . . It must be made perfectly clear that no American soldiers . . . can ever be engaged in war or ordered anywhere except by the constitutional authorities of the United States.

Senator Henry Cabot Lodge

Excerpt A is from a speech by President Woodrow Wilson urging the Senate to approve the treaty. Although he does not state it, Wilson's comments allude to the provision of the treaty which called for the United States to enter into the League of Nations.

What is Wilson's argument? He claims the United States is now a world power and must continue to assume that responsibility. What support did he use? He points out that the United States began overseas expansion, ending a period of isolation. It had annexed Hawaii, and had been involved in the Spanish-American War, events in Mexico, and the Great War. Why would Wilson hold the point of view he expresses—urging the Senate to ratify the treaty and join the League of Nations?

Excerpt B is taken from a speech against ratification by Senator Henry Cabot Lodge. As you have read, Lodge was a leading opponent of the treaty. His view is that the United States should not enter the League. What reasons does he give for his opposition?

As you know, the United States did not ratify the treaty or join the League of Nations. Why do you think Lodge's arguments were successful?

For independent practice, see Practicing the Strategy on page 353.

The Granger Collection

After the U.S. Senate refused to ratify the Versailles Treaty, an American cartoonist in 1920 drew "The Accuser," showing the treaty stabbed by the Senate. What is this cartoonist's message? Why do you suppose editorial cartoonists so often portrayed their subjects in a Roman fashion, especially those dealing with government?

advantages of territorial conquest. There is nothing of those things in this treaty.[1] **"**

Then, in September 1919, while he was trying to rally support for the League, he suffered another stroke. This time there was no mistake about it. His left side was partially paralyzed.

For weeks Wilson was an invalid in the White House. As he slowly recovered, his advisers pleaded with him to compromise with the moderate Republicans. Otherwise the treaty, which required a two-thirds majority to pass, was sure to be defeated. Wilson refused. It was better "to go down fighting," he told his friends.

On November 19, 1919, the treaty, with the Lodge Reservations attached, came to a vote in the Senate. It was defeated by Democratic votes. Then it was voted on without reservations. This time the Republicans defeated it. The following March, after further debate, the Senate again voted on the treaty with reservations. This time some Democratic senators refused to follow Wilson's urging. They voted for ratification. Not enough of them did so, however, and for a third and final time the treaty was rejected.

The Election of 1920

Wilson had hoped that the presidential election of 1920 would prove that the people of the United States wanted to join the League. The

[1]From *War and Peace: The Public Papers of Woodrow Wilson*, Vol. 1

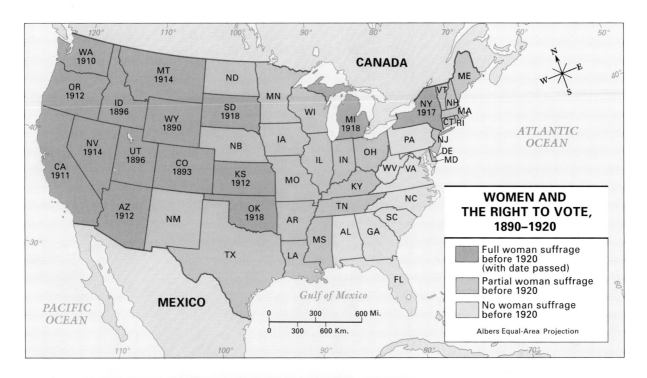

WA
1910

OR
1912

ID
1896

MT
1914

ND

MN

CANADA

ME

VT

NH

NY
1917

MA

CT RI

ATLANTIC
OCEAN

NV
1914

UT
1896

WY
1890

SD
1918

WI

MI
1918

PA

NJ

DE

MD

CA
1911

CO
1893

NB

IA

IL

IN

OH

WV

VA

KS
1912

MO

KY

NC

AZ
1912

NM

OK
1918

AR

TN

SC

MS

AL

GA

TX

LA

FL

PACIFIC
OCEAN

MEXICO

Gulf of Mexico

WOMEN AND THE RIGHT TO VOTE, 1890–1920

- Full woman suffrage before 1920 (with date passed)
- Partial woman suffrage before 1920
- No woman suffrage before 1920

Albers Equal-Area Projection

0   300   600 Mi.
0   300   600 Km.

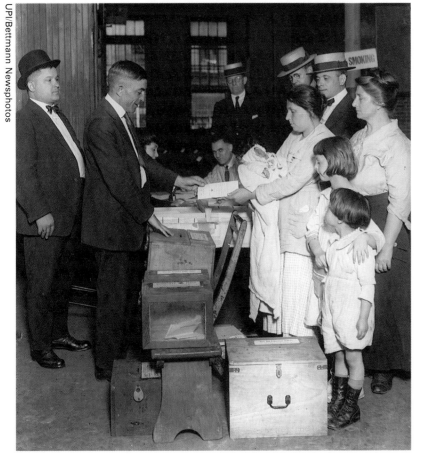

UPI/Bettmann Newsphotos

SMOKING

LEARNING FROM MAPS. *As you can see from this map, women's right to vote spread slowly between 1890 and the ratification of the 19th Amendment in 1920. What four states first granted women the right to vote? Why do you think this movement started in the West?*

The vote theirs at last—after carrying the water, toting the firewood, ironing the clothes, and keeping the family together—these ladies have come forward to claim what is rightfully theirs by the Nineteenth Amendment.

The Tragedy of Woodrow Wilson   317

Both, UPI/Bettmann Newsphotos

The 1920 presidential campaign was between Warren G. Harding and James M. Cox, both of Ohio. On the right Cox and his running mate Franklin D. Roosevelt (a year before his crippling polio) lead a parade through Columbus, Ohio, after receiving official word of their nomination. Harding, below, campaigns from his front porch in Marion, Ohio. His wife, whom critics and Harding both called Duchess, had great political aspirations for him but his "friends" took advantage of his presidency with shady schemes.

Return to the Preview & Review on page 312.

Democratic candidate, Governor James M. Cox of Ohio, campaigned on a platform which called for joining.

The Republican candidate, Senator Warren G. Harding, refused to take a clear position on the issue. Harding was an expert at avoiding controversial questions. Instead, he urged Americans to vote for the Republicans and a return to "normalcy." By this he meant that the U.S. should turn away from Europe and concentrate on domestic issues.

During the presidential campaign Harding used a technique called "bloviating." This meant talking about a subject in a way that sounded intelligent but which actually made little or no sense. Citizens who favored the League could think that Harding favored it. Those who opposed it could interpret his statements the other way.

On Election Day, Harding won by a huge majority. The new **Nineteenth Amendment,** which gave women the vote in national elections, caused a larger voter turnout in 1920. The vote for president was nearly 9 million more than it had been in 1916. Harding got 61 percent of the total, over 16 million votes to Cox's 9.1 million.

Once elected, Harding made it clear that he did not want the United States to join the League. Since the League could not be separated from the Versailles Treaty, Congress simply passed a resolution in the summer of 1921 declaring that the war was over. 🔲

2. AMERICAN REACTION TO THE WAR

Foreign Policy in the 1920s

The American people were not ready to assume the kind of international responsibilities that Wilson called for, but they really had little choice. The United States had become the leading industrial and financial power in the world. After the huge foreign loans made by the United States during the war, the rest of the world owed the United States $13 billion. America could not retreat into an isolated cocoon.

In practice the presidents of the 1920s tried to follow a middle road between the narrow view of **isolationism** and the broader view of **internationalism.** They wanted to enjoy the benefits of America's commanding economic position in the world. Yet they did not want to make binding promises to other countries. This attitude was clearly revealed in the way President Harding approached the question of reducing the size of the navy.

After the huge cost of the Great War the public was eager to avoid building still more warships. In 1921 Harding invited nine European and Asian nations to Washington to discuss **disarmament—** limiting the manufacture of weapons of war. Far Eastern issues were also discussed at this Washington Disarmament Conference.

Several treaties were negotiated by the delegates. The most important was the **Five-Power Naval Treaty.** In this treaty the United States, Great Britain, Japan, France, and Italy agreed to a ten-year

Culver Pictures

PUTTING HIS FOOT DOWN.

Preview & Review

Use these questions to guide your reading. Answer the questions after completing Section 2.
Understanding Issues, Events, & Ideas. Describe the postwar reaction in America using the following words: isolationism, internationalism, disarmament, Five-Power Naval Treaty, Open Door, postwar reaction, anarchists, Big Red Scare, Palmer raid, ghetto, Emergency Quota Act, National Origins Act, American Civil Liberties Union. Explain the major changes in American society after the war using these words: prohibition, dry state, Eighteenth Amendment, Volstead Act, bootlegger, repeal, Twenty-first Amendment, fundamentalism.
1. Why did American presidents in the 1920s try to find a middle ground between isolationism and internationalism?
2. What effect did peacetime have on industry? Why?
3. Why was prohibition difficult to enforce?
4. How was the fundamentalist movement a part of the postwar reaction in America? How was the Sacco-Vanzetti case a part?
Thinking Critically.   1. You have read that after the Great War, Americans "wanted peace without the responsibility of maintaining it." Do you think that Americans still have that attitude? Give reasons to support your answer.
2. Write two editorials about the Scopes trial: one from the point of view of a person who favored the advances of science and technology being taught and the other from the point of view of a fundamentalist against teaching about them.

In this editorial cartoon, "Putting His Foot Down," Uncle Sam holds a copy of the "Trade Treaty with China" that began America's Open Door Policy. For a complete discussion of the Open Door Policy, see pages 228–29. What did the policy provide? Why did Americans consider such an agreement important in the 1920s?

"holiday" on the construction of battleships. They also agreed to maintain a fixed ratio, or balance, on all major warships. The United States and Great Britain were to have no more than 525,000 tons of such vessels. Japan's limit was 315,000 tons, France and Italy's 175,000 each. In another agreement all nine nations promised to uphold the principle of the **Open Door** in China. This was the policy which assured all nations equal trade rights with an independent China.

President Harding insisted that the Washington Conference treaties did not commit the United States "to any kind of alliance, entanglement, or involvement." This was true enough. The treaties were backed only by the good will of the nations that signed them. This satisfied most Americans. They wanted peace without the responsibility for maintaining it. They could accept the treaties and still believe that they could remain isolated in the old way from foreign "entanglements."

The Postwar Reaction

Isolation was an aspect of a larger **postwar reaction** in the United States. The Great War had been a Great Mistake, most people now thought. Millions of lives had been lost. Billions of dollars had been wasted. And for what purpose? The world had certainly not been made safe for democracy, as Wilson had promised.

In 1919 most Americans seemed more worried about making the United States safe for themselves. Many seriously believed that a communist revolution might break out in the United States at any moment. They were mindful that a tiny group of communists had taken over all of Russia in 1917. Now there were perhaps seventy thousand communists (called Reds) in the United States.

Communists wanted workers to raise the red flag of revolution, take up arms, and destroy the capitalist system. At the same time **anarchists,** who wanted all governments violently abolished, stirred up workers. But most workers were simply trying to keep their jobs. Going from war to peace had been difficult for American industry. Without contracts for war supplies, many plants shut down temporarily or slowed down their operations. Hundreds of thousands of wage earners were thrown out of work. Soldiers returning to civilian life found it almost impossible to get jobs. Many of the workers found their jobs had been filled by African Americans who had moved from the South during the war to work in factories. This added fuel to racial tensions that erupted in situations like the race riots in Washington and Chicago.

As a result a wave of strikes spread over the land. At one time or another during 1919, 4 million workers were on strike. Seattle was paralyzed. In Boston even the police walked off their jobs. Strikes by police were unheard of at that time. With the streets of Boston

The Chicago Steel Strike of 1919 was one of the disturbing postwar demonstrations. Even police went on strike in Boston. Most people blamed these strikes on "creeping Bolshevism"—Russian communism—as we see in the Red Scare cartoon below.

unprotected, looters began breaking into stores. The governor of Massachusetts, Calvin Coolidge, finally called in troops to restore order in the city.

At the same time a series of bombings by terrorists took place. To this day no one knows who was responsible for most of the bombings. But the tendency was to blame "the Reds." A **Big Red Scare** swept over America.

President Wilson's attorney general, A. Mitchell Palmer, became convinced that a massive communist plot to overthrow the federal government was being organized. He ordered raids on the headquarters of suspected radical groups. These **Palmer raids** were often conducted without search warrants. Many suspected communists were held for weeks without formal charges. There was no evidence of a nationwide uprising. Yet in 1921 Palmer announced that such a revolution would take place on May 1, the communist Labor Day. When May 1 passed quietly, Americans realized that the danger of a revolution had been only in their minds. As quickly as it had begun, the Big Red Scare ended.

The nervous mood of the 1920s then took other forms. One was a revival of the Ku Klux Klan. Klan membership grew between 1920 and 1923 from about 5,000 members to several million. Unlike the Klan of Reconstruction days, not black people but immigrants and religious minorities, especially Jews and Catholics, were the new Klan's primary targets. This helps explain why it was an important political and social force in northern cities in the early 1920s.

Of course, the Klan persecuted African Americans too. And the

The hooded figures are but a handful of the millions nationwide who joined the Ku Klux Klan in the 1920s. They burned crosses and lynched African Americans in the dead of night, some of their victims still wearing their uniforms from the Great War.

blacks also faced hostility from many less openly prejudiced people. In the South, hard times were causing thousands of sharecroppers and tenants to abandon the land and move north in search of work. But in the northern cities most could find only low-paying jobs such as dishwasher, servant, and garbage collector. Blacks were segregated in crowded **ghettos,** which were dirty, unhealthy slums.

Racial tensions sizzled. Mobs in the South lynched more than 60 African Americans, 10 of them Great War veterans still in uniform. Race riots erupted in Washington, D.C., Chicago, and other northern cities. The NAACP now urged blacks to stand firm, to fight back. The violence increased throughout the country.

Some people blamed the communists for stirring up the racial trouble. Meanwhile black leaders and liberal whites pushed for anti-lynching laws. And many African Americans were attracted to the Universal Negro Improvement Association of Marcus Garvey. He appealed to African American traditions and religious values. Both God and Christ were black, Garvey claimed. He wanted African Americans to return to Africa, where he hoped to create a black-controlled kingdom. Meanwhile, he started several black businesses, including a company that manufacured black dolls and the Black Star Line steamship company. His movement boosted the pride and dignity of hundreds of thousands of followers. ''Up you mighty race,'' he urged, ''you can accomplish what you will.''

Garvey's ideas also had great influence in Central America, the Caribbean, and Africa. Even the African National Congress in southern Africa is a direct outgrowth of Garvey's movement.

At the same time the NAACP continued to battle for equal rights. Seeking to unify African Americans—in fact all Americans—the organization issued a national statement of its aims in 1919:

“ 1. A vote for every Negro man and woman on the same terms as for white men and women.

2. An equal chance to acquire the kind of an education that will enable the Negro everywhere wisely to use this vote.

3. A fair trial in courts for all crimes of which he is accused, by judges in whose election he has participated without discrimination because of race.

4. A right to sit upon the jury which passes judgment upon him.

5. Defense against lynching and burning at the hands of mobs.

6. Equal service on railroad and other public carriers. This to mean sleeping car service, dining car service, Pullman service, at the same cost and upon the same terms as other passengers.

7. Equal right to use of public parks, libraries and other community services for which he is taxed.

8. An equal chance for a livelihood in public and private employment.

9. The abolition of color-hyphenation and the substitution of 'straight Americanism.'

If it were not a painful fact that more than four-fifths of the colored people of the country are denied the above

The flag passes by as a member of the 309th Colored Infantry pays his respects.

Grant Wood was one of America's finest 20th-century painters. In "Daughters of the Revolution" he posed the three in front of a print of Washington crossing the Delaware.

named elementary rights, it would seem an absurdity that an organization is necessary to demand for American citizens the exercise of such rights. . . . Has not slavery been abolished? Are not all men equal before the law? Were not the Fourteenth and Fifteenth Amendments passed by the Congress of the United States and adopted by the states? Is not the Negro a man and a citizen?[1] **"**

The NAACP also made a strong statement of principles and observations of the plight of blacks in America. In part it said:

" When the fundamental rights of citizens are so wantonly denied and that denial justified and defended as it is by the lawmakers and dominant forces of so large a number of our states, it can be realized that the fight for the Negro's citizenship rights means a fundamental battle for real things, for life and liberty.

This fight is the Negro's fight. 'Who would be free, himself must strike the blow.' But, it is no less the white man's fight. The common citizenship rights of no group of people, to say nothing of nearly 12,000,000 of them, can be denied with impunity [freedom from harm] to the State and the social order which denies them. . . . Whoso loves America and cherishes its institutions, owes it to himself and his country to join hands with the members of the National Association for the Advancement of Colored People to 'Americanize' America and make the kind of democracy we Americans believe in to be the kind of democracy we shall have in *fact*, as well as in theory.[2] **"**

[1]From "The Task for the Future—A Program for 1919" by the NAACP
[2]*Ibid.*

Despite these efforts, little progress was made in ending discrimination in America.

America's postwar mood was also reflected in new immigration laws. In 1921 Congress reacted to the isolationism of the times by taking steps to control the entry of foreigners into the United States. This made some sense at the time. The frontier had disappeared. In a machine age the nation no longer needed to import large numbers of unskilled laborers. The **Emergency Quota Act** limited the number of immigrants by nationality, reducing the number of newcomers from eastern and southern Europe. A still stiffer quota law, the **National Origins Act,** was passed in 1924. Beginning in 1929, a total of only 150,000 immigrants a year could enter the United States. In practice the number of actual immigrants fell below 100,000 every year from 1931 to 1946.

The Sacco-Vanzetti Case

Such xenophobia—the fear of foreigners—led to the Sacco-Vanzetti case. In April 1920 two men in Massachusetts killed a paymaster and a guard during a daring daylight robbery of a shoe factory. Shortly thereafter, Nicola Sacco and Bartolomeo Vanzetti were charged with the crime, and in 1921 they were convicted of murder. Sacco and Vanzetti were anarchists who believed that government was unnecessary and should be violently overthrown. They were also Italian immigrants. Their trial was a travesty of justice. There was little real evidence against them. Much of what was presented at the trial had been manufactured by the prosecution. In addition, the judge seemed prejudiced against the two, especially in his comments outside the courtroom.

Prominent people all over the world praised the dignity Sacco and Vanzetti showed throughout the trial. The noted lawyer Felix Frankfurter helped found the **American Civil Liberties Union** to fight for the two men. Other defenders of justice, including the novelist John Dos Passos and the poet Edna St. Vincent Millay, joined worldwide protests that for years kept Sacco and Vanzetti alive through efforts to obtain a new trial. Vanzetti's dignified words are still remembered:

> ❝ You see me before you, not trembling. I never commit a crime in my life. . . . I am so convinced to be right that if you could execute me two times, and if I could be reborn two other times, I would live again and do what I have done already.❞

In August 1927 Sacco and Vanzetti were electrocuted. Historians now suspect that at least Sacco was guilty, but the truth and shame of the incident remain: at the time Sacco and Vanzetti paid with their lives for being radicals and foreigners as much as for any crime.

Ben Shahn, *The Passion of Sacco and Vanzetti,* 1931-32, tempra on canvas, 84 ½ x 48", Collection of Whitney Museum of American Art, Gift of Mr. and Mrs. Milton Lowenthal in memory of Juliana Force, 49.22.

Were these two humble Italian immigrants—Nicola Sacco and Bartolomeo Vanzetti—guilty of a bold daylight robbery and killing a paymaster? Or were they simply guilty of being foreigners at a time when xenophobia—fear of foreigners—swept over America in the 1920s? Those who believed them innocent hung Ben Shahn's lithograph, "The Passion of Sacco and Vanzetti," right in the living room for all to see.

Thomas Hart Benton depicts the dark side of prohibition in "The Bootleggers," painted in 1927. Planes, trains, and fast cars bring the customers to buy liquor in a scene sadly suggestive of city streets today when people come to buy drugs.

Prohibition

During the Progressive Era there had been strong popular support for prohibiting the manufacture, transportation, and sale of alcoholic beverages. This temperance movement, like the one in the 1840s, was led by American religious groups who saw liquor as the devil's tool. By 1914 prohibition was in force in more than a quarter of the states, known as the dry states. Most of the dry states were in the South and rural areas, where many of the people were members of fundamentalist Protestant religious groups.

The outburst of moral and religious concern caused by the war gave energy to a national prohibition movement. Some saw it as an attack on the German custom of drinking beer; others as an attack on the drinking habits of European Catholics. What tipped the scales was a very effective campaign to protect young servicemen from the sale of alcohol on or near army bases. This fit closely with the prohibitionist charge that drinking was a cause of poverty and social disorder. As a result, in 1919 the **Eighteenth Amendment** was ratified, making the entire nation dry. This amendment was enforced by the **Volstead Act.**

People who favored prohibition pointed to the sharp decline in arrests for drunkenness and to the lower number of deaths from alcoholism in the 1920s. Fewer workers spent their hard-earned dollars on drink. However, prohibition was impossible to enforce, even with the tough Volstead Act. Private individuals bought liquor smuggled by **bootleggers** or drank gin from teacups in "speakeasies"—secret bars or clubs.

Crime statistics soared in the 1920s. Most of the liquor was sold by gangsters such as "Scarface" Al Capone of Chicago. Hoodlums fought for territories with guns and bombs, killing innocent bystanders as well as their rivals. The scene was not much different from the one on some city streets today where drug deals are common. Dealers, like the bootleggers, fight over territory, often killing one another and innocent bystanders as well.

Still, in the 1920s powerful "dry" forces kept politicians in both parties from proposing that prohibition be lifted, or **repealed.** It remained in force until December 1933, when it was repealed by the **Twenty-first Amendment.**

The Fundamentalist Movement

America was rapidly changing in the postwar years. Over 19 million people moved from the farm to the city in the 1920s. Problems such as crime, gambling, and corruption seemed to be all too common, especially in the cities. The progressive spirit had died in the disillusionment following the Great War. Many Americans searching for a system of values in this time of rapid change found it in the

In the purity of her white robe a woman baptized on a farm in Kansas may feel she walks with Jesus at Galilee. Study this painting by John Steuart Curry, who painted to show the "struggle of man against nature." How does he show the depth of feeling of the fundamentalist onlookers?

John Steuart Curry, *Baptism in Kansas* (1928), oil on canvas, 40 × 50", Collection of Whitney Museum of American Art, 31.159.

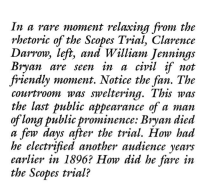

In a rare moment relaxing from the rhetoric of the Scopes Trial, Clarence Darrow, left, and William Jennings Bryan are seen in a civil if not friendly moment. Notice the fan. The courtroom was sweltering. This was the last public appearance of a man of long public prominence: Bryan died a few days after the trial. How had he electrified another audience years earlier in 1896? How did he fare in the Scopes trial?

Protestant religious movement called **fundamentalism.** It was strongest on the farms and in the small towns of America. Many people in these rural areas blamed society's economic and social problems on modern urban culture. Fundamentalists believed that the King James translation of the Bible was God's truth. They took its words literally.

Fundamentalists thought that the science and technology of the machine age were challenging the traditional values and beliefs they held dear. Every year new discoveries seemed to question ideas held for centuries. As an example they seized on Charles Darwin's theory of evolution described in *The Origin of Species*. They campaigned vigorously for laws banning all mention of Darwin's theory, especially in textbooks and classrooms. Darwin, a British naturalist, had theorized that modern species of plants and animals had evolved from a few earlier ones. From Darwin's theory came the idea that human beings had slowly evolved from ape-like creatures, which of course had gradually evolved from even lower life-forms. This idea directly opposed the fundamentalist's view of God having created the heavens and the earth in six days. Didn't the Bible describe how and when God created each of his creatures, including humans?

In their battle against evolution, the fundamentalists found a leader in William Jennings Bryan, the forceful orator who had been Wilson's secretary of state. Bryan went about the country charging that modern Americans had "taken the Lord away from the schools." He even offered $100 to anyone who would admit in public that he was descended from an ape as he claimed Darwin had said.

In 1925 the fundamentalists won a victory when Tennessee passed a law forbidding instructors in the state's schools and colleges to teach "any theory that denies the story of the Divine Creation of man taught in the Bible." Many people were shocked at the law, which they felt restricted academic freedom, maybe even the freedom of speech. The American Civil Liberties Union, a nonprofit group whose stated purpose was to protect the basic freedom of the people, offered to defend any Tennessee teacher who would challenge the constitutionality of the law. A young biology teacher in the Tennessee mountain town of Dayton, John T. Scopes, agreed to violate the law and teach Darwin's theory. He was taken to court by the state. Clarence Darrow, perhaps the greatest lawyer of the time, headed Scopes' defense. Darrow put the issue this way:

> 66 Scopes isn't on trial. Civilization is on trial. The prosecution is opening the doors of a reign of bigotry equal to anything in the Middle Ages. No man's belief will be safe if they win. 99

The prosecuting attorney was no less than William Jennings Bryan himself. Overnight the Dayton "Monkey Trial" attracted national attention. Sensing a story, big-city reporters like H. L. Mencken flocked to the trial.

The trial took place in a sweltering courtroom. The prosecution took every opportunity to state its view of creation. Bryan even testified as an expert witness on the Bible. On the stand he explained that he believed that the earth had been created in 4004 B.C., that a whale had swallowed Jonah, that Joshua had stopped the sun in its course, and that Eve had been created from Adam's rib, all as the Bible said. Under intense questioning by Darrow, Bryan showed an almost complete ignorance of modern scientific thought. And he doomed his own cause when he agreed that creation took hundreds of years, that a "day" in the Bible might actually be centuries.

This admission had no effect on the trial. The conviction of Scopes was a foregone conclusion. After rousing arguments from both sides, Scopes was found guilty and fined $100. That decision was soon overturned by the state supreme court. More important, Bryan had contradicted the fundamentalists' argument.

Still, the fundamentalism that prompted the trial had vigor throughout the country. Crusaders such as Billy Sunday found audiences over the airwaves.

And the vigor has not left the movement. Conservative church groups are the most rapidly growing segment of American Protestantism. Although their message and methods are different today, fundamentalists still seek to be heard by the American people. Through television they reach their widest audience ever. Many of the groups have become politically involved, taking active roles in a variety of movements.

The Scopes trial symbolized something larger than a controversy over Darwin's theory. It emphasized the divisions within American society—rural versus urban, traditional versus modern. The rising fortunes of the late 1920s made these divisions seem deeper. Business owners and urban laborers raked in the money. Yet prosperity seemed to pass by farmers and people in small towns, leaving many of them hostile to the new urban society. ▣

Return to the Preview & Review on page 319.

American Reaction to the War   329

Use these questions to guide your reading. Answer the questions after completing Section 3.
Understanding Issues, Events, & Ideas. Describe the Roaring Twenties using the following words: jazz, Jazz Age, flappers, Harlem Renaissance, Golden Age of Sports, Harlem Globetrotters, expatriates.
1. What was the origin of jazz? How did jazz reflect the 1920s?
2. Name five heroes of the Golden Age of Sports and the sport for which each was famous.
3. How did movies influence people? What advantage did radio have over movies? Why did radio become a giant industry?
4. Who were the "lost generation?" Why does this name seem appropriate?
Thinking Critically. **1.** Compose a poem or song about the changing values of women during the 1920s. **2.** Why might someone want to become an expatriate? What reasons, if any, do you think are legitimate reasons to permanently leave America?

3. THE ROARING TWENTIES

The Jazz Age

Not all Americans were so troubled in the 1920s. Many were finding new ways to enjoy life. Industry continued to grow, producing new wealth and providing more leisure time for many millions of people. Change was in the air, and the speed of change was increasing. People everywhere were casting off old ways and seeking new ways to express themselves.

Consider the typical music of the period. The music that most Americans listened to and danced to during the 1920s was called **jazz.** Jazz was created by African American musicians in New Orleans in the late 1800s. It grew out of the "blues"—music that reflected the hard life of most blacks in America and the tough-minded humor that many displayed in trying to cope with it. W. C. Handy of Alabama was the "father of the blues." His most famous composition was "St. Louis Blues" (1914).

Most of the early African American jazz musicians had little or no formal training in music. Yet they were superb performers. Their music was often the only outlet for their emotions. Bessie Smith, a leading singer of the 1920s, sang movingly about her own sorrowful experiences. Louis "Satchmo" Armstrong was the most famous jazz musician of the day. He won international fame as a trumpeter, a singer, and as an ambassador of goodwill to other countries.

Jazz musicians *improvised* much of their music. Taking a theme or musical idea, they chased a tune up and down the scales as they played. This gave musicians and listeners alike a sense of freedom.

Both, Brown Brothers

Bessie Smith and W.C. Handy are two of the great jazz musicians who gave America its own music. Bessie Smith lived only 40 years but is fondly remembered as the "Empress of the Blues." Handy composed "Memphis Blues" and "Beale Street Blues" and dozens of other jazz standards. What made jazz spread so quickly in the United States?

"Jazz" by Romare Bearden practically makes its own music with its colors and wonderful composition. Notice how the artist combines all kinds of textures to make one unified image. How is that like jazz itself?

Jazz spread from New Orleans to Chicago and New York and then throughout most of the world. White musicians as well as black performed it. It became in its own way a powerful force for breaking down racial barriers, both among the players and for those who simply listened.

The decade of the 1920s is sometimes called the **Jazz Age.** In part the popularity of its music is enough to explain this. But jazz also symbolized the way many young people of the time felt about life in general. They sought to break away from rigid, conventional rules and traditions, just as jazz trumpeters and saxophonists departed from written notes in order to express themselves.

This new spirit of freedom also influenced the other arts. Isadora Duncan became world-famous for her beautiful and graceful free-form dancing. Frank Lloyd Wright expressed the same spirit in his architecture. Perhaps the most extreme expression of this break with the conventional was dadaism, an outrageous art movement started as a protest against all artistic and civilized standards.

Young women in particular seemed determined to free themselves from restricting "out-of-date" ideas and rules. They cast off uncomfortable (and unhealthy) corsets and thick petticoats in favor of short skirts and loose-fitting clothing. They cut their hair short. They wore makeup. They drank and smoked in public.

The behavior of these "new women" shocked older people deeply. They called them **flappers** and predicted they would come to a bad end. Actually most of these young women were just trying to liberate themselves. Not all of them were conscious feminists. Some were merely trying to keep up with the latest fads and fashions. Still, consciously or not, they were demanding the right to behave the same way men behaved.

Point of View

Two stanzas from "Homage to the Empress of the Blues," show how much the poet admired Bessie Smith.

> **She came out on the stage in yards of pearls, emerging like a favorite scenic view, flashed her golden smile and sang.**
> . . . .
> **She came out on stage in ostrich feathers, beaded satin, and shone that smile on us and sang.**
> Robert Hayden, 1966

The Roaring Twenties   331

Langston Hughes, the most important poet of the Harlem Renaissance, also invented a character he called Jess B. Semple ("Simple" to his friends) who spoke out on life in Harlem in all its many aspects.

The Harlem Renaissance

The disappointments of the 1920s faced by African Americans produced the "New Negro," as they called themselves. These African Americans were determined to build pride and a better life for themselves and their children. Langston Hughes, one of the great poets of the era, expressed what life must have been like for African American children:

Merry-Go-Round

" *Colored child at carnival:*

Where is the Jim Crow section
On this merry-go-round,
Mister, cause I want to ride?
Down South where I come from
White and colored
Can't sit side by side.
Down South on the train
There's a Jim Crow car.
On the bus we're put in the back—
But there ain't no back
To a merry-go-round!
Where's the horse
For a kid that's black?[1] "

Although to an outsider who did not know better, Harlem looked like a typical segregated slum, it was in reality a very special neighborhood. It was a place where African Americans could be themselves, mostly free of white prejudices, the largest black community in the entire world. In the 1920s Harlem became the center of a cultural outburst known as the **Harlem Renaissance.** Musicians and artists such as Aaron Douglas, William H. Johnson, Palmer Hayden, and Meta Warwick Fuller found there an audience that unleashed their creativity. Poets and writers like Hughes, Claude McKay, James Weldon Johnson, and Countee Culleen put the black experience into words. The novelist Zora Neale Hurston urged respect for black folk religion, music, and customs. Newspapers and magazines along with theater troupes and libraries owned and operated by African Americans flourished.

The Golden Age of Sports

The 1920s had its full share of gangsters, corrupt politicians, and other villains. It also had its heroes. Athletes were among the most popular. Spectator sports boomed. Public relations ballyhoo and the magic of radio created larger-than-life performers who attracted thousands to sporting events. The 1920s was truly the **Golden Age of Sports.**

[1]From "Merry-Go-Round" by Langston Hughes

THE LONE EAGLE

The most popular American hero of the 1920s was Charles A. Lindbergh. On May 20, 1927, Lindbergh took off from a muddy, rain-drenched airfield near New York City in a tiny, one-engine plane, the *Spirit of St. Louis.* He was headed for France. Alone, hour after hour, he guided his plane eastward across the Atlantic. He flew with a map in his lap and only some coffee and a few sandwiches to keep up his strength. Staying awake called for a tremendous feat of willpower. If he dozed off, even for a minute, the *Spirit of St. Louis* might crash into the sea. But Lindbergh did not doze off. About 33 and a half hours after takeoff he landed safely at Le Bourget airport on the outskirts of Paris. He was the first aviator to fly nonstop across the Atlantic—and he had done it alone.

Lindbergh's achievement captured the imagination of the entire world. Here is how *The New York Times* described his landing at Le Bourget:

> PARIS, May 21—Lindbergh did it. Twenty minutes after 10 o'clock tonight suddenly and softly there slipped out of the darkness a gray-white air-

Culver Pictures

plane as 25,000 pairs of eyes strained toward it. At 10:24 the *Spirit of St. Louis* landed and lines of soldiers, ranks of policemen and stout steel fences went down before a mad rush as irresistible as the tides of the ocean.

Lindbergh returned home a grinning, modest hero. The idol of millions, he was given a tremendous ticker tape parade through New York City. The newspapers named him "The Lone Eagle." He was also known as "Lucky Lindy," but his success was due far more to courage and skill than luck.

Now that dozens of giant jets fly across the Atlantic every day, Lindbergh's flight may not seem very important. But his flight marked the coming of age of the airplane. Lindbergh himself is the perfect symbol of the Air Age. He was two years old when Wilbur and Orville Wright made the first successful airplane flights at Kitty Hawk, North Carolina, in 1903. Those flights lasted only a few seconds and covered only a few hundred yards at most. Yet before Lindbergh died, American astronauts had landed on the moon.

Some 91,000 boxing fans paid a total of more than $1 million in July 1921 to watch the heavyweight champion, Jack Dempsey, knock out Georges Carpentier of France. Every fall weekend thousands of people jammed football stadiums to cheer for players like Harold "Red" Grange, the "Galloping Ghost" of the University of Illinois. One Saturday afternoon in 1924 Grange took the University of Michigan's opening kickoff 95 yards for a touchdown. He scored three more touchdowns in the first quarter and another before the game ended, Illinois winning 39-14. Grange carried the ball 21 times and gained an incredible 402 yards.

The most famous football coach of the 1920s was Knute Rockne of Notre Dame's "Fighting Irish." He began the decade with an

Four of the greatest sports heroes of the 1920s were, clockwise from the bottom, Red Grange, Jack Dempsey, Helen Wills, and Babe Ruth.

undefeated season. For many the 1920 highlight was Notre Dame's defeat of Army, 27-17, owing largely to the 357 yards gained by the team's captain, George Gipp. Years later, at halftime of an important game, Rockne implored his team to "win one for the Gipper," who had died of pneumonia. The locker room speech, recreated in a popular movie starring Ronald Reagan as Gipp, would later add to Reagan's enormous popularity as president.

In 1927 one of the most famous barnstorming, or traveling, basketball teams in the world was formed by Abe Saperstein. He recruited most of his players from the slums of Chicago's South Side, but he called his team of black athletes the **Harlem Globetrotters.** They became magicians with the basketball and drew fans throughout the world, as they continue to do today.

Baseball was the national game. Its most famous hero at the time was Babe Ruth, the "Sultan of Swat." Ruth was originally a pitcher—and a very good one. He was also a tremendous hitter. The Boston Red Sox quickly made him an outfielder so he could play every day. Thereafter, year after year, he was baseball's home run leader. In 1927 he hit 60, a record that stood until Roger Maris hit 61 in 1961. By the end of his career he had knocked out 714 home runs, most of them for the New York Yankees.

Americans were good at nearly all sports. Tennis players William "Big Bill" Tilden and Helen Wills both won many national and international championships. Johnny Weismuller held a dozen world swimming records. Gertrude Ederle became the first woman to swim across the English Channel.

Motion Pictures

Lindbergh's solo flight to Paris combined his own human abilities and the mechanical perfection of his plane. This combination was characteristic of the period. It explains the rapid growth of motion pictures, which, like the airplane, came of age in the 1920s.

Movies were popular even before the Great War. The early movie theaters were often installed in vacant stores. These "nickelodeons"—the usual admission charge was five cents—showed jerky, badly lit scenes. In the 1920s motion pictures became an important art form and one of the ten largest industries in the nation. In 1922, 40 million people a week went to the movies. By 1930 weekly attendance was averaging 100 million.

Every large city had its movie palaces—large, elaborate theaters seating several thousand people. Hollywood, California, became the motion picture capital of the world. The state's warm, sunny climate was ideal for outdoor movie making.

Americans in the 1920s flocked to every kind of film. There were historical pictures and the most durable of all movies—westerns. The leading actors and actresses were loved by millions. Movie fans followed the careers and personal lives of their favorites as though they were members of their families.

Movies influenced the way people dressed and talked. Women styled their hair like Greta Garbo or Mary Pickford. Men tried to copy Rudolph Valentino, the great lover of *The Sheik*, or Douglas Fairbanks, the sword-fighting hero of *The Three Musketeers*.

The greatest star of the 1920s was Charlie Chaplin. He wrote and directed his own films. In 1915 he created his world-famous character, the sad-looking "little tramp" who wore baggy pants and a battered derby hat and carried a springy bamboo cane. Chaplin

Millions of people flocked to the movies to see their favorite stars. Three of the most glittering are seen here: swashbuckling Douglas Fairbanks, bottom left, romantic idol Rudolph Valentino, bottom right, and Charlie Chaplin, below, the most famous actor in the world. Why do you think sports and movies were so popular in the 1920s?

All, Culver Pictures

was a marvelous slapstick comedian and a gifted mimic. He was also a superb actor, who could literally make audiences laugh and cry at the same time.

For years the movies were silent. Usually a pianist in each theater played mood music to accompany the action on the screen. Then, in 1927, Warner Brothers, a major film company, released the first "talkie," a film that projected the actors' voices as well as their movements. This film was *The Jazz Singer,* starring Al Jolson. He sang three songs and then told the film audience, "You ain't heard nothin' yet, folks." The next year Walt Disney made the first sound cartoon, *Steamboat Willie,* which introduced Mickey Mouse to the world.

Radio

Radio had an even more powerful hold on the public in the 1920s than movies. Like the movies, it could not have been developed without the remarkable scientific and technological advances of the times.

Everyone could enjoy and profit from radio, even sick and bed-ridden people who could not get to the movies. Radio could be listened to without admission cost and in the privacy of one's home. It was also "live." What people heard was taking place at that very moment: a politician making a speech, the crack of the bat when Babe Ruth hit another home run, the roar of the crowd at a football game, the sound of a jazz band or a symphony orchestra. More people than ever before became interested in sports and music.

The first commercial radio station was KDKA in Pittsburgh. It was operated by the Westinghouse Electric Company. KDKA began broadcasting in 1920. Two years later there were more than 500 commercial stations. The National Broadcasting Company (NBC) began combining local stations into a nationwide radio network in 1926. A year later the Columbia Broadcasting System (CBS) created a competing network. Thereafter, people all over the country could hear the same program at the same time. Audiences grew to the millions.

Radio became still another giant industry. Large companies sprang up to manufacture radio sets and broadcasting equipment. Department stores devoted entire floors to radios. Repairing radios became an important craft. By 1922, 3 million families already had radios. In the single year 1929, 5 million sets were sold.

Radio brought an enormous variety of information and entertainment into American homes. News, music, plays, political speeches, and sports events filled the airwaves. Radio also influenced what Americans bought in stores. Audiences were bombarded with commercials by manufacturers of all sorts. These advertisers paid large sums to broadcast their "sales pitches."

Postwar American Writers

The Great World War had shocked and disillusioned people all over the world. This was especially true of Americans who had resisted the war at first, only to be drawn in by promises of a better future, one made safe for democracy. It was Gertrude Stein, an **expatriate** writer who had left America to live permanently in Europe, who gave these young people a name. She told a young American writer, Ernest Hemingway, about a mechanic who took a very long time to repair her Model T. The owner of the garage reprimanded him: "You are a génération perdue! (lost generation!)." "That's what you are," Stein told Hemingway, "That's what you all are. All of you young people who served in the war, you are a lost generation." To these people progressive ideals that had been so important before the war seemed less so now. Many writers expressed this loss of values in their works.

Culver Pictures

The Metropolitan Museum of Art, Bequest of Gertrude Stein, 1946.

Ernest Hemingway survived a wound while driving an ambulance in Italy; was nearly gored by bulls running in Pamplona, Spain; and later walked away from an airplane crash in Africa. For all his manly exploits, he paid close attention to Gertrude Stein at her home in Paris where she critiqued his writing and urged him to use only the "perfect word." Of her portrait by Pablo Picasso, she complained that it didn't look like her. The confident Picasso replied, "It will."

The Fitzgeralds, Zelda and Scott, pose with their daughter Scottie. Fitzgerald wrote some of his best work in Paris, including his classic novel The Great Gatsby, *at the end of which the narrator sees how America has changed: "And as soon as the moon rose higher the inessential began to melt away until gradually I became aware of the old island here that flowered once for Dutch sailor's eyes—a fresh, green breast of the new world."*

Ernest Hemingway spent much of his youth hunting and fishing with his father in northern Michigan and had been wounded in the Great War while driving an ambulance for the Red Cross. These Michigan memories and his wartime experiences were the subjects of his early writing.

Hemingway's style is probably the most widely imitated of all American authors. He took considerable pains to choose exactly the right word and no other, writing prose the way poets write poetry. He wanted very badly, he said, to write "one true sentence." In one of his first major novels, *A Farewell to Arms,* we can see the result of Hemingway's painstaking effort:

> " In the late summer of that year we lived in a house in a village that looked across the river and the plain to the mountains. In the bed of the river there were pebbles and boulders, dry and white in the sun, and the water was clear and swiftly moving and blue in the channels. Troops went by the house and down the road and the dust they raised powdered the leaves of the trees. The trunks of the trees too were dusty and the leaves fell early that year and we saw troops marching along the road and the dust rising and leaves, stirred by the breeze, falling and the soldiers marching and afterward the road bare and white except for the leaves.
>
> The plain was rich with crops; there were many orchards of fruit trees and beyond the plain the mountains were brown and bare. There was fighting in the mountains and at night we could see the flashes from the artillery. In the dark it was like summer lightning, but the nights were cool and there was not the feeling of a storm coming.[1] "

Hemingway gave the writing of fiction a new rhythm of action and simple, straightforward dialogue. He also developed the image of life as a battlefield on which a new type of hero suffers with grace and dignity and accepts gratefully life's few moments of pleasure. In 1954 Hemingway received the Nobel prize for literature for such works as *The Sun Also Rises, For Whom the Bell Tolls,* and *The Old Man and the Sea.*

Francis Scott Key Fitzgerald, more than any other author, gave a voice to the "lost generation." His greatest work—for many *the* great American novel—was *The Great Gatsby*. In it the American dream of wealth and power goes terribly and tragically wrong. Throughout the novel Fitzgerald used the glitter of Gatsby's life to symbolize the purposeless lives of the rich and powerful. Nick Carraway, the narrator, notes after a spectacular party at Gatsby's:

[1]From *A Farewell to Arms* by Ernest Hemingway

" The caterwauling [noisy crying] of horns had reached a crescendo and I turned away and cut across the lawn toward home. I glanced back once. A wafer of a moon was shining over Gatsby's house, making the night fine as before, and surviving the laughter and the sound of his still glowing garden. A sudden emptiness seemed to flow now from the windows and the great doors, endowing with complete isolation the figure of the host, who stood on the porch, his hand up in a formal gesture of farewell.[1] "

[1]From *The Great Gatsby* by F. Scott Fitzgerald

Fitzgerald also wrote *Tender Is the Night*, an account of his own despair. He died in 1940 while writing *The Last Tycoon*.

While Fitzgerald and Hemingway wrote in Europe, William Faulkner in his native Mississippi invented a mythical county called Yoknapatawpha. He spent his life populating it with fallen southern aristocrats, new arrivals (all named Snopes), and the long-suffering blacks who tended what was left of the land. In this setting—the American South—he explored such universal themes as human suffering, the passions of the heart, and the destruction of the natural wilderness.

In Faulkner's novels the sudden shifts in time, frequent use of symbolism, and unusual syntax reveal the confused emotions of his characters and the disorder that surrounds them. His most noted works include *The Sound and the Fury, As I Lay Dying, Absalom, Absalom,* and *Light in August*.

Faulkner received a Nobel Prize for literature in 1950. In his acceptance speech at the ceremony in Stockholm, Sweden, he described his view of the writer:

" . . . I decline to accept the end of man. It is easy enough to say that man is immortal simply because he will endure; that when the last ding-dong of doom has clanged and faded from the last worthless rock hanging tideless in the last red and dying evening, that even then there will still be one more sound: that of his puny inexhaustible voice, still talking. I refuse to accept this. I believe man will not merely endure: he will prevail. He is immortal, not because he alone among the creatures has an inexhaustible voice, but because he has a soul, a spirit capable of compassion and sacrifice and endurance. The poet's, the writer's, duty is to write about these things. It is his privilege to help man endure by lifting his heart, by reminding him of the courage and pity and sacrifice which have been the glory of his past. The poet's voice need not merely be the record of man, it can be one of the props, the pillars to help him endure and prevail. "

William Faulkner, the inventor of a fictional world called Yoknapatawpha County, emerged into the real world to surprise and delight listeners with his acceptance speech in Stockholm after being awarded the Nobel Prize for literature.

Return to the Preview & Review on page 330.

4. AN AUTOMOBILE CIVILIZATION

Preview & Review

Use these questions to guide your reading. Answer the questions after completing Section 4.
Understanding Issues, Events, & Ideas. Explain how the automobile changed America, using the following words: Model T, mass production, moving assembly line, Model A, tourism, suburb, air pollution.

1. How did Henry Ford change the automobile industry? How did the growth of the automobile industry affect the entire economy?
2. How did the automobile bring freedom to ordinary people?
3. What effects, both good and bad, did the automobile have on family life?

Thinking Critically. Write an obituary for Henry Ford that might have appeared in a newspaper or magazine; or compose an advertisement for Henry Ford's Model T.

Henry Ford's Automobile

Of all the forces reshaping American life in the 1920s, the automobile probably had the most influence. The first gasoline-powered vehicles were built in the 1890s. By the time the United States entered the Great War, over 1 million cars a year were being produced. In the 1920s an average of more than 3 million a year were turned out.

Henry Ford was the key figure in this new industry. Ford had come to Detroit, Michigan, because he hated farm work. He had talent for all kinds of mechanical projects. While working in Detroit for the Edison Illuminating Company in the 1890s, Ford designed and built an automobile in his home workshop. A little later he built a famous racing car, "999," which set several speed records. In 1903 he founded the Ford Motor Company.

The first American automobiles were very expensive. They were toys for the rich. Henry Ford dreamed of producing cars cheaply so that ordinary people could own them. (The name of the well-known German automobile, the *Volkswagen*, or "people's car," expresses his idea exactly.) In 1908 he achieved his goal with his **Model T** Ford. It sold for only $850. And by 1916 Ford had reduced the cost of the new Model T's to $360.

Ford's secret was **mass production** achieved through the use of the **moving assembly line.** His cars were put together, or assembled, while being moved past a line of workers. Each worker or team performed only one fairly simple task.

This method of production was highly efficient. Prices were also held down by Ford's policy of keeping his cars simple and making the same basic model year after year. The Model T was not changed in any important way until 1928, when the **Model A** replaced it. According to a joke of the day, you could have a Model T in any color you wanted as long as you chose black.

Other automobile manufacturers copied Ford's methods. But most made more expensive cars. In prosperous times many customers were willing to pay for larger and more comfortable cars than the Model T. By the end of the 1920s Ford was no longer the largest manufacturer. The General Motors Company had taken the lead.

New Wealth from the Automobile

The automobile fueled an economic boom. The 3 million or more cars produced each year were worth about $3.5 billion even before the car dealers added their expenses and profits. This was only part of the new wealth the automobile created. A huge rubber industry sprang up to produce tires, belts, and hoses for cars. Manufacturers

Culver Pictures

Henry Ford is as spare as his famous Model T in this photograph. How did the Model T resemble the more recent German Volkswagen?

of steel, glass, paint, and dozens of other products greatly increased their output.

The automobile revolutionized the petroleum-refining industry. Before the war the most important petroleum product was kerosene. By 1919 ten times as much gasoline as kerosene was being refined. The total amount of petroleum refined in the United States soared from about 50 million barrels to 1 billion barrels a day.

Then there were the effects of the automobile on road building and on **tourism.** So long as people traveled no faster than a horse could pull a coach or wagon, the bumps and ruts of dirt and gravel roads did not matter much. By the 1920s, however, ordinary cars could speed along at 50 or 60 miles an hour or more. Such speeds were impossible on uneven surfaces. Hundreds of thousands of miles of smooth paved roads had to be built. Great amounts of asphalt and concrete were manufactured to surface them. New road-building machinery was designed and constructed. Thousands of new jobs were created in this road-building industry.

Better roads for cars meant more traveling, both for business and for pleasure. Gasoline stations appeared alongside each new highway. Roadside restaurants opened side by side with motor ho-tels—a new way of housing travelers, soon to be known as motels.

Point of View

Two of Henry Ford's biographers, Peter Collier and David Horowitz, tell of the first excursions in what Ford called the "baby carriage."

"Seeing the strange little car coughing and wheezing along the narrow streets during the next few days, people would sometimes yell out the nickname his obsessive drive to build a horseless carriage had earned Ford—'Crazy Henry!' But whenever he stopped, crowds immediately surrounded his invention, examining it with such enthusiasm that he finally had to begin chaining it to lightposts for fear they would carry it off. 'Yes, crazy,' he sometimes said, tapping his temple with a forefinger. 'Crazy like a fox.'"

From *The Fords: An American Epic,* 1987

An Automobile Civilization   341

Culver Pictures

Sunday, after church and Mom's fried chicken, plans for a suburban cruise go awry in this early traffic jam outside St. Louis, Missouri. Notice the large number of Model T's. How did the automobile bring Americans both freedom and dependence?

Automobiles and American Life

For thousands of years the power to move about freely and easily was a sign that a person had social status. That is why in ancient times and throughout the Middle Ages ownership of a horse meant that a person belonged to the upper class. Now, because of Henry Ford and the other pioneers of the auto industry, nearly everyone in the United States could afford a car. A *new* Model T could cost as little as $300 in the early 1920s. A secondhand Ford still capable of good service could be bought for $25 to $50.

Automobiles freed ordinary people. Cars let them travel far more widely and rapidly than medieval knights had traveled. They could live in **suburbs** outside the cities, surrounded by trees and green fields, and drive daily to jobs in the cities. They could visit places hundreds of miles away on weekends or cover thousands of miles on a two-week summer vacation.

Little wonder that automobiles became status symbols—objects associated with the upper classes of society—for many people. Owners spent Saturday mornings washing and polishing their cars the way a trainer grooms a racehorse or a pedigreed dog before a show. Car owners decorated their autos with shiny hood ornaments and put flowers in small vases on the inside.

The personalities of many car owners seemed to be affected by their vehicles. Once behind the wheel, drivers were in command of half a ton or more of speeding metal. They often became "roadhogs" who turned into cursing bullies when another driver got in their way or tried to pass them on the road.

Automobiles had both good and bad effects on family life. Family picnics and sightseeing trips brought parents and children closer together. However, crowding five or six people into a small space on a hot summer afternoon hardly made for family harmony. Quarrels developed about where to go and how to get there. People complained about "backseat drivers"—those passengers who made a habit of criticizing the driver.

The automobile also tended to separate family members. Once children were old enough to drive, they generally preferred to be off by themselves or with friends their own age. Soon "two-car" and "three-car" families came into being. In extreme cases the home became little more than a motel or garage. Family members rested there before zooming off again in their Fords and Chevrolets or, if they were wealthy, in their Packards and Pierce-Arrows.

The new automobile civilization had other unfortunate side effects. Between 1915 and 1930 the number of road accidents soared. By 1930 automobile crashes caused more than half the accidental deaths in the nation.

As the number of cars on the roads increased, traffic tie-ups became common. The exhaust fumes of millions of cars caused serious **air pollution** in some areas.

Because of the automobile, the oil resources of the nation were being used up at a rapidly increasing rate. Anyone who thought about the question realized that there was only so much petroleum in the ground. It had taken millions of years to be formed and could never be replaced. Still, the supply was so large that most people assumed that it would last practically forever. During the 1920s huge new oil fields were discovered in Texas and Oklahoma. Only a tiny percentage of the petroleum used in America then came from foreign sources. That percentage was actually declining in those years.

The nation was becoming more and more dependent upon gasoline and other petroleum products. Giant industries could not exist without oil in one form or another. Neither could the new life style that was developing in the United States. Yet in the 1920s few people worried about these matters. Gasoline was cheap. There was plenty of it. Let us enjoy life while we can, most people reasoned. 📧

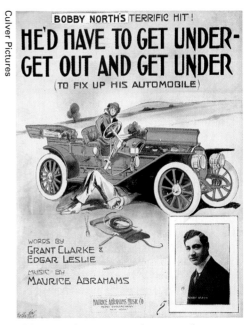

This song sheet cover takes a good-natured view of the plight of most car owners, who had to be their own mechanics. Scarcely a trip was made without at least patching a tire.

Return to the Preview & Review on page 340.

An Automobile Civilization 343

Use these questions to guide your reading. Answer the questions after completing Section 5.
Understanding Issues, Events, & Ideas. Use the following words to describe American politics and the economy of the 1920s: Elk Hills, Teapot Dome, chain store, synthetic, sick industry, Farm Bloc, subsidy, Black Tuesday, Great Stock Market Crash.
1. How did the political mood of the 1920s differ from the way people behaved?
2. What changes took place in business in the 1920s? Which were the sick industries in the 1920s? Why were they sick?
3. Why did the Republicans win the election of 1928 so easily?
4. Why did people tend to adopt a "get-rich-quick" attitude in the 1920s?
Thinking Critically. 1. Imagine that you are a Wall Street reporter on October 29, 1929. Interview several people on the street and use their comments to write your newspaper article. 2. You are a farmer in the South in 1921. Write a letter to your congressman, a member of the Farm Bloc, explaining the troubles you are having. Conclude your letter by describing what the government could do to solve your problems.

5. AMERICA HEADS FOR A CRASH

Harding and Coolidge

The 1920s were a time when politics seemed to have little connection with how people lived and thought. While society was changing in dramatic and significant ways, most political leaders were conservative, slow moving, and lacking in imagination.

President Warren G. Harding looked like a statesman. He was friendly, good looking, firm jawed, and silver haired. He worked for conservative policies that favored big business. But he was not a creative leader. His programs included high protective tariffs on manufactured goods, lower taxes for the wealthy, and reduction of the national debt, the same policies as earlier Republican presidents. Nor was he a strong leader. Harding was careless about the appointments he made to important public offices. Some people he appointed were incompetent. Others were plainly corrupt.

Harding died of a heart attack in 1923. Soon thereafter a series of government scandals was uncovered. Harding himself was not involved. It turned out that various members of his administration had stolen money intended for a veterans' hospital, mishandled government property, and accepted bribes.

The worst scandal involved Albert Fall, Harding's secretary of the interior. Fall leased government-owned land containing rich deposits of oil to private companies at very low rents. These included the **Elk Hills** reserve in California and the **Teapot Dome** reserve in Wyoming. In return the heads of the oil companies gave Fall bribes amounting to $400,000. When the facts were discovered by a government investigation in 1923, Fall was convicted and put in prison.

It was fortunate for the Republican party that Harding died before the scandals broke. His successor, Vice President Calvin Coolidge, had nothing to do with the corruption. Coolidge's personality was almost the exact opposite of Harding's. He was quiet and very reserved. He hated to spend money. Indeed, he was the only modern president who was able to save part of his salary while in office. He was thoroughly honest. His no-nonsense attitude made it difficult for the Democrats to take political advantage of the scandals.

In 1924 Coolidge easily received the Republican nomination for a full term. The Democratic nomination was decided only after a long and bitter struggle. The eastern wing of the party supported Governor Alfred E. Smith of New York. Most southern and western delegates favored William G. McAdoo, who had been President Wilson's secretary of the treasury.

Under the rules of the convention, a candidate needed a two-thirds majority to be nominated. Since neither Smith nor McAdoo could get two thirds, a deadlock developed. It lasted for days. Finally,

Both, National Portrait Gallery

At left is Warren G. Harding by Margaret Lindsay Williams. Right is Calvin Coolidge. A man of few words, Coolidge was once told at a White House dinner that a lady believed she could coax at least three words from him. "You lose," he replied. Howard Chandler Christy painted Grace Goodhue Coolidge, the popular first lady, and her collie Rob Roy.

on the 103rd ballot, the exhausted delegates nominated John W. Davis, a conservative lawyer from West Virginia.

The deadlock between Smith and McAdoo reflected the basic divisions within the Democratic party and within the nation itself. Smith was a Catholic. Many people were prejudiced against Catholics and would not vote for a Catholic for president. Some even feared that such a person would be a servant of the pope rather than a servant of the American people.

Many rural people disliked Smith because he had been raised "on the sidewalks of New York." Yet the nation was becoming more and more urban. By the 1920s farmers no longer made up the majority of the population. Many resented this fact. In Smith's candidacy they saw a symbol of the shift from a rural to an urban nation.

In addition to Coolidge and Davis, Senator Robert La Follette of Wisconsin ran for president in 1924. La Follette had been a leading progressive before the Great War. He found both the major parties too conservative for his taste after the war. He therefore formed a new Progressive party. La Follette campaigned on a platform calling for government ownership of railroads, protection of the right of workers to bargain collectively, aid for farmers, and other reforms. "The great issue before the American people," La Follette believed, was "the control of government and industry by private monopoly."

America Heads For a Crash   345

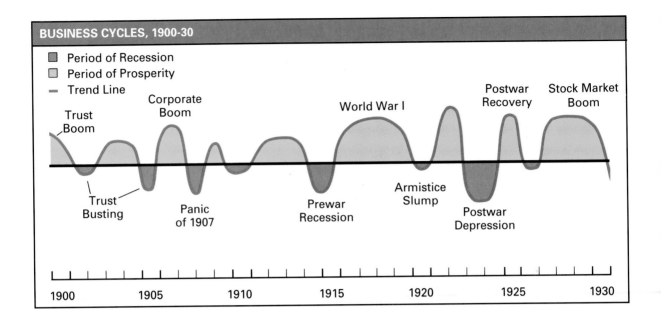

BUSINESS CYCLES, 1900-30

■ Period of Recession
□ Period of Prosperity
— Trend Line

Trust Boom

Corporate Boom

World War I

Postwar Recovery

Stock Market Boom

Trust Busting

Panic of 1907

Prewar Recession

Armistice Slump

Postwar Depression

1900   1905   1910   1915   1920   1925   1930

LEARNING FROM GRAPHS. *The graph above shows American business cycles between 1900 and 1930. What happened to the economy during the war? Why? What happened to the economy after the war ended? Why?*

Coolidge won the election easily. He received more than 15 million votes to Davis' 8.4 million and La Follette's 4.8 million. Clearly the national mood was politically conservative at a time when society was going through tremendous changes.

Business Growth in the 1920s

The policies of the federal government in the 1920s had large effects on the economy. These policies greatly influenced the lives of nearly everyone. President Coolidge believed that "the business of America is business." He also said, "The man who builds a factory builds a temple." His policies were designed to help business interests and other large investors.

Coolidge presided over one of the most business-minded administrations in American history. Its chief architect was Andrew Mellon, the secretary of the treasury. Mellon believed prosperity depended on the ability of Americans to invest and reinvest in business. He sponsored a tax cut that favored the wealthy and businesses by reducing the taxes for people making $60,000 a year or more. Within 3 years money was pouring into business investments.

To make up for the reduced revenues, the government raised tariffs and increased excise taxes slightly. The higher tariffs benefited businesses in two ways, allowing them to raise their prices while cutting down on their competition. The slight increases in excise taxes on consumer goods and a new tax on automobiles was paid primarily by the middle class.

The friendly attitude of the government encouraged businesses to make new investments. Once the switch back to peacetime production had been completed, the American economy certainly prospered. Many industries that had been established before the Great War expanded rapidly. Coolidge and his advisers expected this to create more jobs and a better standard of living for all.

Between 1915 and 1930 the number of telephone users in the United States doubled. Dial phones and improved switchboards speeded communication and cut costs. Electric light companies prospered. As more and more homes were hooked up for electricity, the electric appliance industry grew. Most families now had electric irons. Many had electric vacuum cleaners and washing machines and refrigerators as well. Electricity also became an important source of power for industry. By 1930 the United States was using more electricity than all the rest of the world *combined*.

Chain stores grew rapidly in the 1920s. The A&P grocery chain expanded from 400 outlets in 1912 to 15,000 in 1932. Woolworth "five and tens" were opened by the dozens in big cities and small towns. By the end of the decade Americans were buying more than 25 percent of their food and clothing in chain stores. With more and more people living in cities, sales of canned fruits and vegetables rose rapidly.

Even more impressive was the growth of entirely new industries. Chemical plants began turning out many **synthetics**—artificial substances such as rayon for clothing and Bakelite, a hard plastic, for radio cases. Other new mass-produced products included wristwatches, cigarette lighters, improved cameras, and Pyrex glass for cooking.

Some of the wonderful new labor-saving devices being advertised in the 1920s include the vacuum, refrigerator, and washing machine. Think how each made life a bit simpler.

All, The Granger Collection

"Sick" Industries

Despite the general economic expansion of the 1920s, there were several weak areas in the economy. **Sick industries** like coal and textiles did not prosper at all. Coal was meeting stiff competition from oil, natural gas, and electricity. Over 1,000 coal mines were shut down in the 1920s, and nearly 200,000 miners lost their jobs.

Manufacturers of cotton and woolen cloth did not prosper either. Partly because of competition from rayon, the new synthetic textile, these manufacturers were soon producing more cloth than the public was buying. Their profits therefore shrank, and the number of unemployed textile workers rose.

American agriculture also suffered. Once the Great War was over, European farmers quickly recaptured their local markets. The price of wheat and other farm products fell sharply. Farmers' incomes declined, but their expenses for mortgage interest, taxes, tractors, harvesters, and supplies did not.

In 1921 a group of congressmen from the South and West organized an informal **Farm Bloc.** (A bloc is a common interest group.) Their purpose was to unite congressmen from farm districts behind legislation favorable to agriculture. The Farm Bloc pushed through a bill providing for **subsidies** for farmers through government purchase of farm surpluses. President Coolidge was not sympathetic to proposals to subsidize farm prices. He vetoed the bill.

But the tremendous growth of the 1920s also had a down side. Business owners pushed their factories to produce more, faster. New and improved products continued to attract buyers, and old models wore out and had to be replaced. But by the late 1920s businesses were producing more than the public demanded. By the end of the decade warehouses were full of consumer goods waiting to be purchased.

LEARNING FROM GRAPHS. *Early America was a nation of farmers. Even as late as 1879 more than half of the value of the gross national product came from agriculture. But what trend does the graph illustrate? Why do you think this happened?*

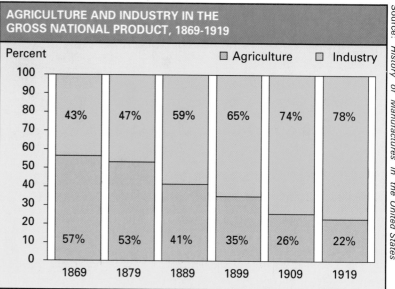

AGRICULTURE AND INDUSTRY IN THE GROSS NATIONAL PRODUCT, 1869-1919

Source: *History of Manufactures in the United States*

The Election of 1928

President Coolidge played down the problems of farmers and workers in the "sick" industries. He believed the future was bright. In his 1928 State of the Union message he said:

> **❝** No Congress has met with a more pleasing prospect than that which appears at the present time. **❞**

Most people agreed with Coolidge. Americans were enjoying the greatest period of prosperity in their history. Most were earning more money and working shorter hours than ever before. They had cars, radios, and household gadgets. Life was easy. It seemed likely to become easier still. The Republican party naturally took the credit for the good times.

In the 1928 presidential campaign, Herbert Hoover, the secretary of commerce, received the Republican nomination. The Democratic candidate was Alfred E. Smith. Smith had a record of solid accomplishment as governor of New York. He could not be denied the nomination. But his Catholic religion and his "big city" background hurt him in rural areas.

Hoover won the election with 21 million votes to Smith's 15 million. The electoral vote was 444 to 87. Smith even lost his own state of New York as well as several Democratic states in the once Solid South. The main cause of Smith's defeat was the prosperity issue. A majority of the American people had come to believe that

Herbert Hoover, candidate for president in 1928, says "hello" to Elizabeth, New Jersey, where a large and enthusiastic crowd greets him. What made him so popular at the time?

America Heads For a Crash   **349**

the Republican party was the symbol of economic progress and the guardian of good times.

The Great Crash

Prosperity tended to make people ambitious and optimistic. A "get-rich-quick" attitude developed in the United States as the decade advanced. More and more people set out to make fortunes in the stock market. They followed the prices of stocks in the newspapers as closely as they followed Babe Ruth's batting average. By mid-1929 stocks had been climbing steadily in price for several months. The profits of most corporations were on the rise. By 1929 the companies listed on the New York Stock Exchange, one market where stocks were bought and sold, were paying out three times as much money in dividends as they had in 1920. A newspaper writer of the day made fun of the stock buying frenzy.

"Sold Out." How can this woman comfort her husband who in a day has lost their savings in the Stock Market Crash of 1929?

❝ But nowadays the bores I find
Are of a single, standard kind:
For every person I may meet
At lunch, at clubs, upon the street,
Tells me, in endless wordy tales,
Of market purchases and sales;
Of how he bought a single share
Of California Prune and Pear;
Or how he sold at 33
A million shares of T. & T.
How McAvoy and Katzenstein°
Told him to sell at 99;
Of the thousands lost and millions made
In this or that egregious°° trade;
How bright he was to buy or sell
EP, GM, X or GL.
In herds, in schools, in droves, in flocks
The men and women talk of stocks.[1] **❞**

This boom could not go on forever. Speculation—investing money in hopes of making a profit—ran on the false belief that no matter how much a person paid for stock, someone would buy it from them. But once stock prices reached a certain level, there would be no more buyers. The market reached that peak in September. Nervous speculators realized prices could only come down.

Quite suddenly, on October 24, 1929, thousands of investors wanted to sell stocks instead of buy them. Investors jammed tele-

°A Wall Street investment firm
°°Notable
[1]From *Christopher Columbus and Other Patriotic Verses* by Franklin P. Adams

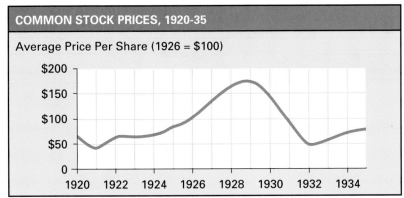

COMMON STOCK PRICES, 1920-35

Average Price Per Share (1926 = $100)

Source: *Historical Statistics of the United States.*

LEARNING FROM GRAPHS.
The graph shows the average price of a share of common stock for each year between 1920 and 1935. Because the graph shows the average *price, remember that some stocks sold for much more and others for much less. What was the general trend in stock prices in the 1920s? What was the trend between 1930 and 1932? Why did the trend change?*

phone lines and crowded into brokers' offices, desperate to turn their stocks into cash. With many sellers and few buyers, the prices of stocks plunged. People even began to sell at a loss in order to get something before prices fell still lower. General Electric Company shares dropped from $315 to $283 in that one day. U.S. Steel skidded from $205 to $193.

Then, on October 29, a day known as **Black Tuesday,** came an even steeper decline. The **Great Stock Market Crash** reached panic proportions. Day after day the drop continued. By the middle of November General Electric stock was down to $168, U.S. Steel to $150.

The Granger Collection

The prosperity of the 1920s was over. Overproduction and overspeculation—investing too much money in hopes of making a profit—had caught up with the American people. The country was about to enter the Great Depression.

Return to the Preview & Review on page 344.

CHAPTER 8 REVIEW

1917
America enters
the Great War

1918
The Great War
ends

1919
Treaty of Versailles

★
Palmer raids

1920
Prohibition begins

★
Senate rejects
Versailles Treaty

★
Nineteenth Amendment

★
First radio broadcast

1921
Emergency Quota Act

Chapter Summary
Read the statements below. Choose one, and write a paragraph explaining its importance.
1. Republican opposition to the Versailles Treaty, especially to the League of Nations, caused Wilson political troubles.
2. Wilson's failing health added to the problems of getting the treaty ratified. It was eventually rejected.
3. The Nineteenth Amendment gave women the vote in national elections. The large voter turnout in 1920 elected Warren Harding.
4. The United States steered a middle course between isolationism and internationalism in the 1920s.
5. At home, Americans worried about anarchists and communists. This led to a series of actions aimed at limiting foreign influences in the United States. Other examples of the American reaction to the war included prohibition, the fundamentalist crusade, and the Sacco-Vanzetti Case.
6. Most Americans enjoyed life during the "Roaring Twenties." Music, sports, motion pictures, and the radio began their golden ages. Writers of the Lost Generation produced works that gave a voice to both the despair and the dazzle of the postwar period.
7. America also became an "automobile civilization" during the Twenties.
8. Despite the prevalent "get-rich-quick" attitude, problems of farmers and "sick" industries slowed the economy. The bubble of speculation burst in October 1929 when the stock market crashed, causing panic throughout the American economy.

Understanding Chronological Order
Number your paper 1–5. Then study the time line above and place the following events in the order in which they happened by writing the first next to 1, the second next to 2, and so on.
1. Sacco and Vanzetti executed
2. Teapot Dome
3. Senate rejects Versailles Treaty
4. Stock market crash
5. Lindbergh flies across the Atlantic

Understanding Main Ideas
1. Why was the Versailles Treaty rejected? Who were the mild reservationists? The strong reservationists? The irreconcilables?
2. What was meant by the term "the Jazz Age?" Why was jazz music a symbol for the times?
3. What were some reasons the 1920s was the Golden Age of Sports?
4. What methods did Henry Ford use to produce automobiles that ordinary people could afford?
5. Which were the "sick" industries of the 1920s? Why were they called "sick"?
6. What caused the price of stocks to plunge after October 24, 1929?

Thinking Critically
1. **Solving Problems**. If you were President Wilson, how would you have acted differently to ensure that the Senate would approve the United States joining the League of Nations?
2. **Imagining**. If you could be a celebrity during the Twenties, would you rather be a jazz musician, a poet living in Harlem, an athlete, an airplane pilot, a movie star, a radio comedian, or a writer living in Paris? Why?
3. **Determining Cause and Effect**. You know that Henry Ford's Model T dominated the automobile market until the end of the 1920s, when General Motors gained the lead. What changes would you have advised Ford to make in 1925 in order to maintain his advantage?

Writing About History: Informative
Write a report on the great hero of the 1920s, Charles A. Lindbergh. You might wish to focus on topics such as a) Lindbergh's barnstorming days, b) the planning and building of the *Spirit of St. Louis,* c) the day before the transatlantic flight, d) the May 1927 flight itself, e) the reception in Paris, and f) Lindbergh's welcome home. Conclude your report by explaining how Lindbergh's flight was a triumph for both man and machine.

1923	1924	1925	1927	1928	1929
Harding dies suddenly ★ Coolidge succeeds Harding	National Origins Act ★ Teapot Dome ★ Coolidge elected president	Scopes "Monkey Trial"	Harlem Globetrotters formed ★ Ruth hits 60 home runs ★ Lindbergh's solo flight ★ Sacco and Vanzetti executed	Hoover elected president ★ Ford introduces Model A	Stock market crash ★ Great Depression begins

Practicing the Strategy

Review the strategy on page 315.

Comparing Points of View. Reread the comments of Senator Borah and President Wilson on pages 313–14. Then answer the following questions.

1. How does Wilson's statement about the League of Nations differ from Borah's?
2. Would you consider Borah an expert on American foreign affairs? Why? Do you consider President Wilson an expert? Why?
3. Which view of the League of Nations do you agree with? Why?
4. Use your historical imagination to explain how Americans in 1919 might have had a different view of an international peace-keeping organization than people today.

Using Primary Sources

The 1920s were a time of drastic social change. Two social scientists, Robert S. Lynd and Helen M. Lynd, wrote a book called *Middletown,* which was a study of the way people lived in a mid-sized American town. The following quotations from the book indicate how people felt about the automobile. As you read the comments, think about how the automobile transformed America.

> *'We don't have no fancy clothes when we have the car to pay for,' said another. 'The car is the only pleasure we have.'*

> *'I'll go without food before I'll see us give up the car,' said one woman.*

> *'Our daughters [eighteen and fifteen] don't use our car much because they are always with somebody else in their car when we go out motoring,' lamented one business class mother.*

1. Why do you think someone would go without food or clothing before they would give up their car?

2. What does the last quotation suggest about how the automobile changed family life?
3. Do you think cars are as important to people today as they were in the 1920s? Why or why not?

Linking History & Geography

Throughout the nation's history, improvements in transportation and communication have helped bring Americans closer together. The automobile, the airplane, and the radio came of age in the 1920s. To understand how these developments reshaped Americans' sense of geography, answer the following questions.

1. How did the automobile affect the number and quality of roads, the distances between where people lived and worked, and the amount of the country the average person visited?
2. What advantages did the airplane have over other types of transportation? What disadvantages did it have?
3. What advantages did the radio have over the telegraph and the telephone?
4. What generalization can you state about the effects of the automobile, the airplane, and the radio on regional differences in the U.S.?

Enriching Your Study of History

1. **Individual Project.** Prepare a classroom display to show how the automobile changed American life.
2. **Cooperative Project.** Have your group use its historical imagination to prepare and present on tape a radio broadcast from the 1920s. Each of you should select one of the following topics: news of the day, music, interviews with famous persons, comedy routines, and commercials. Then combine your parts into a radio program. Research the 1920s carefully so that your broadcast seems true to the times.

Chapter 8 Review   353

The Great Depression and the New Deal

The stock market crash of 1929 was the first major event of what we call the Great Depression. There had been many earlier depressions in the United States, but the Great Depression lasted longer and was more severe than any before in the nation's history. Human suffering was widespread. Shopkeepers lost their businesses. Farmers lost their farms. Banks failed and investors lost their savings. Finally, in 1932, the nation turned to Franklin Delano Roosevelt, a man of wealth who understood suffering after his own struggle with the paralysis of polio he suffered in 1921. As president, could the popular FDR pull the nation from "the depths of depression"?

National Academy of Design

An American playwright wrote in his autobiography that "boredom is the keynote of poverty." Look carefully at this picture, "Unemployment," by Paul Starrett Sample. Then ask yourself which must be worse: hunger? physical discomfort? lack of shelter? disease? Or is the meaningless milling about the street below the worst consequence of the Great Depression, at least for the able bodied?

1. THE COSTS OF DEPRESSION

The "Normal" Business Cycle

The crash was the start of the Great Depression but not its cause. Stocks actually regained some of their October losses, and the economy did not decline steeply until the following spring. In any case, the depression was worldwide, not merely an American collapse. It was an indirect result of the destruction of lives and property during World War I. In addition, the boom in the United States in the 1920s had enabled a relatively small number of people to obtain a very large percentage of the nation's purchasing power. Production increased more rapidly than the income of the average family. After a time the mass of consumers could not afford to buy all the many goods pouring forth from the factories.

When the depression first became noticeable, no one expected it to be particularly serious. People had come to accept depressions as a regular part of the **business cycle.** This is how business cycles worked:

In good times economic activity tended to expand. More goods were produced. Prices rose. More workers were hired. Eventually output increased faster than goods could be sold. Surpluses then piled up in company warehouses and in retail stores. Manufacturers had to slow down their production. They let go some of their workers. These unemployed people had less money to buy goods. More manufacturers then had to reduce output and lay off more workers. Prices fell. Producers who were losing money began to go out of business. The general economy was in a state of **depression.**

People believed that depressions were self-correcting. When output became very low, the surpluses were gradually used up. Then the efficient producers who had not gone out of business increased output. They rehired workers. These workers, with wages in their pockets, increased their own purchases. Demand increased. Prices rose. The economy entered the **recovery** stage. Recovery eventually led to **prosperity**—a time of high prices, full production, and almost no unemployment.

The Great Depression

A complete business cycle might last anywhere from two or three to five or six years. What made the **Great Depression** different was that it lasted for more than ten years. The economy declined steeply from late 1929 until the winter of 1932-33. Then it appeared to be stuck. Recovery was slow and irregular. The output of goods remained far below what it had been in 1929. Only in 1940, after the outbreak of the Second World War, did a strong recovery begin.

Throughout this long period at least 10 percent of the work force was unemployed. At the low point, early in 1933, about 25 percent

Preview & Review

Use these questions to guide your reading. Answer the questions after completing Section 1.
Understanding Issues, Events, & Ideas. Use the following words to describe the depression: business cycle, depression, recovery, prosperity, Great Depression, soup kitchens and breadlines, public works, Bonus March.
1. How were depressions supposed to be self correcting?
2. How did the Great Depression differ from other depressions in the nation's history?
3. How did President Hoover try to stimulate the economy?
4. Why did the Bonus Marchers come to Washington? How did Hoover respond to them? Why did Hoover's popularity suffer from that response?

Thinking Critically. Imagine you are a newspaper editor in 1932. Write an editorial in which you either criticize or praise Hoover's handling of the depression.

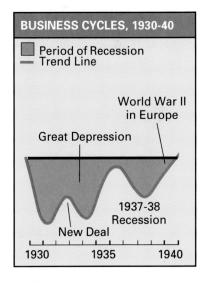

BUSINESS CYCLES, 1930-40

▨ Period of Recession
— Trend Line

World War II in Europe

Great Depression

1937-38 Recession

New Deal

1930   1935   1940

LEARNING FROM GRAPHS. *What effect did the New Deal have on the Great Depression? How can you tell?*

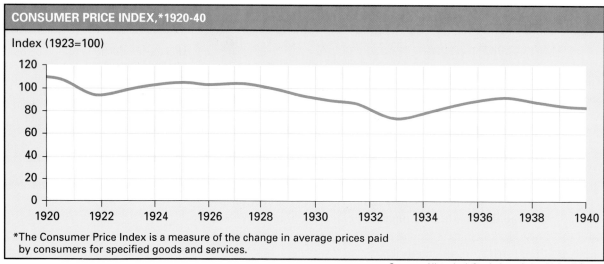

CONSUMER PRICE INDEX,*1920-40

Index (1923=100)

*The Consumer Price Index is a measure of the change in average prices paid by consumers for specified goods and services.

Source: *Historical Statistics of the United States*

LEARNING FROM GRAPHS. *The Consumer Price Index, or CPI, is a statistic that tells economists how much a typical American can afford. What happened to the CPI during the Great Depression? Why?*

of all Americans were without jobs. Americans spent $10.9 billion in food stores in 1929. But although the population increased in every year, Americans did not spend that much on food again until 1941. This was true also of money spent on furniture, clothing, automobiles, jewelry, recreation, medical care, and nearly all other items.

These cold figures tell us little about the human suffering and discouragement that the Great Depression caused. Shopkeepers who had worked for years to develop their businesses lost everything. People lost their savings in bank failures. Workers who had risen through the ranks to well-paid jobs found themselves unemployed. Those who had developed skills found that their skills were useless. Students graduating from schools and colleges could find no one willing to hire them.

The weakest and poorest suffered most. Many married women lost their jobs because employers thought they did not need to work. Unemployment was far higher among African Americans, Hispanics, and other groups than among whites. In the southwestern states thousands of Mexican-born farm laborers and their children born in the United States were gathered up by federal authorities and shipped back to Mexico when they were unable to find work. Officials excused this cruel policy by arguing that there was not enough relief money to care for them. Many Mexican-born workers who had *not* lost their jobs were also shipped back. In this case the excuse was that they were holding down jobs that United States citizens needed.

The term "depression" describes the mood of the people as well as the state of the economy. Until the middle of the 1930s there was no system of unemployment insurance and no national welfare assistance program to help the unemployed and their families. People in desperate need had no sure place they could turn to. After 54 homeless men were arrested for sleeping in the New York City subway, they told a reporter from *The New York Times* that they were lucky because being in jail meant "free meals yesterday and shelter last night."

Great efforts were made to assist the jobless. State and city governments and private charities raised money to feed the poor and provide them with a little cash for their other needs. Special "charity drives," many led by churches and religious groups, were conducted to collect clothing for the unemployed and their families. There were **soup kitchens** and **breadlines** where hungry people could get a free meal and lodging houses where the homeless could spend the night. One woman, a teenager during the Great Depression, recalled:

" My mother'd send us to the soup line. And we were never allowed to curse. If you happened to be one of the first ones in line, you didn't get anything but the water that was on top. So we'd ask the guy that was putting the soup into the buckets—everybody had to bring their own bucket to get the soup—he'd dip the greasy watery stuff off the top. So we'd ask him to please dip down to get some meat and potatoes from the bottom of the kettle. But he wouldn't do it. So we learned to curse.

Then we'd go across the street. One place had bread, large loaves of bread. Down the road just a little way was a big shed, and they gave milk. My sister and me would take two buckets each. And that's what we lived off for the longest time.[1] "

[1]From *Hard Times: An Oral History of the Great Depression* by Studs Terkel

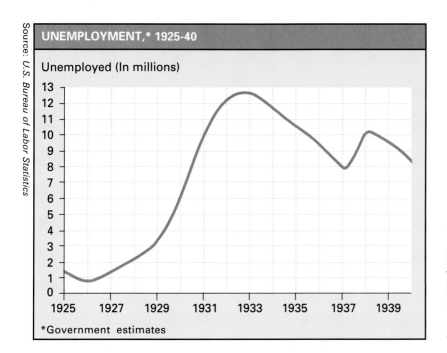

Source: U.S. Bureau of Labor Statistics

UNEMPLOYMENT,* 1925-40

Unemployed (In millions)

*Government estimates

LEARNING FROM GRAPHS. *Note the ups and downs of unemployment figures between 1925 and 1940. They are usually much more stable. What event caused them to soar in 1929–30? What helped bring them down in the mid-1930s?*

These crowds have not come to see the latest movie by the popular Wallace Beery, in which a little boy gets a prizefighter back on his feet. They stand on line in the hope that there will be some work when their turn comes. "We all had an understanding that it wasn't our fault," recalled one survivor of the 1930s, but who to blame?

Many victims of the depression received help from relatives and friends. Malcolm Little, who later became the black radical known as Malcolm X, recalled such instances in his *Autobiography*. "No one we knew had enough to eat or live on," he explained. "Some old family friends visited us now and then. At first they brought food. Though it was charity, my mother took it."

Others stood on street corners trying to sell apples or pencils. Some simply held out their hands, begging for a few pennies. Some became tramps, wandering aimlessly around the country, stealing rides on railroad freight cars. Some became thieves. And some people actually starved to death. In 1931, for example, four New York City hospitals reported treating 95 cases of severe malnutrition, and 20 of these patients died of starvation.

Hoover Fights the Depression

Herbert Hoover's work during the Great World War seemed good training for dealing with the depression. He had helped the Belgians after the Germans invaded their country. He had run the American food program after 1917. As secretary of commerce during the 1920s he had won the confidence of most business leaders.

"Woman of the High Plains, Texas Panhandle" was taken by Dorothea Lange in 1938. It is one of the most lingering images of the depression. Dignity and despair are matched in this touching photograph. The drought will come again to this desolate field, crops will fail. What can she do?

Hoover also understood economics better than most politicians. When he realized that the nation had entered a serious depression, he tried to stimulate recovery quickly. He urged Congress to lower taxes so that people would have more money to spend on goods and services. He called for more government spending on **public works,** such as road construction or building dams. These measures would increase the demand for goods and put jobless people back to work, he said. Congress passed each of these measures. Unfortunately they were too limited to end the Great Depression.

Farmers in particular were hard hit by the depression. The price of most farm products fell sharply. Hoover urged farmers to form cooperatives and to raise smaller crops until prices rose. He also favored holding down interest rates so farmers and the businesses they supported could borrow money more easily. Neither bankers nor farmers were willing to follow these voluntary guidelines in the face of the crisis.

Above all, the president recognized that the American people

Louis Ribak, *Home Relief Station*, (1935-36), oil on canvas, 28 x 36", Collection of Whitney Museum of American Art, 36.148.

"Home Relief Station" reminds us that waiting and humiliation are often part of private charity. The victims await their turns in front of the woman who will investigate (probably in too loud a voice) their claims. Louis Ribak painted the scene. Imagine what you would say to this minor bureaucrat when your time came.

had lost confidence in the economic system. This was part of their psychological depression. He tried to encourage them to have faith in the future. "Prosperity," he said, "is just around the corner."

But Hoover's strength as an organizer in wartime proved to be a weakness during the depression. Voluntary cooperation would not solve the nation's problems this time. During the war people knew who the enemy was and what to do to protect themselves. In the depression they could not identify any particular enemy. Therefore they did not know how they could protect themselves.

Hoover displayed still another weakness. He believed that the federal government should not increase its authority just because times were hard. If the United States took over powers that normally belonged to state and local governments, it would become a "superstate." Even when city after city proved unable to raise enough money to take care of the unemployed, Hoover opposed federal grants for relief purposes. Such aid would destroy the "real liberty" of the people, he said.

Hoover supported federal assistance to banks and big industries. These loans were sound investments, he said. The money would be used to produce goods and earn profits. Then the loans could be repaid. Lending money to a farmer to buy pig feed or more seed or a tractor was also proper, according to Hoover's theory. But he opposed giving federal aid to farmers so that they could feed their children. That would be giving them something for nothing. He believed charity was the business of state and local governments and private organizations like the Red Cross and the Salvation Army.

As the Great Depression dragged on, Hoover became more and more unpopular. People began to think that he was hardhearted. He seemed not to care about the sufferings of the poor. His critics even claimed that he was responsible for the depression.

Both charges were untrue. Hoover cared deeply about the suffering the depression was causing. He sincerely believed that his policies were the proper ones. These policies had certainly not caused the depression. After all, every industrial nation in the world had high unemployment at the time. The Great Depression affected all of Europe and most of the rest of the world.

The economies of nations that depended on agriculture were badly depressed. There was a depression in wheat-growing Australia and in beef-raising Argentina. The price of Brazilian coffee fell so low that farmers there burned the coffee beans in cookstoves. Coffee made a cheaper fuel than coal or kerosene.

Still, even if he was not responsible for the long depression, Hoover's rigid policies were not working. But he was too convinced that they were correct to try something different. He was in charge of the government. Therefore people tended to blame him.

The Bonus Army

Public opinion turned further against Hoover after the **Bonus March** of the summer of 1932. Some years earlier Congress had passed a law giving veterans of the Great World War an adjusted compensation bonus. Its purpose was to make up for the low pay that soldiers had received during the war while workers at home were earning high wages. The bonus money, however, was not to be paid until 1945.

During the depression veterans began to demand that the bonus be paid at once. As you can see in this excerpt from a letter to the veteran's committee, this issue was turning public opinion and anger against Hoover and the government.

    66 Now that our income is but $15.60 a week (their are five of us My Husband Three little children and myself). My husband who is a world war Veteran and saw active service in the trenches, became desperate and applied for Compensation and was turned down and that started me thinking. . . . Oh why is it that it is allways a bunch of overley rich, selfish, dumb, ignorant money hogs that persist in being Senators, legislatures, representatives Where would they and their possessions be if it were not for the Common Soldier, the common laborer that is compelled to work for a starvation wage, for I tell you again the hog of a Landlord gets his there is not enough left for the necessities if a man

Brown Brothers

UPI/Bettmann Newsphotos

Federal troops use tear gas and bay-onets in 1932 to clear the tent city set up by the Bonus Army. Who super-vised the work? General Douglas MacArthur, left, and his aide Dwight D. Eisenhower. Were the Bonus Marchers dangerous radicals to be driven from the capital?

has three or more children. . . . Oh for a few Statesmen, oh for but one statesman, as fearless as Abraham Lincoln, the amancipator who died for us. . . .[1]**”**

[1] From *Down and Out in the Depression: Letters from the "Forgotten Man,"* edited by Robert S. McElvaine

Then in July 1932 about 20,000 former soldiers marched on Washington to demonstrate before the Capitol. When Congress re-fused to change the law, some of the marchers settled down on vacant land on the edge of Washington. They put up a camp of tents and flimsy tar-paper shacks. They announced that they would not leave until the bonus was paid.

Hoover had opposed the bonus to begin with. Such giveaways threatened to destroy the "self-reliance" of the people, he said. He believed, wrongly as it turned out, that the Bonus Marchers were being led by dangerous radicals. When trouble broke out, Hoover ordered army units to assist police in driving out the veterans.

Troops commanded by General Douglas MacArthur went into action. Infantrymen backed by cavalry units and five tanks swiftly cleared the camp. No shots were fired and no one was killed. How-ever, news film of steel-helmeted, rifle-bearing soldiers firing tear gas grenades at ragged, unarmed war veterans shocked millions of Amer-icans. Hoover's popularity hit rock bottom. 🖳

Return to the Preview & Review on page 355.

362   THE GREAT DEPRESSION AND THE NEW DEAL

2. ROOSEVELT COMES TO POWER

Franklin D. Roosevelt

It is safe to say that in 1932 any Democratic presidential candidate could have defeated the Republican Hoover. Somewhere between 13 and 16 million workers were unemployed. The total income of all Americans had fallen from $87 billion in 1929 to $42 billion in 1932. All the shares of the stocks listed on the New York Stock Exchange were worth only a quarter of their value before the Great Crash.

The particular Democrat who profited from this situation was Franklin D. Roosevelt, the governor of New York. Roosevelt came from a wealthy family. He had graduated from Harvard College, studied law, and gone into politics. As we have seen, he had run for vice president in 1920 on the ticket with James M. Cox, who was defeated by Warren G. Harding.

The next year Roosevelt spent his usual vacation at his summer home in Campobello, Canada. One day in August 1921 he helped put out a brush fire while on an outing with his children. He returned home tired and chilled in his wet swimming suit. That night he burned with fever. Within a few days his legs were almost completely paralyzed. He had a severe case of polio. He recovered from the disease, but for the rest of his life he could walk only with the aid of metal braces and two canes. More often he was carried or used a wheelchair.

Roosevelt's usual high spirits sagged, but only briefly. He went on with his political career. In 1928, when Governor Alfred E. Smith of New York ran for president against Hoover, Roosevelt was chosen by the Democrats to run for governor. Hoover defeated Smith in the race for electoral votes in New York, but Roosevelt, the Democrat, was elected governor. Two years later he was reelected by a huge majority. This evidence of popular support won him the 1932 Democratic presidential nomination.

Roosevelt was almost the exact opposite of Hoover. Hoover was restrained, stiff, and by 1932, very glum. Roosevelt had a cheerful, relaxed, almost carefree personality. Indeed, in 1932 many observers thought he had more style than substance. He was no more radical than Hoover, but he was a much less rigid person. Hoover worked out careful theories and tried to apply them to the practical problems of government. Roosevelt mistrusted theories. Yet he was willing to apply any theory to any particular problem if there seemed a good chance it would work.

Roosevelt turned out to be a most popular political campaigner. He made excellent speeches. He had tremendous energy. Moreover, he was an optimist. At a time when most people were deeply depressed, his cheer encouraged and uplifted millions. The crowds that gathered when he campaigned seemed to inspire him as well. "I have

Use these questions to guide your reading. Answer the questions after completing Section 2.
Understanding Issues, Events, & Ideas. Use the following words to trace Roosevelt's first moves to counter the depression: New Deal, relief, recovery, reform, Hundred Days, Bank Holiday, Federal Deposit Insurance Corporation, National Industrial Recovery Act, minimum wage, National Recovery Administration, Agricultural Adjustment Act, Tennessee Valley Authority, Federal Securities Act, Home Owner's Loan Corporation, Federal Emergency Relief Administration, Civil Works Authority, Civilian Conservation Corps.
1. Contrast the personalities of Herbert Hoover and Franklin Roosevelt.
2. How did the banking crisis turn out to be an advantage for the entire country?
3. What was the overall effect of the flood of laws passed during the Hundred Days?
Thinking Critically. Which do you think was the most important law passed during the Hundred Days? Why?

Vanity Fair, *a witty and popular magazine, in 1934 offered this cover of FDR "breaking in" the rambunctious country. If the horse stands for the United States, how is Roosevelt doing?*

looked into the faces of thousands of Americans," he confided to one friend. "They are saying: 'We're caught in something we don't understand; perhaps this fellow can help us out.'"

Roosevelt had no clear idea of how to provide what the voters wanted. When he discussed farm policy, balancing the budget, and other economic problems in his speeches, he was vague. Sometimes he contradicted himself. In his campaign speeches, he attacked Hoover for not balancing the budget and at the same time promised to unbalance it further if necessary to care for any Americans who were in "dire need." But he was deeply moved by the trust he sensed that people had in him. He sought ideas from all kinds of experts: college professors, social workers, reporters, old-fashioned political bosses.

At no point during the campaign did Roosevelt claim to know exactly how to end the depression. He offered a point of view, not a specific plan. "The country needs bold, persistent experimentation," he said. "It is common sense to take a method, and try it. If it fails, admit it frankly and try another. But above all, try something." He called this policy "a New Deal," and the term described his approach exactly. In a game of bridge or poker or pinochle, no one can know how the cards will fall. But if one is dealt a poor hand, there is always the chance that the next will be better.

Roosevelt's New Deal argument proved to be what millions of voters wanted to hear. In November he defeated Hoover easily. His electoral majority was 472 to 59. The popular vote was 22.8 million to 15.8 million. The voters also gave the Democrats large majorities in both houses of Congress.

"Nothing to Fear but Fear Itself"

Roosevelt was elected in November, but he could not by law take his oath as president until March 4. Meanwhile, the economy seemed to drift downward aimlessly, like a falling leaf in a winter forest. Between December 1932 and February industrial production hit an all-time low. This, together with continuing news of bank failures, caused Americans to panic. Suddenly, in February, people all over the country began to rush fearfully to withdraw their savings from the banks. This banking panic forced even most of the soundest banks to close their doors.

The banking crisis turned out to be a great advantage for Roosevelt and indirectly for the entire country. It forced people to put politics aside and treat the depression as a great national emergency.

Inauguration Day in Washington was cold and damp. In this dark hour Roosevelt's speech came like a ray of summer sunshine. He said:

66 This great nation will endure as it has endured, will revive, and will prosper.

So, first of all, let me assert my firm belief that the only thing we have to fear is fear itself—nameless, unreasoning, unjustified terror which paralyzes needed efforts to convert retreat into advance. . . .

Happiness lies not in the mere possession of money; it lies in the joy of achievement, in the thrill of creative effort.

We face the arduous [hard] days that lie before us in the warm courage of national unity; with the clear consciousness of seeking old and precious moral values; with the clean satisfaction that comes from the stern performance of duty by old and young alike. . . .[1] 」」

Roosevelt spoke only generally about measures for fighting the depression. But he made his approach crystal clear. He was going to do something. ''Action, and action now,'' was his theme. His first priority would be to put people back to work, he said.

The Hundred Days

In his inaugural address the president called upon Congress to meet in a special session on March 9 to deal with the emergency. From March 9 to June 16, when this special session ended, was 100 days. No one planned to have the session last exactly 100 days. The fact that it did dramatized how much that Congress accomplished.

In his campaign for president, Roosevelt had called for a **New Deal**. Roosevelt's New Deal had three general aims—relief, recovery, and reform. **Relief** came first and was aimed at all Americans in

[1]From *The Public Papers and Addresses, 1933* by Franklin D. Roosevelt

The Bank Panic in 1933 brought lines of New Yorkers to withdraw their savings from the American Union Bank. Even the soundest banks had to close their doors to stop "runs." What event of the 1980s reminded many people of the panic?

economic distress. **Recovery** would then spur the economy and get the country out of the depression. **Reform** would prevent another severe depression from happening. The flood of new laws passed during the **Hundred Days** had the effect of convincing people that old ways were indeed being tossed out, like a worn deck of cards. The country seemed to be making a fresh start.

Even before Congress met, Roosevelt declared a **Bank Holiday,** closing all the banks so that a general plan to protect the savings of the public could be developed. Congress then passed new banking laws, the most important being a measure which created the **Federal Deposit Insurance Corporation** (FDIC). The FDIC insured everyone's savings up to $5,000. Runs on banks stopped. Depositors knew that even if their bank failed, they would get their money back. Nothing did more than this measure to restore public confidence. As one of Roosevelt's advisers said:

    66 The bank rescue of 1933 was probably the turning point of the Depression. When people were able to survive the shock of having all the banks closed, and then see the banks open up, with their money protected, there began to be confidence. Good times were coming. Most of the legislation that came after that didn't really help the public, the public helped itself, after it got confidence.

    It marked the revival of hope. . . .[1]99

But new banking laws could not create jobs or cause farm prices to rise or stimulate business activity directly. So Congress quickly passed laws to accomplish these objectives. The most important and controversial measure was the **National Industrial Recovery Act** (NIRA).

The NIRA was supposed to stimulate private business by permitting manufacturers to cooperate with one another without fear of violating the antitrust laws. Firms in every industry were to draw up rules, called codes of fair competition. The firms were allowed to set limits on how much each could produce in order to avoid flooding markets with goods that could not be sold. They could also fix prices to avoid cutthroat competition.

In addition the codes provided certain benefits for workers. One was the right to freely join unions. Through these unions workers could bargain collectively with their employers. **Minimum wage** rates and maximum hours of work were also guaranteed under the codes. Each industrial code had to be approved, supervised, and enforced by the government through the **National Recovery Administration** (NRA). Roosevelt selected the enthusiastic Frances Perkins as his secretary of labor. She became the first woman cabinet member and an active advocate of workers' rights.

In this Vanity Fair *cover Uncle Sam is rescued by the Blue Eagle. Why was it a hopeful symbol?*

[1] From *Hard Times: An Oral History of the Great Depression* by Studs Terkel

Brown Brothers

Frances Perkins, the first woman cabinet member, greets workmen of Carnegie Steel. This is a far cry from the ugly scene of the Homestead Strike against Carnegie years earlier. How did the Great Depression bring a truce to labor, management, and government?

NRA officials made great efforts to persuade workers and employers to accept the new system. "We Do Our Part" was the slogan of the NRA. Its symbol was a picture of a Blue Eagle. Soon Blue Eagle stickers were being displayed in the windows of giant factories and small shops all over the country. This symbol was also printed on the labels of products of all kinds.

The NRA was expected to get the sluggish industrial economy moving again. Congress next dealt with the farm problem by passing the **Agricultural Adjustment Act** (AAA). During the depression farm prices had fallen even further than the prices of manufactured goods. The basic idea of the AAA was to push prices up by cutting down on the amount of crops produced.

Under this law the government rented some of the land that was normally planted in so-called basic crops, such as wheat, cotton, tobacco, and corn. No crops were planted on the land the government

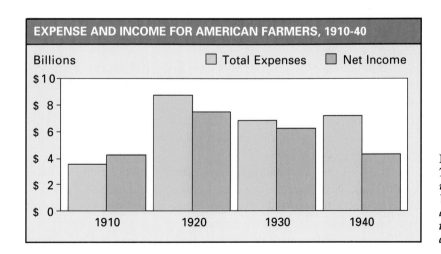

EXPENSE AND INCOME FOR AMERICAN FARMERS, 1910-40

Billins — ☐ Total Expenses ☐ Net Income

LEARNING FROM GRAPHS. *The fortunes of American farmers had risen to new heights after the Great War, although expense still outdistanced income. What had happened to the difference between expense and income by 1940?*

Roosevelt Comes to Power   367

Millie Wong, a ten-year-old girl in Brooklyn, received more Blue Eagles than any other individual. She wrote Washington to request 10 Blue Eagles for father, mother, and her 7 sisters and brothers. She wanted to prove that all members of the Wong family were good citizens, although some were born in China and not naturalized. Her request was granted.

Senator George W. Norris of Nebraska was the father of the TVA, the program of flood control that brought electricity to the rural South.

rented. Farmers benefited in two ways. They got the rent money from the government, and they got higher prices for what they grew on the rest of their land because the total amount grown was smaller and therefore more valuable.

The AAA raised the money to rent the land taken out of production by what were called processing taxes. These were taxes paid by each business that processed, or prepared, the basic crops for general use—the miller who ground wheat into flour, the cotton manufacturer, and so on.

Congress also created the **Tennessee Valley Authority** (TVA) during the Hundred Days. This New Deal agency had no direct relation to the fight against the depression. Its "father" was Senator George W. Norris of Nebraska. During the 1920s, before the depression, Norris had fought efforts to get the government to sell to private interests the dam it had built at Muscle Shoals on the Tennessee River. He wanted the electricity produced at Muscle Shoals to be used as part of a broad plan to develop the resources of the entire Tennessee Valley.

Although Norris was a Republican, Roosevelt accepted his proposal. Under the TVA, Muscle Shoals was an efficient producer of electricity. The TVA had accurate information about how much electricity should cost consumers. The project therefore served as a kind of "yardstick" for measuring the fairness of prices charged by private electric power companies.

The TVA also manufactured fertilizers, built more dams for flood control, and developed a network of parks and lakes for recreation. It planted new forests and developed other conservation projects. It also provided jobs throughout the region.

Another achievement of the Hundred Days was the passage of

the **Federal Securities Act,** which regulated the way companies could issue and sell stock. Still another was the creation of the **Home Owners' Loan Corporation** (HOLC), which helped people who were unable to meet mortgage payments to hold on to their homes. Thousands of letters bombarded the president and officers of HOLC. Most showed tremendous loyalty and love for Roosevelt and begged for his help. One man wrote:

> **"** I sincerely *hope* and *pray* you will come to my aid and help me save my home for my family, if I should loose it I don't know what I'll do as I have *no other place to go.* . . .
>
> I believe God will see us through some way but it has been the hardest thing I have had to go through, this may be His way so I'm writing to you asking and praying that you will do something to save our home.
>
> I am sure the President, if he only knew, would order that something be done, God Bless him. he is doing all he can to relieve the suffering and I am sure his name will go down in history among the other great men of our country. . . .[1] **"**

These measures brought many benefits. Still, many people became homeless. Men left their families to find work. Whole families were forced out onto the street to search for shelter.

The greatest benefits of the New Deal came from what was done about the unemployed and the poor. The poor faced problems that

[1]From *Down and Out in the Great Depression: Letters from the "Forgotten Man,"* edited by Robert S. McElvaine

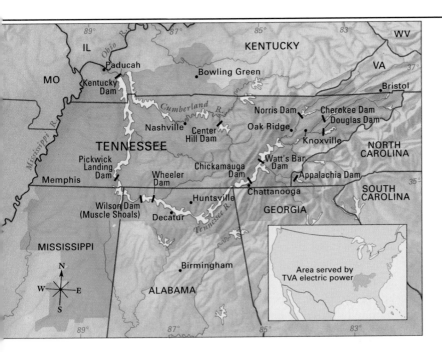

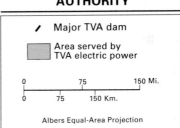

TENNESSEE VALLEY AUTHORITY

↗ Major TVA dam

▨ Area served by TVA electric power

0   75   150 Mi.

0   75   150 Km.

Albers Equal-Area Projection

LEARNING FROM MAPS. *One major aim of the Tennessee Valley Authority was flood control and river navigation. Which rivers were the heart of the TVA? The TVA stretched over vast areas in several southern states. What states were served by TVA electric power?*

Roosevelt Comes to Power   369

THE DUST BOWL

Nature had seemed to smile upon the young nation in the 1830s. In the 1930s nature seemed particularly cruel. As times got harder, weather and even the land seemed to turn against the poor. Perhaps the hardest hit were the farmers of the high plains—the states from Texas and Oklahoma to South and North Dakota. This region rarely gets much rain. In the early 1930s almost none fell.

By 1934 the drought had become so bad that winds picked up powder-dry topsoil and blew it across the plains in dense, black clouds. The region came to be known as the Dust Bowl. It was impossible to grow anything on this shifting land.

Broke and discouraged, many Oklahoma farm families loaded seemed almost overwhelming—no job, little food, no home. Yet many hoped and prayed that they could hold on to what they had and that better days were ahead. A woman wrote:

> Phila., Pa.
> November 26, 1934
>
> Honorable Franklin D. Roosevelt
> Washington, D.C.
> Dear Mr. President:
>
> I am forced to write to you because we find ourselves in *a very serious condition*. For the last three or four years we have had depression and *suffered* with my *family* and little children *severely*. . . . There has been unemployment in my house for more than three years. You can imagine that I and my family have suffered from lack of water supply in my house for more than two years. Last winter I did not have coal and the pipes burst in my house and therefore could not make heat in the house. Now winter is here again and we are suffering of cold, no water in the house, and we are facing to be forced out of the house, because I have no money to move or pay so much money as they want when after making settlement I am mother of little children, am

into their secondhand Model T Fords and headed west toward California. There they became migrant workers, picking fruit, vegetables, cotton, and other crops. They followed the harvest in their overheated cars and spent their nights in roadside camps. Old people died alongside unfamiliar roads. Babies grew up hungry, their eyes big with suspicion.

One of the people who came to California was a young folk-

The human and physical consequences of the depression meet here. Alexandre Hogue painted "Drouth Stricken Area" with the thirsty cow, reduced to skin and bones, in the thin shadow of the windmill. The photograph of the **Migrant Mother** *in California, was taken in one quick ten-minute session by Dorothea Lange in 1936.*

singer named Woodrow Wilson Guthrie, who arrived from Oklahoma in 1937. Californians

"needed more and more people to pick their fruits," Woody Guthrie said. "But they looked down for some reason on the people that came in there from other states to do that kind of work." The times were dangerous. "In most towns . . . it is a jailhouse offense to be unemployed," he wrote.

One of Woody Guthrie's songs put the plight of the migrant workers in this way:

California is a garden of Eden,
A paradise to live in or see.
But, believe it or not, you
*   won't find it so hot,*
If you ain't got the do-re-mi°[1]

°"do-re-mi" is money
[1]From "Do Re Mi," words and music by Woody Guthrie. TRO © copyright 1961 and 1963 Ludlow Music Inc., New York, N.Y. Used by permission.

A tenant farmer poses with his family during the Great Depression. Why would Americans of the 1830s have welcomed such a family?

Roosevelt Comes to Power   371

Brown Brothers

Civilian Conservation Corpsmen are clearing brush from scrubland in the western United States to lessen the risk of fire. Below is Harry Hopkins, a close friend of Roosevelt's, who conceived many of the attempts to remedy the Great Depression.

Culver Pictures

sick and losing my health, and we are eight people in the family, and where can I go when I don't have money because no one is working in my house. . . . Now I have *no money, no home* and *no wheres to go.* I beg of you to please help me and my family and little children for the sake of a sick mother and suffering family to give this your immediate attention so we will not be forced to move or put out on the street.

Waiting and Hoping that you will act quickly.
Thanking you very much I remain

Mrs. E.L.[1]

[1]From *Down and Out in the Great Depression: Letters from the "Forgotten Man,"* edited by Robert S. McElvaine

In response to such suffering Roosevelt rejected Hoover's ideas about what the federal government could and could not do about unemployment and poverty. Soon after Roosevelt took office, the **Federal Emergency Relief Administration** was created. This agency was headed by Harry Hopkins, a New York social worker. It distributed $500 million in federal grants among state organizations that cared for the poor. The following fall and winter another New Deal agency, the **Civil Works Authority,** also headed by Hopkins, found jobs for more than 4 million people out of work.

During the Hundred Days, Congress also created the **Civilian Conservation Corps** (CCC). This agency put unemployed young men from poor families to work on various conservation projects. CCC workers lived in camps run by the army. They cleared brush, planted trees, built small dams, and performed dozens of other useful tasks. The CCC provides a good example of how swiftly New Deal measures were put into effect. The law that created the program passed Congress on March 31, 1933. By July there were 300,000 corpsmen at work in 1,300 camps all over the country. 🔲

Return to the Preview & Review on page 363.

3. THE NEW DEAL

Why the New Deal Was Popular

The New Deal was very popular. Democrats increased their majorities in Congress in the 1934 elections. When Franklin D. Roosevelt ran for a second term in 1936, against Alfred Landon of Kansas, he won every state in the Union except Maine and Vermont. He did so despite the fact that New Deal legislation had not ended the depression. Unemployment remained extremely high. Industrial production picked up, but only very slowly.

The personality of FDR, as the newspapers came to call him, had a great deal to do with the success of the New Deal. He was an optimist. His hope for better conditions was always cheerful and encouraging, but never silly or foolish. This excerpt from a popular song of 1936 tells how the people felt about their president:

> ❝No more breadlines we're glad to say, the donkey won election day,
> No more standing in the blowing, snowing rain;
> He's got things in full sway, we're all working and getting our pay,
> We've got Franklin D. Roosevelt back again.[1]❞

Roosevelt had a way of reaching people that was truly remarkable. He spoke frequently on the radio. These **fireside chats** were not speeches in the usual sense. The president seemed to come right into the room with his listeners. He explained what problems lay before the nation, how he proposed to deal with them, and what people could do to help him.

Roosevelt made great use of experts. His close advisers, mostly college professors, were known as the **Brain Trust.** Yet ordinary citizens never got the idea that Roosevelt was listening to theories that were not practical and down to earth.

The president never put all the nation's eggs in one basket. This made sense to most people. The economic mess was so complicated that no single plan or project was likely to untangle it. Roosevelt's way was to experiment with many things at once. This created the impression that the best minds in the country were hard at work fighting the depression. They were not winning an immediate victory. But what seemed important was that *something* was being done.

The New Deal was also popular because it made large groups of people feel that the government was genuinely trying to improve their lives. This had little to do with the depression itself. For example, workers in industries like steel and automobiles were not organized in 1933. It was not the policy of the federal government to

[1]From "Franklin D. Roosevelt's Back Again," in *This Singing Land*, compiled and edited by Irwin Silber

Preview & Review

Use these questions to guide your reading. Answer the questions after completing Section 3.
Understanding Issues, Events, & Ideas. Use the following words to explain the New Deal: fireside chat, Brain Trust, Rural Electrification Administration, Works Progress Administration, National Youth Administration, Second New Deal, Wagner Labor Relations Act, National Labor Relations Board, Social Security Act.
1. How did the New Deal help relieve much of the human suffering caused by the depression?
2. On what grounds did the Supreme Court rule that some New Deal measures were unconstitutional?
3. How did Roosevelt change his tactics in his battle against the depression?
Thinking Critically. Imagine that you are the owner of a large corporation in 1935. Write a letter to President Roosevelt explaining why you think that the New Deal will hurt your business. Cite specific measures in your letter.

COMPOSING AN ESSAY

You are often asked to prepare a written report or to answer an essay question on a test. An essay is a short composition on a specific topic. It should always contain three parts: an introduction, a body of information, and a closing.

You have already learned the preliminary steps to composing an essay: Writing About History (page xx) and composing paragraphs (page 266). Once you have mastered that strategy, the next step is the actual writing of an essay.

How to Compose an Essay

Before learning the steps for analzying economic statistics, review Composing Paragraphs on page 266. Then to compose an essay, follow these steps.

1. **Focus on the topic.** Make sure you understand what you are to write about. The topic should be broad enough to provide enough material for an essay but not too broad to be dealt with in a short composition.
2. **Organize your ideas.** Remember that your essay should have three parts. Organize your thoughts accordingly.
3. **Compose your essay.** Clearly state your topic in the introduction. Present your evidence and supporting details in the body of the essay. Your closing should briefly sum up what you have said in the essay.

Applying the Strategy

Suppose you were given an assignment to write an essay according to the following directive:

Explain briefly what the aims and outcomes of the three parts of the New Deal were.

Your first task is to identify the topic of your essay: *the aims and outcomes of the three parts of the New Deal.* You might organize your thoughts in a manner similar to the following outline:

The New Deal

I. Introduction
II. Three Parts of New Deal
  a. Relief
    1. Aims
    2. Outcomes
  b. Recovery
    1. Aims
    2. Outcomes
  c. Reform
    1. Aims
    2. Outcomes
III. Closing

For independent practice, see Practicing the Strategy on page 393.

INTERPRETING HISTORY: The New Deal

When Franklin D. Roosevelt became president in 1933, the United States was on the verge of economic collapse. People were desperate for the government to take action. Roosevelt and his advisers quickly drafted the New Deal to ease the nation's terrible financial distress.

Americans in the 1930s had different opinions about the New Deal. Many people welcomed the plan because it brought needed and immediate relief. Others disliked the expanding role government was to play in the daily lives of American citizens.

Historians also have debated the effects of the New Deal on government and society. Basil Rauch divided the New Deal into two phases. In *History of the New Deal 1933-1938* (1944) he argued that each part had a different set of goals and achievements. The First New Deal, from 1933 to 1935, worked to bring about recovery from the depression by helping the unemployed and raising prices for industry and agriculture. During the Second New Deal, from 1935 to 1938, reform was more important than recovery. The Second New Deal aimed at changing the economic system to avoid severe depressions in the future.

Arthur Schlesinger's three-volume study of the New Deal, *The Age of Roosevelt* (1957-1960), offered another assessment of Roosevelt's program. Schlesinger claimed that the New Deal was part of a continuing conflict between conservatives and liberals that had been going on for generations. During the 1920s the government failed to live up to the reform impulses of the Populists and the progressives. The New Dealers were liberals who promoted reform measures in order to reverse the conservative trend. And to Schlesinger, the First New Deal was far more radical than the Second and included far greater government control of the economy than ever before. This was directly opposite the individualism and free competition of an earlier America. The Second New Deal recalled legislation of the early 1900s—collective bargaining and government attacks on monopoly.

In the 1960s scholars known as the New Left historians challenged the positive assessments of the New Deal by previous historians. Barton J. Bernstein's essay in *Towards a New Past: Dissenting Essays in American History* (1968) characterized the New Deal as being too conservative. For example, Roosevelt's unwillingness to question private enterprise or nationalize the banks is seen as evidence that the New Deal was a conservative program. The national mood at the time was desperate. Financial institutions were in such confusion that the American people would have approved very drastic measures if Roosevelt had proposed them. But he did not, recommending laws that helped the bankers.

Bernstein and other New Left historians criticize the New Deal because it failed to redistribute wealth in the United States, promote racial and social equality, or make business more responsible for the public welfare.

Government actions usually cause a wide range of reactions. Historians who study such actions and their effects often reach an equally wide range of interpretations.

promote unions, but the spirit of the New Deal encouraged many workers to join unions. Roosevelt certainly wanted workers to be treated more fairly and with greater respect by their employers than had been common in the past.

President Roosevelt's greatest sympathy was for farmers. New Deal farm legislation was aimed at increasing their shrunken incomes and improving the quality of rural life. The **Rural Electrification Administration,** which brought electricity to remote farm districts, is a good illustration of how the lives of farmers could be improved.

Most important, the New Deal relieved much of the human suffering caused by the depression. The Civil Works Administration, and later the **Works Progress Administration** (WPA), found useful work for millions of idle men and women. Most of the jobs were of

U.S. Department of the Interior, Uniphoto

Many students had libraries for the first time under this WPA project. The advantages to society are obvious. Above, the work of a muralist in the Federal Arts Project.

the pick-and-shovel type, but not all of them. Harry Hopkins insisted that the full skills of the unemployed be used whenever possible.

In the city of Boston, for example, New Deal work projects included building a subway, expanding the East Boston Airport, and improving a municipal golf course. Other Boston relief workers taught in nursery schools, cataloged books in the Boston Public Library, and read to blind people. College students employed by the **National Youth Administration** graded papers and did office chores in their schools. Singers performed in hospitals. Musicians gave concerts. Troupes of actors put on plays, including a revival of *Uncle Tom's Cabin*. Artists designed posters and painted murals on the walls of schools and libraries.

UPI/Bettmann Newsphotos

Criticism of the New Deal

The laws passed during the Hundred Days greatly increased the power of the federal government and particularly of the president. Many day-to-day decisions had to be made under these laws. The president and his appointees seemed the logical persons to make them. New Deal laws are full of such phrases as ''The president is authorized . . .'' and ''The secretary of agriculture shall have the power to . . .'' and ''The Board shall have power, in the name of the United States of America, to . . .''

Some people found this trend alarming. Business leaders in particular objected to the new restrictions placed on how they conducted their affairs. The New Deal would destroy the free enterprise system, they charged. They therefore brought suits against the government in the courts, claiming that the new laws were unconstitutional.

In 1935 and 1936 the Supreme Court ruled that the National Industrial Recovery Act and the Agricultural Adjustment Act were indeed unconstitutional. The Court also declared unconstitutional some important state laws regulating economic affairs, such as a New York minimum-wage law. In the NIRA case, *Schechter v. U.S.* (1935), the Court decided unanimously that Congress had delegated too much of its law-making power to the boards that watched over industrial codes. In *U.S. v. Butler* it ruled that the AAA processing tax was not really a tax but a method of regulating farm production.

Conservatives charged that the New Deal was trying to do too much. Other critics argued that the government was not doing enough. As time passed, the excitement of the Hundred Days disappeared. Perhaps prosperity was ''just around the corner,'' but the corner never seemed to be reached.

Library of Congress

OLD RELIABLE!

With a wave of his wand Roosevelt performs his trick ''Old Reliable.'' What is this magic rabbit expected to do? Why does the cartoonist say it never fails?

The New Deal

Three very strong critics of President Roosevelt were, from left, Huey Long of Louisiana; Father Charles Coughlin; and Dr. Francis E. Townshend. Which one of their ideas is with us to this day?

Some people who had originally supported Roosevelt now turned against him. One was Senator Huey Long of Louisiana, who ruled like a king in his home state. The "Kingfish," as he was called, had great pity for the little person. He claimed that the president had become a tool of Wall Street investors. Long wanted to tax away all incomes of more than $1 million a year. With that money, he said, everyone would be guaranteed a large enough income to own a house, a car, and everything else needed to live decently. Long's Share-Our-Wealth organization had over 4.6 million members in 1935.

Francis Townshend, a California doctor, called for granting Old-Age Revolving Pensions to every American over 60. He attracted a very large following. A Catholic priest, Father Charles E. Coughlin, spoke to millions in his weekly radio broadcasts. He criticized various New Deal programs. Eventually he made bitter personal attacks on President Roosevelt.

There were even critics within the Roosevelt administration. Some were complaining by 1935 and 1936 that the president was not fighting the depression vigorously enough. They wanted the government to spend more money in order to stimulate the economy and put more people to work.

The Second New Deal

Roosevelt responded to the criticisms of the mid-1930s by proposing more reforms. We call his new program the **Second New Deal.**

After the Supreme Court struck down the National Industrial Recovery Act, Congress passed the **Wagner Labor Relations Act** of 1935. This law again gave labor unions the right to organize and bargain collectively. It set up a **National Labor Relations Board** (NLRB) to run union elections and settle disputes. When a majority of the workers in the plant voted to join a union in an NLRB election,

Library of Congress

How could Roosevelt not have been a favorite for editorial cartoonists? "New Deal Remedies" shows how Roosevelt was able to try another approach if the first failed, but it hardly meant to pay him a compliment. How many remedies on the table can you identify?

that union became the representative of all the workers in the plant, not merely of those who had voted to join it.

In 1935 Congress also passed the **Social Security Act.** This law set up a system of old-age insurance, paid for partly by workers and partly by their employers. This system paid retired people 65 years of age and over a pension. The amount of the pension was based on the number of years a worker had paid into the system. The act provided for unemployment insurance too. This supplied money for workers who had lost their jobs and were looking for new ones. Many workers, such as farmhands and maids, were not covered by the original Social Security Act. Nevertheless, the law marked a great turning point for American society.

Other laws passed in 1935 included a "soak-the-rich" income tax and an act regulating banks more strictly. Another law was aimed at breaking up combinations among electric light and gas companies.

These measures marked a change of tactics in Roosevelt's battle against the depression. In 1933 he had tried to unite all groups and classes. By 1936 he had given up on holding the support of big business and rich people. During his campaign for reelection he attacked these people, whom he called "an enemy within our gates." He and his campaign managers turned instead to the labor movement; to women voters; and to blacks, Hispanics, and other such groups for support. Their efforts were successful. As we have already noted, Roosevelt was reelected by a landslide in 1936.

Return to the Preview & Review on page 373.

Understanding Issues, Events, & Ideas. Use the following words to describe some of the effects of the New Deal: Black Cabinet, Urban League, Supreme Court Reform Plan, deficit spending, Commodity Credit Corporation, Fair Labor Standards Act, industrial union, Congress of Industrial Organizations, welfare state, federal deficit.

1. What accounted for the political shift that occurred among black voters between 1932 and 1936?
2. How did many New Deal programs discriminate against blacks and Hispanics either directly or indirectly? Why did many blacks and Hispanics continue to support the New Deal?
3. Why did the Supreme Court Reform Plan produce a bitter fight?
4. How did labor unions change during the New Deal?

Thinking Critically. 1. Imagine you are a young black artist in 1934. Write a diary entry explaining why you want to move to Harlem. 2. Do you think President Roosevelt took on too much power and responsibility during the New Deal years? Why or why not?

4. EFFECTS OF THE NEW DEAL

African Americans Vote Democratic

In 1936 a majority of African American voters cast their ballots for Roosevelt and other Democratic candidates. This marked one of the most significant political shifts of the 20th century. Before the New Deal most blacks had supported "the party of Lincoln." The Republicans had not done much to win or hold the loyalty of blacks since Lincoln's day. The southerners who dominated the Democratic party had usually offered blacks nothing at all.

During the 1920s African Americans lost many of the gains they had won during the Great World War when their labor had been so much in demand. The revived Ku Klux Klan was a constant source of worry. The migration of southern blacks to northern cities continued. Indeed, African Americans were the immigrants of the 1920s. They replaced the European immigrants, whose numbers had declined because of the new immigration laws.

So many African Americans moved to northern cities that they were crowded into slums, or ghettos. Harlem, in New York City,

UPI/Bettmann Newsphotos

Joe Louis, the world heavyweight champion, on his honeymoon with his wife Marva strolls the streets of Harlem. Most blacks, like these onlookers, were proud rather than jealous of his great show of prosperity.

National Museum of American Art, Smithsonian Institution.

One of the finest paintings of the Harlem Renaissance is "The Janitor Who Paints" by Palmer Hayden.

was the best known of the black ghettos. By the end of the 1920s 165,000 blacks were crowded into Harlem's run-down row houses and decaying tenements.

Like the earlier immigrants, most black newcomers were able to get only the dirtiest, most exhausting, and lowest-paid work. Most labor unions shut out black members. This kept blacks from working in industries and crafts where organized labor was strong.

Yet, as you have read, even in segregated sections like Harlem, blacks were able to improve their situation. In such places they were actually the majority. They did not have to stand aside for white people. They could vote and elect black officials. Blacks came to have considerable influence on the larger politics of the city and state. They became more self-confident and more conscious of their rights.

Black writers, musicians, actors, and journalists had found audiences in Harlem. Black doctors and lawyers and other professionals practiced and prospered too. New York City blacks had experienced the Harlem Renaissance in the 1920s. Harlem had become the black intellectual and cultural capital of the nation. And it remained so throughout the depression. Ambitious young blacks from other states moved there, believing Harlem was the best place to develop their talents.

However, the Great Depression took much of the glitter from this revival of confidence. It struck African Americans with cruel force, as it did Hispanic Americans. As always in hard times, these workers were "the last hired and the first fired." By 1932 more than 30 percent of all black and Hispanic workers were unemployed.

Still, most African Americans voted the Republican ticket in 1932. In Chicago, for example, Hoover got 76 percent of the black vote. In Cincinnati he got 71 percent. But in 1936 most blacks in Chicago and Cincinnati voted for Roosevelt.

Black Support of the New Deal

Today it is hard to understand why African Americans and Hispanic Americans found Roosevelt and the New Deal so attractive. Many of the most important New Deal programs did little or nothing to help them. Most of the NRA industrial codes permitted employers to pay lower wages to black and Hispanic workers than to whites. New Deal farm policy badly hurt black tenant farmers and sharecroppers in the South. The AAA payments went to land *owners*. They were paid for taking tobacco land out of production. The tenants and sharecroppers who had farmed these acres lost their jobs and often their homes as well. It did nothing to help Hispanic farmers in the Southwest. Unemployed blacks and Hispanics in all parts of the country rarely got a full share of federal relief money or jobs.

The social security program did not discriminate directly against African Americans or Hispanics. However, it left out farm laborers and household workers. The millions of blacks and Hispanics who did work of this kind received no share of the new pension and unemployment benefits.

Yet African Americans and Hispanic Americans liked the New Deal. Many became enthusiastic admirers of Franklin Roosevelt. Thousands of black and Hispanic parents in the 1930s named babies after the president. The reasons for such strong feelings are best understood by keeping in mind how white society treated these groups at that time. This is another example of the need to use historical imagination. For example, the Civilian Conservation Corps camps in the South were segregated. If black youths had *not* been sent to separate camps when they joined the CCC, the program could not have functioned in the southern states. More important, the program almost certainly would not have been created by Congress. Blacks realized this. Most blacks therefore accepted the segregation of the camps as a lesser evil than being without work.

Most African Americans and Hispanic Americans thought the

main point was that they were included in New Deal programs and that some effort to treat them fairly was being made by important officials. Because so many of the unemployed and poor were black or Hispanic, WPA and the federal relief programs were particularly important to them. President Roosevelt ordered state relief officials not to "discriminate . . . because of race or religion or politics" in distributing government aid. This order was not always obeyed, but Harry Hopkins and other key WPA officials tried hard to enforce it.

With the approval of Roosevelt, Harold L. Ickes, the secretary of the interior, appointed Clark Foreman to his staff. Ickes instructed Foreman to seek out qualified blacks and try to get them jobs in the Interior Department and other government bureaus. Foreman also served as a kind of watchdog, checking on cases of racial discrimination in various New Deal programs. Among other distinguished African Americans whose government service began in New Deal agencies were Robert Weaver, who became the first head of the Department of Housing and Urban Development in the 1960s, Ralph Bunche, who later became the first African American to win the Nobel Peace Prize, and William Hastie, later a federal judge. These appointees made up what became known as Roosevelt's **Black Cabinet.**

One of the most prominent members of the Black Cabinet was Mary McLeod Bethune. She was the 15th child of former slaves. Some of her brothers and sisters had been sold away from her parents before the Civil War. Mary McLeod was fiercely independent. After completing her education in South Carolina, she taught at several schools for blacks in the South. In 1898 she married Albertus Bethune, also a teacher. She then founded a school in Florida.

In 1936 Mary McLeod Bethune was put in charge of the Office of Minority Affairs in the National Youth Administration. As with male black officials, her role was broader than her title indicated. She always had access to President Roosevelt. During the New Deal period, she later recalled, she conferred with him privately about six or seven times a year.

In a way their relationship points up the strengths and weaknesses of Roosevelt's way of dealing with his black supporters. His intentions were good, but he was unwilling to take the political risk. Once Mary Bethune asked him to act quickly on some important matter. He refused. "Mrs. Bethune, if we must do that now, we'll hurt our progress," he said. "We must do this thing stride by stride."

Mary McLeod Bethune worked strongly for equal rights for African Americans and other groups. She served as president of the National Association of Colored Women. She was a vice president of the two most important organizations in the United States that worked for racial equality—the NAACP and the **Urban League.** Yet she was not offended by Roosevelt's attitude. Indeed, she admired him enormously. Her reaction tells us a great deal about racial attitudes and the problems faced by minorities at that time.

It is not surprising that Mary Mc-Leod Bethune is quietly dignified in her portrait by Betsy Groves Reyneau. What did Roosevelt think of Mary Bethune?

Effects of the New Deal   383

UPI/Bettmann Newsphotos

Eleanor Roosevelt, the first lady, had worked to improve the treatment of African Americans long before her husband became president. And no prominent white person in the United States worked harder than she during the New Deal in the struggle for racial equality.

She urged her husband to press for more legislation. Although FDR hesitated to do so because he feared losing southern support, the First Lady did score one significant, if symbolic, victory.

In early 1939 Marian Anderson, a famous African American singer, was planning a concert in Constitution Hall in Washington, D.C. But when the owners of the hall, the Daughters of the American Revolution (DAR), heard of the plans, they canceled the concert, saying that no blacks were allowed to sing there. Outraged, Eleanor Roosevelt resigned from the DAR and arranged for Anderson to sing in front of the Lincoln Memorial in Washington, D.C., instead.

Before an audience of 75,000, which included Supreme Court justices, cabinet members, and members of Congress, Anderson delivered a concert that brought the cheering audience to its feet. Many rushed to congratulate the singer immediately afterward. Walter White of the NAACP noted that one of the members of the audience was a small black girl with tears streaming down her face. White later remarked, "If Marian Anderson could do it, the girl's eyes seemed to say, then I can, too."

The End of the New Deal

Despite his great victory in the election of 1936, President Roosevelt feared that much of the important New Deal legislation would be declared unconstitutional by the Supreme Court. These laws had greatly increased the powers of the federal government. The more conservative justices of the Supreme Court believed, for instance, that Congress had no right under the Constitution to control the negotiations of workers and their employers. Nor could it force workers to contribute to an old-age pension fund without their consent.

Roosevelt was not a constitutional expert. He felt that the election had proved that the people were behind the New Deal. Necessary reforms should not be held up by technical legal questions. He therefore proposed that Congress enable him to increase the number of Supreme Court justices. He would fill these new seats with his appointees. That way he could be sure that a majority of the Court would uphold key New Deal laws. This **Supreme Court Reform Plan** of 1937 produced a bitter, long, drawn-out fight. Roosevelt had misjudged the attitude of Congress and the public. The plan seemed to most people to threaten the independence of the Court. Roosevelt tried hard, but Congress rejected the plan.

However, the justices who had opposed New Deal laws eventually died or resigned. Roosevelt then appointed justices favorable to his program to replace them. The Wagner Labor Relations Act,

This 1937 cartoon recalls the Biblical warning "It is easier for a camel to go through the eye of a needle than for a rich man to enter the Kingdom of God." What is the political inspiration for this cartoon?

Effects of the New Deal 385

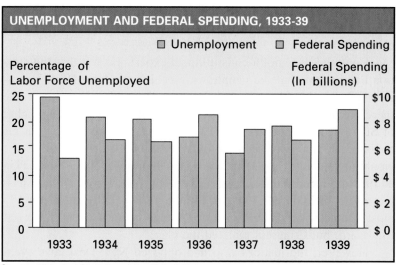

UNEMPLOYMENT AND FEDERAL SPENDING, 1933-39

Source: *Historical Statistics of the United States*

the Social Security Act, and all other New Deal laws attacked in the courts were eventually declared to be constitutional. Nevertheless, the Court fight was a serious setback for Roosevelt.

Another setback soon followed. Roosevelt had never understood modern economics. When the important English economist John Maynard Keynes [pronounced KANES] urged him to have the government spend more than it took in, called **deficit spending,** he ignored Keynes's advice. Roosevelt had never given up the hope of cutting government expenses and eventually reducing the national debt.

During 1936 and early 1937 the economy had been gradually improving. In June 1937 Roosevelt therefore decided to cut back sharply on federal money spent for relief.

The result was to bring the recovery to a sudden stop. Business activity fell off sharply. Unemployment increased. This recession in 1937 and 1938 was deeply discouraging. Just when prosperity appeared to be *really* around the corner, things turned again for the worse. Was the Great Depression going to last forever?

Roosevelt quickly agreed to increase government spending again. Congress provided money for a big new public works program to pick up the economy. At about this time Congress also passed a new Agricultural Adjustment Act. This established the **Commodity Credit Corporation.** It provided that when prices were low, producers of wheat, cotton, and certain other crops could store their crops in government warehouses instead of selling them. The Corporation would lend them money for their crops in storage.

When prices rose, the farmers could take their crops out of storage, sell them, and pay back the loans. This new system was called the ever-normal granary. (A granary is a storehouse for grain and other farm crops.) The new system raised prices by keeping surpluses off the market. Then, in years of bad harvests, there would be reserves to prevent shortages.

Another important law passed in 1938 officially outlawed child labor. This measure was the **Fair Labor Standards Act.** It also set the length of a normal work week at 40 hours and established a national minimum wage. Many New Dealers were uneasy with this law. It contained many loopholes "protecting" particular industries such as farming and family-operated businesses from having to meet "fair standards." Still, the principles the law established were important. Eventually most of the loopholes were closed.

The Fair Labor Standards Act was the last important New Deal law. In 1939 a new world war broke out in Europe. As during the Great World War (which now became known as World War I), European purchases caused the American economy to pick up.

Significance of the New Deal

All laws passed by Congress during the New Deal and all the new agencies and boards did not end the Great Depression. Why then is the New Deal considered so important? One reason is that it produced a revolution in relations between workers and their employers.

Under the National Recovery Administration and then under the National Labor Relations Board, industrial workers formed strong national unions. The old-fashioned AFL unions had been organized along craft lines. Carpenters were in one union, plumbers in another, machinists in a third, and so on. This system made organizing the workers of a large industry, such as steel or rubber or farm machinery, very difficult. The New Deal laws encouraged workers to form new **industrial unions.** Industrial unions represented all the workers in a particular industry, regardless of their specialty. These unions joined together in a **Congress of Industrial Organizations** (CIO), which soon rivaled the AFL in importance.

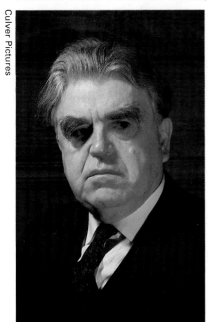

Culver Pictures

John L. Lewis

There were some bitter strikes during the New Deal. In 1937 workers staged "sit-down" strikes in which they took over plants and refused to leave until their demands were met. New Deal legislation protected workers' rights and established orderly methods of settling labor-management disputes. Labor became a force that manufacturers could neither ignore nor hold back.

In Jonathan Swift's famous satire Gulliver's Travels Captain Lemuel Gulliver is staked to the ground by tiny people called Lilliputians. The same fate has here befallen Uncle Sam. New Deal agencies form the bonds, so we may assume that the artist thought the 'alphabet soup' of the New Deal had become a burden.

Labor became a force in politics too. Unions made contributions to candidates for public office. Union leaders campaigned for candidates who supported policies favorable to organized labor. Union lobbyists put pressure on Congress to pass pro-labor legislation.

The New Deal also created what we think of as the **welfare state.** The popularity of New Deal relief programs and programs to create jobs was so great that it was impossible to depend only on state and local agencies after the depression was over. After the New Deal nearly all people agreed that the federal government ought to do whatever was necessary to advance and protect the general welfare. Later Republican administrations accepted this idea as enthusiastically as the Democrats, although Ronald Reagan, once a supporter and admirer of Roosevelt, was unrelenting in his efforts to dismantle much of the legacy of the New Deal.

Increasing the power of the federal government meant that state and local governments had less power. It also meant that the federal government had more control over individuals and over private organizations. Looking back, most Americans lost some freedom. Federal agencies became involved in more and more aspects of life. This seems to have been a necessary price to pay if such a complex society was to function smoothly. Still, the loss was large.

The New Deal years also saw a shift in the balance of power within the federal government. Congress came to have less power as the presidency grew stronger. Ever since it created the Interstate Commerce Commission in 1887, Congress had relied on special agencies and boards to carry out and enforce complicated laws. Since the presidents appointed the members of these organizations, the White House had gained more power and influence.

Under Franklin Roosevelt this trend became an avalanche. The crisis atmosphere of the times encouraged Congress to put more responsibility on the shoulders of Roosevelt and his appointees. Dozens of new agencies, each known by its initials, such as NRA, AAA, TVA, CCC, and NLRB, made up the confusing "alphabet soup" of the New Deal.

Roosevelt's great power and remarkable personal popularity made the presidency the strongest force in the government. At the time most liberals considered this both necessary and desirable. Conservatives such as Herbert Hoover were greatly alarmed by this trend. We shall see in a later chapter that both liberals and conservatives eventually changed their attitudes.

One more change that resulted from the New Deal was not fully clear until a number of years later. Economists and political leaders learned from their experiences during the Great Depression that the economy could be stimulated by unbalancing the federal budget.

The normal reaction of people during depressions had always been to cut down on their expenses. Most ordinary citizens believed that the government should also economize in hard times.

The long depression of the 1930s demonstrated that government economizing only made things worse. When as Keynes had recommended, the government took a greater role in the economy and engaged in deficit spending, it put money into the pockets of citizens. When people spent this money they encouraged producers to increase output. Indirectly they were causing employers to hire more workers. This was soon fairly obvious. However, most economists and political leaders hesitated early in the New Deal era to carry the technique far enough. Roosevelt's decision to reduce spending in 1937 illustrates this point very well. Greater government spending would probably have ended the depression sooner.

After their experience with unbalanced budgets during the Second World War, most governments got over their fear of the **federal deficit** which resulted from deficit spending. Everyone learned this lesson of the Great Depression. However, as we also shall see in a later chapter, attitudes on this subject would once again change with the passage of time. 🖳

Return to the Preview & Review on page 380.

LINKING HISTORY & GEOGRAPHY

DUST FROM THE GREENHOUSE

Half a century ago huge areas of the Great Plains blew away, leaving in the wake enormous human suffering and untold damage to the land. Many geographers and scientists wonder if we are heading in that direction again.

Breadbasket of America

1. Why had the Great Plains become a great farming region?

At the beginning of the 1900s the Great Plains was a region just starting to blossom. Rain fell in abundance, and farming techniques allowed farmers to turn the fields into the "breadbasket of America." No one foresaw a coming drought even though the region had had a history of drought and dust for centuries, even before the land was plowed. Indeed, many had come to believe that the more the land was plowed, the greater would be the rainfall.

Farmers poured into the region. The soil was broken, and just as forecasted, rain fell and wheat flourished. In the Texas panhandle some 82,000 acres had been planted in wheat in 1909. Twenty years later nearly 2 million acres were lush with ripening wheat.

This seeming miracle of agriculture was made possible by the tractor. Tractors enabled farmers to cultivate more and more of the grassland. As they moved westward, they came dangerously closer to the edges of the desert region. The plow that the tractor pulled pulverized the soil into powder. This to most farmers appeared ideal. They thought the layer of dust over the top of a hard-packed base would keep the moisture in the soil from evaporating. The tragedy of this, as we look back, is that it seemed to work. So by 1930 a layer of dust covered 5 million acres of wheat land stretching from Montana and the Dakotas in the north to Texas.

The Dust Bowl

2. What caused the Dust Bowl of the 1930s?

There have been many theories about the causes of the Dust Bowl of the 1930s. Certainly drought and wind were major physical factors. But they were aided by people and their greed.

Into the 1930s the rains continued to fall and the wheat thrived. In 1931 many plains farmers harvested as much as 50 bushels an acre. Then came the day of reckoning. Once-dependable rains suddenly stopped. Drought began to spread over the land. From 1933 to 1936, 20 states set records for dryness. (Those records still stand today.) Wheat withered. The carpeting of dust that covered the landscape was no longer held in place by moisture and a dense mantle of wheat. Dry winds lifted the dust from the fields in great clouds that swept across the sky.

This dust was so dense that people couldn't see. They had to string ropes from their barns to their houses to keep from getting lost in the swirling dust. It seemed like the whole landscape was on the move. Dust seemed to infiltrate everything. It covered dishes inside closed kitchen cabinets. It had to be scooped out of bathtubs before bathing. People slept with damp cloths over their faces to keep from choking.

Lessons of the Past

3. What can we learn from the tragedy of the Dust Bowl of the 1930s?

There are many lessons to be learned from that 1930s experience if we are to prevent its recurrence in the future. In the more than 50 years since those terrible days a great deal has been learned about managing land in areas subject to drought. Today's plows dig deeply into the soil, breaking it into large clods. This keeps the topsoil from blowing away. Marginal lands are not plowed. Many farmers do not plow at all but drill their seed into soil that is still covered by the stubble of last year's crop. Some plains farmers feel their techniques will prevent another dust bowl.

Many geographers disagree. The problem in the future, they admit, may not come from either the farmers or their agricultural practices. Rather, it is more likely to come from changes in the earth's atmosphere, changes that in the 1990s are well underway. The cause of these changes is the greenhouse effect.

The greenhouse effect is the name given to the process by which natural and humanmade gases trap solar heat in the earth's atmosphere. The process works like a greenhouse. In a greenhouse the sun's rays penetrate the glass but the glass keeps the heat from escaping. The sun's rays penetrate the earth's atmosphere like they do the glass of a greenhouse and strike the

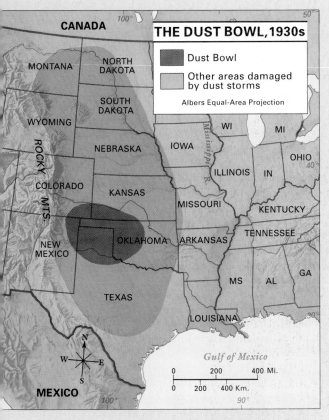

THE DUST BOWL, 1930s

- ■ Dust Bowl
- ▨ Other areas damaged by dust storms

Albers Equal-Area Projection

CANADA

MONTANA

NORTH DAKOTA

SOUTH DAKOTA

WYOMING

ROCKY MTS.

NEBRASKA

WI

MI

IOWA

OHIO

ILLINOIS

IN

COLORADO

KANSAS

MISSOURI

KENTUCKY

TENNESSEE

NEW MEXICO

OKLAHOMA

ARKANSAS

TEXAS

MS

AL

GA

LOUISIANA

Mississippi R.

Gulf of Mexico

MEXICO

N
W E
S

0   200   400 Mi.
0   200   400 Km.

earth. Some of the heat is absorbed, but most is radiated back into the atmosphere. Carbon dioxide, a gas in the atmosphere given off by burning fossil fuels such as coal, oil, natural gas, and wood traps some of this heat, keeping it close to the earth's surface.

The greenhouse effect is a natural occurrence. Were it not for it, life on earth would be a nightmare of subzero temperatures. But since the Industrial Revolution there has been greatly increased use of fossil fuels, spewing more and more carbon dioxide in the atmosphere. Consequently, this atmospheric blanket is now capturing far more of the earth's radiated heat than at any time in the past. The result has been a gradual warming of the earth.

Future Effects

4. What can be done to slow or stop the greenhouse effect?

Droughts in the late 1980s showed Americans what they could expect if the warming trend continues. Summers will be hotter and drier than they are today. Crops will wilt in the fields. Many areas will become unproductive. Can nothing be done? The answer is decidedly *yes,* if people are willing to pay the price.

The first and most useful step is to eliminate the production and use of chlorofluorocarbons (CFCs). CFCs are used primarily in air-conditioners and fast-food containers. In the atmosphere they trap 10,000 times as much heat as carbon dioxide. In 1990 President Bush called an international conference on CFCs. Most of the world nations agreed to totally stop the production of CFCs by the end of the 1990s. This should cut the greenhouse effect by 15 percent.

The biggest problem, however, will still be the amount of carbon dioxide pouring into the atmosphere as a byproduct of burning fossil fuels.

Unfortunately fossil fuels are comparatively cheap, and supplies are quite huge. It will be difficult and expensive to find alternatives to them. Certainly we could increase the use of solar power, hydroelectric power, and nuclear power. But these have drawbacks.

We also must stop burning the world's tropical forests to provide room for settlement and farming. Their destruction adds carbon dioxide to the atmosphere. In addition, trees naturally convert carbon dioxide into oxygen. Destroying the rain forests ruins this natural defense against the greenhouse effect.

Not all scientists and geographers agree on the extent of the greenhouse effect or the severity of its consequences. All do agree, however, that if we want to be sure to avoid the dust bowl conditions of the 1930s—which might be worldwide this time—people everywhere must awaken to the consequences of remaining ignorant of their environment.

APPLYING YOUR KNOWLEDGE

You will be organized into five groups. Each group will research and report on one of the following topics: the greenhouse effect, solar power, hydroelectric power, nuclear power, and the tropical forests. Reports should contain information on the most current research and prospects for the future. Your class will assemble the reports in a display for all the students in the school.

CHAPTER 9 REVIEW

1929
Hoover becomes president
★
Stock market crash
★
Great Depression begins

1932
Bonus March
on Washington
★
Roosevelt elected president

1933
New Deal begins
★
FDIC, NIRA, NRA, AAA, TVA, CCC

Chapter Summary

Read the statements below. Choose one, and write a paragraph explaining its importance.

1. A normal business cycle has periods of recession, depression, recovery, and prosperity.
2. The Great Depression lasted longer, was steeper, and had more severe consequences than other depressions.
3. Human suffering during the depression was great. People lost their jobs and their savings. Many were hungry. In general the poor suffered most.
4. Hoover attempted to stimulate the economy, but he believed that the federal government should not provide direct relief. This attitude and his handling of the Bonus Army ruined his public image.
5. Franklin D. Roosevelt defeated Hoover and was inaugurated in the midst of a banking panic.
6. Roosevelt's New Deal was aimed at relief, recovery, and reform.
7. Roosevelt's personality and the feeling of action made the New Deal popular with most Americans, including blacks and other disadvantaged groups.
8. Some critics complained that the president had not gone far enough to end the depression more quickly. Others claimed he had gone too far.
9. The New Deal produced a revolution in employer-employee relations, created a "welfare state," and changed thinking about deficit spending.

Reviewing Chronological Order

Number your paper 1-5. Then study the time line above and place the following events in the order in which they happened by writing the first next to 1, the second next to 2, and so on.

1. Social Security Act
2. Roosevelt elected president
3. National Industrial Recovery Act
4. New Deal begins
5. Stock market crash

Understanding Main Ideas

1. Describe how the business cycle works.
2. What were some of the actions taken by Congress during the Hundred Days?
3. Describe these New Deal agencies or laws: Civilian Conservation Corps (CCC), Agricultural Adjustment Act (AAA), Works Progress Administration (WPA).
4. How did the Second New Deal differ from the first?
5. Give examples to show how most blacks responded to the New Deal.
6. What was the "welfare state" created in the 1930s?

Thinking Critically

1. **Synthesizing.** Imagine that you are General Douglas MacArthur writing your memoirs. Compose a brief account of your view of the Bonus March and your part in the events that followed in the summer of 1932.
2. **Analyzing.** Of the FDIC, the NRA, the AAA, the TVA, the CCC, or the WPA, which program of the New Deal do you think raised American morale the most? Why?
3. **Relating.** The year is 1938. Write a letter to the president of the NAACP nominating Mary McLeod Bethune for Woman of the Year and explaining why you think she should be chosen for this honor.
4. **Evaluating.** In your opinion, what was the most important result of the New Deal? Explain your answer and support it with sound reasoning.
5. **Distinguishing Fact from Opinion.** Review the excerpt from a letter to the veteran's committee in Section 1. Name two facts and two opinions included in the letter.

Writing About History: Classificatory

Evaluate the advantages and disadvantages of the programs contained in the New Deal. Use the information in Chapter 9 to help you write your evaluations. You also may wish to interview people who lived during the New Deal to get their impressions of the programs.

1935
REA, WPA
★
NIRA ruled
unconstitutional
★
Wagner Act, Social Security Act
passed; CIO established

1936
AAA ruled
unconstitutional
★
Roosevelt reelected

1937
Supreme Court
Reform Plan defeated
★
Recession slows
recovery

1938
New AAA is passed
★
Fair Labor Standards Act

1939
Second World War begins in Europe
★
Depression ends

Practicing the Strategy

Review the strategy on page 374.
Composing an Essay. Study the Chapter Summary on page 392. Choose one of the statements as your topic, then compose a short essay.

Using Primary Sources

Langston Hughes was one of the most famous writers of the Harlem Renaissance. Hughes greatly admired the work of Carl Sandburg, especially Sandburg's ability to capture the voice of the people. Hughes' "I, Too" is a response to a song millions of school children have sung: "My Country, 'tis of thee/Sweet land of liberty/Of thee I sing." As you read the following poem think about how the poet captures the voice of black Americans of the time.

I, Too

I, too, sing America.
I am the darker brother.
They send me to eat in the
kitchen
When company comes,
But I laugh,
And eat well,
And grow strong.
Tomorrow,
I'll be at the table
When company comes,
Nobody'll dare
Say to me,
"Eat in the kitchen,"
Then.
Besides,
They'll see how beautiful I am
And be ashamed—
I, too, am America.

1. To whom does the word *they* in line three refer? What do you think "the kitchen" symbolizes?
2. How does the last line differ from the first line?

Why do you think the poet changed the wording? Do you think Eleanor and Franklin Roosevelt would have agreed with the poet?
3. What prediction does the poet make? Do you think Hughes' prediction has come true? Explain your answer.

Linking History & Geography

In many ways the forces of nature were as hard on the American landscape as the economy was on the American people. Several of the programs of the New Deal were aimed at improving land use and conserving nature. To understand the impact of the New Deal on the geography of America, review President Roosevelt's first inaugural address and information on the CCC and TVA, especially the TVA map on page 369. Then answer these questions.

1. How does Roosevelt's inaugural address indicate he was concerned about the environment?
2. What did the CCC do to help conserve the nation's resources and natural environment?
3. Some critics claimed the TVA ruined rather than improved the environment. Why might they say this? Do you agree or disagree? Explain.

Enriching Your Study of History

1. **Individual Project.** Use an almanac to find unemployment figures, average income, or other economic statistics for the years 1929-39. Plot the numbers on a graph large enough to be seen by the entire class. Use the graph to illustrate how the economy changed in the 1930s.
2. **Cooperative Project.** Present-day historians sometimes record *oral history*. These are tape recorded (and sometimes video recorded) interviews that are later set down on paper. Oral history gives us the actual words of a person who recalls a period of history firsthand. Your group will prepare an oral history titled "The Great Depression: Personal Views." Group members will interview people in your community who lived through the events of 1929-39. You will then combine your interviews into a report, an audiotape, or a videotape and present it to the local library.

Chapter 9 Review   **393**

UNIT THREE REVIEW

Unit Summary

Read the summary of main ideas in Unit Three below. Choose one statement, then write a paragraph predicting its outcome or future effect.

1. A variety of factors caused Europe to erupt in 1914 in the largest war in history.
2. The United States eventually declared war on the Central Powers in 1917.
3. The Treaty of Versailles reflected many of Wilson's 14 Points, including the League of Nations. But it was not the peace without victory he felt was so essential to future peace.
4. The United States rejected the Versailles Treaty and the League of Nations. American reaction to the war led to a series of actions aimed at limiting foreign influences in the United States.
5. Most Americans enjoyed the "Roaring Twenties." The automobile, jazz, sports, motion pictures, and the radio brought zest to life.
6. Despite the prevalent "get-rich-quick" attitude, problems of farmers and "sick industries" slowed the economy.
7. The Great Depression lasted longer and was steeper than other depressions, and human suffering was great, especially for the poor.
8. Roosevelt's New Deal was aimed at relief, recovery, and reform. It did not immediately end the depression, however.
9. The New Deal changed many things in American society, most importantly the role of government in business and everyday life.

Connecting Ideas

1. You know that radio became a powerful influence on American life in the 1920s. Do you think that television has less, the same, or more influence today than radio did then?
2. From what you have learned of the political ideas of Alexander Hamilton and Thomas Jefferson, how do you think each of them would have viewed President Roosevelt's use of power during the New Deal? In your answer cite some specific New Deal programs.
3. Choose any presidential election in this unit and either draw a political cartoon representing the point of view about an issue of the campaign or a candidate or create a campaign slogan for each party in that election.

Practicing Critical Thinking

1. **Analyzing.** As you have read, Oliver Wendell Holmes declared that if something said or written presents a "clear and present danger" to the war effort, the speaker or writer may be punished by law. Do you think this interpretation should also apply to peacetime crises such as the depression? Why or why not?
2. **Drawing Conclusions.** You know that during the 1920s American life was changed by the automobile. How do you think the widespread use of cars affected regional differences in the nation? Give specific examples.
3. **Synthesizing.** You are a reporter who can interview one of the following people: Herbert Hoover, Franklin Roosevelt, or Eleanor Roosevelt. Choose one, and make a list of five questions that you would ask during your interview.

Exploring History Together

1. Your group will study the time lines at the end of each of the chapters in Unit Eight. Then you will create two time lines, one illustrating the most important domestic events in the unit and the other showing the major international events. Some group members may illustrate the time line by adding sketches or pictures. Display your time lines in the classroom.
2. Your group will create a chart to display in the classroom, showing the "alphabet soup" of the New Deal. Group members will research each agency and briefly describe its function. Others may illustrate the chart with appropriate symbols for the various agencies.
3. Make a model of a battlefield on the Western Front, using clay or plaster of paris. Include trenches, barbed-wire mazes, and no man's land.

Reading in Depth

Allen, Frederick Lewis. *Only Yesterday*. New York: Harper & Row. Provides a highly readable account of life in the 1920s.

Hiebert, Roslyn and Ray Hiebert. *Franklin Delano Roosevelt, President for the People*. New York: Watts. Presents a closeup picture of the man who led America through the Great Depression.

Horan, James David. *The Desperate Years: A Pictorial History of the Thirties*. Portland, ME: Walch. Contains a dramatic visual portrayal of the decade through photographs and paintings.

Richards, Kenneth. *Babe Ruth*. New York: Children's Press. Traces the life and career of one of baseball's greatest stars.

The peaceful use of atomic power came with the race for space between the Soviet Union and the United States. Here Norman Rockwell, in "Apollo 11 Space Team", shows American astronauts with eager watchers, awaiting their expeditions into the unknown heavens.

A GLOBAL AMERICA UNIT 4

T he Great War finally ended and the weary soldiers returned home. But spectres of another war rose from the foul trenches and poisoned battlefields to move stealthily among the survivors, spreading the vision of a world that would be Heaven for the strong, Hell for the weak and different. In the years following the Great War powerful leaders in Italy and Germany took iron-fisted control. In Spain a violent civil war erupted. In the Soviet Union Stalin began his bloody purge of some 1 million citizens. Japan began to arm for war. Americans wondered if they would be drawn once again into war across the seas. This happened in 1941 when the Japanese bombed Pearl Harbor. That war concluded with the apocalyptic firestorms of the atomic bomb. Soon after, the Soviet Union and the United States began the standoff that came to be known as the Cold War.

World War II

On September 1, 1939, an enormous German army of 1.7 million men invaded Poland. Two days later Poland's allies—Great Britain and France—responded to this attack by declaring war on Germany. The Second World War had begun. This great world conflict immediately affected the United States. It ended the economic depression. It forced President Roosevelt to direct nearly all of his attention to foreign affairs. And it caused the American people to look once again at their alliances in Europe and the Pacific.

Culver Pictures

Il Duce, Benito Mussolini, and the Führer, Adolf Hitler, ruled their countries with iron fists. Mussolini, here saluting his troops, wanted Italy to again have greatness. Hitler played on the emotions of the German people in their defeat after the Great War to forge a war machine fueled by hatred and prejudice. By 1945 both these leaders were dead, one hanged in a public square in Milan after being shot, the other a suicide in Berlin. Why do you think neo-Nazi and other groups continue to express hatred for Jews and other ethnic and racial groups?

1. AMERICAN NEUTRALITY

Preview & Review

The Totalitarian States

The **Second World War** resulted from the efforts of three nations—Germany, Italy, and Japan—to conquer and control new territories. These nations developed what are called **totalitarian** governments. Their basic principle was that the state was everything, the individual citizen nothing. Totalitarian governments stamped out opposition. The only political party was controlled by the state. All power was in the hands of one leader, or **dictator.** The dictators allowed no criticism of their policies. They claimed absolute authority over the lives of their citizens.

Totalitarianism first developed in Italy in the 1920s. Benito Mussolini became the country's dictator. He called his political system **fascism.** The name came from the ancient Roman symbol of authority, the *fasces,* a bundle of rods tied tightly around an ax. The rods and ax represented the power of the state. Binding them closely together represented national unity. Mussolini, a swaggering, domineering leader, dreamed of controlling the entire Mediterranean region.

The Japanese system was somewhat different. The official head of the Japanese government was the emperor, Hirohito. He was considered to be a god, and he took no part in the day-to-day running of the government. In practice, however, the Japanese government was equally committed to the idea that the interests of the state were all-important.

The Japanese warlords who controlled the Japanese government in the late 1920s also dreamed of expansion and military glory. Seizing lands for raw materials for rapidly growing Japanese industries was the first step in a plan to control east Asia and the Pacific.

The Soviet Union witnessed the rise of a dictator during the 1920s too. Joseph Stalin replaced V.I. Lenin, founder of the Communist party in Russia and leader of the Communist Revolution in 1917. Stalin began a ruthless purge of all his opponents. He then openly showed his intention to spread communism throughout the world.

There were other dictators, including General Francisco Franco, who came to power in Spain in 1939 after a bloody civil war. Many Americans had watched the civil war closely, for it was the testing ground for the war machine of the European aggressors.

In Germany the National Socialists, or **Nazis,** led by Adolf Hitler, established a totalitarian government in 1933. In rousing speeches and rallies Hitler drew on the bitterness of the German people over the Versailles Treaty and the psychological effects of the postwar depression to captivate followers. Once in power he began ruthless expansion by conquest.

Hitler was a dictator who used terror and brute force to crush those Germans who opposed him. Democratic principles such as

Use these questions to guide your reading. Answer the questions after completing Section 1.
Understanding Issues, Events, & Ideas. Use the following words to describe the state-controlled governments of the 1930s: Second World War, totalitarian, dictator, fascism, Nazis, concentration camp, pacifist, conscientious objector, merchant of death, neutrality act, quarantine, collective security.
1. How did Hitler gain support for his rise to power?
2. Why did most Americans favor a policy of isolationism?
3. What events caused Congress to pass the neutrality acts?
4. Why did Roosevelt urge a quarantine of aggressor nations by peaceful nations?
Thinking Critically. 1. Imagine that you lived in a totalitarian nation such as Germany, Italy, or Japan during the 1920s-1930s. Write a letter to an American friend, describing what your life is like in that nation. **2.** If you had been a member of Hoover's cabinet when Japan invaded China, would you have recommended the policy of nonrecognition? Why or why not?

When Berlin hosted the 1936 Olympic Games, an African American, Jesse Owens, won four gold medals. Hitler, in a sulk, did not award the medals as is the custom for the leader of the host nation.

freedom of speech and the press were destroyed in Germany and wherever the Nazis were victorious in the war.

Hitler believed that the Germans belonged to a special breed of humans, a "master race" that was supposed to be superior to all others. When Jesse Owens, an African American athlete from the United States, began winning gold medals in the 1936 Olympics held in Berlin, Hitler stopped publicly congratulating the winners. The government persecuted political opponents, Gypsies, homosexuals, the mentally retarded, and anyone else that Hitler considered inferior. But Hitler reserved most of his hatred for Jews, whom he considered subhuman. Early in the Nazi dictatorship, Hitler decreed that Germany's Jews were no longer citizens. He then systematically deprived them of all their political and human rights. When thugs ransacked Jewish homes or businesses, the police stood idly by. Jews were not allowed to work for the government or in any profession. Jewish children could not attend public schools. All Jews had to wear a yellow star of David—a Jewish religious symbol—on their clothes so that everyone would know who they were.

As persecution continued, many Jews hastened to leave Germany. Even in leaving, however, discrimination against them continued. It was illegal for them to take property out of the country. Those who could not ship money out secretly often arrived in other countries penniless. The Nazis threw tens of thousands of those who remained in Germany into horrifying **concentration camps.**

Japanese Aggression

In 1931 a Japanese army marched into Manchuria, a province in northern China. This action gave Japan control of rich coal, oil, and iron ore deposits and blocked Soviet designs on the region. Although the attack challenged the Open Door policy, President Herbert Hoover refused to take either military or economic measures against Japan. He instead announced that the United States would not recognize Japan's right to any Chinese territory seized by force.

This policy of nonrecognition had no effect on Japan. In 1932 the Japanese navy attacked the Chinese port of Shanghai. On March 4, 1933, the same day that Franklin D. Roosevelt took his oath of office as president, the Japanese marched into Jehol, a province in northern China.

American Isolationism

Totalitarian ideas had little appeal to Americans. Totalitarian states silenced their political opponents and stormed over the borders of weaker nations during the 1930s. This shocked and angered nearly everyone in the United States. When a totalitarian nation attacked another country, the danger of war spreading was on everyone's mind. Americans nearly always sympathized with the victims of the

invaders. But they did not want to become involved in another foreign war. Most Americans once again favored a policy of isolationism. Charles Lindbergh voiced their sentiments:

     66 No one can make us fight abroad unless we ourselves are willing to do so. . . . Over one hundred million people in this nation are opposed to entering the war. If the principles of democracy mean anything at all, that is reason enough for us to stay out. If we are forced into a war against the wishes of an overwhelming majority of our people, we will have proved democracy such a failure at home that there will be little use fighting for it abroad.[1] 99

Also urging isolation were a large number of American **pacifists.** These people believed war for any cause was wrong. Throughout American history pacifists had objected to United States involvement in war. Many based their beliefs in religious teachings. Among the most notable pacifists were the Quakers. Most Quakers had refused to enter the armed forces during the Great War. War was against their religion, they said. These **conscientious objectors** had served in the medical corps in the war. The human suffering they witnessed further strengthened their belief that war was wrong.

[1]From a speech by Charles A. Lindbergh, Jr., in *The New York Times*, April 24, 1941

Never has the "civilized" world known such hatred as that of Hitler for the Jews of Eastern Europe. His deadly policy was genocide—the systematic elimination of 6 million Jews and their ancient culture. Here soldiers drive terrified women and children from the Warsaw ghetto. They will most likely be sent to a concentration camp. Hitler's soldiers also rounded up thousands of political enemies and members of other outcast groups to be hauled off to prisons.

American Neutrality   **399**

In Elsa Morante's powerful novel of World War II, a poor widow, Ida, witnesses the train that will take its Jewish occupants to the concentration and death camps.

> **Perhaps ten paces from the entrance she began to hear, at some distance, a horrible humming sound, but for the moment she couldn't understand precisely where it was coming from.**
>
> **The invisible voices were approaching and growing louder, . . . as if they came from an isolated and contaminated place. The sound suggested certain dins of kindergartens, hospitals, prisons; however all jumbled together. . . . At the end of the ramp on a straight, dead track, a train was standing which to Ida seemed of endless length. The voices came from inside it.**
>
> **There were perhaps twenty cattle cars. . . . The cars had no windows except a tiny grilled opening up high. At each of these grilles two hands could be seen clinging, or a pair of staring eyes.**
>
> From *La Storia (History)*, 1974

The movement for disarmament and antiwar feelings were quite strong throughout the 1930s. When the ten-year naval holiday negotiated after the Great World War expired in 1932, Dorothy Dexler and the Women's International League for Peace and Disarmament doggedly insisted that Americans negotiate another. Antiwar groups spread the word in every way possible, as the following excerpt from an antiwar song shows:

> " I'll sing you a song, and it's not very long
> It's about a young man who never did wrong
> Suddenly he died one day
> The reason why no one could say
>   . . . Only one clue as to why he died
>   —A bayonet sticking in his side.[1] "

In fact, fighting the Great World War to make the world safe for democracy now seemed a terrible mistake. The totalitarian governments that arose after the war were enemies of democracy. America's allies had failed to pay back the money that the United States had lent them in their hour of desperate need. Looking back, the only Americans who appeared to have profited from the war were the manufacturers of guns and other munitions. It became popular to refer to these manufacturers as **merchants of death.**

The Neutrality Acts

Japan's attacks in China worried Roosevelt. Still, he could not ignore the strong isolationist and antiwar sentiment in the United States. On the 18th anniversary of America's entrance into the Great World War, 50,000 veterans paraded through Washington in a march for peace. A few days later some 175,000 college students across the country staged a one-hour strike against war. The government should build "schools not battleships," they claimed.

In August 1935 Congress responded by passing the first of a series of **neutrality acts.** This law prohibited the sale of weapons to either side in any war. Later neutrality acts directed the president to warn American citizens that if they traveled on the ships of warring nations, they did so at their own risk.

The idea behind the neutrality laws was to keep the country from repeating what now seemed to be the mistakes of the 1914–17 period. At that time, it will be remembered, President Wilson had insisted on American neutral rights. American ships, citizens, and goods, he stated, had the right to travel without interference on the high seas. That policy had led to the deaths of Americans in submarine attacks and eventually to America entering the war.

[1] From an antiwar song by the Almanac Singers, cited in *America in the Twentieth Century* by James T. Patterson

Roosevelt's Strategy

Soon after the passage of the first neutrality act, Italian troops invaded the African nation of Ethiopia. Roosevelt immediately applied the neutrality law. Nearly all Americans sympathized with the Ethiopians, who had done nothing to provoke Italy. Yet because the Ethiopians had few modern weapons to use against the heavily armed Italians, the neutrality act hurt them far more than their enemy.

Therefore, when Japan launched an all-out attack against China in 1937, Roosevelt refused to apply the neutrality law. Using the technicality that Japan had not formally declared war, he allowed the Chinese to buy weapons from American manufacturers.

Roosevelt was looking for a way to check the totalitarian nations without getting involved in a shooting war. In a speech in October 1937 he warned that "mere isolation or neutrality" was no protection. Peaceful nations must work together to isolate, or **quarantine,** aggressor nations. He was talking about what was called **collective security.** Safety required that democratic countries cooperate in the effort to prevent the aggressors from seizing whatever they wanted. However, the speech alarmed many citizens, Congress took no action, and Roosevelt let the matter drop.

Roosevelt's annual message to Congress in January 1939 shows how difficult the situation was becoming. Americans knew the actions of the aggressors were wrong and that they must be prepared. But officially they must remain neutral. Roosevelt said:

     There comes a time in the affairs of men when they must prepare to defend not only their homes alone but the tenets of faith and humanity on which their churches, their governments, and their very civilizations are founded. The defense of religion, of democracy, and of good faith among nations is all the same fight. To save one we must now make up our minds to save all. . . .

     The world has grown so small and weapons of attack so swift that no nation can be safe in its will for peace so long as any other single powerful nation refuses to settle its grievances at the council table.

     For if any government bristling with implements of war insists on policies of force, weapons of defense give the only safety. . . .

     Obviously we must proceed along practical, peaceful lines. But the mere fact that we rightly decline to intervene with arms to prevent acts of aggression does not mean that we must act as if there is no aggression at all. Words may be futile, but war is not the only means of commanding a decent respect for the opinions of mankind. . . .[1]

[1]From "Message of the President of the United States," January 4, 1939, *Congressional Record,* Vol. 84, Part 1

Return to the Preview & Review on page 397.

Use these questions to guide your reading. Answer the questions after completing Section 2.
Understanding Issues, Events, & Ideas. Use the following words to explain American attempts to help battle totalitarianism while remaining neutral: cash-and-carry policy, Dunkirk, Battle of Britain, internationalist, Four Freedoms, Lend-Lease Act, wolf pack, Battle of the Atlantic, Atlantic Charter, convoy.
1. What was Poland's fate in 1939? What had Hitler done before the invasion of Poland?
2. What was Roosevelt's destroyers-for-bases trade?
3. What promise about the war did President Roosevelt make during his campaign for a third term?
4. What were Roosevelt's Four Freedoms?
5. What was the purpose of the Atlantic Charter?
Thinking Critically. 1. Imagine that it is the fall of 1940, and you are Edward R. Murrow. Write an outline for a radio news report to broadcast from London to the United States. **2.** Construct a time line of the events that led to America's undeclared war with Germany. Start your time line with the Battle of Britain.

2. THE EUROPEAN WAR

Western Europe Falls to Hitler

After 1933 Hitler systematically violated the Versailles Treaty. His troops occupied the Rhineland and he annexed Austria. A famous American journalist had this to say about the German aggressions:

❝ Why does Germany want Austria? For raw materials? It won the world war, and . . . Nazism started on the march across all of Europe east of the Rhine.

Write it down that the world revolution began in earnest—and perhaps the world war. . . .

Why does Germany want Austria? For raw materials? It has none of any importance. To add to German prosperity? Austria is a poor country with serious problems. But strategically it is the key to the whole of central Europe. Czechoslovakia is now surrounded. The wheat fields of Hungary and the oil fields of Rumania are now open. Not one of them will be able to withstand the pressure of German domination.

It is horror walking. Not that 'Germany' joins with Austria. We are not talking of 'Germany.' We see a new Crusade, under a pagan symbol, worshiping 'blood' and 'soil,' preaching the holiness of the sword and glorifying conquest. It hates the Slavs, whom it thinks to be its historic 'mission' to rule. It subjects all life to a militarized state. It persecutes men and women of Jewish blood. . . .

Today, all of Europe east of the Rhine is cut off completely from the western world. . . .[1] ❞

Then in the summer of 1939 Hitler and Stalin signed a non-aggression treaty, known as the Nazi-Soviet Pact. This treaty frightened many Americans who now began to believe that the United States should take a more active role in European affairs. Nevertheless, isolationism remained strong in America.

The Nazis and Soviets never made public the fact that the treaty included provisions for carving eastern Europe into German and Soviet spheres of influence. Hitler, who had pledged publicly that he

[1] From *Let the Record Speak* by Dorothy Thompson

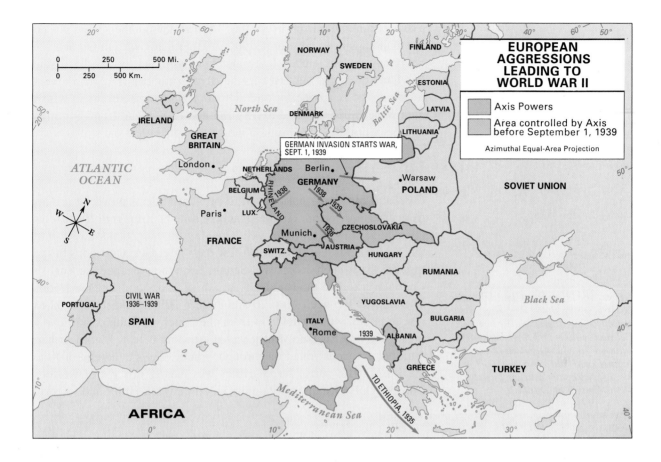

EUROPEAN
AGGRESSIONS
LEADING TO
WORLD WAR II

Axis Powers

Area controlled by Axis
before September 1, 1939

Azimuthal Equal-Area Projection

GERMAN INVASION STARTS WAR,
SEPT. 1, 1939

had no further territorial ambitions, then invaded Poland on September 1, 1939. In a little more than a month, Poland was swallowed up. The Second World War, also called World War II, had officially begun, although Japanese, Italian, and German armies had been on the move throughout the 1930s.

In September President Roosevelt called Congress into special session to revise the neutrality laws. After several weeks of debate Congress agreed to allow warring nations to purchase arms and other goods provided that they paid for them in cash and transported their purchases in foreign ships. This **cash-and-carry policy** favored the Allies. As in the Great World War, now called the First World War or World War I, the British and French navies controlled the Atlantic Ocean. German merchant ships could not reach American ports.

The Draft Lottery

In September 1940, as the United States moved closer to war, Congress voted to draft men between the ages of 21 and 35 for military service. This was the first peacetime draft in American history.

On October 16 more than 16 million men reported to their local draft boards to register for a possible call to military duty. Each was

LEARNING FROM MAPS. *German and Italian actions eventually brought on World War II. Italy hoped to claim an empire in Africa. What country did they attack there? Why do you think the first German aggressions were in the areas shown on the map? Which action was the immediate cause of World War II?*

assigned a number from 1 to 8,500. Then all the numbers were placed in small capsules and dropped into a large fishbowl. On October 29 Secretary of War Henry L. Stimson, blindfolded, reached into the bowl and drew out the first capsule. It was number 158. Then others took out the rest, one by one. This determined the order in which men were called up for duty. By the end of the war 10 million men had been drafted and 6 million men and women had enlisted.

Hitler's War Machine Rolls On

Cash and carry was not enough to prevent Hitler's powerful armies from crushing Poland. His war machine rolled on. In April 1940 Hitler invaded Denmark and Norway. On May 10 Nazi tanks swept into the Netherlands and Belgium. A few days later German troops broke through the French defenses at Sedan. Soon they reached the English Channel, trapping thousands of British, French, and Belgian troops at **Dunkirk.** Between May 26 and June 4 British ships managed to rescue about 340,000 soldiers from the beach at Dunkirk and carry them safely to England. But it was a crushing defeat. Swift German armored divisions rolled on through France. Before the end of June the French had surrendered. Hitler was master of most of western Europe. Only Britain and its navy stood between Hitler and victory.

Across the English Channel come boats of every shape and size in the spring of 1940. British, French, and Belgian soldiers had their backs to the channel as the Germans advanced. France was lost, but 340,000 men were saved by the courage and mettle of the British at Dunkirk.

Nearly everyone in the United States was horrified by the thought of such a victory. Hitler was both cruel and power mad. If he conquered Great Britain, would the United States be safe from his mighty armies? Without massive American aid, Great Britain seemed in danger of being invaded and overwhelmed. German U-boats and bombers had sunk many British destroyers needed to protect Atlantic shipping and prevent a German invasion of England. In July 1940 British Prime Minister Winston Churchill appealed to President Roosevelt for help. He needed 40 or 50 American destroyers. These vessels were not being used because the United States had replaced them with more modern ships.

Roosevelt wanted to help the British. He knew that it would take time to get Congress to act. Therefore he issued an executive order turning over 50 destroyers to the British in exchange for 99-year leases on several naval and air bases in the British West Indies. This destroyers-for-bases trade was acceptable to those people who would have objected to simply giving the ships to Great Britain.

The Election of 1940

Hitler expected to crush British resistance with massive air raids and then invade the shattered island. The Nazi bombings brought the war uncomfortably close to the United States. In the fall of 1940 an American news commentator, Edward R. Murrow, began a series of radio broadcasts from London.

    “ *September 13, 1940*
This is London at 3:30 in the morning. This has been what might be called a 'routine night'—air-raid alarm at about nine o'clock and intermittent bombing ever since. I had the impression that more high explosives and fewer incendiaries [fire bombs] have been used tonight. . . .

September 18, 1940
You can have little understanding of the life in London these days—the courage of the people, the flash and the roar of the guns rolling down the streets where much of the history of the English-speaking world has been made, the stench of air-raid shelters in the poor districts. These things must be experienced to be understood. . . .

September 22, 1940
I'm standing again tonight on a rooftop looking out over London, feeling rather large and lonesome. . . . At the moment there's an ominous silence hanging over London. But at the same time a silence that has a great deal of dignity. . . .[1]**”**

[1]From *In Search of Light* by Edward R. Murrow

Hitler is the Grim Reaper in this caricature, slaughtering all who oppose his ravishing of Europe.

Edward R. Murrow's broadcasts held Americans spellbound as they leaned closer to their radios to hear news of the war from London. He became America's most distinguished broadcaster and fighter for truth. Geographically, why were Americans so concerned with England's fate?

St. Paul's Cathedral, the masterpiece of famed architect Sir Christopher Wren, was so badly damaged by the nightly bombings and fires that it was not fully restored for twenty years.

The English, even school children, went about their business in spite of the deadly German bombings. In London children learned how to use gas masks and where the nearest shelters were. These youngsters wait in a trench for the German planes to once more fly home, after failing again to crush the English spirit.

John Topham/Black Star

The **Battle of Britain** formed the background of the presidential election of 1940. Republicans could not decide between Senator Robert A. Taft, the son of former president William Howard Taft, and Thomas E. Dewey of New York. After six ballots the convention turned to a dark horse, Wendell Willkie of Indiana. Willkie, a former Democrat, was the head of a large public utility corporation. He had led the opposition to the creation of the Tennessee Valley Authority in 1933. Willkie was a strong supporter of aid to Britain. His nomination was a victory for the Republican **internationalists** over the isolationist wing of the party, led by Senator Taft.

When the Democratic convention met in Chicago, not even Roosevelt's closest advisers knew if he would seek renomination. No president had ever run for a third term. However, Roosevelt felt he was needed because of the critical international situation. He won the nomination easily.

Roosevelt ran on his record. Willkie tried to play up the third-term issue and the failures of the New Deal to get the economy moving. Late in the campaign he also accused the president of planning to involve the United States in the war. "If you reelect him," Willkie told one audience, "you may expect war in April 1941."

Roosevelt responded quickly. "I have said this before, but I shall say it again and again and again: your boys are not going to be sent into any foreign wars." In the November election Roosevelt received 449 electoral votes, Willkie only 82.

The Lend-Lease Act

Roosevelt interpreted his reelection as an endorsement of his policy of aiding Great Britain. The British were now running desperately short of money to pay for American supplies. Therefore Roosevelt proposed lending them the weapons and goods they needed to continue the struggle against Hitler. In a fireside chat he told the people that the United States "must become the great arsenal of democracy." He asked them to support increased aid to Great Britain even at the risk of becoming involved in the war.

In January 1941 Roosevelt called for support for those who were fighting in defense of what he called the **Four Freedoms**—freedom of speech and religion, freedom from want and fear. A few days later he asked Congress to pass his program for aid to Britain, the **Lend-Lease Act.** This measure gave the president authority to sell or lend war supplies, or matériel, to any nation whose defense was essential to America's security.

The Lend-Lease bill aroused fierce opposition. "Lending war equipment is a good deal like lending chewing gum," said Senator Taft. "You don't want it back." But the public was behind the president. One poll showed that 70 percent of those questioned supported aid to Britain—even at the risk of war. Congress passed the Lend-Lease Act in March.

The Battle of the Atlantic

To stop the flow of supplies to Britain, swarms of German U-boats, called **wolf packs,** ranged the Atlantic. Hitler also shifted part of his air force to attack Atlantic shipping. The **Battle of the Atlantic** was a desperate struggle. During the first half of 1941, U-boats sank ships faster than the British could build them. Roosevelt authorized the United States naval yards to repair damaged British ships, and he transferred ten Coast Guard cutters to the British navy.

In April the United States set up bases in Greenland. American naval vessels began to patrol the Atlantic. These American ships did not try to sink German submarines. Their purpose was to track the submarines and radio their location to British planes and destroyers.

On June 22, 1941, Hitler broke his 1939 nonaggression agreement with Joseph Stalin and invaded the Soviet Union. Roosevelt quickly

To cover the war in Europe—and later in the Pacific—magazines like Life *sent artists as well as photographers. This painting shows what the camera at night might not show so well: the* Campbell, *training its searchlights on a U-boat being shelled. The U-boat was sunk, but the* Campbell *was so badly damaged it had to be towed 800 miles to safety.*

announced that lend-lease aid would be extended to the Soviet Union. In July he ordered 4,000 Marines to Iceland. This move pushed the area under American protection farther into the Atlantic.

The Atlantic Charter

In August 1941 President Roosevelt met with Prime Minister Churchill aboard the destroyer *Augusta* at Argentia Bay in Newfoundland. There the two leaders outlined their aims for the postwar world. This **Atlantic Charter,** as it became known, is an inspiring statement of eight democratic principles. In the conclusion the president and the prime minister called for gradual disarmament:

“ Eighth, they [the United States and Great Britain] believe that all of the nations of the world, for realistic as well as spiritual reasons, must come to the abandonment of the use of force. Since no future peace can be maintained if land, sea, or air armaments continue to be employed by nations which threaten, or may threaten, aggression outside of their frontiers, they believe, pending the establishment of a wider and permanent system of general security, that the disarmament of such nations is essential. They will likewise aid

and encourage all other practicable measures which will lighten for peace-loving peoples the crushing burden of armaments.[1] **"**

[1]From *The Atlantic Charter* by Franklin D. Roosevelt and Winston S. Churchill, August 14, 1941

Franklin Roosevelt and Winston Churchill, leaders of the free world, met at sea in 1941 to plan for the postwar world and to declare the Atlantic Charter. What did they mean when they wrote, "lighten for peace-loving peoples the crushing burden of armaments?"

The Undeclared War

In September 1941 a German submarine fired a torpedo at the United States destroyer *Greer* off Iceland. The destroyer had been trailing the U-boat and relaying its position to a British plane, which had dropped four depth charges. Although the *Greer* provoked the attack, Roosevelt called the attack "piracy legally and morally." He compared Hitler to a rattlesnake. He ordered naval vessels to escort, or **convoy,** merchant ships carrying lend-lease goods across the Atlantic. And he ordered naval vessels to "shoot on sight" any German submarines they encountered.

After a submarine sank the destroyer *Reuben James* on October 30, killing over 100 sailors, Congress authorized the arming of merchant ships. All restrictions on American commerce were removed. The United States was now engaged in an undeclared war with Germany.

Return to the Preview & Review on page 402.

Use these questions to guide you reading. Answer the questions after completing Section 3.
Understanding Issues, Events, & Ideas. Use the following words to describe the situation in America at the outbreak of World War II: Tripartite Pact, Rome-Berlin-Tokyo Axis, Pearl Harbor, National War Labor Board, withholding system, G.I. Bill of Rights, internment camp, Tuskegee Airmen, Fair Employment Practices Committee, bracero.
1. What economic steps did Roosevelt take to check Japan?
2. What was the extent of the damage done by the Japanese attack on Pearl Harbor? How did the United States react?
3. How did the war finally bring the Great Depression to an end?
4. What problems were there for black and Hispanic Americans in the military during the war? in labor? What advances were there?
Thinking Critically. 1. Write an eye witness account of the attack on Pearl Harbor. **2.** Imagine that you are a young Japanese American who will soon be placed in an internment camp. Explain why you think the government's reasons for this treatment are unfair.

3. THE PACIFIC WAR

Negotiations with Japan

Meanwhile Japan continued to increase its control in east Asia. In September 1940 Japanese troops had conquered part of French Indochina, now Southeast Asia. Later that month Japan, Germany, and Italy signed a mutual defense treaty, the **Tripartite Pact.** This treaty created what was called the **Rome-Berlin-Tokyo Axis.**

Roosevelt hoped to check Japanese aggression with economic weapons. In July 1940 he stopped the export of aviation gasoline and scrap iron to Japan. To prevent a total breakdown of communications with Japan, he did not cut off oil, which Japan needed most. Japan depended upon the United States for 80 percent of its oil.

In July 1941, after Hitler invaded Russia, Japanese troops moved into French Indochina (now Vietnam), obviously preparing to attack the Dutch East Indies, where there were important oil wells. Roosevelt then cut off all oil shipments to Japan.

The oil embargo stunned the Japanese. Japan had no oil supply for their rapidly growing industries. They would either have to come to terms with the United States or strike for an independent supply. Since the United States insisted that Japan withdraw from China and Indochina, Japan decided to attack the United States.

Attack on Pearl Harbor

The Japanese planned a surprise air attack to destroy the American fleet stationed at **Pearl Harbor** in Hawaii. They believed that by the time the United States could rebuild its Pacific forces, Japan would have further expanded its control of the Far East. Then it would be able to defeat any American counterattack. The attack date was set for Sunday, December 7.

American intelligence experts had broken Japan's diplomatic code. Decoded radio messages indicated that war was near. As early as November 22 one dispatch from Tokyo revealed that ''something was going to happen'' if the United States did not lift the oil embargo and stop demanding that Japanese troops leave China.

On November 27 all American commanders in the Pacific were warned to expect a ''surprise aggressive move'' by Japan. The Americans thought the attack was coming in southeast Asia, possibly in the Philippines. Hawaii seemed beyond the range of Japanese forces. The commanders at Pearl Harbor, Admiral Husband E. Kimmel and General Walter C. Short, took precautions only against sabotage by Japanese secret agents in Hawaii.

By the early morning hours of December 7 the Japanese naval task force was in position about 200 miles (320 kilometers) north of the Hawaiian Islands. The aircraft carriers' crews sent their planes

off with shouts of "Banzai! Banzai!"—the Japanese battle cry which means "10,000 years!" The first wave of 183 planes headed for Pearl Harbor.

The lead pilots reached their target about 7:30 on a peaceful and quiet Sunday morning in Honolulu. On the ships some sailors were still asleep. Others were getting breakfast or lounging on deck. Many were on their way to church services. Some were getting ready to go ashore for a swim at Waikiki Beach. Admiral Kimmel and General Short had a date to play a game of golf.

At 7:55 the Japanese struck. Screaming dive bombers swooped down for the kill. Explosions shattered the air. Fortunately, the American aircraft carriers were all at sea. But seven battleships were lined up on Battleship Row in the harbor. The bombers came so low over these ships that sailors could see the faces of Japanese pilots as they released their bombs.

The destruction was terrible. The worst blow came when the

Never was the United States so surprised as by the Sunday morning attack on Pearl Harbor by the Japanese. Now the U.S. had to enter the war. Apparently the attack was anticipated, but no one knew when it would come—and with what savagery. Read on and then report on the extent of the destruction. In spite of the heroic efforts of the sailors on the fireboat in the lower left, do you think this ship was saved?

The Pacific War 411

On December 9, the day after the president had asked for a declaration of war, he spoke to the nation in perhaps his saddest "Fireside Chat."

"We are now in this war. We are all in it—all the way. Every single man, woman, and child is a partner in the most tremendous undertaking of our American history. We must share together the bad news and the good news, the defeats and the victories—the changing fortunes of war."

Franklin D. Roosevelt

U.S.S. *Arizona* blew apart and sank, trapping more than a thousand men inside. The Japanese planes rained bombs on every ship in the harbor. They ranged up and down the coast, attacking airfields and barracks. In less than two hours 19 warships were sunk or disabled. Three others were damaged. One hundred and fifty planes were destroyed, most of them on the ground. Then the Japanese returned to their carriers. The task force sped back to Japanese waters. The attack on Pearl Harbor was by far the worst defeat the United States navy has suffered in all its history.

Americans were shocked and angered by the attack on Pearl Harbor. President Roosevelt went before Congress on December 8 to ask that war be declared on Japan. He called December 7, 1941, "a date which will live in infamy." He had the whole country behind him. Germany and Italy, in turn, carried out the terms of their Tripartite Pact and, on December 11, declared war on the United States.

The Home Front

The United States was much better prepared to fight World War II than it had been to fight the Great World War. Long before the attack on Pearl Harbor, Roosevelt had established councils to oversee the production and distribution of war matériel. After war was declared, similar boards were given broad powers to control the distribution of raw materials to manufacturers and to stop the production of many nonessential goods. The government rationed scarce foods, such as meat, butter, and sugar, to make sure that all citizens got their fair share.

The demand for weapons and supplies finally ended the Great Depression. American industry had slowly been climbing out of the depression, helped by European war needs. Now greatly expanded production was needed. Suddenly steel, aluminum, rubber, and other raw materials needed to make weapons were in extremely short supply. There was no serious shortage of gasoline, but gas was rationed in order to discourage unnecessary travel. Gasoline rationing also saved rubber by keeping drivers from wearing out their tires.

Many manufacturers shifted their plants from the production of consumer goods to weapons. A typical example was the producer of orange juice squeezers who made bullet molds during the war. The automobile companies, of course, turned out tanks and trucks, and airplanes too. The output of airplanes increased from less than 6,000 in 1939 to 96,000 in 1944.

Hundreds of thousands of new workers were needed to produce the tools of war. Unemployment ceased to be a national problem for the first time since 1929. Men and women flocked from farms, towns, and great cities to the East Coast shipyards, to the steel plants and former automobile factories of the Midwest, and to the aircraft plants of the West.

The famous photographer Margaret Bourke-White composed unique and striking images of the war. Note the angle she used to show these women helping to build tanks in 1943. The women enjoyed knowing they could handle this "man's work."

About 6 million women were employed during the war. Songs like "Rosie the Riveter" helped persuade women to take jobs traditionally held only by men. One woman remembered her job as a riveter and the pride and confidence it brought her:

    ❝ I loved working at Convair [an aircraft factory]. I loved the challenge of getting dirty and getting into the work. I did one special riveting job, hand riveting that could not be done by machine. I worked on that job for three months, ten hours a day, six days a week, and slapped three-eighths- or three-quarter-inch rivets by hand that no one else would do. I didn't have that kind of confidence as a kid growing up, because I didn't have that opportunity. Convair was the first time in my life that I had the chance to prove that I could do something, and I did.[1] ❞

[1]From *The Homefront: America During World War II* by Mark Jonathan Harris, et al.

The Pacific War   **413**

Amazing changes in the nature of warfare took place between 1918 and 1941. Tanks, which had served mostly as shields for advancing infantry, became swift and powerful offensive weapons. Airplanes, which had been used mainly as scouts and observation posts, now served more as bombers and as mobile machine gun nests. They could drop deadly loads of high explosives on distant factories, railroad yards, and troop concentrations. They also carried supplies to troops in the field and dropped specially trained soldiers called paratroopers behind enemy lines. These daring fighters would slip one after another from planes high over Hitler's Europe and scramble to reassemble on the ground below.

Air power revolutionized naval warfare. A new kind of warship, the aircraft carrier, served as a kind of seagoing airport. Squadrons of carrier-based planes could fly great distances and drop their bombs accurately on enemy ships and shore positions. They could then return to the carrier to refuel and take on another load of bombs. Many crucial naval battles were fought and won in World War II without any warship actually coming within sight of an enemy vessel.

Another new weapon was the rocket. Rockets differed from bullets and explosive shells in that they carried the fuel that drove them. In this respect they were like the torpedoes fired by submarines. Large rockets could be fired like artillery at far-distant targets. Smaller ones were fired from planes. There were even small rocket launchers called bazookas that two-man infantry teams used against tanks and armored vehicles.

Two British inventions were extremely important in helping to locate enemy planes, ships, and submarines. One was radar, which stands for "radio detection and ranging." Radar, perfected in 1941, bounces radio waves off objects. The reflected waves reveal the shape of the object and its distance from the source. The other tracking device, sonar, short for "sound navigation ranging," locates objects that are underwater, where radar is useless. Developed in 1945, sonar machines bounce sound waves off objects and record the echoes, thus indicating where the object is. Sonar devices can also pick up the vibrations caused by the propellers of submarines.

A trained technician "reads" the presence and position of planes and ships on this giant radar screen. Surveillance under water was by sonar. Both were British inventions that aided the war effort. Behind the transparent expanse of the giant circle we see other enlisted men noting the incoming flow of information. How have radar and sonar proved to be among the most durable new weapons of war—and peace?

U.S. Navy Photo

Movies pictured the wives and sweethearts of servicemen working at these jobs while their loved ones fought against the Germans and the Japanese. It was all so new and exciting for many. One woman, who was only 18 at the time, recalled her experience as a machinist in an airplane engine plant:

> **"** I was very unsophisticated at the time, but I was very zealous, probably overzealous. I remember some of the older guys who had been there for years used to say, 'Hey kid, don't be in such a hurry!'
>
> But I'd get into the thing and geared up for it and I'd just keep plugging away, measuring and grinding, measuring and grinding, and they'd say, 'Hey kid, take it easy.' . . .[1] **"**

The wartime labor shortage cemented the gains that organized labor had made under the New Deal. A **National War Labor Board** was established in 1942 to regulate wages and prevent labor disputes.

Farmers experienced boom times. The demand for food to feed American and Allied troops was enormous. Farm income more than doubled during the war. Farmers who had suffered during the 1920s and 1930s were soon able to pay off their mortgages, improve their property, and put aside savings too.

During the war Congress adopted the **withholding system** of payroll deductions for collecting income taxes. Employers withheld a percentage of their workers' pay and sent the money directly to the treasury. The withholding system made paying taxes a little less painful. It also supplied the government with a steady flow of funds and made evading taxes almost impossible.

High taxes on personal incomes (up to 94 percent) and on the profits of corporations helped persuade Americans that no one was benefiting too much from the war while soldiers were risking their lives overseas. To boost the morale of those in uniform, Congress passed the Serviceman's Readjustment Act of 1944. This **G.I. Bill of Rights** made low-cost loans available to veterans who wished to buy houses or start new businesses. It also provided money for expenses such as tuition and books for those who wished to resume their education after the war.

Suspicion of Japanese Americans

World War II had great popular support. Almost no one questioned the decision to fight the Axis powers. Assured of the solid backing of the people, the Roosevelt administration adopted a relaxed attitude toward freedom of speech in wartime. There was little persecution of German Americans as had occurred during the Great World War.

The major blot on the Roosevelt record of civil liberties was the

[1]From *Americans Remember the Home Front: An Oral History* by Roy Hoopes

Along with most Japanese Americans, these two generations of the Mochida family, tagged for evacuation from their home in Hayward, California, would be interned until the war ended—even though many were U.S. citizens. Read some of the accounts by these victims on this page and the next.

treatment of Japanese Americans. About 112,000 lived on the West Coast. They were forced to move to **internment camps** in barren sections of the country. The government was afraid that some were disloyal and would try to interfere with the war effort and help Japan. Others were placed in the camps for their own protection.

The white population of the American West had always been suspicious of the Chinese and Japanese who settled there. Partly this was the typical dislike of immigrants with different customs. Partly it was a matter of racial prejudice. The suspicion was greatly increased by the sneak Japanese attack on Pearl Harbor. Many people were convinced that unless everyone of Japanese origin was cleared out of the Pacific Coast region, the Japanese would soon be bombing San Francisco.

There was absolutely no evidence that the Japanese Americans were less loyal than other Americans. Most of them had been born in the United States. Immigration from Japan had been ended by the so-called Gentlemen's Agreement of 1907. Nevertheless, all were forced to sell their homes and property and leave for the camps. One woman, a college student in Seattle, Washington, at the time of her internment, described a relocation camp:

❝ Camp Minidoka was located in the south-central part of Idaho, north of the Snake River. It was a semidesert region. When we arrived I could see nothing but flat prairies, clumps of greasewood shrubs, and jack rabbits. . . .

Our home was one room in a large army-type barracks, measuring about 20 by 25 feet [6 by 7.5 meters]. The only furnishings were an iron pot-belly stove and cots.

Our first day in camp we were given a rousing welcome by a dust storm. We felt as if we were standing in a gigantic sand-mixing machine as the gale lifted the loose earth up into the sky, hiding everything. Sand filled our mouths and nostrils and stung our faces and hands like a thousand darting needles. . . .

Idaho summer sizzled on the average of 100 degrees [43 degrees Celsius]. For the first few weeks I lay on my cot from morning to night, not daring to do more than go to the mess hall three times a day. . . .

Winter in Minidoka was as intense an experience as summer had been. . . .[1]

Another victim of the internment remembered his confusion over what was happening to him and his family.

I remember the pain of being labeled a 'dirty Jap' and a 'dangerous enemy.' For me, a Los Angeles teenager of 17, it was a time when my entire value system was thrown out of kilter. If we, good Christians and loyal American citizens, could be stripped of our civil rights, it seemed that all of the values and ideals I held most dear would need to be reexamined. . . .[2]

After the war many Americans regretted their treatment of Japanese Americans. In 1948 Congress passed an act to help those interned to recover part of the losses. Court decisions in the 1980s further awarded retribution to the families sent to the camps.

African Americans and Hispanic Americans in Wartime

African Americans also had a difficult time during the war. About 1 million enlisted or were drafted. Black servicemen were expected to risk their lives for the country. Still they were kept in segregated units and frequently treated with disrespect by both officers and enlisted men. Yet by comparison with their treatment during earlier wars, there was some improvement. More black officers were commissioned. A number of blacks became pilots in the air force. For example, the **Tuskegee Airmen,** trained at segregated quarters in Tuskegee, Alabama, flew missions throughout Europe and North Africa.

As during the Great World War, the labor shortage benefited

[1]From *Nisei Daughter* by Monica Stone
[2]From "Point of View: A Sorry Part of Our History" by Daniel Kuzuhara, from *The Chicago Tribune,* August 26, 1981

Point of View

Roosevelt's biographer writes of the decision to intern Japanese Americans.

During January the climate of opinion in California turned harshly toward fear, suspicion, intolerance. Clamor arose for mass evacuation and other drastic action. The causes of the change have long been studied and defy easy explanation. Partly it was the endless Japanese advance in the Pacific, combined with a spate of false alarms . . . of attacks on the coast, stories of secret broadcasting equipment, flashing signals, strange lights and the like. . . . But the main ingredient that fired and fueled the demand for "cleaning out the Japanese" was starkly obvious. The old racism— economic, social, and pathological—toward the Japanese on the West Coast simmered a few weeks after Pearl Harbor and then burst into flames.

James MacGregor Burns, 1970

Gordon Coster/Life Picture Service

Asa Philip Randolph was a writer and editor of the Messenger. *He had planned a march on Washington when racial discrimination did not end in wartime service. Roosevelt persuaded him not to protest because it would disrupt the war effort. After reading further and using historical imagination, which man do you think had the stronger argument?*

UNITED WE WIN

Return to the Preview & Review on page 410.

black workers. Thousands got a chance to learn new skills and therefore earn higher wages. Yet racial discrimination did not end. For this reason, early in 1941 a black leader, A. Philip Randolph, decided to organize a march on Washington to protest the way blacks were being treated.

President Roosevelt feared that such a march would split public opinion at a time when national unity was essential. To persuade Randolph to cancel the march, he issued an executive order prohibiting racial discrimination in defense plants. This rule was enforced by a **Fair Employment Practices Committee.** Randolph then called off the march.

This did not mean that African Americans were satisfied with their treatment after 1941. Many whites resented the concessions Roosevelt had made. There was a good deal of racial trouble in the armed services and in industrial plants throughout the war years. In 1943 it erupted in riots involving attacks on blacks in New York City and Detroit. More and more African Americans were demanding their rights as members of a democratic society. It was clear that when the war ended, demands for fair treatment were sure to increase.

The situation for Hispanic Americans was similar. Almost 400,000 of them served in the armed forces during the war. A higher percentage saw combat duty overseas than any other ethnic minority. They also received more military medals—12 earned the Congressional Medal of Honor. Yet like black soldiers and sailors, Hispanic Americans suffered discrimination. On the other hand, for many it was the first chance to experience life outside their neighborhoods. When they returned home, Hispanic Americans were determined to fight for a better life.

The war brought many new opportunities for Hispanic Americans on the home front despite a vicious riot against them in Los Angeles in 1943. Hispanic American women gained jobs in many industries, especially in the West and Southwest. In July 1942 the United States and Mexico signed a treaty that allowed **braceros,** Mexican farm workers, to enter temporarily and work in the United States. Their efforts helped keep up vital food production during the war.

A Move Toward Religious Toleration

The war had an important effect on religion in America. American society moved toward religious pluralism, or the acceptance of different religions. People from all denominations found themselves supporting the war. The open hatred for Jews led by Adolf Hitler and his Nazi followers shocked Americans. People of various faiths sang *God Bless America* as they united in the struggle to win against their common enemy. By the end of the war the various religions had grown more tolerant of each other. 🖻

4. THE ALLIES REGAIN EUROPE

Preview & Review

Use these questions to guide your reading. Answer the questions after completing Section 4.

Understanding Issues, Events, & Ideas. Use the following terms to describe the Allied victory in Europe: Allies, Operation Torch, Battle of Kasserine Pass, Sicily, Operation Overlord, D-Day, Normandy, Battle of the Bulge, Bastogne, Berlin, V-E Day.

1. What was the Allies' overall war strategy?
2. In what ways was Operation Overlord a massive military operation?
3. Why did Roosevelt run for a fourth term?
4. What did the Germans hope to accomplish at the Battle of the Bulge? Why were they not successful?
5. Which allied nations marched on Berlin to end the war?

Thinking Critically. 1. Why do you think the author says that Churchill was mistaken when he called Italy "the soft underbelly of Europe"? Give reasons to support your answer. **2.** Imagine that you are a member of the American Third Army. Write a letter to your family, describing your impressions of General Patton.

The Invasion of North Africa

The nations that fought the Axis powers in World War II were known as the Allies. Chief among the Allies were the United States, Great Britain, France, the Soviet Union, China, Australia, and Canada. Joint planning among the Allies eventually led to an overall war strategy. Stated simply it was "Europe first, then the Far East." Allied military strategists hoped to hold the line against further Japanese advances in the Pacific. Their first major effort would be to defeat Germany. By early 1942 Hitler controlled nearly all of Europe and most of North Africa as well.

In June 1942 President Roosevelt put General Dwight D. Eisenhower in command of American troops in Europe. "Ike" was a first-rate military planner. He also got on well with all kinds of people. Managing and directing the huge and complicated Allied war machine required diplomacy as much as military talent.

Frank Scherschel/Life Picture Service

The commanders of the Allied troops in North Africa, Eisenhower of the U.S., and Montgomery of Britain—"Ike" and "Monty"—showed the stuff generals are made of by presenting a united front to their troops despite personal differences. Why is this particularly important in all team efforts?

The Allies Regain Europe   419

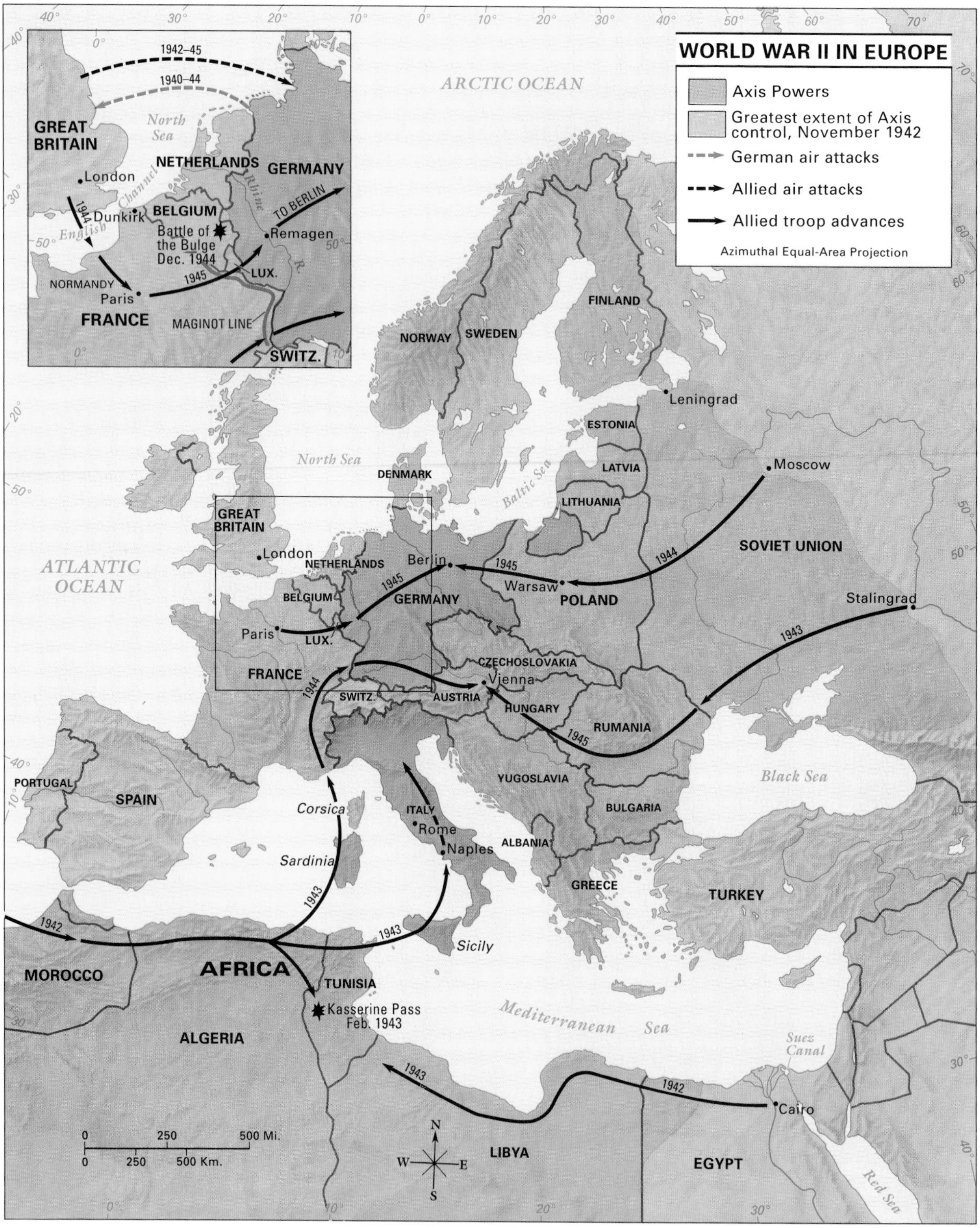
WORLD WAR II IN EUROPE
Axis Powers
Greatest extent of Axis control, November 1942
German air attacks
Allied air attacks
Allied troop advances
Azimuthal Equal-Area Projection
ARCTIC OCEAN
ATLANTIC OCEAN
North Sea
Baltic Sea
Black Sea
Mediterranean Sea
Red Sea
Suez Canal
GREAT BRITAIN
London
NETHERLANDS
BELGIUM
LUX.
GERMANY
Berlin
FRANCE
Paris
SWITZ.
DENMARK
NORWAY
SWEDEN
FINLAND
Leningrad
ESTONIA
LATVIA
LITHUANIA
Moscow
SOVIET UNION
Stalingrad
POLAND
Warsaw
CZECHOSLOVAKIA
AUSTRIA
Vienna
HUNGARY
RUMANIA
YUGOSLAVIA
BULGARIA
ALBANIA
GREECE
TURKEY
ITALY
Rome
Naples
Corsica
Sardinia
Sicily
PORTUGAL
SPAIN
MOROCCO
AFRICA
ALGERIA
TUNISIA
Kasserine Pass Feb. 1943
LIBYA
EGYPT
Cairo
1942
1943
1944
1945
0 250 500 Mi.
0 250 500 Km.
N
S
E
W
1942–45
1940–44
North Sea
English Channel
Rhine R.
NORMANDY
Dunkirk
Battle of the Bulge Dec. 1944
Remagen
TO BERLIN
MAGINOT LINE

LEARNING FROM MAPS. *Allied plans called for the defeat of Germany first. German defenses were strong, but the Allies eventually won. What countries were under Axis control by November 1942?*

Allied leaders did not feel an invasion of Europe was possible until more troops and supplies had gathered in England. So the first major campaign that Eisenhower directed was **Operation Torch,** an attack in North Africa, where the British had been battling the Axis powers for two years. On November 8, 1942, three forces—one American—landed in Morocco. About 110,000 troops, mostly American, were put ashore quickly and efficiently. There was little resistance, and Morocco and Algeria were soon in Allied control.

Then, in February 1943, the first real battle between the Americans and the Germans in North Africa took place at Kasserine Pass in Tunisia. The brilliant German general, Erwin Rommel, deployed his *Afrika Korps* tanks against American tanks in desert warfare. This **Battle of Kasserine Pass** ended in a standoff. But soon the Germans were driven out of the rest of North Africa.

The Italian Campaign

In July 1943 Eisenhower's forces invaded the Italian island of **Sicily,** the first step in an attack on what Prime Minister Churchill mistakenly called "the soft underbelly of Europe." In a little more than a month Sicily was conquered. The Italians then revolted against the dictator Mussolini and tried to surrender. Unfortunately, the German army in Italy simply took over control of the country. The Americans made a successful landing on the Italian mainland. But the conquest of Italy against fierce German resistance was a long and bloody process.

War correspondents kept Americans informed about the day-to-day events of the war, including the horrors of the battlefield. Ernie Pyle, one of the most outstanding war correspondents, spent months at the front with American troops, as did the famous photographer Margaret Bourke-White, the first woman war correspondent accredited by the U.S. army. American novelist John Steinbeck was also a war correspondent. He had this to say about the job:

"The Desert Fox," German General Erwin Rommel, effectively used his **Afrika Korps** *to stall the Allies for months and keep them from landing on the European mainland.*

66 What the correspondent really saw was dust and the nasty burst of shells, low bushes and slit trenches. He lay on his stomach, if he had any sense, and watched ants crawling among the little sticks of the sand dune. . . .

Then he saw an advance. Not straight lines of men marching into cannon fire, but little groups scuttling like crabs from bits of cover to other cover, while the deep chatter of machine guns sounded, . . .

He might have seen the splash of dirt and dust that is a shell burst, and a small Italian girl in the street with her stomach blown out, and he might have seen an American standing over a twitching body, crying. He probably saw many dead mules, lying on their sides, reduced to pulp. He saw the wreckage of houses, with torn beds hanging like shreds out of the spilled hole in a plaster wall. There were red carts and stalled vehicles of refugees who did not get away.

The stretcher-bearers come back from the lines, walking in off step, so that the burden will not be jounced too much, and the blood dripping from the canvas, brother and enemy in the stretchers, so long as they are hurt. And the walking wounded coming back with shattered arms and bandaged heads, the walking wounded struggling painfully to the rear.

He would have smelled the sharp cordite [gunpowder] in the air and the hot reek of blood if the going has been rough. The burning odor of dust will be in his nose and the stench of men and animals killed yesterday and the day before. . . .[1]"

D-Day

Now the long-awaited invasion of France, **Operation Overlord,** was about to begin. For months the United States and British air forces had been bombing industrial targets and railroad yards in Germany in preparation for the invasion. Now, on **D-Day**—June 6, 1944—4,000 landing craft and 600 warships carried 176,000 soldiers across the English Channel. They went ashore at several beaches along the coast of **Normandy,** a province in northern France. Naval guns and 11,000 planes bombarded the German defense positions. By nightfall 120,000 men were ashore. The reconquest of Europe had begun.

The Germans fought skillfully and bravely, but the Allies held the beaches. Reinforcements were brought over. In a single week 326,000 men, 50,000 tanks and trucks, and over 100,000 tons of supplies were ferried across the Channel. By the end of July more than 1 million Allied soldiers were safely landed and established on French soil.

The opening of this second front was truly the beginning of the end for the Germans. Until D-Day they had been able to concentrate their forces in eastern Europe, driving deep into the Soviet Union. Millions of Soviet soldiers and citizens died in the onslaught. Stalin became more and more frustrated as the Americans and British planned the assault. Each hesitation led to tremendous losses by Soviet forces and opened a rift among the Allies. But after D-Day the Germans had to fight on two fronts.

The Allies Enter Paris

In August, after fierce fighting, the American Third Army under General George S. Patton broke through the German defenses and raced toward Paris. Patton was a colorful and controversial general. He wore ivory-handled pistols more suitable to a cowboy than a

"God help me, but I love it," said General George S. Patton of war. What emotions he must have felt during Operation Overlord, shown in panorama on the facing page. In this huge military operation the Allies, on D-Day, June 6, 1944, invaded Normandy to begin their advance on Berlin.

[1]From *Once There Was a War* by John Steinbeck

lieutentant general. He insisted that all his soldiers, in or out of combat, wear a combat helmet and tie. He once slapped one battle-weary soldier because he thought he was a coward seeking to avoid combat. But Patton had a first-rate military mind. He was a master of tank warfare. Troops under General Patton's command moved quickly and decisively. They won victories.

Allied troops entered Paris amid great rejoicing in late August. By the end of September almost all of France was liberated. Everyone expected that the invasion of Germany would soon follow.

The Election of 1944

With victory in sight Roosevelt had to decide whether to run for a fourth term in 1944. He should not have done so because he was in very poor health. He had a bad heart, high blood pressure, and other physical ailments. Still, he was determined to bring the war to a victorious conclusion. The need for a new world organization to replace the League of Nations was also on his mind.

The president was renominated by the Democrats without opposition. Senator Harry Truman of Missouri was chosen as his running mate. The Republican candidate was Governor Thomas E. Dewey of New York. Dewey was not a particularly effective campaigner, but no one could have defeated the popular Roosevelt on the eve of victory in the war. The election was never in doubt. The popular vote was 25.6 million for Roosevelt, 22 million for Dewey. The electoral count was 432 to 99.

The Battle of the Bulge

In December 1944 the Allied armies were poised along the German border from Holland to Switzerland. On December 16, before the Allies could march, Hitler threw his last reserves—250,000 men—into a desperate counterattack. The Germans hoped to break through the Allied line and drive on to the Belgium port of Antwerp. That would split the Allied force in two.

The German attack was a total surprise. Within ten days the Germans had driven a wedge, or bulge, 50 miles (80 kilometers) deep into the Allied lines. This attack was called the **Battle of the Bulge.** American troops of the 101st Airborne Division were surrounded at the important road junction of **Bastogne.** The Germans demanded that the American commander, General Anthony C. McAuliffe, surrender his troops. "Nuts!" replied the general. Bastogne was held and the German advance stopped.

Elsewhere along the bulge every available American soldier, including platoons of black volunteers, were thrown against the German surge. For the first time white and black soldiers fought side by

Robert Capa/Magnum Photos

side, breaking the barriers of segregation that still existed in the armed services. By January the bulge had been flattened. The Allies were now ready to storm into Germany.

The Battle of the Bulge was Hitler's last attempt to break through Allied lines in Belgium. His troops succeeded in driving a wedge, or bulge, in the lines, but the Allies held.

Victory in Europe

The Battle of the Bulge shattered Hitler's hope of winning the war. The end came swiftly. In March 1945 Allied forces crossed the Rhine River into Germany. By the middle of April American, British, and French troops were within 50 miles (80 kilometers) of **Berlin,** the German capital. Russian armies were approaching the city from the east. On April 25 American and Russian troops met at the Elbe River. Five days later Adolf Hitler killed himself in his bombproof air raid shelter in Berlin. On May 8 Germany surrendered. This became known as **V-E Day**, for Victory in Europe.

American joy at the ending of the war was restrained, for President Roosevelt was dead. On April 12, while working on a speech at his winter home in Warm Springs, Georgia, he had died of a massive stroke. The burdens of the presidency were now upon the shoulders of Harry S Truman.

Return to the Preview & Review on page 419.

Use these questions to guide your reading. Answer the questions after completing Section 5.
Understanding Issues, Events, & Ideas. Describe the Allied victory in the Pacific, using the following words: Philippine Islands, Battle of the Coral Sea, Battle of Midway, island-hopping, Guadalcanal, Battle of Leyte Gulf, Iwo Jima, Okinawa, kamikaze, atomic bomb, Manhattan Project, Hiroshima, Nagasaki, V-J Day.

Explain Nazi attitudes toward Jews, using the following words: Final Solution, Holocaust, genocide.

1. What had General MacArthur pledged in 1942? When did he keep his pledge?
2. What was the American strategy in the Pacific? What was General MacArthur's role? What was Admiral Nimitz's role?
3. How did Japanese troops in the Pacific resist the American advance?
4. How did the Second World War bring home the horrors of war to people around the world?

Thinking Critically. Write a conversation between two people. One person should argue in support of the atomic bombing of Hiroshima and Nagasaki. The other person should argue against the bombing.

5. THE ALLIES WIN IN THE PACIFIC

The War in the Pacific

The war against Japan was slowly approaching its climax. The strategy, it will be recalled, was first to prevent further Japanese advances. After Pearl Harbor the Japanese had conquered the **Philippine Islands,** capturing large numbers of American troops. An army nurse described the last days before the Japanese took over:

❝ Conditions at Hospital Number 1 were not too good during the last few weeks we spent there. Patients were flooding in. We increased from 400 to 1,500 cases in two weeks time. Most of them had serious wounds, but nine out of ten patients had malaria or dysentery besides.

We were out of quinine [a drug to fight malaria]. There were hundreds of gas gangrene cases, and our supply of vaccine had run out months before. There were no more sulfa drugs. There weren't nearly enough cots, so triple-decker beds were built from bamboo, with a ladder at one end so we could climb up to take care of the patients. They had no blankets or mattresses.

There was almost no food except carabao [water buffalo]. We had all thought we couldn't eat carabao, but we did. Then came mule, which seemed worse, but we ate that too. . . .[1] ❞

General Douglas MacArthur, the commander in the Philippines, was evacuated by submarine on the order of President Roosevelt before his troops surrendered. "I shall return," he promised.

Japan, confident of victory, next prepared to invade New Guinea and Australia. But in the great naval **Battle of the Coral Sea** in May 1942 the Japanese fleet was badly damaged. The Japanese were forced to give up their planned invasion.

Then, in June 1942, a powerful Japanese fleet advanced toward American-owned Midway Island west of Hawaii. The plan was to force a showdown with the American Pacific fleet. But the Japanese ships never reached Midway. The Americans broke their secret codes and scout planes spotted their movements. On June 4 dive bombers from American aircraft carriers pounded the Japanese vessels. They sank four Japanese aircraft carriers and destroyed 275 Japanese planes. Again the Japanese fleet had to withdraw. This **Battle of Midway** gave the United States control of the central Pacific.

[1] From "An Army Nurse at Bataan and Corregidor," as told by Annalee Jacoby in *History in the Writing* by Gordon Carroll

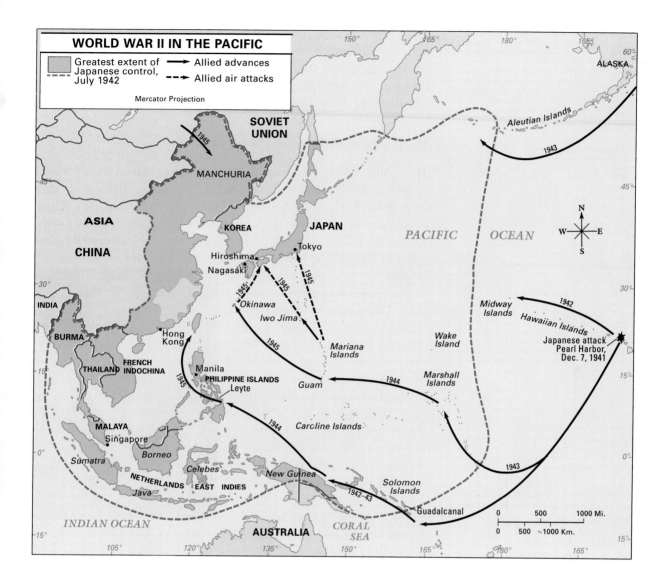

WORLD WAR II IN THE PACIFIC

Greatest extent of Japanese control, July 1942

Allied advances

Allied air attacks

Mercator Projection

ALASKA

SOVIET UNION

MANCHURIA

Aleutian Islands

1943

ASIA

CHINA

KOREA

JAPAN

Tokyo

Hiroshima

Nagasaki

PACIFIC OCEAN

INDIA

Okinawa

Iwo Jima

Midway Islands

Hawaiian Islands

1942

BURMA

Hong Kong

Wake Island

Japanese attack Pearl Harbor, Dec. 7, 1941

FRENCH INDOCHINA

THAILAND

Manila

PHILIPPINE ISLANDS

Leyte

Guam

Mariana Islands

Marshall Islands

MALAYA

Singapore

Caroline Islands

1944

Sumatra

Borneo

Celebes

NETHERLANDS EAST INDIES

Java

New Guinea

Solomon Islands

1943

INDIAN OCEAN

AUSTRALIA

CORAL SEA

Guadalcanal

1942–43

0   500   1000 Mi.

0   500   1000 Km.

The Pacific Campaign

As victory in Europe seemed assured, the Allies turned their full attention to Japan. To defeat Japan, the strategists believed, the Japanese islands must be invaded. But how to get there? The Japanese controlled thousands of small islands in the Pacific—the Bismarcks, the Carolines, the Gilberts, the Solomons, the Marshalls, and others. Capturing all these islands would be too costly, both in lives and in time.

General MacArthur, the commander of the army forces in the Pacific, was set on returning to the Philippines. He favored a sweep through the Bismarck Islands to the Philippine Sea. The Philippines could then be regained and the captive American soldiers set free.

Admiral Chester W. Nimitz, commander of the Pacific fleet,

LEARNING FROM MAPS. *After defeating the Germans, the Allies turned their attention to the Pacific, where the U.S. navy had held the Japanese in check. The Allies used a tactic called "island hopping." This called for driving the Japanese from some islands while bypassing others. Why does this seem like a good strategy in the Pacific?*

argued for advancing directly toward Japan itself. The military planners in Washington, the Joint Chiefs of Staff, decided on a two-pronged campaign. MacArthur was to clean out the Bismarcks and then head for the Philippines. Nimitz would attack the Japanese-held islands in the central Pacific and press on toward Japan.

From Guadalcanal to Leyte

The Allied strategy was called **island hopping.** Allied forces would seize key Japanese-held islands while bypassing others that were then isolated. First the Solomon Islands had to be captured. Early in August 1942 American troops landed on three islands of the group. Two of the islands were captured quickly. But on **Guadalcanal** Island some of the hardest fighting of the Pacific war took place. For six months the Americans struggled slowly ahead through dense jungles. The Japanese troops resisted stubbornly. They were ready to die to the last man for their country. Japanese sharpshooters tied themselves high in trees. Machine gun teams set up their weapons in caves from which retreat was impossible. Before Guadalcanal was finally reclaimed in February 1943, 20,000 Japanese were killed.

Culver Pictures

Fleet Admiral Chester W. Nimitz was made commander of the Pacific Fleet after Pearl Harbor.

As Nimitz's forces advanced, every island they attacked was defended with equal determination. The Japanese fought desperately for every inch of ground. When American marines went

LEARNING FROM TABLES. *Most people believed there would never be a war as destructive as the Great War. They were wrong. How do the statistics in this table compare with those from the Great War in the table on page 301?*

MILITARY CASUALTIES IN WORLD WAR II

ALLIES		AXIS	
Soviet Union	7,500,000	Germany	3,500,000
China	2,200,000	Japan	1,219,000
United States	405,399	Italy*	307,448
Great Britain	329,208	Others	912,000
France	210,671		
Others	300,000		
Total	10,945,278	Total	5,938,448
	Total	16,883,726	

*Italian losses: 294,297 as member of Axis;
  13,151 against Germany after Sept. 8, 1943

ashore on the island of Tarawa, they were opposed by 4,500 troops. Only 17 of these Japanese soldiers were taken prisoner. All the rest died in battle.

To the south MacArthur's army was carrying out its part of the plan. In October 1944 it recaptured the Philippines. In the **Battle of Leyte Gulf** the navy destroyed the last major Japanese fleet. Now the United States had complete control of Philippine waters.

Iwo Jima and Okinawa

The Allies next secured the bases needed for the invasion of Japan. The marines first fought hard to capture the tiny island of **Iwo Jima,** 750 miles (1,200 kilometers) south of Japan. The fight to capture Iwo Jima was bitter. On February 23 the victorious marines reached the top of Mount Suribachi, a volcano on the southern tip of the island.

Island-hopping forces moved determinedly across the Pacific as they closed in on Japan. Here American fighters signal the conquest of this small island by hanging an American flag on a shattered palm tree.

The Allies Win in the Pacific 429

Driven from the Philippines early in the war, in 1944 Douglas MacArthur returned as he had promised. Soon the U.S. had complete control of the Philippines and surrounding waters.

As they crawled toward the rim of the crater, they came under fire from Japanese soldiers dug in on the other side of the mountain. A fierce fight developed. To rally his men one marine picked up an iron pipe, bound a small American flag he was carrying to it, and held it for the men to see. Later another marine arrived with a larger flag and pole. The victorious marines proudly planted it at the top of the mountain. A photographer took a picture of this famous second flag raising over Iwo Jima. That picture has become the most reproduced image—in paintings and sculptures—of the Second World War.

Two weeks after taking Iwo Jima, American troops went ashore on **Okinawa,** a much larger island only 350 miles (560 kilometers) from Japan. Before the battle for Okinawa ended in June 1945, the Japanese had suffered over 100,000 casualties, the Americans over 11,000.

The United States now had complete control of both air and sea. From airfields throughout the Pacific, American planes bombed Japan mercilessly. American battleships and cruisers moved in closer to pound industrial targets with their heaviest guns. Soon every important Japanese city was a smoking ruin.

As American forces neared Japan, they were repeatedly pestered by **kamikaze** attacks. These suicide pilots, who crashed their planes

into the approaching American fleet, had pledged their lives to protect Japan. They took their name from a divine wind believed to have foiled an invasion of Japan centuries before.

All Americans take pride in this moment as the flag is raised on Mt. Suribachi on the island of Iwo Jima.

The Atomic Bomb

Victory was now certain. Although Japanese leaders had begun trying to arrange a surrender, progress was extremely slow. Military experts expected that Japan would have to be invaded, at tremendous cost. Japanese soldiers had demonstrated repeatedly that they would fight every battle to the last man. Some authorities believed that the United States would suffer 1 million more casualties before Japan was conquered.

This was the situation President Truman faced when he learned that American scientists had produced a new and terrible weapon—

STRATEGIES FOR SUCCESS

EVALUATING DECISIONS

Many key decisions made by world leaders have worldwide consequences, both at the time and for the future. Such decisions are debated endlessly by historians. By using historical imagination to understand the situation at the time and analyzing the consequences, it is possible to evaluate the decision. This evaluation will help you learn to make better decisions.

How to Evaluate Decisions

To evaluate decisions, follow these steps.

1. **Determine the nature of the decision to be made.** Use research and historical imagination to take into account the conditions that existed at the time the decision was made.
2. **Identify the alternatives available.** Note the possible choices the decision maker had.
3. **List the risks and benefits of each alternative.** Note the short-term and long-term effects of each choice.
4. **Weigh the costs and benefits of each alternative.** Compare the possible benefits and costs. Don't overlook possible future benefits or costs.
5. **Evaluate the decision.** Determine if, all things considered, the decision was a good one or a bad one. Remember that the long-range effects may not have been evident at the time the decision was made.

Applying the Strategy

Read the following paragraphs about Truman's decisions concerning the end of World War II.

Victory was now certain. Still, military experts expected that the cost of invading Japan would be enormous. Japanese soldiers had demonstrated repeatedly that they would fight every battle to the last man. Some authorities believed that the United States would suffer 1 million more casualties before Japan was conquered.

This was the situation President Truman faced when he learned that American scientists had produced a new and terrible weapon—the atomic bomb. . . . President Truman had to make an extremely difficult decision. Dropping an atomic bomb on a Japanese city would kill thousands of innocent civil-

ians. He also feared use of the terrible force would turn international sentiment against the United States. Yet Truman felt that he had no choice. Without the atomic bomb far more people would be killed before the war was over. He believed that the only way to convince the proud Japanese that further resistance was useless was to use this revolutionary bomb against them.

Let's evaluate Truman's decision making. What was the nature of the decision to be made? Truman had to decide how to end the war as quickly and with as few losses as possible. What were his alternatives? He could invade Japan. Or he could use the terrible new atomic bomb. What were the risks and benefits of each alternative? Invading Japan might cost 1 million more American casualties. But it followed the practices of conventional warfare. Using the atomic bomb might end the war much more quickly, sparing hundreds of thousands of lives on both sides. But unleashing the horrible destruction might turn international furor against the United States. How do the risks and benefits of each alternative compare? Truman chose to use the bomb to end the war quickly, thus avoiding a bloody invasion of Japan. The following paragraphs describe the situation further.

On August 6, 1945, in one blinding flash 75,000 people died. Another 100,000 were injured. Another atomic bomb was dropped on the city of Nagasaki. The radioactivity released by the explosions caused hundreds of persons to die horrible, lingering deaths. Later many children were born deformed because of radioactive damage suffered by their parents. Was there no way that the Japanese could have been shown the power of the bomb without using it on human beings?

On the other hand, the bomb may have saved lives—Japanese as well as American. Far more people would have died in an all-out invasion than died in the atomic blasts. There was also the hope that a demonstration of the horrors of atomic warfare would convince the entire world that such a weapon must never be used again. So far none has.

Do you think President Truman made the correct decision? Support your position.

For independent practice, see Practicing the Strategy on pages 438-39.

the **atomic bomb.** On orders from President Roosevelt, scientists had been working on the top-secret **Manhattan Project** since early 1942. Now they had produced a weapon with the explosive force of 20,000 tons of TNT. This tremendous power was released by the breaking of the chemical bonds that held together the atoms of uranium and plutonium, two highly radioactive elements.

President Truman had to make an extremely difficult decision. Dropping an atomic bomb on a Japanese city would kill thousands of innocent civilians. He also feared use of the terrible force would turn international sentiment against the United States. Yet Truman felt that he had no choice. Without the atomic bomb far more people might be killed before the war was over. He believed that the only way to convince the proud Japanese that further resistance was useless was to use this revolutionary bomb against them.

The mushroom cloud of nuclear destruction rose twice over wartime Japan. Such a sight recalls the address to the UN by Pope Paul VI: "Ne jamais plus la guerre": "Never again war."

INTERPRETING HISTORY:
Truman and the Atomic Bomb

Use of the atomic bomb in 1945 changed the course of modern history. President Harry S Truman approved the military use of the atomic bomb to end World War II. Yet the reasons for dropping the bomb on Japan have long been a subject of controversy among historians. They have sought to answer the following questions: Did Truman believe the bomb was necessary to end the war with Japan? Was Truman's decision influenced by his desire to limit the postwar power of the Soviet Union?

In *The Atomic Bomb and the End of World War II* (1966) Herbert Feis presented evidence that the Japanese were unwilling to surrender in 1945. Military advisers convinced Truman that nothing short of a huge land invasion of Japan would bring a surrender. But such an invasion would cost at least half a million American casualties and could not be accomplished before November.

Feis claimed that Truman's main concern was ending the war any way he could. Truman sought Soviet help in defeating Japan, meeting with Stalin at Potsdam, Germany, in July. He learned shortly after the conference began that tests on the atomic bomb had been successful and realized that the atomic bomb gave the United States the means to end the war quickly. However, because his chief aim was to end the war, Truman continued to shape a military alliance with the Soviets.

Feis dismissed the argument that Truman wanted to use the bomb as a postwar threat. He claimed that Truman knew the bomb might alter the postwar relationship between the United States and the Soviet Union. But many government advisers were already trying to devise ways to control further production of the bomb and to ban its future use as a weapon.

Gar Alperovitz interprets Truman's decision differently in *Atomic Diplomacy: Hiroshima and Potsdam* (1965). He argued that American leaders knew that Japanese officials were discussing surrender during the spring and summer of 1945. However, the Americans failed to take the information seriously. Truman wanted to end the war before the Soviets could enter it. Truman knew that if the Soviets helped defeat Japan they would expect to have a say in the postwar occupation and reconstruction of Japan. If Truman could obtain a quick surrender from Japan by using the atomic bomb *before* the Soviet Union entered the war in Asia, he could limit postwar Soviet influence in that part of the world. Alperovitz suggested that the atomic bomb gave Truman the chance to end the war quickly.

Alperovitz also claimed that the United States used the atomic bomb more as a symbol of American power than as a tool to end the war with Japan. For support of this theory he points to Truman's behavior at the Potsdam conference, where the president was unnecessarily rigid with a seemingly more moderate Stalin.

As you can read, historians continue to debate Truman's decision. Why he chose to use the atomic bomb—and what the world might have been like if he had not—remain provocative questions even today.

On August 6, 1945, an American bomber dropped the first atomic bomb on **Hiroshima,** a city of 344,000. In one blinding flash 75,000 people died. Another 100,000 were injured. John Hersey collected accounts such as the following from the survivors of the explosion.

“ Then a tremendous flash of light cut across the sky. Mr. Tanimoto has a distinct recollection that it traveled from east to west, from the city toward the hills. It seemed a sheet of sun. . . . Mr. Tanimoto took four or five steps and threw himself between two big rocks in the garden. He . . . did not see what happened. He felt a sudden pressure, and then splinters and pieces of board and fragments of tile fell on him. . . .

As Mrs. Nakamura stood watching her neighbor, everything flashed whiter than any white she had ever seen. . . . The reflex of a mother set her in motion toward her children. She had taken a single step . . . when something picked her up and she seemed to fly into the next room over the raised sleeping platform, pursued by parts of her house.

Timbers fell around her as she landed, and a shower of tile pommelled her; everything became dark, for she was buried. The debris did not cover her deeply. She rose and freed herself. She heard a child cry, ''Mother, help me!,'' and saw her youngest—Myeko, the five-year-old—buried up to her breast and unable to move. As Mrs. Nakamura started to frantically claw her way toward the baby, she could see or hear nothing of her other children.[1]**

[1]From *Hiroshima* by John Hersey

When the Japanese still hesitated to surrender, another atomic bomb was dropped on the city of **Nagasaki.** This convinced the Japanese. On September 2, **V-J Day** (Victory in Japan), the Japanese signed terms of surrender. World War II was finally over.

The terrible destruction caused by the atom bombing of Hiroshima and Nagasaki has resulted in a long controversy about President Truman's decision. Even today, people disagree on whether or not the president did the right thing. Aside from the immediate loss of so many lives, the radioactivity—emissions harmful to humans—released by the atomic explosions caused hundreds of people to die horrible, lingering deaths. Later many children were born deformed because of radioactive damage suffered by their parents. Was there no way that the Japanese could have been shown the power of the bomb without using it on human beings?

The bomb may have saved lives—Japanese as well as American. Most people thought that far more Americans would have died in an all-out invasion. There was also the hope that a demonstration of the horrors of atomic warfare would convince the entire world that such a weapon must never be used again. So far none has.

The final judgment on President Truman's decision lies in the future. It depends upon what all of us and all our descendants do with our knowledge of the atomic bomb and the dreadful consequences of atomic explosions.

The Horrors of War

The Second World War made Americans see how horrible war really is. Photographs of survivors of the Bataan Death March in the Philippines and of the barren landscapes of Hiroshima and Nagasaki

A joint study by Japanese and Americans a few months after World War II revealed the extent of the atomic bombing of Hiroshima.

"In the case of an atomic bombing . . . a community does not merely receive an impact; the community itself is destroyed. Within 2 kilometers of the atomic bomb's hypocenter all life and property were shattered, burned, and buried under ashes. The visible forms of the city where people once carried on their daily lives vanished without a trace. The destruction was sudden and thorough; there was virtually no chance to escape. . . . Citizens who had lost no family members in the holocaust were as rare as stars at sunrise. . . ."

From *The Making of the Atomic Bomb,* Richard Rhodes, 1986

made the point clearer than ever before. People around the world began to feel that the world could not survive another global war.

The most shocking aspect of the entire war was revealed when Allied forces liberated Nazi concentration camps such as Auschwitz, Treblinka, and Maidanek. To carry out what Hitler called the **Final Solution** and the rest of the world called the **Holocaust,** the Nazis had constructed death camps throughout occupied Europe for the express purpose of murdering millions of Jews and other ''nondesirables.'' These innocent people had been rounded up, crammed into cattle cars, and transported to the camps. Those who survived the journey were lined up and examined by Nazi officials. Those who were sick, over the age of 40, or too young to work were sent to the gas chambers and immediately murdered. The others were housed in barracks and forced to work long hours under brutal conditions. When they became too weak to work, they too made the final trip to the gas chambers.

In his book *Never to Forget,* Milton Meltzer quoted a German soldier who witnessed the gas chambers in operation:

    " They walked along the path, . . . and entered the death chambers. A sturdy SS man [member of an elite corps of Nazi soldiers] stood in the corner and told the wretched people in a clerical tone of voice: 'Nothing at all is going to happen to you! You must take a deep breath in the chambers. That expands the lungs. This inhalation is necessary because of illness and infection.' . . .

    This gave some of these poor people a glimmer of hope that lasted long enough for them to take the few steps into the chambers without resisting. The majority realized—the smell told them—what their fate was to be. So they climbed the steps and then they saw everything. . . . They hesitated, but they went into the gas chambers, pushed on by those behind them, or driven by the leather whips of the SS. . . . Many people were praying. . . .

    The SS forced as many in together as was physically possible. The doors closed. . . . After 28 minutes only a few were still alive. At last, after 32 minutes everyone was dead.

    Men of the work squad opened the wooden doors from the other side. . . . The dead were standing upright . . . pressed together in the chambers. . . . One could see the families even in death. They were still holding hands. . . . Two dozen dentists opened the mouths with hooks and looked for gold. . . . The . . . corpses were carried in wooden barrows just a few meters away to the pits.[1] **"**

[1] From *Never to Forget* by Martin Meltzer

Before the end of the war, about 6 million Jews—men, women, and children alike—were murdered on Hitler's orders. The Nazis also executed millions of Poles, Slavs, Gypsies, homosexuals, and political opponents in the camps.

The Holocaust is an example of **genocide,** the deliberate elimination of a people, their heritage and traditions. How could the world permit the Holocaust to happen without coming to the defense of the Jews? As early as 1938 world leaders met at a conference in Evian, France, to discuss what might be done to help the Jews. They could reach no decision. By this time authorities in the United States and other European nations knew of the horrors that were going on, but they did nothing to help. In fact, the United States made immigration laws even more restrictive, and the British government cut down on the number of Jews it allowed into Palestine because Great Britain did not want to offend the Arabs.

Historians have listed several reasons why these nations failed to help the Jews. First, in the 1930s the world was in the depths of the Great Depression. With high unemployment, many governments did not want more immigrants coming to their countries. At that time the United States would only accept immigrants who had enough money to support themselves until they found jobs. But most Jews could leave Germany only with the clothes on their backs. So because they had no money, these Jews did not qualify for immigration to America.

When news of the death camps reached the outside world, many people simply did not believe the stories. To them, such stories were simply too horrible to be true. Some people also remembered the exaggerated stories of German atrocities that circulated during World War I. After the war these stories had proved to be false. Finally, there was little that could be done during the war to rescue the prisoners in the camps. Most Allied leaders believed that the only way to help the Jews was to defeat the Germans.

Despite the inaction of Allied governments, the Holocaust did spark heroic acts in defense of the Jews. Many Jews resisted being taken to the camps. In Warsaw, for example, Jews rose up against the Nazis in 1944. Fighting German tanks and machine guns with revolvers and homemade bombs, these Jews held out for more than a month. Throughout occupied Europe, many people hid Jews from the Nazis, though to do so was to risk death. Today the Avenue of the Righteous near Tel Aviv, Israel, memorializes these non-Jews, many of whom the Nazis murdered. The government of Israel awards to these heroes medals inscribed with a verse from the *Talmud*, the holy book of Judaism:

66 He who saves one life is considered as having saved the whole world.99 🗐

Return to the Preview & Review on page 426.

CHAPTER 10 REVIEW

1922
Mussolini takes power in Italy

1931
Japan seizes Manchuria

1932
Roosevelt elected president

1933
Hitler becomes dictator
of Germany

Chapter Summary
Read the statements below. Choose one, and write a paragraph explaining its importance.
1. Despite the rise of totalitarian governments, most Americans believed in isolationism.
2. Hitler insisted Jews were an inferior people. He set up concentration camps for the Jews and murdered nearly 6 million of them. This genocide is called the Holocaust.
3. Roosevelt sought ways to check the aggressors without becoming involved in a shooting war.
4. Hitler's war machine invaded Poland, starting World War II.
5. Japanese bombing of Pearl Harbor brought the United States into World War II.
6. Allied efforts focused on Europe first. By early 1945 Allied armies had retaken Europe and Germany had surrendered.
7. In the Pacific the Allies then island-hopped toward Japan. Atomic bombs dropped on Japan in 1945 ended the war.
8. The horrors of World War II made many people realize that global war must now be avoided.

Reviewing Chronological Order
Number your paper 1-5. Then study the time line above and place the following events in the order in which they happened by writing the first next to 1, the second next to 2, and so on.
1. V-E Day
2. Lend-Lease Act
3. Germany invades Poland
4. V-J Day
5. Atomic bomb dropped on Hiroshima

Understanding Main Ideas
1. What was the reaction of most Americans to the aggressions of the 1930s? How were the neutrality acts part of this reaction?
2. Describe U.S. actions that showed the step-by-step movement away from the neutrality of the 1930s to open aid for the Allies by 1941.
3. By 1942 which were the major Axis and Allied countries?
4. How were minorities affected by World War II, including Japanese Americans?

5. Explain the importance of Operation Overlord and the battles of the Coral Sea and Midway.

Thinking Critically
1. **Synthesizing.** You are either a pacifist or a conscientious objector during World War II. Write a handbill explaining why you think war is wrong.
2. **Creating.** Create a poster, poem, song, or short story about the historic raising of the American flag on the island of Iwo Jima.
3. **Evaluating.** Choose either the topic of Japanese internment or the use of the atomic bomb. Discuss whether you think the correct decision was made by the United States. If you think the decision was incorrect, suggest an alternate course of action. Support your position.

Writing About History: Expressive
With your classmates, use historical imagination to write letters about the war. Some of you might write letters home to your families from the front. Tell of your experiences and describe one of the U.S. generals. Other classmates might write letters to you from home telling of their work in the U.S. for the war effort. Use the information in Chapter 10 to help you write your letters.

Practicing the Strategy
Review the strategy on page 432.
Evaluating Decisions. Study the sections titled "Negotiations with Japan" and "Attack on Pearl Harbor" on pages 410–12, then answer the following questions.
1. Why did Japan attack Pearl Harbor?
2. What response did the United States make to the attack on Pearl Harbor? Do you think that the Japanese expected the United States to respond in this way? Why or why not?
3. What alternate course of action, if any, could Japan have taken? What alternate course could the U.S. have taken? If you do not think that there were alternate courses, explain why.

| **1935**
First neutrality act

1936
Roosevelt reelected | **1939**
Germany
invades
Poland
★
Second
World War
begins | **1940**
Battle of
Britain
★
U.S.
institutes
draft
★
Roosevelt
elected to
third term | **1941**
Lend-Lease Act
★
Japanese attack
Pearl Harbor
★
U.S. declares
war on Japan

1942
Battles of Coral Sea,
Midway, and Guadalcanal
★
Operation Torch | **1943**
Italian campaign

1944
Operation Overlord
★
MacArthur returns
to Philippines
★
Roosevelt wins
fourth term | **1945**
Roosevelt dies, Truman takes over
★
Germany surrenders (V-E Day)
★
Hiroshima and Nagasaki
★
Japan surrenders; the war ends (V-J Day) |

4. Evaluate the decisions made by Japan and by the United States. Support your position.

Using Primary Sources

During World War II the American people were asked to show their loyalty to the United States. If families worked together to help the war effort, they earned a V-Home certificate, which they received from their local Defense Council and which they could place in their windows. As you read the following text of the V-Home certificate, think about how the war changed people's lives.

THIS IS A V-HOME!

We in this house are fighting. We know this war will be easy to lose and hard to win. We mean to win it. Therefore we solemnly pledge all our energies and all our resources to fight for freedom and against fascism. We serve notice to all that we are personally carrying the fight to the enemy, in these ways:

I. This home follows the instructions of its air-raid warden, in order to protect itself against attack by air.

II. This home conserves food, clothing, transportation, and health, in order to hasten an unceasing flow of war materials to our men at the front.

III. This home salvages essential materials, in order that they may be converted to immediate war uses.

IV. This home refuses to spread rumors designed to divide our nation.

V. This home buys War Savings Stamps and Bonds [stamps and bonds sold by the U.S. government to help finance the war] regularly. We are doing these things because we know we must to Win This War.

1. In what ways did the war change the everyday lives of ordinary people?

2. Do you think that the war emergency justified these changes?

3. Why do you think that it was necessary for people to conserve their health?

Linking History & Geography

The conflict that began in the 1930s erupted into the Second World War. Many nations were involved, and fighting raged throughout the world. To understand the global nature of the war and the tremendous distances involved, with your classmates prepare a world map showing the United States and the areas of North Africa, Europe, and the Pacific involved in the fighting. Then create two large maps to show the war in Europe and in the Pacific. Label the sites of the major battles and give short reports on each.

Enriching Your Study of History

1. Individual Project. On April 12, 1945, Franklin D. Roosevelt died suddenly in Warm Springs, Georgia. The new president, Harry S Truman, told reporters, "I felt like the moon, the stars, and all the planets had fallen on me." Use historical imagination to interview Truman on his first day in the White House. Discuss with him some of the major decisions he must make, such as his plans for ending the war.

2. Cooperative Project. Your group will create an oral history of one of the following: a person who fought in World War II or a person who worked on the home front. Each person in your group should prepare five questions that will lead the interview in a purposeful way. Get permission from the subject to tape the interview. Play your taped oral history for the class.

Chapter 10 Review 439

America in the Cold War

The Cold War began before World War II was over. The United States and the Soviet Union, marching toward Berlin to crush Hitler's capital, already distrusted each other. Like master chess players each side played up the other's weaknesses and for the next half century they held one another in wary check. Americans criticized the Soviets for building the Berlin Wall and for violations of human rights. The Soviets challenged America to resolve its racial inequalities and to redistribute its great wealth more fairly among the people. Sympathy for communist satellite countries such as Poland, Hungary, and Czechoslovakia was strong in America. Would this Cold War rivalry erupt into a global war?

Preview & Review

Use these questions to guide your reading. Answer the questions after completing Section 1.
Understanding Issues, Events, & Ideas. Describe world politics in the late 1940s, using the following words: San Francisco Conference, United Nations, Big Three, Yalta Conference, puppet government, communist, Cold War, capitalism.
1. What was the result of the San Francisco Conference?
2. How was the United Nations created?
3. Why did the Big Three meet at Yalta in 1945?
Thinking Critically. What do you think is the most important sentence in the preamble to the United Nations Charter? Give reasons to justify your decision.

1. THE UNITED NATIONS

The Search for World Peace

Any war as widespread and destructive as World War II was bound to cause difficulties and conflicts that would not disappear simply because the shooting had stopped. President Roosevelt had realized this. During the war he prepared to face postwar problems. In particular he hoped to avoid the mistakes that Woodrow Wilson had made after World War I. Wilson's policies had led to the rejection of the Versailles Treaty by the Senate.

In 1943 Congress had agreed to commit to American participation in an international peace-keeping organization. In July 1944 the United States, Great Britain, the Soviet Union, and China met to outline plans for such an organization. Then in 1945 delegates from 50 nations met in San Francisco to draft a charter for the organization to be called the United Nations.

Roosevelt succeeded in avoiding Wilson's mistake of not consulting the opposition party about the peace treaty. He made Senator Arthur Vandenberg of Michigan, who was the leading Republican on the Foreign Relations Committee, a delegate to the **San Francisco Conference** to draft the **United Nations** (UN) charter. As a result the

UPI/Bettmann Newsphotos

Flanked by the flags of 50 nations, Secretary of State Edward Stettinius signs the United Nations Charter on behalf of the United States. President Truman stands to his right. With your classmates name some of the actions taken and programs sponsored by the United Nations since its founding in 1945.

Senate approved the treaty that made the United States a member of the UN by a vote of 87 to 2.

The new international organization was created to replace the League of Nations. The United Nations did not have the power to make the United States or any other major power do anything it did not want to do. Under the UN charter the United States, Soviet Union, Great Britain, France, and China all had the right to block any UN Security Council action by their veto power.

The United Nations had wide appeal in America. Politicians, scholars, even religious figures such as evangelist Billy Graham, Rabbi Joshua Loth Liebman, and Monsignor Fulton J. Sheen, supported it. All conducted enormously popular television programs. They urged Americans to accept their place as leaders of the world community.

The United Nations Charter

The delegates in San Francisco represented three fourths of the people on the planet. Long weeks of discussion and debate were necessary for the delegates to agree on the wording of the charter. It was then ratified by the separate nations. On October 24, 1945, the world organization officially came into being.

Olive branches—traditional symbols of peace—surround a map of the world on the United Nations flag.

The preamble to the charter is a fine statement of the hopes of the postwar world:

“ We the peoples of the United Nations, determined to save succeeding generations from the scourge of war, which twice in our lifetime has brought untold sorrow to mankind, and

To reaffirm faith in fundamental human rights, in the dignity and worth of the human person, in the equal rights of men and women and of nations large and small, and

To establish conditions under which justice and respect for the obligations arising from treaties and other sources of international law can be maintained, and

To promote social progress and better standards of life in larger freedom,

And for these ends

To practice tolerance and live together in peace with one another as good neighbors, and

To unite our strength to maintain international peace and security, and

To ensure, by the acceptance of principles and the institution of methods, that armed force shall not be used, save in the common interest, and

To employ international machinery for the promotion of the economic and social advancement of all peoples,

Have resolved to combine our efforts to accomplish these aims.[1] ”

The Yalta Conference

President Roosevelt and Prime Minister Churchill worked closely together on military and diplomatic problems during the war. Both also consulted frequently with the Soviet dictator Joseph Stalin. The most important meeting of the **Big Three,** as they were called, took place at the Soviet seaside resort of Yalta in February 1945.

At the time of this **Yalta Conference** the war in Europe was almost over. The war had started back in 1939 when Germany had invaded Poland. The Allies had entered the war with the intention of restoring an independent Polish government. Yet by 1945 Poland had been entirely occupied by the Soviet troops who were driving the Germans out. Roosevelt and Churchill hoped to prevent the Soviet Union from keeping too much territory in Poland.

Stalin, however, was determined to prevent any government unfriendly to the Soviet Union from controlling Poland. The Germans had invaded his country from Poland in 1941. Many times in the past other enemies had crossed Poland to attack Russia.

[1]From the preamble to *The United Nations Charter*

From this meeting on Yalta on the Crimean Peninsula in the Soviet Union came the compromises of the Cold War. Left to right are Winston Churchill, soon to lose power in England; Franklin Roosevelt, gravely ill after 12 years as president of the United States; and the ruthless Soviet dictator Joseph Stalin. The Big Three worked out the plan that allowed most of Eastern Europe to remain under Soviet control. Why do you think the United States and Great Britain allowed the Soviets to dominate Eastern Europe?

The difficulty was that no freely elected Polish government was likely to be friendly to the Soviet Union. After all, the Soviet Union had joined Germany in dividing up Poland before the Great World War and again in 1939. Soviet troops had treated the Poles brutally. Thousands of Polish officers had been murdered in cold blood by the Soviets in the Katyn Forest Massacre of 1940.

After considerable discussion the Big Three worked out a compromise. The Soviet Union was to add a large part of eastern Poland to its territory. In the rest of Poland free elections were to be held. The Poles could choose whomever they wished to govern them.

The trouble was that Stalin did not keep his promise to permit free elections in the new Polish republic. Instead he set up a **puppet government,** one that he could control as completely as a puppeteer controls a puppet. This government was bitterly resented by the vast majority of the Polish people.

Probably nothing could have prevented the Soviet Union from dominating Poland. Soviet troops had already occupied the country. The Allies could have driven them out only by going to war. And war with the Soviet Union at that time was unthinkable. Rather, the Allies hoped to convince the Soviets to join them in defeating Japan, a nation the Soviets were not at war with.

The United Nations   443

During the siege of Leningrad by the Germans and what Napoleon once called "General Winter," a woman pulls scraps of firewood across the snowy square. The poster behind her says "Death to the Murderers of Children!" The poster reminds us of a pietà—Mary holding the crucified Christ. The most famous pietà, by Michelangelo, may be seen in the Vatican. You might be startled by the similarity to the Soviet poster if you can find a picture of the sculpture. Why would the Soviets choose such a subject to rally the people during the terrible siege?

Sovfoto

Most Americans admired and respected the Soviets in 1945, even though the Soviet Union was a **communist** society in which the government controlled the economy and was ruled by a dictator. The Soviets had defended their country bravely and had contributed their full share to the Allied destruction of the Nazi armies. Indeed, more than 7 million—perhaps as many as 20 million—Soviets died in the war, many of them civilians who starved during the two-year Siege of Leningrad by the Germans.

General Eisenhower referred at this time to the long record of "unbroken friendship" between the United States and the Soviet Union. He said, "The ordinary Russian seems to me to bear a marked similarity to what we call an 'average American.'"

However, the seeds of what was called the **Cold War** were planted in these broken promises and suspicions. It became a standoff between western **capitalism,** in which individuals control the economy, and communism, between democracy and totalitarianism.

Return to the Preview & Review on page 440.

2. TRUMAN IN THE COLD WAR

Preview & Review

Getting Back to "Normal"

President Roosevelt died a few weeks after returning from Yalta. Less than a month later Germany surrendered. The Soviets then declared war on Japan, keeping a promise Stalin had made to Roosevelt at Yalta. However, their contribution to the defeat of Japan was not needed because the United States ended the war by dropping the atomic bomb.

The new president, Harry S Truman, was more suspicious of Soviet motives than Roosevelt had been. He believed that the Soviets expected the United States to suffer a serious postwar economic depression. They were "planning to take advantage of our setback," he later wrote.

Truman was eager to frustrate Soviet plans by preventing a depression. But could he handle the complicated task of converting the economy from wartime to peacetime production?

Truman had grown up on a Missouri farm. He had been an artillery captain in World War I. During the 1920s he got involved in Missouri politics. He served as a local judge, and in 1934 he was elected to the United States Senate. He received the 1944 Democratic vice presidential nomination because party leaders needed a likable candidate without any enemies to replace Vice President Henry A. Wallace, whom they considered too radical.

Truman had a reputation for being honest and reasonably liberal, but he seemed a rather ordinary politician. Yet no one had ever accused him of being unwilling to accept responsibility. When he became president, he put a sign on his desk in the White House that said, "The Buck Stops Here." However, many people, including Truman himself, wondered whether he would be "big enough" to fill Franklin Roosevelt's shoes.

The depression that Truman feared never occurred. War contracts were canceled and thousands of war workers lost their jobs. However, millions of consumers had saved money during the war when there were few civilian goods to buy. The demand for all sorts of products from houses and automobiles to washing machines and nylon stockings was enormous. No automobiles had been manufactured for civilian use since 1941. Millions of people wanted to replace their worn-out cars. Returning soldiers and laid-off war workers quickly found new jobs.

Unfortunately, the huge demand for goods could not be satisfied quickly. Shortages developed. A period of confusion and bickering followed. After four years of going without and paying high taxes, people wanted to enjoy themselves. They believed that they had sacrificed enough for the common good and the national interest. Now they hoped to concentrate on their own interests. Workers

Use these questions to guide your reading. Answer the questions after completing Section 2. **Understanding Issues, Events, & Ideas.** Use the following words to discuss Truman's domestic programs: Fair Deal, wage and price controls, Twenty-second Amendment, Taft-Hartley Act, closed shop, "cooling-off period."

Explain Truman's foreign policy, using these words: Iron Curtain, Truman Doctrine, Marshall Plan, satellite nation, human rights, Federal Republic of Germany, Berlin Airlift, North Atlantic Treaty Organization, Warsaw Pact, containment policy.
1. Why didn't a postwar depression occur?
2. How did Truman respond to the Taft-Hartley Act?
3. What caused the communist parties in Europe to grow stronger?
4. What effect did the Marshall Plan have on the economy of Europe? On the politics?
5. What agreements were made by signers of the NATO treaty?
Thinking Critically. Define each word in the phrase "Iron Curtain." Then explain why you think Churchill used this phrase to describe the political division between Western and Eastern Europe.

UNEMPLOYMENT, 1945-60

Percent of Civilian Labor Force

Source: Board of Governors of the Federal Reserve System

LEARNING FROM GRAPHS. *Why did unemployment rise between 1945 and 1950?*

The CIO Political Action Committee sponsored this 1944 poster by Ben Shahn, an artist who portrayed important social issues.

for full employment after the war
REGISTER・VOTE
CIO POLITICAL ACTION COMMITTEE

For Full Employment After War Register Vote. Offset lithograph, 30 × 39⅞.
Collection, Museum of Modern Art, New York. Gift of CIO Political Action Committee.

PURCHASING POWER*, 1940-60

$2.20
$2.00
$1.80
$1.60
$1.40
$1.20
$1.00
$0.80
$0.60
$0.40
$0.20
0

1940   1950   1960

*Purchasing power is computed using the average prices of specific goods and services.

LEARNING FROM GRAPHS. *Statistics on purchasing power are often a good measure of the value of money and the overall effects of inflation on consumers. For statistical purposes, 1957 was chosen as the base year. In that year the value of $1.00 was $1.00. The purchasing power of all the other years are compared to that year. How much was $1.00 worth in 1960? You may wish to find what it would buy today.*

demanded higher wages but protested angrily against increases in consumer prices. Manufacturers wanted all controls lifted and their taxes reduced.

President Truman tried to resist these demands. He proposed a group of reforms he called the **Fair Deal** to balance national and personal interests. It called for larger social security benefits, a national health insurance plan, a higher minimum wage, money for public housing, and a continuation of the Fair Employment Practices Committee. At the same time the president resisted efforts to do away with **wage and price controls**—limits the government had set during the war.

Congress refused to pass most of the laws Truman requested. Few workers or employers supported any of Truman's proposals except those that benefited them directly. The president became more and more frustrated and less and less popular.

Finally, in late 1946 nearly all wartime economic controls were removed. Prices then rose sharply. Workers responded by demanding higher wages. When they got them, their increased spending caused prices to go up again. An upward spiral of wages and prices was set in motion, one that has continued almost without interruption to the present day.

Turning Out the Democrats

By the fall of 1946 even large numbers of Democrats had decided that Truman was incompetent. "To err is Truman," became a commonly heard wisecrack. "Had enough?" Republican candidates asked during the 1946 Congressional campaign, "Vote Republican."

A majority of the voters in 1946 did just that. The Republican party won control of both houses of Congress for the first time since the 1920s.

This new Congress set out to reverse the trend toward liberal legislation that had begun with the election of Franklin Roosevelt. First it passed the **Twenty-second Amendment** to the Constitution, limiting future presidents to two terms. This was a slap at Roosevelt's legacy. The Congress also reduced appropriations for many social welfare programs. It tried to lower the income taxes of people with large incomes, but Truman vetoed that bill.

The most controversial measure of the session was the **Taft-Hartley Act,** passed in June 1947 to curb powers of unions. It outlawed the **closed shop**—the clause in many labor contracts that required job applicants to join the union before they could be hired. It also allowed court injunctions that forced striking unions to call off their strikes for an 80-day **"cooling-off" period.** The president could only seek these injunctions when strikes threatened the national interest. Yet judges seldom refused to grant injunctions. Truman vetoed the bill, but Congress passed it over his veto.

Senator Robert Taft was known throughout Washington as "Mr. Republican." He was the son of the 27th president of the United States and sponsor of the Taft–Hartley Act.

The Truman Doctrine

Truman's domestic difficulties did not prevent him from developing a determined foreign policy. Because he was suspicious of Stalin's motives, he worried a great deal about the danger of Soviet expansion and the spread of communism.

In Europe the change from war to peace had not been easy. While the American economy had expanded during the war, in Europe the reverse was true. More than 30 million Europeans had been killed. The loss of so many potential workers was a terrible blow to the economies of every nation. More millions were homeless and hungry. Such people could not produce very effectively. In every country railroads had been wrecked, bridges blown up, factories smashed. About 25 percent of all the wealth of Great Britain was destroyed during the war. In Germany there were shortages of everything. A package of American cigarettes cost as much as a German laborer could earn in a month.

These conditions caused a rapid increase in the strength of communist parties in several Eastern European countries. Whether or not the Soviet government had anything to do with this trend, it was certainly willing to take advantage of it. Truman reasoned that once the communists got control of a government, as they had in Russia in 1917, they would do away with free elections. Then their opponents could get back into power only through revolt and bloodshed. Truman noted, for example, that when the Communist party in Hungary won only 17 percent of the vote in the 1945 elections, Stalin snuffed out opposition and installed communists in power.

Harry S Truman's oil portrait was painted by Martha Kempton. Behind the president is the Capitol. What did Truman's famous sign, "The Buck Stops Here," tell visitors to the Oval Office in the White House?

Johnny Florea/Life Picture Service

Robert Capa/Magnum Photos

Two images of postwar Germany: A woman with all her belongings sits not far from the badly bombed cathedral in Cologne. At right is the Brandenburg Gate in Berlin, later closed by the infamous wall built to separate East and West Germany.

It therefore seemed absolutely necessary to Truman that the spread of communism in Europe be checked. But how could this be done without starting another war? The question became urgent in early 1947. Greece seemed about to fall behind what Churchill described as the **Iron Curtain**—the striking image he used to show the political division between democratic and communist territories in western and eastern Europe. Communist guerrillas in Greece were seeking to overthrow the conservative Greek government. Great Britain had been providing aid to that government. In February 1947 the British informed President Truman that because of their own economic problems they could no longer afford to help Greece.

Truman believed that if Greece became communist, its neighbor, Turkey, might also fall under Soviet influence. He thought this would give the Soviets the confidence to move against Italy and perhaps France. He apparently believed this even though the Soviets were not supporting the Greek guerrillas. Truman was sure the communists would then seize American businesses in these countries, ruining American economic interests in Europe. The president therefore asked Congress for $400 million to aid Greece and Turkey. He said:

❝ It must be the policy of the United States to support free peoples who are resisting . . . outside pressures. . . . I believe that we must assist free peoples to work out their destinies in their own way. . . . Our help should be primarily through economic and financial aid. . . .[1] ❞

[1]From speech to Congress by Harry S Truman, March 12, 1947

448   **AMERICA IN THE COLD WAR**

STRATEGIES FOR SUCCESS

ANALYZING HISTORICAL INTERPRETATIONS

How and why did the Cold War begin? Historical interpretations of how and why it began are varied. A historical interpretation is an explanation by a historian about why an event happened as it did. One historian may emphasize a different cause or effect than another, or they may disagree completely. This difference occurs, in part, because historians bring different points of view to their interpretations. To effectively interpret historical accounts, you must analyze historical interpretations and evaluate their supporting evidence.

How to Analyze Historical Interpretations

Before learning the steps for analzying historical interpretations, review Comparing Points of View on page 315. Then to analyze historical interpretations, follow these steps.

1. **Identify the main points of the interpretation.** Determine the main points and conclusions.
2. **Determine the historian's point of view.** Identify circumstances that might have influenced the historian's interpretation. Note whether the historian was a participant or observer, or wrote a later interpretation.
3. **Assess the evidence and reasoning.** Study the information provided. Check the logic of the historian's reasoning.
4. **Compare the interpretation with other interpretations of the event.** Note similarities and differences among interpretations. If there are differences, ask yourself why such differences exist.
5. **Evaluate the interpretation.** Based on your analysis of the interpretation, assess its reliability. Accept or reject its main points.

Applying the Strategy

Read the following excerpts that offer different interpretations of how and why the Cold War began. Excerpt A is from an article written in 1947 by George Kennan, at the time Counsellor of the United States Embassy in Moscow. Excerpt B is from *The Holy Crusade: Some Myths of Origin* written in 1969 by Michael Parenti.

Excerpt A

Belief is maintained in the basic badness of capitalism, in the inevitability of its destruction, and in the obligation . . . to assist in that destruction [and in

an] antagonism between capitalism and socialism.

Basically, the antagonism remains. . . . And from it flow many of the phenomena which we find disturbing in . . . foreign policy: the secretiveness, . . . the wary suspiciousness and the basic unfriendliness.

This means that we are going to continue for a long time to find the Russians difficult to deal with.

Excerpt B

It was Harry Truman who succeeded to the Presidency before the war's end, and no reading of his opinions or actions would uphold the view that the United States was motivated by a sincere intention to extend friendly cooperation, only to be taken by surprise by Russian aggressiveness. If Truman brought anything to the White House, it was an urgency . . . "to get tough" with the Kremlin. "Unless Russia is faced with an iron fist and strong language, another war is in the making," he concluded, "The Russians would soon be put in their places" and the United States would then "take the lead in running the world in the way that the world ought to be run. . . ." What is overlooked is the probability that Truman's own belligerent, uncompromising, and ungracious approach was a major factor in actualizing [causing] the struggle and in preventing the kind of accommodation [agreement] between the United States and the Soviet Union that is just beginning to emerge today.

Note that these historians differ greatly in their interpretations. Kennan stated that the Cold War resulted from communist antagonism toward capitalism. This caused the Soviets to see Americans as the enemy. What in Kennan's background influenced his point of view? He was a high-ranking official of the United States embassy in the Soviet Union, writing in 1949 as the Cold War began. He was considered an authority on Soviet-U.S. relations.

How does Parenti's interpretation differ? He claims the Cold War started with Truman's "get-tough" policies. Parenti's point of view differs almost as much as his interpretation. He is a political analyst writing in 1969, more than 20 years after the event. What other information would help you analyze these interpretations to allow you to assess their reliability?

For independent practice, see Practicing the Strategy on pages 486–87.

This idea became known as the **Truman Doctrine.** Of course, Truman's reference to outside pressures, namely the Soviets, was either mistaken or a deliberate falsehood. But in the mood of the day Congress appropriated the money and the communist threat to Greece and Turkey was checked.

The Marshall Plan

The Truman Doctrine was popular in the United States because it appealed to both liberals and conservatives. Liberals liked the idea of helping the people of other countries defend their independence and rebuild their war-torn economies. Conservatives liked the idea of resisting communism and thus preserving the free enterprise system. Nearly everyone took pride in the great influence and prestige that came to the United States in other parts of the world.

Critics of the Truman Doctrine argued that it was a disguised form of imperialism. They saw it as a revived form of dollar diplomacy, similar to the old technique of encouraging American investments in nations like Nicaragua and Haiti before World War I. They also thought that the doctrine aimed too much at attacking communism and not enough at helping people in need.

To counter these objections, George C. Marshall, whom Truman had appointed secretary of state, proposed his **Marshall Plan** in a speech at Harvard University in June 1947. All the nations of Europe, including the Soviet Union, needed American help in rebuilding their war-damaged societies, Marshall said. But they also had to help themselves. The plan could not be imposed on the Europeans from the outside. The United States would provide money once the European nations had developed a European recovery plan.

Marshall's offer to include the Soviet Union was a bluff, or at least a gamble. If the Soviets had accepted it, Congress would probably not have provided the money to make the plan work. But Marshall did not think the Soviets would accept this plan, and he was right. They also forced the countries under its control to pull out of the meeting. The communists had no desire to contribute to the revival of the capitalist nations.

While the Soviet Union and the countries of eastern Europe under its control rejected the Marshall Plan, western Europeans adopted it eagerly. They soon created the Committee for European Economic Cooperation (CEEC) to decide what needed to be done and how much it would cost. Over the next few years the United States gave CEEC about $13 billion to carry out its plans.

The Marshall Plan was a brilliant success. By 1951 the economies of the participating nations were booming. Still, the plan had further divided Europe into two competing systems. When Czechoslovakia showed signs of accepting Marshall Plan aid, the local communist party seized power with Soviet support. Democracy was destroyed.

National Portrait Gallery

In 1953 General George C. Marshall was awarded the Nobel Peace Prize. How did this selection pay tribute to the Truman Doctrine as well as the Marshall Plan?

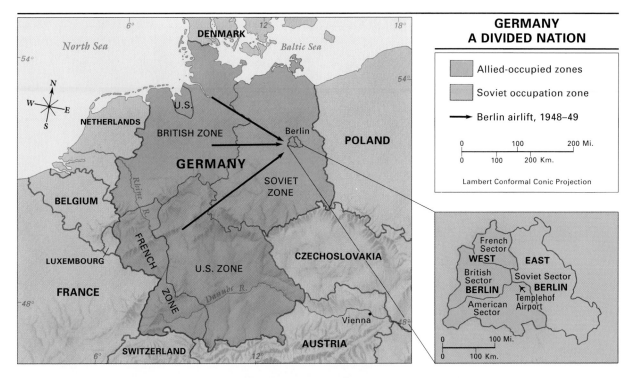

Allied-occupied zones

Soviet occupation zone

Berlin airlift, 1948–49

Lambert Conformal Conic Projection

French Sector
WEST   EAST
British Sector   Soviet Sector
BERLIN   BERLIN
American Sector   Templehof Airport

Czechoslovakia, like Poland, Hungary, and the other states of eastern Europe, fell into the Soviet orbit. The countries dominated by the Soviet Union became known as **satellite nations.** In all of these nations, the communist governments deprived the citizens of basic **human rights** such as freedom of speech, assembly, movement, and religion.

The Berlin Airlift

After the war the victors had divided Germany into four zones. One zone was controlled by the United States, one by Great Britain, one by France, and one by the Soviet Union. Berlin, the capital city, was located in the Soviet zone. Because of Berlin's large size and importance, however, it too was divided into four zones.

In 1948 the United States, Great Britain, and France announced plans to create an independent **Federal Republic of Germany** from the part of Germany they controlled. This step led the Soviets to close all the roads leading across their zone to Berlin. They could not block the formation of the West German republic. But they might force the Allies to give up their zones in the capital city.

The Soviet action caused a serious crisis. If the Americans tried to ship supplies to Berlin by truck or train, they would run into a Soviet roadblock. Then they would either have to turn back or start a fight. Truman therefore decided to *fly* supplies to Berlin.

Truman's **Berlin Airlift** turned the tables on the Soviets. There was no way to block the air lanes. Now the Soviets would have to

LEARNING FROM MAPS. *The victorious Allies—the United States, Great Britain, France, and the Soviet Union—divided defeated Germany for purposes of administration. Soon after the war, however, the iron curtain clanged down across the country, separating West Germany from Soviet-dominated East Germany. The situation was even graver within the divided city of Berlin. West Berliners, surrounded by East Berlin and its Soviet presence, felt seriously threatened.*

Truman in the Cold War   451

Through the clouds over Berlin a C-47 swoops down with its supplies to keep the 2 million residents of West Berlin alive. Why had the Soviets blocked all highways and railroads to Berlin?

decide whether to allow the supplies to reach West Berlin or start fighting.

The Soviets chose to do nothing. They probably believed that it would be impossible to keep the 2 million residents of West Berlin supplied with food and other necessities by air alone.

The Berlin Airlift was assigned to the United States air force. Bulky products usually shipped by river barge or freight car had to be flown in on military planes. At one point General Lucius D. Clay, who had charge of the airlift, telephoned an American air force general in Frankfurt, Germany, "Have you any planes that can carry coal?" he asked.

"We must have a bad phone connection," the air force general replied, "It sounds like you are asking if we have any planes for carrying coal."

"Yes, that's what I said—coal."

"The air force can deliver anything," the astonished general then responded. And he proved that it could indeed. Over the next 11 months American and British planes flew some 277,000 missions into Berlin. Their cargoes kept West Berliners fed and working.

In May 1949 the Soviets gave up trying to squeeze the western powers out of Berlin. They lifted the land blockade. The city, however, remained divided into Soviet and Allied zones.

Containment

The United States and its western European friends responded to the communist takeover of Czechoslovakia and the blockade of Berlin by strengthening their own alliance. In April 1949 the United States, Great Britain, France, Italy, and eight other nations signed a treaty creating the **North Atlantic Treaty Organization** (NATO). The signers agreed to defend one another in case of attack and to form a unified military force for this purpose. By the time the NATO force was organized, the Soviet Union had exploded its first atomic bomb. The American monopoly on nuclear weapons had been broken. Soon after the Soviet Union and its satellites signed the **Warsaw Pact,** pledging mutual defense as NATO members had.

Rivalry between the communist and capitalist worlds grew steadily more intense. Neither side dared risk open warfare in the atomic age. Instead they waged the Cold War. For American leaders the main objective of the Cold War was to prevent the expansion of Soviet influence in every way possible short of all-out war. In 1947 George F. Kennan, a professional diplomat who had served for many years at the American embassy in Moscow, explained how the Cold War could be won. America must build up its armed forces and be prepared to *contain* Soviet expansion wherever it was attempted.

This **containment policy,** according to Kennan, President Truman, and most other Americans, was purely defensive in purpose. The Soviets, on the other hand, felt that the containment policy,

COLD WAR IN EUROPE, 1950s

- NATO members*
- Communist nations
- Nonaligned nations
- Not controlled by the Soviet Union

*North Atlantic Treaty Organization; other members: U.S., Canada, Iceland.

0   300   600 Mi.
0   300   600 Km.

Azimuthal Equal-Area Projection

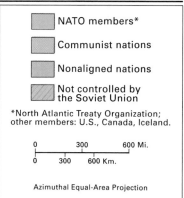

LEARNING FROM MAPS. *Soviet refusal to leave the Eastern European countries it had liberated from Germany in World War II helped trigger the Cold War. What countries in Eastern Europe became Soviet satellites? Which have moved away from Soviet domination in recent years?*

INTERPRETING HISTORY: The Cold War

Have you ever been involved in a disagreement that lasted for a long time and that ended in an argument over who started it in the first place? If so, you have a background to help you understand the historical controversy over the origin of the Cold War.

For more than 40 years after World War II the United States and the Soviet Union engaged in a Cold War, a war without direct military conflict but bitterly contested. It began after the Yalta Conference while the two were still allies and intensified after 1950 when conflicts broke out in Korea and Vietnam.

Historians agree that there was a Cold War, but they have disagreed about which nation started the war and why it did so.

In 1950 Thomas A. Bailey claimed in his book *America Faces Russia* that the Soviet Union bore complete responsibility for the onset of the Cold War. Aggressive Soviet military actions aimed at spreading communism in Eastern Europe brought the Soviet Union into direct conflict with the United States. According to Bailey, the United States had no choice but to oppose this threat and develop a policy of containment. Many historians of the 1950s agreed.

Historian William Appleman Williams presented a different interpretation in *American-Russian Relations* (1952). Williams argued that the United States thought that Soviet domination of Eastern Europe was a threat to American economic interests in the area. To Williams, Gabriel Kolko, and other "revisionist" historians, the Cold War was not a conflict between communism and democracy but a conflict over trade and investment. In other words, it was a result of expanding United States economic interests in those countries that the Soviet Union came to dominate after the war.

Other historians offered a third interpretation. As early as 1948 British physicist and historian P.M.S. Blackette stated in *Fear, War and the Bomb* that the United States' use of the atomic bomb on Japan was "not so much the last military act of the Second World War as the first major operation of the cold diplomatic war with Russia." Historian Gar Alperovitz agreed in *Atomic Diplomacy,* published in 1965. He insisted that the United States started the Cold War in order to demonstrate its power and keep the Soviets from having an influence in the occupation of Japan after the Japanese surrender. According to Alperovitz, President Truman used the atomic bomb against Japan not only to avoid the heavy loss of life that would have resulted during a conventional invasion, but also to overawe the Soviets and make their participation in the war with Japan unnecessary.

Still later historians have insisted that both the Soviet Union and the United States are to blame for the long conflict. John L. Gaddis in *The United States and the Origins of the Cold War* (1972) and Thomas G. Paterson in *Soviet-American Confrontation* (1973) and *On Every Front* (1979) argue that the Soviets were overly suspicious and that the Americans were too eager to influence the course of events everywhere and too confident of the correctness of their world view. "Neither side can bear sole responsibility for the Cold War," Gaddis has written.

Although world events have brought the Cold War to an end, historians have surely not finished writing about it. We know a great deal about what caused it and about the crises that marked its development. But there is still too much to be learned about the motives of the participants.

particularly the NATO force, would provoke war. Each side suspected the other of preparing all kinds of threatening schemes. In part the tensions of the Cold War were caused by poor communications between the communist and noncommunist diplomats. For this the secretive and overly suspicious Soviets were chiefly to blame.

The containment policy worked well. It enabled the western European nations to rebuild their economies and preserve their democratic political systems. It may even have helped prevent a major war. The chief difficulty with containment was that it tended to prolong the Cold War. A policy of negotiation and compromise might have ended it or at least avoided some of the tension and crises it produced.

Return to the Preview & Review on page 445.

3. TRUMAN SURVIVES HIS CRITICS

The Election of 1948

While the success of the Berlin Airlift was still in doubt, the 1948 presidential election campaign took place. The Democratic party was badly divided. Almost none of its leaders wanted to renominate Truman. Some supported Henry A. Wallace, who was running as the candidate of a new **Progressive party.** Wallace had been Truman's secretary of commerce. He believed that the Soviets' intentions were good—they wanted to help the countries of Eastern Europe as well as themselves—and that Truman's aggressive Cold War strategy was likely to lead to a real war. When Wallace criticized the Truman Doctrine, the president had forced him to resign. Wallace went on to attack the Marshall Plan and fight every aspect of Truman's containment policy.

Conservative southern Democrats opposed Truman because of his civil rights policy. In 1947 his **Civil Rights Committee** recommended laws protecting the right of African Americans to vote and banning segregation on railroads and buses. It also called for a federal law punishing lynching and the creation of a permanent Fair Employment Practices Committee.

Truman had urged Congress to adopt all these recommendations. He issued executive orders ending segregation in the armed forces and prohibiting job discrimination in all government agencies. After much discussion and a fruitless search for another candidate, the Democratic convention nominated Truman and made his proposals part of the party platform. Southern Democrats who were known as Dixiecrats then organized a **States' Rights party** and nominated Strom Thurmond, the governor of South Carolina, for president.

With three Democrats running, the Republican candidate, again Thomas E. Dewey, seemed sure of victory. Dewey's strategy was to avoid taking stands on controversial issues while the Democrats fought among themselves. But Truman conducted a hard-hitting campaign. In his exhausting whistle-stop tour by train he attacked the record of the "do-nothing" Republican-controlled Congress. The Republican party, he claimed, wanted to "turn the clock back" and do away with all the reforms of the New Deal era.

These tactics worked well. Organized labor supported Truman because of his veto of the Taft-Hartley Act. African Americans backed him because of his civil rights stand. Many farmers were persuaded by his argument that Congress had refused to provide adequate storage space for surplus farm products. Former New Dealers responded to his charge that the Republicans intended to repeal important New Deal laws.

Preview & Review

Use these questions to guide your reading. Answer the questions after completing Section 3. **Understanding Issues, Events, & Ideas.** Use the following words to describe the Cold War atmosphere at home and abroad in the early 1950s: Progressive party, Civil Rights Committee, States' Rights party, McCarthyism, North Korea, South Korea, Inchon, Yalu River, Korean War, McCarran Internal Security Act.

1. Who were the four candidates for president in 1948? For what reasons was Truman elected?
2. What events in 1949 and 1950 prompted a widespread fear of communism among the American people?
3. What kinds of accusations did Joseph McCarthy make? Why did many Americans believe him?
4. What provoked the Korean War? How did Truman respond?

Thinking Critically. Imagine that you witnessed a speech by Truman during his whistle-stop campaign. Explain why you would or would not vote for Truman in the election of 1948.

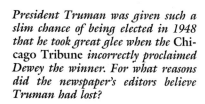

President Truman was given such a slim chance of being elected in 1948 that he took great glee when the Chicago Tribune *incorrectly proclaimed Dewey the winner. For what reasons did the newspaper's editors believe Truman had lost?*

Still, nearly all the experts continued to predict that Dewey would be elected. How could Truman win with two other candidates competing with him for Democratic votes? The editor of the *Chicago Tribune* was so sure that Dewey would win that he approved the headline "DEWEY DEFEATS TRUMAN" and went to press on election night before all the votes had been counted.

But the experts were wrong. Truman received over 2 million more votes than Dewey and won a solid majority in the electoral college. The States' Rights ticket won in only four southern states. Wallace's Progressive party was swamped everywhere. Truman had proved himself a clever politician. His energy, courage, and determination in fighting so hard when his cause seemed hopeless was part of the reason for his success. Another reason was that a majority of the voters wished to continue the policies of the New Deal.

The New Red Scare

Despite his remarkable victory, Truman was unable to get much of his Fair Deal program passed by Congress during his second term. More and more, the Cold War was occupying everyone's attention. A number of events in 1949 and 1950 produced widespread fear of communism similar to the Red Scare of 1919-20. One was the sensational trial of Alger Hiss, the president of the Carnegie Foundation for International Peace. Hiss had been a state department official before and during World War II. Whittaker Chambers, a former associate, charged that Hiss had been a member of the Communist party and had given him secret state department documents to pass on to the Soviets. When Hiss denied this, he was tried and found guilty of lying. He was sentenced to five years in prison.

Next came the arrest and conviction of several Americans accused of turning over secret information about the manufacture of atomic bombs to the Soviets. People panicked. Some believed that Soviet spies were hiding in every pumpkin patch and that the American government was a nest of traitors.

Then came what many called the loss of China to communism. In 1949 Chinese communists, called the Red Chinese, had defeated the armies of General Chiang Kai-shek. Chiang and his supporters were forced to flee to the island of Formosa (Taiwan). China, with its hundreds of millions of people, was now part of the communist world.

In the feverish atmosphere caused by the spy trials, many Americans believed that conspiracy lay behind the communists' victory in China. During the Chinese civil war state department experts had reported that the Chiang government was hopelessly corrupt and inefficient. Now these same experts were accused of being secret communists who helped cause the Chiang government's overthrow by cautioning against giving Chiang more money. The fact that their

Generalissimo Chiang Kai-shek sits astride his Mongolian pony. His followers (below) are in retreat from mainland China to the island of Formosa (Taiwan).

Truman Survives His Critics   457

When the playwright Lillian Hellman was asked to testify to the House Committee on Un-American Activities, she wrote these lines.

66 I am not willing, now or in the future, to bring bad trouble to people who, in my past association with them, were completely innocent of any talk or any action that was disloyal or subversive. I do not like subversion or disloyalty in any form and if I had ever seen any I would have considered it my duty to have reported it to the proper authorities. But to hurt innocent people I knew many years ago is, to me, inhuman and indecent and dishonorable. I cannot and will not cut my conscience to fit this year's fashions, even though I long ago came to the conclusion that I was not a political person and could have no comfortable place in any political group. . . . 99

From *Scoundrel Time*, Lillian Hellman, 1976

reports had been accurate did not protect them. If the United States had given more military and economic aid to Chiang, the critics claimed, he could have defeated the Red Chinese forces.

The Rise of McCarthyism

Early in 1950 a Republican senator, Joseph R. McCarthy of Wisconsin, charged that the state department was riddled with traitors. He claimed to know the names of 205 communists who held policy-making posts in the department.

This accusation naturally caused a sensation. McCarthy had been almost unknown outside Wisconsin. Suddenly he was making headlines in newspapers all over the country. He quickly took advantage of his new fame by making even more astonishing charges. For example, General Marshall had for a time been a special ambassador to China. Now McCarthy accused him of being part of the conspiracy to turn that country over to the communists.

McCarthy was a total fraud. His charges were false. One of the first Americans to see through McCarthy was Edward R. Murrow, the news commentator who described the Battle of Britain. Another early critic was one of McCarthy's fellow senators, Margaret Chase Smith, who in June 1950 questioned McCarthy's tactics:

66 I think it is high time that we remembered that we have sworn to uphold and defend the Constitution. I think it is high time that we remembered that the Constitution, as amended, speaks not only of freedom of speech but also of trial by jury instead of trial by accusation. . . .

Wide World Photos

The "Whispering Gallery" was what some called the almost continual conferences of Senator Joseph McCarthy and his lawyer Roy Cohn during the Army-McCarthy hearings. Why did so many people believe McCarthy at first?

The American people are sick and tired of being afraid to speak their mind lest they be politically smeared as Communists or Fascists by their opponents. . . .[1]"

Still, thousands of Americans assumed that no high public official would make such serious charges without evidence. Politicians often exaggerated. Sometimes they deliberately misled people. But flagrant lying was a different matter. If McCarthy announced that he had a list of 205 or 81 or even 57 communists, people thought surely there must be *some* truth in what he was saying.

In this atmosphere McCarthy did not have to prove his charges. He never showed anyone the 205 names or told anyone where he had obtained this information. The people whom he accused of being "soft on communism" found their careers in government ruined. This was **McCarthyism.** When he attacked other politicians who tried to expose his lies, he was believed, not they. For a time McCarthy became one of the most powerful men in the entire United States.

The Korean War

McCarthy's rise came at a time when war broke out in Korea, a nation on the east coast of Asia. Japan had absorbed the Kingdom of Korea, a nation with a long history and a distinct and unique culture, in 1910. After World War II Korea was freed from Japanese control and divided in two along the 38th parallel of north latitude. **North Korea** was supported by the Soviet Union, **South Korea** by the United States.

Efforts to reunify Korea after the war were unsuccessful. The Soviet Union blocked free elections because two thirds of the people lived in the South, which would easily control the elections. The Soviets would have liked a unified Korea if they could have dominated it, but not otherwise. In 1948 and 1949 the Americans and Soviets pulled their troops out of Korea, but the Soviets left behind a well-armed North Korean army, a force much superior to the force defending the south.

The two Korean governments each threatened to attack the other. "Tension along the 38th Parallel was extreme," historian Clay Blair, wrote, "the border area was like a war zone." Although the United States supported South Korea, official policy considered Korea too far away to be essential to American defense. This alarmed the South Koreans and with good reason. On June 25, 1950, the North Korean army suddenly struck across the border in force.

President Truman assumed that the Soviet Union was behind the invasion. Whether or not he was correct is still not known. In any case Truman was intent on maintaining United States prestige in the face of growing communist threats and felt he had no time to

[1]From *Congressional Record*, 81st Congress, 2nd Session, June 1, 1950

Carl Mydans/Life Picture Service

Five-star General Douglas Mac-Arthur. At right a helicopter picks up marines in the harbor of Inchon.

Point of View

American Caesar was the title General Douglas MacArthur's biographer gave to him.

"He was a great thundering paradox of a man, noble and ignoble, arrogant and shy, the best of men and the worst of men, the most protean, most ridiculous, and most sublime. No more baffling, exasperating soldier ever wore a uniform. . . . He carried the plumage of a flamingo. . . . Yet he was also extraordinarily brave. His twenty-two medals—thirteen of them for heroism—probably exceeded those of any other figure in American history."
William Manchester,
1978

investigate the situation in detail. He decided to apply the containment policy to the situation. In the name of the United Nations he ordered American forces stationed in Japan into Korea. General MacArthur was put in command of the campaign.

Truman did not ask Congress to declare war, and his right to send American troops to Korea was challenged by Robert Taft, the leading Republican in Congress. He claimed Truman had "usurped," or illegally seized, Congress' power to declare war. However, Congress took no further action. Perhaps if it had, circumstances in Vietnam 14 years later would have been different.

The North Koreans had the advantage of surprise. By September they had conquered nearly all of South Korea. Then the UN army, which consisted mainly of Americans and South Koreans, managed to check their advance. Next General MacArthur planned and executed a brilliant counterattack. He landed troops at **Inchon,** far behind

Wide World Photos

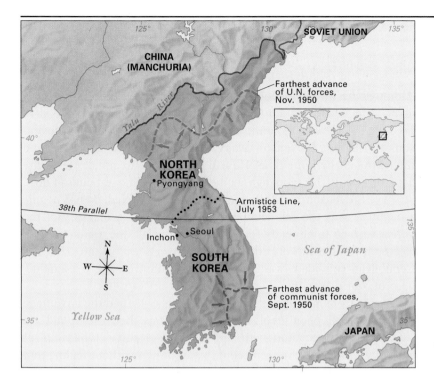

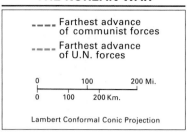

- - - - Farthest advance of communist forces
- - - - Farthest advance of U.N. forces

| 0 | 100 | 200 Mi. |
| 0 | 100 | 200 Km. |

Lambert Conformal Conic Projection

LEARNING FROM MAPS. *The division of Korea after World War II left North Korea with most of Korea's mineral resources and heavy industry, but with scarce agricultural resources. South Korea, on the other hand, found itself with most of the country's people, commerce, farmland, and food production but almost no industrial raw materials. Since the Korean War almost no trade between the two countries has crossed the 38th parallel. How does North Korea's relative location seem to assure it would become communist?*

the North Korean lines. The tide of battle turned swiftly. The North Koreans, attacked from two sides, retreated. Soon MacArthur's troops had driven the invaders out of South Korea.

However, instead of stopping at this point, MacArthur obtained permission from Truman to invade North Korea. By November his troops were approaching the **Yalu River,** the boundary between North Korea and China. This action caused the Chinese to enter the war. Striking suddenly and with tremendous force, they routed Mac-Arthur's army, driving it back into South Korea. Finally, in the spring of 1951, the battle line was stabilized along the original border between the two Koreas.

MacArthur then requested permission to bomb China and to use anticommunist Chinese troops from Taiwan in Korea. President Truman refused to allow this expansion of the war. Still, MacArthur continued to argue for his plan. Truman was forced to remove him from command. The fighting in Korea continued.

The **Korean War** added to the public's worry about communist spying and therefore to the influence of Senator McCarthy. Early in the war Congress passed the **McCarran Internal Security Act.** This law required all communist organizations to register and open their financial records to the government. A special board was set up to investigate organizations that might be subversive—that is, out to overthrow the government. By 1952 Senator McCarthy was describing the Roosevelt and Truman administrations as "20 years of treason."

Return to the Preview & Review on page 455.

4. THE EISENHOWER LEGACY

The Election of 1952

Use these questions to guide your reading. Answer the questions after completing Section 4.
Understanding Issues, Events, & Ideas. Use the following words to describe the key events of the Eisenhower years: massive retaliation, brinksmanship, Army-McCarthy Hearings, East Germany and Hungary, Vietnam, Israel, Suez Canal, Summit Meeting, U-2 Affair, St. Lawrence Seaway, Federal Highway Act, Interstate System, Warren Court, *Brown v. Board of Education of Topeka,* Little Rock, Montgomery Bus Boycott, nonviolent resistance, sit-in.

1. Why did Stevenson have little chance of defeating Eisenhower in the 1952 election?
2. Why did the Eisenhower-Dulles foreign policy tend to prolong the Cold War?
3. How was Eisenhower's domestic policy conservative? How was it liberal?
4. Why was it important that the decision of the Warren Court in *Brown v. Board of Education* be unanimous?
5. What prompted the Montgomery Bus Boycott? What was its outcome?

Thinking Critically. 1. Argue either for or against President Eisenhower's response to various world trouble spots in the 1950s. 2. Imagine that you are one of the nine black students attending the previously all-white high school in Little Rock. Write a poem or short story describing your feelings on your first day of school.

Although the Twenty-second Amendment did not apply to him, President Truman decided not to seek reelection in 1952. Instead he gave his support at the Democratic convention to Governor Adlai Stevenson of Illinois. Stevenson was an excellent speaker, witty and thoughtful at the same time. He had the courage to attack McCarthy head-on during the campaign, something few Democrats dared do.

Yet Stevenson had little chance of being elected. Many people thought he was too intellectual. More important, a majority of the voters seemed to be ready for a change. After all, the nation had not elected a Republican president since Hoover's victory in 1928. The Republican candidate was Dwight D. Eisenhower, the outstanding hero of World War II.

Aside from his fame as a general, Eisenhower had the advantage of never having been involved in party politics. Because he did not have a long association with the Republican party, thousands of normally Democratic citizens could vote for him without feeling that they were voting for a Republican. As a matter of fact, before deciding to back Stevenson, President Truman had tried to persuade Eisenhower to run on the Democratic ticket!

In addition, Eisenhower's warm, easygoing personality appealed to millions. The campaign slogan "I like Ike" perfectly expressed the general reaction. Liberals of both parties who were worried about

The opponents in the 1952 presidential election, Adlai Stevenson, left, and Dwight Eisenhower, right, share a friendly handshake after the heat of the campaign.

Wide World Photos

Dwight D. Eisenhower Presidential Library

Senator McCarthy voted for Eisenhower in hopes that he would be able to silence or control the senator. Further, Eisenhower announced during the campaign that if elected he would go to Korea to negotiate a settlement of the war there. Any last doubts about his victory evaporated. Eisenhower won by more than 6 million votes.

When asked how he felt after being so badly beaten, Stevenson said that he felt like a small boy who had stubbed his toe—too grown-up to cry but too hurt to laugh. These were the same words used to concede defeat in 1858 by another candidate from Illinois, Abraham Lincoln.

Eisenhower's Foreign Policy

President Eisenhower made no basic changes in the containment policy. But he was under great pressure from conservative Republicans to reduce government spending. He and his secretary of state, John Foster Dulles, developed a strategy called **massive retaliation.** In simple terms, massive retaliation meant threatening to respond to Soviet aggression anywhere in the world by dropping nuclear bombs on Moscow and other Soviet cities. It meant being willing to go ''to the brink'' of all-out war to contain communism. This policy came to be known as **brinksmanship.**

Atom bombs were replacing ''what used to be called conventional weapons,'' Dulles said. There was no need, he argued, to spend huge amounts on tanks, battleships, and other expensive ''military hardware.''

Dulles' policy was pure bluff. By 1953 both the Soviets and the United States had made hydrogen bombs hundreds of times more deadly than the bomb that destroyed Hiroshima. Neither Dulles nor

A biographer of the Dulles family wrote these lines.

''During all but the final months of the Eisenhower era it was the Dulles family which managed and manipulated the foreign affairs of the United States, and, in consequence, decidedly influenced the policies of the rest of the world. John Foster Dulles was at the peak of his powers, a Secretary of State so powerful and implacable that no government in what was then fervently referred to as the Free World would have dared to make a decision of international importance without first getting his nod of approval. . . .''
Leonard Mosley, 1978

Carl Mydans/Life Picture Service

John Foster Dulles

Eisenhower ever seriously considered dropping a nuclear bomb on anyone. It would have been suicidal to do so because a nuclear strike would almost surely have caused the world to erupt in nuclear war.

The warlike language Dulles used tended to keep Cold War tensions high at a time when the Soviets were taking a less aggressive position. Joseph Stalin died in 1953. The new Soviet leaders claimed to favor "peaceful coexistence and competition" with the western nations. This gave them an advantage in the worldwide competition to influence public opinion, for Dulles seemed unable to back off from his policy of brinksmanship.

The Eisenhower-Dulles foreign policy also increased Senator McCarthy's influence in the United States because it focused attention on the danger of a clash with the communist powers. The popular President Eisenhower detested McCarthy and his tactics, but he was unwilling to criticize the senator openly.

Eisenhower stiffened the already harsh loyalty program that Truman had set up to clean out possible communist sympathizers in the government. Employees found to be "security risks" were to be fired even if they had not actually done anything wrong. For example, persons who had been convicted of crimes in the past might be classified as security risks. The idea was that communist agents might threaten to expose such people's pasts unless they turned over secret information. Under this program about 3,000 employees were fired.

Joseph Welch, seated, represented the Army in the Army-McCarthy hearings. After a vicious McCarthy smear of a young aide, millions of television viewers heard Welch ask, "Have you no decency left, sir?" How was Mc-Carthy's spell broken?

Robert Phillips/Black Star

An even larger number resigned. Yet almost none of these people had actually done anything disloyal.

McCarthy finally went too far. Early in 1954 one of his assistants was drafted into the army. McCarthy tried unsuccessfully to get him excused from service. Out of spite he then announced an investigation of "subversive activities" in the army. These **Army-McCarthy Hearings** were televised. They destroyed McCarthy's prestige completely. Day after day the emptiness of his charges and his snarling cruelty and insensitivity were seen by millions of viewers. The people he attacked were aware that they were being watched and judged by this enormous audience. They *had* to fight back. When they fought and survived, McCarthy's spell was broken.

The hearings produced no specific political or legal results. Later, in August 1954, the Senate voted to investigate McCarthy's behavior. In December the Senate voted to censure him. By a vote of 67 to 22 the Senate resolved "that the conduct of the Senator from Wisconsin, Mr. McCarthy, is contrary to senatorial traditions and is hereby condemned." McCarthy's power to do harm was gone. He remained in the Senate until his death in 1957, ignored if not forgotten.

Eisenhower and the Cold War

During his campaign Eisenhower had promised to go to Korea. Soon after his victory, and before becoming president, he flew to Korea to meet with U.S. commanders to discuss strategy. Eisenhower and Dulles decided on a "peace or else" policy. Early in 1953 the U.S. increased air attacks on North Korea while hinting to the Chinese that if peace talks did not start soon they would send bombers across the Chinese border—perhaps carrying nuclear weapons. Finally in July 1953 a truce was signed. Although peace talks have continued, no final treaty has ever been signed. Armies continued to face each other across a narrow demilitarized zone near the 38th parallel. The United States has refused to remove its soldiers until a final settlement has been reached. United States soldiers still guard the border.

Elsewhere President Eisenhower avoided military solutions to international problems. Dulles had spoken of "liberating" the people of eastern Europe who had been forced to accept communist governments after World War II. There were revolts against these governments in **East Germany** in 1953 and in **Hungary** in 1956. But Eisenhower did not intervene.

When the French, who had colonized Southeast Asia in the 1860s, were being driven out of **Vietnam** by local communists in 1954, Eisenhower rejected the suggestion that the air force bomb communist positions. Instead the United States supported the division of Vietnam into a northern, procommunist section and a southern, pro-Western government. This United States position was contrary to the Geneva Accords signed in 1954 by the French and the leaders of

Nearly a boy himself, this Hungarian freedom fighter stands guard in Budapest. The crowd seems to be waiting to see what will happen next. What sad lesson did supporters of a free Hungary learn in 1956? How many years did it take to win true freedom?

rival Vietnamese groups. That agreement called for a unified and independent Vietnam by 1956.

Another example of Eisenhower's restraint occurred in 1956 in the Middle East. In 1948 the state of **Israel**, which had formerly been the British mandate, or colony, of Palestine, declared its independence. Many Jews who had escaped Hitler's Holocaust flocked to Israel after the war to start a new life. So did thousands of Jews from all over the world, many of them former residents of the United States.

However, the Arab nations surrounding Israel took up arms to prevent what they considered an invasion of their territory. A series of wars resulted. Although outnumbered, the Israelis overcame the Arabs. Nearly 1 million Arabs who had lived in the area when it was Palestine fled to neighboring regions. They then conducted raids and terrorist attacks on Israel, determined to recover their homeland and drive the Jews from the Middle East.

A crisis erupted in 1956 when Egypt stepped up its raids against Israel and seized control of the **Suez Canal,** which was an international waterway. Israel fought back, joined by Great Britain and France, who wanted to reopen the canal.

Eisenhower faced a serious dilemma. The United States had supported the independence of Israel from the start. Most Americans felt that the Jews were entitled to a country of their own after their terrible suffering during World War II. In addition, Great Britain and France were also allies of the United States. But Eisenhower objected to their using force to regain the canal. He demanded that the invaders pull back. So did the Soviets, who threatened all-out war. As a result the allies withdrew, and Egypt kept control of the Suez Canal.

By 1954 Nikita Khrushchev had become the head of the Soviet government. Khrushchev was a difficult person to understand. At one moment he was full of talk about peace, at the next he was threatening to use nuclear bombs. One historian described Khrushchev as a mixture of Santa Claus and a "wild, angry Russian bear."

Eisenhower and the heads of the British and French governments met with Khrushchev in Geneva, Switzerland, in July 1955. They accomplished little at this Geneva **Summit Meeting,** or gathering of world leaders, but their discussions were friendly. Experts spoke hopefully of a possible end of the Cold War. Yet, little more than a year later, Khrushchev threatened to bomb Great Britain and France if they did not pull back from their war with Egypt over the Suez Canal.

Soviet scientists then shocked the world on October 4, 1957, when they sent into orbit around the earth a small satellite called *Sputnik.* (Sputnik is the Russian word for "traveling companion.") In November they launched a larger satellite, *Sputnik II,* which carried a dog. These amazing feats shattered American self-confidence and provided a great propaganda boost for the Soviet Union and communism. Soon "rocket fever" swept the United States. After repeated embarrassing failures the Americans hurled a grapefruit-sized satellite into space in January 1958. The United States and the Soviet Union were now in the space race.

The success of *Sputnik* sent shock waves through American society. Americans felt they led the world in science and technology. Now many people blamed the educational system for falling behind the Soviets in the space race. Courses in science and mathematics were added to school and college curriculums, and valuable scholarships were awarded to promising students in these fields. America was determined to "catch up."

Perhaps the most serious Cold War test of Eisenhower was the **U-2 Affair.** In 1960 the Soviets scored a second propaganda victory over the United States when they shot down an American U-2 "spy plane" which was illegally taking photographs high over Soviet territory. President Eisenhower at first denied that the plane had been on a spying mission. Later, when Premier Khrushchev revealed that the pilot had survived the plane crash, the president was forced to admit the truth about the U-2 mission.

MINIMUM HOURLY WAGE RATES 1950-91	
Year	Minimum Hourly Wage Rate
1950	$0.75
1955	$0.75
1960	$1.00
1965	$1.25
1970	$1.60
1975	$2.10
1980	$3.10
1985	$3.35
1990	$3.80
1991	$4.25

Source: Statistical Abstract of the United States, 1989

LEARNING FROM TABLES. *The minimum hourly wage rate, set by the government after studying statistics on inflation, purchasing power, and other economic indicators, influences the wages of both hourly and salaried employees. What might explain the unusually large increase in the rate between 1975 and 1980?*

Eisenhower's Domestic Policies

President Eisenhower stood halfway between the conservative domestic policies of the Republicans of the 1920s and the liberal policies of the New Deal. He was eager to reduce government spending. He favored measures designed to help private enterprise. He hoped to turn over many federal programs to the individual states.

Yet Eisenhower was unwilling to do away with most of the social welfare legislation of the 1930s. He agreed that it was the government's job to try to regulate economic growth and stimulate the economy during hard times.

While Eisenhower was president, 11 million more workers were brought into the social security and unemployment system. The minimum wage was raised. A start was made in providing public housing for low-income families. Eisenhower also established the new cabinet-level Department of Health, Education, and Welfare. The first head of this important department was Oveta Culp Hobby, the former director of the Women's Army Corps.

Although Eisenhower genuinely wished to hold federal spending to a minimum, he approved two very large new projects. One was the construction of the

Myron Davis/Life Picture Service

Oveta Culp Hobby

LEARNING FROM GRAPHS. *As you can see from the graph, the business cycle entered strong periods of prosperity during World War II and the Korean War. What economic problem troubled both Truman and Eisenhower, and had a negative effect on the business cycle as well?*

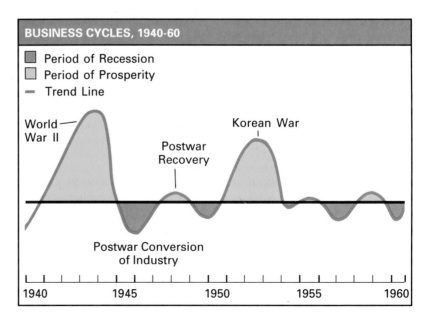

BUSINESS CYCLES, 1940-60

■ Period of Recession
□ Period of Prosperity
— Trend Line

World War II

Korean War

Postwar Recovery

Postwar Conversion of Industry

1940   1945   1950   1955   1960

St. Lawrence Seaway, which deepened the channel of the St. Lawrence River so that ocean-going ships could sail directly into the Great Lakes. The other was the Federal Highway Act of 1956. This measure authorized the construction of an enormous network of superhighways, the Interstate System. Eisenhower considered both these projects necessary for defense in case of war. Yet it was also Eisenhower who in his Farewell Address warned against the rising power of the "military-industrial complex." By this he meant the economic power and prestige of defense industries that had developed during World War II and had grown during the Cold War.

While Eisenhower was president, the last of the 50 states were added to the Union. Alaska became a state in January 1959 and Hawaii was admitted in August of the same year.

School Desegregation

In 1956 Eisenhower again defeated Adlai Stevenson for president. His margin was even larger than in 1952. Clearly a majority of the voters approved of his middle-of-the-road philosophy.

Yet Eisenhower's most important action during his first term produced radical social changes. Eisenhower himself strongly disapproved of some of these changes. No better modern example exists of how difficult it is to understand the historical significance of events until long after they have occurred.

The action in question was Eisenhower's appointment of Governor Earl Warren of California as Chief Justice of the United States in 1953. Warren had served three terms as governor. He had also run for vice president in 1948 on the ticket with Thomas E. Dewey.

Although Warren had never been a judge before, he quickly became the most important member of the Supreme Court. Under his leadership the Court became a solid unit, at least where civil rights cases were concerned.

In 1954 this Warren Court made one of the most important decisions in the history of the Supreme Court. It decided in the case known as Brown v. Board of Education of Topeka (Kansas) that it was unconstitutional for states to maintain separate schools for black and white children. This case overturned the "separate but equal" doctrine established in *Plessy v. Ferguson* in 1896. The decision said:

❝ Today, education is perhaps the most important function of state and local governments. Compulsory school attendance laws and the great expenditures for education both demonstrate our recognition of the importance of education in a democratic society. It is required in the performance of our most basic public responsibilities, even the armed forces. It is the very foundation of good citizenship. Today, it is a principle instrument in awakening the child to cultural values, in preparing him for later professional training, and

Yousuf Karsh/Woodfin Camp

Chief Justice Earl Warren, who had been the Republican governor of California, was appointed by President Eisenhower. But the Warren Court's growing liberalism and strong stance against segregation scattered the American landscape with "Impeach Earl Warren" signs. Eisenhower was not as strongly criticized when he enforced the Court's decision to integrate schools in Brown v. Board of Education. *Explain how the president proved to be a defender of the Constitution in this action.*

The Eisenhower Legacy   469

The American flag of fifty stars and thirteen stripes has gone through many changes. The early colonies had a variety of flags depicting patriotic themes, such as one showing Benjamin Franklin's advice: "Join, or Die." Others showed rattlesnakes with the warning "Don't tread on me." By the 1750s many of the flags were using 13 alternating stripes, usually red and white, to symbolize the 13 colonies.

As conflicts with England drew the colonies closer together, the desire for a colonial flag grew. The 1775 Continental Colors was the first national flag. It had 13 alternating red and white stripes (7 red, 6 white) and the British flag in the upper left. After the Declaration of Independence, the Continental Congress acted to remove the British flag from the American flag. In 1777 Congress resolved that "the Flag of the united states be 13 stripes alternate red and white, and the Union be 13 stars white on a blue field representing a new constellation." This was the original American flag.

No one knows for sure who designed this flag, or who made the first one. Soon after it was adopted, Congressman Francis Hopkinson of Pennsylvania said he was its designer. In 1870 William J. Canby claimed that his grandmother, Betsy Ross, a Philadelphia seamstress and flag maker, had designed and sewn the first flag. Historians are unable to support either claim.

The stripes were probably taken from the most popular patriotic flag of the Revolution, the flag of the Sons of Liberty. On it the stripes represented the 13

America's strong young navy showed a "rattlesnake" ensign in 1775. Its warning seems perfectly clear.

An early flag of the Revolutionary period, with thirteen stars in the pattern of twelve stars in a wreath and one star at center that was first adopted by the famed Third Maryland Regiment and flown by them at the Battle of Cowpens in 1781.

"Beautiful as a flower to those who love it, terrible as a meteor to those who hate it." This unique "Great Flower" flag was made in 1861.

This ensign has 38 stars displayed in a "double-wreath" pattern, 13 in the inner ring and the balance for states joining the Union until 1876.

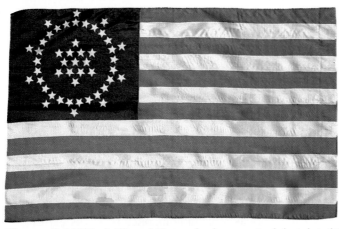

The so-called Whipple Flag of 48 stars having a central six-pointed "Great Star" for the 13 colonies, was designed by Wayne Whipple.

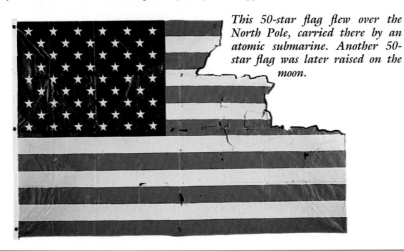

This 50-star flag flew over the North Pole, carried there by an atomic submarine. Another 50-star flag was later raised on the moon.

original colonies. This part of the flag's design has changed little over the years. The first flags after independence added stripes as well as stars for new states. The flag of 1795, for example, had 15 of each. But the flag of 1818 went back to 13 stripes, the standard for all flags afterward.

The stars in the first design stood for the states. The Continental Congress in 1777 stated there should be 13 of them. But it did not indicate how they should be arranged. The most common arrangement of the time was alternating rows of three stars, two, three, two, and three. Another flag had twelve stars in a circle around the 13th star. And still another had all thirteen stars in a circle. In 1818 Congress ordered that a new star be added on the July 4th after a state joined the Union. It still did not say how the stars should be arranged. So many arrangements were seen until 1912. Since then presidential orders have fixed the positions of the stars as new ones are added.

The Continental Congress also never stated why red, white, and blue were chosen for the flag's colors. But later when designing the nation's seal— also red, white, and blue—they listed the following meanings: *red* for courage and hardiness, *white* for purity and innocence, *blue* for justice, vigilance, and perseverance.

The flag is saluted by the Pledge of Allegiance:

"I pledge allegiance to the flag of the United States of America and to the Republic for which it stands, one Nation under God, indivisible, with liberty and justice for all."

The Eisenhower Legacy 471

in helping him adjust normally to his environment. In these days, it is doubtful that any child may reasonably be expected to succeed in life if he is denied the opportunity of an education. Such an opportunity, where the state has undertaken to provide it, is a right which must be made available to all on equal terms.

We come then to the question presented: Does segregation of children in public schools solely on the basis of race, even though the facilities and other 'tangible' factors may be equal, deprive the children of the minority group of equal educational opportunities? We believe it does. . . .

We conclude that in the field of public education the doctrine [idea or principle] of 'separate but equal' has no place. Separate educational facilities are inherently [by nature] unequal. . . .[1]"

The Court ruled that a separate education was by its very nature an unequal education. This would be true even if the conditions in the separate schools were identical. Segregation, in other words, suggests that the people kept out are inferior. As Chief Justice Warren wrote, segregation had harmful effects on all children, white as well as black.

In 1954 all the southern states had separate school systems for whites and blacks. Many northern schools were also segregated in fact if not by law. Putting the *Brown v. Board of Education of Topeka* decision into effect was bound to be time consuming and difficult. Therefore, a year later the Court announced that the states must go ahead "with all deliberate speed." This actually meant that they could change slowly. Still, they must begin to change promptly and move steadily toward single, racially integrated school systems.

The *Brown* decision was a unanimous one. This was extremely important. If even one of the nine justices had written a dissenting opinion arguing against the ruling, opponents of desegregation could have used his reasoning to justify resisting the law.

Even in the face of a unanimous Court, many southern whites were unwilling to accept school integration, no matter how slowly carried out. There was talk of "massive resistance." This was not mere bluff as in the case of Dulles' "massive retaliation." In 1957 the school board of **Little Rock,** Arkansas, following a court order to integrate schools, voted to admit nine black students to a high school for whites. Governor Orville Faubus called out the Arkansas National Guard to prevent the children from entering the school.

President Eisenhower was not personally opposed to school integration. He believed, however, that it was "just plain *nuts*" to force white parents to send their children to integrated schools be-

[1]From *Brown v. Board of Education of Topeka,* Supreme Court of the United States, 347 U.S. 483, 1954

Burt Glinn/Magnum Photos

cause of the problems such a move would cause. But Faubus' act was a direct challenge to federal authority. The president promptly sent 1,000 soldiers to Little Rock. With this force behind them, the black children were admitted to the school. The president of the Arkansas chapter of the NAACP described the day:

❝ At 9:22 A.M. the nine Negro pupils marched solemnly through the doors of Central High School, surrounded by twenty-two soldiers. An army helicopter circled overhead. Around the massive brick schoolhouse 350 paratroopers stood grimly at attention. Scores of reporters, photographers, and TV cameramen made a mad dash for telephones, typewriters, and TV studios. Within minutes a world that had been holding its breath learned that the nine pupils, protected by the might of the United States military, had finally entered the 'never-never land.'

When classes ended that afternoon, the troops escorted the pupils to my home. . . .

I asked if they had a rough day. Not especially, they said.

President Eisenhower ordered U.S. troops to escort the young black students into Central High School in Little Rock, Arkansas. Why had they been denied admission to the school? What effect did photographs such as this one have on the American public in the late 1950s?

The Eisenhower Legacy   473

In *Parting the Waters* the Montgomery Bus Boycott is seen in two perspectives.

" Only the rarest and oddest of people saw historical possibilities in the bus boycott. Of the few people who bothered to write the *Advertiser* at first, most were women who saw it as a justifiable demand for simple decent treatment. One woman correspondent did speculate that there must be a Communist hand behind such strife, but the great mass of segregationists did not bother to address the issue. . . . As for the boycotters themselves, the religious fervor they went to bed with at night always congealed by the next morning into cold practicality, as they faced rainstorms, mechanical breakdowns, stranded relatives, and complicated relays in getting from home to job without being late or getting fired. . . . "
Taylor Branch, 1988

'Then why the long faces?' I wanted to know.

'Well,' Ernest [Green] spoke up, 'you don't expect us to be jumping for joy, do you?'

Someone said, 'But, Ernest, we *are* in Central. . . .'

'Sure we're in Central,' Ernest shot back, somewhat impatiently. 'But how did we get in? We got in, finally, because we were protected by paratroops. Some victory!' he said sarcastically.

'Are you sorry,' someone asked him, 'that the President sent the troops?'

'No,' said Ernest. 'I'm only sorry it had to be that way.'[1] "

Photographs and motion pictures showed the nine black youngsters being taunted by crowds of angry adults or walking beside army paratroopers in battle dress. These scenes had a powerful impact on millions of people, southerners as well as northerners.

The Struggle for Equal Rights

African Americans had been fighting for their rights since long before *Brown v. Board of Education*. After the Supreme Court declared school segregation unconstitutional, African Americans began to speak out even more vigorously against all forms of racial

[1]From *The Long Shadow of Little Rock* by Daisy Bates

UPI/Bettmann Newsphotos

Rosa Parks sits at the front of a Montgomery, Alabama, bus one year after she refused to give up her seat to a white man. What emotions do you suppose she felt when this picture was taken?

discrimination. In August 1955, 14-year-old Emmett Till was senselessly murdered in Mississippi for speaking to a white woman. When the all-white jury returned a verdict of "not guilty" in the trial of those accused of Till's death, blacks protested in many cities.

Then in December 1955, Rosa Parks, a black woman in Montgomery, Alabama, was arrested because she refused to give up her seat on a city bus to a white man. Her arrest led the blacks of Montgomery to refuse to ride the buses until the rule requiring blacks to sit in the rear was changed. This boycott was a heavy financial loss for the city's bus system.

The **Montgomery Bus Boycott** lasted for nearly a year. It ended with a victory for the African Americans. The Supreme Court ruled that the Alabama segregation laws were unconstitutional. It was in leading the strike that a young African American clergyman, Martin Luther King, Jr., first became well known. When asked why Rosa Parks had refused to move, he explained how she and many African Americans felt:

> No one can understand the action of Mrs. Parks unless he realizes that eventually the cup of endurance runs over, and the human personality cries out, 'I can take it no longer.' Mrs. Park's refusal to move back was her intrepid affirmation [brave statement] that she had had enough. It was an individual expression of a timeless longing for human dignity and freedom. . . .[1]

[1]From *Stride Toward Freedom* by Martin Luther King, Jr.

Throughout the long contest he advised blacks to avoid violence no matter how badly provoked by whites.

King believed in **nonviolent resistance,** what he called nonviolent direct action, for basically religious reasons. He argued that love was a more effective weapon than hate or force. There were also practical reasons for nonviolence. African Americans were a minority in the United States. To obtain fair treatment, they needed the help of white moderates. They were more likely to get that help by appeals to reason and decency than by force.

By the end of Eisenhower's second term real progress had been made. School desegregation was moving ahead slowly. Other forms of segregation were being ended. In 1960, African Americans began an attempt to desegregate lunch counters and similar facilities by staging **sit-ins.** A group would enter a place that served only whites, sit down quietly, and refuse to leave. They were either served or arrested. In either case their actions attracted wide attention and strengthened the drive for fair treatment. By 1960, new organizations such as the Southern Christian Leadership Conference, founded by Reverend King, and the Student Nonviolent Coordinating Committee (SNCC) had sprung up to direct the battle for equal rights.

"Say I was a drum major for justice," said Martin Luther King, Jr., seen here marching in Montgomery in 1956. What philosophy did he preach and practice?*

Return to the Preview & Review on page 462.

Use these questions to guide your reading. Answer the questions after completing Section 5.
Understanding Issues, Events, & Ideas. Use the following words to discuss the Kennedy years: New Frontier, Cuba, Central Intelligence Agency, Bay of Pigs, Peace Corps, Alliance for Progress, Berlin Wall, Cuban Missile Crisis, "hot line," Camelot.

1. What were Nixon's strengths and weaknesses as a candidate for president in 1960? What were Kennedy's strengths and weaknesses?
2. Why did President Kennedy hesitate to allow the CIA to carry out its invasion of Cuba? What happened to his prestige after the invasion failed?
3. Why did Khrushchev build the Berlin Wall?
4. What provoked the Cuban Missile Crisis? What was Kennedy's response? What was Khrushchev's response?

Thinking Critically. 1. Nixon and Kennedy were the first presidential candidates to hold a televised debate. Suppose you were a member of the studio audience. List five topics that you would have liked to hear the candidates debate. **2.** Imagine that you had been able to interview President Kennedy. What three questions would you have wanted to ask him?

5. A YOUTHFUL COLD WARRIOR

The Election of 1960

In 1960 the Republicans nominated Richard M. Nixon for president. Nixon was Eisenhower's vice president. Before that he had been a congressman and a senator from California.

In Congress Nixon had been a leading communist-hunter. Long before most people took the charges against Alger Hiss seriously, Nixon was convinced of Hiss' guilt. He worked closely with Senator McCarthy in his search for traitors in the government. He was almost as reckless in his charges as McCarthy. While running for vice president in 1952, for example, Nixon claimed that Adlai Stevenson was "soft on communism."

Nixon was a clever politician, but victory was more important to him than fair play. He was an intelligent and hard-working legislator. He sympathized with the civil rights movement, and he had strongly supported President Truman's foreign policy. While vice president he had toned down his talk about traitors in the government. He tried to act more like a statesman. This "new Nixon" persuaded Eisenhower and other Republican leaders to back him for president.

Still, many people did not trust Nixon. Nixon tried hard to explain his controversial reputation. "I believe in battle," he said. "It's always been there, wherever I go." He wrote that his life had been a series of crises. In each one, he claimed, he had triumphed by being "cool and calm" and working hard. But he may have appeared quarrelsome along the way, he admitted.

The Democratic candidate for president in 1960 was Senator John F. Kennedy of Massachusetts. Kennedy was young, handsome, intelligent, and rich. He was a war hero, seriously injured in a rescue mission in the Pacific. He was a Pulitzer prize-winning author and a shrewd politician. And he was an excellent campaigner. Kennedy appealed to liberals because he seemed imaginative and forward looking. Many conservatives supported him too because his policies were moderate.

Kennedy's major handicap was his Catholic religion. Al Smith's crushing defeat by Herbert Hoover in 1928 suggested that the anti-Catholic prejudices of voters in normally Democratic states might be difficult to overcome.

During the campaign Kennedy argued that Eisenhower had been too cautious and conservative. The economy was not growing rapidly enough. The nation needed new ideas. He called his program the **New Frontier.** He would open up new fields for development by being imaginative and vigorous. Nixon, on the other hand, defended Eisenhower's record and promised to follow the same lines. In the election the popular vote was extremely close. Kennedy won by only

UPI/Bettmann Newsphotos

100,000 votes out of a total of more than 68 million. But in the electoral vote his margin was 303 to 219.

In his inaugural address on January 20, 1961, the president stirred the nation with these words:

> We observe today not a victory of party but a celebration of freedom—symbolizing an end as well as a beginning—signifying renewal as well as change. For I have sworn before you and Almighty God the same solemn oath our forebears prescribed nearly a century and three quarters ago.
>
> The world is different now. For man holds in his mortal hands the power to abolish all forms of human poverty and all forms of human life. And yet the same revolutionary beliefs for which our forebears fought are still at issue around the globe—the belief that the rights of man come not from the generosity of the state but from the hand of God.
>
> We dare not forget that we are the heirs of that first revolution. Let the word go forth from this time and place, to friend and foe alike, that the torch has been passed to a new generation of Americans—born in this century, tempered by war, disciplined by a hard and bitter peace, proud of our ancient heritage—and unwilling to witness or permit the slow undoing of those human rights to which this nation has always been committed, and to which we are committed today at home and around the world.

Crowds press forward to see John F. Kennedy during his campaign for president in 1960. Both Kennedy and his opponent Richard Nixon traveled widely between Labor Day, when campaigns traditionally began, and Election Day. Kennedy's presidential portrait is by Aaron Shikler.

A Youthful Cold Warrior   477

Let every nation know, whether it wishes us well or ill, that we shall pay any price, bear any burden, meet any hardship, support any friend, oppose any foe to assure the survival and success of liberty. . . .

And so, my fellow Americans: Ask not what your country can do for you—ask what you can do for your country. . . .

With good conscience our only sure reward, with history the final judge of our deeds, let us go forth to lead the land we love, asking His blessing and His help, but knowing that here on earth God's work must truly be our own.[1] 🙿

Close listeners could hear behind such golden rhetoric the old challenges of the Cold War hurled down by this young leader.

The Bay of Pigs

Kennedy's nemesis, Fidel Castro, the dictator of Cuba, is surrounded by the flags of his country as he speaks in Havana. In Greek mythology Nemesis is the goddess of vengeance. Why is it a good word to describe the relationship between the president and the dictator?

President Kennedy had stressed domestic economic issues in the 1960 campaign. But shortly after he took office, foreign problems began to occupy most of his time. During President Eisenhower's second term there had been a revolution in **Cuba** led by Fidel Castro. Castro set up a communist-type government on this island just 90 miles (144 kilometers) off the tip of Florida. Americans had invested heavily in Cuba, and Castro now claimed that property for Cuba. The Eisenhower administration had cut off trade with Cuba. Castro took an increasingly unfriendly attitude toward the United States and established close ties with the Soviet Union.

Meanwhile, the **Central Intelligence Agency** (CIA), a government bureau created in 1947, began to train a small army of Cuban refugees. The plan was to have this force invade Cuba from Central America in order to overthrow Castro. Of course this was done in complete secrecy.

When Kennedy learned of the plan, he hesitated to allow the CIA to put it into effect. He had criticized Eisenhower for supporting conservative governments in Latin America only because they were anticommunist. Should he now encourage the overthrow of a government only because it was procommunist?

Kennedy decided to go ahead with the CIA scheme. But he altered the plan. He encouraged the Cuban patriots to invade the island, but he withheld American air cover for them. On April 17, 1961, the Cuban force was put ashore in southern Cuba, at a place known as the **Bay of Pigs.** The invaders hoped to be joined by other Cubans. Instead they met only Castro's army. All were captured or killed.

The Bay of Pigs dealt a terrible blow to the prestige of the United States and to Kennedy in particular. Was the youthful new president

[1]From *Public Papers of the Presidents of the United States: John F. Kennedy,* 1961

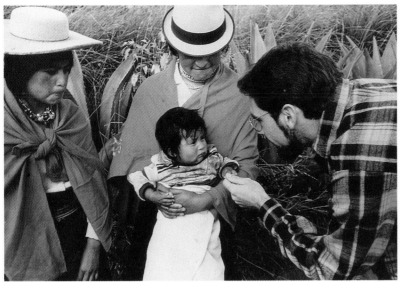

P. Meyer/Black Star

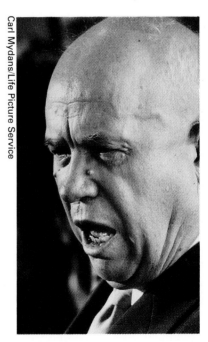

A Peace Corps volunteer in Ecuador brings his gentle mercies to this child.

Carl Mydans/Life Picture Service

a reckless adventurer? Could he stand up to his clever communist opponents? Citizens who had voted for Kennedy because they did not trust Nixon were especially shocked by the mission's secrecy. Everyone was shocked by its failure.

The disaster in Cuba all but hid the fact that Kennedy was eager to develop good relations with Latin American countries and to help them improve the lives of their poor. In early 1961 he created the **Peace Corps,** an organization that sent volunteers to help the people of needy countries. It earned tremendous worldwide goodwill for the U.S. as it still does today. Kennedy also proposed what he called an **Alliance for Progress** to provide economic aid for Latin American countries.

The Berlin Wall

The Soviets had taken advantage of Eisenhower and the United States with the publicity of the U-2 Affair. They had pointed their finger at the United States, claiming it was the aggressor, not the Soviet Union. Now Khrushchev decided to take advantage of the Bay of Pigs Affair and test Kennedy's will to resist Soviet pressure.

Without consulting the western authorities in Berlin, Khrushchev suddenly had a wall built across the city, sealing the Soviet zone off from the three western zones. This **Berlin Wall** was actually a sign of communist weakness. Thousands of people from East Germany had fled to the West by way of Berlin since the end of World War II. They went in search of greater personal freedom and the higher wages they could earn there.

The wall reduced this flow to a trickle. But it also reminded the world that large numbers of people in the eastern European countries were captives of communism.

The powerful Soviet premier Nikita Khrushchev is shown here at the time of the U-2 Affair.

A Youthful Cold Warrior   479

Flip Schulke/Black Star

President John F. Kennedy watches his air force leave Miami for Cuba in 1962.

The Cuban Missile Crisis

The United States let the Berlin Wall stand. Khrushchev then apparently decided to test Kennedy still further. The Soviets began to build bases in Cuba from which rocket-powered missiles could be fired. When Kennedy inquired about the purpose of these weapons, the Soviets assured him that only defensive, antiaircraft missiles were being installed.

This was a bald-faced lie, and Kennedy knew it. American U-2 planes had secretly photographed the new installations. The Soviets were preparing longer-range offensive missile bases from which they could fire nuclear warheads at American targets.

Now came the most dangerous moment in the long Cold War. If the United States destroyed the missile bases, a third world war might result. If the Americans did nothing, they risked destruction.

On October 22, 1962, Kennedy appeared on television to tell the public about the **Cuban Missile Crisis.** He demanded that the Soviets remove all their offensive weapons from Cuba and close down the new missile bases. The United States navy would stop and search all ships approaching Cuba to make sure that no more weapons were brought in. If atomic missiles were fired from Cuba, the United States would launch an all-out attack on the Soviet Union.

For three days the world held its breath. Then Khrushchev agreed to remove the missiles. Kennedy won a great personal victory. More important, the possibility of a nuclear war between the United States and the Soviet Union seemed less likely. Both sides had finally come to the brink that John Foster Dulles had foreseen but never actually faced in the 1950s. Both sides had stepped back rather than risk the destruction of the whole world. The United States pledged never to invade Cuba and to remove some missile bases in Turkey, pledges it kept.

Following the Cuban Missile Crisis, a **"hot line"** telephone connection was set up between Washington and Moscow. In any future crisis American and Soviet leaders could talk to each other directly. In the summer of 1963 the two nations took a small first step toward disarmament. They agreed to stop testing nuclear weapons above ground, where the explosions would release dangerous radioactivity into the atmosphere.

Triumph and Tragedy

His success in dealing with the missile crisis made Kennedy seem sure of being reelected in 1964. After years of wartime austerity and the modest styles of Truman and Eisenhower, Americans were captivated by the style of the new administration. French chefs now prepared their specialties at White House dinners for dazzling people from the arts and sciences who mingled with world leaders, listening to musicians such as the great cellist Pablo Casals. This side of the Kennedy administration later came to be known as **Camelot,** a reference to the mythical Court of King Arthur. In his travels to France with his wife Jacqueline and to Berlin, Kennedy proved what a popular international figure he had become. But at their summit meeting in Vienna in 1961 the wily Khrushchev demonstrated that the youthful president still had much to learn about international politics. Determined to regain his forceful image, Kennedy prepared more carefully for the international stage. In divided Berlin he electrified the huge crowd:

> ❝ All free men, wherever they may live, are citizens of Berlin. And therefore, as a free man, I take pride in the words *'Ich bin ein Berliner'* ['I am a Berliner']. ❞

Before his famous speech in Berlin, President Kennedy gazed into the world enslaved by communism beyond the Berlin Wall.

John Dominus/Life Picture Service

Nevertheless, Kennedy was not able to get Congress to enact much of his domestic program into law. For example, in 1963 he supported a large tax cut. Reducing taxes would stimulate the economy, he claimed. If people paid lower taxes, they would have more money left to spend on goods. Their purchases would cause producers to increase output. More workers would be hired. Unemployment would go down. Personal and business incomes would rise.

In the long run, the president argued, the lower tax rates would actually produce more income for the government. But conservative members of Congress in both parties objected to lowering taxes while the government's budget remained in the red.

Kennedy also introduced a strong civil rights bill in 1963. His proposal outlawed racial discrimination in all places serving the public, such as hotels, restaurants, and theaters. Like the tax reduction, it failed to pass Congress.

Kennedy tried repeatedly to inspire the stubborn Congress. In a typical Cold War challenge, the president told Congress on May 25, 1961:

66 I believe that this nation should commit itself to achieving the goal, before this decade is out, of landing a man on the moon and returning him safely to earth. 99

Congress agreed to fund this venture and two presidents later, in July 1969—six months before Kennedy's deadline—American ingenuity prevailed. Apollo 11 with its crew of three astronauts—Neil Armstrong, Edwin ''Buzz'' Aldrin, and Michael Collins—settled into orbit around the moon. While Collins remained in the command module, Armstrong and Aldrin landed on the moon in an area known as the Sea of Tranquillity. Millions watching on TV saw them step from the lunar lander and heard Armstrong say:

66 That's one small step for a man, one giant leap for mankind. 99

To try to smooth local political matters before the election of 1964, the president and his wife visited Texas in November of 1963. On November 22, 1963, while riding through Dallas in an open car, President Kennedy was shot dead. The deed was done so quickly that onlookers scarcely saw the president slump into his wife's lap. The governor of Texas, riding in the front of the car, was wounded. Vice President Johnson, two cars behind in the motorcade, was safe. He was sworn in as president two hours later on *Air Force 1* as it carried the slain president's body home for burial in Arlington National Cemetery. Millions saw the orderly transfer of power on television, as well as the stately funeral procession of world heads of state led by the president's widow Jacqueline.

The man accused of assassinating the president was Lee Harvey Oswald, a mysterious figure who, it turned out, had at one time lived

Fred Ward/Black Star

The riderless horse, boots reversed, in President Kennedy's funeral procession symbolizes a leader's death.

NASA

The historical significance of this picture will come with time. In its way it is as rare as Columbus' journal describing the first sighting of the Americas. To report "Man Walks on Moon," The New York Times *had to make special headline type large enough for the biggest story of the 20th century. Neil Armstrong took the picture of Edwin Aldrin, his fellow walker on the moon.*

in the Soviet Union. Before Oswald could be properly questioned, *he* was murdered while being transferred from one jail to another. This amazing incident caused many people to believe that Oswald had been killed to keep him from confessing that he was acting with a group of enemies of the president. There have been many investigations of the assassination and many theories put forth to explain it. But none have ever been proved. ☞

Return to the Preview & Review on page 476.

LINKING HISTORY & GEOGRAPHY

POLITICAL GEOGRAPHY: UNCLE SAM'S ISLANDS

Political geographers have long been interested in the connections between mother countries and their colonies, especially their locations and the movements between them. The aftermath of World War II and the accompanying tide of independence movements all but ended colonialism. Yet, surprisingly, the United States found itself in possession of an "empire."

An American Empire

1. How did the United States find itself in control of an "empire"?

Few Americans actually like the idea of colonies. After all, our nation once held that status, and we fought a war over 200 years ago to end it. Military conquest and strategic needs have created an American Empire that is a collection of island colonies.

Most American islands have their own governments and fly their own flags. But they are not independent countries. They use American currency, but are not actually part of the United States. They have no direct say in the decisions made for them by Congress. So, while the U.S. has never officially labeled its possessions as colonies, they are precisely that politically.

The total population of Uncle Sam's islands is just a little under four million persons. The total amount of land they occupy is a modest 4,000 square miles [10,360 square kilometers], less than the area of our third-smallest state, Connecticut. These islands stretch from the Pacific to the Caribbean.

Colonial Status and Benefits?

2. What advantages does colonial status provide for islanders?

The five largest American island colonies—Puerto Rico, the Virgin Islands, Samoa, the Northern Marianas, and Guam—are democracies in the sense that they all have locally elected governors and legislators. But they are definitely not independent, self-governing political entities. To varying degrees each possession answers to some branch of the federal government in Washington, D.C., and each is subject to American laws. Although considered citizens of the United States, islanders cannot vote in presidential elections. They elect as their representative in Washington one *non-voting* delegate to the United States House of Representatives.

The United States does not collect federal income taxes from the residents of its possessions. Instead, it allows the local governments of the islands to claim these monies. In addition, islanders do enjoy the opportunity to travel, live, and work in the states. More than 2 million Puerto Ricans have moved to the mainland, especially to New York, although many return to Puerto Rico when they retire. Some 85,000 Samoans, more than twice the population of American Somoa itself, now reside in Hawaii, California, and the state of Washington.

American Islands in the Caribbean

3. What islands in the Caribbean does America control?

Puerto Rico is both the largest and most populous of Uncle Sam's islands. Its people are American citizens, and they are generally proud of it. Many would like to see Puerto Rico become the 51st state. A small but vocal minority would rather see it become an independent nation.

Puerto Rico enjoys a key economic benefit in its relationship with the U.S. Tax laws give American companies exemptions from United States taxes on business done in Puerto Rico. These laws also allow the profits earned in Puerto Rico to go back to mainland offices without incurring taxes. Such laws are powerful incentives for American companies to build plants in Puerto Rico and to employ large numbers of Puerto Rican workers.

In 1917, during World War I, the United States bought some of Puerto Rico's neighboring islands, the Virgin Islands, from Denmark. The purpose of the purchase was to protect the Panama Canal from possible German submarine attack. The American Virgin Islands consist of 50 small islands and three larger ones—St. Thomas, St. Croix, and St. John.

Although poor in many natural resources, the American Virgin Islands are all rich in natural beauty and climate. Virgin Islanders have made the most of these. Each year nearly two million tourists visit the islands. The money they spend equals half the islands' total income.

The Pacific Possessions

4. Why do these islands welcome their present colonial status?

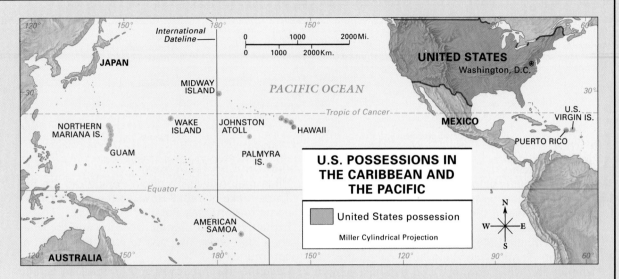

U.S. POSSESSIONS IN THE CARIBBEAN AND THE PACIFIC

United States possession

Miller Cylindrical Projection

Far to the west, in the South Pacific Ocean, is American Samoa. Its 38,000 people have been generally satisfied with how the American government has administered the island. Although many Samoans have left the island, they keep close ties to home. They send money home to supplement local incomes, most of which are earned from U.S. businesses. And even though the average income earned by American Samoans is less than that of Puerto Ricans or Virgin Islanders, it is three and one-half times that of residents of independent Western Samoa just 80 miles away. This is a powerful incentive to retain its current colonial status.

Guam is the most populous and largest American possession in the Pacific. Most Guamanians are proud to be Americans. Yet they are not entirely happy with the present relationship. In particular Guam would like the opportunity to operate more like Puerto Rico in encouraging American businesses to open in Guam.

Guam is an important military base. Much of its income is from military spending. But tourism is growing. Half a million tourists a year now visit the island, most of them from Japan. Meeting the needs of this booming industry is spurring development on Guam, which seems headed for a more secure economic future.

Few Americans have even heard of the Northern Mariana Islands. After being liberated from the Japanese in World War II, many of the islands in the Pacific were turned over to the United States. Most of these territories have

since voted for independence. The Northern Marianas, a group of 16 islands, on the other hand, feel they benefit from their status. The United States department of the interior is responsible to the United Nations for the islands' finances, communications, education, public health, agriculture, and legal problems. The islands receive about $33 million dollars a year for development. And they, like Guam, are attracting large numbers of Japanese tourists. Their sun-drenched beaches are just 1,400 miles (2,240 kilometers) south of Tokyo.

Beyond these larger possessions, the American empire consists of a handful of sparsely populated dots in the Pacific, most of which are important as military bases. Wake Island is a base for the air force. The Midway Islands and Kingman Reef are naval bases. Johnston Atoll is property controlled by the Defense Nuclear Agency, and Palmyra, about 1,000 miles (1,600 kilometers) south of Hawaii, is privately owned. Thus, in the 1990s, the United States is actually one of the few nations in the world retaining colonies. Interestingly, our "colonies" seem unlikely to want this to change in the near future!

APPLYING YOUR KNOWLEDGE
Your class will work in groups to report on U.S. possessions. Each group's report will include maps, pictures, and information on the people, geography, and economy of the possession. Display the reports in the school library.

CHAPTER 11 REVIEW

1945
World War II ends
★
United Nations is formed

1947
Truman Doctrine
★
Taft-Hartley Act
1948
Marshall Plan enacted
★
Berlin Airlift begins
★
Truman elected president

1949
NATO is formed
★
Communists control China

1950
McCarran Internal Security Act
★
Korean War begins
1951
Twenty-second Amendment

1952
Eisenhower elected president
1953
Department of Health, Education, and Welfare created
★
Truce halts the Korean War

1954
Brown v. Bo of Education
★
Communists attack in Vietnam
1955
Montgomer Bus Boycott

Chapter Summary
Read the statements below. Choose one, and write a paragraph explaining its importance.
1. After World War II the search for world peace led to the establishment of the United Nations, with the United States as a leading member.
2. President Truman concentrated on getting America back to "normal," and established a program called the Fair Deal. Congress, however, refused to pass most of the legislation.
3. Despite the help of the Marshall Plan to war-ravaged countries, communists gained power in Europe and China, leading the United States to adopt a policy of containment and involvement in the Korean War. It also led to McCarthyism at home.
4. The Cold War between capitalism and communism caused widespread tension.
5. President Eisenhower's foreign policy threatened massive retaliation based on brinksmanship, but avoided direct conflict.
6. Eisenhower's domestic policies were moderate, sometimes liberal, sometimes conservative. He supported the Constitution after *Brown v. Board of Education of Topeka* and sent troops to keep the Little Rock schools open.
7. John Kennedy's victory in 1960 brought the nation to a New Frontier. He was more assertive toward the communists than either Truman or Eisenhower. Kennedy's leadership, however, was cut short by an assassin's bullet.

Reviewing Chronological Order
Number your paper 1-5. Then study the time line above and place the following events in the order in which they happened by writing the first next to 1, the second next to 2, and so on.
1. Berlin Airlift
2. Korean War erupts
3. Cuban Missile Crisis
4. Fighting in Vietnam erupts
5. Kennedy elected president

Understanding Main Ideas
1. What major decision about Poland did the Big Three make at Yalta? How did the Soviet Union come to dominate Poland?
2. Explain how the Truman Doctrine and the Marshall Plan were intended to stop the spread of communism.
3. Describe the three-way split in the Democratic party in the election of 1948.
4. Why did President Truman order U.S. troops into Korea? Why did he remove General MacArthur from command?
5. Explain the case of *Brown v. Board of Education*. What did the Supreme Court direct in its unanimous decision?

Thinking Critically
1. **Resolving Issues.** Imagine that you are a delegate to the United Nations when it is first created. What three world problems would you most like to see resolved?
2. **Analyzing.** President Truman was not affected by the Twenty-second Amendment. Read the amendment and explain why the amendment did not apply to him.
3. **Synthesizing.** You are a magazine reporter who has been assigned to cover the meeting at Yalta in 1945. Write an article describing the meeting and explaining its historical significance.

Writing About History: Informative
Use historical imagination to write a thank you letter from a Berliner for the airlift of 1948-49. Use the information in Chapter 11 and other accounts of the airlift to help you write your letter.

Practicing the Strategy
Review the strategy on page 449.
Analyzing Historical Interpretations. Read the following passage by historian John Lewis Gaddis on the origins of the Cold War. Then answer the questions that follow.

956
Hungarians revolt against Soviets
★
Egypt seizes Suez Canal
★
Eisenhower reelected

957
Civil Rights Act passed

1959
Castro comes to power
in Cuba
★
Alaska and Hawaii
become states

1960
Kennedy elected president

1961
Alliance for Progress
established
★
Peace Corps established
★
Bay of Pigs invasion fails

1962
Cuban Missile Crisis

1963
Kennedy is assassinated

Historians have debated at length the question of who caused the Cold War. . . . Too often they view that event only as a series of actions by one side and reactions by the other. . . . officials in Washington and Moscow brought to the task of policy making a variety of fixed ideas, shaped by personality, ideology, political pressures, even ignorance and irrationality, all of which influenced their behavior. . . . it becomes clear that neither side can take complete responsibility for the Cold War.

1. Do you agree with Gaddis' reasoning that brings him to the conclusion that neither side was completely responsible for the Cold War? Why or why not?
2. Would you say that Gaddis' analysis was biased? Why or why not?

Using Primary Sources

The following excerpt is from an interview with Diane Nash, who led the movement to desegregate lunch counters in Nashville's department stores. The interview was published in *Eyes on the Prize: America's Civil Rights Years, 1954–1965.* As you read the excerpt, think about how the civil rights movement accomplished social change.

I think it's really important that young people today understand that the movement of the sixties was really a people's movement. The media and history seem to record it as Martin Luther King's movement, but young people should realize that it was people just like them, their age, that formulated goals and strategies, and actually developed the movement. When they look around now, and see things that need to be changed, they should say: "What can I do?"

1. How does Diane Nash offer encouragement to young people today?
2. What do you see that needs to be changed? How could you help to make that change?
3. The civil rights movement used nonviolent direct action. Why do you think the movement chose this strategy?

Linking History & Geography

Geographers often study the earth by dividing it into regions that share similar features, including similar political goals. During the Cold War in Europe, three separate regions developed—NATO members, communist nations of the Warsaw Pact, and neutral nations. Study the map on page 453 and similar maps in reference atlases. Then on an outline map of Europe show the members of NATO and the Warsaw Pact. You may also wish to create a map that illustrates the European Community, the Council for Mutual Economic Assistance, and the European Free Trade Association.

Enriching Your Study of History

1. **Individual Project.** Complete *one* of the following projects: Listen to recordings of the Army-McCarthy Hearings of 1954 and prepare a class report; prepare a report on the life of Martin Luther King, Jr., and his long struggle for equal rights; prepare a large version of the map on page 453 to show Europe during the Cold War. Use the map to illustrate a series of written reports on major events of the Cold War. Topics should include the Marshall Plan, containment, Churchill's Iron Curtain speech, the Berlin Airlift, uprisings in East Germany and Hungary, the establishment of NATO and of the Warsaw Pact, the brinksmanship of John Foster Dulles, and the 1955 Geneva Summit Conference.
2. **Cooperative Project.** Your class will use library periodicals and reference books to find out how meetings of the Security Council of the United Nations are conducted. Some of your class will represent the members of the council and discuss a matter of current world interest. Try to bring the matter to some resolution. The permanent council members are: the United States, China, Great Britain, France, and the U.S.S.R. Other members of your class will represent African and Asian countries, Eastern Europe, Latin America, and Western Europe.

Chapter 11 Review   487

UNIT FOUR REVIEW

Summing Up and Predicting
Read the summary of the main ideas in Unit Four below. Choose one statement, then write a paragraph predicting its outcome or future effect.
1. Most Americans believed in isolationism after the Great World War.
2. Totalitarian governments in Italy, Japan, and Germany began aggressive actions in both Europe and Asia. President Roosevelt sought ways to check them without becoming involved in a shooting war.
3. Hitler's war machine invaded Poland, touching off World War II. Japanese bombing of Pearl Harbor brought the U.S. into the war.
4. The Allies first defeated Hitler in Europe. They then turned their full attention on the Japanese. Atomic bombs dropped on Hiroshima and Nagasaki ended the war.
5. The horrors and inhumanity of the Second World War made people realize that war must now be avoided at all costs.
6. After World War II the search for world peace led to the establishment of the United Nations, with the United States as a leading member.
7. At home after the war, American presidents—Truman and Eisenhower—concentrated on getting America back to "normal."
8. Meanwhile communists gained power in Europe and China, leading to a Cold War between capitalism and communism.
9. John Kennedy's victory in 1960 brought the nation to a New Frontier. Kennedy's leadership, however, was cut short by an assassin's bullet.

Connecting Ideas
1. If you could have been a member of the White House staff during the Roosevelt, Truman, Eisenhower, or Kennedy administrations, which would you have chosen to work for? Why?
2. Describe the incident at Little Rock High School in constitutional terms. Explain the conflict between state and federal powers. How was the conflict resolved? Cite the part of the Constitution that explains how conflicts of this nature should be solved.

Practicing Critical Thinking
1. **Predicting.** What do you think might have happened if Germany had developed the atomic bomb before the United States?
2. **Analyzing.** One of the arguments for the internment of Japanese Americans was that the constitutional rights of citizens are suspended during wartime. Do you think that the constitutional rights of all citizens should be suspended during wartime? Why or why not?
3. **Evaluating.** The Cuban Missile Crisis brought the United States to the brink of war with the Soviet Union. Do you agree with Kennedy's decision to stand tough? Support your view.

Exploring History Together
1. Your group will prepare a multimedia presentation on one of the following: the *Brown* decision and school desegregation, Martin Luther King, Jr.'s, struggle for equal rights, the assassination of John Kennedy, or the fears and reactions in America during the height of the Cold War. Reports should include pictures and recordings when possible.
2. On April 12, 1945, President Franklin Roosevelt died suddenly. The new president, Harry Truman, told reporters, "I felt like the moon, the stars, and all the planets had fallen cn me." One member of your group will play the part of Truman, and the rest of your group will act as reporters. Stage a press conference for the class. The reporters will interview President Truman on his first day in office. Reporters should ask the president about some of the major decisions he will have to make.

Reading in Depth
Barker, Elisabeth. *The Cold War.* New York: Putnam. Contains a description of the beginnings of tensions between the United States and the Soviet Union.

Frank, Anne. *Diary of a Young Girl.* Garden City, NY: Doubleday. Provides a vivid account of a Jewish girl and her family as they hide from the Nazis.

Hichiya, M. *Hiroshima Diary.* Chapel Hill, NC: University of North Carolina Press. Presents eyewitness accounts of the devastation caused by the atomic bomb.

Litz, Richard. *Many Kinds of Courage: An Oral History of World War II.* New York: Putnam. Contains interviews with the men and women who took part in the Second World War.

Savage, Katherine. *The Story of the United Nations.* Portland, ME: Walck. Provides accounts of the international movement for peace and the beginnings of the UN.

Mikhail Gorbachev and Ronald Reagan meet in one of their several summits.

MODERN AMERICA

UNIT 5

Lyndon Johnson was determined to complete President Kennedy's civil rights agenda, and at last got his voting rights bill. Johnson fought an unpopular war in Vietnam and tried to build a Great Society by waging war on poverty. Both took staggering sums of money, even for the Affluent Society. His successor, Richard Nixon, continued the war in Vietnam despite growing American protests. Next came the revelation that the president was covering up a petty burglary at the Democratic headquarters in the Watergate building. When the president refused to turn over evidence, a congressional committee passed articles of impeachment against him. Nixon resigned and Gerald Ford became president. Ford was succeeded by Jimmy Carter, a former governor of Georgia, who was plagued by a hostage crisis in Iran. Ronald Reagan became president partly because many shared his suspicions of the Soviets. But before he left office, progress had been made in ending the Cold War. George Bush succeeded Reagan and continued many of his policies. Events in the Western Hemisphere and the Middle East quickly captured the new president's attention.

The Great Society

Point of View

Lyndon Johnson's first address to Congress as president.

❝ No memorial oration or eulogy could more eloquently honor President Kennedy's memory than the earliest possible passage of the civil rights bill for which he fought so long. We have talked enough in this country about equal rights. We have talked for one hundred years or more. It is time now to write the next chapter—and to write it in the books of law.

I urge you again, as I did in 1957 and again in 1960, to enact a civil rights law so that we can move forward to eliminate from this nation every trace of discrimination and oppression that is based upon race or color. . . .❞
Lyndon Johnson, 1963

Lyndon B. Johnson takes the oath from Judge Sarah T. Hughes, Lady Bird and Jacqueline Kennedy at his side.

Once again an assassin's bullet claimed an American president when John F. Kennedy was shot in 1963. And again the transfer of power to the vice president, clearly outlined in the Constitution, was orderly as Lyndon Baines Johnson succeeded to the presidency.

Perhaps no man has come to the presidency with greater qualifications than Johnson. He had served President Kennedy faithfully. Now he would be an active president. No one knew Washington more intimately. He decided to try to get President Kennedy's legislation passed by Congress as a memorial. He would build a Great Society to improve the lives of all people, but especially the poor and the powerless. And Lyndon Johnson, a Son of the South, would preside over the passage of the Civil Rights Act. For some the Johnson presidency reminded people of the early days of Johnson's great hero Franklin Delano Roosevelt. Could Johnson truly build a great society where others had failed?

Wide World Photos

1. THE JOHNSON PRESIDENCY

Preview & Review

Use these questions to guide your reading. Answer the questions after completing Section 1.
Understanding Issues, Events, & Ideas. Use the following words to describe the economic and social programs proposed by Lyndon Johnson: Civil Rights Act, Economic Opportunity Act, Head Start, Job Corps, VISTA, Great Society, Medicare, Immigration Act of 1965, Housing Act, Highway Safety Act.
1. Why was Lyndon Johnson considered highly qualified for the presidency?
2. For what reasons was Johnson determined to get President Kennedy's programs adopted by Congress?
3. What was contained in the Civil Rights Act of 1964?
4. What were some Great Society measures passed by Congress?
Thinking Critically. **1.** Imagine that you are an American citizen who has benefited from one of the Great Society programs. Write a letter to a friend in which you describe how this program has improved your life. **2.** If you had been a voter in 1964 would you have supported Johnson or Goldwater for president? Explain what factors you considered as you made your decision.

A Whirlwind of Energy

Before becoming vice president, Johnson served for many years in the House and Senate. A lifelong Democrat, he worshipped Franklin Roosevelt and admired Harry Truman. Yet as majority leader of the Senate he had worked with President Eisenhower, a Republican, on most legislative matters. His years in Washington taught him much about government and how to get things done.

In personality and style Johnson resembled Andrew Jackson more than any other president. He was both warm hearted and hot tempered. And like Jackson, he was energetic. He seemed to be everywhere—inspecting offices, signing bills, greeting tourists, settling disputes.

Johnson's first goal as president was to make sure there was no disruption in leadership. He was also determined to get Kennedy's program adopted by Congress. This would honor Kennedy's memory and establish Johnson's own reputation. Here Johnson's long service in Congress was an enormous advantage. He bullied, wheedled, and bargained. He had a way of brushing aside or smothering other people's objections and doubts. He would call in a hesitating lawmaker, rise intimidatingly to his full height of nearly six and a half feet, grab him by the lapels of his suitcoat, and say, "Come, let us reason together." More often than not the legislator would do what Johnson wanted, moved by a combination of awe and fear.

As a result of Johnson's hard work, Congress passed in 1964 a bill reducing taxes by over $10 billion and a **Civil Rights Act** prohibiting racial discrimination in restaurants, theaters, hotels, hospitals, and public facilities of all sorts. This Civil Rights Act also made it easier and safer for southern blacks to register and vote.

Congress also passed the **Economic Opportunity Act** of 1964 at Johnson's urging. This law sought to help poor people improve their ability to earn money. It attacked the problem at every level. It set up the **Head Start** program to give extra help to children at risk even before they were old enough to go to school. There was a **Job Corps** to train school dropouts as well as an adult education program and **VISTA,** a domestic parallel to the overseas Peace Corps.

Johnson wanted to leave his own legacy, as well. He tended to dislike the "Harvard intellectuals" left over from the Kennedy presidency. He gradually replaced most of them with people he had selected.

The Great Society

Lyndon Johnson easily won the Democratic nomination for president in 1964. Although there had been great popular support for choosing

Senator Barry Goldwater became the chief spokesman for the conservative wing of the Republican party. In the early 1960s his firm stand against communism earned him national prominence. His widely read 1962 book The Conscience of a Conservative: Why Not Victory? *was a statement of his views on American foreign policy and the use of force against communism. How did Goldwater's ideas differ from Johnson's?*

Robert Kennedy for vice president, Johnson chose Hubert Humphrey, a liberal senator from Minnesota. His Republican opponent was Senator Barry Goldwater of Arizona. Even people who disliked Goldwater's ideas tended to like him personally. He was sincere and frank, not the kind of politician who adjusts positions to the mood and the prejudices of the voters. Goldwater was extremely conservative. He spoke critically of such basic policies as the social security system. He favored selling all the facilities of the Tennessee Valley Authority to private companies. He wanted to cut back or eliminate many other long-established functions of the federal government.

In his acceptance speech at the Republican National Convention, Goldwater frightened many of his listeners when he said:

    " Extremism in the defense of liberty is no vice. And . . . moderation in the pursuit of justice is no virtue."

Most voters found Goldwater's ideas *too* extreme. Johnson defeated him easily. The Democrats increased their majorities in Congress as well.

Johnson then proposed what he called the **Great Society** program. With typical energy he sent Congress 63 messages calling for legislation in a single year. He stated his vision of the Great Society:

    " The Great Society is a place where every child can find knowledge to enrich his mind and to enlarge his talents. It is a place where leisure is a welcome chance to build and reflect, not a feared cause of boredom and restlessness. It is a place where the city of man serves not only the needs of the body and the demands of commerce but the desire for beauty and the hunger for community.

    It is a place where man can renew contact with nature. It is a place which honors creation for its own sake and for what it adds to the understanding of the race. It is a place where men are more concerned with the quality of their goals than the quantity of their goods.

    But most of all, the Great Society is not a safe harbor, a resting place, a final objective, a finished work. It is a challenge constantly renewed, beckoning us toward a destiny where the meaning of our lives matches the marvelous products of our labor.[1] "

[1]From *History of U.S. Political Parties* by Arthur M. Schlesinger

Congress approved nearly everything Johnson asked for. It created **Medicare,** providing health insurance for people over 65. It supplied huge grants to improve elementary and secondary education. The **Immigration Act of 1965** abolished the system of favoring immigrants from the nations of northern and western Europe. Future admission to the United States was to be based on the skills and abilities of the newcomers, regardless of nationality. There was also

INTERPRETING HISTORY: The Great Society

President Lyndon Johnson's program for "a Great Society" had ambitious and noble goals. The legislative package he proposed in 1964 offered something for everyone. Historian Doris Kearns described its scope in *Lyndon Johnson and the American Dream* (1976):

> "Medicare for the old, educational assistance for the young, tax rebates for business, a higher minimum wage for labor, subsidies for farmers, vocational training for the unskilled, food for the hungry, housing for the homeless, poverty grants for the poor, clean highways for commuters, legal protection for the blacks, improved schooling for the Indians, rehabilitation for the lame, higher benefits for the unemployed, reduced quotas for the immigrants, auto safety for drivers, pensions for the retired, fair labeling for consumers, conservation for the hikers and campers, and more and more and more."

The cornerstone of Johnson's program was his "war on poverty," which drew on his personal views and experience. As a young man in his native Texas he had seen firsthand the effects of poverty on farmers and on the students he taught in the state's public schools. Johnson's political beliefs were in the New Deal and populist traditions. He insisted that the government had a responsibility to try to make life better for all citizens.

Many factors influenced the passage of the Great Society legislation. Johnson was a master both at sensing and at influencing the public's mood. He reminded voters and Congress that John Kennedy had favored the Great Society programs. People were eager to honor the slain president by supporting them now that he was gone. Congressmen and women who had rejected reforms when Kennedy had proposed them hastened to push them through when pressed to do so by the public and Johnson.

Improved relations between the United States and the Soviet Union were also important because they allowed Congress to concentrate attention and money on domestic matters. The majority of Americans were quite well off but it was painfully obvious that poor Americans were not.

However, the personality of Lyndon Johnson was probably the most important reason why the Great Society laws passed so easily. Historians, journalists, and political observers have stressed Lyndon Johnson's ability to persuade people of different backgrounds to do what he wanted them to do. He was a master of the game of politics, rewarding those who backed his program, "punishing" legislators who did not. He believed totally in himself and in the idea of the general good. And he convinced wealthy and middle-class Americans that they too would benefit from programs benefitting the poor. He appealed to the desire of Congressmen and women to be remembered as having contributed to the public good. In his State of the Union message in January, 1965, he said: "A president's hardest task is not to do what is right but to know what is right." Johnson believed that the Great Society represented all that was "right."

---

a **Housing Act** to help pay the rent of poor people and a **Highway Safety Act.**

Under the leadership of Earl Warren, the Supreme Court continued to champion individual rights during these years. In the 1963 case of *Gideon v. Wainwright*, the Court ruled that the government must provide an attorney free of charge to anyone who is accused of a crime but is too poor to afford a lawyer. In the 1966 case of *Miranda v. Arizona*, a majority of the justices ruled that persons accused of crimes must be informed of their rights as soon as they are arrested. These rights include the right to have a lawyer present when being questioned by police and the right to remain silent. Police must also inform prisoners—in English or in the accused's native language if other than English—that anything they say can be used against them in a court of law. 🖎

Return to the Preview & Review on page 491.

Use the questions to guide your reading. Answer the questions after completing Section 2.
Understanding Issues, Events, & Ideas. Explain America's progress in the 1950s and 1960s, using the following words: standard of living, Affluent Society, factors of production, AFL-CIO, nuclear energy, synthetic textile, transistor, antibiotic, polio vaccine, white-collar worker, blue-collar worker, television, computer, fiscal policy, monetary policy.

1. What was the standard of living in America by the mid-1960s? What is meant by the Affluent Society?
2. What were some of the reasons that Americans were so optimistic after World War II?
3. What peacetime use of nuclear energy began in the 1950s?
4. What were some products developed after World War II?

Thinking Critically. Americans were optimistic about the future of their society in the 1950s and 1960s. Do you think that Americans in the 1990s still have this feeling of optimism about their country's future? Give reasons to support your answer.

2. A PROSPEROUS AMERICA

The Affluent Society

The 1950s had seemed settled and comfortable. Americans were enjoying the great prosperity that had developed after World War II. Yet some who looked forward warned Americans about potential problems. The Cold War and the space race had placed new and greater demands on American science, technology, and education. Not all Americans shared equally in the nation's prosperity, and the rising protests of African Americans and others against discrimination and poverty called for government action.

The election of the vigorous and energetic John F. Kennedy in 1960 had signaled that the nation was ready to take up the challenges of change. Kennedy had promised a bold new course for the nation. Lyndon Johnson's first actions as president showed he planned to follow a similar course.

In the mid-1960s the United States seemed to be entering a new Golden Age. Looking back over the 20 years since the end of World War II, most observers were struck by the tremendous advances that had been made. The **standard of living** of the nation as a whole—the measure of the necessities, comforts, and luxuries available—had never been so high. The percentage of poor people had fallen sharply and would probably be further reduced by President Johnson's Great Society program. The worst tensions of the Cold War with the Soviet Union seemed over. Science and technology had produced many new marvels and promised still further advances. America was the most productive country in the world. The question now, wrote the economist John Kenneth Galbraith in 1958, was how to use the abundant wealth created by this **Affluent Society.**

The dominant mood of the 1950s and early 1960s was one of optimism. This does not mean that everyone was satisfied with the state of American society. On the contrary, optimism made many people dissatisfied. They felt that society had serious weaknesses, especially the unequal distribution of wealth. But because they were optimistic, they believed that these weaknesses could be eliminated.

This hopeful, forward-looking mood had many roots. Victory in World War II was certainly one of the most important. Millions of soldiers and sailors came home confirmed optimists, if only because they had survived amid the death and destruction of battle. They and other millions who had not actually fought in the war found that victory strengthened their belief that the American way of life was superior to all others. The contrast between the United States and war-torn Europe further strengthened this belief, as did the dependence on American aid of both the Allies and the defeated Germans and Japanese.

So optimistic were the times that some people believed the Great Society would eliminate poverty from America. The resources to do so existed.

Although it may look like a foreclosure and bankruptcy auction of the 1980s, this family has on display every item purchased with the new easy credit available in the Affluent Society.

The Growing Economy

The unprecedented period of prosperity the United States had created by 1960 was built on what economists call "an economy of abundance." This meant that American businesses were able to produce more goods and services than Americans could consume. In the late 1950s a group of distinguished economists described the growing economy:

> America today has the strongest, most productive economic system in human history. . . . The United States, with little more than 6 percent of the world's population and less than 7 percent of the land area, now produces well over one third of the world's goods and services and turns out nearly half of the world's factory-produced goods. "

There were many reasons for America's remarkable prosperity. The United States had the key **factors of production**—the resources used to produce goods and services. The nation enjoyed abundant natural resources, an excellent transportation network, and a large and skilled labor force. In addition, businesses and industries became more highly organized and efficiently managed. More effective methods of distribution overcame problems of getting products to customers. Advertising created new ways to convince Americans they needed more and better goods and services. And American capitalism

Point of View

In *Henderson the Rain King* a Nobel Prize-winning novelist wrote of the desire for more.

> There was a disturbance in my heart, a voice that spoke there and said, *I want, I want, I want!* It happened every afternoon and when I tried to suppress it it got even stronger. . . . It never said a thing except *I want, I want, I want!* "
>
> *Saul Bellow, 1958*

The American Federation of Labor merged with the Congress of Industrial Organizations in 1955. What do you think the illustration on the seal is meant to symbolize?

The latest in clock-radios does more than wake you up as we can see in this picture.

and the new prosperity rewarded both individual effort and team-work.

The steadily improving relations between labor and management also helped spur economic growth. Naturally the labor force grew in size as the population increased. The two major branches of the labor movement—the American Federation of Labor (AFL) and the Congress of Industrial Organizations (CIO)—united to form the **AFL-CIO,** with George Meany, head of the AFL Plumbers Union, as president. The new union had 16 million members. American workers were convinced unions would protect their rights, and management showed a willingness in many instances to negotiate. Politicians eagerly sought union backing.

The Wonders of Science

New scientific and technological advances caused America's economy to boom. Increasingly efficient and complex power-driven machinery became common in almost every business and industry. Farms, mines, offices, even homes benefited. New goods and services poured out of American factories and businesses in ever-increasing quantities.

Scientific advances caused American farm production to soar. Fertilizers and insecticides and other applications of science to agriculture as well as advances in farm management provided Americans with the abundant and varied diet that made them among the best-fed people in the world. The United States exported huge amounts of farm products each year.

Many industries experienced explosive growth. The aircraft industry became a multibillion-dollar industry. Thousands of men and women were employed in plants producing huge new jets. Thousands more were employed by airlines as pilots, ticket agents, maintenance workers, and flight attendants. The electronics industry expanded in similar fashion. It had been spurred by the need during World War II for radio transmitters, radar, and other military equipment. After the war it continued to grow. The production of radios, phonographs, and countless new appliances for homes and offices made electronics one of the fastest-growing American businesses. Then in the 1950s the industry skyrocketed with the popularity of television and demand for television sets.

The products of the new technology that these discoveries made possible added to the general optimism. One of the most exciting was **nuclear energy.** The same laws of physics that had led to the atom bomb could be used to produce controlled nuclear reactions instead of violent explosions. The enormous energy released by these reactions could be converted into electricity. Some experts predicted that energy would soon be almost as plentiful as water and air. What

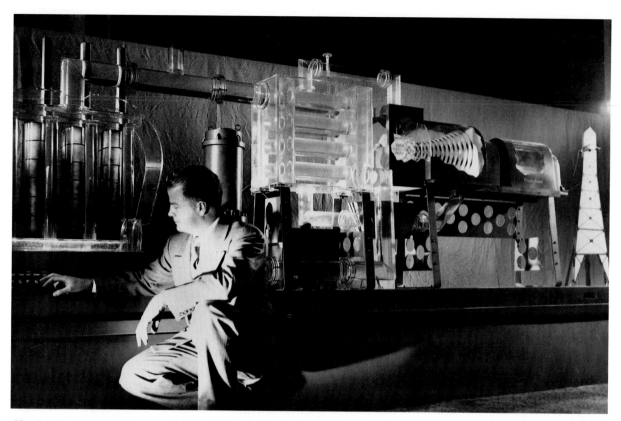

Charles H. Weaver, manager of the Westinghouse atomic power division, explains a station's workings.

this would mean in more wealth and leisure for everyone was easy to imagine. The United States had launched the nuclear-powered submarine *Nautilus* in 1954. By 1956 nuclear power plants could make and distribute electricity, and they began to do so in the United States in 1957. Few people then understood the problems that the nuclear age could bring.

Dozens of products and techniques that made life more comfortable and interesting were introduced in the years after World War II. Television and jet airliners and home air conditioners changed the way people used their spare time and where they lived and worked. New products included such **synthetic textiles** as Orlon and Dacron, water-based latex paint, small portable radios, and even smaller hearing aids. These radios, hearing aids, and a host of other devices used tiny **transistors** instead of bulky vacuum tubes.

Medical advances contributed to the general optimism. Penicillin, first used in military hospitals during World War II, became available to everyone. Along with other new **antibiotics,** penicillin practically eliminated many infectious diseases as major causes of death. The discovery by Dr. Jonas Salk of a **polio vaccine** virtually eliminated infantile paralysis, a particularly frightening crippler of children and some adults, like Franklin D. Roosevelt.

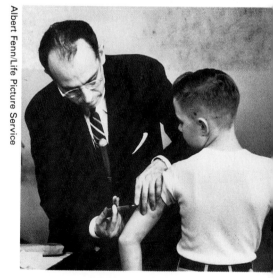

Dr. Jonas Salk gives 10-year-old Randy Bazilausakas his first innoculation of polio vaccine. How was the vaccine a godsend?

A Prosperous America   497

WOMEN IN THE LABOR FORCE, 1890-1990		
Year	Number of Women Employed Outside the Home	Percentage of the Total Labor Force
1890	3,600,000	16.8
1900	5,000,000	17.0
1910	7,700,000	19.5
1920	8,300,000	20.0
1930	10,600,000	20.4
1940	13,800,000	27.1
1950	18,300,000	29.6
1960	23,200,000	33.4
1970	32,500,000	38.1
1980	45,400,000	42.4
1990*	51,900,000	44.0
*Estimated		

Source: *U.S. Bureau of Labor Statistics*

A Changing Labor Force

The labor force that created the products of this period of American prosperity was significantly different from the American labor force before World War II. Many more women were now employed outside the home. In 1940 about 25 percent of the employees were women. By 1960 the percentage had risen to about 35 percent.

This rapid rise, the largest ever to that point, was the result of several developments. The demand for workers on the home front during World War II had helped break down prejudices against women, and it allowed women to show they could handle the same tasks as men in many jobs. Even more importantly, the rapidly growing economy created many more and new jobs. Most did not require sheer muscle. Because labor-saving devices had freed many women from household chores, they filled a large portion of these new jobs.

There was also a striking increase in the number of white-collar workers. In 1956 **white-collar workers**—teachers, doctors, lawyers, sales persons, secretaries, clerks, and others who worked in offices—for the first time outnumbered **blue-collar workers**—those who worked in factories or did other types of manual labor. Many of these workers held jobs in government. By 1960 nearly one of every seven workers was employed by the federal, state, or local government.

The Impact of Television and Computers

Even before World War II inventors had developed a way to transmit pictures similar to the way sound is transmitted by radio. As you know, this technique was called **television.** Only in the late 1940s, however, did manufacturers first offer reliable television sets—appliances to receive television signals—at prices that many people could afford. The demand for television sets proved to be tremendous. Throughout the 1950s television sets were sold at a rate of about 7 million a year. By 1960 nearly every family in America had at least one set. Television was one modern advance that even the poorest people seemed able to afford.

Television combined the virtues of radio and motion pictures. Techniques for broadcasting realistic sound combined with the newest visual techniques from the movies to make television an instant hit. Sports events such as baseball and football games were popular from the start. So were musical programs, comedy hours, and serial dramatic shows. Serials were known as soap operas because many of them were sponsored by manufacturers of soap and similar household products. News programs kept viewers informed and used pictures and maps to illustrate their reports. For the first time people could watch images of the news of the day.

Television soon became a force that influenced public opinion and events as well as one that reported them. For example, televised hearings exposed Senator McCarthy for the bully he was. Many observers believed that John F. Kennedy won the 1960 presidential election because he made a better impression before the TV camera than Richard Nixon. It was even suggested that if Nixon had used better makeup, the election might have gone to him. This was almost certainly an exaggeration. Still, the fact that people could think it was so shows how important television had become. And, as we shall see in the next chapter, when live television began bringing into American homes the war in Southeast Asia and inner cities torn with riots and looting, ordinary people were shocked to see this dark side of America.

The power of television and its almost hypnotic effect on viewers quickly became apparent. Critics warned of the potential hazards of watching what they called "the one-eyed monster." They claimed people would read less, even socialize less, as they locked themselves

TELEVISIONS IN AMERICA		
Year	Number of Households with Televisions	Percentage of American Homes with Televisions
1945	5,000	Less than 0.1
1950	3,880,000	9.0
1955	30,700,000	64.5
1960	45,750,000	87.1
1970	59,550,000	95.2

Source: *Bureau of the Census*

LEARNING FROM TABLES. *Americans soon fell in love with television. In which five-year period did television "come of age"?*

The Thomas Knox family of Cornelius, North Carolina, watches with delight the Ed Sullivan Show—*a popular program that brought vaudeville to television. Here Elvis Presley and the Beatles were introduced to the American television-viewing public. Why did the Chairman of the FCC call television "a vast wasteland?"*

in with their "TV dinners" to watch "the tube." The head of the Federal Communications Commission (FCC) challenged broadcasters in these early days to improve the quality of television. Would his review be much different today?

“ I am the Chairman of the FCC. I am also a television viewer and the husband and father of other television viewers. I have seen a great many television programs that have seemed to me eminently worthwhile. When television is good, nothing—not the theater, not magazines or newspapers—nothing is better.

But when television is bad, nothing is worse. I invite you to sit down in front of your television set when your station goes on the air and stay there without a book, magazine, newspaper, profit-and-loss sheet or rating book to distract you—and keep your eyes glued to that set until the station signs off. I can assure you that you will observe a vast wasteland.

You will see a procession of game shows, violence, audience participation shows, formula comedies about totally unbelievable families, blood and thunder, mayhem, violence, sadism, murder, Western badmen, Western good men, private eyes, gangsters, more violence, and cartoons. And most of all boredom. True, you will find a few things you will enjoy. But they will be very, very few. . . .[1]”

[1]From *Equal Time: The Private Broadcaster and the Public Interest* by Newton N. Minnow, edited by Lawrence Laurent

Perhaps equal to the impact on American life of the television was that of the electronic **computer.** People began to refer to the computer revolution. The first computers were huge, cumbersome, and slow. But advances in computer technology were startlingly rapid, and by 1960 there were 5,000 computers in use in the United States. In a fraction of a second these computers performed tremendously complex calculations. By the 1960s they could perform nearly 360,000 additions or subtractions or 180,000 multiplications in one second. Laboratories used them to analyze complex technical information. Computers took over many of the mental and manual tasks once performed by men and women. They measured, counted, filed, and stored information—usually more efficiently than humans. Banks and businesses used them for bookkeeping and billing. The government used them to collect statistics and to check income tax returns. And there were many other business uses for these fantastic machines. The flights into space would have been unthinkable before the computer came of age.

Eventually the United States would become a computerized society. Schools, businesses, laboratories, hospitals, banks, government offices, hundreds of other organizations, even private homes would come to rely on computers.

Advances in computer technology also led to developments such as robots which seemed straight out of science fiction. Robots—machines that perform the tasks usually done by humans—became commonplace in some factories. These industrial robots worked on assembly lines run by computers. Scientists and engineers have worked to develop robots for every setting in which humans work—even the home. In 1983 one science writer foresaw the development of household robots that seemed somewhat humanlike.

" Times change fast, especially on the technological landscape. . . . The development of the microcomputer [a very small computer] bolstered [supported] the belief that intelligent machines, able to work and act as well as ponder, could be built.

Today they are with us. . . . The Japanese are calling it a "robolution," a revolution that extends from factory spot welders to devices that slice sushi [cold rice cakes usually topped with raw fish] for overworked chefs to piano-playing home robots (available, with many other talents and a price tag of $42,000, from a leading Tokyo department store).

Robotics is breeding a new generation of machines that we may soon meet as pets. . . . BOB, short for Brain On Board . . . scuttles across the room, relying on ultrasonic detectors to avoid walls. When it senses a warm body with infrared detectors, it stops, swaying ever so slightly. BOB does get disoriented, a feature that makes it slightly human.

A bop on the head and it speaks—20 words with a mild robot accent.[1]"

Household robots have not yet become common. But who knows what the future holds?

Of course, the wonders of science are the result of human effort and creativity. As one robotics engineer told the science writer of the *Smithsonian* article:

"BOB is cute, a delightful gimmick, but even among those robotics engineers working on more serious problems, there is a singular awe and admiration of the human organism. . . . 'The only ones who really appreciate how smart people are, are those who try to do some of these things [get them to perform human tasks] with a robot.'[2]"

[1]From "Robots are playing new roles as they take a hand in our affairs" by Jeanne McDermott in *Smithsonian*, November 1983
[2]*Ibid.*

This very interesting double exposure shows one consequence of the computer revolution. A single operator in the foreground does the work of the 31 bank clerks in the background. Why did computers make many people apprehensive?

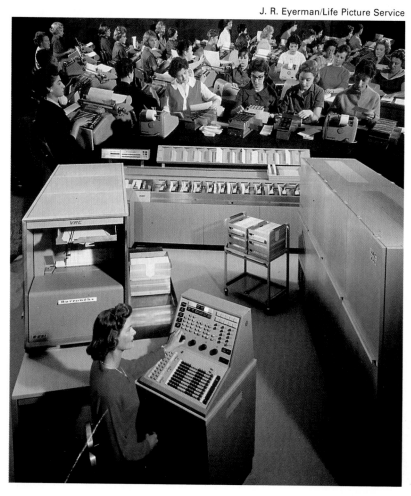

Fine-tuning the Economy

In another important advance economists seemed to have figured out a way to prevent depressions. When business activity began to slow down, they said, the government should stimulate it. There were two ways to do this. One, called **fiscal policy,** involved the federal budget. The government must increase spending and lower taxes. Its spending would increase the demand for goods and services through direct purchases by the government and through increased buying by businesses and individuals who received government money. Lower taxes would leave consumers with more money to buy goods.

The other method for preventing economic recessions or depressions involved **monetary policy.** It called for having the Federal Reserve Board lower interest rates. Then businesses and consumers could borrow money more easily in order to expand business output and increase consumer consumption.

If the economy began to grow too rapidly, causing prices to rise, fiscal and monetary policies could be reversed. If that happened, economists said, the government should reduce its expenditures, increase taxes, and raise interest rates. Economists claimed that it was possible to ''fine-tune'' the economy by shifting these policies back and forth. A steady rate of economic growth would follow.

For the most part in the 1950s and 1960s these methods worked. The Federal Reserve Board and government economic analysts kept an eye on indicators of business activity such as the rate of inflation, unemployment, and the prime rate—the rate of interest banks charged on loans to their best customers. They then worked to coordinate fiscal and monetary policies to keep the economy growing steadily. 🖻

The popular cartoonist Oliphant takes a dimmer view than the Federal Reserve Board of efforts to fine-tune the economy. Is this cartoon critical of fiscal policy or monetary policy?

Return to the Preview & Review on page 494.

Use these questions to guide your reading. Answer the questions after completing Section 3.

Understanding Issues, Events, & Ideas. Use the following words to explain the direction of American society in the 1950s and 1960s: baby boom, Sun Belt, National Aeronautics and Space Administration, suburb, development, shopping center, public housing project, shopping mall, Elementary and Secondary Education Act.

1. What were some of the reasons for the shift in population to the Sun Belt?
2. What changes did the shift to the suburbs bring in housing and shopping? How did this shift put a strain on the finances of city governments?
3. Why did suburban schools benefit from the education boom? Why did city schools suffer?
4. What caused college enrollments to jump between 1946 and 1960?
5. What were some of the ways that Americans used their leisure time in the 1950s and 1960s?

Thinking Critically. Imagine that you are living in a major U.S. city in the early 1960s. Your city is suffering from urban decay and you are very concerned about this situation. Write a letter to the mayor and city council suggesting ways to keep middle class families and businesses from moving to the suburbs.

3. A SOCIETY OF MANY MEMBERS

The Population Explosion

One result of prosperity and public optimism was a rapid increase in the population of the United States. During the Great Depression many people had been too poor to marry and have children. During the war millions of men were overseas. Between 1929 and 1946 the population rose quite slowly, from about 122 million to about 145 million. This was a rate of a little more than 1 million people a year.

In 1946 the depression was over and soldiers had returned home from the war. In that year the population increased by nearly 3 million. The new trend continued for about 20 years. By the end of 1965 the population of the United States had reached 195 million. We call this leap in the birth rate the **baby boom.**

The Sun Belt

After World War II the entire population distribution of the United States shifted. The American population had been moving westward since the first colonists arrived. But the shift in the 1950s and 1960s was as dramatic as that of the westward movement 100 years before. The territories of Alaska and Hawaii were admitted to statehood in 1959. This was a sign of their population growth and economic development. Western states also grew rapidly, and there was a similar population shift to the South. Florida and other southern states soon had population growth rates that rivaled those of western states.

The South and Southwest came to be called the **Sun Belt** because so many people were being drawn there by the warm climate. Retired people in particular moved to Florida and the Southwest to avoid the harsh northern winters. Home air conditioners, which became available in the 1950s, made the hot southern summers more bearable. By the late 1960s nearly 20 million homes were air-conditioned.

There were other reasons for the migration to the West and South. Many firms in the aircraft and electronics industries tended to locate in these regions where lower taxes and living costs meant reduced production costs. Thousands of young families followed, attracted by the high wages and pleasant working conditions in specially designed and newly built offices and factories these industries provided. The new federal highway network made it possible for people to move long distances easily.

The federal government encouraged the shift by establishing huge new facilities in the Sun Belt. The best known were the John F. Kennedy rocket-launching base at Cape Canaveral in Florida and the headquarters of NASA—the **National Aeronautics and Space Administration** in Houston, Texas.

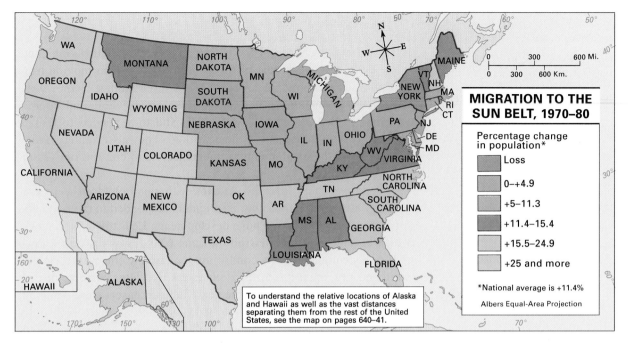

MIGRATION TO THE
SUN BELT, 1970–80

Percentage change
in population*

- Loss
- 0–+4.9
- +5–11.3
- +11.4–15.4
- +15.5–24.9
- +25 and more

*National average is +11.4%

Albers Equal-Area Projection

To understand the relative locations of Alaska and Hawaii as well as the vast distances separating them from the rest of the United States, see the map on pages 640–41.

LEARNING FROM MAPS. *What parts of the United States gained population during the 1970s? Why?*

Blast-off from Cape Canaveral as another Apollo mission is launched to land astronauts on the moon.

Point of View

From her book *Cities on a Hill*, this observation:

"In a sense, the residents of Sun City Center and their peers across the United States are living on a frontier. Not a geographical frontier but a chronological one. Old age is nothing new, of course, but for an entire generation to reach old age with its membership almost intact is something new. . . . In seventeenth-century France, for example, a quarter of all human beings died before the age of one, another quarter died before the age of twenty . . ."
Frances Fitzgerald, 1986

A Society of Many Members   **505**

The Shift to the Suburbs

A second major change in the nation's population distribution came when people in every part of the United States began moving from cities to their surrounding suburbs. These suburbanites, as they were called, were looking for the space, fresh air, privacy, and contact with nature that country life provided. Still they needed to remain near the cities where most of them worked. They also wanted to take advantage of the excitement, conveniences, and cultural opportunities of city life.

Young, recently married couples with small children were particularly attracted to the suburbs. Builders responded to their demand for homes by constructing huge **developments.** Levittown, New York, which became a suburb in itself on Long Island, was the best known of these developments. Its comfortable, relatively cheap tract houses stretched row upon row with a sameness that later came to disturb many Americans. But at the time nearly all purchasers were delighted with the houses. Most had three bedrooms and an extra bathroom. Dishwashers, washing machines, and dryers were already installed. Between 1950 and 1960 nearly a million new homes and apartments were built each year. The construction of schools, hospitals, roads, and offices accompanied this housing boom.

In and around the developments **shopping centers** sprang up, complete with supermarkets, department store branches, movie theaters, and dozens of small shops. The shopping centers were surrounded by acres of paved parking lots, for suburbanites traveled everywhere by automobile. Almost any product that local residents might want could be purchased in these shopping centers. Bulldozers busily cleared an estimated 3,000 acres (1,200 hectares) of land a day for these developments.

Joe Schershel/Life Picture Service

Jumprope and counting-out songs will be found wherever there are children. The game below is in Levittown, one of the first suburbs. On the opposite page children play in front of their Chicago housing project. How might the lives of the schoolchildren in each of these groups differ?

Few poor people lived in the new suburbs. The poor could not afford even the smallest tract homes. There were almost no apartment houses or other places to rent. In other words, suburbs were mostly for members of the middle class—office workers, shopkeepers, teachers and government employees—and well-paid blue-collar wage earners such as carpenters, electricians, and automobile assembly-line workers.

The government tried to improve the living conditions of poor people in the cities by putting up large **public housing projects.** These nonprofit apartments were rented at relatively low rates. Usually the rents were based on the income of the tenants.

The problem was that when the percentage of poor people in the cities increased, more and more middle-class people moved out to the suburbs. This seriously strained the finances of city governments because when the well-to-do left, income from taxes collected by cities fell off. Sales tax receipts dwindled as less and less money was spent on goods and services in cities, and property tax collections sagged as residents vacated more expensive city housing. Because cities had less money, public housing projects were largely neglected and soon become unsafe places to live and raise children.

Many manufacturers shifted to the suburbs to find room to expand and because property taxes were lower. This shift caused many of their employees to become suburbanites. Stores built suburban branches—**shopping malls**—and followed their customers to the suburbs. Each of these moves from the city to the suburbs also meant decreased city tax revenues.

Since many of the poor who remained in the cities were nonwhites, a new kind of segregation developed. The worst effects of this segregation were not felt until after 1965. Until then well-meaning people had high hopes that President Johnson's Great Society programs would solve this problem along with others.

A Society of Many Members   507

Jan Branneis/Life Pictures Service

Commencement at the University of California at Berkeley in 1962. There is no sign here of the free speech and protest movements that will shut down this university in the 1970s.

The Education Boom

With so many children being born after the war, thousands of new schools had to be built. Most schools in the suburbs were low, light, and airy brick buildings. In addition to ordinary classrooms, space was provided for teaching arts and crafts and for sports activities. Teachers' salaries rose, for the increased enrollments created a teacher shortage.

As wealthy and middle-class residents moved out of cities, schools there suffered when the tax revenues that supported them declined. The **Elementary and Secondary Education Act** of 1965 supplied large amounts of federal money to improve these schools.

Changes in higher education were even more dramatic in the affluent society of the 1950s. College enrollments jumped from 1.6 million in 1946 to 3.5 million in 1960. Clearly, many young people, whose parents had not had the opportunity, were going to college. Making a college education available to so many more people had important economic and social effects. There was a close relationship between the amount of education people got and the kinds of lives they led when their training was completed.

In business and in many other fields people with intelligence, imagination, and energy often succeeded brilliantly with little formal schooling. Education helped, but it was not essential. College training, however, was required for entry into the professions such as

STRATEGIES FOR SUCCESS

USING THE CENSUS

April 1, 1990 marked the bicentennial of the first census of the population of the United States, taken in 1790. In that year 17 U.S. marshals and 200 assistants went door-to-door to count the number of people in the brand-new American nation. The Constitution, ratified in 1788, called for a census within three years of the first Congress and every tenth year thereafter. The 1990 Census was the 21st such survey.

The most important reason for taking a census then (and now) was to ensure that citizens were fully represented in the federal government. Under the one person, one vote principle, states must redraw their Congressional election districts to reflect population shifts. (By law the number of representatives is set at 435.)

The census provides a wealth of other information about the American people. The 1990 census included questions about race and ethnic backgrounds, the disabled population, income and medical costs, energy use, housing, and much more. All the information is closely studied by various groups, especially those who work in various local, state, and federal government agencies.

The census contains an amazingly rich resource about trends in American society. Using the census data will give you a picture of the nation's people and insights into changes the nation and its people are undergoing.

How to Use the Census

To use the census, follow these steps.
1. **Select a topic.** Because the information collected by the census is almost overwhelming, it is necessary to focus on a specific body of information.
2. **Study the census data.** Check all the data about your topic. Remember that information may be provided in a variety of forms—in narrative descriptions, on maps, charts and tables, and on graphs.
3. **Note the trends.** Study the changes reflected by the data.
4. **Use the census information.** Draw conclusions and form hypotheses based on census figures. Remember that the statistics portray American society.

Applying the Strategy

Study the table of census data below. It illustrates information for the years 1970 and 1980 in three categories: land area, population, and population density. By how much did the urban population increase between 1970 and 1980? As you can see, it increased by over 17 million people. By how much did the rural population increase between 1970 and 1980? It increased by over 5 million. What is one conclusion you can draw from the data in this table?

For independent practice, see Practicing the Strategy on page 523.

CHANGES IN URBAN AND RURAL POPULATION DENSITIES, 1970-80						
	1970			1980		
	Land Area (sq. mi.)	Population (in millions)	Density (per sq. mi.)	Land Area (sq. mi.)	Population (in millions)	Density (per sq. mi.)
Total	3,540,023	203,212	57	3,539,289	226,546	64
Urban	54,103	149,325	2,760	73,930	167,051	2,260
Rural	3,485,920	53,887	15	3,465,360	59,495	17

Tears rolled down the cheeks of young boys and old men alike the day the decision was announced—the Dodgers were leaving Brooklyn. The team led by Jackie Robinson and Duke Snider was moving west. The fabled and successful franchise—four National League championships and one World Series crown in five years—was moving to Los Angeles in 1958. And to add to the shock of New Yorkers their Giants were heading for San Francisco that same year. Why were these teams leaving their loyal fans?

Teams had moved throughout baseball's history. Usually a team moved when attendance sagged sharply. New cities meant more fans—baseball's life blood. But before World War II these moves were limited to the East Coast and the Middle West. Most western cities were not as large and the West Coast was just too far away. It would take too long for opposing teams to travel there to play.

But the same changes that swept the rest of American society after the war affected baseball. Large numbers of people were moving to booming cities in the West and the Sun Belt, creating huge markets for sports franchises. Technology was producing rapid modes of transportation that pulled the widespread parts of the country more closely together. With the coming of television baseball entered the homes of millions of viewers who quickly became fans. Soon television revenues became a major source of income for a team. Suddenly the West Coast didn't seem so far away—or such a bad investment for team owners.

The Boston Braves had moved to Milwaukee in 1953 and the Philadelphia Athletics to Kansas City in 1955. (Both would move again—the Braves to Atlanta and the Athletics to Oakland—in search of fans and dollars.) But the Dodgers and Giants took the biggest step, moving across the continent to bring baseball to California and the West. Soon major league baseball had spread to all the corners of the nation—and the continent. Teams now play in Seattle in Washington, Houston and Arlington (near Dallas) in Texas, even Montreal and Toronto in Canada.

Other sports have followed baseball's lead. Major league sports teams now represent San

Los Angeles Dodgers on parade.

Wide World Photo

medicine, law, and teaching. Easier access to a college education after World War II opened the professions to a much broader section of the population than ever before.

Leisure Time

Advances in technology created an unexpected benefit for many workers: shorter workweeks. Between 1940 and 1960 the average workweek decreased from 44 to 40 hours. In some of the skilled trades it actually dropped to 35 hours. At the same time the average paid vacation increased from one to two weeks.

Americans began to look for ways to spend their increased free time and money. Millions bought new cars—nearly 50 million during the 1950s. By 1960 nearly 75 percent of all American families owned at least one car, and more than 15 percent owned two or more.

Antonio, Salt Lake City, San Diego, Portland, and Phoenix.

Technology has continued to influence baseball. In 1965 the Houston baseball team—then called the Colt .45's—moved into the engineering masterpiece of its day, an indoor stadium called the Astrodome. Baseball and football teams now play in huge indoor arenas in such places as Minneapolis, New Orleans, and Seattle. Several other teams, along with many college and university teams, play on the artificial surface created to replace the grass that simply would not grow under the Astrodome's roof. Most of those same college teams now use aluminum bats, which have replaced breakable wood bats on every level below the highest minor and major leagues.

Baseball, all America's traditional game, is part of American culture. As such it reflects many of the changes that influence society—the shifting populations, technological advances, and social changes.

The Astrodome with its artificial turf.

These families climbed into their cars and headed for vacations at the beach, the mountains, or the country. More and better roads were needed to handle the growing traffic. The Highway Act in 1956 provided funding for the eventual construction of 42,500 miles (68,400 kilometers) of new superhighways. State and local funds paid for thousands of miles of roads and streets. Motels, fast-food restaurants, and service stations soon lined these roads and highways.

Hundreds of golf courses and bowling alleys were built and were soon crowded. People bought boats of all descriptions. These soon appeared on lakes and harbors throughout the country. Attendance at spectator sports grew tremendously as well. Baseball and football teams built new stadiums to hold the crowds that numbered in the tens of thousands.

At home families gathered around their wonderful new television sets. By 1960 the television was turned on for at least 5 hours a day

Point of View

From *God's Country and Mine.*

"Whoever wants to know the heart and mind of America had better learn baseball, the rules and realities of the game—and do it by watching first some high school or small-town teams."
Jacques Barzun, 1954

TRANSCONTINENTAL TRAVEL*	
Vehicle	**Time It Took To Make Journey**
Covered Wagon	5 months
Steamship through Panama Canal	30 days
Overland Stagecoach	23 days
Railroad, 1875	7 days
Railroad, 1900	4 days
Railroad, 1945	2.5 days
Airplane, propeller	7.5 hours
Airplane, jet	4 hours
*From East Coast to West Coast	

LEARNING FROM TABLES. *As you can see from the table, the changing technology of travel has made the United States "smaller". Now you can travel coast to coast in a few hours. How long did it take by covered wagon? What changes do you think more rapid transportation has brought to America?*

in the average home. But television did not claim all of Americans' new leisure time. Sales of magazines, books, and records climbed steadily in the 1950s and early 1960s.

The New Generation

A major concern of many Americans in the midst of all these changes was the direction being taken by the young men and women reaching adulthood in the 1950s and early 1960s. Their goals appeared to be having plenty of money, a good job, a house in the suburbs, and comfortable retirement. Critics accused them of a lack of concern about politics and the issues confronting the United States and the world.

Critics even went so far as to claim that this tendency to avoid controversy and to conform was not confined to young people. They said that all age groups, men and women alike, seemed to share the same attitude of conformity. Among other critics, John Kenneth Galbraith and Rachel Carson warned Americans that they were neglecting the poor, causing the environment to deteriorate, and permitting cites to decay. In *Silent Spring*, Carson said,

❝ As the tide of chemicals born of the Industrial Age has arisen to engulf our environment, a drastic change has come about in the nature of the most serious health problems.[1]❞

She challenged people to protect the earth from the hazards

Rachel Carson wrote so movingly of the natural environment that not all her readers realized at first that she was warning America to change its ways before the environment deteriorated and cities decayed. Explain the title Silent Spring.

Return to the Preview & Review on page 504.

❝ created by radiation in all its forms, born of the never-ending stream of chemicals of which pesticides are a part, chemicals now pervading the world in which we live, acting upon us directly and indirectly, separately and collectively.[2]❞

[1]From *Silent Spring* by Rachel Carson
[2]*Ibid.*

It is a challenge Americans still face.

4. MOVEMENTS FOR EQUAL RIGHTS

Women Seek Equal Rights

Women in the 1960s continued their long struggle for equal rights. The 1964 Civil Rights Act had banned discrimination on the basis of sex as well as race. Still, women's organizations pressed for a Constitutional amendment that would guarantee their equality under law.

Tens of thousands of women from relatively poor families had always had to work. Middle-class women, however, had tended to work in the home after marriage. In the 1950s more and more of these women took jobs outside the home. They discovered that in nearly every field the wages and salaries paid to women were lower than those earned by men doing the same work. Moreover, the best jobs were rarely open to women. It was much harder for women to gain admission to law schools and medical colleges. In the business world women were rarely promoted to important positions, especially to those where they might be issuing orders to men.

Most male employers justified their practice by claiming that women usually worked only while waiting to be married. There was no use in promoting women, they said, because most would soon leave in order to marry and raise a family. When it was pointed out that more and more married women were working away from home, employers shifted their argument. They claimed that it was all right to pay married women less than men because married women did not have to support a family on their own!

Women naturally resented being discriminated against in the job market. When their numbers increased in the 1950s and 1960s, their resentment burst forth in the **Women's Liberation Movement.** The movement first attracted widespread public attention with the publication in 1963 of *The Feminine Mystique* by Betty Friedan. By ''feminine mystique'' Friedan meant the image of women society holds and the specific attributes of femininity.

Friedan had become interested in the problems of well-educated women after she made a study of graduates of Smith College, one of the nation's leading women's colleges. She discovered that a large percentage of these women were unhappy. Why, she wondered, were so many intelligent women so dissatisfied with their lives?

The answer, Friedan concluded, was that women felt held back by family responsibilities. They did not see themselves as individuals. In her own mind the typical woman was ''Mrs. Jones'' or ''Billy Jones' mother.'' Not even her name could she call her own.

Most women thought that they *ought* to be completely satisfied with their roles as wives and mothers, Friedan wrote. Were not popular magazines like the *Ladies' Home Journal* full of articles describing the satisfactions of raising a large family?

Preview & Review

Use these questions to guide your reading. Answer the questions after completing Section 4.

Understanding Issues, Events, & Ideas. Discuss the movements for equal rights that took place in the 1960s, using the following words: Women's Liberation Movement, consciousness-raising, National Organization for Women, Red Power, Indian Rights Act, American Indian Movement, Wounded Knee, poverty line, nonviolent direct action, Birmingham, March on Washington, Voting Rights Act, ghetto, Black Muslims, Black Panther party, white backlash.

1. What did Betty Friedan discover in her survey of women?
2. What were some of the goals of the National Organization for Women?
3. How did the Indian Rights Act of 1968 cause problems for tribal governments?
4. What did Dr. Martin Luther King, Jr., hope to accomplish by his policy of nonviolent direct action?
5. What did the formation of the Mississippi Freedom Democratic Party show about African Americans and politics?

Thinking Critically. **1.** Imagine that you are one of the founders of the National Organization for Women or the American Indian Movement. Write a list of goals which you would like to see the organization carry out in order to help the people for whom it was founded. **2.** Write an eyewitness account of the March on Washington and Dr. King's speech, Freedom Summer, or the Selma demonstrations. Be sure to include your reaction to the events you are witnessing.

Among the marchers for Women's Rights are Bella Abzug in her hat and Betty Friedan, right.

Many women who read *The Feminine Mystique* experienced what has come to be called **consciousness-raising.** They became aware that their personal doubts and dissatisfactions were shared by others.

Betty Friedan was not a radical. She did not argue that caring for a family was a bad thing. While she was writing her book, she was also bringing up three children of her own. But she insisted that the way to have a satisfying life was the same for women as for men: they must find some sort of "creative work."

In 1966 Friedan helped found the **National Organization for Women** (NOW). Its purpose was to end legal restrictions on women and see that they got equal employment opportunities in all fields. The government should provide day-care centers and other assistance for working women with small children, NOW officials argued. What would come of all this we shall see in a later chapter.

The American Indian Movement

Other American groups also struggled for equal rights, among them American Indians. During the New Deal period the federal government had given up the effort begun with the Dawes Act of 1887 to force Indians to copy white ways and adopt white values.

Instead, the Indian Reorganization Act of 1934 encouraged the revival of tribal life. Indians should choose their own leaders and run their own affairs, supporters of the new policy believed. Many Indians did so.

Indian schools began to teach Indian languages and history. Ancient arts and crafts were relearned and developed. A National Indian Youth Council, founded in 1961, pressed for the return of Indian lands in many parts of the nation. Some Indians coined the term **Red Power** to rally supporters.

Point of View

In *The Feminine Mystique* we read:

> **❝** Who knows what women can be when they are finally free to become themselves? Who knows what women's intelligence will contribute when it can be nourished without denying love? . . . The time is at hand when the voices of the feminine mystique can no longer drown out the inner voice that is driving women on to become complete.**❞**
>
> Betty Friedan, 1963

In 1968 Congress passed the **Indian Rights Act.** This law was intended to protect Indians against discrimination and mistreatment. But it had the unintended effect of weakening the governments the tribes had set up under the Indian Reorganization Act. These were often dominated by powerful chiefs who did not respect the needs and opinions of other tribe members. Many Indians used the new law to have these chiefs removed.

In 1972 a new organization, the **American Indian Movement (AIM)** began to use more radical tactics. The most dramatic of AIM's actions occurred in 1973 at the town of **Wounded Knee**, South Dakota. AIM leaders chose to publicize their demands at Wounded Knee because white soldiers had massacred Indian women and children there in 1890. The Indians held the town for weeks before laying down their arms.

The Struggle Continues

African Americans did not receive their fair share of the new affluence. As late as 1960 about half were still either poor or barely keeping their heads above the so-called **poverty line.** But in 1965 the economic condition of the average black seemed to be improving. More opportunities were opening up. The new AFL-CIO labor federation had promised "to encourage all workers without regard for color" to join their organization. Although some unions shut out black workers, the leaders of the AFL-CIO spoke out strongly against this practice. The United Automobile Workers and a number of other big unions achieved excellent records in promoting harmony between black and white workers. Perhaps even more promising, Jackie Robinson became the first black player in major league baseball. This quickly opened opportunities for blacks in many sports.

Jim Cartier/Photo Researchers

Seminole Indians in Big Cypress, Florida, work with their teacher at the Ahfachkee School.

> ❝ You suddenly find your tongue twisted and your speech stammering as you seek to explain to your six-year-old daughter why she can't go to the public amusement park that has just been advertised on television, and see tears welling up in her little eyes when she is told that Funtown is closed to colored children. . . .❞
> Martin Luther King, Jr., 1963

"Injustice anywhere is a threat to justice everywhere," said Martin Luther King, Jr., who knew, as did his followers, that an assassin would someday take his life. Try to listen to his famous speeches on records or tapes.

Martin Luther King, Jr.

The greatest leadership for blacks was provided by a Baptist minister, the Reverend Martin Luther King, Jr. After his success in leading the Montgomery bus boycott, King became a national figure. Everywhere he preached the idea of **nonviolent direct action,** as the best way to achieve racial equality. "Nonviolent resistance is not a method for cowards," he said. One must "accept blows from the opponent without striking back." Love, not hate or force, was the way to change people's minds.

The movement also used songs to tell its aim and hopes—songs of protest, adaptations of spirituals, and newly composed songs.

C. Ray Moore/Black Star

These expressed what King felt was fundamental to the movement's success: determination. The unofficial theme song of the movement was "We Shall Overcome," which was adapted from a version of an old spiritual by the staff at the Highland Folk School in Tennessee. It was sung everywhere the movement went. Here are the first three verses:

> ❝ We shall overcome, we shall overcome,
> We shall overcome someday.
> Oh, deep in my heart, I do believe,
> We shall overcome someday.
>
> We are not afraid, we are not afraid,
> We are not afraid today.
> Oh, deep in my heart, I do believe,
> We shall overcome someday.
>
> We are not alone, we are not alone,
> We are not alone today.

Oh, deep in my heart, I do believe,
We are not alone today.[1] ""

Protesters in Birmingham, Alabama,
are turned back by fire hoses.

In April 1963 King led a campaign against segregation in
Birmingham, Alabama. The police turned fierce dogs on the peaceful demonstrators and drove them from the streets with jets of water
from powerful fire hoses. King was thrown into jail. Yet this incident
proved the value of King's approach. Millions of Americans who
saw reports of the events on television were impressed by the demonstrators' courage and outraged by the brutality of the police. They
reacted strongly on the behalf of the blacks, writing letters to the
editors of their local newspapers and even joining protest marches.

Later in 1963, 200,000 people gathered in Washington to demonstrate peacefully in favor of President Kennedy's civil rights legislation. During the proceedings King made his famous "I Have a
Dream" speech. He dreamed of a time, he told the huge audience
who had come to this **March on Washington,** when all white and black
Americans could live together in peace and harmony. The printed
page can scarcely do justice to the moving and powerful speech King
delivered. But part of it is reproduced on the following pages:

[1]New words and music arrangement by Zilphia Horton, Frank Hamilton, Guy Cara-
wan, and Pete Seeger. TRO Copyright © 1960 and 1963 by Ludlow Music, Inc.

Movements for Equal Rights 517

The crowd of more than 200,000 that assembled in front of the Lincoln Memorial in Washington, D.C., marched to support President Kennedy's civil rights legislation. The speech Dr. King delivered that day seemed truly inspired by the heavens.

" Five score years ago, a great American, in whose symbolic shadow we stand today, signed the Emancipation Proclamation. This momentous decree came as a great beacon light of hope for millions of Negro slaves who had been seared in the flames of withering injustice. It came as a joyous daybreak to end the long night of their captivity.

But one hundred years later the Negro is still not free. One hundred years later, the life of the Negro is still badly crippled by the manacles of segregation and the chains of discrimination. One hundred years later, the Negro lives on a lonely island of poverty in the midst of a vast ocean of material prosperity. One hundred years later, the Negro is still languishing in the corners of American society and finds himself an exile in his own land. So we have come here today to dramatize a shameful condition. . . .

I say to you today, my friends, even though we face the difficulties of today and tomorrow, I still have a dream. It is a dream deeply rooted in the American dream. I have a dream that one day this nation will rise up and live out the true meaning of its creed: 'We hold these truths to be self-evident, that all men are created equal. . . .'

I have a dream that one day on the red hills of Georgia, the sons of former slaves and the sons of former slaveowners will be able to sit down together at the table of brotherhood.

I have a dream that one day, even the State of Mississippi, a state sweltering with the heat of oppression, will be transformed into an oasis of freedom and justice. . . .

I have a dream that one day, down in Alabama, with its vicious racists . . . little black boys and black girls will be able to join hands with little white boys and white girls as sisters and brothers.

I have a dream today!

I have a dream that one day every valley shall be exalted, every hill and mountain shall be made low, the rough places will be made plain and the crooked places will be made straight and the glory of the Lord shall be revealed and all flesh shall see it together.

This is our hope. This is the faith that I go back to the South with. With this faith we will be able to hew out of the mountain of despair a stone of hope. With this faith we will be able to transform the jangling discords of our nation into a beautiful symphony of brotherhood. With this faith we will be able to work together, to pray together, to struggle together, to go to jail together, to stand up for freedom together, knowing that we will be free one day. . . .

From every mountainside, let freedom ring. And when we let freedom ring, when we let it ring from every village and every hamlet, from every state and every city, we will be able to speed up that day when all of God's children, black men and white men, Jews and Gentiles, Protestants and Catholics, will be able to join hands and sing in the words of the old Negro spiritual: 'Free at last! Free at last! Thank God almighty, we are free at last!'[1] 99

[1]From Martin Luther King, Jr.'s "I Have a Dream" speech. Copyright © 1963 by Martin Luther King, Jr. Reprinted by permission of Joan Daves.

King was an exceptional person, but his optimism was typical of the times. "The believer in nonviolence has deep faith in the future," he once said.

No one knew better than Martin Luther King, Jr., that American society was far from perfect. Yet he believed sincerely that the nation was making progress toward the goals that he was seeking. Millions of other Americans, black and white alike, faced the future in the mid-1960s as hopefully as he did.

Freedom Summer

Yet despite Reverend King's optimism and even though President Johnson had signed the Civil Rights Act into law in 1964, many civil rights activists were impatient with the pace of reform. These activists sought to increase black political power, so they organized a massive voter registration drive in the summer of 1964. Nicknamed "Freedom Summer," the drive attracted volunteers from all over the country who came to the South to register black voters. As usual, segregationists vowed to prevent them from doing so.

Freedom Summer greatly increased the number of African Americans who were qualified to vote. African Americans then founded the Mississippi Freedom Democratic Party (MFDP). Led by Fannie Lou Hamer, a former sharecropper, the MFDP challenged the white delegation to the 1964 Democratic presidential convention. Although Democratic national leaders refused to seat the MFDP delegates, Hamer and her supporters had proved that the newly registered African Americans had considerable political clout.

At about the same time civil rights workers were organizing a voter registration drive in the town of Selma, Alabama. Almost half of the residents of Selma were African Americans, yet only one percent were registered voters. Martin Luther King, Jr., arrived at Selma in early 1965 to lead the campaign. Local police did everything in their power to block the demonstrations. Their attacks were so brutal that President Johnson sent in troops to preserve order. Under the watchful eyes of soldiers, more than 4,000 demonstrators—black and white—left Selma for Montgomery. By the time the marchers reached Montgomery, their numbers had swelled to more than 40,000.

Meanwhile, influenced by the lobbying of Clarence Mitchell of the NAACP and other civil rights leaders, Johnson demanded that Congress pass a **Voting Rights Act** that would outlaw literacy tests. Congress acted quickly, and in August 1965. Johnson signed the bill into law. Along with the Twenty-Fourth Amendment outlawing poll taxes in federal elections, ratified in 1964, this law finally guaranteed African Americans the right to vote.

Black Frustration

Legal segregation was dead. African Americans could vote and use public facilities without restriction. Yet many were unemployed or could get only low-paying menial jobs. Many lived in urban areas called ghettos. Their children attended substandard schools.

In the mid-1960s destructive riots erupted in many urban areas. There were outbursts in New York and Philadelphia in 1964. The next year six days of rioting in Watts, a black section of Los Angeles, left 34 people dead. Eleven people were killed during the riots in 1966, 83 more in 1967.

Most of these riots did not take place in the South, but in parts of the country where legal segregation was not an issue. But they showed the depth of black frustration and rage. Many young blacks began to call for racial separation, not integration.

The first black separatist leader of the 1960s was an eloquent ex-convict named Malcolm Little. While in prison, he had been converted to an anti-white religious sect, the Nation of Islam, whose members called themselves **Black Muslims.** Little changed his name to Malcolm X, the *X* standing for his long-lost African last name. He urged African Americans to take pride in being black. They should reject white society, he said, and refuse to play any part in it. And they should arm themselves in order to protect their rights. As he wrote in his autobiography:

> " I *am* for violence if non-violence means we continue postponing a solution to the American black man's problem— just to *avoid* violence. I don't go for non-violence if it also means a delayed solution. To me a delayed solution is a non-solution. Or I'll say it another way. If it must take violence to get the black man his human rights in this country, I'm *for* violence. . . . no matter what the consequences. . . .[1]"

[1]From *The Autobiography of Malcolm X* by Malcolm X

In 1964, Malcolm X changed drastically. He began to call for *cooperation* with whites. Shortly after he did so, however, he was assassinated by Black Muslim gunmen. But the idea of black separatism became increasingly popular among radicals. A new leader, Stokely Carmichael, called for "Black Power!," usually accompanied by a clenched-fist salute. Another black-power group that gained widespread attention was the **Black Panther party,** which for a few years attracted many recruits among black teenagers.

Veteran black leaders such as Bayard Rustin, a former Freedom Rider, argued that black separatism was a dead end. And black separatism was never an important political movement. But it was a powerful expression of anger and frustration. By wearing African dress and hairstyles, American blacks displayed a pride in their ancestry. By withdrawing from social relationships with whites, they expressed their unease about participating in a society that had been cruel to their people for centuries. In aggressive speeches, they gave voice to the pent-up anger toward the heritage of insult and indignity that whites had imposed on them.

Although the black power movement was quite small in size and relatively short lived, it caused great uneasiness among whites. Hadn't African Americans made enough progress, some asked. A **white backlash** developed, causing a coolness between members of both races. The spirit of dedication to a just cause that had united white and black civil rights activists began to fade from sight. 🖅

Point of View

Lerone Bennett, Jr. described the riots of the 1960s in *Before the Mayflower.*

> "Events hurried on now at an ever-dizzier pace. Everywhere there was whirling movement, confused cries, burglar alarms, screaming sirens, shouting teenagers, the crunch of billy clubs, the whang of rifles, a thunderous, thousand-tongued tumult of blood and fire and steel. At first blush it seemed that all was confusion and disorder. But underneath there was a wild kind of order that made Watts a major insurrection comparable in its day and time to Nat Turner's historic attack 134 years before. Beneath the surface disorder, shielded from the eyes of reporters and history, there were even nameless leaders—bold young men and even bolder women who left their imprint on a rebellion staged for the purpose of asserting that black people would no longer submit to the degradations forced on them."
> Lerone Bennett Jr., 1988

Return to the Preview & Review on page 513.

CHAPTER 12 REVIEW

1957
Nuclear
power plants
begin to
generate electricity

1958
The Affluent Society published

1963
March on Washin
and "I Have a
Dream" speech
★
*The Feminine
Mystique* publishe
★
Kennedy
assassinated;
Johnson becomes
president

1964
Civil Rights Act
★
Johnson elected
president

Chapter Summary

Read the statements below. Choose one, and write a paragraph explaining its importance.

1. Lyndon Johnson used forceful personality and his experience in government to accomplish many of his goals as president.
2. As a result of Johnson's hard work, Congress passed the laws which enacted his domestic program called the Great Society.
3. The unprecedented period of prosperity in the 1950s and early 1960s led to a mood of optimism in the United States.
4. The labor force changed following World War II as the number of women and percentage of white-collar workers increased.
5. Television and the computer had a significant impact on American life in the 1950s and 1960s.
6. A shift in population occurred following World War II when many Americans moved to the Sun Belt and from the cities to the suburbs.
7. The Women's Liberation Movement gained momentum following the publication of *The Feminine Mystique* in 1963.
8. Red Power became a rallying point for Indian Rights activists in the 1960s.
9. Reverend King continued to gain support for the civil rights movement through nonviolent direct action. But other leaders, such as Malcolm X and Stokely Carmichael, sought faster progress through more radical methods.

Reviewing Chronological Order

Number your paper 1–5. Then study the time line above and place the following events in the order in which they happened by writing the first next to 1, the second next to 2, and so on.

1. American Indian Movement founded
2. National Organization for Women founded
3. Johnson elected president
4. March on Washington
5. Elementary and Secondary Education Act passed

Understanding Main Ideas

1. Explain why the United States was called the Affluent Society in the mid-1960s.
2. What were some wonders of science that were developed after World War II?
3. Explain the difference between monetary policy and fiscal policy. Tell how economists planned to use each to prevent future depressions.
4. What were the good and bad effects of the growth of the suburbs following World War II?
5. Describe the efforts of African Americans, women, and Indians in the 20 years following World War II to secure equal rights.

Thinking Critically

1. **Evaluating.** Television began to greatly influence public opinion in the United States in the 1950s, and it continues to do so today. Discuss whether you think television has had a positive or negative effect on society. If you think its effect has been negative, suggest several ways that the television industry could improve its programming.
2. **Problem Solving.** Imagine that you are an African American in 1963 and have just participated in the March on Washington. You heard Dr. King's "I Have a Dream" speech which has greatly inspired you. Make a list of some of the problems faced by African Americans in the early 1960s and suggestions for how these problems may be solved.
3. **Comparing Ideas.** A major concern of many adult Americans in the 1950s and early 1960s was the direction taken by many young people who were becoming adults during this period. Their goals appeared to be having plenty of money, a good job, a house in the suburbs, and comfortable retirement. They were accused of

965
Great Society program
proposed and passed
★
Immigration Act
★
Elementary and Secondary Education Act

966
National Organization for Women formed

1968
Indian Rights Act

1972
American
Indian Movement

1973
Wounded Knee

conforming and lacking in concern for the poor and the environment. Would you say that this description could be used to describe America's youth today? Why or why not?

Writing About History: Classificatory

America's Affluent Society is discussed in this chapter. Write a newspaper editorial in which you outline how America's abundant wealth and resources can be put to better use so that all of its people benefit from them. Conclude your editorial by mentioning which of America's riches you most appreciate and how they have benefited you and your family.

Practicing the Strategy

Review the strategy on page 509.
Using the Census. Study the census data on page 509 and answer these questions.

1. Did the total of square miles increase or decrease in urban areas between 1970 and 1980?
2. Did urban density increase or decrease from 1970 to 1980?
3. What conclusion can you draw from the information you found regarding square miles and density?

Using Primary Sources

In 1963 during an attempted nonviolent campaign against segregation in Birmingham, Alabama, Dr. Martin Luther King, Jr., was arrested. He drew severe criticism from local white clergymen, who accused Dr. King of being an outside agitator. They claimed his demonstrations ignited violence by forcing a confrontation between demonstrators and police. In answer to these accusations Dr. King wrote his now famous "Letter from a Birmingham Jail" while imprisoned in that city. As you read the following excerpt from Dr. King's letter, think about the wisdom of his words and the impact they had on those who continued using nonviolent methods in their campaign for civil rights.

In your statement you assert that our actions, even though peaceful, must be condemned because they precipitate [cause] violence. But is this a logical assertion [statement]? Isn't this like condemning a robbed man because his possession of money precipitated the evil act of robbery? . . . We must come to see that, as the federal courts have consistently affirmed, it is wrong to urge an individual to cease his efforts to gain his basic constitutional rights because the quest may precipitate violence. Society must protect the robbed and punish the robber.

1. Who do you think Dr. King is referring to when he uses the term "robber?"
2. What is it that Dr. King implies is being stolen by the robber?
3. Do you agree or disagree with Dr. King that it is wrong to tell people not to seek their constitutional rights because it "may precipitate violence?" Explain your answer.

Linking History & Geography

People moved from rural to urban areas in ever-increasing numbers in the decades following World War II. To better understand the dramatic impact of this population shift, study the map on page 505. Then with your classmates prepare a map of the United States showing the major urban areas in 1940 and in 1980. You may need to refer to an historical atlas, the *Statistical Abstract of the United States*, or other reference books for the years 1940 and 1980 to complete your maps.

Enriching Your Study of History

1. **Individual Project.** Prepare an oral report on *one* of the following changes or trends that occurred in the 1950s and 1960s: advances in science and technology; population growth and shifts; higher standard of living. Tell how these changes affected American life in the 1950s and 1960s.
2. **Cooperative Project.** Your group will make a collage that illustrates leisure time activities enjoyed by Americans today. Each of you should contribute to the collage by bringing in as many pictures from magazines and newspapers as you can find on the subject or subjects chosen by your group.

Chapter 12 Review   **523**

The Vietnam Era

In August 1964 President Johnson announced that North Vietnamese gunboats had attacked the American destroyer *Maddox* in the Gulf of Tonkin, off the coast of Southeast Asia. He called upon Congress to approve and support in advance "the determination of the president, as commander in chief, to take all necessary measures to repel any armed attack against the forces of the United States." Congress voted for this resolution almost unanimously. As we shall soon see, this is another example of how an event that seems unimportant at the time can have far-reaching and unexpected historical significance. What consequences would commitment to the war in Vietnam have for America and its people?

Larry Burrows/Collection

American troops land at Da Nang to pit their sophisticated weaponry against the tunnels and jungle hideouts of the Viet Cong. What vehicle did the U.S. commonly use to move men about in the war? This picture gives you a hint. After reading about the war in this section, explain why the U.S. used that vehicle.

1. WAR IN VIETNAM

The Domino Theory

In the summer of 1964 the former French colony of Vietnam was torn by war. Communist North Vietnam was supplying aid to pro-communist South Vietnamese guerrillas, who were known as the **Viet Cong.** The Viet Cong had been seeking to overthrow the government of South Vietnam, which was pro-American, ever since Vietnam had been divided into two countries in 1954. They controlled large parts of the country, especially the rural regions.

While Dwight Eisenhower was president, a small number of American military advisers had been sent to South Vietnam to help train the South Vietnamese army. The United States also gave South Vietnam large sums of money for military supplies and economic aid. President Kennedy continued this policy.

The president of South Vietnam, Ngo Dinh Diem, was incompetent and unpopular. Many of the men around him were openly corrupt. Shortly before President Kennedy was assassinated, a group of Vietnamese army officers overthrew the Diem government and killed Diem. Unfortunately, they proved no better than he at defeating the Viet Cong.

President Johnson did not change American policy toward Vietnam until the Gulf of Tonkin affair. Even then he was mainly interested in *appearing* to be more aggressive. His Republican opponent in the 1964 presidential election, Senator Barry Goldwater, demanded that the United States make a bigger effort to "check communism" in Vietnam. Johnson hoped that the **Tonkin Gulf Resolution** which gave him broad war powers would convince the voters that he was pursuing that objective vigorously. But he made a special point of not getting *too* involved in Vietnam. He insisted that he "would never send American boys to do the fighting that Asian boys should do themselves."

After winning the election, however, Johnson decided to step up American military activity in Vietnam. This would restore morale to the South Vietnamese. President Eisenhower had warned of a "falling domino" effect if communist expansion were allowed to go unchallenged. He had said in 1954:

❝ You have a row of dominoes set up, you knock over the first one, and . . . the last one . . . will go over very quickly. ❞

According to the **domino theory,** if South Vietnam was controlled by the communists, its neighbors, Laos and Cambodia, would also become communist. Then all Southeast Asia, and perhaps even India with its hundreds of millions of people, would follow.

Use these questions to guide your reading. Answer the questions after completing Section 1.
Understanding Issues, Events, & Ideas. Use the following words to describe American involvement in Vietnam: Viet Cong, Gulf of Tonkin Resolution, domino theory, escalation, doves, hawks, Saigon, Tet offensive.
1. How did Johnson respond to communist expansion in Southeast Asia after the Tonkin Gulf Resolution?
2. How was Johnson's Vietnam policy different from the policies of Eisenhower and Kennedy?
3. Why did President Johnson and his advisers believe they were acting with restraint in Vietnam?
4. What effect did the Tet offensive have on Americans?
Thinking Critically. 1. Why do you think Congress passed the Tonkin Gulf Resolution so easily? 2. What do you think the American officer meant when he said that "we had to destroy it in order to save it?" Imagine that you are Vietnamese. How would you react to such a remark?

A priest and an army sergeant come to tell Gene and Peg Mullen that their son has been killed in Vietnam.

"Gene looked beyond Father Shimon to the sergeant and asked again, "Is my boy *dead?*"

"Let's go into the house, Gene," Father Shimon said. "I want to talk to you there."

"No!" Gene said, not moving. "I want to *know!* Tell me, *is my boy dead?*"

"I can't tell you here," Father Shimon said, his hand fluttering up toward Gene's shoulder. "Come into the house with us please?"

Gene spun away before the priest's pale fingers could touch him.

Peg Mullen heard the back door open, heard Gene rushing up the stairs into the kitchen, heard him shouting, "It's Mikey! It's Mikey!" his voice half a scream. . . ."
From *Friendly Fire*,
C.D.B. Bryan, 1976

Recent events in Korea and the Cuban Missile Crisis seemed to show that the way to check communist expansion was by firmness and force. President Johnson, urged on by a military with unprecedented power and prestige, felt he could not waver. He said:

"We could tuck our tails between our legs and run for cover. That would just whet the enemy's appetite for greater aggression and more territory, and solve nothing."

The assumption behind this reasoning was that the fighting in South Vietnam was between local Vietnamese patriots and "outside" communists. If the outsiders were allowed to conquer the country, the argument ran, they would be encouraged to press farther. In reality the struggle in South Vietnam was a civil war between supporters of the government and the Viet Cong. "Outside" communists from China and the Soviet Union were supplying the Viet Cong with weapons and advice, just as the United States was helping the anti-communist government of South Vietnam. The communist government of North Vietnam was deeply involved too. Its objective was to unite the two Vietnams under a communist regime.

America Escalates the War

In February 1965 Johnson made a fateful decision. After Diem's assassination in late 1963, the Viet Cong had gained control of more and more South Vietnamese villages. The war now became a test of the president's will. "I will not be the President who saw Southeast Asia go the way China went," he said, referring to the communist takeover in China in 1949. He ordered the air force to bomb selected targets in North Vietnam. In March he sent two battalions of marines to Vietnam. Their job was to protect the air base from which the bombers were operating. Soon more troops had to be sent in to reinforce the marines!

A few months later the American forces in Vietnam were given permission to seek out and attack Viet Cong units. Still, many restrictions on how American troops could fight the war remained. Nonetheless, more troops were shipped to Vietnam. By the end of 1965 there were 185,000 American fighting men in the country.

This steady **escalation,** or increase, in American military strength and involvement in Vietnam went on for three years. Each increase brought more North Vietnamese into the conflict in support of the Viet Cong. By 1968 more than half a million Americans were fighting in Vietnam. Yet Congress never officially declared war. Johnson instead waged war by the authority of the Tonkin Gulf Resolution, which had seemed to have little historical significance when it was passed by Congress in 1964.

The president and his advisers thought they were acting with great restraint. The enormous difference in size and wealth between

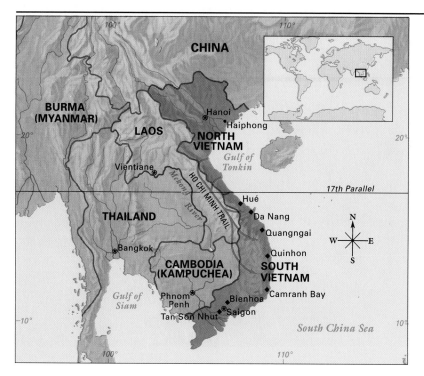

→ Ho Chi Minh Trail

◆ U.S. base

0   200   400 Mi.

0   200   400 Km.

Mercator Projection

LEARNING FROM MAPS. *Compare this map to the one of Korea on page 461. Note that the geography of Vietnam is strikingly similar to that of Korea. Describe how the geography—especially aspects of relative location—are similar. After reading about President Nixon's decision to extend U.S. bombing into Cambodia, study this map. What was the geographic reasoning behind Nixon's decision?*

the United States and North Vietnam lulled them into believing that the United States could win the war whenever it chose. How, asked the advisers, could a tiny country like North Vietnam successfully resist the United States? They wanted to risk the lives of as few Americans as possible. When each escalation proved to be not enough, they hoped just one more increase would do the job.

But North Vietnam was successful because the war in Vietnam was like no other war Americans had fought. Much of it was guerrilla warfare. The enemy, the Viet Cong, wore no uniforms and fought by ambush and by night. By day they blended with the rest of the population. Much of the war was fought in dense jungles and rugged mountains where tanks, even jeeps, were almost useless. Small squads of American soldiers slowly worked their way through vegetation so thick they could see only a few feet in any direction. The enemy could be hiding anywhere. Snipers would pick off one or two men and then disappear. One soldier recalled an attack in the jungle:

  ❝ Men all around me were screaming. The fire [shooting] was now a continuous roar. We were even being fired at by our own guys. No one knew where the fire was coming from, and so the men were shooting everywhere. Some were in shock and were blazing away at everything they saw or imagined they saw. . . .[1] ❞

[1]From "Death in the Ia Drang Valley" by Jack Smith in the *Saturday Evening Post,* January 28, 1967

War in Vietnam   **527**

The United States became mired in a land war in Asia, just as the French had before them. Critics sharply opposed the war. Much of the antiwar sentiment focused on American soldiers. Later came a time of reconciliation. Many efforts today are directed at helping Vietnam veterans find their place in society. Do you think the government has this responsibility after a war?

Mines and booby traps—hidden explosive devices—made movement through the countryside terrifying. Added to these difficulties were the limits placed on American troops. They often could not fire until fired upon, could not pursue the enemy in many places, could not bomb certain areas. And while American forces struggled in Vietnam, large numbers of people at home turned against the war, focusing much of their opposition on the soldiers fighting the war on the orders of others.

Time passed without victory. Large numbers of Americans decided that the war was a terrible mistake. Some claimed that keeping the government of South Vietnam, which was weak and very unpopular with the South Vietnamese people, in power was not worth the cost in American lives and money. Others argued that it was wrong for Americans to be killing people in a small country that was quite literally on the other side of the world.

The fighting in Vietnam was savage. Both sides were capable of extreme cruelty. Prisoners were sometimes killed or tortured. Hundreds of civilians died in air raids. Peaceful villages were burned to the ground to root out possible Viet Cong sympathizers. Local South Vietnamese officials were murdered by Viet Cong terrorists.

Americans who wanted to stop the war were called **doves,** after the traditional bird of peace. Those who insisted that the war must be fought until it was won were known as **hawks.** For a long time the hawks were in the majority. National pride and hatred of communism made many of the hawks believe that it would be cowardly and shameful to pull out of South Vietnam.

Both sides grew more vocal as escalation proceeded. President Johnson expressed the determination of the United States government to see victory in Vietnam. Early in 1965 he said:

> " Tonight Americans and Asians are dying for a world where each people may choose its own path to change.
>
> Why must we take this painful road?
>
> Why must this nation endanger its ease, and its interest, and its power for the sake of a people so far away?
>
> We fight this war because we must fight if we are to live in a world where every country can shape its own destiny [future]. And only in such a world will our own freedom be secure. . . .
>
> Why are we in South Vietnam?
>
> We are there because we have a promise to keep. Since 1954 every American president has offered support to the people of South Vietnam. We have helped to build, and we have helped to defend. Thus over many years have we made a national pledge to help South Vietnam defend its independence.
>
> And I intend to keep that promise.
>
> To dishonor that pledge, to abandon this small and brave nation to its enemies, and to the terror that must follow, would be an unforgivable wrong. . . .[1] "

Equally determined opponents spoke out against American involvement in the war. One opponent, Senator J. William Fulbright of Arkansas, chairman of the Senate Foreign Relations Committee, said:

> " We [the U.S.] are in a war to 'defend freedom' in South Vietnam. . . .
>
> One wonders how much the American commitment to Vietnamese freedom is also a commitment to American pride—the two seem to have become part of the same package. When we talk about the freedom of South Vietnam, we may be thinking about how our pride would be injured if we settled for less than we set out to achieve. We may be thinking about our reputation as a great power, fearing that a compromise settlement would shame us before the world, marking us as a second-rate people with failing courage and determination.
>
> Such fears are senseless. They are unworthy of the richest, most powerful, most productive, and best educated people in the world. . . .[2] "

[1]From "Peace Without Conquest," a speech by Lyndon B. Johnson on April 7, 1965
[2]From *The Arrogance of Power* by J. William Fulbright

STRATEGIES FOR SUCCESS

DRAWING CONCLUSIONS

One of the most important ways to use the information you read and study is as a basis to draw conclusions. A conclusion is a reasoned judgment arrived at by studying evidence. Historians draw conclusions based on evidence from primary and secondary sources, maps, charts and graphs, the census, and many other sources.

How to Draw Conclusions

To draw conclusions, follow these steps.

1. **Study the evidence carefully.** Note all trends and other relationships.
2. **Read "between the lines."** Make inferences by using your reasoning abilities to look for implied or suggested meanings. (But be sure to treat all inferences with caution. Use them carefully to support or refute the solid evidence you collect.
3. **Continually test your conclusions and revise if necessary.** Collect additional evidence. Refine your conclusion to fit the additional information. The more supporting facts you have, the more likely the conclusion you have drawn is correct.
4. **Use your conclusions.** Apply the conclusions you draw to the topic you are studying to help you understand the topic.

Applying the Skill

Read the following excerpt. It contains conclusions by a historian. See if you can identify one of the conclusions.

President Johnson did not change American policy toward Vietnam until the Gulf of Tonkin Affair. Even then he was mainly interested in appearing to be more aggressive. His Republican opponent in the 1964 presidential election, Senator Barry Goldwater, demanded that the United States make a bigger effort to "check communism" in Vietnam. Johnson hoped that the Tonkin Gulf Resolution would convince the voters that he was pursuing that objective vigorously. But he made a special point of not getting too involved in Vietnam. He insisted that he "would never send American boys to do the fighting that Asian boys should do themselves."

The most obvious conclusion stated by the historian in the excerpt is that President Johnson only wanted to appear more aggressive. The historian has reached this conclusion based on his research into this situation. Now read the following except and draw at least two conclusions based on your reading.

After winning the election, however, Johnson decided to step up American military activity in Vietnam. . . . In February 1965 Johnson made a fateful decision. He ordered the air force to bomb selected targets in North Vietnam. In March he sent two battalions of marines to Vietnam. Their job was to protect the air base from which the bombers were operating. Soon more troops had to be sent in to reinforce the marines!

A few months later the American forces in Vietnam were given permission to seek out and attack Viet Cong units. More troops were shipped to Vietnam. By the end of 1965 there were 185,000 American fighting men in the country.

This steady escalation, or increase, in American military strength in Vietnam went on for three years. Each increase brought more North Vietnamese into the conflict in support of the Viet Cong. By 1968 more than half a million Americans were fighting in Vietnam. Yet Congress never officially declared war. Johnson instead waged war by the authority of the Tonkin Gulf Resolution, which had seemed to have little historical significance when it was passed by Congress in 1964.

The president and his advisers thought they were acting with great restraint. The enormous difference in size and wealth between the United States and North Vietnam lulled them into believing that the United States could win the war whenever it chose. How, asked the advisers, could a tiny country like North Vietnam successfully resist the United States? They wanted to risk the lives of as few Americans as possible. When each escalation proved to be not enough, they hoped just one more increase would do the job.

What conclusions can you draw from this information? You might conclude that Johnson took his election victory as a sign that the American people supported escalated American involvement in Vietnam. Another conclusion you might draw is that Johnson's advisers did not portray an accurate picture of what it would take to win the war. What are some other conclusions you can draw from this excerpt?

For independent practice, see Practicing the Strategy on page 550.

In New York's Washington Square Park protestors of the war light candles during a candlelight vigil calling for a moratorium. What does the word moratorium *mean?*

Point of View

The author of *A Bright Shining Lie* brings a historical perspective to the Tet offensive.

> **"**Yet to turn the war decisively in [the Viet Cong's] favor they had to achieve a masterstroke that would have the will-breaking effect on the Americans that Dien Bien Phu had had on the French. The masterstroke was Tet, 1968. . . . In cities and towns all across South Vietnam, tens of thousands of Communist troops were launching . . . a 'panorama of attacks.' . . . The goal was to collapse the Saigon regime with these military blows. . . . Ho Chi Minh and his confederates hoped to knock the prop out from under the American war, force the United States to open negotiations under disadvantageous conditions, and begin the process of wedging the Americans out of their country. . . .**"**
>
> Neil Sheehan, 1988

Early in 1968 the American commander in Vietnam, General William C. Westmoreland, announced that victory was near. Soon the Viet Cong would be crushed. But on January 30, the Vietnamese New Year's Day (*Tet*), the Viet Cong suddenly attacked cities all over South Vietnam. They even briefly gained control of parts of **Saigon,** the capital. They held a number of important cities for weeks.

The American and South Vietnamese troops fought back, as one historian has put it, "with the fury of a blinded giant." Eventually they regained control of the cities. In doing so, however, they destroyed even more of Vietnam. In a remark that soon became famous, an American officer justified the smashing of the town of Ben Tre. "We had to destroy it in order to save it," he said.

The American counterattack crushed the **Tet offensive.** Viet Cong and North Vietnamese losses were enormous. Still, the American public was profoundly shocked at the strength shown by the communists after so many years of war. The tide of opinion turned against the war. When General Westmoreland asked for another 200,000 men, President Johnson turned him down.

Return to the Preview & Review on page 525.

1. How did Lyndon Johnson acknowledge that his Vietnam policy had failed?
2. How did many Americans react to the assassination of Martin Luther King, Jr.?
3. What caused the riots at the 1968 Democratic convention?
4. Why did many Americans think Nixon would never be president? How did he get another chance in 1968?
5. Why was the selection of Agnew as Nixon's running mate a key to the 1968 election?

Thinking Critically. 1. Imagine you are a delegate to the Democratic National Convention in 1968. Write an article for your local newspaper explaining who you are supporting and why. 2. Imagine that Martin Luther King, Jr., and Robert Kennedy had not been assassinated in 1968. How might this have changed events in the years after 1968?

Leonard McCombe/Life Picture Service

Senator Eugene McCarthy in his Children's Crusade—so called because his supporters were young and had yet to vote for president—was the first candidate to challenge President Johnson. How did the Tet offensive make McCarthy's candidacy a serious challenge?

2. A YEAR OF TRAGEDY

1968 Shocks Americans

In March 1968 President Johnson acknowledged that his Vietnam policy had failed. He had been planning to run for a second full term in 1968. Senator Eugene McCarthy of Minnesota had announced that he would oppose Johnson for the Democratic nomination. McCarthy was a leading dove. Before the Tet offensive no one gave him any chance of defeating Johnson.

After Tet, however, the situation changed. McCarthy almost defeated Johnson in the New Hampshire presidential primary. Then Robert F. Kennedy, brother of the slain president, declared that he too was a candidate. Faced with a difficult fight that would probably divide the country still further, Johnson announced that he would not seek reelection.

On April 4, less than a week after Johnson's withdrawal, came another shock. Martin Luther King, Jr., was murdered in Memphis, Tennessee, where he had gone to support a strike of garbage collectors. King had foreseen the price he might have to pay for his leadership. In a speech delivered in Memphis just before his assassination he observed:

66 Well, I don't know what will happen now. We've got some difficult days ahead. But it really doesn't matter with me now, because I've been to the mountaintop. And I don't mind. Like anybody, I would like to live a long life. Longevity has its place. But I'm not concerned about that now. I just want to do God's will. And He's allowed me to go up to the mountain, and I've looked over, and I've seen the promised land. I may not get there with you. But I want you to know tonight, that we as a people will get to the promised land. And so I'm happy tonight. I'm not worried about anything. I'm not fearing any man. Mine eyes have seen the glory of the coming of the Lord.[1] 99

King's murder caused an explosion of anger in black communities all over the country. Riots broke out in 125 cities in 28 states. Whole sections of Washington were aflame in the shadow of the Capitol.

Robert Kennedy was among those who tried to calm the waters. In a speech in an Indiana ghetto, he described King's assassination with these words:

66 Martin Luther King dedicated his life to love and to justice for his fellow human beings, and he died because of that effort.

[1]From *Bearing the Cross* by David J. Garrow

Declan Haun/Black Star

Flip Schulke/Black Star

In this difficult day, in this difficult time for the United States, it is perhaps well to ask what kind of a nation we are and what direction we want to move in. For those of you who are black—considering the evidence there evidently is that there were white people who were responsible—you can be filled with bitterness, with hatred, and a desire for revenge. We can move in great polarization—black people amongst black, white people amongst white, filled with hatred toward one another.

Or we can make an effort, as Martin Luther King did, to understand and to comprehend, and to replace that violence, that stain of bloodshed that has spread across our land, with an effort to understand with compassion and love. . . .

What we need in the United States is not division; what we need in the United States is not hatred; what we need in the United States is not violence or lawlessness, but love and wisdom, and compassion toward one another, and a feeling of justice towards those who still suffer within our country, whether they be white or they be black. . . .

For Martin Luther King, Jr., a poor man's funeral. His mourners march through the streets of Atlanta behind a farm wagon drawn by mules. How was this a reminder of King's heritage? King's widow, Coretta Scott, and his daughter Yolanda are pictured at his funeral.

A Year of Tragedy   533

At first he was thought to be ruthless and hard—foe of corruption in labor but supporter of Joseph McCarthy. But Robert Kennedy became nearly as popular as his presidential brother when he campaigned for the Democratic nomination in 1968. And his compassion for the poor and disadvantaged grew. What chance had he of winning the nomination?

We've had difficult times in the past. We will have difficult times in the future. It is not the end of violence; it is not the end of lawlessness; it is not the end of disorder.

But the vast majority of white people and the vast majority of black people in this country want to live together, want to improve the quality of our life, and want justice for all human beings who abide in our land.

Let us dedicate ourselves to what the Greeks wrote so many years ago: to tame the savageness of man and to make gentle the life of this world.

Let us dedicate ourselves to that, and say a prayer for our country and for our people.[1] 99

In June Robert Kennedy himself was assassinated by an Arab immigrant who objected to the support the United States was giving the country of Israel. Kennedy had just won the California presidential primary. He had seemed likely to win the nomination at the Democratic national convention in Chicago. His death made Vice President Hubert H. Humphrey the favorite.

Humphrey loyally supported Johnson's policy in Vietnam. (If

[1]From *Robert Kennedy and His Times* by Arthur M. Schlesinger, Jr.

he had not, Johnson would not have supported him for president.) When the convention met, large numbers of antiwar protesters, many of whom favored Senator McCarthy for president, flocked to Chicago to demonstrate. Mayor Richard Daley, a Humphrey supporter, packed the area around the convention hall with city police.

Radicals among the demonstrators insulted and taunted the police. They called them ''pigs'' and other vulgar names. The police responded by rushing into the crowd, clubs swinging. Millions of television viewers who had tuned in to watch the convention debates saw instead burly, helmeted policemen hitting the demonstrators with their night sticks and herding them dazed and bloody into police wagons.

Not many people at the time realized that the protests in Chicago were a continuation of the antiwar and free-speech movements spreading across the land. At the University of California students burned draft cards, and at Columbia University they occupied many campus buildings.

The Election of 1968

Humphrey won the Democratic nomination easily. But thousands of Democrats blamed him, quite unfairly, for the police riot in Chicago. Most of these same Democrats resented his support of the war in Vietnam.

This split in the Democratic party helped the Republican candidate, Richard M. Nixon, the former vice president whom Kennedy had defeated in 1960. Few had expected Nixon to get a second chance to run for president. In 1962 he had run unsuccessfully for governor of California. At the time he seemed a sore loser, blaming reporters for his defeat.

However, Nixon had worked hard for the Republican party during the Kennedy and Johnson administrations. Hundreds of local Republican officials felt that he deserved a second chance for the presidency. When the 1968 Republican convention met, he had a majority of the delegates in his camp and was easily nominated.

Governor George C. Wallace of Alabama, an outspoken foe of racial integration, also ran for president in 1968 on an independent ticket. For this reason Nixon chose Spiro T. Agnew of Maryland as his running mate. Agnew had taken a tough stand against black activists, urban crime, and protesters of all kinds. He was not well known nationally, but his record on several issues made him acceptable to many voters who might otherwise have supported Wallace.

In the three-way contest for president, Nixon won. He got only about 43 percent of the popular vote, less than 1 percent more than Humphrey. But he received a solid majority (61 percent) of the electoral vote. 🖃

From top to bottom: Hubert Humphrey, George Wallace, and Richard Nixon.

Return to the Preview & Review on page 532.

Fred Ward/Black Star

Bettmann Newsphotos

Dennis Brack/Black Star

3. NIXON AS PRESIDENT

Use these questions to guide your reading. Answer the questions after completing Section 3.
Understanding Issues, Events, & Ideas. Use the following words to discuss key events during Nixon's first term in office: wage-and-price freeze, antiwar movement, Vietnamization, Cambodia, Ho Chi Minh Trail, Kent State and Jackson State, Strategic Arms Limitation Treaty, détente, Hanoi, Six Days' War, Arab Oil Crisis, shuttle diplomacy.

1. What was a major cause of the inflation that President Nixon set out to check? How did he attempt to check it?
2. Why did Nixon order American troops into Cambodia? What was the response in the United States to this move?
3. What diplomatic moves did President Nixon make in 1972? What effect did they have on the American people?
4. What were some reasons that Nixon was reelected by such an overwhelming majority?
5. What were the terms of the first Vietnam War peace agreement negotiated by Henry Kissinger? What reasons were given for its failure?

Thinking Critically.   1. Why do you think the United States, with its far greater wealth and technology was unable to win the war in Vietnam? What other lessons do you think Americans can learn from the Vietnam War?   2. Why might it have been easier for Nixon to visit China and initiate regular diplomatic relations than it would have been for Eisenhower or Kennedy?

Nixon and the Economy

The new president favored moderation. He sought to please middle-income voters and persons who were neither radicals nor reactionaries. (Politically, radicals favor extreme change; reactionaries resist change or want to return to old-fashioned ways, an extreme change in itself.) These moderates and middle-income people were worried about high taxes and rising prices. Inflation in particular seemed the most alarming economic issue of the times. President Nixon set out to end it.

President Johnson was partly responsible for the inflation. Each time he ordered an escalation of the war in Vietnam, the government had to spend billions of additional dollars on weapons and other supplies. Government purchases put huge sums of money into the economy, but the economy was not producing more consumer goods. So people had money but a limited supply of goods to spend the money on. The prices of goods rose sharply. In addition, Johnson had not asked Congress to increase taxes to pay for the war, partly because he feared that his domestic programs would be cut back if he did so. (He also wished to avoid the congressional debate on the war that asking for a tax hike would cause.) In a popular expression of the day, he refused to choose between guns and butter, or between spending money on the war and on domestic programs. Therefore the federal budget was badly unbalanced.

Nixon used both fiscal and monetary policies to check inflation. He reduced government spending and persuaded the Federal Reserve Board to raise interest rates to discourage borrowing. The economy slowed down. These policies caused unemployment to go up. Plants cut back production and people were laid off as consumer buying dropped off. But for some reason prices continued to go up too. Economists were as puzzled by the trend as the president. Throughout 1969 and 1970 the trend continued.

Finally, in August 1971, Nixon took a drastic step. He suddenly ordered a **wage-and-price freeze.** During the 90-day period he set up new government boards to supervise wages and prices. Then he announced guidelines which placed maximum limits on future increases in wages and prices. This program did not stop inflation, but it did slow it down.

Nixon and the War

Nixon also sought a middle-of-the-road solution to the war in Vietnam. He was unwilling to give up the American goal of keeping the communists from conquering South Vietnam. Yet every report of

Robert Ellison/Black Star

This Vietnamese army nurse attends a fallen soldier as American fighters offer assistance. The picture was taken during the Vietnamization of the war. Why was there doubt from the start about this policy?

new American casualties in Vietnam increased the strength of the American **antiwar movement**—the organized effort to stop war. Nixon's problem was how to reduce the casualties without losing the war.

He decided to shift the burden of fighting the Viet Cong and North Vietnamese to the South Vietnamese army. Gradually, as that army grew stronger, American troops could be withdrawn. This was called the **Vietnamization** of the war.

Whether Vietnamization would work was doubtful from the start. After all, the escalation of the American effort in Vietnam had

> **"We are people of this generation, bred in at least modest comfort, housed now in universities, looking uncomfortably at the world we inherit."**
>
> Tom Hayden, 1962

been necessary because the South Vietnamese had not been able to defeat the communists on their own. At best, Vietnamization would take a long time. The first reduction of American strength amounted to only 25,000 out of an army of more than 540,000.

As time passed, however, Nixon was able to reduce the size of the American force in Vietnam considerably. By the spring of 1970 it was down to 430,000. Nixon proudly announced that he intended to pull out another 150,000 men within a year.

Instead, only a few days later, on April 30, the president suddenly announced an expansion of the war. He was sending American troops into **Cambodia,** the nation on the western border of Vietnam. The reason for this invasion, Nixon said, was that the North Vietnamese were using Cambodia as a sanctuary, or safe base of operations, from which to launch attacks on South Vietnam. The Americans were going to destroy these bases.

The North Vietnamese had been moving soldiers and supplies into South Vietnam along the **Ho Chi Minh Trail** in Cambodia and Laos for years. (Ho Chi Minh had been the president of North Vietnam.) The Americans had responded by bombing the trail. Since Cambodia was a neutral country, this bombing was done secretly. And like so much in this frustrating war, the bombings were in vain. No large bases were ever found in Cambodia.

Nixon's public announcement of the invasion of Cambodia set off a new storm of protest in the United States. In November 1969 250,000 people had staged a protest demonstration in Washington against the war. But the antiwar movement had become less vigorous as Nixon reduced the number of American soldiers in Vietnam. It now suddenly revived. If Vietnamization was a success, why was it necessary to send Americans into Cambodia?

College students in particular reacted angrily to news of the invasion. Throughout the spring of 1970 there were demonstrations on campuses all over the country. Much property was destroyed. The worst trouble occurred at **Kent State** University in Ohio. Rioting there led the governor of Ohio to send National Guard troops to the campus to preserve order. After several days of troubles in May, an overly tense guard unit opened fire on protesting students. Four students were killed and nearly a dozen more were wounded. Some of the victims had merely been walking across the campus on their way to classes when the guardsmen began shooting.

Several days later two students were shot down by Mississippi state police at **Jackson State.** The killings at Kent State and Jackson State caused still more student protests. Some colleges were forced to close down for the remainder of the school year. Parents were shaken by the spectacle of their children under fire at home in the United States, not on some foreign battlefield of war.

The Cambodian invasion did not lead immediately to much heavy fighting. Nixon depended increasingly on air attacks on North

John Paul Filo

A cry heard round the world. Americans everywhere were deeply shocked by this picture taken in 1970 at Kent State University. There National Guardsmen opened fire on students during a campus protest. What announcement by President Nixon prompted this demonstration?

Vietnam to weaken the communists. Soon the American troops in Cambodia were ordered back into South Vietnam. Nixon continued the troop withdrawals. By the end of 1972 fewer than 100,000 Americans were still fighting the war, and the number was declining steadily.

Nixon Visits China and the Soviet Union

As American soldiers withdrew from Vietnam, President Nixon tried to end the war by diplomacy. His chief foreign policy adviser, Henry Kissinger, entered into secret discussions with North Vietnamese leaders in Paris. In February 1972 Nixon himself made a dramatic trip to China, a nation that supported North Vietnam.

The United States had never officially recognized the communists as the legal rulers of China. At the time of the 1949 civil war that brought the communists to power in China, Nixon had been a leader of the group in Congress that opposed recognizing the new government. Like Senator Joseph McCarthy, Nixon had blamed the state department for the loss of China to the communists. Over the years he had opposed having any dealings with the "Red Chinese."

Now Nixon reversed himself completely. He no longer saw the need for containment. Instead he hoped to establish a balance of power. "It will be a safer world and a better world if we have a

President and Mrs. Nixon prepare to meet Mao Tse-tung, the communist leader of China. This was one of two historic visits abroad made by the Nixons. What was the other?

strong, healthy United States, Europe, Soviet Union, China, Japan— each balancing the other, not playing one against the other, an even balance," he said in 1971. America's withdrawal from Vietnam— where it had been involved since the Eisenhower administration in the early 1950s—also helped open the way.

His visit to China was his boldest step towards a balance of power, and it was a great success. The Chinese leaders greeted him warmly. He agreed to support the admission of Red China to the United Nations in place of Taiwan, which had represented China since 1949. Important trade agreements were worked out. It was clear that the two nations would soon establish regular diplomatic relations.

A few months later Nixon made another important diplomatic move. This time he went to the Soviet Union. Again he was given an extremely friendly welcome. This happened despite the fact that the Soviet Union, like China, was supporting the North Vietnamese in the war. Out of this visit came the first **Strategic Arms Limitation Treaty** (SALT). This treaty placed limits on the use of nuclear weapons by the two powers. The two powers seemed to be entering a period of **détente,** or reduction of tensions between them.

The Election of 1972

President Nixon rose in popularity after his successful diplomatic visits and his sincere efforts to wind down the war in Vietnam. The

Republicans nominated him for a second term without opposition. The Democrats, however, had no obvious leader in 1972. Hubert Humphrey hoped to face Nixon again. Senator Edmund Muskie of Maine had many supporters. But the nomination went to Senator George McGovern of South Dakota, who had campaigned hard in the primaries on an antiwar platform.

McGovern's campaign was bungled from the start. His running mate, Senator Thomas Eagleton of Missouri, was discovered to have been hospitalized in the past for psychiatric treatment. At first McGovern announced that he would stand behind Eagleton "one thousand percent." Then he changed his mind. He asked Eagleton to withdraw. Sargent Shriver, a brother-in-law of John F. Kennedy, was chosen instead. This incident made McGovern seem both indecisive and unfaithful to a loyal supporter.

Bettmann Newsphotos

Shortly before the election, Nixon's negotiator, Henry Kissinger, announced that he had reached an agreement with North Vietnamese leaders. "Peace is at hand," he said. As a result Nixon won an overwhelming victory on election day. He got more than 60 percent of the popular vote and carried every state but Massachusetts.

America Leaves Vietnam

After Kissinger's "peace is at hand" announcement, Nixon stopped the bombing of North Vietnam. The agreement Kissinger had negotiated called for a cease-fire, joint North and South Vietnamese administration of the country, and free elections. Then the last of the

Henry Kissinger, President Nixon's tireless national security adviser and later secretary of state, announced "Peace is at hand" shortly before Nixon stood for reelection in 1972. What happened instead?

American troops would go home and the American prisoners of war held by the North Vietnamese would be released.

After the presidential election this agreement fell through. According to the Americans, the Vietnamese communists backed away from terms they had accepted earlier. But perhaps the main reason the talks ended was the refusal of South Vietnamese president Thieu to cooperate because his government objected to parts of the agreement. President Nixon then resumed the air strikes.

This time the president sent B-52 bombers, the largest in the air force, to strike at **Hanoi,** the capital of North Vietnam. These were far heavier attacks than any launched on Germany in World War II.

While the B-52s pounded Hanoi, peace negotiations were resumed in Paris. Finally, in January 1973, an agreement was signed. So far as the United States was concerned, the war was over. But American policy had been a failure. The United States had lost the war. By the time the last Americans were airlifted out of the newly named capital of Vietnam, Ho Chi Minh City, the war had cost more than $100 billion and the lives of more than 58,175 Americans and a much larger number of Vietnamese. No one then anticipated how great would be the adjustment for the returning veterans, many of whom were deeply shocked by the war. There were few parades for them, few joyous public celebrations. Some Americans saw them as the symbol of all that was wrong with the war. Yet had they not been drafted and sent to that war by the American government, just as soldiers had been sent to previous wars? The veterans deeply resented the treatment they received.

What did the Vietnam War teach us? One of the most important lessons of the war in Vietnam was the effect a truly divided nation has on the war effort and the people fighting it. Antiwar sentiments focused first on government leaders and then on the soldiers themselves. Perhaps just as important is the lesson learned from fighting a war without going "all out." As one article on the war said:

> " Viet Nam veterans argue passionately that Americans must never again be sent to die in a war that 'the politicians will not let them win.' And by win they clearly mean something like a World War II-style triumph ending in unconditional surrender.[1] "

The aftermath of the Vietnam War brought another point to light. It proved the domino theory was wrong. The communist victory in Vietnam did not lead to the long-feared communist control of East and Southeast Asia. The countries of the region, such as Vietnam and Cambodia (also called Kampuchea), began fighting among themselves. The dominoes, instead of falling one after the other against Western democracy, seemed to crash angrily into each other.

[1]From *Time* magazine, April 15, 1985

THE VIETNAM VETERANS MEMORIAL

Etched in the polished black granite are 58,175 names. They are the names of the Americans who died in the Vietnam War. The names are listed in order of death, showing the war as a series of personal sacrifices and giving each person a special place in history.

To most Americans, the Vietnam Veterans Memorial is a symbol of long-overdue public recognition of the Americans who fought in the controversial war. The nation's commitment to the war had never been as intense as it had to previous wars involving American troops. In fact, public opinion about America's involvement in the war was sharply divided. Even many of those who fought in Vietnam came to question why they were there and how the war was being fought.

In other times war-weary veterans were greeted by cheering crowds and parades. Vietnam veterans returned instead to an indifference, almost a hostility. Many buried their memories of the war and kept silent. Some had a difficult time readjusting to life after the stress of combat and their reception at home. Others returned easily and successfully to civilian life. Gradually Vietnam veterans organized and began to insist on public recognition of their war efforts.

In July 1980 Congress selected a site for a Vietnam memorial in the Constitutional Gardens near the Lincoln Memorial in Washington, D.C. The memorial's design would be chosen through a national competition open to all American citizens 18 years of age or older. The only criterion set by the committee was that the memo-

rial must display the names of the Americans who had died in the war.

In May 1981 a jury of eight internationally famous artists, designers, and architects announced their unanimous first choice from the 1,421 entries. The winning entry had been submitted by Maya Ying Lin of Athens, Ohio. At the time she was a 21-year-old student at Yale University. In March 1982 ground was broken and construction began. The memorial was dedicated on November 13, 1982.

Maya Lin's design creates a park within a park—a quiet and peaceful place. The mirrorlike

surfaces of the polished black granite reflect the surroundings—trees, flowers, and the faces of the people who search the memorial for names. The memorial's walls point to the Lincoln Memorial and the Washington Monument.

Flowers, pictures, and other mementos cover the ground at the base of the walls. They are remembrances brought by parents, friends, and lovers. But the most striking feature of the memorial is the list of names. As Lin had planned, the names became the memorial. They are the ultimate honor to those who died in America's most controversial war.

Christopher Morris/Black Star

Source: World Book Encyclopedia

THE COSTS OF AMERICA'S WARS

War	Military Deaths	Financial Costs
Revolutionary	25,324*	$101,100,000
War of 1812	2,260	$90,000,000
Mexican	13,283	$71,400,000
Civil	529,332	$5,183,000,000
Spanish-American	2,446	$283,200,000
The Great War	126,000	$18,676,000,000
World War II	405,399	$263,259,000,000
Korean	54,246	$67,386,000,000
Vietnam	58,132*	$150,000,000,000
*Estimated		

LEARNING FROM TABLES. *This table contains the number of military deaths and financial costs of each of America's wars. In what war did the most Americans die? Why? Why do you think the expenditures for World War II and the Vietnam War were so high?*

Middle Eastern Diplomacy

Vietnam was not the only trouble spot to attract America's attention. The Arab states of the Middle East continued to present perplexing problems, mostly because they remained opposed to the very existence of Israel. In 1967 Israel had won a smashing victory over Egypt in the **Six Days' War.** A precarious peace, broken by Arab raids and Israeli reprisals, had held until October 6, 1973. On that day, Yom Kippur, the Jewish holy day of atonement, Egypt and Syria again attacked Israel. While the war raged, the Arab-controlled Organization of Petroleum Exporting Countries (OPEC) banned all oil shipments to the United States, Japan, and Western Europe in retaliation for their support of Israel.

The impact surprised many Americans. Petroleum products, most notably gasoline, were rationed. Long lines of cars waited at gas pumps all over America.

This **Arab Oil Crisis** caused Americans to realize that an extended ban would threaten the American economy and life style. They had known petroleum was a limited and nonrenewable resource since the automobile boom of the 1920s. They had learned to conserve petroleum during the emergency of World War II. Now they began to conserve petroleum in their everyday lives. People were encouraged to use carpools or mass transit. Gasoline prices were raised, in part to discourage extra driving. Schools and public buildings closed on the coldest or hottest days to conserve the electricity or oil needed to heat or cool the building.

Nixon realized that America's two Middle Eastern interests—Israel and oil—created a complex situation. He sent his master negotiator, Henry Kissinger, into action. Kissinger visited the Middle East nearly every month. His **shuttle diplomacy** brought Egypt and Israel to a cease-fire. He kept the region from erupting into the flames of war and reestablished the flow of Middle Eastern oil to the United States.

Return to the Preview & Review on page 536.

4. THE WATERGATE AFFAIR

Preview & Review

Use these questions to guide your reading. Answer the questions after completing Section 4.

Understanding Issues, Events, & Ideas. Use the following words to explain Nixon's fall from power: Watergate Affair, executive privilege, Saturday Night Massacre, Twenty-fifth Amendment, articles of impeachment.

1. What three articles of impeachment were passed by the House Judiciary Committee against Nixon?
2. How was the Supreme Court involved in the case against Nixon?
3. Why were the transcripts of the White House tapes unable to prove the president's claim of innocence?
4. In your opinion, should the president be allowed to resign to avoid impeachment? Explain your view.

Thinking Critically. Do you think that President Ford should have offered Nixon a pardon? Why or why not?

Nixon's Power Begins to Crumble

The ending of the war and his landslide victory in the 1972 election made Richard Nixon seem one of the most powerful of American presidents. He used his power to cut back sharply on various New Deal and Great Society programs designed to help poor people, blacks, and other disadvantaged groups. He hoped the cut in government spending would slow inflation. He also announced that it was time to crack down hard on crime. He criticized what he called the "permissiveness" of many Americans.

Yet, at the very moment of his great election success, Nixon's power began to crumble. The cause was the **Watergate Affair,** one of the strangest episodes in the entire story of America.

On the night of June 17, 1972, shortly before the presidential nominating conventions, five burglars were arrested in the headquarters of the Democratic National Committee in Washington, D.C. The headquarters were located in the Watergate, a modern office building and apartment house complex on the Potomac River.

The burglars had large sums of money in new $100 bills in their wallets when they were arrested. They were carrying two expensive cameras, 40 rolls of film, and a number of tiny listening devices, or "bugs." They had obviously intended to copy Democratic party records and attach the bugs to the office telephones.

Suspicion naturally fell on the Republican party. One of the men arrested was James W. McCord, a former CIA employee who was working for Nixon's campaign organization, the Committee for the Reelection of the President (CREEP). Soon it was discovered that two other campaign officials had been involved in the break-in. Other CREEP techniques came to light. CREEP workers had joined the campaign of Senator Muskie in 1972 and disrupted it by leaking damaging and false rumors to the press and mixing up schedules so that Muskie and his supporters missed several important appearances and appointments.

Both Nixon's campaign manager, former Attorney General John Mitchell, and the president himself denied that anyone on the White House staff had anything to do with Watergate. Nixon's press secretary described it as a "third-rate burglary." Vice President Spiro Agnew suggested that the *Democrats* might have staged the affair to throw suspicion on the Republican party. Most people accepted the president's denial. The Watergate Affair had no effect on the election.

The Cover-up

Early in 1973 the Watergate burglars were put on trial in Washington. Most of them pleaded guilty. This meant that they could not be

All of Washington sought passes to the Watergate hearings held to determine whether or not the president of the United States should be impeached. Here John Dean, the president's lawyer, is sworn in. How did Watergate provoke the Constitutional crisis of the 20th century?

questioned about the case. But one of them, James McCord, told the trial judge, John Sirica, that a number of important Republican officials had been involved in planning the burglary.

McCord's charges were found to be true. The Justice Department renewed its efforts to locate the people behind the break-in. One by one, important members of the Nixon administration admitted that they had known about the incident. The head of the FBI confessed that he had destroyed documents related to the affair. Clearly there had been a cover-up of evidence. The Senate began an investigation.

John Dean, the president's lawyer, provided particularly damaging evidence to investigators. The president fired Dean, whom he considered a traitor. Nixon's two closest aides, H. R. Haldeman and John Ehrlichman, were forced to resign. Still, Nixon insisted that they were loyal public servants who had done nothing wrong.

As the Senate investigation proceeded, witnesses brought out more and more details about Watergate and other illegal activities connected with Nixon's campaign for reelection. Evidence suggested that many large corporations had made secret contributions to the campaign fund. Such gifts were illegal. John Dean testified that the president had helped plan the cover-up from the beginning. When he had gone on television to deny that anyone in the White House was involved, the president had lied, Dean said.

Dean's testimony was extremely important because it so directly involved the president. He appeared to be telling the truth. When details of his testimony could be checked against other sources, they proved to be correct. But Nixon denied the charges. It seemed to be his word against Dean's.

Then another witness revealed to the startled investigators that Nixon had been secretly recording all the conversations that had taken place in his office. These tape recordings would show whether or not Dean had told the truth! At once the Senate investigators demanded that the president allow them to listen to these and other White House tapes that might reveal important information.

Nixon refused to allow anyone to listen to the tapes. He claimed what he called **executive privilege**—the right to keep information secret when it related to presidential business.

More and more people came to the conclusion that Nixon was lying. Charges that he had cheated on his income taxes while president by claiming large illegal deductions further turned public opinion against him. Yet how could the full truth be discovered while people Nixon had appointed ran the Justice Department? To end the criticism, Nixon agreed to the appointment of a distinguished law professor, Archibald Cox, as a special prosecutor for the Justice Department to take charge of the case. Cox was promised a free hand and told to pursue the truth wherever the facts led him.

Professor Cox also demanded that the White House tapes be turned over to his investigators for study. Again Nixon refused. A federal judge then ordered him to give Cox the tapes. Instead of doing so, Nixon ordered Attorney General Elliot L. Richardson, head of the Justice Department, to fire Cox!

Richardson resigned rather than carry out this order. So did the assistant attorney general. But Nixon persisted and finally a third member of the Justice Department, Robert G. Bork, discharged Cox. These events occurred on the evening of Saturday, October 20, 1973. The affair was called the **Saturday Night Massacre.**

Nixon's entire administration seemed riddled with scandal. Only ten days before the Saturday Night Massacre, Vice President Spiro Agnew admitted that he had been cheating on his income taxes. He resigned from office. Actually, the official record of his case revealed that he had also accepted $200,000 in bribes while serving as a public official in Maryland. To avoid the national shame of having a vice president in prison, government lawyers had allowed him to plead nolo contendere (no contest) only of income tax evasion. Agnew was fined and placed on probation.

The **Twenty-fifth Amendment** of the Constitution, ratified in 1967, includes a provision that when the vice presidency falls vacant, the president shall appoint a new vice president. Nixon chose Congressman Gerald R. Ford of Michigan. The appointment was approved by Congress and Ford became vice president.

Nixon Falls from Power

The Saturday Night Massacre led many people to demand that Nixon be impeached. (*Impeachment* is the legal process of charging a high

The House Judiciary Committee left little doubt how they felt about Nixon's behavior during the Watergate investigation.

Article I

"... Richard M. Nixon, has prevented, obstructed, and impeded the administration of justice. . . .

Article II

. . . Richard M. Nixon . . . has repeatedly engaged in conduct violating the constitutional rights of citizens, . . . contravening [blocking] the laws of governing agencies. . . .

Article III

. . . Richard M. Nixon . . . has failed without lawful cause or excuse to produce papers and things, as directed by duly authorized subpoenas [writs commanding a person to turn over evidence or to testify]. . . .

Wherefore, Richard M. Nixon, by such conduct, warrants impeachment and trial, and removal from office."

From *Articles of Impeachment,* August 4, 1974

official with wrongdoing.) To quiet those demanding his impeachment, Nixon promised to cooperate with Cox's successor as Watergate prosecutor, Texas lawyer Leon Jaworski. Nevertheless, the Judiciary Committee of the House of Representatives began an investigation to see if there were grounds for impeaching Nixon.

While the Judiciary Committee studied the evidence of Nixon's involvement, prosecutor Jaworski proceeded against the others involved in CREEP's illegal activities. One after another, men who had been involved in Nixon's campaign for reelection were charged and convicted of crimes. Some had lied under oath, others had obstructed justice, one had raised money for the campaign in an unlawful manner.

Late in April 1974 Nixon released edited transcripts of some of his taped conversations. These, he said, would prove his innocence. However, important parts of conversations were left out in these printed versions. At many places the typescripts contained blanks because, Nixon claimed, the tapes had not recorded what was said clearly enough to be understood. Still he refused to let others check on the editing by listening to the tapes.

Both what the transcripts revealed and what they left out led to increased demands that the president allow investigators to listen to the key tapes themselves. Nixon still refused. He would not turn them over to either the House Judiciary Committee or to special prosecutor Jaworski.

Jaworski therefore asked the Supreme Court to order the president to give him the tapes of 64 specific conversations known to have taken place in the White House. While the Court considered the matter, the Judiciary Committee decided to allow its sessions to be broadcast and televised. In July 1974 the committee passed three **articles of impeachment,** or charges against the president. One accused Nixon of obstructing justice. Another accused him of misusing the powers of the presidency. The third concerned his refusal to let the committee listen to the tapes.

Under the Constitution the Judiciary Committee's report would be submitted to the full House of Representatives. If the report was accepted, the House would then impeach Nixon by presenting the articles of impeachment to the Senate. The Senate would act as a court hearing the charges. If two thirds of the senators voted in favor of any of the three articles, Nixon would be removed from office.

While the Judiciary Committee was still debating, the Supreme Court ruled that Nixon must turn the tapes over to prosecutor Jaworski. Nixon hesitated. If he defied the Court's order, it was difficult to see how it could be enforced. But Nixon's advisers convinced him that if he refused to obey the court order, the Senate was certain to remove him from office. Therefore he gave up the tapes.

The tapes proved conclusively that Nixon had known about and even ordered the Watergate cover-up from the start. Only one day after he had said on television that no one in the White House had anything to do with the affair, he had ordered his chief assistant, H. R. Haldeman, to persuade the FBI not to investigate the break-in too vigorously. The FBI could be told that national security was involved, the president suggested.

Meanwhile the Judiciary Committee voted on their recommendation to impeach the president. It was a somber evening as committee members cast their votes. One writer recalled:

> The room is utterly still except for the call of the roll and the sound of cameras clicking. The moment has taken over the members; they know what they are doing, and they are physically, mentally, and emotionally spent [worn out]. They have been through a long period of strain. . . . One can barely hear the members as they respond to the clerk.
>
> The clerk announces, 'Twenty-seven members have voted aye, eleven members have voted no.' All twenty-one Democrats—including three Southerners—and six Republicans have voted to impeach the President for the cover-up. . . .
>
> The room is utterly silent, and then, at a few minutes after seven, Rodino [committee chairman Peter Rodino] announces, 'Article I . . . is adopted and will be reported to the House.'[1]

[1]From *Washington Journal: The Events of 1973–1974* by Elizabeth Drew

Nixon now had the choice of resigning before the House voted to impeach him or going on trial in hopes that the Senate might not remove him. He resigned. On August 9, at noon, he officially surrendered his powers. Gerald R. Ford then took the oath of office and became president of the United States.

One of President Ford's first actions was to offer Nixon a pardon for any crimes he may have committed. He offered the pardon, he said, because Nixon would have a difficult time getting a fair trial. It would also save America the embarrassment of having an ex-president on trial. "My conscience tells me clearly and certainly that I cannot prolong the bad dreams that continue to reopen a chapter that is closed. My conscience tells me that only I, as President, have the constitutional power to firmly shut and seal this book." Thus Ford "shot himself in the foot" as far as his future political plans went. Nixon promptly accepted the pardon.

Here we close this sad chapter with the full truth about the Watergate Affair still not known. And while many Americans look on the incident with shame, others point out that it is an example of how the American system of government worked—a powerful president was forced to resign when he lost the faith of the people.

Shortly before Gerald Ford took the oath as president, he and his wife, Betty, escorted Patricia and Richard Nixon from the White House. How would you summarize President Nixon's strengths and weaknesses as a national leader?

Return to the Preview & Review on page 545.

CHAPTER 13 REVIEW

1964
Johnson elected President
★
Tonkin Gulf Resolution

1965
American involvement in Vietnam escalate
1967
Twenty-fifth Amendment ratified

Chapter Summary
Read the statements below. Choose one, and write a paragraph explaining its importance.
1. The Tonkin Gulf Resolution gave President Johnson the power to escalate American involvement in Vietnam. By 1968 more than 500,000 Americans were in Vietnam.
2. At home, antiwar sentiments grew rapidly after the 1968 Tet offensive.
3. Americans were shocked in 1968 when President Johnson admitted his Vietnam policy was a failure, Martin Luther King, Jr., and Robert Kennedy were murdered, riots scorched American cities, and violence disrupted the Democratic National Convention in Chicago.
4. Richard Nixon began the withdrawal of American troops. Finally, in 1973, a treaty was signed and the war was over.
5. Nixon improved foreign relations with the Soviets, the Chinese, and in the Middle East.
6. The Watergate Affair caused Nixon's power to crumble. He eventually resigned rather than face impeachment proceedings.

Understanding Chronological Order
Number your paper 1–5. Then study the time line above and place the following events in the order in which they happened by writing the first next to 1, the second next to 2, and so on.
1. Burglars break into the Watergate
2. Vietnam War ends
3. Shootings at Kent State and Jackson State
4. Tet offensive
5. Martin Luther King, Jr., murdered

Understanding Main Ideas
1. What role did each of the following play in the Vietnam War: South Vietnam, North Vietnam, and the Viet Cong?
2. What events made 1968 a year of tragedy for the United States?
3. What was Vietnamization? Why did Nixon send American troops into Cambodia? What reaction did this set off in the United States?

4. What was the extent of President Nixon's victory in his reelection in 1972? How was the Democratic campaign bungled?
5. What was the Watergate Affair?

Thinking Critically
1. **Using Historical Imagination.** Suppose you are an adviser to President Johnson. Write him a memorandum recommending either escalation of American involvement in the war or American withdrawal from it.
2. **Citing Historical Significance.** Imagine you are a historian. Explain the historical significance of Nixon's visit to the Soviet Union to events in Eastern Europe today.
3. **Evaluating Ideas.** You are a personal friend and adviser to President Nixon. Write him a letter in which you encourage him to surrender the Watergate tapes.

Writing About History: Informative
As secretary of state under President Nixon, Henry Kissinger won the Nobel Peace Prize in 1973. Research one of these secretaries of state: John Hay (pages 222, 228, 231), John Foster Dulles (463–65), or Henry Kissinger (539, 541, 544) and write a report on their activities as secretary.

Practicing the Strategy
Review the strategy on page 530.
Drawing Conclusions. Read "America Escalates the War" on pages 526–31. Then answer the following questions.
1. What conclusion does the author draw about how the president and his advisers viewed their actions in fighting the Vietnam War?
2. What evidence does the author present to support this conclusion?
3. What information in this section suggests some Americans disagreed with this conclusion?

58
offensive

1970
Nixon decides to bomb Cambodia

★
Shootings at Kent State and Jackson State

1971
Wage-and-price freeze

1972
Nixon reelected

★
Nixon travels to China and Soviet Union

★
Watergate Affair begins

1973
Agnew resigns; Nixon appoints Gerald Ford

★
Final U.S. troops leave Vietnam

★
OPEC announces oil embargo

1974
Kissinger's shuttle diplomacy in Middle East

★
Nixon resigns

★
Ford pardons Nixon

rtin Luther King, Jr., murdered

bert F. Kennedy killed

on elected president

59
tnamization and American withdrawal begins

Using Primary Sources

While many people the world over applauded the new détente between the United States and the Soviet Union, others cautioned Americans to beware of Soviet tricks. One was famous Soviet writer Aleksandr Solzhenitsyn, who had spent many years in detention and labor camps for writings that were critical of Stalin and later Soviet leaders. Finally in 1974 he was forced to leave the Soviet Union and live in exile. As you read the excerpt from a 1975 speech by Solzhenitsyn, consider his warning in light of more recent events in the Soviet Union.

America—in me and among my friends and among people who think the way I do over there [in the Soviet Union], among all ordinary Soviet citizens—brings forth a mixture of admiration and compassion. You're a country of the future; a young country; a country of still unused possibilities; a country of tremendous geographical distances; a country of tremendous spirit; a country of generosity. But these qualities—strength and generosity—usually make a person and even a whole country trusting. This already has done you a disservice several times.

I would like to call upon America to be more careful with its trust and prevent those people who are falsely using the struggle for peace and social justice to lead you down a false road. They are trying to weaken you. They are trying to disarm your strong and magnificent country.

1. According to Solzhenitsyn, what makes Americans particularly trusting?
2. Do you agree with Solzhenitsyn that being trusting has done America a disservice several times? Give examples to support your answer?
3. What do you think Solzhenitsyn is warning Americans against?

Linking History & Geography

The Middle East has been an area of concern for the United States since World War II. To better understand its relative location and the countries of the region, create two maps. On an outline map of the world, label the Mediterranean Sea, the Nile River, Egypt, Israel, and the Middle East. Then draw or use an outline map of the Middle East to label all the countries, their capitals, major bodies of water, and the Suez Canal.

Enriching Your Study of History

1. **Individual Project.** Create a map of the Vietnam War. Your map should show the two Vietnams and the surrounding countries, major cities and towns, battle sites, and physical features. Display your map on the bulletin board or use it to illustrate a discussion of the war.
2. **Cooperative Project.** As an oral history project, have members of your group ask family members to describe their reactions to major events of the late 1960s and early 1970s. Topics should include the Vietnam War and the antiwar movement; the assassinations of Martin Luther King, Jr., and Robert Kennedy in 1968; the Chicago riot between antiwar demonstrators and police; the opening of China by President Nixon; and the Watergate Affair and Nixon's resignation. Compile the responses into a group report, either written or on tape. Combine members' reports into a single commentary on the late 1960s and early 1970s.

Chapter 13 Review 551

Modern Times

The last four presidents of the United States have had to grapple with increasingly complex domestic problems. How will the famous American melting pot accommodate all the newcomers to the United States? How shall the crisis in America's cities be resolved as homeless people and decaying housing drive other city dwellers farther out into the suburbs? How can America cope with pollution—smog, oil spills, acid rain, the destruction of forests—and preserve its fragile environments? How will Americans cope with growing energy needs? What is the future of nuclear energy after accidents at power plants in Pennsylvania and the Soviet Union? Will women and men be fairly treated in the workplace? And, finally, with the pace of world affairs quickened by an inspired Soviet leader and peoples' revolts, what will be the stance of the United States, the longtime protector of freedom and guardian of democracy?

Cross/Miami Herald/Black Star

Flags fly in this celebration of citizenship in Miami. Cuban immigrants swear to uphold the Constitution. Even though they are relative newcomers, Cubans have contributed greatly to the nation's culture and prosperity.

1. TWO CENTURIES OF DEMOCRACY

The Ford Presidency

Before he became president, Gerald Ford was known as an honest, hard-working politician. Nearly everyone in Congress liked him. He got along easily with people. But he had never been noted for vision or originality. When he became president, he announced that he would work closely with Congress. Because both Ford and his vice president, Nelson Rockefeller, had been appointed rather than elected by the people, Ford's style seemed the proper one to adopt.

Dennis Brack/Black Star

Economic Slowdown

Ford's biggest problem was the economy. By 1974 business activity had slowed down, caused for the most part by cutbacks in government programs and rising inflation. Unemployment was increasing. The Democrats wanted to increase government spending in order to speed recovery. On the other hand, most Republicans feared the economic slump less than they feared inflation. Even when the economy was slowing down, prices had continued to rise. More government spending would push prices still higher, Republicans predicted.

Cartoon by S.C. Rawls, reprinted by permission of N.E.A., Inc.

Preview & Review

Use these questions to guide your reading. Answer the questions after completing Section 1. **Understanding Issues, Events, & Ideas.** Use the following words to describe important events that occurred during the presidency of Gerald Ford: stagflation, Bicentennial, Operation Sail.

1. Why did President Ford's style seem a proper one for him to adopt when he assumed the presidency?
2. What were some of the bills passed by the Democratic-controlled Congress during Ford's administration? How did President Ford react to them?
3. What helped to end the economic stagflation that occurred in the mid-1970s?
4. In what ways did the tall ships symbolize pride and hope? **Thinking Critically.** Imagine that you are present at one of the following events on July 4, 1976: the swearing in ceremony in Miami Beach; the president's speech in either Valley Forge or at Independence Hall; the celebration at the Mall in Washington, D.C.; Operation Sail in New York Harbor; a ceremony in your community or anywhere in the U.S. Write a brief eyewitness account of what you see going on around you. Include a description of your participation, and how you feel as an American on this day.

Gerald Ford was a popular president. Much was made of his days as a college football player. Hence the cartoon, "Bad Tackle, Jer," showing the override of Ford's veto of spending bills by Congress.

Two Centuries of Democracy 553

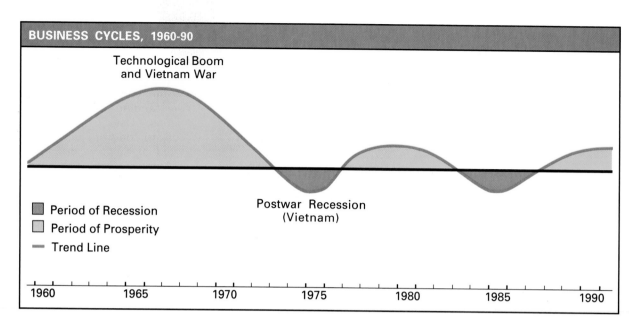

BUSINESS CYCLES, 1960-90

Technological Boom
and Vietnam War

Postwar Recession
(Vietnam)

☐ Period of Recession
☐ Period of Prosperity
— Trend Line

1960   1965   1970   1975   1980   1985   1990

LEARNING FROM GRAPHS.
How would you describe the rise and fall of the business cycle since 1975? What factors might account for such behavior?

Charles Gatewood/Magnum Photos

Hopes for a rollback in the costs of food during the stagflation of the Ford administration were dashed by presidential vetoes. How was the recession finally ended?

In the 1974 Congressional elections voters expressed their negative reactions to scandals such as Watergate linked to the Republicans. As a result, the Democrats increased their majorities in both houses of Congress. When the new Congress met, it passed bills designed to help poor people and to create new jobs. Measures providing for construction of public housing, aid to education, and health care were also sent to President Ford. He vetoed all of them. Spending so much more money, he argued, would lead to greater inflation. In most cases the Democrats were not able to get the two-thirds majorities needed to override the president's veto.

The recession continued. Economists began to describe the country as passing through a period of **stagflation**—a word coined by combining "*stag*nation," which means not developing or advancing, and "in*flation*." Finally, in the spring of 1975, Ford reluctantly signed a bill reducing taxes, a step he had avoided for fear it would fuel greater inflation. The cut put more money in circulation and helped to end the downturn. By early 1976 the recession was over.

The Bicentennial

American spirits were lifted by the recession's end. In 1976 the United States also celebrated its **Bicentennial,** the 200th anniversary of the signing of the Declaration of Independence. The celebration was carried out in grand style. Communities all over the country organized and carried out hundreds of special programs.

In Miami Beach, Florida, 7,000 immigrants were sworn in as citizens of the United States in a mass ceremony at Convention Hall. A man in Oro Grande, California, unfurled a giant American flag measuring 102 by 67 feet (about 30 by 20 meters). There was a balloon

Dan Budnik/Woodfin Camp

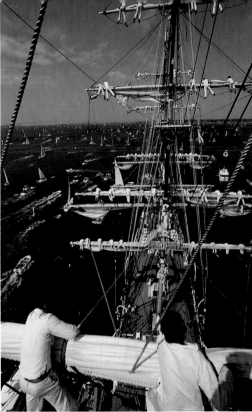

Kenneth Garrett/Woodfin Camp
A burst of fireworks over New York Harbor and the Statue of Liberty salute the nation's Bicentennial in 1976. At right, crew members secure the rigging of a tall ship as it enters the Hudson River. What did the tall ships symbolize?

race to celebrate the occasion in San Antonio, Texas, and a cherry-pie eating contest in Traverse City, Michigan. In other cities and towns there were parades, fireworks, and reenactments of Revolutionary War battles.

President Ford spoke at Valley Forge, where Washington's army had spent the hard winter of 1777, and at Independence Hall in Philadelphia, where the Declaration had been signed.

The highlight of the Bicentennial was **Operation Sail,** a majestic procession of gaily decorated ships in New York harbor. No fewer than 16 great, high-masted sailing ships from different nations participated. Millions of people lined the New York waterfront and crowded the windows of skyscrapers to watch these "tall ships" and the hundreds of other craft that accompanied them.

Somehow the tall ships became a symbol of pride and hope. They had come to New York from all over the world, sent by nations with close ties to the United States as well as those with not-so-close ties to help celebrate the anniversary. This was a recognition of the importance of the United States and even more of what America had meant over the centuries to the people of other nations.

And the tall ships had endured, just as the United States had endured, through a time of enormous change. They were old but still strong, sound, and very beautiful. Although dwarfed by the great Verrazano Bridge across the harbor entrance and by the skyscrapers of Manhattan, they seemed to tower over their surroundings. They had a quiet dignity in contrast to the noise and bustle of the tugs, ferries, and other craft that swarmed about them. They stood for the value of tradition, for past achievements, for history. Better than any military parade or other display of modern power, they reflected the strength of the American people. 🔲

Return to the Preview & Review on page 553.

Two Centuries of Democracy 555

Use these questions to guide your reading. Answer the questions after completing Section 2.
Understanding Issues, Events, & Ideas. Use the following words to describe immigration and social changes in American society from the 1960s to the 1990s: National Farm Workers Association, United Farm Workers Organizing Committee, barrios, affirmative action, Equal Rights Amendment.

1. For what reasons did immigrants come from Korea, the Philippines, and Vietnam after 1965?
2. How were the Puerto Rican immigrants similar to the European immigrants before the Great World War?
3. Why were restrictions for immigration set aside for Cubans?
4. What Supreme Court rulings in 1969 and 1971 supported the Brown decision? How did some whites react?
5. How did the status of women improve in the 1970s and 1980s?
6. What were some of the problems faced by Indians on reservations in the 1980s?

Thinking Critically. Imagine that you are a member of the United Farm Workers during the great *huelga* against the California grape growers. Write a newspaper editorial explaining why you are striking, what you hope to achieve by the strike, and why you support César Chávez as your leader.

2. THE MELTING POT BUBBLES OVER

Immigration and Social Change

The flow and makeup of the American people celebrating the nation's bicentennial had changed after the passage of the Immigration Act of 1965. Europeans no longer accounted for the majority of new immigrants. In their place were immigrants from Latin America (Mexico, the Caribbean, and Central and South America) and Asia. Under the old regulations, the entire continent of Asia supplied only 20,000 immigrants to America in 40 years. In 1973 over 124,000 Asians entered the country.

The Korean War and the stern policies of the South Korean government led thousands of Koreans to migrate to the United States. Most settled in California and Hawaii, but considerable numbers came to New York City and other eastern cities.

Still larger numbers of Filipinos became Americans. When the islands became independent after World War II, the immigration slowed to a trickle. Under the 1965 act it soared again. As with the South Koreans, many Filipinos came for political reasons. Many were skilled workers and professional people.

After the Vietnam War large numbers of South Vietnamese who had been friendly to the Americans came to the United States to escape persecution by the victorious communists. The United States government helped these refugees settle in the country.

The growth of the Asian American population has been dramatic. Although Asian Americans currently make up only about 3 percent of the population, it is estimated that their numbers will increase to

Borrell/Sipa Press

Cambodian refugees leave Phnom Penh in their 1975 exodus after the city fell to the Khmer Rouge. Some of these refugees eventually reached the United States, setting out on boats that were not seaworthy. Report on the "boat people" who reached America.

nearly 10 million by the year 2000. This means there will be nearly ten times as many Asian Americans as in 1970. Why are so many people attracted to the United States? One observer said:

> **"** New immigrants are trying all over again to integrate themselves into the system. They have the same hunger. On any given day, there are about three million throughout the world who are applying to come to the United States and share the American Dream. . . .
>
> The Vietnamese boat people [who fled Vietnam after the communist takeover in 1975] express it as well as anyone. They don't know if they're gonna land, if the boat's gonna sink. They don't know what's gonna happen to 'em, but they've a hunch they might make it to the U.S. as the 'freedom place.'
>
> There is the plain hard fact of hunger. In order to eat, a person will endure tremendous hardship. . . .[1] **"**

Nina Barnett

The flag of his country proudly drawn in school, this Chinese American boy celebrates democracy with his parents. How is this family representative of the new immigration of the last two decades?

Mexican Americans Increase Their Numbers

Hispanic Americans are now the fastest growing segment of the United States population. During the 1980s the Hispanic population of the United States grew by 30 percent. In comparison the overall population of the United States increased by only 6 percent. Today Hispanic Americans account for about 8 percent of the American population. Census experts estimate that by the year 2025 Hispanic Americans may constitute as much as 20 percent of the nation's total population.

By far the largest group among the new immigrants came from Mexico. Before World War II the ebb and flow of Mexican immigration had depended almost entirely on economic conditions. During the Great Depression, when jobs were scarce, far more Mexicans left the United States than came in. When the United States entered World War II, however, the demand for labor in the Southwest soared. The United States and Mexico signed an agreement allowing Mexicans to work temporarily in this country. These workers were called *braceros,* a name that comes from the Spanish word for "arm." The *braceros* came north to harvest crops and returned to Mexico when the season ended. Between 1942 and 1964 almost 5 million Mexicans came to the United States under the *bracero* program. Each year many stayed rather than return to Mexico.

As with immigrants all through history, many of the Mexicans who settled permanently in the United States found it to be a true land of opportunity. Many obtained farms of their own. Others found good jobs. Some became successful professionals. Their example caused thousands of other Mexicans to want to come to the United States. After the 1965 immigration law put a limit on the number of

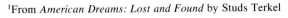

[1]From *American Dreams: Lost and Found* by Studs Terkel

The Melting Pot Bubbles Over   557

Michael Rougier/Life Picture Services

The plentitude of food on your family's kitchen table comes in part from these Mexican-born harvesters called bra-ceros. When this photo was taken, many Mexicans had to cross the bor-der illegally to find work until a pub-lic amnesty program was approved by Congress. Below is César Chávez, whose fasts for the National Farm Workers drew worldwide attention. Huelga means "strike."

Paul Fusco/Magnum Photos

newcomers from the Western Hemisphere, many Mexicans entered the United States illegally. They came north because there was no work for them in Mexico.

Throughout the postwar years Mexican-born workers harvested most of the crops grown in California and the rest of the Southwest. Gradually a leader, César Chávez, emerged among these migrant workers who followed the harvest. Chávez had grown up in the migrant camps of California. Hoping to call attention to conditions in the camps, he founded a labor union, the **National Farm Workers Association.** This group joined with an organization of Filipino farm laborers to form the **United Farm Workers Organizing Committee.** He remembered his first days of organizing the workers:

" The idea was to set up a meeting and then get each attending person to call his own house meeting [in the organizer's home], inviting new people—a sort of chain letter effect. After a house meeting I would lie awake going over the whole thing, playing the tape back, trying to see why people laughed at one point, or why they were for one thing and against another. I was also learning to read and write, those late evenings. I had left school after the 7th grade after attending 67 different schools, and my reading wasn't the best. . . .

I found that if you work hard enough you can usually shake people into working too, those who are concerned. You work harder and they work harder still, up to a point and then they pass you. Then, of course, they are on their own. . . .[1] "

The committee worked hard to improve wages and the poor conditions of migrant camps. Most workers received less than half the

[1]From "The Organizer's Tale" by Luis Valdez in *Ramparts*, July 1966

minimum wage, which at the time was $1 dollar an hour. The camps were usually no more than rough cabins, often without indoor plumbing and no garbage pickup. To attract attention to these problems, Chávez called for a great *huelga,* or strike, against the California grape growers.

The strikers won a great deal of public sympathy. Chávez's personal dedication was almost as important as anger over the low wages paid the pickers in winning public support. Eventually the grape growers recognized the union and settled the strike.

Chávez inspired migrant workers with a sense of their own worth. "We . . . stood tall outside the vineyards where we had stooped for years," the grape pickers stated proudly.

Some who called themselves Chicanos spoke of *La Causa* (the cause) which was to make all members of *La Raza* (the race) conscious of their common history and culture. Rodolfo "Corky" Gonzales captured that spirit in the last verses of the poem "I am Joaquín." Following are the verses in Spanish and in English.

Yo Soy Joaquín

. . . Y en todos los terrenos fértiles
los llanos átidos,
los pueblos montañeros
cuidades ahumadas
  empezamos a AVANZAR.
¡La Raza!
¡Mejicano!
  ¡Español!
    ¡Latino!
      ¡Hispano!
        ¡Chicano!
o lo que me llame yo,
  yo parezco lo mismo,
  yo siento lo mismo
  yo lloro
  y
  canto lo mismo
Yo soy el bulto de mi gente y
yo renuncio ser absorbida.
    Yo soy Joaquín
Las desigualdades son grandes
pero mi espíritu es firme
  mi fé impenetrable
  mi sangre pura.
Soy príncipe Azteca y Cristo cristiano
    ¡YO PERDURARÉ!
    ¡YO PERDURARÉ!

[1]From "I am Joaquín" by Corky Gonzales

I am Joaquín

And in all the fertile farmlands,
  the barren plains,
the mountain villages,
smoke-smeared cities
  we start to MOVE.
  La Raza!
Mejicano!
  Espanol!
    Latino!
      Hispano!
        Chicano!
or whatever I call myself,
  I look the same
  I feel the same
  I cry
    and
  sing the same
I am the masses of my people and
I refuse to be absorbed.
    I am Joaquín
The odds are great
but my spirit is strong,
  my faith unbreakable
  my blood is pure.
I am Aztec Prince and Christian Christ
  I SHALL ENDURE!
  I WILL ENDURE![1]

David Margolin/Black Star

Jason Laure/Photo Researchers

Two marchers in New York's Puerto Rican Day Parade. Baseball is the national pastime on the island. The girl smiling shyly is holding the Puerto Rican flag. Do you think Puerto Rico might become the 51st state? What arguments are made for and against statehood?

Other Hispanic Newcomers

Another major group of Hispanic immigrants was from Puerto Rico. Since Puerto Rico was part of the United States, these people were already American citizens. The immigration laws did not apply to them. Hundreds of thousands of Puerto Ricans had come north in search of work and better pay. Most settled in New York City, which soon had a larger Puerto Rican population than San Juan, the capital of Puerto Rico.

In many ways the Puerto Ricans were like the European immigrants of the years before the Great World War. Most were very poor. Most came from rural backgrounds and were not accustomed to city life. Few could speak English. Few had the skills needed to get well-paid jobs. Many were crowded into neglected pockets of the city called **barrios.**

Yet many Puerto Ricans were able to improve their lives. Herman Badillo came to New York from Puerto Rico in 1941, when he was 12. He worked as a dishwasher and as a pin boy in a bowling alley. He went to college and earned a law degree. In 1965 he was elected borough president of the Bronx, the part of New York City with the largest Puerto Rican population. In 1970 he was elected to Congress.

Since 1960 increasing numbers of people have immigrated to the United States from other areas of Latin America. More than 750,000 people have immigrated to the United States from Cuba since 1960. Many opposed the new government of Fidel Castro in 1959 and emigrated to the United States. After Castro announced that he was a communist and made an alliance with the Soviet Union, these Cubans were admitted to the United States under laws that allowed refugees from communist countries to come in without regard for any limits set by the immigration laws. About half settled in southern Florida in and around Miami.

For the next 20 years Castro made it next to impossible for Cubans to leave their country. In 1980, however, he changed his mind. In a few weeks' time more than 100,000 Cubans entered the United States. As with the Vietnamese in 1975, restrictions on immigration were temporarily set aside. Today Cuban Americans account for over 5 percent of all Hispanic Americans.

Even more Hispanic people have immigrated from Central and South America over the last three decades. Since 1960 over 1 million legal immigrants have come to the United States from Central and South America. Today over 11 percent of all Hispanic Americans trace their origins to Central or South America.

Hispanic political influence has continued to grow. In 1990 there were 10 Hispanics in the House of Representatives. But Hispanics have not shared equally in America's wealth. They have lagged behind in educational attainment and income. Yet great variations exist within the Hispanic American population. Cuban Americans have reached levels close to non-Hispanic Americans in average years of schooling, average family income, and the percentage of families living above the poverty level. Puerto Rican Americans, on

Source: Current Population Reports, Series p-20, No. 416, 1987

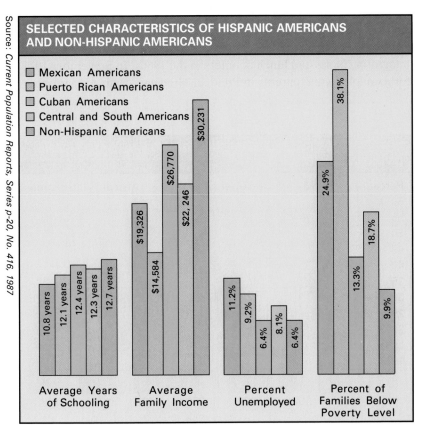

SELECTED CHARACTERISTICS OF HISPANIC AMERICANS AND NON-HISPANIC AMERICANS

☐ Mexican Americans
☐ Puerto Rican Americans
☐ Cuban Americans
☐ Central and South Americans
☐ Non-Hispanic Americans

Average Years of Schooling: 10.8 years, 12.1 years, 12.4 years, 12.3 years, 12.7 years

Average Family Income: $19,326, $14,584, $26,770, $22,246, $30,231

Percent Unemployed: 11.2%, 9.2%, 6.4%, 8.1%, 6.4%

Percent of Families Below Poverty Level: 24.9%, 38.1%, 13.3%, 18.7%, 9.9%

LEARNING FROM GRAPHS. *The label Hispanic American encompasses people from many different backgrounds. This graph shows certain characteristics of the largest groups of Hispanic Americans. Compare the data on the graph. Then state a comparison of the four Hispanic American groups. How do these groups compare to non-Hispanic Americans?*

The Melting Pot Bubbles Over   561

V. S. Naipaul, who grew up in Trinidad, observed this about the American South today.

"'Nearly sixteen millions of hands will aid you in pulling the load upward, or they will pull against you the load downward. We shall constitute one-third and more of the ignorance and crime of the South, or one-third of its intelligence and progress; we shall contribute one-third to business and industrial prosperity of the South; or we shall prove a veritable body of death, stagnating, depressing ... the body politic.'

The words read like special pleading. They come from the speech Booker T. Washington made in Atlanta in 1895, when he was only thirty-nine: a famous speech that ... calmed white people down and offered hope to black people at a time of near hopelessness. ... Those words now read like prophecy."

From *A Turn in the South*, 1989

LEARNING FROM GRAPHS. *This graph shows the number of white Americans and African Americans below the poverty level. What trend do you note for African Americans? Is the trend the same for white Americans? Explain any differences you find.*

the other hand, have a poverty rate nearly four times that of non-Hispanics.

African Americans Continue Their Struggle

White backlash continued into the 1970s. One major cause of the white resentment was the use of busing to achieve integration in the nation's schools. The Supreme Court had declared segregated schools unconstitutional in 1954. Yet, in the late 1960s, many of the nation's school systems remained segregated because students usually attended schools closest to their homes. Since most neighborhoods in towns and cities throughout America were either all-white or all-black, these schools were often segregated.

In yet another historic decision, the Supreme Court in the 1969 case of *Alexander v. Holmes* decreed that integration must proceed at once. To do so, the federal courts would have to approve integration plans submitted by school districts. More often than not, these plans included busing students from white neighborhoods to schools in black neighborhoods and students from black neighborhoods to schools in white neighborhoods. Although many of these plans were challenged in court, the Supreme Court declared in 1971 in the case of *Swann v. Charlotte-Mecklenburg Board of Education* that busing was a constitutional way to promote school integration.

As more and more schools adopted busing plans, white northerners objected as strongly as white southerners had objected to integrating buses and lunch counters in the 1960s. In September 1971, for example, white parents in Pontiac, Michigan, chained themselves

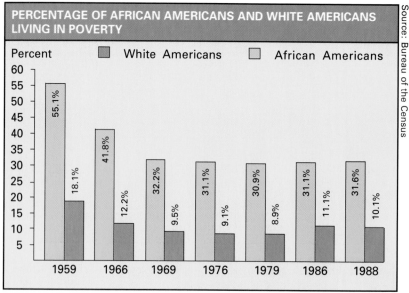

PERCENTAGE OF AFRICAN AMERICANS AND WHITE AMERICANS LIVING IN POVERTY

Percent — White Americans — African Americans

Year	White Americans	African Americans
1959	18.1%	55.1%
1966	12.2%	41.8%
1969	9.5%	32.2%
1976	9.1%	31.1%
1979	8.9%	30.9%
1986	11.1%	31.1%
1988	10.1%	31.6%

Source: Bureau of the Census

Eli Reed/Magnum Photos

Constantine Marcos/Magnum Photos

to fences to protest school busing. In the following days, 10 buses were firebombed, and many parents kept their children out of school. In Boston in 1974 thousands of white parents organized protest marches and boycotted schools when a busing plan was put into effect. Despite the protests of whites, however, the nation's schools speeded up integration plans.

Another example of white backlash concerned the government's programs of encouraging minority hiring. Known collectively as **affirmative action,** these programs required that employers recruit more African Americans as well as other minority workers. Many whites considered this an example of reverse discrimination. That is, they believed that affirmative action discriminated against whites.

Despite violence and white backlash, the civil rights movement that began in the 1950s transformed the United States. Gone were the "for whites only" signs that had been common throughout the South. Gone too in both the North and the South were all-black or all-white school systems. Many more African Americans were taking their rightful places in society, free of the stigma of racial discrimination. More and more African Americans were being elected to public office. More were attending medical schools and becoming lawyers and owners of important businesses. Their examples encouraged other disadvantaged groups—Hispanics, Native Americans, women—to demand fair treatment too.

Despite the progress of the civil rights movement, however, much remained to be done. The incomes of African Americans and Hispanics lagged behind those of whites. The nation's cities remained segregated in fact if not in law, with large numbers of poor African Americans living in run-down ghettos. Lacking education and job

The frustration of African Americans is shown by these marchers. Study the signs carried by the young mother and the Harvard students. What are their complaints?

The Melting Pot Bubbles Over   563

Source: Bureau of the Census

LEARNING FROM GRAPHS. *Years of schooling completed has a dramatic effect on income, as this graph shows. How much more on average does a white college graduate make than a white American who only completed elementary school? What is the difference for African Americans in the same categories? Why do you think this is true?*

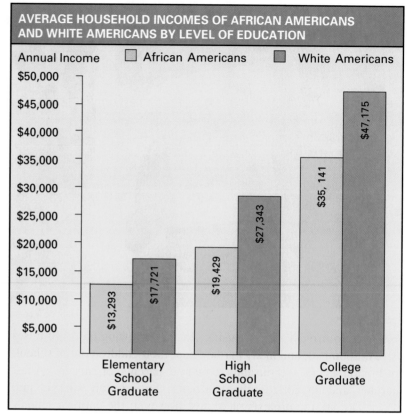

AVERAGE HOUSEHOLD INCOMES OF AFRICAN AMERICANS AND WHITE AMERICANS BY LEVEL OF EDUCATION

Annual Income — ☐ African Americans   ☐ White Americans

	African Americans	White Americans
Elementary School Graduate	$13,293	$17,721
High School Graduate	$19,429	$27,343
College Graduate	$35,141	$47,175

skills, many ghetto dwellers found it almost impossible to improve their lot in life.

Problems for American Indians

Like African Americans, American Indians continued to search for ways to revive their lost cultures. But the violence of the confrontation at Wounded Knee in 1973 drained some of the public's sympathy from the American Indian Movement.

In the late 1970s courts began to award millions of dollars in damages to tribes who sued the government over broken treaties. These rulings provided some small sense of justice. But by the 1980s Indians on reservations faced several disastrous problems. Life on many reservations had deteriorated. Unable to recapture past ways, many Indians were forced to rely on government welfare and help from religious and charitable groups. The demoralizing effects of this led to rates of alcoholism and suicide far higher than the national average. This was especially true of Indian teenagers. In addition, many Indians dropped out of both reservation and public schools. One Hopi girl described the feelings of many younger Indians:

❝ We would like to leave the reservation. We wouldn't mind seeing how Indians live in cities. A lot of Hopis say you stop being a Hopi when you go into a city and live in big buildings and forget about our land, and our hills, and the sky over us. Maybe. I don't know. The Indian can't just sit and think of his past. My mother says it's a pity; our people were happy here for so long. Now, a lot of us want to leave. . . .[1]"

For Indians who were not on reservations, life was somewhat better. Many were successful members of the professions and leaders of their communities. But most still felt the loss of their culture, and in schools and the job market they still faced discrimination.

[1]From *Eskimos, Chicanos, Indians: Volume IV of Children in Crisis* by Robert Coles

The Equal Rights Amendment Fails

Another group within American society that became more vocal at this time was women. As you have read, many women fought to keep the gains they made after World War II. After much debate Congress passed an **Equal Rights Amendment** (ERA) in 1972. This amendment provided that "equality of rights under the law shall not be denied or abridged by the United States or by any state on account of sex." It was submitted to the states for ratification.

The proposed amendment had wide support among women and men from all walks of life. But opposition to the proposed Equal Rights Amendment proved to be strong. It did not win the approval

This young Crow in tribal regalia helps us recall the past. Yet what does the speaker quoted on the previous page say about the past?

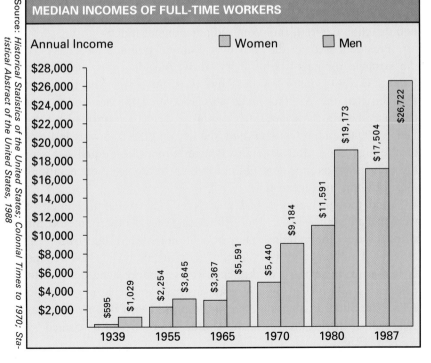

MEDIAN INCOMES OF FULL-TIME WORKERS

Annual Income   ☐ Women   ☐ Men

Year	Women	Men
1939	$595	$1,029
1955	$2,254	$3,645
1965	$3,367	$5,591
1970	$5,440	$9,184
1980	$11,591	$19,173
1987	$17,504	$26,722

Source: *Historical Statistics of the United States; Colonial Times to 1970; Statistical Abstract of the United States, 1988*

LEARNING FROM GRAPHS. *Although women have begun to claim more higher-paying jobs than ever before, a gap between the average salary for women and men still exists. What was that gap in 1987? How would you explain the difference?*

The Melting Pot Bubbles Over   565

Members of the Supreme Court in early 1991 are, front row from left to right: Associate Justices John Paul Stevens, Thurgood Marshall, Chief Justice William H. Rehnquist, Associate Justices Byron R. White, and Harry A. Blackmun. Back row from left to right: Associate Justices David Souter, Antonin Scalia, Sandra Day O'Connor, and Anthony M. Kennedy.

of three fourths of the state legislatures, even after the deadline for ratification was extended. Some people considered ERA unnecessary because laws against discrimination already existed. Others feared that it would do more harm than good by doing away with laws providing special benefits and protections for women, such as those limiting the hours of women workers. Women would have to be drafted into the armed services in the event of war, opponents of the ERA claimed.

Thus hope dimmed for supporters of the ERA. In 1980 the Republican party refused to endorse the amendment. When the second deadline expired, the proposed amendment failed.

President Reagan did, however, show a political awareness of the struggle for equal rights early in his presidency by appointing Sandra Day O'Connor to the Supreme Court. Still, the president stressed that the Arizona judge was appointed for her ability, not because she was a woman. O'Connor was easily confirmed by the Senate, 99-0, and in October 1981 she became the first woman to sit on the high court. But generally Reagan's record on equal rights in his eight years as president did not live up to the great expectations raised by this appointment.

And though progress had been slow, the economic status of women had improved. In the 1970s and 1980s women entered the work force by the millions. They bought and started their own businesses—4 million by 1990. In fact, women-owned businesses was the fastest-growing segment of the American economy. One out of four businesses was owned by a woman, up from only one in twenty in 1980. The Small Business Administration predicted that by the year 2000 half of the businesses in the United States would be owned by women. 🖳

Sandra Day O'Connor was the first woman appointed to the Supreme Court. How was her appointment received by the Senate?

Return to the Preview & Review on page 556.

566   MODERN TIMES

3. THREE AMERICAN TRAGEDIES

Preview & Review

Crisis in America's Cities

Americans faced other problems as well. By the 1970s about three quarters of the American people were living in cities and their surrounding suburbs. As these metropolitan areas expanded, they began to meet one another to form supercities.

One such **megalopolis** (from the Greek for "great city") stretched from Portland, Maine, through Boston, New York City, Philadelphia, Baltimore, and Washington to Richmond, Virginia. It was known as BosWash. Another, ChiPitt, reached from Chicago to Pittsburgh. A third, SanSan, extended from San Francisco to San Diego along the California coast.

The central areas, or **inner cities,** of these regions wasted away as well-to-do and middle-class residents moved to the suburbs. Poor city dwellers, many of them African Americans, Puerto Ricans, or Mexican Americans, remained behind.

A vicious circle of decay resulted from this population shift. When the people with money to spend began to leave, department stores and other businesses followed. This meant that there were fewer jobs for inner-city residents. It meant also that city tax collections fell off.

Michael Weisbrot/Black Star

Use these questions to guide your reading. Answer the questions after completing Section 3. **Understanding Issues, Events, & Ideas.** Use the following words to explain three major problems that faced the American people in the 1970s and 1980s: megalopolis, inner cities, dropouts, urban decay, pollution, smog, acid rain, greenhouse effect, Environmental Protection Agency, nuclear energy, Three Mile Island, Chernobyl.
1. What causes a megalopolis to develop?
2. Describe the vicious circle of decay that developed when the urban population shifted to the suburbs.
3. What was one of the causes for the growing number of homeless in America's cities in the 1970s and 1980s?
4. Why did it become necessary to establish the Environmental Protection Agency?
5. Why was the construction of nuclear power plants halted?
Thinking Critically.   1. Imagine that you have just become the mayor of a large American city. Outline plans for how you intend to solve the problem of homelessness in your city.
2. Write a letter to your Representative or Senator in Congress suggesting ways for solving the problems of pollution.

Urban decay and blight such as this have spread through whole areas of America's cities.

The Reverend Jesse Jackson presented this view of environmental concern.

"The question is not, 'will we start treating our environment better?' The question is, 'will we start treating ourselves better by not contaminating the environment that we live in and are part of?'

This is, at its very heart, a spiritual question. Ultimately we must decide how much respect and love we have for other human beings. . . .

The environment is, in the final analysis, a political question. That means we must organize across and against lines of race, class, gender, nation and geography in order to save the earth. . . . If we can take down the Berlin Wall, we can take down the wall that prevents us from seeing what must be done to leave our children a livable world."

Greenpeace, 1990

Public services then declined. If the city governments raised tax rates to make up for the loss, more middle-income citizens moved away. Higher property taxes also made it difficult for landlords to make a profit. They skimped on maintaining their buildings. Heating systems broke down in winter. Roofs leaked. Corridors were dark and dirty. Buildings soon deteriorated beyond repair, and decent neighborhoods became slums. As the population of the inner cities fell, whole neighborhoods were abandoned.

This decline made life harder for the people who had to remain in the inner cities. Their children had little hope of getting decent jobs when they completed their schooling. Because the cities had less money, the schools began to suffer too. Classes were overcrowded. Supplies were inadequate. Equipment broke down. Faced with such conditions many students lost interest in school. They became **dropouts.** Unable to find jobs, many of these dropouts idled about causing trouble. Hopeless and resentful, some turned to crime.

One of the worst examples of this **urban decay** was the section of New York City called the South Bronx. In 1977 when the president of the United States visited this district, he was deeply shocked. The area looked as though it had been bombed in an air raid. Most of the buildings were fire-blackened, empty shells. Yet just a few minutes' drive from the South Bronx, fashionable shoppers bought gold cuff links at Tiffany's and perfume at Saks Fifth Avenue.

An astonishing number of people became homeless in the 1980s, living in the streets and parks with only a shopping bag to hold their belongings. Visitors to American cities were shocked by these people, who slept in cardboard boxes or doorways when weather was bad. The problem was serious under the Democrats and continued to grow under President Reagan. The problem was compounded during the Reagan administration when many mental patients were "deinstitutionalized"—that is, put out on the street with the notion that they would be better off "free" and that local communities would supply the shelter and medication they needed. In every major city passersby stepped over homeless people, but no one seemed able to devise a policy that would allow the homeless to retain their dignity and human rights and also receive the therapies that at least one third of the homeless needed.

Coping with Pollution

Beginning in the 1960s the crowding of so many people and so much manufacturing into metropolitan areas caused serious **pollution.** Millions of automobiles, buses, and trucks poured harmful exhaust fumes into the air in increasing amounts. The furnaces of factories and utility companies released clouds of smoke and cinders. The mile-high city of Denver, Colorado, was veiled in haze. At certain times in Los Angeles polluting substances called **smog** (the word comes from *smoke* plus *fog*) were so thick that venturing outside could be dangerous. Some people with heart trouble, allergies, and lung diseases took to wearing gas masks outdoors to protect themselves! Wastes from U.S. industry were sometimes carried by winds to Canada, and the chemicals came back to earth as **acid rain,** causing much destruction.

Many factories were dumping poisonous chemical waste products into rivers and lakes. Accidents to off-shore oil wells and to huge oil tankers released tons of thick, black crude oil into the oceans. The oil killed birds and fish and covered miles of beaches with tar and grease.

Chemicals used to kill insects and to fertilize the soil proved dangerous too. Scientists claimed that the gases used in spray cans caused damage to the upper atmosphere by weakening the ozone layer that protects the earth from dangerous radiation from the sun. Weather experts believed that the earth was growing warmer because of what they called the **greenhouse effect.** The increase in the burning of coal, oil, and other fuels in homes, factories, and automobiles was increasing the amount of carbon dioxide in the air. This, the experts said, was preventing the radiation of heat from the earth from escaping into space.

Public support for the fight against pollution was vigorous. As early as 1955, Congress had passed a law to improve air quality. Over the next 35 years, this act was strengthened several times. In 1969 Congress passed the National Environmental Policy Act, which set up a council to advise the president on environmental matters and

The City of Angels, Los Angeles, lies smothered in the smog created in part by the movement of traffic along the freeways. But environmentalists with activities such as Earth Day, right, have fought for 20 years to awaken the consciences of polluters.

Ken Biggs/After Image

Werner Wolff/Black Star

Chris Harris/Gamma-Liaison

Mike Maple/Woodfin Camp

This pair of photos shows a nuclear power plant from cooling tower (top) to the central core (bottom). Explain briefly how a nuclear reactor produces energy.

Return to the Preview & Review on page 567.

oversee pollution controls. Environmentalists were further encouraged in 1970 when Congress established the Environmental Protection Agency to monitor pollution and seek ways to eliminate it. But its efforts were seldom successful. Automakers and other large manufacturers delayed deadlines to clean up the environment.

The problems of air and water pollution and the greenhouse effect went beyond national boundaries. People and concerned groups began to seek global solutions. Delegates to international conferences on environmental problems, such as the hole in the ozone layer, offered suggestions to all world nations.

Coping with Energy Shortages

As you have read, in the 1970s Americans experienced a severe shortage of energy. By 1980 they had been forced to cut back hard on their consumption of petroleum products. Americans began to buy smaller, lighter automobiles to replace the "gas guzzlers" they had previously favored. Eventually conservation and the discovery of new oil fields in non-OPEC nations caused the price to fall considerably—but not nearly to what it had been in 1973.

Meanwhile, the search for other sources of energy went on. One source, **nuclear energy,** was already producing large amounts of electricity. Nuclear plants make electricity by controlled splitting of atoms of uranium, the same element used in atom bombs. When uranium atoms are slowly broken, instead of exploding they release enormous amounts of heat. The heat turns water into steam, just as coal or oil are used to heat water into steam in conventional power plants. The steam turns the turbines that create electricity.

Nuclear power plants are very expensive to build. And an accident that allowed the uranium to overheat might cause an explosion and release death-dealing radioactive particles over wide areas. In 1979, an accident at **Three Mile Island** nuclear plant near Harrisburg, Pennsylvania, did great damage to the plant and caused a near panic in surrounding communities. In 1986 the explosion of a Soviet plant at **Chernobyl,** near Kiev, spewed huge amounts of radiation into the air. Its effect was felt over thousands of miles. Plans to construct and operate more nuclear power plants were cut back sharply.

The search for new, safe sources of energy such as sunlight slackened when the price of oil fell. But in the long run, such new sources will have to be found, because oil reserves will eventually be consumed.

4. THE DEMOCRATS TAKE A TURN

The Election of 1976

In the mid-1970s the United States faced these serious problems as well as a loss of faith in its leadership as a result of Watergate. The Democratic convention, which met in New York City in July nominated James Earl Carter, Jr., for president. Jimmy Carter, as he preferred to be known, had been a little-known governor of Georgia, peanut farmer, and businessman. His political experience had been limited to service in the Georgia legislature and one term as governor.

At the Republican convention in Kansas City, President Ford won a narrow victory by beating back the challenge of Ronald Reagan, a Hollywood actor and the former governor of California.

In the campaign Carter's strategy was to picture himself as an "outsider" who had no connection with the corruption and scandal that seemed to surround Washington in the age of Watergate. He stressed his sincerity, his honesty, and above all, his deep religious faith. He would run the federal government efficiently, he said, and he would balance the budget. In one campaign speech he voiced the concerns of many Americans and his vision of the nation:

      66 Can our government in Washington, which we love, be decent? Is it possible for it to be honest and truthful and fair and idealistic, compassionate, filled with love? Is it possible for our government to be what the American people are, or what we would like to be? Can it once again be a source of pride instead of apology and shame and embarrassment?

      A lot of people think the answer is no. I think the answer is yes.

      We still have a system of government that's the best on earth. The vision that was ours 200 years ago is still there. Our Constitution still says the same thing. Equality, equity, fairness, decency, are still aspects of our government. Freedom, liberty, individualism, are still integral aspects of our government. We have a nation of which we ought to be proud. . . .

      We ought to be searching for a way to make our nation more decent and more fair.[1] 99

Ford emphasized his political experience. He compared his 27 years in national politics to Carter's brief stint at the state level.

Neither candidate presented imaginative solutions to the nation's problems. So public interest in the campaign was low. Barely half the eligible voters actually went to the polls. It was particularly

[1]From *A Government as Good as Its People* by Jimmy Carter

The Carters appear at one of the inaugural balls celebrating the return of the Democrats to the White House. Report to your classmates on the most recent evaluations of the Carter presidency. Predict whom the woman registering to vote below cast her ballot for: Carter or Ford?

discouraging that relatively few of the 18- to 20-year-olds who had been given the vote by the **Twenty-Sixth Amendment** (ratified in 1971) bothered to cast ballots.

The election was very close. Carter won in the electoral college by 297 votes to 240. He carried the northern industrial states and the South. A major reason for his victory was the support he received from Mexican Americans, particularly in south Texas, and from African Americans. Almost 95 out of every 100 African American voters cast their ballots for Carter.

The low **voter participation rate**—the percentage of eligible voters who vote—reflected the start of a discouraging trend that has continued. Today the United States has one of the lowest voter participation rates among democratic nations. Only about 50 percent of the voting-age population has bothered to cast ballots in presidential elections since 1972. In contrast, Italy has a voter participation rate of 94 percent and many European countries have rates of over 80 percent. Yet today more than 25 percent of Americans of voting age are not even registered to vote. This is particularly discouraging because democracy is based on people's choices. Americans, through their power to elect government representatives and through their right to openly express their views, can bring about social change.

The election of Carter, who publicly affirmed his religious convictions, also represented a change that had been taking place in American society since World War II. He symbolized the reawakening of American religious spirit. Despite radical movements of the 1960s and unprecedented scientific breakthroughs in the 1970s and 1980s, the tide of popular religion had continued to rise. Many people—among them political candidates and even Catholic priests—described experiences something like a traditionally Protestant "new birth." These "born again" Americans spread the experience both publicly and privately.

Carter at Home

Jimmy Carter tried to make himself more available to ordinary people than most recent presidents. Instead of riding to the White House in a limousine after his inauguration, he and his wife and small daughter walked down Pennsylvania Avenue at the end of the inaugural parade, waving and smiling to the crowd.

In office Carter continued to stress this informal style. He appeared on television wearing a sweater instead of a suit coat. He had a "call in" in which he answered questions phoned in by citizens.

Carter began his presidency by ruffling the feathers of members of Congress. He displayed a kind of petulance—seeming arrogant and superior—and although he was a good orator, he often spoke to the American people about things they could not feel or understand. Carter claimed there was "a growing malaise of the American spirit."

By this he meant a vague illness that would be hard to treat. This dark view could hardly console troubled Americans waiting for the economy to improve and for foreign tensions to ease. Carter also stressed that with American **citizenship**, or legal membership in society, came certain obligations such as obeying the law. How bright the future would be depended in large part on how actively each American worked toward creating a just and prosperous society.

As the months passed, critics began to claim that Carter was a poor leader, his economic policies were ineffective, and his civil rights measures were not strong enough. Within his own party some Democrats insisted that to stimulate the economy and reduce unemployment, Carter should urge Congress to increase government spending. Instead he attempted to slow the economy by cutting government spending. He set out with zeal to protect the environment, the workplace, the consumer, and the nation's highways. But each new regulation brought protests from businesses who feared losing profits trying to comply with the new laws. He named three women to his cabinet, and more women, blacks, and Hispanics received federal jobs and judgeships than ever before. Still, many African Americans and Hispanics complained that Carter had not appointed enough of their members to posts in his administration.

Carter and Foreign Relations

Although Carter's intentions were good, his inexperience in foreign relations caused continual problems. He bravely set the tone for his foreign policy in his inaugural address:

> ❝ Because we are free we can never be indifferent to the fate of freedom elsewhere. . . . Our commitment to human rights must be absolute. . . .[1] ❞

[1]From his inaugural speech by Jimmy Carter, January 20, 1977

Securing worldwide human rights, however, proved easier said than done. Pressure for human rights weakened American ties with anticommunist nations such as Iran and Nicaragua, where autocratic governments regularly violated the human rights of citizens. It threatened détente with the Soviets. Then Carter's mishandling of negotiations for a new Strategic Arms Limitation Treaty (SALT II) and his firm stand against the Soviet invasion of Afghanistan in 1979 sent détente gasping its last breaths.

But the president did win much praise for his efforts to bring peace to the troubled Middle East. He brought Israel's premier, Menachem Begin, and Egypt's president, Anwar Sadat, to Camp David, the presidential retreat. With Carter's help, Begin and Sadat hammered out an agreement to work for peace, known as the **Camp David Accords.** 🖥

Own D.B./Black Star

The triumph of the Carter presidency was bringing together the leaders of two ancient rivals: Egypt represented by Anwar Sadat and Israel represented by Menachem Begin. What agreement did they reach at Camp David before this handshake?

Return to the Preview & Review on page 571.

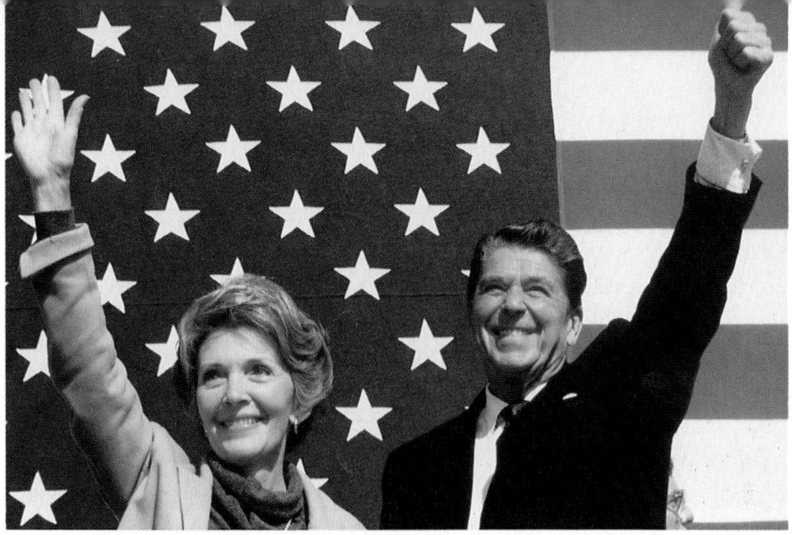
Bettmann Newsphotos

Even his sharpest critics concede that Ronald Reagan, shown here with his wife, Nancy, restored the country's pride in its flag. Once again patriotism was in fashion.

Preview & Review

Use these questions to guide your reading. Answer the questions after completing Section 5.

Understanding Issues, Events, & Ideas. Use the following words to describe the presidential elections of 1980, 1984, and 1988, as well as the Reagan years and the beginnings of the Bush presidency: inflation rate, supply-side economics, Sandinistas, Income Tax Act, Contras, Boland Amendment, *glasnost, perestroika,* strategic defense initiative.

1. What international crisis helped cause the defeat of Jimmy Carter in the 1980 presidential election?
2. What is supply-side economics?
3. Why did Reagan send aid to the El Salvador government and the anti-government Nicaraguans?
4. How did candidate Mondale compare to candidate Reagan in the 1984 election?
5. What were some of the alarming changes occurring in American society at the end of the 1980s?

Thinking Critically. Imagine that you are a member of Congress in the early 1980s. Write a press statement in which you either attack or defend Reagan's policy of sending military and economic aid to the anti-government Nicaraguans.

5. THE REPUBLICANS TRIUMPHANT

The Election of 1980

The energy crisis of the 1970s aggravated the problem of inflation. The skyrocketing price of gasoline, heating oil, and everything made from petroleum pushed the **inflation rate** to 13 percent by 1979. Inflation became the main issue in the 1980 presidential election.

President Carter won the Democratic nomination after a hard campaign against Senator Edward M. Kennedy, a brother of President John F. Kennedy. Carter was helped in the primaries by an international crisis that had broken out in November 1979. A mob in Teheran, the capital of Iran, invaded the American embassy and held the people in the building hostage. The leaders demanded that the United States turn over to them the former shah, or king, of Iran, who had been deposed a year earlier and who had been admitted to the United States to receive treatment for cancer.

The United States government refused to return the shah, and a stalemate resulted. For months the Iranians held 53 Americans prisoner in the embassy in Teheran. In desperation President Carter ordered a team of marine commandos flown into Iran by helicopter at night to rescue the hostages. The commandos landed in the desert near Teheran without being detected. However, the mission had to be called off because several of the helicopters broke down. Eight commandos died when two helicopters collided on the ground. The Iranians shocked the world with a ghoulish display of the dead. The effort earned Carter praise. But the hostages remained in captivity. This was a severe blow to Carter and to the prestige of the United States.

The Republicans nominated Ronald Reagan. John Anderson, a liberal Republican congressman from Illinois entered the race as the candidate of the Independent party.

Reagan won a sweeping victory, 43.9 million popular votes to

35.5 million for Carter. Anderson received 5.7 million popular votes. Reagan's electoral majority was even more stunning: 489 to Carter's 49. The Republican party also made large gains in both houses of Congress.

The hostages held in Iran shown on their arrival on free soil were given a boisterous ticker tape parade a few days later in New York City.

On January 20, 1981, Ronald Reagan took the oath of office as president. At a luncheon shortly afterward he announced that the hostages in Iran had been freed. The Iranians claimed they had delayed the release until after the inauguration to punish President Carter for invading their country.

After leaving office Jimmy Carter devoted himself to world peace and sheltering the homeless. Many of his former critics saw him in a new light, some nearly conferring sainthood on him. But the fact remains that he seemed unequal to the challenges put forth during his term as president.

Reagan as President

President Reagan believed that the federal government had grown too big and was involved in too many aspects of everyday life. He said in his inaugural address, "It is my intention to curb the size and influence of the Federal establishment." He hoped that by 1988 more than 40 federal programs would have been taken over by the states. He called his plan "The New Federalism."

Reagan was determined to increase the amount of money spent

The Republicans Triumphant 575

This picture was taken to reassure Americans that President Reagan was recovering from a would-be assassin's bullet. How did the president react to the shooting?

on defense but to cut back on other government spending. He also wished to reduce taxes. He argued that the budget could be balanced despite the lower taxes. Americans would invest the money they saved on taxes in new business enterprises. This would cause the economy to boom. More jobs would be created, and profits would rise. Tax *revenues* would go up even though tax *rates* were lower. This theory was known as **supply-side economics.**

If the theory did not work, Reagan's program would result in a large increase in the national debt. Democratic leaders opposed the program, especially the tax cut.

Reagan proved to be a determined leader and an extremely skillful politician. By midsummer 1981 both the Reagan budget and bills reducing the federal income tax by 25 percent over three years had been enacted into law.

In the midst of the budget fight a would-be assassin shot the president in the chest as he emerged from a Washington hotel. Reagan showed great courage as well as a sense of humor in the face of near death. When he was wheeled into the operating room, he said to the doctors, "I hope you fellows are all Republicans." When his wife arrived at his side, he told her, "Honey, I guess I forgot to duck." Fortunately, he recovered from the wound quickly, although his injuries were far worse than the nation knew.

Despite Reagan's economic policies, the nation's economic problems persisted for a time. A serious recession developed, called by Reagan supporters "the Carter Depression." Business activity lagged. Unemployment rose to over ten percent and interest rates remained high. With tax revenues down and the government spending billions on defense, the deficit rose to nearly $200 billion in 1983.

The recession did have one good result—the inflation rate tumbled from over 12 percent to below 4 percent by early 1984. With that, business began to pick up. Thousands of idle workers found new jobs.

But the huge budget deficit remained. Some advisers urged Reagan to reduce it by cutting down on military spending. He refused to do so because he believed that the Soviet Union was an "evil empire" out to dominate the world. Only if the Soviets knew the United States was as strong as they were, would they restrain themselves, the president believed.

This policy caused Reagan to take a particularly strong stand against possible Soviet "penetration" of Central America. Some years earlier, rebels in Nicaragua known as **Sandinistas** had overthrown a reactionary dictator. These Sandinistas had set up a government friendly to the Soviet Union. They were also supporting rebel forces in the nearby nation of El Salvador. Reagan provided advisers and military and economic aid to the government of El Salvador and ordered the CIA to organize anti-government Nicaraguans who were seeking to defeat the Sandinistas.

The Election of 1984

Reagan's Central American policy was controversial, but he remained personally popular. In 1984 the Republican convention unanimously nominated him for a second term as president. The fight for the Democratic nomination was long and drawn out, but in the end Walter Mondale, who had been Carter's vice president, was victorious. For the first time an African American, the Reverend Jesse Jackson, waged a serious campaign for the nomination. Jackson attracted wide support by denouncing Reagan's economic policies as harmful to the poor.

Mondale electrified the country by selecting a woman, Representative Geraldine Ferraro of New York, as his running mate. He also announced that if elected he would ask Congress to raise taxes in order to reduce the budget deficit. This was a direct challenge to President Reagan, who had sworn not to increase taxes under any circumstances.

In the campaign Mondale emphasized the difficulties the nation faced. He claimed that Reagan was taking *too* tough a stand toward the Soviets. He charged that the Republicans had been unfair to poor people and those outside the mainstream of American society.

Mondale made a good argument for these propositions. But his tone was quarrelsome, his mood dark. Reagan, on the other hand, was the eternal optimist. His tone was friendly, his mood sunny. He won powerful support from religious fundamentalists and from other conservatives, who were concerned about communism, forced school busing, the toleration of homosexuals, the drug problem, and rising crime rates.

The result was a Reagan landslide. Reagan won nearly 60 percent of the popular vote. The electoral college vote was even more lopsided: 525 to 13. Mondale carried only his home state, Minnesota, and the District of Columbia. African Americans were the only traditionally Democratic group to support Mondale. The Democratic tactic of nominating a woman for vice president failed. Women did not automatically vote for a woman. Though Mondale would have lost in any case, far more women voted for Reagan than for Mondale.

The Mondale/Ferraro ticket failed to catch the imagination of American voters. In spite of Geraldine Ferraro's presence on the Democratic ticket, whom did most women vote for?

The Reagan "Revolution"

In his second term President Reagan continued to try to cut back on government spending on social welfare projects and to lower taxes still further. The **Income Tax Act** of 1986 relieved 6,000,000 low-income people from all income taxes and lowered the maximum rate for everyone else to 28 percent. The taxes paid by corporations were also reduced.

The president also pursued his policy of appointing as many conservatives as possible to public office. When Chief Justice Warren

Marchers for Women's Equal Rights come to Washington. Just above is Norma McCorvey, who used the name "Jane Roe" of Roe v. Wade *to protect her identity.*

Burger resigned in 1986, Reagan nominated Associate Justice William Rehnquist, an extremely conservative judge, to the top post on the Supreme Court. Rehnquist's position was filled by Antonin Scalia, another conservative judge. The next year, when another justice retired, Reagan offered the seat to Robert Bork, a judge so conservative that the Senate refused to confirm him. It later did confirm the conservative but more moderate Anthony Kennedy.

The makeup of the high court was particularly important to those on both sides of the issue of abortion. Right to life advocates argued that all life is sacred, and only in the most extreme cases should an unborn child be taken from its mother. They were challenged by the pro-choice movement, which claimed a woman had the constitutional right to protect her own physical and mental health, even if a pregnancy had to be ended in the first three months. The Court was drawn into the argument by the 1973 landmark case, *Roe v. Wade,* in which the court ruled that women have a constitutional guarantee of personal privacy that includes the right to have an abortion during the first three months of pregnancy. In the late 1980s, however, the more conservative Supreme Court upheld some state laws that put various restrictions on the right of abortion. Abortion remained a controversial issue into the 1990s.

The president's many successes were partly due to his personal popularity and partly a matter of the famous Reagan luck. His appointments were clearly moving the government in the conservative

STRATEGIES FOR SUCCESS

EXPRESSING A POINT OF VIEW

You may often be called upon to express and defend your point of view on a topic—in class discussions, essay tests, research papers, or debates. At such times you need to clearly state your positions and provide support.

How to Express a Point of View

To express a point of view, follow these guidelines.

1. **Research the issue.** Make sure you know what you are talking about. Find out what the opposing points of view are.
2. **Decide on your position.** Study the evidence and evaluate the situation. Decide how you stand on the issue. Begin to collect support for your position.
3. **State your position simply and clearly.** Prepare an introduction that identifies the issue and states your position in simple and clear terms.
4. **Support your position.** When writing your point of view, develop additional paragraphs that provide support for your position. End with a concluding paragraph briefly restating your position and reasoning.

Applying the Strategy

Today the issue of gun control raises a controversy in many parts of the United States. The basic question is: To what degree should the government regulate and limit the sale and ownership of guns? Those who are against gun control point for their defense to a portion of the Second Amendment which guarantees a "right of the people to keep and bear arms." However, those who favor gun control point out that the amendment cites the right to bear arms as part of a "well-regulated Militia." They also cite the rise in violent, gun-related crimes. State your point of view on gun control. Be sure to support your position.

For independent practice, see Practicing the Strategy on page 587.

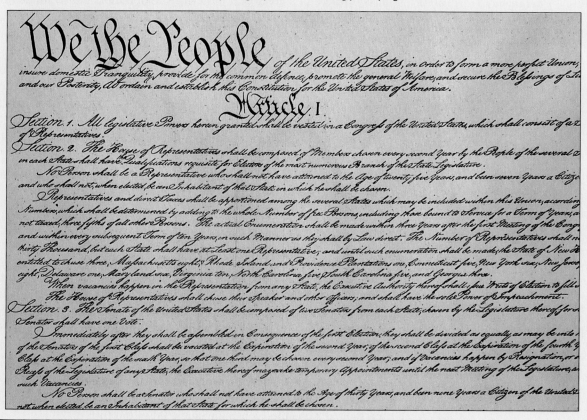

Realization that mothers could pass the deadly AIDS virus to their unborn children came slowly. The children who contracted the disease were sometimes abandoned. Mother Hale, pictured above, cares for such children. The disease has no cure nor vaccine. Your families, schools, and churches can help you understand how the AIDS virus is spread.

direction he favored. But at the same time new and sometimes deadly social problems began to change the face of America. Many Americans were shocked by almost daily news reports of abused and neglected children. Physically and emotionally scarred, such children had little chance of living well-adjusted, productive lives.

Despite efforts to get tough on criminals, crime rates actually rose. Illegal habit-forming drugs flooded the country, and many addicts, once "hooked," would stop at nothing to obtain money to purchase them. "Crack," a particularly potent form of cocaine, was especially troublesome because it was cheap and widely available.

More frightening still was the sudden appearance of a deadly new disease, acquired immune deficiency syndrome, or AIDS. AIDS was caused by a virus that prevents the body from fighting off pneumonia and other diseases. Because there was (and is) no known cure for AIDS, almost everyone who contracted it eventually died.

Although the economy was booming in the late 1980s, many people were not sharing in the wealth being produced. The rich were getting richer, but many of the poor were getting poorer. Many were victims of technological unemployment. That is, extremely efficient computers and automated machinery began to replace human workers at the lower end of the wage scale.

Reagan's policy of eliminating government restrictions on business resulted in a great deal of healthy competition. But competition could be painful to the inefficient, who were swallowed up by the more successful. Ending government regulation also encouraged recklessness. Banks in particular, freed from strict control, sometimes invested in extremely risky ventures. In addition, when falling oil prices caused a severe depression in Texas and other oil-producing states, many companies could not repay their loans and area banks went "belly up" by the dozens.

Another problem resulted from the flood of cheap but high quality imports from Japan and other countries of Asia, such as South Korea and Taiwan. The imports were snapped up by American consumers, but competing American businesses suffered.

Iran Contra

Reagan's policies were only indirect causes of these economic problems. But in two foreign areas he pursued policies that made his last years in office unhappy ones. One involved the Central American nation of Nicaragua. Reagan, of course, disapproved of the pro-Soviet Sandinistas. In 1981 he persuaded Congress to provide weapons and other supplies to the **Contras** (from the Spanish *contra*, meaning "against") who were seeking to overthrow them. However, the Contra revolt made little progress. Fearing that continued military assistance might lead to "another Vietnam," in 1984 Congress passed the **Boland Amendment** banning such aid in the future.

John Ficara/Woodfin Camp

Meanwhile a savage war had broken out in the Middle East between Iran and Iraq. Like most Americans, President Reagan had no love for the Iranians because of the hostage crisis of the Carter years. But there were a number of Americans being held captive somewhere in Lebanon by radicals under the influence of Iran. Reagan was eager to obtain their release. In 1986, despite his dislike of the Iranian government and his known opposition to bargaining with hostage takers, he authorized the secret sale of American arms to Iran, expecting that the hostages would be freed in exchange.

The man who arranged the Iranian arms deal was Oliver North, a marine colonel assigned to the White House. After the passage of the Boland Amendment, North had also been given the job of persuading foreign countries and well-to-do individuals to contribute money for the support of the Contras. North, with the knowledge of his immediate superiors, used the profits of the arms sale to Iran ($12 million) to supply the Contras in Nicaragua. This, of course, was illegal because of the Boland Amendment. When the secret sales became known in late 1986, North and Reagan's national security adviser were forced from office. They and others involved in the transactions were indicted and in the first of a series of trials, North was found guilty.

During the Iran-Contra hearings, Senators grilled members of the Reagan administration about their knowledge of the secret events. Name another of the Washington hearings you've read about in The Story of America *that attracted wide interest.*

New American-Soviet Relations

The main foreign policy development of Reagan's second term was the dramatic shift that occurred in the Soviet Union after Mikhail Gorbachev became premier in March 1985. Soviet leaders were forced to deal with the failing communist economic system, a failure

Point of View

The magazine *Vanity Fair* published this profile of Mikhail Gorbachev after the collapse of the communist governments in Russia's eastern satellites.

"The eyes. Everyone is struck by the gleam that blazes behind his dark eyes. Presidents, Soviet-ologists, resident C.I.A. psychologists, Wall Street deal makers—all come away talking about some strange chemical reaction, as if with the intensity of his belief Mikhail Gorbachev had burned his image of a new world onto their own retinas and they will never be the same.

'His eyes convey an intensity that is slightly abnormal,' muses a senior analyst . . . 'It's as though his temperature is a little higher than normal, and he's running a little faster than anybody else.'"

Gail Sheehy, 1990

that had spread in one degree or another to all the Soviet satellite nations. Gorbachev encouraged people to discuss public issues and even to criticize government actions (the policy called *glasnost*). He also tried to stimulate the Soviet economy by encouraging individual enterprise. This was called *perestroika*.

At first Reagan was suspicious of these new Soviet policies. He urged Congress to appropriate large sums to build a **strategic defense initiative** (called "Star Wars" by some), a complicated and extremely expensive computerized system designed to destroy incoming missiles before they could reach the United States. Such a system would only be needed in case of a Soviet attack. But by 1986 it was clear that Gorbachev was really interested in reducing international tensions. Disastrously small harvests had forced the Soviets to sign trade agreements with many nations, including the United States. Other breakdowns in the Soviet economic system followed soon after. Now Gorbachev conceded that the Soviet Union needed help in rebuilding its economy as it turned its back on the communism it had adopted when Stalin became the Soviet leader.

At a summit meeting in 1988 Reagan and Gorbachev finally signed a treaty eliminating medium-range nuclear missiles, a major step toward reducing the danger of nuclear war. Americans and people all over the world cheered the efforts of the two world leaders.

Bill Fitzpatrick/The White House

Arm in arm in the Kremlin are Ronald Reagan, Raisa Gorbachev, Mikhail Gorbachev, and Nancy Reagan.

Bettmann Newsphotos

Steve Liss/Time Picture Syndication

The Election of 1988

According to polls, most Americans disapproved of the Iran-Contra deal and believed that President Reagan knew about it. However, they continued to admire him personally. In any case his final term was ending.

The Republican candidate to succeed Reagan was his vice president, George Bush. There were so many candidates battling for the Democratic nomination that it was hard at the start to tell them apart. As the primaries proceeded, the field shrank to two: the Reverend Jesse Jackson and Governor Michael Dukakis of Massachusetts. Jackson, who ran another exciting campaign, attracted more white support than in 1984. But Dukakis had a solid majority of the delegates at the convention and was nominated on the first ballot.

The Democrats hoped to take advantage of the Iran-Contra scandal and of George Bush's reputation for seeming weak and easily dominated by others. Dukakis was not glamorous, but presented himself as the efficient governor of a prosperous state. At the start of the campaign he seemed the likely winner.

But the race for president did not turn out as expected. Instead of being weak, Bush attacked Dukakis at every turn, whereas Dukakis proved to be not as strong as expected—more like a punching bag than an efficient manager. Actually neither candidate aroused much popular enthusiasm, partly because they did not disagree much about really important issues. But as time passed, it became increasingly clear that a majority of the people preferred Bush. On election day he won easily, carrying the electoral college by 426 to 112.

Rivals for the Democratic nomination in a friendly moment, Jesse Jackson and Michael Dukakis. Both had a formidable opponent in George Bush, who promised to continue much of the Reagan legacy. The Bush inaugural and the grandeur of the Capitol are seen on the left.

Return to the Preview & Review on page 574.

LINKING HISTORY & GEOGRAPHY

FATAL ERROR: OIL ON WATER

Prince William Sound is an emerald jewel, one of Alaska's scenic wonders. It is a bay with 1,000 miles of shoreline. Its waters teem with fish. It is the playground of hundreds of thousands of sea otters, seals, sea lions, and whales. Sea birds and bald eagles nest along its rocky shores. Surrounding the sound are snow-capped peaks and enormous glaciers that send icebergs floating off into the crystal-clear water. This is how it had been for centuries. Then, a little after midnight, on March 24, 1989, a fatal error was made.

The Disaster Begins

1. What caused the *Exxon Valdez* to snag on the rocks in the sound?

Late Thursday night, March 23, the *Exxon Valdez,* a supertanker as long as three football fields, left the port of Valdez filled with crude oil. There was nothing unusual about the impending voyage. Since 1977 some 8,700 loaded tankers had made the trip out of Valdez with virtually no incidents. Visibility was 10 miles or more and the seas were calm that night. All electrical and mechanical systems aboard the ship were working perfectly.

The captain radioed the Coast Guard for permission to cross from the outbound lane to the inbound lane to avoid some small icebergs. It was a routine request. The Coast Guard gave permission. Within 10 minutes the huge ship had swung into the inbound lane. But instead of following the lane to the southwest, it headed due south. Fifteen minutes later it had completely crossed the inbound lane and had sailed into waters closed to oil tankers.

Half an hour later the *Exxon Valdez* passed close to Busby Island, far outside the well-established and clearly marked tanker lanes. Suddenly the unlicensed third mate commanding the ship realized that an error had been made. He frantically gave orders to turn sharply to the west to reenter the traffic lanes. Meanwhile, the captain was asleep in his cabin.

But the mate's orders came too late. At four minutes after midnight the *Exxon Valdez* scraped the rocks of Bligh Reef. The enormous tanker crunched to a halt, balanced on a pinnacle of rock. From its ripped hull 10.1 million gallons of thick crude oil gushed into the pristine waters of Prince William Sound.

The Disaster Grows

2. Why did emergency plans fail?

In 1973, when Congress approved the Alaska pipeline, all of the oil companies involved made solemn promises in writing to do everything possible to protect Alaska's fragile environment. Yet on that tragic night, Alyeska Pipeline Service Company had no emergency crew on hand and little equipment ready for use. It did virtually nothing for three days. During those first few critical days the sound's waters were flat calm, there was almost no wind, and it was unseasonably warm and sunny. Conditions for clean-up were ideal. The spill spread to cover only a five-square mile area, and it was entirely manageable.

Then, 66 hours after the accident, rapidly rising winds and seas sent the main mass of oil racing southwestward. It surged forward at more than a mile per hour, churning the sound into a foamy mixture of oil and water.

By the second week the oil had sunk to depths of more than 90 feet, making the water hazardous even for bottom-feeding marine life. It had spread across more than 3,000 square miles of water. In the cold water, the surface of the spill had weathered into a heavy, tar-like substance. Under this coating was a 6- to 18-inch layer of oil with the consistency of peanut butter. The annual spring migration of salmon and herring was on a collision course with black, oily death.

Fourteen days after the ship hit the reef just 630,000 gallons out of 10.1 million gallons of oil had been picked up. The western beaches along the sound were covered with oozing, stinking tar. The poisoned bodies of otters and seabirds lay matted and almost unrecognizable in the gooey mess. Five weeks after the accident the spill covered an area the size of Massachusetts.

The Disaster's Effects

3. What human and environmental toll did the spill take?

The sound's fishing industry had been among Alaska's most productive. It had yielded about $100,000,000 annually. Now it was ruined.

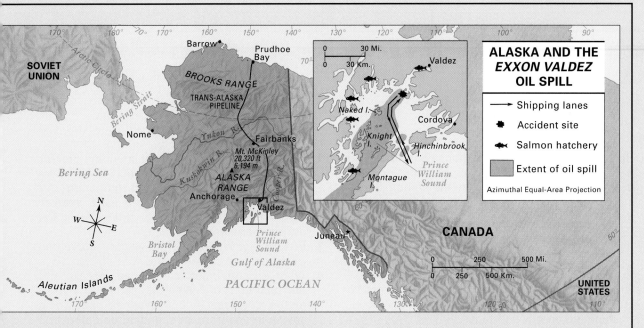

ALASKA AND THE *EXXON VALDEZ* OIL SPILL

→ Shipping lanes
✹ Accident site
🐟 Salmon hatchery
▨ Extent of oil spill

Azimuthal Equal-Area Projection

Despair tore at the hearts of the residents of tiny fishing villages. Their way of life was disappearing before their eyes. Not only were millions of fish dying, but there was danger that toxins in the oil might become embedded in the still-living fish, making them unfit to eat. The public would fear eating fish, shrimp, or crab from the sound. They knew it would be years before they could rebuild their industry, if ever.

Lessons to be Learned

4. What lessons can we learn from this disaster? One of things that makes the situation difficult to analyze is that the issues are so loaded with emotion. Oil spills and dying animals make a powerful case against current methods of transporting dangerous materials.

But it should be remembered that for 12 years oil had flowed safely through the pipeline and had been safely transported out of Prince William Sound. Also for 12 years the oil industry had assured the public that through technological feats it could handle any emergency.

For 12 years few people worried. A large number of Alaskans make their living from the oil industry. The state's economy rests comfortably on the money received in taxes from the oil industry. Many schools, symphonies, and museums were handsomely financed by donations from large oil companies. Oil was good for Alaska!

Perhaps the most valuable long-term lesson to be learned is that alertness, when untested for too long, deteriorates into complacency. Human failing is the thing to attack, not oil exploration or oil transportation. The world needs oil.

History shows clearly that the oil-shipping industry is basically safe. There have been amazingly few spills considering the enormous volume of oil that has been transported around the world. But the industry seemed so safe that responsible people forgot that they are still required to run it properly. Environmental protection demands constant vigilance. Powerful incentives must keep that protection on task. Human errors must be made harder to repeat and too expensive and too dangerous to be tolerated.

APPLYING YOUR KNOWLEDGE

Your class will study environmental concerns in your local community. Each group will select or will be assigned a concern to research. The group will then create a display or presentation that informs others about the concern. Donate your display to the local library or perform your presentation for the city or county council.

Linking History & Geography   585

CHAPTER 14 REVIEW

1971
Twenty-Sixth
Amendment ratified

1973
Roe v. Wade

1974
Nixon resigns;
Ford becomes
president

1976
U.S. Bicentennial
★
Carter elected president

1979
Three Mi
Island
★
Hostages
seized
in Iran

Chapter Summary
Read the statements below. Choose one, and write a paragraph explaining its importance.
1. In 1976 people throughout the United States celebrated the nation's Bicentennial.
2. As president, Jimmy Carter was often seen as a weak leader. However, a triumphant moment in his presidency occurred when he brought the leaders of Egypt and Israel together to sign the Camp David Accords.
3. During the 1970s and 1980s Americans had to cope with the problems of urban decay, pollution, and energy shortages.
4. Many of the immigrants of the 1970s came from Asia and Latin America.
5. Many modern blacks were eager to recover their lost heritage and preferred to be known as African Americans.
6. The problem of searching for ways to revive their lost culture continued to plague many American Indians in the 1980s.
7. In 1972 Congress passed the Equal Rights Amendment, but it was not ratified by the states.
8. President Reagan proved to be a determined leader and a skillful politician.
9. At the beginning of the 1990s America faced difficult problems with even more difficult solutions, such as a rising crime rate, drug abuse, and the devastating AIDS virus.

Reviewing Chronological Order
Number your paper 1–5. Then study the time line above and place the following events in the order in which they happened by writing the first next to 1, the second next to 2, and so on.
1. Sandra Day O'Connor becomes first woman on the Supreme Court
2. Eastern European countries begin to allow free elections
3. Iran Contra deal becomes known
4. George Bush becomes the forty-first president of the United States
5. Twenty-Sixth Amendment ratified

Understanding Main Ideas
1. Why did President Ford veto spending projects approved by Congress in the mid-1970s? What action did he later take to end stagflation?
2. Why do you think the United Farm Workers won public sympathy in their strike against California grape growers?
3. In what ways did the civil rights movement transform the United States?
4. What economic actions did Reagan take after his 1980 election? What happened as a result of the decrease in tax revenues and the increase in government spending on defense?
5. Describe some of the changes that took place in the world in the late 1980s and 1990.

Thinking Critically
1. **Hypothesizing.** Throughout *The Story of America* you have been encouraged to use your historical imagination. You have also been asked to think about historical significance. Two good examples of historical significance are the Monroe Doctrine and the Tonkin Gulf Resolution. Neither seemed particularly important when first announced. Yet 35 presidents have based Latin American policy on the Monroe Doctrine. And Lyndon Johnson waged war in Vietnam under the Tonkin Gulf Resolution. What government actions in recent years do you think might have historical significance? Explain.
2. **Analyzing.** Prepare a brief essay in which you describe what you think is the most important challenge facing America today. Include a paragraph in which you tell how you think our sense of American history can help us meet the challenge.
3. **Evaluating Ideas.** If you were a member of Congress would you have voted for the Reagan budget? The Income Tax Act of 1986? The Boland Amendment? Why or why not?

Writing About History: Informative
Imagine that it is the year 2040. Write a letter to your grandchildren describing what it was like

The Reagan Presidency					
980	MODERN TIMES				1990

1980
Reagan
elected
President

1981
Hostages in
Iran freed

★
Sandra Day O'Connor becomes
first woman Supreme Court Justice

1984
Reagan
reelected
as president

1985
Gorbachev
becomes
Soviet premier

1986
Iran-Contra deal
becomes known

1988
Reagan-
Gorbachev
summit

★
Bush elected
president

1989
Berlin Wall comes
down; democratic
movements in
Eastern Europe

1990
Nelson Mandela
released in
South Africa

growing up in the 1980s and 1990s in America. Include descriptions of your family life, school, leisure-time activities, and styles in clothes and music. It might be interesting to save your letter and read it in the year 2040.

Strategies for Success

Review the strategy on page 579.

Expressing a Point of View. Reread the section titled "The Equal Rights Amendment" on pages 565–66. Then write an essay in which you answer the following questions.

1. What is your position on the Equal Rights Amendment?
2. Why do you take that position?
3. How would American society have changed if the ERA had been ratified? What were the effects of its being rejected?

Using Primary Sources

Like his hero, Dr. Martin Luther King, Jr., African American leader Reverend Jesse Jackson also has a dream for a better America. The following is an excerpt from Jackson's autobiography, *Straight from the Heart,* in which he implores young people to dream.

I am more convinced than ever that we can win. We'll vault up the rough side of the mountain—we can win. But I just want the youth of America to do me one favor. Exercise the right to dream. You must face reality—that which is. But then dream of the reality that ought to be, that must be. Live beyond the pain of reality with the dream of a bright tomorrow. Use hope and imagination as weapons of survival and progress. Use love to motivate you and obligate you to serve the human family. . . .

Young people, dream a new value system. . . . Dreams of authentic leaders who will mold public opinion against a headwind, not just ride the tailwinds of opinion polls. Dream of a world where we measure character by how much we share and care, not by how much we take and consume. Preach and dream. Our time has come.

We must measure character by how we treat the least of these, by who feeds the most hungry people, by who educates the most uneducated people, by who cares and loves the most, by who fights for the needy and seeks to save the greedy. We must dream and choose the laws of sacrifice, which lead to greatness, and not the laws of convenience, which lead to collapse.

1. What does Reverend Jackson mean when he says, "We'll vault up the rough side of the mountain?"
2. Do you agree with Reverend Jackson that we need "a new value system?" Explain.
3. Do you find Reverend Jackson's words inspirational? Why or why not?

Linking History & Geography

As the American population continued its shift to urban areas, major metropolitan regions expanded to the point where they met one another. To comprehend the size and to identify the location of these supercities, with your classmates prepare a map of a megalopolis mentioned in this chapter. On your map you should label the most important city or cities, suburbs, and transportation links. You may need to use an atlas or gazetteer to prepare your map. Discuss with your classmates the impact that these supercities have had on America.

Enriching Your Study of History

1. **Individual Project.** Prepare a classroom display to show various forms of energy in use today, and those proposed for tomorrow. Prepare an oral report to go along with the display in which you describe the strengths and weaknesses of each.
2. **Cooperative Project.** Your group will make a collage on the theme that America is a country of many peoples and special interest groups. Each group member should participate in preparing the collage by bringing in as many pictures from magazines and newspapers as he or she can find on this subject.

Chapter 14 Review   587

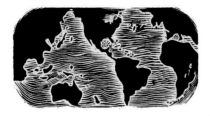

America in the World

Ever since President James Monroe issued his Monroe Doctrine in 1823, most American diplomats have insisted that a "special relationship" has existed between the United States and the other nations of the Western Hemisphere: Canada and the countries of Latin America, which includes the islands of the Caribbean.

Certainly the countries of the "New World" have many things in common. They share a connected landmass—North and South America—that is separated by broad oceans from the nations of the "Old World." They also share most of the values of Western culture, including belief in the importance of democracy. President John F. Kennedy described the idea of a special relationship in a speech to Latin American leaders in 1961:

" We meet together as firm and ancient friends, united by our determination to advance the values of American civilization. For this new world of ours is not merely an accident

"Hail Kennedy, the Defender of the Americas" says this sign in Rio de Janiero, Brazil. Many Latin Americans favored President Kennedy's strong opposition to Soviet involvement in Cuba. Signs like this one suddenly appeared throughout Rio after Kennedy announced the naval blockade of Cuba on October 29, 1962.

SALVE KENNEDY

O DEFENSOR DAS AMERICAS

Bettmann Newsphotos

of geography. Our continents are bound together by a common history—the endless exploration of new frontiers. Our nations are the product of a common struggle—the revolt from colonial rule. And our people share a common heritage—the quest for dignity and the freedom of man.[1］"

Nevertheless, many people have questioned whether there really is a "special" relationship between the nations of the hemisphere. The countries of the Americas are all different from one another. Each has its own distinct society and its own goals and interests, which do not exactly match those of the United States. In short, the notion that a special relationship unites the nations of the hemisphere is partly true, partly myth. Although the United States has a long history of trying to work with the countries of the hemisphere to solve common problems, there are still many differences to resolve.

1. OUR NORTHERN NEIGHBOR: CANADA

A History of Friendship

Since the United States and Canada have usually enjoyed good relations, their relationship has often been used as a model for the rest of the world. The two countries share the world's longest undefended border, running all the way from the Atlantic coast of Maine westward to the state of Washington on the Strait of Juan de Fuca. Every year some 70 million citizens of both countries cross this border. Doing so is almost as simple as entering another state of the Union or another province of Canada. Both countries have democratic governments, and each is the other's largest trading partner.

Yet, as in any relationship, there are difficulties. As former President Lyndon Johnson once said, "Canada is such a close neighbor and such a good neighbor that we always have plenty of problems here. They are kind of like the problems in a hometown." Although Canada is the world's second-largest country in land area (larger than the United States) and an important industrial nation, the economy of the United States is 10 times larger than that of Canada, and the United States has 10 times as many people as Canada does. Eight out of 10 Canadians live within 100 miles of the U.S. border, and they have become highly influenced by American popular culture: television, radio, magazines, movies, sports. The influence of American culture has created a certain resentment among Canadians who feel that they are losing their national identity.

Furthermore, the United States does not always consider the

[1]From *U.S. Policy Toward Latin America: From Regionalism to Globalism* by Harold Molineu

Preview & Review

Use these questions to guide your reading. Answer the questions after completing Section 1.

Understanding Issues, Events, & Ideas. Use the following words to describe U.S. relations with Canada: reciprocity, Permanent Joint Board on Defense.

1. What caused tensions between the United States and Canada before 1910?
2. Why did Canadians reject the Reciprocity Treaty of 1911?
3. How have Canada and the United States cooperated since World War II?

Thinking Critically. State in your own words what former Prime Minister Pierre Trudeau meant when he compared the United States to an elephant.

Mike Yamashita/Woodfin Camp and Associates

This bridge in the Thousand Islands between New York and Canada is part of the border between Canada and the United States.

impact of its actions on Canada. Nor does it always grant Canada the attention Canadians feel their nation deserves. As former Canadian Prime Minister Pierre Trudeau once told an American audience: "Living next to you is in some ways like sleeping with an elephant. No matter how friendly or even-tempered is the beast, if I may call it that, one is affected by every twitch and grunt."

In the 18th and 19th centuries, Canada's relations with the United States were strongly influenced by American relations with Britain, because Canada was a British colony. During the American Revolution (1775–1781) and the War of 1812, Canada and the United States were enemies. On both occasions American troops invaded Canada, while British troops from Canada crossed the border into American territory. During the Civil War, when Britain first expressed sympathy for the Confederacy, the Union again threatened to attack Canada. Since then, however, there has been little danger of armed conflict between the two nations.

Early Issues in U.S.-Canada Relations

One of the most critical issues in early U.S.-Canada relations was fishing rights, a problem that continues to this day. Fishing is an important economic activity and way of life in Canada and in the states of New England. In the 1800s the American and Canadian governments were frequently involved in disputes over rights to the rich fishing grounds off eastern Canada and the New England states. At times fishing boats were seized and angry words were exchanged, but the two governments eventually managed to reach an agreement.

The Granger Collection

In this 18th-century engraving, Newfoundlanders from Canada's eastern coast dry and cure codfish.

In the late 1970s and early 1980s, the dispute over fisheries and maritime boundaries in the Atlantic flared again. This time the two countries agreed to submit the case to the World Court of the United Nations, based in the Netherlands. Despite this step, however, the dispute has not been finally resolved.

Another problem concerned Canada's boundary with Alaska, which was not well defined when the United States purchased Alaska from Russia in 1867. The issue did not become important until 1897, when gold was discovered in Alaska and in Canada's Yukon Territory. With prospectors flocking into the disputed territory, something had to be done. In 1903 the two countries agreed to submit the case to a commission made up of American, British, and Canadian members.

President Theodore Roosevelt warned that he would not accept the loss of any American territory. As it turned out, the warning was unnecessary because the British member of the commission, Lord Alverstone, supported the American claim. He did so because the British government needed American support on other international issues of that time. The Canadians were furious and, with some justice, called Lord Alverstone's vote a betrayal. But they had no real choice. They had to accept the decision.

The border between Alaska and Canada stretches through miles of wilderness and in the late 1800s was even less clearly defined than the strip of cleared forest in this drawing. What event caused the boundary to become an important issue?

In this editorial cartoon, John Bull and Uncle Sam (Britain and the United States) hammer out an agreement defining the boundary between Alaska and Canada. Why is Canada pictured as a crying baby?

Canadian resentment over the Alaskan boundary issue did spoil the chances of negotiating an important trade pact between the two nations in 1911. For years Canada had wanted more trade with the United States and had backed the idea of **reciprocity,** the lowering or eliminating of tariffs on many goods traded between the two countries in order to promote the freer flow of goods between the two. The United States was ready to approve a trade agreement in 1911, but Canada rejected the proposed agreement. On top of resentment over the Alaskan boundary question, Canadians feared American economic and even political domination. Many Americans wanted to make Canada a part of the United States, and Canadians felt that the trade pact might be a first step toward doing so. As Sir James Whitney, premier of Ontario, said at the time:

      There is not an American who does not hope way down in his heart that Canada will some day be a part of the United States and feel that reciprocity is the first step in this direction. It is the means by which annexation will be reached most quickly.[1]

Despite the defeat of the reciprocity agreement, trade between Canada and the United States continued to grow, largely because each nation produced goods that the other needed. After World War I, the United States replaced Great Britain as Canada's leading economic partner.

[1]From *Canada and the United States* by Hugh L. Kennleyside

Wartime Allies

World War II cemented relations between the United States and Canada even further. In 1939 the two countries formed the **Permanent Joint Board on Defense** to coordinate the collective defense of northern North America. They built airfields in Canada and Alaska and began construction of the Alaska Highway, which now connects Alaska with the lower 48 states. They also worked out arrangements for joint economic assistance, especially the supply of war materials. And the two countries collaborated on Allied war strategy in Europe and the Pacific.

Relations with Canada continued to evolve. After World War II, Canada joined NATO and helped create NORAD, the North American Aerospace Defense Command, which is a network of radar, aircraft, and missile installations set up for the defense of the North American continent. Canada and the United States also cooperated in the building and operation of the Saint Lawrence Seaway. Completed in 1959, the Seaway opened the Great Lakes to oceangoing vessels for the first time.

But in the 1970s Canada increasingly separated itself from American foreign policy. It criticized American involvement in Vietnam

The Alaska Highway stretches across British Columbia and continues as far north as Fairbanks, Alaska.

NORAD's Cheyenne Mountain command post lies underground in Colorado. Technicians monitor any aircraft or missiles that approach North America.

Our Northern Neighbor: Canada 593

Regis Bossu/Sygma

The effects of acid rain on the vegetation of southern Canada are easily seen in these photographs, taken (from left to right) in 1970, 1980, and 1990. How would you describe the change?

Return to the Preview & Review on page 589.

and established diplomatic relations with Communist China. It also provided a refuge for American draft evaders and deserters during the Vietnam War.

Canada also criticized the United States over the problem of acid rain. This is rain that has been made poisonous to plants and fish by industrial pollution, produced in this case on the U.S. side of the border. Acid rain polluted Canadian lakes and forests, harming Canadian fisheries and the state-subsidized timber industry. Canada demanded more stringent American controls on industrial emissions, and late in 1990 Congress passed ''clean air'' laws aimed at solving the problem.

Meanwhile, the United States and Canada found common ground more easily in 1988 when they agreed to phase out all tariffs on their products over the next 10 years. 🖎

2. LATIN AMERICA AND THE CARIBBEAN

A Stormy Relationship

Relations between the United States and the countries of Latin America have been much more difficult than those between the United States and Canada. Over the years, the United States, seeing that many of the governments in the region were undemocratic and unstable, has often tried to control or "reform" them. For their part, Latin Americans may admire American democracy and respect American economic achievements, but many resent the power the United States wields over their countries.

In general, the United States has pursued two goals in the region: to prevent foreign encroachment, originally from Europe but later from the communist world, and to expand markets for American goods.

The Monroe Doctrine of 1823 set the tone for U.S. relations with the newly independent nations of Latin America. Monroe warned European nations that any attempt to form new colonies or extend their influence in the hemisphere would be seen as a threat to the United States. Most Latin American governments initially welcomed this statement. Later they saw it as saying, in effect, "keep off, this is ours."

The United States first expanded into Latin American territory when the Republic of Texas approved a treaty annexing Texas to the United States. Although the Texans had declared their independence from Mexico in 1836, Mexico still considered Texas a province and

Preview & Review

Use these questions to guide your reading. Answer the questions after completing Section 2.
Understanding Issues, Events, & Ideas. Use the following words to describe changes in United States relations with Latin America before 1960: Platt Amendment, Good Neighbor policy, Montevideo Pact, Trade Agreements Act, nationalize, Organization of American States, Alliance for Progress.

1. How did gunboat diplomacy differ from dollar diplomacy?
2. How did U.S.–Latin American relations improve during Franklin Roosevelt's administration?
3. Why did World War II create an economic boom for many Latin American countries?
4. Why did the Alliance for Progress fall short of its goals?

Thinking Critically. Imagine that you are a Cuban citizen who has just learned of the passage of the Platt Amendment. Write a letter to the editor of your local newspaper explaining whether you support or oppose the amendment. Give reasons to justify your opinion.

Culver Pictures

UNCLE SAM—THAT'S A LIVE WIRE, GENTLEMEN!

"That's a live wire, gentlemen," says Uncle Sam in this editorial cartoon that refers to the Venezuela Boundary Dispute (see pages 205-06). Who do the other characters in the picture represent? For more than a century the United States used the Monroe Doctrine to discourage European interference in the Western Hemisphere. What does Uncle Sam imply would happen if they stepped on the live wire?

Latin America and the Caribbean   **595**

considered the annexation an act of war. In the Mexican War (1846–1848) the United States defeated Mexico. Under the terms of the treaty ending the war, Mexico ceded one third of its territory to the United States. Then, after the Spanish-American War (1898) the United States took over Puerto Rico and occupied Cuba. The U.S. Congress granted Cuba its independence in 1901, but it also passed the **Platt Amendment.** This amendment allowed the United States to keep naval bases on the island, from which the U.S. navy could protect American interests in the Caribbean. The amendment also limited Cuba's power to accumulate debts and make treaties. Most important, it gave the United States the right to intervene in Cuba "for the purpose of preserving order and maintaining Cuban independence." Over the years, the United States often cited the Platt Amendment to justify involvement in Cuban affairs.

Gunboats and Dollars

During the Progressive Era of the early 1900s, the United States became more and more involved in Central America and the Caribbean. Marines and naval units were used to protect American investments that seemed threatened by political unrest and to reorganize the finances of countries like Haiti, the Dominican Republic, and Nicaragua. Theodore Roosevelt established this policy with the Roosevelt Corollary to the Monroe Doctrine in 1904. Roosevelt said:

    ❝ Chronic wrongdoing, or an impotence [weakness] which
        results in a general loosening of the ties of civilized society,

In 1901 President Theodore Roosevelt said, "Speak softly and carry a big stick; you will go far. If the American nation will speak softly and yet build and keep at a pitch of the highest training a thoroughly efficient navy, the Monroe Doctrine will go far." In this 1904 cartoon TR uses that navy to patrol the Caribbean, which has become an American pond. What locations surround the pond? Why are those particular places shown?

596   AMERICA IN THE WORLD

may in America, as elsewhere, ultimately require intervention by some civilized nation, and in the Western Hemisphere the adherence of the United States to the Monroe Doctrine may force the United States, however reluctantly, in flagrant cases of such wrongdong or impotence, to the exercise of an international police power.[1] **99**

In other words, the United States would act as the "policeman" of the hemisphere. This policy was sometimes referred to as "gunboat diplomacy." In 1903 Roosevelt used the threat of force to help Panama gain its independence from Colombia, leaving the United States free to build and control the Panama Canal.

The next president, William Howard Taft, adopted a slightly different approach known as "dollar diplomacy." Taft wanted to increase American investment in Latin America. By substituting "dollars for bullets," he thought that the economic power of American businesses and banks would result in political stability and make

[1]From *The United States and Latin America: An Historical Analysis of Inter-American Relations* by Gordon Connell-Smith

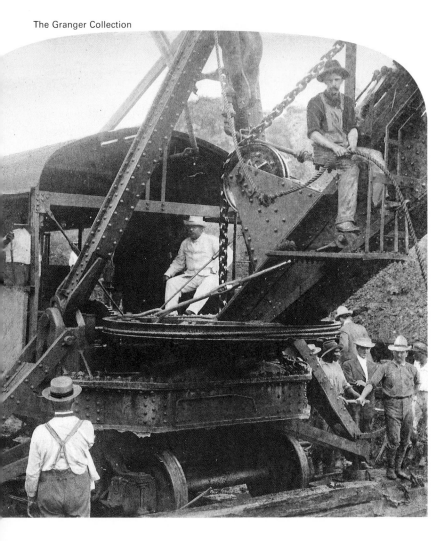

In 1906 President Theodore Roosevelt—operating the steam shovel—visited work crews digging the Culebra Cut of the Panama Canal. Cut is an engineering term for an artificial channel. It took seven years to blast through the mountains of rock to complete the cut, which was renamed the Galliard Cut in 1913 in honor of the engineer in charge of digging it.

597

This advertisement for the United Fruit Company Steamship Service appeared in Life magazine in 1913. The United Fruit Company gained control of large portions of the most productive land in many Central American countries, and it came to have strong influence on many of the governments in the region. How does the advertisement attempt to make a voyage into the troubled waters of the Caribbean seem safe?

military intervention unnecessary. The United Fruit Company, for example, came to dominate several Central American governments. Nations like Honduras became known as "banana republics," weak states controlled by corrupt leaders in league with foreign interests. In the end, such conditions only contributed to instability because the mass of the people did not share in the wealth produced by U.S. investments.

In 1912 Taft sent the marines to Nicaragua when civil war threatened to break out. The marines remained for many of the next 21 years, ensuring pro-U.S. rule, but also causing deep resentment throughout Latin America toward what was seen as uninvited U.S. intervention.

When Woodrow Wilson became president, he promised a different Latin American policy. He intended to carry out a "moral" foreign policy and to promote democracy in Latin America. But his actions sometimes contradicted his words. The United States became involved in Latin America more often under Wilson than under Roosevelt and Taft combined.

For years Central American countries had been ruled by dictators who overthrew one another in an endless cycle of military coups. Wilson hoped to end this undemocratic and wasteful system by refusing diplomatic recognition to any government taking power by force. In 1914 he sent troops into Mexico to influence the course of the Mexican Revolution and to overthrow Victoriano Huerta, whom he considered to be an evil dictator. Many Americans wanted him to send even more troops, but Wilson recognized the Mexican right to self-determination and domestic reform. Although the presence of American troops caused some conflict, by the late 1920s relations between the United States and Mexico were quite good, in part owing to Wilson's policies.

Wilson also sent the marines to occupy Haiti in 1915 and the Dominican Republic in 1916. World War I was raging and Wilson feared a German takeover of these nations and a resulting threat to the Panama Canal. The troops remained in the Dominican Republic until 1924 and in Haiti until 1934.

Latin Americans considered Wilson's policy of nonrecognition simply another form of interference. They also viewed it as another way the U.S. planned to keep pro-Yankee governments in power.

Shifting Policies

By the 1920s, the United States began to change its Latin American policy. One of the most important nations in this respect was Mexico, still in some turmoil from the Mexican Revolution that began in 1910. President Plutarco Elías Calles' government was popular, but his reforms were posing a threat to American business interests and to the Catholic church. But instead of sending troops, President Calvin Coolidge sent a sympathetic new ambassador, Dwight Morrow, to

Both: The Granger Collection

These two pictures symbolize the change in the United States' Latin America policy. Above, U.S. marines, sent by President Wilson in 1914, raise the American flag over Veracruz, Mexico. Wilson hoped this action would prompt the overthrow of Mexican dictator Victoriano Huerta. Left, Dwight Morrow (left) shakes hands with Mexican president Plutarco Calles in 1927. Morrow, an investment banker appointed by President Coolidge as ambassador to Mexico, tried to understand the Mexican point of view and repair the damage that past U.S. policies had done. Mexican leaders soon viewed him as an "ambassador of goodwill."

The U.S. government declared rebel leader Augusto César Sandino (center) an outlaw when he and his followers seized American property in Nicaragua. He battled U.S. marines for six years, declaring that he wanted to end American involvement in his homeland. The last marines left in 1933. Sandino then accepted amnesty from the U.S.-backed Nicaraguan government but was assassinated in 1934. His chief aide, Augustin F. Marti, (right) later led a popular uprising in El Salvador.

AP/Wide World Photos

Historical Picture Service

Henry Stimson, U.S. Secretary of State from 1929 to 1933, helped shape policy toward Latin America.

Mexico. Morrow negotiated agreements that greatly improved relations between the two countries.

In 1925 Coolidge withdrew the marines from Nicaragua, only to send them back a year later when unrest threatened the American-backed government. Calling for a "free country or death," a patriot leader named Augusto César Sandino demanded new elections and the withdrawal of American forces. For six years Sandino's ragtag army fought the much more powerful Americans. As time passed, U.S. support for the war eroded. In 1931 Coolidge's successor, Herbert Hoover, began the gradual withdrawal of troops from Nicaragua.

President Hoover continued the shift away from involvement in Latin America, even when American business interests seemed threatened. In 1930 the United States government announced that the Roosevelt Corollary was dead. As Secretary of State Henry L. Stimson put it: "The Monroe Doctrine was a declaration of the United States versus Europe—not of the United States versus Latin America." Another official added that the Monroe Doctrine "conferred no superior position on the United States." A new era seemed to be dawning in U.S.–Latin American relations.

600   AMERICA IN THE WORLD

Warmer Relations

In 1933, shortly after his inauguration, President Franklin Roosevelt announced a new Latin American policy, Pan-Americanism. It would be based on nonintervention, a fair and objective recognition policy, and greater cooperation among all the nations of the hemisphere. Roosevelt said:

“ The essential qualities of a true Pan Americanism must be the same as those which constitute a good neighbor, namely, mutual understanding and, through such understanding, a sympathetic appreciation of the other's point of view. It is only in this manner that we can hope to build up a system of which confidence, friendship, and good will are the cornerstones.[1] ”

Under this **Good Neighbor policy,** Roosevelt took steps to improve inter-American relations. He removed the last U.S. troops from Haiti and Nicaragua, and he renounced the Platt Amendment.

[1]From *The United States and Latin America: An Historical Analysis of Inter-American Relations* by Gordon Connell-Smith

President Franklin Roosevelt greets Latin American leaders at the Inter-American Peace Conference in Buenos Aires in 1936. At that historic meeting the United States finally agreed to a policy of nonintervention. After you have completed this section, tell whether or not the United States kept that agreement.

However, the United States retained its naval base at Guantanamo, Cuba, and continued to exert great influence on economic and political events in the island nation.

Under FDR the United States took part in a number of important conferences with Latin American leaders. The first meeting took place in Montevideo, Uruguay, in 1933 and resulted in the historic **Montevideo Pact** with the Latin American states. Its key feature was a nonintervention clause: "No state has the right to intervene in the internal affairs of another." Although the United States reserved the right to intervene under certain conditions, the Montevideo Pact was a major step forward in inter-American relations. At the Buenos Aires Conference in 1936, the United States finally gave unqualified support for nonintervention.

With war threatening in Europe, the United States and the Latin American countries began to discuss the idea of a collective response to outside aggression. This "Pan-Americanization of the Monroe Doctrine" implied that the United States was not solely responsible for the defense of the hemisphere. This idea was strengthened at follow-up inter-American meetings in 1938 and 1939.

In the 1930s all the nations of the hemisphere were in the grips of the Great Depression. Roosevelt realized that more trade within the hemisphere would work to everyone's advantage. In 1934 Congress passed the **Trade Agreements Act,** which lowered or eliminated tariffs on many Latin American products imported into the United States.

In 1938 the Good Neighbor policy faced its most critical test when the government of Mexico under the leadership of President Lázaro Cárdenas **nationalized,** or put under government ownership, the holding of foreign oil companies operating in that nation. Cárdenas argued that the companies had refused to negotiate new labor contracts with their Mexican employees in good faith, and he offered to pay them a fair price for their holdings. Cárdenas also felt that the Mexican government would operate the companies' facilities so that the Mexican people, rather than foreign owners, would benefit from the profits. In the past the United States might have sent in troops on behalf of the oil companies because many of them were American-owned, but in this case Roosevelt refused to do so.

Of course there were still areas of friction between the United States and its neighbors. The United States continued to provide military and economic aid to dictators who ensured stability and supported U.S. policies. One such dictator was Rafael Trujillo, who controlled the Dominican Republic from 1930 to 1961. Trujillo ruled the country as if it were his private estate and treated ordinary Dominicans almost like slaves, but the United States supported him for three decades.

Another dictator was Anastasio Somoza García of Nicaragua. Somoza headed the National Guard, which was trained by U.S.

Raphael L. Trujillo (right) solicits votes on horseback in his successful 1947 campaign for reelection as president of the Dominican Republic. Thirteen years later in New York, exiles from the Dominican Republic voice their hatred for Trujillo, who was a repressive dictator. He was assassinated in 1961.

officers. It was created to preserve order and democracy in Nicaragua after the American withdrawal in 1933. Instead, Somoza used the Guard to take over the country in 1937 and to hold power until 1956, when he was assassinated. His sons maintained a Somoza dynasty until the Sandinista Revolution of 1979.

Wartime Partners

During World War II, the United States worked to ensure that the Latin American countries joined in the Allied war effort or at least remained neutral. At a 1940 conference in Havana, Cuba, Latin American leaders reaffirmed their pledge of collective security in the hemisphere. Several also allowed the establishment of U.S. military bases on their soil.

In 1942 at a conference in Rio de Janeiro, Brazil, the United States persuaded most Latin American countries to break ties with Germany. An Inter-American Defense Board was also formed, much like the one created by Canada and the United States. By 1943, 14 Latin American countries had declared war on the Axis powers. Although only Brazil and Mexico sent troops into battle, citizens from several Latin American countries enlisted in the American armed forces and fought the Axis powers.

World War II fueled an economic boom in Latin America. The Allied powers needed food and other raw materials, and Latin American nations provided them. New industries were developed in the region to supply manufactured goods for the war effort. When the

Under dictator Anastasio Somoza García, shown here in 1940s, mineral and agricultural production increased but all opposition was crushed.

Latin America and the Caribbean   603

war ended, however, the market for war goods almost disappeared, and Latin America slid into depression. When these nations sought economic assistance, the United States did little to help them. It was providing massive aid to Western European democracies under the Marshall Plan and said it could not afford to help Latin America. Many Latin American countries then began to question the special relationship that had been built up through the Good Neighbor policy and wartime cooperation.

The Onset of the Cold War

The Cold War between the United States and the Soviet Union had great influence on inter-American relations. The United States was determined to prevent the spread of communism in the hemisphere. At a meeting in Mexico City in 1945 the United States and the countries of Latin America extended their pledge of collective security through the Act of Chapultepec. This agreement called for a collective response to aggression not only from outside the hemisphere but by one American country against another. This act also discussed possible sanctions, including the use of armed force, that might be taken under such circumstances.

Another agreement was the Inter-American Treaty of Reciprocal Assistance, or Rio Treaty, which was signed in Rio de Janeiro in 1947. This treaty, an extension of the previous inter-American agreements, called for a collective response to aggression from within or outside the hemisphere. "An armed attack by any State against an American State shall be considered as an attack against all the American States."

The following year brought the creation of the **Organization of American States** (OAS). The OAS is a regional agency within the United Nations, its membership open to all nations in the hemisphere. Its principal goals are to promote the peaceful resolution of disputes, democracy, and economic development. The OAS is based in Washington, D.C., and currently has 30 members.

Although the creation of the OAS was an important achievement, the results have been mixed. The body does provide a forum for member states to discuss issues and problems and to settle disagreements peaceably. On the other hand, OAS members have often used the organization for their own ends. As with the United Nations itself, strong differences of opinion within the OAS have sometimes made it ineffective in times of crisis.

As Cold War tensions mounted, the United States continued to prop up unpopular dictators like Trujillo in the Dominican Republic and the Somozas in Nicaragua because they were anticommunist. The United States also became suspicious of noncommunist reformers, fearing that their reforms might lead to instability and increased communist influence.

The first major Cold War clash in Latin America occurred in Guatemala, a Central American country that had been ruled by dictators for most of its history. A tiny group of landowners possessed most of the nation's wealth, while the people—mainly Mayan Indian farmers—lived in dire poverty. In 1944, however, Guatemala entered a period of democratic rule and social change. President Jacobo Arbenz launched a land-reform program designed to make land available to some of the landless farmers. Arbenz was not a communist, but some of his associates were. That, along with his reforms, caused concern in Washington. When Arbenz's government took over land owned by the United Fruit Company, President Dwight D. Eisenhower authorized the funding and training of a small group of Guatemalan rebels. In 1954 this group invaded the country from Honduras and overthrew the Arbenz government. For the next 32 years Guatemala was ruled by a succession of military leaders who blocked social reform and crushed all opposition.

The overthrow of the Arbenz government sent a strong message to Latin America. Despite its pledge of noninvolvement, the United States would seek to topple governments it considered communist inspired. Many Latin Americans believed that Washington might even oppose democratic reform on the grounds that it might lead to communist gains. Reformers such as José Figueres in Costa Rica and Rómulo Betancourt in Venezuela urged the United States to support democratic changes and more social reform. A number of

Heroes of Latin American revolutions look over the shoulders of delegates meeting in Bogotá, Colombia, in 1948 to charter the Organization of American States.

The president of Guatemala, Guzman Arbenz, delivers his inaugural address on March 15, 1951.

Latin America and the Caribbean   605

reform-minded Latin Americans even began to think that real change would only come through violent revolution.

In 1958 Vice President Richard Nixon made a goodwill tour of South America. Most of the trip went smoothly, but in Peru and Venezuela Nixon was met with violent demonstrations. In Caracas, Venezuela, a rock-throwing mob trapped Nixon in his car and he barely escaped unharmed. The American government blamed these events on communist agitators, but analysts suggested that the mobs were reacting to the economic hardship and political oppression imposed by American-backed dictators.

Both: Bettmann Newsphotos

A wide range of reactions greeted Vice President Richard Nixon on his goodwill tour of South America in 1958. Nixon waves to a friendly crowd in Bogotá, Colombia (left). However, later in the day anti-American protestors clashed with pro-American supporters in Bogotá. Violence also marred Nixon's last stop, in Caracas, Venezuela, where residents protesting Americans' involvement in Guatemala threw rocks at the vice president's car (right). What U.S. actions in Guatemala were Latin Americans protesting?

The Cuban Revolution

In 1959 an event took place in Cuba that profoundly affected the United States and the rest of the hemisphere. A small band of revolutionaries led by a young lawyer named Fidel Castro overthrew the government of dictator Fulgencio Batista.

No country in Latin America had been more closely tied to the United States than Cuba. Ever since the Spanish-American War in 1898, the United States had played a major role in Cuban life. Cuba's leaders were generally corrupt and depended heavily on Americans' political and economic support to maintain their control over the people. Americans owned more than half of Cuba's farmland, much of the tobacco output, and many of its most important businesses. And the island was a vacation playground for many Americans.

Cuba was one of the wealthiest and most developed nations in Latin America, but its wealth was poorly distributed. While a few wealthy Cubans and Americans lived in luxury, most people on the island were poor. It was these conditions, along with Batista's brutal rule, that finally sparked Castro's revolution.

The United States expressed the hope that Castro's government would pursue moderate reforms and protect American business interests on the island. However, the two countries soon clashed because Castro took over American-owned land and businesses and forged close ties with the Soviet Union. In October 1959 the United States imposed a trade embargo on Cuba, and in January 1961, shortly before he left office, President Eisenhower broke diplomatic relations with Cuba.

Hostility between the United States and Castro's Cuba may well have been inevitable. Castro was probably not a communist when he took power, but he was determined to improve social conditions in Cuba and end the island's historical dependence on the United States. Washington was bound to be alarmed by his ties with the communist world. The Cold War atmosphere of the time made trouble almost certain.

Early in 1960 Eisenhower approved plans to overthrow the Castro government by training a secret force of anti-Castro Cubans.

Cuban newspapers herald the success of Castro's revolution with the headline "Batista Flees."

Supporters of Cuban revolutionary leader Fidel Castro raise their hands in salute as he steps to the speaker's platform in front of the presidential palace in January 1959. What sparked Castro's revolution?

607

President John F. Kennedy carried through with those plans in the disastrous Bay of Pigs invasion of 1961. The invaders were easily crushed, and this humiliating defeat of the United States only strengthened Castro's hold on Cuba. The following year Kennedy and Soviet premier Nikita Khrushchev faced off in the Cuban Missile Crisis. Thereafter, the United States worked to isolate Cuba from other Latin American countries. Cuba was ousted from the Organization of American States, and many Latin American countries broke relations with Cuba. At the same time, Cuba tried to promote revolution and undermine U.S. interests in the hemisphere.

Fidel Castro shakes hands with Soviet premier Nikita Khrushchev in Moscow after signing the Joint Soviet-Cuban Declaration on May 23, 1963. Why did Cuba's growing relationship with the Soviet Union worry many Americans?

AP/Wide World Photos

The Alliance for Progress

To counter the Cuban Revolution and to strengthen relations with Latin America, President Kennedy launched an ambitious program of aid and social reform called the **Alliance for Progress.** In announcing the program, Kennedy said:

❝ To our sister republics south of our border, we offer a special pledge—to convert our good words into deeds—in a new alliance for progress, to assist free men and free governments in casting off the chains of poverty.[1]❞

Kennedy felt that reform in Latin America would ease discontent and eliminate the causes of revolution. As he put it, "Those who make peaceful revolution impossible will make violent revolution inevitable." In Kennedy's view a program of economic development and social reform would protect U.S. interests in the long run. Under the Alliance for Progress the United States was to provide economic aid and technical assistance. In return the Latin Americans were to

[1]From *Latin American–United States Relations* by Federico G. Gil

Columbus Memorial Library/OAS

carry out reforms in agriculture, housing, health, education, tax policy, and other areas.

The Alliance for Progress made possible many reforms. Schools, roads, and hospitals were built, and land-reform programs enacted. But in the end the alliance fell far short of its goals. The deep-rooted social and economic problems of Latin America were more than any such program could overcome. The funds provided by the United States—$20 billion—were not enough. More important was the long-standing resistance to change in Latin America. The wealthy classes who had traditionally controlled those countries were able to block the changes that might have undermined their power and their wealth.

In the 1960s widespread protests against repressive governments broke out in many Latin American countries. To prevent the spread of revolutionary movements, the United States doubled its military aid in the region. Protests were frequently crushed, the rights of the protestors denied. In hopes of providing stability, protecting U.S. investments, and halting the spread of communism, the United States strengthened Latin American military regimes that undermined democratic institutions. 🖰

Vice President Lyndon Johnson and Congressional leaders—including future president Gerald Ford and future vice president Hubert Humphrey—look on as President John Kennedy signs the Alliance for Progress into law. According to Kennedy, what was the aim of the "Alianza"?

Return to the Preview & Review on page 595.

Use these questions to guide your reading. Answer the questions after completing Section 3.
Understanding Issues, Events, & Ideas. Use the following words to discuss U.S.–Latin American relations from 1960 to the present: leftist, developing nations, Central American Common Market, Contras, right wing, Contadora Group, Caribbean Basin Initiative.
1. How did President Carter's policy toward Latin America differ from that of earlier presidents?
2. What policies did the Reagan administration follow to oppose the Sandinistas?
3. Why did President Duarte's attempts to bring peace to El Salvador meet with little success?
4. What did President Bush do to halt the drug trade?
Thinking Critically. 1. Imagine that you are a member of Chile's working class or middle class in 1970. Explain why you support or oppose Salvador Allende for president. **2.** Explain why you support or oppose the American invasion of Panama in 1990.

Salvador Allende holds a press conference in Santiago, Chile, days before the presidential election.

3. LATIN AMERICA: 1960s–1990s

New Involvements

American preoccupation with hemispheric security was heightened in 1965, when a revolt broke out in the Dominican Republic. President Juan Bosch had been ousted by the military two years earlier. When his supporters took up arms to demand his return, President Johnson, believing that communists were behind the revolt, sent American troops to the island. Johnson declared that the United States "cannot, must not, and will not permit the establishment of another communist government in the Western Hemisphere." The United States gained backing for this action from the Organization of American States, and the soldiers were withdrawn after restoring order. But many Latin Americans saw the Dominican incident as a return to the United States' involvement policies of the past.

In 1970 another major challenge to American policies in the hemisphere arose, this time in Chile. Chilean voters elected a Marxist president, Salvador Allende, who set out to transform the Chilean economy. Allende intended to nationalize key industries, some of which were controlled by American corporations.

Alarmed by Allende's **leftist** policies—those aimed at the radical reform of established institutions—and his ties to Cuba, the United States set out to destabilize his government in hopes of toppling it. The United States cut back on trade with Chile and blocked international loans to the country. Agents of the Central Intelligence Agency (CIA) provoked strikes and disorder. They also provided

Ernest Maneway/Black Star

Christopher Morris/Black Star

money to Chilean opposition forces. It was these forces that overthrew Allende in a bloody coup on September 11, 1973. Allende was
assassinated, and a new military government, led by General Augusto
Pinochet, was installed.

Although the United States did not participate directly in the
coup that toppled Allende's government, it helped create the circumstances that resulted in his fall. The result was considered a success
for American policy. Without sending troops, the United States had
helped prevent the rise of a ''second Cuba'' in the hemisphere.
Others, however, saw the events in Chile as a shocking abuse of
American power. The United States had supported the overthrow of
a freely elected leader and had helped undermine Chile's long tradition of democratic rule. General Pinochet's military government soon
amassed one of the worst human rights records in recent history,
executing thousands of political opponents.

General Augusto Pinochet speaks to the Chilean people after taking control of the government. Pinochet established a military dictatorship that brutally crushed opposition. How was the United States involved in Pinochet's takeover?

Increasing Independence

In the 1970s many countries in South America became increasingly
independent of the United States. The military regimes of Argentina
and Brazil even developed ties with Cuba, the Soviet Union, and
communist China as well as with democratic nations outside the
hemisphere. Although they remained anticommunist, they wanted
the benefits that broader economic and political relations would
bring.

These efforts to carve out a more independent position in world
affairs were part of a broader movement among many of the poorer
nations of the world. So-called **developing nations**—poor countries in
Africa, Asia, and Latin America—were determining their own interests without taking sides in the Cold War.

The Carter Years

When President Jimmy Carter took office in 1977, he promised a new approach to foreign relations. Much like Woodrow Wilson, he favored a moral policy that respected the rights of the smaller, less-powerful nations. In a speech, Carter said:

“ In the aftermath of Vietnam and Watergate and the CIA revelations, our Nation's reputation was soiled. Many Americans turned away from our own Government, and said: 'It embarrasses me.' The vision, the ideals, the commitment that were there 200 years ago when our Nation was formed, have somehow been lost. One of the great responsibilities that I share with you is to restore that vision and that degree of cleanness and decency and honesty and truth and principle to our country.[1] ”

In his Latin American policy, Carter stressed human rights. "We can live with diversity in governmental systems, but we cannot look away when a government tortures people or jails them for their belief," he said. The Carter administration put pressure on governments that jailed or even executed citizens who dared oppose their policies. Among these governments were the military regimes of Chile, Argentina, Brazil, and Guatemala. Human rights activists praised Carter's policy. They claimed that it saved the lives of many victims of military repression. But the policy was inconsistently applied, and in many cases it only stiffened the resistance of foreign governments to American policies.

Carter's most controversial achievement was the signing of the Panama Canal treaties. Many Panamanians resented American

[1]From *United States Policy in Latin America: A Quarter Century of Crisis and Challenge, 1961–1986*, edited by John D. Martz

At a historic meeting of the Organization of American States President Jimmy Carter and Panamanian president Omar Torrijos sign the Panama Canal Treaties. Why did some Americans oppose the treaties?

Alon Reininger/Contact Press Images/Woodfin Camp and Associates

control of the Canal Zone. Riots in Panama in the 1960s had finally awakened the United States to this problem, and Carter was determined to seek an agreement that would restore friendly relations.

In 1977 Panama and the United States signed a treaty providing for joint operation of the canal until the year 2000. Thereafter it would come under full Panamanian control. A second treaty guaranteed the permanent neutrality of the canal, but also the right of the United States to make sure the canal remained open. Many Americans opposed the treaties as a "giveaway" of American property and a sign of American weakness. For Latin Americans, however, the canal treaties seemed to signal an end to the pattern of U.S. involvement begun by Theodore Roosevelt.

It was in Central America, however, that President Carter faced his most difficult test. In 1979 revolutionaries in Nicaragua known as Sandinistas overthrew Anastasio Somoza Debayle, the last of the Somoza dictators. The Sandinistas, named after nationalist hero Augusto César Sandino, wanted to end their country's long dependence on the United States, just as Castro had ended Cuba's. Carter attempted to get along with the Sandinistas, but mistrust on both sides soon soured relations. Under President Ronald Reagan, relations deteriorated further.

Supporters of the Sandinistas rally in Managua, the capital of Nicaragua. Their signs warn against imperialist intervention by the United States and praise the junta *set up by the Sandinistas to rule the country. Why did President Reagan oppose the Sandinistas?*

Revolutions in Central America

In the 1970s the economies of Central American nations benefited from a regional agreement known as the **Central American Common Market** that lowered tariffs and developed other forms of economic cooperation. As in the past, however, many of the gains were absorbed by the region's small ruling class. The harsh military governments of the region curbed protest and blocked meaningful reform.

Latin America: 1960s–1990s   613

As a result, revolutionary movements gained more and more support. In Guatemala leftist guerrillas had been battling the military since the 1960s. In turn in nearby El Salvador the Sandinista Revolution of 1979 encouraged radicals. All Central America seemed on the verge of radical upheaval.

President Reagan came into office in 1981 determined to stem this tide of revolution. In his view, its main cause was not poverty and oppression but Soviet and Cuban interference. Reagan believed that the United States had to draw the line against communist expansion in Central America. He explained:

> " If Central America were to fall, what would be the consequences for our position in Asia and for our alliances such as NATO? . . . The national security of all the Americas is at stake in Central America. If we cannot defend ourselves there, we cannot expect to prevail elsewhere. Our credibility would collapse, our alliances would crumble.[1] "

Opposing the Sandinistas

Reagan's concern centered on Nicaragua. He accused the Sandinistas of trying to spread their revolution throughout Central America, pointing to their military buildup and their support of the rebels in El Salvador. He began a campaign to undermine the Sandinista government. Although the United States never broke relations with Nicaragua, it put severe economic and political pressure on the Sandinistas, just as it had on the Allende government in the early 1970s. The president also authorized the CIA to support the opponents of the Sandinistas.

Most important, the United States aided a rebel army made up of Nicaraguan opponents of the Sandinista regime known as the **Contras** (from the Spanish word *contra*, meaning "against") who were seeking to overthrow it. Throughout the 1980s the Contras made raids into Nicaragua from bases in neighboring Honduras and Costa Rica. They killed thousands of Nicaraguan soldiers and civilians and caused millions of dollars in economic damage.

At first Congress agreed to fund the aid. But fearing "another Vietnam," Congress outlawed funding to the Contras in 1984. Top officials in the Reagan administration violated these restrictions, however, giving rise to the Iran-Contra scandal.

The Sandinistas denied American charges that they intended to make Nicaragua a communist state and then export their revolution to other countries. They did invite Cuban advisers to the country and instituted socialist reforms, but they did not outlaw private enterprise. And they took some steps toward making the government more democratic. They also announced plans to hold a presidential

[1]From *The Central America Fact Book* by Tom Barry and Deb Preusch

Jason Bleibtreu/Sygma

election in February 1990. By that date, the country was on the brink of economic collapse.

In the election, Violeta Chamorro was the winner. The United States cheered the selection and claimed that the vote vindicated American policy toward Nicaragua. The Sandinistas accepted their defeat but argued that they had lost because the United States had crippled the Nicaraguan economy by its economic sanctions and support of the Contras. In any case, it was clear that Nicaraguans wanted a change.

President Chamorro promised to unify the nation and revive the economy. But the Sandinistas remained the most powerful of the many political parties in Nicaragua. The military, the labor unions, and other important sectors of society supported them. Nicaragua struggled to get back on its feet after more than a decade of turmoil.

Nicaraguan Contras train in a jungle camp along the Nicaragua-Honduras border. The United States provided money, supplies, and advisers to the Contras.

AP/Wide World Photos

Newly inaugurated Nicaraguan president Violeta Barrios de Chamorro gives the "V" sign to supporters. Former president Daniel Ortega (left) applauds after placing the presidential sash on her during inaugural ceremonies in Managua.

Latin America: 1960s–1990s   **615**

STRATEGIES FOR SUCCESS

Preparing an Oral History

To bring a period alive, historians often seek our personal accounts of the events and attitudes of the time. They interview participants and eyewitnesses, then record the interview either in writing or with a tape recorder. Such interviews are called oral histories, and they add much to a historian's treasury of information. Such oral histories can be considered primary sources. Of course, people's memories of events may change slightly over time. For this reason, the time lapse between an event's occurrence and the interview is an important consideration in evaluating the reliability of the account.

Preparing an oral history can be easy and enjoyable. But it does require planning and research.

How to Prepare an Oral History

There are three main parts to compiling a useful oral history: preparation, interviewing, and post-interview analysis and reporting. To prepare an oral history, follow these guidelines.

1. **Identify the topic.** Determine the information you will need and from whom the information can be obtained.
2. **Research the topic.** Gather available information on the topic on which to base your questions.
3. **Set up an interview.** Identify yourself and state clearly the purpose of the interview. Arrange a time when the interview can be conveniently scheduled.
4. **Prepare questions.** Develop questions that will elicit the information you need. Determine a direction for the interview so that one question leads logically to the next.
5. **Conduct the interview.** Explain again the purpose of the interview. Be an active listener, paying close attention to the responses and interacting when appropriate. Talk only as much as absolutely necessary. Be sure to record the responses accurately. (This can be done most easily through the use of a tape recorder or video camcorder.)
6. **Prepare the oral history.** Accurately transcribe the information collected in the recorded interview or edit the audio or video tape.
7. **Analyze the interview.** Use the information gathered in the interview to draw conclusions about the event. Then prepare a summary of your experience.

Applying the Strategy

Suppose you have been assigned to find out the effects of one of the Latin American revolts of the 1980s on the people of the country in which it happened. To research the uprising you might refer to newspaper and magazine articles or one of the following books: *Inevitable Revolutions* by Walter LaFeber; *The Central America Fact Book* by Tom Barry & Deb Preusch; *Distant Neighbors,* Alan Riding. Then carefully prepare questions for your interview. You might include some of the following questions:

1. Why did the uprising take place?
2. Were you in favor of the revolt or did you oppose it?
3. How did the unrest affect you personally? How did it affect the members of your family?
4. What were the results of the uprising? Did these results improve your life? How did it affect the members of your family?

Remember to analyze the information you have collected to prepare a summary of it.

For independent practice, see Practicing the Strategy on pages 630–31.

The Struggle in El Salvador

El Salvador was engulfed in civil war in the 1980s. As in other Latin American countries, the conflict had its roots in the nation's unbalanced distribution of land, wealth, and political power. El Salvador was dominated by a tiny group of wealthy landowners, the "14 Families." One visitor in 1931 noted that these families owned "nearly everything in the country. They live in almost regal style. The rest of the population has practically nothing."

In the 1970s, with the help of the Catholic church, Salvadoran peasants and workers began to organize. Their efforts were crushed by the dictatorship. In 1980 Archbishop Oscar Romero, a revered supporter of the poor, was murdered by assassins determined to protect the status quo. This caused many Salvadorans to take up arms. Guerrilla groups came together under the banner of the Farabundo Martí National Liberation Front, or FMLN, named for the leader of a 1932 revolutionary movement.

To prevent a leftist victory, the United States funneled massive aid to the Salvadoran government. It also persuaded the Salvadoran military to hand power over to a civilian administration, headed by President José Napoleón Duarte. With American support, Duarte tried to carry out democratic reforms and bring peace to the nation, but he had little success. **Right-wing** "death squads" supported by the established order tortured and killed anyone they suspected of having leftist sympathies.

In 1989 a presidential election resulted in victory for the right-wing Arena party. Human rights abuses continued, and the war dragged on with no victory in sight for either side. In 11 years of fighting, more than 70,000 Salvadorans lost their lives, while countless others live as refugees outside their country.

One sign of the economic problems that plague many Latin American countries is the vast slums, such as Villa El Salvador on the outskirts of Lima, Peru (left). Home to unemployed farm workers and their families, they go up overnight near most large cities in the region. War disrupts the economy, causing part of the problem. For example, civil war has torn El Salvador periodically for more than 20 years. Leftist guerillas, one shown here in his red mask, continue to fight for change. The ruling junta appointed José Napoleón Duarte (below) president in 1980. In 1986 he was elected to the office. Despite U.S. support, Duarte was unable to end the fighting or revive the economy.

Voices in Opposition

Many Americans opposed the Reagan administration's Central American policy, which they thought was prolonging and even creating conflict in the region. They argued that the United States should pursue diplomatic and economic rather than military solutions to the region's problems.

In 1982 a group of Latin American countries known as the **Contadora Group** came out in opposition to American policy. They called for a negotiated peace in the region. After a series of meetings of Central American leaders, peace accords were signed in 1987. These agreements called for democratic reforms and an end to outside influence in the region. For his role in arranging the accords, Costa Rican president Oscar Arias won the 1987 Nobel Peace Prize. Yet despite these encouraging developments, Central America remains a deeply troubled region.

Cindy Karp/Black Star

Oscar Arias, shown here greeting supporters, was elected president of Costa Rica in 1986. Arias worked hard for peace in the war-torn region of Central America. He said, "In the Americas peace must be democratic, pluralistic, tolerant, and free. . . . Working together for democracy, freedom, and development is working together for peace." How is the peace Arias describes different from that achieved in many Latin American countries in recent decades?

Facing Other Challenges in the Hemisphere

The small island nations of the Caribbean face the same difficulties plaguing Central America: deep-rooted poverty, unequally distributed wealth, undemocratic governments, and sluggish economies. To address these problems, President Reagan announced the **Caribbean Basin Initiative** (CBI) in 1982. The CBI was designed to promote economic stability by developing private enterprises. The United States would encourage investment to help the region's export industries expand. It would also lower American tariffs on some products so they could be sold more cheaply in the United States. Unfortunately, the CBI had little effect. Critics claimed that more direct financial aid was needed to overcome the region's problems.

One country excluded from the CBI in 1982 was Grenada, a tiny island with a socialist government. The United States accused Grenada of becoming a Soviet-Cuban military base. Tensions increased in 1983 when Grenada's government was overthrown by an even more radical group. After being asked by neighboring Caribbean islands to help, President Reagan sent 7,000 American troops to seize the island and install a new government.

Being more distant, the nations of South America had a lower priority in American policy during the 1980s, but there were problems there too. In 1982 Argentina invaded the Falkland Islands, a British colony in the South Atlantic. The Argentines had long claimed the islands, which they call the Malvinas. They assumed that Great Britain would not go to war over the islands, and that the United States would support Argentina's claim against a European power.

They were wrong on both counts. Great Britain did go to war, and the Reagan administration supported its European ally. When the British quickly conquered the islands, Argentina's military government collapsed. Argentina then returned to civilian rule. But during the Falkland war, other Latin American countries backed Argentina and criticized the United States for supporting Great Britain and betraying its pledge of respecting hemispheric solidarity.

The Falkland war was a much less important cause of trouble than the traffic in illegal drugs, especially cocaine. Large amounts of

United States troops, together with troops from six Caribbean nations, invaded Grenada in 1983. Their mission was to protect Americans there and to restore order. Among the Americans rescued from Grenada were more than 600 students at St. George's University School of Medicine, who were airlifted back to Charleston, South Carolina (right).

Randy Taylor/Sygma

Perry Baker/Sygma

The war on drugs throughout the Americas has been difficult and costly. Drug enforcement agents in Bolivia burn cocaine seized in a bust.

According to the latest estimates, people clear 100 acres of tropical rain forest every minute of every day. Why? Just as in the United States, the promise of open land attracts thousands to Brazil's vast interior wilderness. More than 12,000 settlers arrive in the rain forest each month. Scientists fear this might reduce worldwide rainfall and oxygen levels.

cocaine grown and refined in Peru, Bolivia, and Colombia were being smuggled to drug dealers in the United States and Europe. At times the illegal drugs entered through third countries, such as Panama and Brazil. This drug traffic was a multi-billion-dollar enterprise controlled by powerful criminals, such as the Medellín Cartel, named after the city in Colombia that became the group's headquarters. Governments were corrupted, and entire economies came under the sway of the "drug lords."

In 1989 President George Bush announced a war on drugs and set out to stem the international drug traffic. He offered American money and law-enforcement assistance to Latin American governments willing to crack down on the traffic. Colombia, in particular, pursued the drug lords diligently but paid a high price for its efforts. The Medellín Cartel declared war on the Colombian government and killed hundreds of law-enforcement officials, judges, politicians, and journalists.

In 1989 Bush sent American troops to Panama to capture that nation's ex-president, General Manuel Noriega, who Bush claimed was involved in drug trafficking. Noriega was captured and sent to the United States for trial. A properly elected government Noriega had refused to accept was restored to power. But economic damage resulting from the invasion left this Panamanian government in a weakened state and in dire need of American assistance. Some people charged that drug dealing was still taking place in Panama.

Environmental issues also gained increasing importance in inter-American relations in the late 1980s. Chief among these was Brazil's rapid destruction of the Amazon rain forest, the largest tropical forest in the world. The United States strongly opposed this action. Finally in November 1990 the president of Brazil announced that the Amazon Basin was to be protected forever.

The Debt Crisis

Another problem plaguing U.S.–Latin American relations was the growing debt being accumulated by many Latin American countries. The roots of the debt crisis go back to the 1970s. Rising oil prices had caused a worldwide economic slump, and Latin American countries were having trouble selling their products abroad. They began to borrow heavily. Foreign banks encouraged this borrowing, often showing little concern about how the money would be used or repaid. In some Latin American countries, the money was spent on unneeded projects, and some of it ended up in the pockets of corrupt officials. Frequently, these countries had to borrow more money just to pay the interest on their existing debt.

In 1982 the Mexican government announced that it could not make payments on its $80-billion debt. The news struck like a bombshell. A Mexican default could ruin many major world banks that had provided substantial loans. So many bank failures could then threaten the stability of the international financial system. The United States quickly patched together an emergency loan, but the problem did not go away. Many international banks cut back on their lending. United States banks raised interest rates and forced Latin American governments to reduce their expenditures drastically. These cuts in government spending affected such things as housing, health care, and food subsidies. They had disastrous effects on poor people. Unemployment, homelessness, and crime increased sharply throughout Latin America, causing massive protests.

The turmoil in Latin America had a ripple effect in the United States. It limited the ability of those countries to buy American goods. Deteriorating social conditions also added to the already large numbers of people migrating to the United States from the area "south of the border."

Left, Guatemalan refugees fleeing economic woes and war huddle outside Casa Romero, a church-sponsored shelter in Texas. Right, other Central American refugees—many of them farm workers—head northward through Texas looking for work.

Return to the Preview & Review on page 610.

4. THE WORLD IN THE 1990s

Use these questions to guide your reading. Answer the questions after completing Section 4.

Understanding Issues, Events, & Ideas. Use the following word to describe world changes in the 1990s: apartheid

1. What new problems did *glasnost* cause for the Soviet Union?
2. Why was *perestroika* especially difficult to achieve?
3. What chain of events did Gorbachev's policies cause in the Soviet Union's Eastern European satellite nations?

Thinking Critically. Why was the change from the state-controlled Soviet economy to a free market economy not immediately successful? What do you think Soviet leaders could do to make the change easier?

Glasnost, Perestroika, and the Soviet Union

The meaning of events becomes more difficult to interpret as we approach the present day. In the last decades of the 20th century, United States foreign policy experts were faced with a multitude of sudden and totally unexpected events. In China, the communist government that had been moving toward a more open society suddenly reversed itself. Students demonstrating for more democracy were mowed down by government troops merely for demanding the right of free speech. On the other hand, after the United States and other nations applied economic sanctions to South Africa for years because of its refusal to treat the black majority of that country fairly, the South African government repealed its policy of **apartheid**—separation of the races. It also released its best-known political prisoner, Nelson Mandela, from prison.

But the most dramatic upheaval occurred in the Soviet Union in 1985 when Mikhail Gorbachev became premier. Gorbachev set in motion a chain of events that transformed all the countries of Eastern Europe as well as the Soviet Union. In doing so, he brought the long Cold War with the western democracies to a peaceful end. For this he was awarded the 1990 Nobel Peace Prize.

When he took office Gorbachev was faced with the fact that the communist economic system was collapsing. Hoping to encourage the people to work harder and display more initiative, he encouraged them to discuss public issues and even to criticize government actions when they thought its policies were wrong. This was called *glasnost,* meaning "openness." He also called for stimulating the Soviet

David Modell/Woodfin Camp and Associates

Nelson Mandela acknowledges the crowd of well-wishers during a speech to delegates of the African National Congress (ANC), the political party representing South Africa's black majority. Mandela went on a worldwide speaking tour after his release from a South African prison in 1990.

R. Maiman/Sygma

economy by encouraging individual enterprise. The Russian term for this is *perestroika,* which means "economic restructuring."

American officials watched the developments with delight mixed with suspicion and disbelief. *Glasnost* meant ending censorship and political repression. Soviet newspapers began to report on Soviet problems as well as the nation's achievements. Writers were allowed to publish articles and books criticizing past and present Soviet leaders, such as Leonid Brezhnev and even Gorbachev himself. Hundreds of political prisoners were released. Freedom of religion, long denied, was now restored.

Gorbachev expected *perestroika* to revive the stagnant Soviet economy. He pushed through reforms reducing the control of Communist party officials over the production and distribution of goods. He also created a powerful new office—state president—to which he was elected by a new more-representative national legislature.

Glasnost caused many new problems. Freedom to express their political opinions led the people of the separate republics that made up the Union of Soviet Socialist Republics to demand more control of their own affairs. Some, such as the states on the Baltic Sea—Lithuania, Latvia, and Estonia—demanded the right to leave the Soviet Union entirely. Despite *glasnost,* Soviet leaders sent troops to quell these disturbances.

But if *glasnost* posed problems, *perestroika* was extremely difficult to achieve at all. Local communist bureaucrats dragged their feet when asked to give up their control of the economy and the special privileges party officials had possessed for years. Economic restructuring caused farmers and manufacturers to withhold their produce from state stores where prices were fixed by the government and to sell them at higher prices on the free market.

Soviet president Mikhail Gorbachev visits Ottawa, Canada's capital. Reforms instituted by Gorbachev helped end the Cold War. Now the Soviet Union and the Western democracies are forging new relationships. What are the names of the two main reforms begun by Gorbachev?

Stephen Ferry/Gamma-Liaison

Perestroika—economic restructuring—has had many devastating results. Food and consumer goods are scarce, and the shelves of most government stores, such as this meat market in Moscow, are bare. Why has the change from a communist economy to a free enterprise one been difficult?

Gorbachev's economic reforms directly affected United States foreign policy. The Soviet leader wanted to sharply cut back military expenditures and use the money saved to improve the standard of living of the people. In 1987 he and President Reagan signed a treaty limiting nuclear weapons. Gorbachev then reduced the Soviet armed forces by 500,000 men and promised to begin withdrawing all Soviet troops in the satellite nations—Hungary, Poland, Czechoslovakia, and even East Germany.

AP/Wide World Photos

President Bush and Soviet President Gorbachev shake hands in the White House in June 1990 after signing accords to further reduce nuclear weapons. Relations between the United States and the Soviet Union improved significantly in the late 1980s and early 1990s.

624   AMERICA IN THE WORLD

The Transformation of Eastern Europe

Chip Hires/Gamma-Liaison

Because of Gorbachev's policies the people of these satellite nations suddenly realized that they could throw off their Communist party leaders without fear of Soviet attack. A startling political transformation followed in a kind of chain reaction. During 1989, beginning in Hungary, all these nations discarded the communist system and began the process of developing democratic political institutions and free enterprise economies.

As in the Soviet Union, the second of these changes was more difficult to carry out than the first. Their economies were in a shambles, and both producers and consumers lacked experience with free markets. Indeed, they had no free markets at all at the start. Living standards, already low, fell still lower. Unemployment soared. Industrial output fell, on average, 25 percent.

Adam Michnik, a Polish writer, described the problems faced by the countries:

> 66 All of us know how to switch from a market economy to a planned totalitarian economy. Nobody knows how to switch from a totalitarian economy to a market economy. . . . As we say in Poland, we have to distinguish between an aquarium and fish soup. The difference, of course, is that you can make fish soup out of an aquarium, but you cannot make an aquarium out of fish soup. The road to the market must lead through poverty and unemployment. [But] neither the institutions of the state nor the people themselves are psychologically prepared to struggle with reality of this sort.[1] 99

[1]From "The Two Faces of Eastern Europe" by Adam Michnik in *The New Republic*

Anthony Suau/Black Star

Glasnost *has spurred a number of independence movements within the Soviet Union and among its satellite nations in Eastern Europe. Above, Lithuanians demonstrate for independence in the capital of Vilnius. Skirmishes between demonstrators and Soviet troops in January 1990 left 13 Lithuanians dead. Below, Romanians show their support for new democratic reforms and freedom from Soviet domination.*

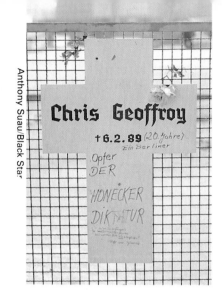

Chris Geoffroy

†6.2.89 (20 Jahre)
Ein Berliner

Opfer
DER
HONECKER
DIKTATUR

While what one American magazine described as "the death of communism" ended the Cold War, it also raised many new problems. Nowhere had the pace of change been more dizzying and its consequences more worrisome than in East Germany, known as the German Democratic Republic (DDR). The government of the DDR, led by Erich Honecker, had been the most hard-line of all the Soviet satellite states. When they realized that the Soviet army would no longer back their government, masses of East Germans arose and forced it from power without firing a shot. Meanwhile, tens of thousands of East Germans had fled to Hungary and Czechoslovakia, whose borders with Western European nations were now open. From there they had gone on to West Germany, where the people welcomed them with open arms. In hopes of stopping the exodus, the East German government then allowed its citizens to travel freely to West

No new memorials will mark where East Berliners died trying to cross the Berlin Wall, for Germans have torn down the hated wall and reunited their country.

Peter Turnley/Black Star

Germany. In November 1989, amid wild rejoicing, the people began tearing down the hated Berlin Wall.

Suddenly the reunification of Germany became inevitable. The nation that had torn Europe apart in World War II, the nation whose military might had come close to dominating the entire continent, now demanded that it be allowed to come back together. The opinion was so nearly unanimous that anyone who believed in democracy could not resist it. At a conference in February 1990 the United States, Great Britain, France, and the Soviet Union—the four Allied powers of World War II that divided Germany—formally agreed to allow the two Germanys to combine. Nevertheless, few could avoid worrying about what the future might hold.

Russia and the Soviet Union

Nowhere is the transformation from a communist state to a free market democracy so difficult to accomplish as in the Soviet Union. As time passed, it was uncertain whether Gorbachev or even the Soviet Union itself would survive the upheavals resulting from *glasnost* and *perestroika*. The United States did what it could to assist the Gorbachev government. But would this be enough? A writer in *U.S. News and World Report* expressed the opinion of many observers when he wrote that "in his efforts to modernize Russia, [Gorbachev] has released long-suppressed pressures, like the violent uncoiling of long-compressed steel springs. Now, Gorbachev himself may be swept away by the very forces he has unleashed."

By late 1990 the state-controlled economy was on the verge of total collapse. Even in Moscow people had difficulty getting enough to eat from the state-owned stores, and prices on the free market were beyond the reach of all but the most well-off citizens. Radical supporters of free enterprise, led by Boris Yeltsin, president of the powerful Russian Republic of the Soviet Union, demanded that Gorbachev adopt their plan for completely transforming the system to a free market economy, which they claimed could be accomplished in a mere 500 days. So drastic a change alarmed conservatives, and Gorbachev, seeking to balance both factions, hesitated to adopt it.

At the same time the separate republics continued to be encouraged by *glasnost* in their demand for more power to determine their own future. Armenia and Georgia, far to the south, declared their independence as the Baltic states had. In these and other republics ethnic and religious differences resulted in violent confrontations.

How to chart a course in these rapidly changing circumstances challenged the wisdom and ingenuity of United States policymakers and those of all the western democracies. The Cold War was no more. The "slave nations" of Eastern Europe were free at last. But if the Soviet Union were to collapse, who could say what the future might bring?

Boris Yeltsin, president of the Russian Federation of the Soviet Union, addresses a session of the Russian republic's Congress of People's Deputies on November 27, 1990. Yeltsin was speaking out against Gorbachev's new Union treaty.

Of course, dramatic events took place outside Eastern Europe and the Soviet Union as well as the 1990s began. When Iraq invaded and conquered Kuwait, the United States demanded that Iraq withdraw its troops. When Iraq refused, the United States reacted by blocking the flow of goods into and out of Iraq, a move supported by many countries and sanctioned by the United Nations. The United States also sent a large military force to the Middle East.

Everyone hoped that the threat of military action would convince Iraq to withdraw from Kuwait. But Iraqi dictator Saddam Hussein refused to pull his troops out or to negotiate. In January 1991 a United Nations force led by the United States launched an attack on Iraqi military targets. The swift U.N. victory forced Iraq to withdraw from Kuwait and created the possibility of lasting peace in the region. 👉

Return to the Preview & Review on page 622.

In response to Iraq's invasion of Kuwait, the United States sent troops and military equipment to the Middle East. A marine light assault vehicle passes a herd of camels in the Saudi Arabian desert (bottom left), while a member of the 325th Airborne Infantry passes the lonely hours in the desert near Jubail, Saudi Arabia, by writing home (top left). The troops took up positions in Saudi Arabia close to the border with Kuwait.

President Bush visited the troops in Saudi Arabia during Thanksgiving 1990 (top left). When war broke out in mid-January 1991 the coalition of countries against Iraq had more than 530,000 troops in the region, more than 475,000 of them American men and women (top right).

CHAPTER 15 REVIEW

1820	1900	1930	1940	

1823
Monroe
Doctrine

1904
Roosevelt
Corollary

1933
Good
Neighbor
policy

1935
Trade
Agreements
Act

1939
Permanent
Joint Board
on Defense

1948
OAS founded

Chapter Summary
Read the statements below. Choose one, and write a paragraph explaining its importance.
1. The United States and Canada have a long history of good relations, although disputes over fishing rights and boundaries have cropped up from time to time.
2. Over the years, the United States has used the Monroe Doctrine as the basis for its policies toward Latin America.
3. President Theodore Roosevelt favored gunboat diplomacy, while President Taft favored dollar diplomacy.
4. During the administration of Franklin D. Roosevelt, the Good Neighbor policy helped make U.S.–Latin American relations more friendly.
5. During the Cold War, the United States aided Latin American governments that were anti-communist.
6. The establishment of a communist regime in Cuba led to tensions between the island nation and the United States.
7. Revolutions rocked Central America in the 1970s and 1980s.
8. The drug trade and mounting national debts plagued Latin American nations in the 1980s.
9. Beginning in 1989, Eastern Europe and the Soviet Union initiated broad reforms, and tensions between the communists and the Western democracies decreased.
10. Iraq's invasion of Kuwait in 1990 led to a worldwide effort to contain Iraqi aggression.

Reviewing Chronological Order
Number your paper 1–5. Then study the time line above and place the following events in the order in which they happened by writing the first next to 1, the second next to 2, and so on.
1. Berlin Wall comes down
2. U.S. sends troops to Panama
3. OAS founded
4. Gorbachev becomes Soviet premier
5. Panama Canal Treaties

Understanding Main Ideas
1. What have been the major causes of tensions between the United States and Canada?
2. What was the main point of the Monroe Doctrine? How did the Roosevelt Corollary support that idea?
3. How did United States relations with Latin America improve after World War I?
4. What have been the main causes of problems in Latin America since the 1960s?
5. What changes did Mikhail Gorbachev bring to the Soviet Union? What chain reaction in the Soviet satellite nations did these changes cause?

Thinking Critically
1. **Solving Problems.** Although the United States and Canada have enjoyed a good relationship, certain problems exist. If you were an American diplomat, how would you improve relations with Canada?
2. **Analyzing.** Why did President Reagan take a strong stand against leftists who sought to bring about change in Latin America? How did he think this action would help the people of Latin America?
3. **Hypothesizing.** How might U.S. relations with the Soviet Union and the countries of Eastern Europe change as those nations continue to undergo the political and economic shifts started by Gorbachev?

Practicing the Strategy
Review the strategy on page 616.
Preparing an Oral History. Suppose you have been assigned to interview a person who was present at the opening of the Berlin Wall on November 9, 1989. Answer the following questions about your preparation for the interview?
1. How would you research the events and emotions surrounding the opening of the wall?
2. What would you like to know about the event?

1960	1970	1980	1990

1959
Castro comes
to power

★
St. Lawrence
Seaway

1961
Alliance for
Progress

1962
Cuban Missile
Crisis

1965
U.S. sends
marines to
Dominican
Republic

1973
Allende
overthrown

1977
Panama Canal
Treaties

1979
Revolution in
Nicaragua

1980
Civil war in
El Salvador

1982
Latin American
debt crisis

1983
U.S. sends
troops to
Grenada

1985
Gorbachev
becomes
Soviet premier

1989
President Bush's
war on drugs

★
U.S. sends
troops to
Panama

★
Berlin Wall
comes down

1990
U.S. sends
troops to
Middle East

3. List at least four questions you would ask the person you are to interview.
4. What will you be looking for in your analysis of the oral history interview?

Writing About History: Expressive

Imagine that you are a newspaper correspondent. Write a report on one of the following: the political unrest in one of the Soviet republics, the reunification of Germany, or the activities of American troops in Saudi Arabia. Use the information in Chapter 15 to help you develop your report.

Using Primary Sources

Even before he was elected president, Jimmy Carter championed human rights. He outlined this concern during a campaign speech on September 8, 1976. As you read the excerpt from the speech, think of how Carter planned to implement his ideas.

"I do not say to you that we can remake the world in our own image. I recognize the limits on our power, but the present administration—our government—has been so obsessed with balance of power politics that it has often ignored basic American values and a common and proper concern for human rights.

Ours is a great and a powerful nation, committed to certain enduring ideals, and those ideals must be reflected not only in our domestic policy but also in our foreign policy. There are practical, effective ways in which our power can be used to alleviate human suffering around the world. We should begin by having it

understood that if any nation . . . deprives its own people of basic human rights; that fact will help shape our own people's attitude toward that nation's repressive government. . . . Now, we must be realistic . . . we do not and should not insist on identical standards. . . . We can live with diversity in governmental systems, but we cannot look away when a government tortures people or jails them for their belief."

1. According to Carter, why has the current administration ignored human rights?
2. How do you think Carter planned to use American power to protect human rights throughout the world?
3. Based upon what you have read in the chapter, was President Carter successful in protecting human rights?

Enriching Your Study of History

1. **Individual Project.** Complete *one* of the following projects: Create a collage or picture essay of Canada or Mexico that includes both historical pictures and pictures from current magazines and newspapers *or* develop a scrapbook of news articles on current events in either Canada or Mexico.
2. **Cooperative Project.** Your class will prepare reports on the current events in the three main parts of Latin America: Central America, South America, and the islands of the Caribbean. Each report should include a map for that part of Latin America.

Chapter 15 Review   631

UNIT FIVE REVIEW

Summing Up and Predicting
Read the summary of the main ideas in Unit Five below. Choose one statement, then write a paragraph predicting its outcome or future effect.

1. Among the successes of the Great Society were Medicare and the Voting Rights Act.
2. By the 1960s the United States was called the Affluent Society because no nation in the world had ever been so productive.
3. Movements for equal rights by women, Native Americans, Hispanics, and African Americans continued.
4. The domino theory led to U.S. involvement in South Vietnam.
5. The year 1968 was a tragedy because of the Tet offensive in Vietnam; the murders of Dr. Martin Luther King, Jr., and Robert Kennedy, and the riots at the Democratic convention in Chicago.
6. The Watergate cover-up led to the resignation of President Nixon.
7. Presidents Ford, Carter, and Reagan struggled with the economy.
8. Relations between the United States and the other countries of the Western Hemisphere—Canada and the nations of Central and South America and the Caribbean—continued to undergo change.
9. By the early 1990s the Cold War had ended as the nations of Eastern Europe, as well as the Soviet Union, introduced multiparty systems and other democratic features to their political processes.
10. In response to the Iraqi invasion of Kuwait, several nations, including the U.S., sent troops to the area and war soon broke out.

Connecting Ideas
1. The author says that by 1960 the impact of computers was beginning to be felt in the United States. He said that "Eventually the United States would become a computerized society." Do you think the author was correct in his prediction and that we have become a "computerized society?" What are some of the ways that we rely on computers?
2. The Twenty-Sixth Amendment to the Constitution, which lowered the voting age to 18, was ratified in 1971. However, in every national election since ratification the voter turnout for 18- to 20-year-olds has been relatively low. How would you account for this? What can be done to encourage 18- to 20-year-olds to vote?

Practicing Critical Thinking
1. **Analyzing.** In his acceptance speech as Republican presidential candidate in 1964 Barry Goldwater said, "Extremism in the defense of liberty is no vice. And . . . moderation in the pursuit of justice is no virtue." Do you agree or disagree with Goldwater? Why do you think many voters were frightened by this statement?
2. **Predicting.** What do you think might have happened if President Nixon had not resigned and had been put on trial by the Senate?
3. **Solving Problems.** Select *one* of the following problems and explain how you would solve it: acid rain, the rising crime rate, the increasing use of illegal drugs, the growing numbers of homeless, or one of the sources of conflict among nations in the Western Hemisphere.

Exploring History Together
1. Your group will prepare a pictorial essay of either a major event that occurred or a policy that was enacted in the United States from 1964 to the present. Your group will prepare an oral report to go along with the essay and choose a member of the group to present the report.
2. Working in two groups, your class will research and then prepare a debate on a current controversial topic. A speaker from each side should be chosen to present the case. After the speakers have finished, each side should present a rebuttal or final argument defending their side's point of view. Present your debate before a civic or community group.

Reading in Depth
Greene, Laura. *Computer Pioneers.* New York: Franklin Watts/First Books. Presents an account of men and women of the electronic age.

Harlan, Judith. *American Indians Today: Issues and Conflicts.* New York: Franklin Watts/Impact Books. Focuses on the problems of Native Americans today.

Lasky, Kathryn. *Home Free.* Soquel, Ca.: Four Winds Press. Contains the story of a fifteen-year-old boy and his valiant effort to protect endangered bald eagles whose home is being threatened by a developer.

Thomas, Joyce Carol. *Water Girl.* New York: Avon Books/Flare Books. Provides an account of an African American teenage girl who unwittingly comes across a piece of her own history.

REFERENCE SECTION

The Reference Section contains a variety of features designed to enhance your understanding of the story of America. *Maps: Portraying the Land* reviews general information about maps and map-reading skills. The atlas includes a world map, maps of Europe, Asia, Africa, and several maps of the United States. A series of graphs and charts presents statistical profiles of major American social and economic changes. For easy reference, a strategy review section provides the *Strategies for Success* presented in Volume 1. *Documents in American History* contains primary source documents. The glossary lists boldfaced words and their definitions. The index provides page references for the topics discussed in *The Story of America*. An acknowledgments page lists the title and publisher of the primary sources.

MAPS: PORTRAYING THE LAND

We use maps to picture the land. When early people traveled, they noticed differences among places. To describe the new places they had seen, they scratched crude maps on rocks or drew them on leather. Today's maps are the geographer's most important tool. As you read, keep these questions in mind:

1. What features do most maps have in common?
2. Why are maps imperfect representations of the earth?
3. What are map projections? Why do they contain distortions?
4. What are the four most common landforms?
5. What are some of the topics about the United States illustrated on maps in this textbook?

UNDERSTANDING MAPS

Perhaps you have used a map to find your way to a place, such as a friend's house for a party. In order to use any map, you must be able to "read" it, or understand its parts.

Maps

Most of the maps in this textbook have similar parts. These include a **title,** a **legend,** a **directional indicator,** and a **scale.** The title tells you what the map is about. Many map titles also include a date and the area shown. The title of this map is Colonial Products, 1775. The title tells you that the subject is items produced in the colonies in 1775.

The legend, or key, explains the meaning of the symbols used on the map. Areas where tobacco was grown are marked with a tobacco leaf, paper mills with a roll of paper, and other activities with a variety of other symbols. The extent of settlement in 1775 is shaded in brown.

A directional indicator, such as the **compass rose,** helps you find directions on a map. The four cardinal directions—north, south, east, and west—are labeled on the compass rose. North is labeled with an N, south with an S, east with an E, and west with a W. As the compass rose shows, you would travel north to get from Newport to Boston.

You can also determine intermediate directions—northeast, southeast, southwest, and northwest—using the compass rose. Often they are indicated but not labeled. The compass rose at the top of the next column shows the four

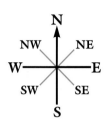

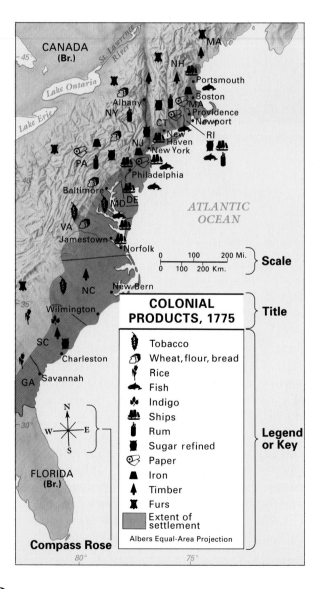

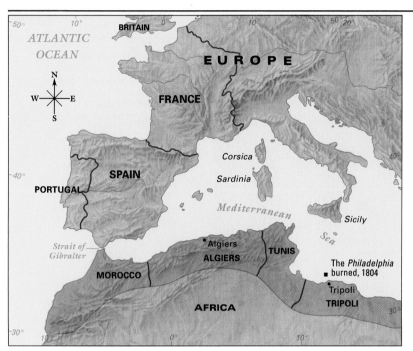

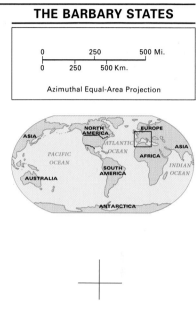

THE BARBARY STATES

| 0 | | 250 | | 500 Mi. |
| 0 | 250 | | 500 Km. | |

Azimuthal Equal-Area Projection

intermediate directions. As you can see on the map, New York City is northeast of Philadelphia.

To help you determine distance, maps have a scale. The distances shown on the map are much smaller than the actual distances on the earth's surface. The scale tells you how to relate the two. The line of the scale is divided into equal intervals and labeled in both miles and kilometers. The scale on the map shows that just less than three-quarters of an inch on the map represents 200 miles on the earth's surface. About how far is it from Jamestown to Philadelphia? You should find that it is about 200 miles. The Strategy for Success on page 658 will help you practice using the parts of a map.

Maps in *The Story of America* contain certain special features to enrich your study of them. Around the edges of each map are marks referring to the global grid. This grid, created by the lines of latitude and longitude, helps you locate places on the map. The Strategy for Success on page 659 provides information about latitude and longitude and offers opportunities to practice using them.

Many of the maps in *The Story of America* also have special maps to help you see the location of the area you are studying in relation to other areas of the United States or the world. Such maps are called **locator maps.** The map above has a world locator map to the right of the main map. A box shows the Barbary States in relation to the rest of the world. As you can see, the Barbary States, on the northern coast of Africa, lay far across the Atlantic Ocean from the United States. In the map on the next page the locator map is in the upper lefthand corner of the main map. It outlines the eastern half of the United States, shows the area of study with a box, and shades the extent of the original colonies for further reference.

Map Projections

Because maps are flat and the earth is a sphere, maps are imperfect representations of the earth's surface. Globes provide a much more accurate picture of the earth. But they are impractical to carry with you. So **cartographers,** or mapmakers, have devised ways of showing the round earth on flat maps. These **map projections** allow us to get a better idea of how the earth really looks. Mapmakers create such projections through complex

Maps: Portraying the Land 635

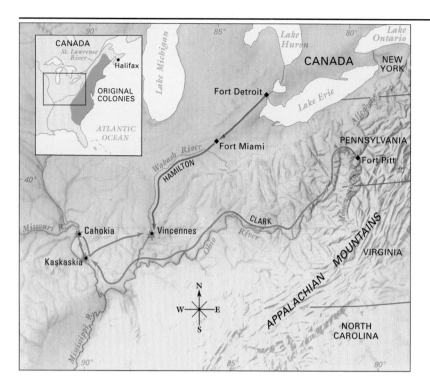

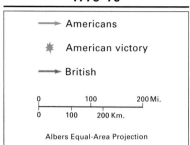

THE WAR IN THE WEST, 1778–79

→ Americans

✳ American victory

→ British

| 0 | | 100 | | 200 Mi. |
| 0 | 100 | | 200 Km. | |

Albers Equal-Area Projection

mathematical formulas, usually using computers to design the maps.

How does a cartographer create a projection? Imagine taking the cover of a softball and using it to make a flat, rectangular picture of the ball. You would have to cut and flatten the cover to fit the rectangle. When you were finished making your picture, parts of the cover would no longer look just as they had when they were on the ball. A cartographer designing a map projection does the same, deciding what to show most accurately and what to twist and shape, or distort. The interrupted projection at top of the next page gives you an idea of how this process works.

Every map projection, and therefore every map, contains distortions. A projection might distort the shapes of land areas, or their sizes, or distances, or directions. Maps generally are most accurate near the center and more distorted around the edges. Maps of large areas tend to be more distorted than maps of smaller areas. To see how different projections make maps look different, compare the two maps at the bottom of the next

page. The map on the left is a Robinson projection; the map on the right uses a Peters projection.

Knowing all this, mapmakers choose the projection that least distorts what they wish to show. One of the earliest projections, the Mercator projection, was used to make maps for sailors. It shows direction accurately—most important for navigation—but it distorts the size of areas away from the equator. The two small maps at the bottom of pages 640–41 are Mercator projections.

Most of the maps in this textbook are equal-area maps. Equal-area maps show relative sizes quite accurately, although they distort shapes somewhat. The map of the United States on pages 646–47 is an Albers Equal-Area projection.

You also will note several world maps that use the Robinson projection. The Robinson projection is a compromise, which means it minimizes distortions in size, shape, distance, and direction but does not preserve complete accuracy in any of those properties. It has become widely accepted for world maps. The world map on pages 640–41 of the Atlas is a Robinson projection.

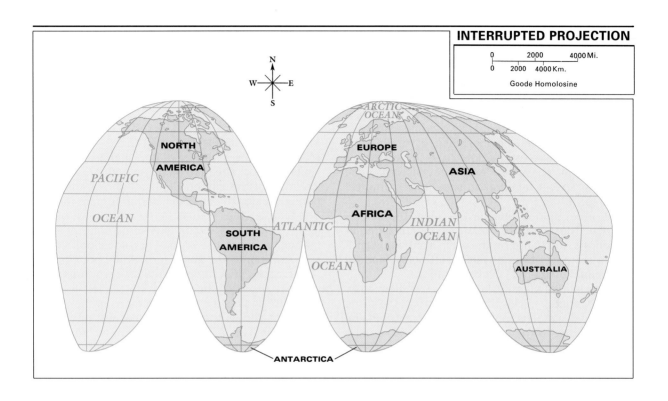

INTERRUPTED PROJECTION

0   2000   4000 Mi.
0   2000 4000 Km.

Goode Homolosine

NORTH AMERICA

EUROPE

ASIA

PACIFIC

OCEAN

AFRICA

INDIAN OCEAN

SOUTH AMERICA

ATLANTIC

OCEAN

AUSTRALIA

ARCTIC OCEAN

ANTARCTICA

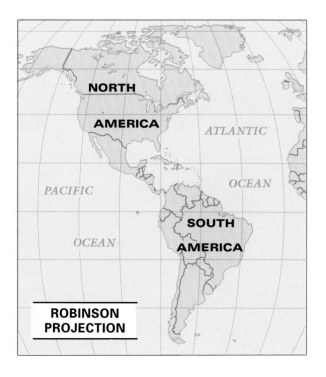

NORTH AMERICA

ATLANTIC

PACIFIC

OCEAN

SOUTH AMERICA

OCEAN

ROBINSON PROJECTION

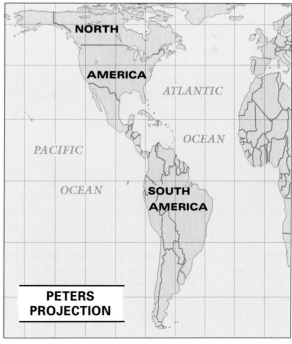

NORTH AMERICA

ATLANTIC

PACIFIC

OCEAN

SOUTH AMERICA

OCEAN

PETERS PROJECTION

Maps: Portraying the Land   637

Types of Maps

Just as there are many map projections, there are many types of maps. Most maps are either political maps or physical maps. Political maps show information such as national and state boundaries and major cities. Physical maps illustrate the natural landscape of an area. They often use shading to illustrate **relief**—the existence of mountains, hills, and valleys—and colors to show **elevation,** or the height above sea level. They also may use colors or special symbols to show other physical features.

Wrinkles, bulges, and gashes mark the earth's surface. These surface variations create different **landforms,** or shapes on the earth's surface. Landforms are part of the **physical setting,** or **natural landscape,** of every place on earth.

Geographers classify landforms by their characteristics. Four of the most common landforms are plains, plateaus, hills, and mountains. **Plains** are nearly flat or gently rolling lands that stretch unbroken to the horizon. The nomadic hunters—those who wandered from place to place—and early explorers who came to America were cheered by the vast plains, knowing they would be easier to cross than mountains. **Plateaus,** too, are relatively flat lands, but unlike plains they rise sharply from the surrounding landscape to 2,000 feet (610 meters) or more on at least one side.

Hills are rounded bulges of land that rise at least 500 feet (152 meters) above the surrounding land to no more than 2,000 feet (610 meters). Various natural forces form hills, but many result from the wearing down, or **erosion,** of mountains. Early settlers found hills obstacles to movement until improvements in wagons and roads in the 1700s made crossing them easier.

The most dramatic landform is the **mountain.** Mountains are often rocky, rugged land that rises sharply from the surrounding land to heights of over 2,000 feet (610 meters). The highest mountain peaks in the United States (not including Alaska and Hawaii) are in the west—the Rocky Mountains, the Sierra Nevada, and the Cascades. Mountain ranges lie near both coasts of the United States. These mountain barriers have influenced American history, from settlement patterns to government policies.

Other maps are called **special-purpose maps** because they illustrate special information. Special-purpose maps include historical maps that show the routes of explorers or boundary changes, population maps that illustrate where the most people live, and economic maps that highlight economic activities.

MAPPING THE UNITED STATES

Maps illustrate a variety of information about the United States. The map on pages 646–47 is a physical map of the United States. It shows the locations of major rivers, lakes, and mountain ranges. Shading on the map illustrates the "lay of the land." This map also contains some political information, such as the names and locations of the states, major cities, and international boundaries.

The Story of America contains several special-purpose maps of the United States. The map on page 109 depicts the climate regions of the United States. It shows that the northeastern quarter of the nation has a continental climate, while the southeastern quarter has a humid subtropical climate. Much of the western half of the country has a semiarid climate. It is interesting to compare the map of climate regions with the one on page 175 that illustrates the agricultural regions of the U.S. The similarities and differences between those two maps will tell you something about the climate conditions needed for a variety of types of farming.

The map on page 144 shows another special category of information about the United States—the sizes and locations of major cities in 1900. The largest cities in 1900 were east of the Mississippi River. Only a few major cities—St. Louis, San Francisco, Denver, and Minneapolis—were west of the river. The information on the map on page 649 of settlement of the United States will help you understand the reasons for this.

The textbook also contains a map of United States cultural regions. The map on page 271 provides one example of the cultural regions that geographers have identified. And there are many other kinds of maps in this textbook.

Map Skills

The ability to read and understand maps can come in handy in your everyday life. You may use a street map to find directions or get information from a weather map. Reading maps is, of course, a key part of studying geography, history, and many other subjects in school. Learning about the global grid, map projections, and types of maps is the first step in learning to read maps. Many of the Strategies for Success in this textbook focus on reading and comparing maps and interpreting the information they contain.

Map Section Review

1. Name and describe the four features most maps have in common.
2. Why have mapmakers created map projections? Why are there different projections?
3. Why do map projections contain distortions?
4. Name and describe the four most common landforms.
5. Study the list of maps in the Table of Contents. What are some of the topics about the United States illustrated on maps in this textbook?

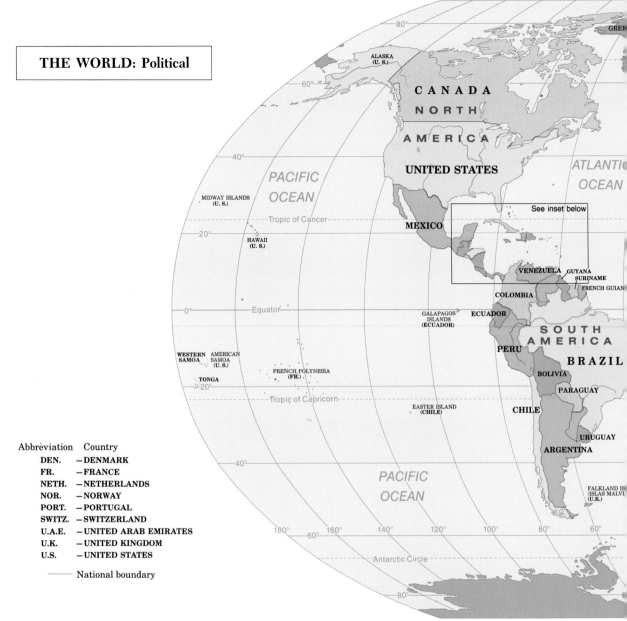

THE WORLD: Political

ALASKA
(U. S.)

GRE[

CANADA

NORTH

AMERICA

UNITED STATES

ATLANTIC
OCEAN

PACIFIC
OCEAN

MIDWAY ISLANDS
(U. S.)

Tropic of Cancer

MEXICO

See inset below

HAWAII
(U. S.)

VENEZUELA GUYANA
SURINAME
FRENCH GUIAN

COLOMBIA

Equator

GALAPAGOS
ISLANDS
(ECUADOR) **ECUADOR**

**SOUTH
AMERICA**

WESTERN AMERICAN
SAMOA SAMOA
(U. S.)

PERU

BRAZIL

TONGA

FRENCH POLYNESIA
(FR.)

BOLIVIA

PARAGUAY

Tropic of Capricorn

EASTER ISLAND
(CHILE)

CHILE

URUGUAY

ARGENTINA

PACIFIC
OCEAN

FALKLAND IS
(ISLAS MALVI
(U.K.)

Abbreviation	Country
DEN.	**–DENMARK**
FR.	**–FRANCE**
NETH.	**–NETHERLANDS**
NOR.	**–NORWAY**
PORT.	**–PORTUGAL**
SWITZ.	**–SWITZERLAND**
U.A.E.	**–UNITED ARAB EMIRATES**
U.K.	**–UNITED KINGDOM**
U.S.	**–UNITED STATES**

—— National boundary

Antarctic Circle

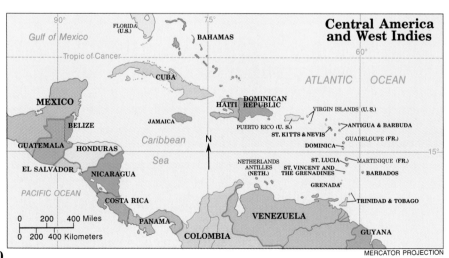

Central America
and West Indies

FLORIDA
(U.S.)

Gulf of Mexico

BAHAMAS

Tropic of Cancer

ATLANTIC OCEAN

CUBA

MEXICO

DOMINICAN
REPUBLIC
HAITI

VIRGIN ISLANDS (U.S.)

BELIZE

JAMAICA

ANTIGUA & BARBUDA

PUERTO RICO (U. S.)
ST. KITTS & NEVIS

GUADELOUPE (FR.)

GUATEMALA HONDURAS

Caribbean

DOMINICA

EL SALVADOR

NICARAGUA

Sea

NETHERLANDS
ANTILLES
(NETH.)

ST. LUCIA
ST. VINCENT AND
THE GRENADINES

MARTINIQUE (FR.)

PACIFIC OCEAN

BARBADOS

GRENADA

COSTA RICA

TRINIDAD & TOBAGO

0   200   400 Miles
0 200 400 Kilometers

PANAMA

VENEZUELA

COLOMBIA

GUYANA

MERCATOR PROJECTION

640

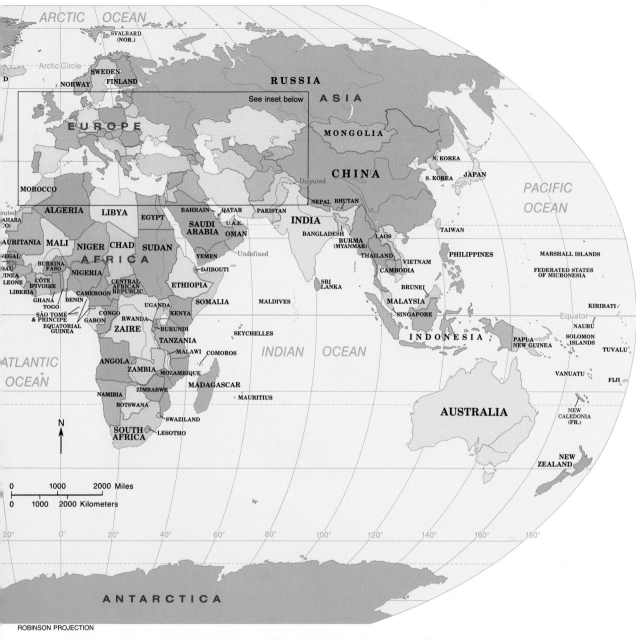

ARCTIC OCEAN

SVALBARD (NOR.)

Arctic Circle

SWEDEN
NORWAY FINLAND

RUSSIA

ASIA

See inset below

EUROPE

MONGOLIA

CHINA

N. KOREA
S. KOREA JAPAN

PACIFIC OCEAN

MOROCCO

Disputed

NEPAL BHUTAN

MOROCCO

ALGERIA LIBYA
EGYPT

BAHRAIN QATAR
SAUDI ARABIA U.A.E.
OMAN

PAKISTAN

INDIA

TAIWAN

SAHARA

AURITANIA MALI
NEGAL
SSAU
UINEA
LEONE
LIBERIA
GHANA
TOGO
SÃO TOMÉ
& PRÍNCIPE
EQUATORIAL
GUINEA

NIGER CHAD
SUDAN

AFRICA

BURKINA
FASO
NIGERIA
CÔTE
D'IVOIRE
BENIN
CAMEROON
CONGO
GABON
ZAIRE

CENTRAL
AFRICAN
REPUBLIC

ETHIOPIA

UGANDA
KENYA
RWANDA
BURUNDI

SOMALIA

YEMEN
DJIBOUTI

Undefined

BANGLADESH
BURMA
(MYANMAR)
THAILAND
LAOS
VIETNAM
CAMBODIA

PHILIPPINES

MARSHALL ISLANDS

FEDERATED STATES
OF MICRONESIA

SRI
LANKA

MALDIVES

BRUNEI

MALAYSIA
SINGAPORE

KIRIBATI

Equator

NAURU
SOLOMON
ISLANDS

TANZANIA
MALAWI COMOROS
ANGOLA
ZAMBIA
MOZAMBIQUE
ZIMBABWE
NAMIBIA
BOTSWANA
MADAGASCAR

SEYCHELLES

INDIAN OCEAN

INDONESIA

PAPUA
NEW GUINEA

TUVALU

VANUATU

FIJI

ATLANTIC
OCEAN

MAURITIUS

AUSTRALIA

NEW
CALEDONIA
(FR.)

N

SWAZILAND
SOUTH
AFRICA LESOTHO

NEW
ZEALAND

0   1000   2000 Miles
0   1000   2000 Kilometers

20°   0°   20°   40°   60°   80°   100°   120°   140°   160°   180°

ANTARCTICA

ROBINSON PROJECTION

15°   0°
NORWAY
SWEDEN
ESTONIA
LATVIA
UNITED
KINGDOM
DENMARK
LITHUANIA
RUSSIA
IRELAND
NETH.
BYELARUS
BELGIUM
GERMANY
POLAND
LUXEMBOURG
CZECHOSLOVAKIA
UKRAINE
LIECHTENSTEIN
FRANCE SWITZ.
AUSTRIA HUNGARY
MOLDOVA
MONACO
ITALY
ROMANIA
ANDORRA
CORSICA
(FR.)
SAN MARINO
YUGOSLAVIA
VATICAN CITY
BULGARIA
PORTUGAL
SARDINA
(ITALY)
ALBANIA
SPAIN
SICILY
(ITALY)
GREECE
MALTA
MOROCCO
TUNISIA
ALGERIA
LIBYA
EGYPT

0   250   500 Miles
0   250   500 Kilometers

Europe and
Central Asia

RUSSIA

KAZAKHSTAN

45°

Black Sea
GEORGIA
ARMENIA
TURKEY
AZERBAIJAN

Caspian
Sea

UZBEKISTAN

KYRGYZSTAN

TURKMENISTAN

TAJIKISTAN

CHINA

N

CYPRUS
SYRIA
LEBANON
ISRAEL
IRAQ
JORDAN
SAUDI ARABIA KUWAIT

IRAN

AFGHANISTAN
PAKISTAN
INDIA NEPAL

30°

Mediterranean Sea

ATLANTIC
OCEAN

MERCATOR PROJECTION

641

Reykjavík
ICELAND

Arctic Circle

FAROE IS.
(DEN.)

SHETLAND IS.
(U.K.)

Trondheim

SWEDEN

NORWAY

Bergen

Oslo
Uppsala
Stavanger
Stockholm

Glasgow • Edinburgh
Belfast
UNITED
KINGDOM
Dublin
IRELAND
Liverpool

Göteborg

North
Sea

DENMARK
Copenhagen

Bornholm
(DEN.)
Kalin
Gdans

Manchester

Birmingham

Hamburg

NETHERLANDS
Cardiff
Bristol Thames R.
London
Dover
Calais

Bremen
Bremen Berlin
Amsterdam
The Hague
Rotterdam
GERMANY

English Channel

BELGIUM
Brussels
Bonn

POLA

Le Havre

Leipzig
Oder
River

Elbe R.

Seine
Paris
LUXEMBOURG
R.
Luxembourg
Frankfurt

Prague
Kra

ATLANTIC

Loire

River

FRANCE
La Rochelle
Dijon

Strasbourg
Stuttgart
Danube
R.
Rhine R.

CZECHOSLOVA

OCEAN

Munich
Vienna

Bay of
Biscay

Bordeaux

Bern
Geneva
Lyon
Zürich
LIECHTENSTEIN
SWITZERLAND
AUSTRIA
Budapes

HUN
Rhône R.

ALPS
Milan
Turin
Po River
Venice
Genoa

Zagreb
Trieste

Porto

PYRENEES
Garonne
R.

Marseille
Nice
MONACO
Florence
Bel
SAN
MARINO
YUGOSLA
Sarajevo

Lisbon

PORTUGAL

Ebro River
ANDORRA

Madrid
Tagus
R.

Barcelona

Corsica
(FR.)

APENNINES
Tiber R.
Rome
ITALY

Adriatic
Sea

SPAIN

Valencia

Sardinia
(IT.)

Tir
AL

Seville

BALEARIC ISLANDS
(SP.)

Naples

Cádiz

Strait of
Gibraltar

Tyrrhenian

Sea

Ion
Se

Mediterranean Sea

Palermo

Sicily

642

AFRICA

MALTA

ARCTIC
OCEAN

URAL MOUNTAINS

White Sea

Arkhangel'sk

North Dvina River

FINLAND

Lake
Ladoga

Helsinki
St. Petersburg

RUSSIA

Tallinn

ESTONIA

Nizhniy Novgorod
(Gor'kiy)

Gulf of Finland

Riga
LATVIA

Moscow

Samara
(Kuybyshev)

River

LITHUANIA

Ural

Vilnius

Minsk

BYELARUS

Warsaw

Kiev

Kharkov

Volgograd

Volga

UKRAINE

Don River

Volga River

ASIA

Dniester

River

R.

Dnieper

60°

MOLDOVA
Kishinev

Sea
of
Azov

Caspian

Odessa

40°

CARPATHIAN

MTS.

CAUCASUS   MTS.

Sea

RUMANIA

Sevastopol

Bucharest

Danube River

Black   Sea

BALKAN MTS.

Sofia

BULGARIA

TURKEY
Istanbul

GREECE

Aegean
Sea

N

EUROPE

Athens

⊛   National capital

•   Other city

Canal

National boundary

Crete

AZIMUTHAL EQUAL AREA PROJECTION

0	100	200	300 Miles
0	100 200 300		Kilometers

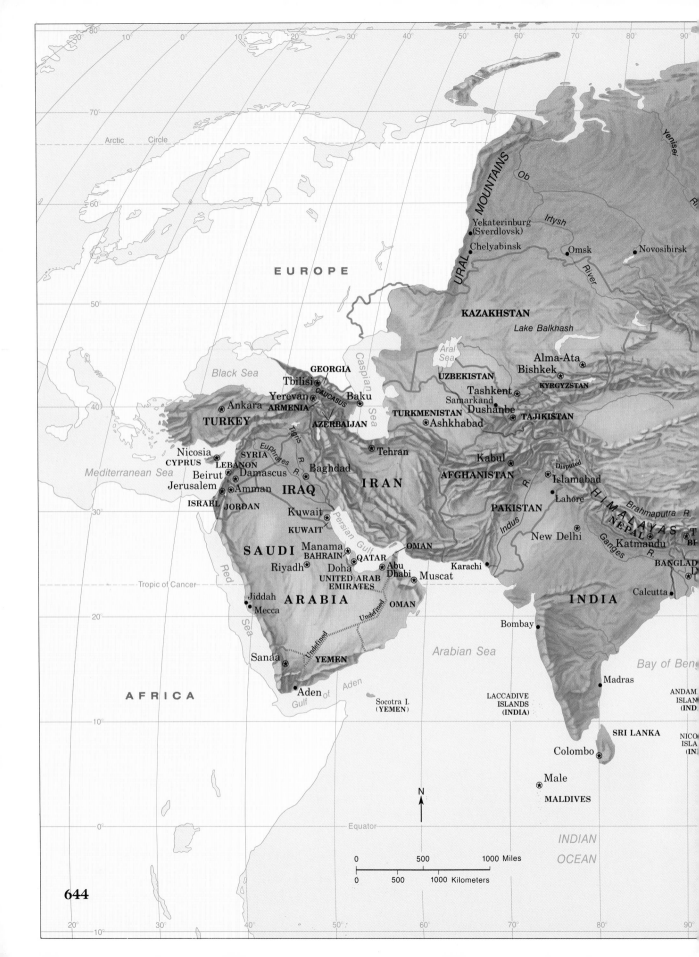

ARCTIC Circle

80° 70° 60° 50° 40° 30° 20° 10° 0° 10° 20° 30° 40° 50° 60° 70° 80° 90°

70°

60°

EUROPE

URAL MOUNTAINS

Ob

Yekaterinburg
(Sverdlovsk)

Irtysh

Chelyabinsk

Omsk

Novosibirsk

River

Yenisei

50°

KAZAKHSTAN

Lake Balkhash

Aral
Sea

Alma-Ata
Bishkek

Black Sea

GEORGIA

Tbilisi
CAUCASUS
Baku

UZBEKISTAN

KYRGYZSTAN

Yerevan
ARMENIA

Ankara

Caspian Sea

Tashkent

Samarkand

Dushanbe

TAJIKISTAN

TURKEY

AZERBAIJAN

40°

TURKMENISTAN
Ashkhabad

Tehran

Kabul

Mediterranean Sea

Nicosia
CYPRUS
SYRIA
LEBANON
Beirut
Damascus
Jerusalem
Amman
ISRAEL
JORDAN

Euphrates R.

Tigris R.

Baghdad

IRAQ

IRAN

AFGHANISTAN

Disputed

Islamabad

Lahore

HIMALAYAS

Brahmaputra R.

30°

Kuwait

KUWAIT

Persian Gulf

PAKISTAN

Indus R.

NEPAL

Katmandu

BANGLAD

New Delhi

Ganges R.

SAUDI

Manama
BAHRAIN
Riyadh

Doha
QATAR

Abu
Dhabi
UNITED ARAB
EMIRATES

OMAN

Muscat

Karachi

INDIA

Calcutta

Tropic of Cancer

Red Sea

Jiddah
Mecca

ARABIA

Undefined

Undefined

OMAN

Arabian Sea

Bombay

Madras

ANDAM
ISLAN
(IND

20°

Sanaa

YEMEN

Aden
Gulf of Aden

Socotra I.
(YEMEN)

LACCADIVE
ISLANDS
(INDIA)

SRI LANKA

NICO
ISLA
(IN

10°

AFRICA

Colombo

N

Male

MALDIVES

0°

Equator

INDIAN

OCEAN

0   500   1000 Miles

0   500   1000 Kilometers

10°

644

20° 10° 20° 30° 40° 50° 60° 70° 80°

ARCTIC OCEAN

80°

70°

Arctic Circle

Lena River

RUSSIA

Lena River

60°

Bering Sea

Sea of Okhotsk

KAMCHATKA PENINSULA

50°

Lake Baikal

Ulaanbaatar

MONGOLIA

GOBI (DESERT)

Amur River

•Harbin

KURIL ISLANDS (U.S.S.R. & JAPAN)

Yalu R.

•Vladivostok

Sea of Japan

40°

Beijing

N. KOREA
P'yongyang

Tianjin

Truce Line

JAPAN

Seoul

S. KOREA

Tokyo

CHINA

Huang He

Yellow Sea

Kobe
•Osaka

Yokohama

PACIFIC

Chang Jiang

•Chongqing

Shanghai

East China Sea

30°

OCEAN

Xi

River

RYUKYU IS. (JAPAN)

Taipei

TAIWAN

Guangzhou

Tropic of Cancer

Hanoi

HONG KONG (U.K.)

20°

LAOS

MACAO (PORT.)

ASIA

⊛ National capital

iane
oon

Mekong R.

South China Sea

Philippine Sea

• Other city

National boundary

THAILAND
Bangkok

VIETNAM

Manila

PHILIPPINES

ROBINSON PROJECTION

CAMBODIA (KAMPUCHEA)

Phnom Penh

•Ho Chi Minh City

10°

BRUNEI

MALAYSIA

Bandar Seri Begawan

Kuala Lumpur

⊛ Singapore
SINGAPORE

Equator

0°

Java Sea

Jakarta

INDONESIA

100°   110°   120°   130°   140°   150°   160°   170°

-10°

645

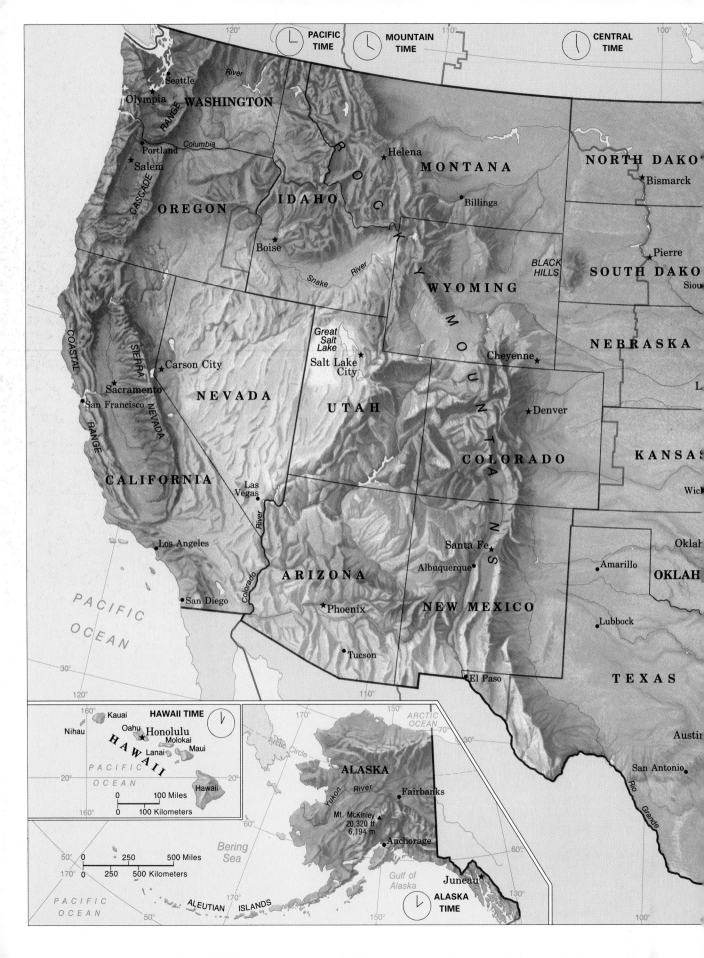

PACIFIC TIME

MOUNTAIN TIME

CENTRAL TIME

120°   110°   100°

Seattle
River
Olympia
WASHINGTON
Helena
MONTANA
NORTH DAKO
*Bismarck
RANGE
Portland
Columbia
Salem
CASCADE
IDAHO
Billings
OREGON
*Boise
ROCKY
WYOMING
BLACK HILLS
SOUTH DAKO
Pierre
Siou
Snake   *River*
NEBRASKA
COASTAL
Great Salt Lake
Cheyenne
Carson City
SIERRA
Salt Lake City
MOUNTAINS
Sacramento
NEVADA
San Francisco
NEVADA
UTAH
Denver
RANGE
COLORADO
KANSAS
Wic
CALIFORNIA
Las Vegas
River
Santa Fe
Amarillo
Oklah
Los Angeles
Albuquerque
OKLAH
Colorado
ARIZONA
NEW MEXICO
San Diego
Lubbock
PACIFIC
Phoenix
OCEAN
Tucson
TEXAS
30°
120°   110°
El Paso

HAWAII TIME
160°
Kauai
Nihau
Oahu
Honolulu
Molokai
HAWAII
Lanai   Maui
PACIFIC
20°
OCEAN
Hawaii
160°
0   100 Miles
0   100 Kilometers

ARCTIC OCEAN
170°   150°   70°
30°
Arctic Circle
ALASKA
Yukon   *River*
Fairbanks
Mt. McKinley
20,320 ft
6,194 m
Anchorage
60°
60°
Bering Sea
50°
0   250   500 Miles
170°   0   250   500 Kilometers
Gulf of Alaska
Juneau
PACIFIC
ALASKA TIME
OCEAN
50°
ALEUTIAN   ISLANDS
170°   150°   130°   100°

Austin
San Antonio
Rio Grande

90° 80° 50° 70°

Lake Superior

Duluth

NESOTA

MICHIGAN

Lake
Huron

eapolis St. Paul
Mississippi

WISCONSIN

Milwaukee

Madison Lansing

River Detroit

Lake
Michigan

Lake
Erie

IOWA

Des Moines

Chicago

Gary

ILLINOIS

INDIANA

OHIO

Cleveland

Columbus

Springfield

Indianapolis

Cincinnati

St. Louis

Ohio River

Louisville

Frankfort

Kansas
City

Jefferson
City

MISSOURI

KENTUCKY

ARKANSAS

River

Memphis

Tennessee River

Little
Rock

TENNESSEE

Nashville

APPALACHIAN MTS

Atlanta

Birmingham

ALABAMA

Jackson

Montgomery

GEORGIA

Savannah

MISSISSIPPI

Mobile

Red River

Baton Rouge

LOUISIANA

Houston

New Orleans

Jacksonville

Tallahassee

FLORIDA

Orlando

Gulf of Mexico

Tampa

Miami

MAINE

Augusta

VERMONT

Montpelier

NEW
HAMPSHIRE

Concord

St. Lawrence River

GREEN MTS.

Lake Ontario

Rochester

Albany

Boston

MASSACHUSETTS

NEW YORK

Hartford

Providence

RHODE
ISLAND

Buffalo

CONNECTICUT

New York

Hudson River

40°

PENNSYLVANIA

NEW
JERSEY

Harrisburg

Philadelphia

Trenton

Pittsburgh

Wilmington

Baltimore

Dover

DELAWARE

WEST
VIRGINIA

Washington

Annapolis

MARYLAND

70°

Charleston

Richmond

VIRGINIA

Norfolk

Chesapeake Bay

ATLANTIC

OCEAN

NORTH

Raleigh

CAROLINA

Charlotte

SOUTH

Columbia

CAROLINA

Charleston

30°

N

0   250   500 Miles

0   250   500 Kilometers

90° 80°

647

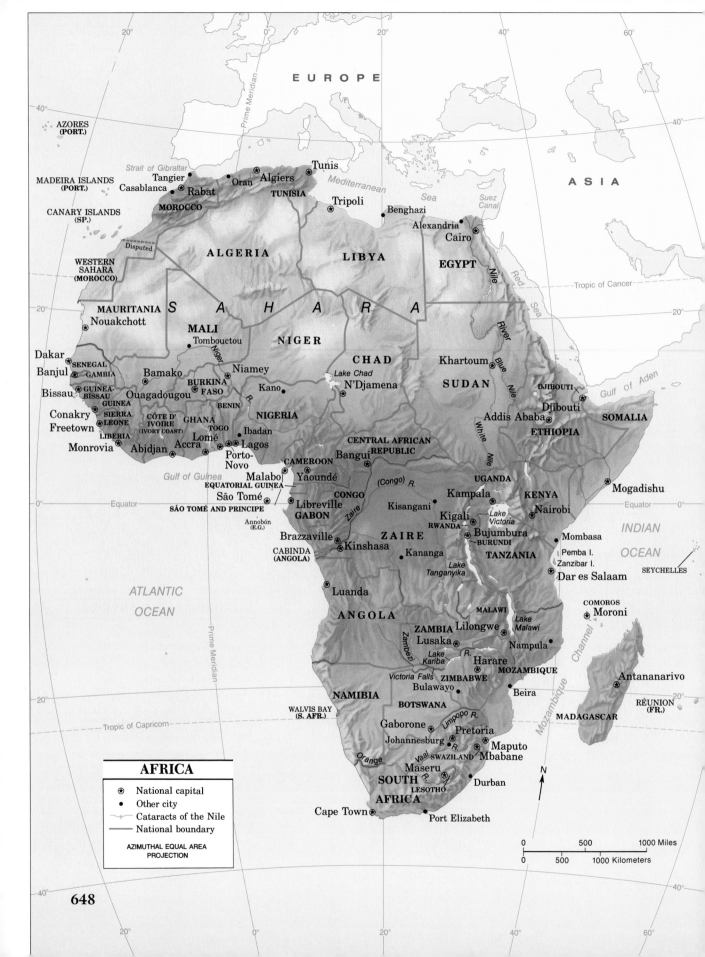

AZORES
(PORT.)

MADEIRA ISLANDS
(PORT.)

CANARY ISLANDS
(SP.)

EUROPE

ASIA

Strait of Gibraltar

Tangier ⊛ Tunis
Oran Algiers
Casablanca ⊛ Rabat
MOROCCO TUNISIA Tripoli Benghazi
Mediterranean
Sea
Suez
Canal

Alexandria
Cairo ⊛

WESTERN
SAHARA
(MOROCCO)

Disputed

ALGERIA

LIBYA

EGYPT

Tropic of Cancer

MAURITANIA S A H A R A
Nouakchott ⊛

MALI
Tombouctou

NIGER

CHAD

Khartoum ⊛

Nile

Red

Sea

River

DJIBOUTI

Dakar ⊛ SENEGAL
Banjul ⊛ GAMBIA
Bissau ⊛ GUINEA-
BISSAU
GUINEA
Conakry ⊛ SIERRA
Freetown ⊛ LEONE
LIBERIA
Monrovia ⊛

Niger R.
Bamako ⊛ Niamey ⊛
BURKINA
FASO Kano
Ouagadougou ⊛
BENIN
CÔTE D'
IVOIRE GHANA
(IVORY COAST) TOGO
Abidjan Accra ⊛ Lomé ⊛
Ibadan
Porto-
Novo

Lake Chad
N'Djamena ⊛

SUDAN

White Nile

Blue Nile

Addis Ababa ⊛

Djibouti ⊛
Djibouti

SOMALIA

ETHIOPIA

Mogadishu ⊛

Gulf of Aden

NIGERIA
Lagos

CENTRAL AFRICAN
REPUBLIC
Bangui ⊛

Malabo ⊛
EQUATORIAL GUINEA
São Tomé ⊛
SÃO TOMÉ AND PRINCIPE
Annobón
(E.G.)

CAMEROON
Yaoundé ⊛

(Congo) R.
CONGO
Libreville ⊛
GABON

Kisangani

UGANDA
Kampala ⊛
Kigali ⊛
RWANDA
Bujumbura ⊛
BURUNDI

Lake
Victoria

KENYA
Nairobi ⊛

Mogadishu ⊛

Equator

Gulf of Guinea

Equator

Zaire

Brazzaville ⊛
Kinshasa ⊛
CABINDA
(ANGOLA)

ZAIRE
Kananga

Lake
Tanganyika

TANZANIA

Mombasa
Pemba I.
Zanzibar I.
Dar es Salaam

INDIAN
OCEAN

SEYCHELLES

ATLANTIC

OCEAN

Luanda ⊛

ANGOLA

MALAWI

COMOROS
Moroni ⊛

ZAMBIA
Lusaka ⊛
Zambezi R.
Lake
Kariba
Victoria Falls

Lilongwe ⊛
Lake
Malawi
Harare ⊛
ZIMBABWE
Bulawayo

Nampula

MOZAMBIQUE

Beira

Mozambique Channel

Antananarivo ⊛

RÉUNION
(FR.)

MADAGASCAR

NAMIBIA

WALVIS BAY
(S. AFR.)

BOTSWANA

Tropic of Capricorn

Orange R.

Gaborone ⊛
Johannesburg
Limpopo R.
Pretoria ⊛
Vaal R.
Maseru ⊛
SWAZILAND
Mbabane ⊛
Maputo ⊛

Durban

SOUTH
AFRICA

LESOTHO

Cape Town ⊛

Port Elizabeth

N

AFRICA

⊛ National capital
• Other city
⊬⊬ Cataracts of the Nile
— National boundary

AZIMUTHAL EQUAL AREA
PROJECTION

0   500   1000 Miles
0   500   1000 Kilometers

648

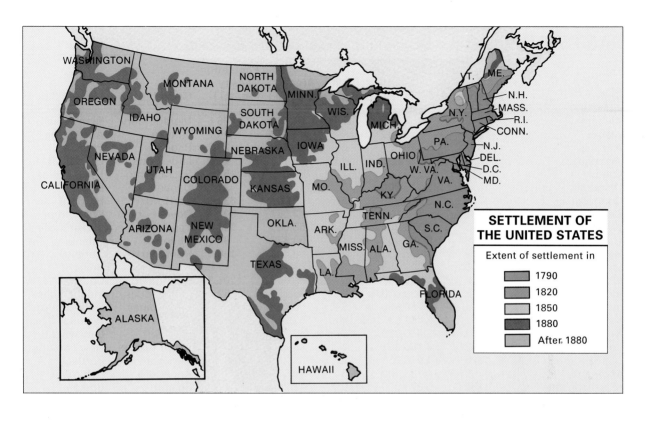

SETTLEMENT OF THE UNITED STATES

Extent of settlement in

- 1790
- 1820
- 1850
- 1880
- After 1880

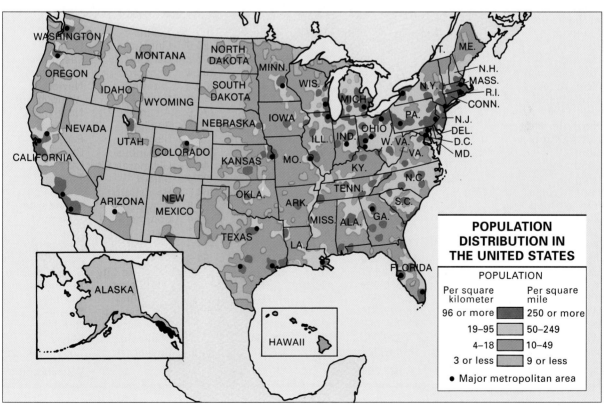

POPULATION DISTRIBUTION IN THE UNITED STATES

POPULATION

Per square kilometer	Per square mile
96 or more	250 or more
19–95	50–249
4–18	10–49
3 or less	9 or less

• Major metropolitan area

FACTS ABOUT THE STATES

State	Year of Statehood	1990 Population	Reps. in Congress	Area (Sq. mi.)	Population Density (Sq. mi.)	Capital	Largest City
Alabama	1819	3,984,000	7	51,609	76.6	Montgomery	Birmingham
Alaska	1959	546,000	1	586,412	0.7	Juneau	Anchorage
Arizona	1912	3,619,000	6	113,909	23.9	Phoenix	Phoenix
Arkansas	1836	2,337,395	4	53,104	43.9	Little Rock	Little Rock
California	1850	29,279,000	52	158,693	151.4	Sacramento	Los Angeles
Colorado	1876	3,272,000	6	104,247	27.9	Denver	Denver
Connecticut	1788	3,226,929	6	5,009	637.8	Hartford	Hartford
Delaware	1787	658,031	1	2,057	307.6	Dover	Wilmington
Florida	1845	12,775,000	23	58,560	180.0	Tallahassee	Jacksonville
Georgia	1788	6,387,000	11	58,876	94.1	Atlanta	Atlanta
Hawaii	1959	1,095,000	2	6,450	150.1	Honolulu	Honolulu
Idaho	1890	1,003,558	2	83,557	11.5	Boise	Boise
Illinois	1818	11,325,000	20	56,400	205.3	Springfield	Chicago
Indiana	1816	5,499,000	10	36,291	152.8	Indianapolis	Indianapolis
Iowa	1846	2,766,658	5	56,290	52.1	Des Moines	Des Moines
Kansas	1861	2,467,000	4	82,264	28.9	Topeka	Wichita
Kentucky	1792	3,665,220	6	40,395	92.3	Frankfort	Louisville
Louisiana	1812	4,180,831	7	48,523	94.5	Baton Rouge	New Orleans
Maine	1820	1,218,053	2	33,215	36.3	Augusta	Portland
Maryland	1788	4,733,000	8	10,577	428.7	Annapolis	Baltimore
Massachusetts	1788	5,928,000	10	8,257	733.3	Boston	Boston
Michigan	1837	9,179,000	16	58,216	162.6	Lansing	Detroit
Minnesota	1858	4,358,864	8	84,068	51.2	St. Paul	Minneapolis
Mississippi	1817	2,534,814	5	47,716	33.4	Jackson	Jackson
Missouri	1821	5,079,385	9	69,686	71.3	Jefferson City	St. Louis
Montana	1889	794,329	1	147,138	5.4	Helena	Billings
Nebraska	1867	1,572,503	3	77,227	20.5	Lincoln	Omaha
Nevada	1864	1,193,000	2	110,540	7.3	Carson City	Las Vegas
New Hampshire	1788	1,103,163	2	9,304	102.4	Concord	Manchester
New Jersey	1787	7,617,418	13	7,836	986.2	Trenton	Newark
New Mexico	1912	1,490,381	3	121,666	10.7	Santa Fe	Albuquerque
New York	1788	17,627,000	31	49,576	370.6	Albany	New York City
North Carolina	1789	6,553,000	12	52,586	120.4	Raleigh	Charlotte
North Dakota	1889	634,223	1	70,665	9.4	Bismarck	Fargo
Ohio	1803	10,778,000	19	41,222	263.3	Columbus	Cleveland
Oklahoma	1907	3,124,000	6	69,919	44.1	Oklahoma City	Oklahoma City
Oregon	1859	2,828,214	5	96,981	27.4	Salem	Portland
Pennsylvania	1787	11,764,000	21	45,333	264.3	Harrisburg	Philadelphia
Rhode Island	1790	988,609	2	1,214	897.8	Providence	Providence
South Carolina	1788	3,407,000	6	31,055	103.4	Columbia	Columbia
South Dakota	1889	693,294	1	77,047	9.1	Pierre	Sioux Falls
Tennessee	1796	4,822,134	9	42,244	111.6	Nashville	Memphis
Texas	1845	16,825,000	30	267,339	54.3	Austin	Houston
Utah	1896	1,711,117	3	84,916	17.8	Salt Lake City	Salt Lake City
Vermont	1791	560,029	1	9,609	55.2	Montpelier	Burlington
Virginia	1788	6,128,000	11	40,817	134.7	Richmond	Norfolk
Washington	1889	4,827,000	9	68,192	62.1	Olympia	Seattle
West Virginia	1863	1,782,958	3	24,181	80.8	Charleston	Huntington
Wisconsin	1848	4,869,640	9	56,154	86.5	Madison	Milwaukee
Wyoming	1890	449,905	1	97,914	4.9	Cheyenne	Cheyenne
District of Columbia		637,651	—	69	10,123.2		Washington

PRESIDENTS OF THE UNITED STATES

No.	Name	Born–Died	Years in Office	Political Party	Home State	Vice President
1	George Washington	1732–1799	1789–97	None	Va.	John Adams
2	John Adams	1735–1826	1797–1801	Federalist	Mass.	Thomas Jefferson
3	Thomas Jefferson	1743–1826	1801–09	Republican*	Va.	Aaron Burr
						George Clinton
4	James Madison	1751–1836	1809–17	Republican	Va.	George Clinton
						Elbridge Gerry
5	James Monroe	1758–1831	1817–25	Republican	Va.	Daniel D. Tompkins
6	John Quincy Adams	1767–1848	1825–29	Republican	Mass.	John C. Calhoun
7	Andrew Jackson	1767–1845	1829–37	Democratic	Tenn.	John C. Calhoun
						Martin Van Buren
8	Martin Van Buren	1782–1862	1837–41	Democratic	N.Y.	Richard M. Johnson
9	William Henry Harrison	1773–1841	1841	Whig	Ohio	John Tyler
10	John Tyler	1790–1862	1841–45	Whig	Va.	
11	James K. Polk	1795–1849	1845–49	Democratic	Tenn.	George M. Dallas
12	Zachary Taylor	1784–1850	1849–50	Whig	La.	Millard Fillmore
13	Millard Fillmore	1800–1874	1850–53	Whig	N.Y.	
14	Franklin Pierce	1804–1869	1853–57	Democratic	N.H.	William R. King
15	James Buchanan	1791–1868	1857–61	Democratic	Pa.	John C. Breckenridge
16	Abraham Lincoln	1809–1865	1861–65	Republican	Ill.	Hannibal Hamlin
						Andrew Johnson
17	Andrew Johnson	1808–1875	1865–69	Republican	Tenn.	
18	Ulysses S. Grant	1822–1885	1869–77	Republican	Ill.	Schuyler Colfax
						Henry Wilson
19	Rutherford B. Hayes	1822–1893	1877–81	Republican	Ohio	William A. Wheeler
20	James A. Garfield	1831–1881	1881	Republican	Ohio	Chester A. Arthur
21	Chester A. Arthur	1830–1886	1881–85	Republican	N.Y.	
22	Grover Cleveland	1837–1908	1885–89	Democratic	N.Y.	Thomas A. Hendricks
23	Benjamin Harrison	1833–1901	1889–93	Republican	Ind.	Levi P. Morton
24	Grover Cleveland		1893–97	Democratic	N.Y.	Adlai E. Stevenson
25	William McKinley	1843–1901	1897–1901	Republican	Ohio	Garrett A. Hobart
						Theodore Roosevelt
26	Theodore Roosevelt	1858–1919	1901–09	Republican	N.Y.	
						Charles W. Fairbanks
27	William Howard Taft	1857–1930	1909–13	Republican	Ohio	James S. Sherman
28	Woodrow Wilson	1856–1924	1913–21	Democratic	N.J.	Thomas R. Marshall
29	Warren G. Harding	1865–1923	1921–23	Republican	Ohio	Calvin Coolidge
30	Calvin Coolidge	1872–1933	1923–29	Republican	Mass.	
						Charles G. Dawes
31	Herbert Hoover	1874–1964	1929–33	Republican	Calif.	Charles Curtis
32	Franklin D. Roosevelt	1882–1945	1933–45	Democratic	N.Y.	John Nance Garner
						Henry Wallace
						Harry S Truman
33	Harry S Truman	1884–1972	1945–53	Democratic	Mo.	
						Alben W. Barkley
34	Dwight D. Eisenhower	1890–1969	1953–61	Republican	Kans.	Richard M. Nixon
35	John F. Kennedy	1917–1963	1961–63	Democratic	Mass.	Lyndon B. Johnson
36	Lyndon B. Johnson	1908–1973	1963–69	Democratic	Texas	
						Hubert H. Humphrey
37	Richard M. Nixon	1913–	1969–74	Republican	Calif.	Spiro T. Agnew
						Gerald R. Ford
38	Gerald R. Ford	1913–	1974–77	Republican	Mich.	Nelson A. Rockefeller
39	Jimmy Carter	1924–	1977–81	Democratic	Ga.	Walter F. Mondale
40	Ronald Reagan	1911–	1981–89	Republican	Calif.	George H. Bush
41	George H. Bush	1924–	1989–	Republican	Texas	R. Danforth Quayle

*The Republican party of the third through sixth presidents is not the party of Abraham Lincoln, which was founded in 1854.

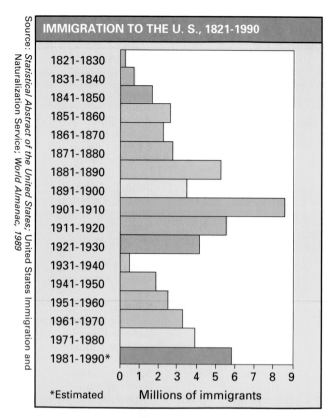

IMMIGRATION TO THE U. S., 1821-1990

Source: *Statistical Abstract of the United States; United States Immigration and Naturalization Service; World Almanac, 1989*

*Estimated   Millions of immigrants

As the graphs on this page indicate, the United States has a rich and varied racial and cultural heritage. This rich heritage is due in large part to immigration. Prior to World War II the majority of immigrants to the United States came from Europe. The Immigration Act of 1965, however, made it easier for non-Europeans to immigrate to the United States. As a result, people from Central and South America, the Caribbean, and Asia now make up the majority of new immigrants.

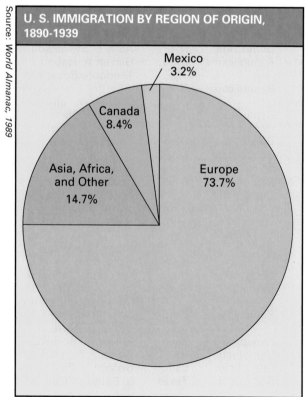

U. S. IMMIGRATION BY REGION OF ORIGIN, 1890-1939

Source: *World Almanac, 1989*

Mexico 3.2%
Canada 8.4%
Asia, Africa, and Other 14.7%
Europe 73.7%

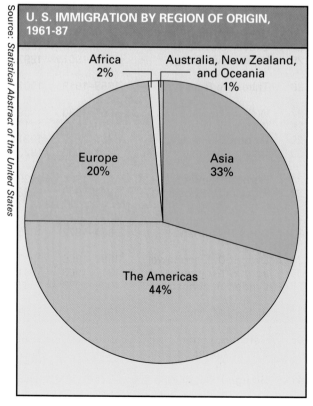

U. S. IMMIGRATION BY REGION OF ORIGIN, 1961-87

Source: *Statistical Abstract of the United States*

Africa 2%
Australia, New Zealand, and Oceania 1%
Europe 20%
Asia 33%
The Americas 44%

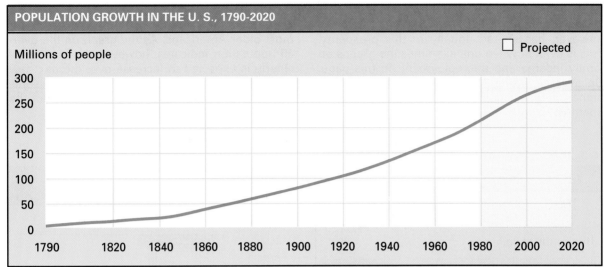

POPULATION GROWTH IN THE U. S., 1790-2020

Millions of people

☐ Projected

Source: Bureau of the Census

Technology also has helped shape American society. The graphs on this page illustrate some of the social consequences of new technologies. Advances in medicine and public sanitation, for instance, have increased the number of years most people live. As a result, the population of the United States has grown. More efficient farming methods have reduced the number of farmers needed to produce food for the American people. This decrease in the demand for farm labor has meant that more workers have been available to fill the jobs created by industrialization. Because these jobs tend to be located in or near cities, the population of the United States has become increasingly urban.

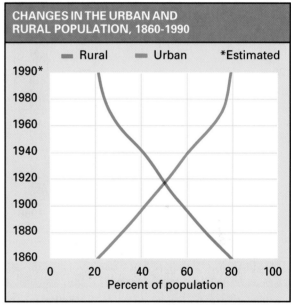

CHANGES IN THE URBAN AND RURAL POPULATION, 1860-1990

— Rural — Urban *Estimated

Percent of population

Source: Bureau of the Census

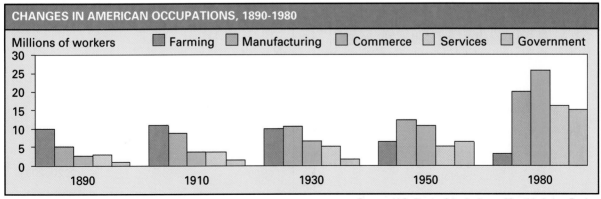

CHANGES IN AMERICAN OCCUPATIONS, 1890-1980

Millions of workers ■ Farming ■ Manufacturing ☐ Commerce ☐ Services ☐ Government

Source: U.S. Dept. of Agriculture; *Monthly Labor Review*

Over its history the United States has enjoyed strong economic growth. Not everyone in society, however, has shared equally in this prosperity. This is evident when one examines the graphs on family income and unemployment on this page. On average, white Americans have enjoyed the highest family incomes and the lowest rates of unemployment.

Social Security and other government programs have made the retirement years more secure for most older Americans. As the graph on the over-65 population indicates, however, the number of elderly is expected to increase over the next few decades. This increase will place new pressures on the government to develop ways to meet the needs of older Americans.

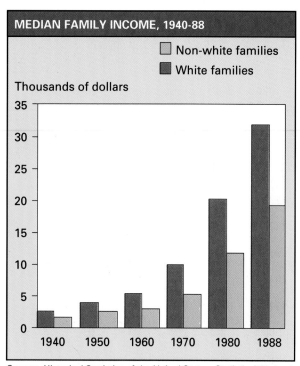

MEDIAN FAMILY INCOME, 1940-88

☐ Non-white families
■ White families

Thousands of dollars

Source: *Historical Statistics of the United States; Statistical Abstract of the United States, 1988;* Bureau of the Census

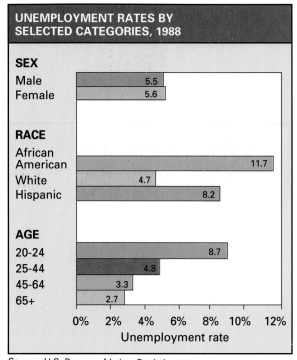

UNEMPLOYMENT RATES BY SELECTED CATEGORIES, 1988

SEX
Male 5.5
Female 5.6

RACE
African American 11.7
White 4.7
Hispanic 8.2

AGE
20-24 8.7
25-44 4.8
45-64 3.3
65+ 2.7

Unemployment rate

Source: U.S. Bureau of Labor Statistics

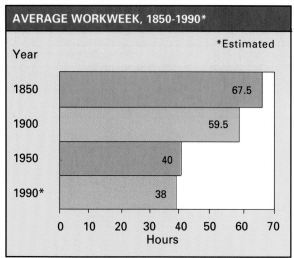

AVERAGE WORKWEEK, 1850-1990*

*Estimated

Year

1850 — 67.5
1900 — 59.5
1950 — 40
1990* — 38

Hours

Source: *Statistical Abstract of the United States, 1989*

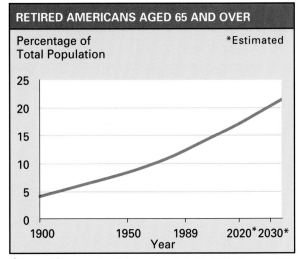

RETIRED AMERICANS AGED 65 AND OVER

Percentage of Total Population   *Estimated

Year

Source: *"Grays on the Go"* in *Time,* Feb. 22, 1988; Bureau of the Census

The federal government must have enough money to finance its programs and activities. The money the government collects for this purpose is called receipts. Most government receipts are in the form of taxes. The money the government spends is referred to as outlays. As can be seen from the graph at the top left, in recent decades the federal government has spent more than it has taken in. This shortfall is called a budget deficit. When the federal government experiences a budget deficit, it must borrow money to finance its spending. This borrowed money is called the national debt. As the graph on the top right shows, paying the interest on the national debt is a major outlay for the federal government.

In recent years, the United States also has experienced a trade deficit. A trade deficit occurs when a nation imports more than it exports. The graph at the bottom of the page shows the relationship between United States import and export values since 1950. The inset traces the rise and fall of United States tariffs.

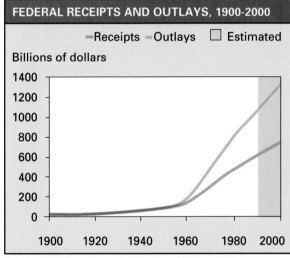

Source: *Statistical Abstract of the United States, 1989*

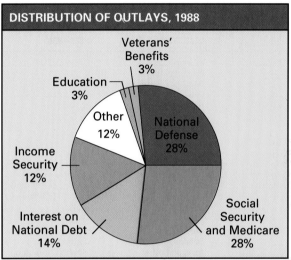

Source: *Statistical Abstract of the United States, 1989*

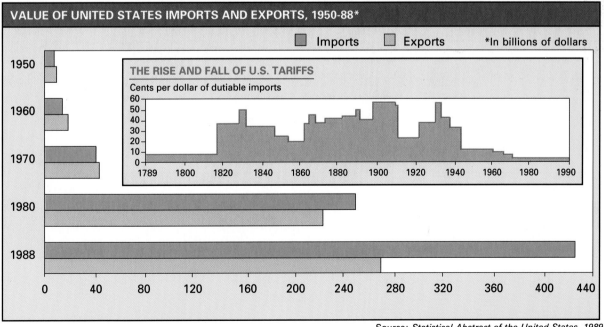

Source: *Statistical Abstract of the United States, 1989*

All societies must face the fact that the resources needed to produce goods and services are limited. Thus each society must decide how best to use its limited resources. A society makes this decision by answering three basic economic questions: (1) What goods and services should be produced? (2) How should these goods and services be produced? (3) For whom should these goods and services be produced?

In the United States these three questions are answered in a free-market environment. By free market, we mean that people are free to produce, sell, and buy whatever they wish and to work for whomever they want. What goods and services are actually produced, however, is determined by the forces of supply and demand. Producers supply those goods and services that are demanded by consumers.

Over time, changes in technology and in the types of goods and services available from other markets around the world have altered the nature of business and industry.

MAJOR ADVANCES IN AMERICAN BUSINESS AND INDUSTRY

	1607-1783	1783-1850	1850-1900	1900-1920	1920-Present
Power	Human muscles Animals muscles Wind and water power	Steam power	Electric power Internal combustion engines		Atomic energy Geothermal energy
Manufacturing Materials	Copper, bronze, iron Wood Clay Plant and animal fibers	Large-scale production of iron	Large-scale production of steel Development of combustion fuels: coal, oil, gas	Large-scale production of light metals and alloys Development of plastics and sythetics	Large-scale production of plastics and synthetics
Factory Methods	Handforges and tools Hand-powered equipment	Machinery powered by water and steam Interchangeable parts	Mass production, with centralized assembly of interchangeable parts	Conveyor-belt assembly line	Automation Computer-operated machinery
Agriculture	Wooden plows Spades and hoes Axes and other hand tools	Iron and steel plows Cotton gin Mowing, threshing, and haying machines	McCormick reaper Barbed-wire fencing	Scientific agriculture	Large-scale mechanized agriculture Corporation farms
Transportation	Horses Animal-drawn vehicles Sailing vessels	Canals Clipper ships Development of railroads and steamships	Large-scale steamship and railroad lines City trolleys, elevated trains	Automobiles, trucks, and buses Development of propeller-driven aircraft	Space exploration Monorail trains Supersonic airplanes
Communication	Hand-operated printing presses Newspapers	Mechanized printing presses Telegraph Mass-circulation books and magazines	Transatlantic cable Telephones Phonographs Typewriters Cameras	Motion pictures Radios	Television Transistors Magnetic tapes Lasers Satellite transmissions
Merchandising and Business Organization	Small shops Peddlers	Individual and family-owned factories and mills General stores	Chain stores Mail-order houses Growth of corporations Trusts	National advertising Holding companies	Shopping centers Conglomerate corporations Multinational corporations

STRATEGIES FOR SUCCESS

READING A TIME LINE

Historians say that "the skeleton of history is chronology." The dictionary defines *chronology* as "the science that deals with measuring time by regular divisions and that assigns to events their proper dates." In other words, historians arrange events in *chronological order,* or the order in which they happened.

One of the best ways to show chronological order is by a *time line.* Time lines appear at the end of each chapter of *The Story of America.* These time lines show the order in which the events mentioned in each chapter happened and complement the written summary.

How to Read a Time Line

In reading a time line, follow these steps.

1. **Determine its framework.** Note the years covered and the intervals of time into which the time line is divided. The time lines in *The Story of America* are divided into years, except those in this first unit, which are divided by 100-year periods (centuries) because they cover such broad spans of time. Colored bars show long-term events.
2. **Study the sequence carefully.** A time line is proportional. The space between each date— the *interval*—is always the same. In this way you can visually see the span of time between events. Remember that sometimes the length of time between events is an important historical fact. (Also note that each year is marked on the time line, even when no event is listed.)
3. **Fill in the blanks.** Time lines usually list only key events. Study those listed. Think about the events and the people, places, and other events associated with them. In this way, you can "flesh out" the framework provided by the time line.
4. **Note relationships.** Ask yourself how each event relates to the other events. This will help you recognize cause-effect relationships.
5. **Use the time line as a summary.** Use the listed events to weave a summary of the time period.

Applying the Strategy

Study the time line below. Note that the years covered are 900 to 1500. The time line has intervals of 100 years. The time line lists events related to the Age of Discovery. As you know from your reading, each journey was built on the experiences of previous journeys. Eventually this spirit of exploration led to the discovery of a "New World." What other relationships among the events can you discover? Remember to "fill in" important events not listed on the time line.

THE AGE OF DISCOVERY

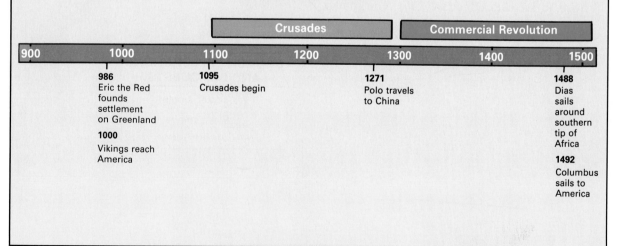

Crusades

Commercial Revolution

| 900 | 1000 | 1100 | 1200 | 1300 | 1400 | 1500 |

986 Eric the Red founds settlement on Greenland

1000 Vikings reach America

1095 Crusades begin

1271 Polo travels to China

1488 Dias sails around southern tip of Africa

1492 Columbus sails to America

STRATEGIES FOR SUCCESS

READING MAPS

Your study of history is greatly enriched by geography. To fully understand geographic information, you must be able to read a map. All of the maps in *The Story of America* have four parts: a *title;* a *key,* or *legend;* a *scale;* and a global *grid.* If you understand the information provided by these four parts, you will be able to read a map with confidence.

How to Read a Map

To gather information from a map, follow these guidelines.

1. **Read the title.** The title of a map tells the subject of the map and what parts of the earth are shown. Some map titles include a date.
2. **Study the key, or legend.** The legend explains what the colors and special symbols on the map mean.
3. **Note the distance scale.** The map scale is used to measure distances. Maps in *The Story of America* have a bar scale. The length of the line on the scale represents that number of miles and kilometers on the earth's surface.
4. **Use the grid.** The grid of latitude and longitude helps you locate places on the earth through a special numbering system based on a unit of measure called a degree. Most of the maps in this textbook have grid "tics" around the map's border to indicate the presence of the complete grid.
5. **Note other map features.** Most maps show other information in special ways as well. The maps in *The Story of America* use a compass rose to indicate direction. *Italic* type marks physical features while regular type labels political features. Be sure to look for all the features of each map.

Applying the Strategy

Study the map below. The title, "Spanish Explorations and Conquests," tells you that the map illustrates the routes of Spanish explorers and areas of conquest in America. Although no special symbols are used on the map, colors mark the locations of the Aztec and Inca empires. You can use the compass rose to determine the directions the explorers moved. For example, Da Vaca and Esteban traveled first generally west, then south. You can use the scale to measure the distance the explorers traveled.

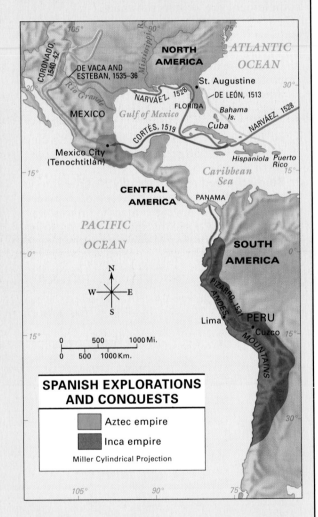

STRATEGIES FOR SUCCESS

USING LATITUDE AND LONGITUDE

One of the basic tasks in both history and geography is to locate exactly what is where on the earth. To do this, you must identify the *absolute location* of each place, or its precise spot on the earth. Cartographers, or map makers, have created a grid system of imaginary lines to make this task easier.

Most maps are drawn with the North Pole at the top and the South Pole at the bottom. The *equator* is the line halfway between the North and South poles. Several shorter imaginary lines circle the earth parallel to the equator and on both sides of it. They are called *parallels*, or *lines of latitude.* Parallels are used to locate places north and south of the equator. They are numbered from zero degrees (0°) at the equator to 90 degrees (90°) north (N) at the North Pole and 90° south (S) at the South Pole.

A second set of imaginary lines called *meridians*, or *lines of longitude,* crisscrosses the parallels. In 1884, an international agreement set the meridian passing through the Royal Observatory in Greenwich, England, near London, as 0° longitude, or the *prime meridian.* The meridian directly opposite the prime meridian, on the other side of the globe, is the 180° meridian. Meridians are used to locate places east and west of the prime meridian. Meridians east of the prime meridian are numbered from 0°E at the prime meridian to 180°E and those to the west are numbered from 0°W to 180°W. By noting latitude and longitude, you can quickly find exact locations on earth.

How to Find Exact Location

To use latitude and longitude to find the exact location of a place, follow these guidelines.
1. **Use the global grid.** The grid provides lines of latitude and longitude marked with corresponding degrees.
2. **Find the equator.** Check the lines of latitude, those running from east to west, until you find 0°. This marks the equator.
3. **Locate the correct parallel.** Continue to check the lines of latitude until you find the one you are looking for. Remember that northern latitudes are above the equator and southern latitudes are below it.
4. **Find the prime meridian.** Check the lines of longitude by reading along the top or bottom of the map. The prime meridian is marked 0°.
5. **Locate the correct meridian.** Continue to read along the grid until you find the meridian you are looking for. Remember that west is to the left of the prime meridian and east is to the right.

Applying the Strategy

Study the map below. It shows the voyages of Cabot and Raleigh and the locations of the first colonies. You can note that Jamestown is located at about 37°N, 77°W while Plymouth is at about 42°N, 70°W. See if you can find the exact locations of other colonies as well.

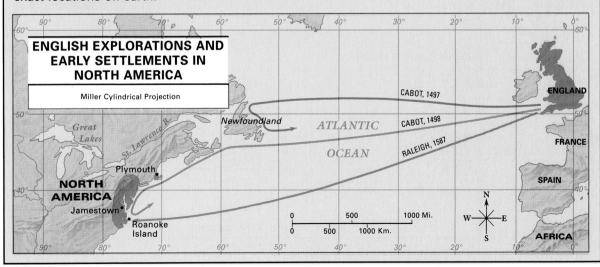

ENGLISH EXPLORATIONS AND EARLY SETTLEMENTS IN NORTH AMERICA

Miller Cylindrical Projection

STRATEGIES FOR SUCCESS

READING GRAPHS

The successful student is able to gather information from a variety of sources, including graphs. *The Story of America* contains many graphs. Graphs present information visually. There are several types of graphs, each used to present a certain type of data. A *pie*, or *circle*, graph is used to show proportions. A *line* graph shows changes in two factors. It most often shows changes over time. A *bar* graph shows comparisons, making highs and lows stand out. A *picture* graph, or *pictograph*, uses pictures to illustrate amounts.

Because graphs can contain so much information and are so common in histories, it is important to know how to read them.

How to Read a Graph

Follow these steps to read a graph.
1. **Read the title**. The title will tell you the subject and purpose of the graph. It may also contain other information, such as dates.
2. **Study the labels**. Line and bar graphs show two sets of data, one set displayed on the horizontal axis and the other on the vertical axis. The *horizontal* axis is the line at the bottom of the graph that runs across the page. The *vertical* axis is at the left side of the graph and runs up and down. Labels on these axes identify the type of data and the unit of measurement, when appropriate.
3. **Analyze the data**. Note all trends, relationships, and changes among the data. Note increases and decreases in quantities.
4. **Put the data to use**. Use the information to form generalizations and hypotheses and to draw conclusions.

Applying the Strategy

You may have heard the expression, "A picture is worth a thousand words." The picture graph may also be worth a thousand words. Study the picture graph below. Note that small figures 🧍 are used to make a simple comparison of the population of the American colonies in 1730. Each symbol stands for 10,000 persons. A partial 🧍 figure represents a fraction of 10,000. For example, the population of Delaware in 1730 was 9,170 persons, so it is represented by part of a figure. What is the population of Virginia? New York? If you said 114,000 for Virginia and 48,000 for New York, you have read the graph correctly!

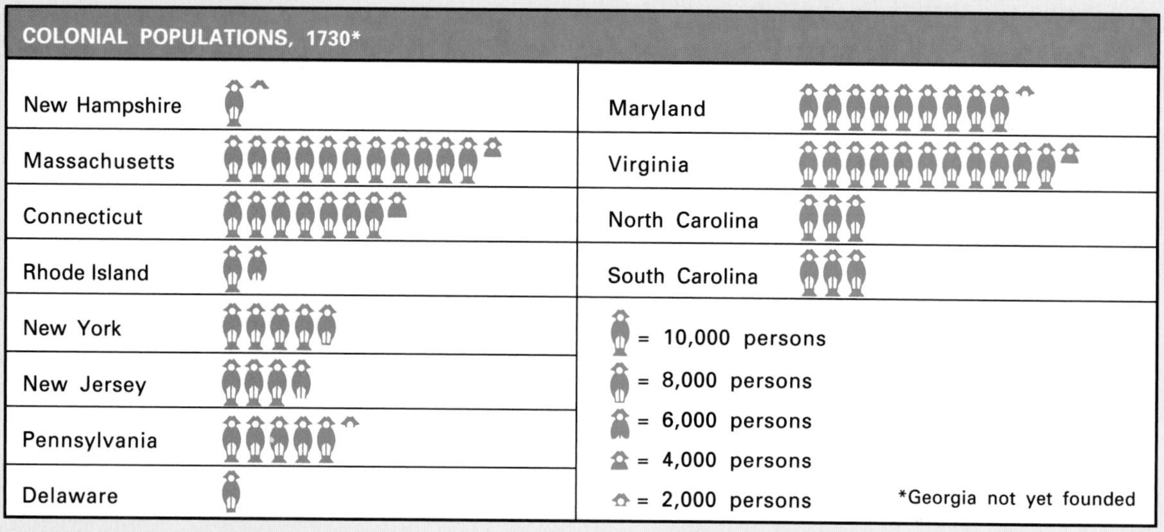

COLONIAL POPULATIONS, 1730*		
New Hampshire	Maryland	
Massachusetts	Virginia	
Connecticut	North Carolina	
Rhode Island	South Carolina	
New York	🧍 = 10,000 persons	
New Jersey	🧍 = 8,000 persons	
Pennsylvania	🧍 = 6,000 persons	
Delaware	🧍 = 4,000 persons	
	🧍 = 2,000 persons	*Georgia not yet founded

Source: *Historical Statistics of the United States*

660   STRATEGIES REVIEW

STRATEGIES FOR SUCCESS

CREATING A GRAPHIC REPRESENTATION

Students are required to read and remember a great deal of information. One of the best ways to help you remember all you read is to develop a graphic representation. A graphic representation is a kind of diagram that links related words, terms, or concepts together, a visual illustration of a verbal statement.

There are many types of graphic representations. You are familiar with several: flow charts, pie charts, and even family trees. Other types include spider maps, continuum scales, and compare/contrast matrices. One of the most useful in American history is a word web.

How to Develop a Word Web

To develop a word web, follow these steps.

1. **Identify the main ideas.** Read the information and list the heading or title of each major idea or topic. If no heading or title is given, create your own.
2. **Note supporting details.** Review the material to identify details that support each main idea.
3. **Structure the headings.** Form a word web by placing each main idea in a circle. Then place supporting details or related ideas in separate circles and connect them to the main idea. Continue to connect ideas and details to complete a web similar to the one to the right.
4. **Use the information.** Note the relationships among the data. Draw conclusions, make inferences, and form hypotheses.

Applying the Skill

Research the beginnings of slavery in America. As you read, make a list of topics about the origins of slavery. Your list might include ideas such as the origins of slavery, slave life, southern agriculture, triangular trade, and the treatment of slaves. To make a word web, place those five ideas in circles.

Your research on the origins of slavery might uncover three main topics: European prejudices, slaves as an improved labor source, and the arrival of the first slaves in 1619. Choose a term to indicate each of these topics, such as "prejudices," "labor source," and "first slaves." Place these terms in circles and connect them to your central term: origins of slavery. A word web for the first topic would resemble the one below. You may wish to expand your web by finding additional terms to include on your web. (For example, "heathens" has been linked to prejudices in the web below.) From your research, create word webs for the other topics about the beginnings of slavery in America.

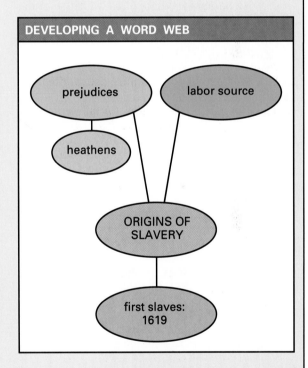

DEVELOPING A WORD WEB

- prejudices
- labor source
- heathens
- ORIGINS OF SLAVERY
- first slaves: 1619

STRATEGIES FOR SUCCESS

RECOGNIZING CAUSE AND EFFECT

Determining cause-and-effect relationships is crucial for the reader of history. A cause is a condition, person, or event that makes something happen. An effect is the outcome of a cause. A cause may have many effects. An effect may itself be the cause of other effects. For example, because of high costs of the French and Indian War, Britain levied taxes on the colonies. The costs were a cause and the taxes were the effect. But the taxes resulted in colonial unrest, becoming a cause of the Revolution. Visually, the relationship would look like this:

CAUSE		EFFECT/CAUSE		EFFECT
Cost of French and Indian War	→	New taxes levied	→	Colonial protests

To fully understand the reasons for an event, you must be able to recognize the cause-effect relationships.

How to Recognize Cause-Effect Relationships

Follow these steps to recognize cause-effect relationships.

1. **Look for cause-effect clues.** Certain words are immediate clues to cause and effect. Cause clues include *led to, brought about, produced, because, as a result of, the source of,* and *the reason why.* Some effect clues are the *outcome of, as a consequence, resulting in, gave rise to,* and *depended on.*

   Remember, however, that writers do not always state the link between cause and effect. Sometimes you must read closely to see the relationship between the events.

2. **Check for complex connections.** Note that many cause-effect relationships have complex connections. A single cause may have many effects. Likewise, a single effect may have root in many causes. And remember that an effect may itself be a cause.

Applying the Strategy

Read the following paragraphs and identify at least one cause-effect relationship. Then draw a cause-effect diagram similar to the one in the first column.

The British eventually defeated the French in the French and Indian War. But peace brought new problems. The British government had borrowed huge sums to pay for the war. The new, larger empire would also be more expensive to maintain and defend. Where was the money to come from?

The British prime minister, George Grenville, had the mind of a bookkeeper. Running the colonies was expensive. Most of the tax money collected in the colonies was also spent there. To Grenville the conclusion was obvious: Parliament should raise the money to run the colonies by taxing the colonists.

Parliament followed his suggestions. In 1764 it passed the Sugar Act, the first of Grenville's tax measures. Americans did not want to pay any new taxes. But most colonists did no more than complain about the Sugar Act. However, when Parliament passed the Stamp Act in 1765, nearly all the colonists spoke out in opposition. They drafted stern resolutions denying Parliament's power to tax them.

The first open resistance to British authority now occurred. Groups calling themselves Sons of Liberty began to organize. These "Liberty Boys" believed in action rather than talk. Grenville had appointed stamp masters who were to receive the stamps and sell them to the public. In Boston the Liberty Boys stormed the house of the stamp master even before he had received any stamps to sell. They broke his windows and made off with many of his valuables. Similar Stamp Act Riots erupted in other colonies. Many of the stamp masters found their very lives in danger. No one could safely distribute the stamps.

Colonists also began to refuse to buy anything English until the law was repealed. This boycott was effective because it hurt the business of exporters in England. These exporters were soon urging Parliament to back down. Finally, Parliament repealed the act.

There are numerous cause-effect relationships in this material. For example, defeating the French gave England more territory in North America—and greater expenses. The British decided to increase colonial taxes to pay those expenses. What other cause-effect relationships, both stated and unstated can you find in the excerpt?

STRATEGIES FOR SUCCESS

TRACING MOVEMENTS ON A MAP
Oftentimes a map shows routes of movement. They may illustrate the paths of explorers or the movements of weather patterns or trade goods. Maps in Chapter 10 of this book show the routes of World War II troop advances in Europe and the Pacific. Studying routes on a map will give you a great deal of information about the course of events and will help you understand how the story unfolded.

How to Trace Movements on a Map
To trace movements on a map, follow these guidelines.
1. **Read the map's title.** The title will tell you what general information is shown on the map.
2. **Study the legend.** Lines indicate routes. Arrows indicate the directions of movement. In the case of troop movements, the routes and arrows may be colored differently to represent each army. Battle sites will be shown and will often indicate by color which army was victorious.

3. **Note the routes and related events carefully.** The routes tell you a great deal about the geography of an area as well as the overall picture of the historical event. For example, by studying troop movements closely you gain a sense of the sweep of an army from battle to battle—the victors in pursuit, the defeated in retreat. You can see where armies gathered strength and where desperate fighters played out their final hours.

Applying the Strategy
Like all good maps, the one on this page tells a story. But the story may be fully appreciated only by carefully reading descriptions of Paul Revere's ride. Then turn to the map to see Revere, Dawes, and Prescott riding across Massachusetts ahead of the advancing British army. Note the site of the American victory at North Bridge near Concord and the retreat of the British troops to Boston.

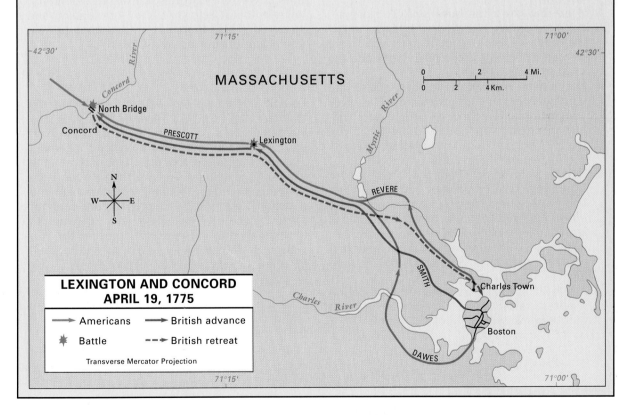

LEXINGTON AND CONCORD
APRIL 19, 1775

→ Americans   → British advance

✦ Battle   --→ British retreat

Transverse Mercator Projection

STRATEGIES FOR SUCCESS

SQ3R—A HELPFUL STUDY PLAN

One of your most important tasks is to remember what you learn. SQ3R is a strategy that makes that task simpler. SQ3R stands for *Survey, Question, Read, Recite,* and *Review.* It is a study plan that can make you a more efficient reader. With practice it will save you time and help you remember important information.

How to Use SQ3R

To use the SQ3R method to study, follow these steps.

1. **Survey the sections.** When you begin a reading assignment in *The Story of America,* skim over the section titles, Preview & Review, boldface words, and illustrations and their captions. Surveying helps you prepare to read the assignment.
2. **Question what lies ahead.** Use the information from your survey to question what lies ahead. Turn section heads into questions. Ask who? what? when? where? why? and how? Write down your questions as a study guide for yourself.
3. **Read to answer the questions.** You needn't try to remember everything you read. Usually the answers to the questions you have formed will give you the main ideas and the most important details.
4. **Recite what you find.** Write down answers to your questions in your own words. This gives you an immediate check on your understanding and helps you not to forget what you read. Using your own words makes you think carefully about the material.
5. **Review your work.** There are two times for useful review—immediately and later. When you finish writing down answers to all your questions, *immediately* answer the questions a second time without looking at your written answers. Reread any parts of the chapter that give rise to questions you still find difficult to answer.

   A few days later, perhaps while preparing for a test, review again by answering your set of questions without looking back to your written answers. Again reread if necessary.

SQ3R GUIDELINES

STEP	WHAT TO DO
Survey	Read the Preview & Review. Read the headings. Scan for specific details. Skim for unfamiliar words. Look at illustrations and their captions.
Question	Make up a set of questions from your survey. Turn titles into questions. Ask who? what? when? where? why? how?
Read	Read to find answers to your questions.
Recite	Write the answers to your questions in your own words.
Review	Immediately answer your questions without looking at your earlier answers. Reread if necessary. Later answer your questions again. Reread if necessary.

SQ3R may seem to take a great amount of time and effort. But as you learn to use it, you will see that it actually saves both reading and study time. Use the chart on this page to help you organize your use of SQ3R.

Applying the Strategy

Use SQ3R to help you study a section of the chapter. The Preview & Review introduces new words and asks you to use them to further help you understand and remember their meaning. The Preview & Review questions indicate the focus of the section. As you skim through the section, pick out the headings and turn them into questions. As you read, prepare answers for these questions. Reviewing your answers to these questions and answering those in the Preview & Review will help you study and remember the information in the section.

STRATEGIES FOR SUCCESS

SEPARATING FACT FROM OPINION

Being able to distinguish fact from opinion is a key strategy for the successful student. Reading history presents us with many facts. A *fact* is something known to be true. Facts about the early days of the American nation might include: "By 1790 the treasury department had 70 people" and "Washington would have preferred to serve without salary as president, as he had served as commander of the army during the Revolutionary War, but Congress voted him a salary of $25,000." These statements are facts. Both can be proven from records that exist.

But history also presents us with opinions. An *opinion* is a personal belief. When the facts are sorted through, it remains for the historian to offer an opinion about larger events. For example, in describing Washington's approach to his responsibilities as president, the author states: "Washington was extremely conscientious." This statement is the historian's opinion that Washington was very conscientious about his duties. People at the time and other historians might disagree with this assessment. It is important to know when the ideas you are reading are facts and when they are opinions.

How to Separate Fact from Opinion

To separate facts from opinions, follow these guidelines.

1. **Ask "can it be proven?"** Determine whether the idea can be checked for accuracy in other sources. If so, it is probably factual. If not, it probably contains an opinion.
2. **Look for context clues.** Opinions are sometimes signaled in writing by words like *believe* or *think*. Other clues that signal opinions include **loaded words** intended to stir your emotions, such as *extremely, ridiculous,* or *most important.*

Applying the Strategy

Read the following excerpt from *The Story of America.* List the sentences that contain the opinions of the historian who wrote the excerpt.

The election of a president to succeed Washington was the first in which political parties played a role. Today we think of political parties as the machinery by which office seekers work out programs and present issues to the voters. The two-party system—today the Demo-cratic and Republican parties—makes it possible for this large country to have an effective national government. If every candidate or local group set up a different organization, no one would ever have a majority. No satisfactory decisions could be made.

The framers of the Constitution, however, disliked and distrusted political parties. They made no provision for them. They called parties factions. The word suggests fringe groups conspiring to dominate the rest of society. The framers believed that individuals representing small districts could arrive at agreements based on the national interest. In their eyes political parties meant corruption. Leaders, they thought, should take personal responsibility for their decisions.

Yet very soon after the Constitution was ratified, political parties began to form. They did so because the Constitution created a strong national government. Because it was powerful, the government made important decisions. National politics therefore mattered. People joined together in parties to attempt to control the decisions of the government.

The first parties were influenced more by personalities than by issues. The principal figures were Secretary of the Treasury Hamilton and Secretary of State Jefferson. Members of Congress who favored Hamilton's financial policies took the name Federalists. They began to vote as a group on most issues, even those not related to Hamilton's program.

Those who opposed Hamilton and his ideas began calling themselves Democratic-Republicans.

You should note that the historian claims that the framers of the Constitution "disliked" and "distrusted" political parties. The author is basing his statements on a consensus of the sources he has studied. It is a valid interpretation of the situation, but it is an opinion because it cannot be proven with absolute certainty.

Continue to reread the discussion of the first American political parties. Note that the historian claims these early parties were more influenced by personalities such as Hamilton and Jefferson than by issues. Is this an example of an opinion? Why or why not? What other examples of opinions can you find in the section?

STRATEGIES FOR SUCCESS

INTERPRETING A PHYSICAL MAP

A *physical map* is a special-purpose map that shows the natural landscape, or *topography,* of an area. It shows the location and extent of physical features such as rivers and mountain chains. It also illustrates the relative locations of various features. Because elevation, access to water, and the "the lay of the land" often influence human activities, a physical map can help you better understand how the history of an area unfolded.

How to Understand a Physical Map

To understand a physical map, follow these guidelines.

1. **Use basic map reading skills.** Review the strategy on page 658. Study the title, key, scale, and grid for important information.
2. **Note the colors used to show elevation.** The distance above or below sea level is *elevation*. Look at the colors on the map to get a "feel" for the landscape. Check the elevation key to associate colors to elevations. Note also that special shading called "cartographic art" highlights mountain and valley areas.
3. **Study shapes.** Look closely at the shapes of the features shown on the map—how steep a mountain range is and how far it stretches, how wide and long a river is.
4. **Read the labels.** Learn the names of the key features.
5. **Note relative locations.** *Relative location* is the position of a feature in relation to other features. Note where each major feature appears in relation to other major features. Use this information to draw conclusions about the effect of the topography on movement, settlement patterns, and economic activity.

Applying the Strategy

Study the physical map to the right. It shows the topography of the lands of the eastern seaboard of the United States. Note that the Appalachian Mountains form a wall to the west of the region. What effect did they have on settlement? Note also that the area is drained by several rivers. What are the major ones? How did they affect settlement? Along which did important cities begin to grow? How did rivers affect farming and transportation for the early settlers?

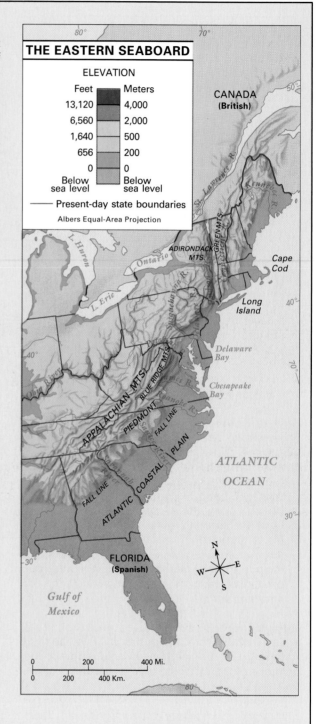

STRATEGIES FOR SUCCESS

SYNTHESIZING INFORMATION

To synthesize information you must combine ideas from several sources. *The Story of America* is a synthesis. The author studied many historical sources and used that information to create this textbook. You, too, are asked to synthesize information in this and other courses. Each time you are directed to read information *and* study a map to gain a new understanding, you are synthesizing information.

How to Synthesize Information

To effectively synthesize information, follow these guidelines.

1. **Select sources carefully.** Make sure that the sources you are studying cover the same information and complement, or add to, each other.
2. **Read for understanding.** Identify main ideas and important supporting evidence in each source.
3. **Compare and contrast.** Note where sources agree or build on each other. More importantly, note where they differ.
4. **Interpret all the information.** Use what you have found to interpret the information. This is the key step in synthesizing.

Applying the Strategy

You know that after the end of the Revolutionary War, settlers moved into the lands beyond the Appalachian Mountains. Here troubles erupted. Study this map and research the movement of settlers across the Appalachians after 1783.

By studying these two sources, you should be able to answer some key questions about these events. Why were so many settlers attracted to these lands? What would most of the settlers do with the land? The map shows the area beyond the Appalachians as gently rolling, with abundant streams and rivers. Could this be what many of the settlers were looking for? As you know, many of these pioneers were farmers. They were looking for fertile soil on which to start farms. Do you think they found what they were searching for?

This surge of land-hungry settlers across the mountains caused trouble with the Indians already there. Why? Synthesize the information by using your prior knowledge about how the Indians and settlers differed on their view of land ownership and the information from your reading and the map to answer this question.

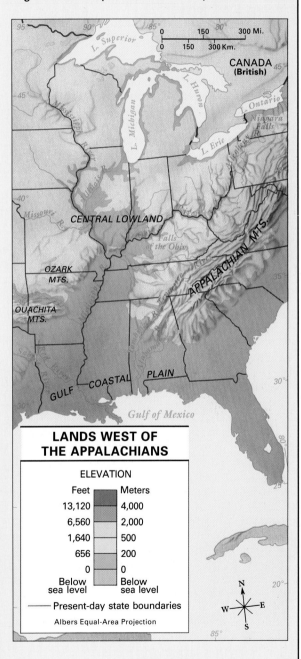

LANDS WEST OF THE APPALACHIANS

ELEVATION

Feet	Meters
13,120	4,000
6,560	2,000
1,640	500
656	200
0	0
Below sea level	Below sea level

——— Present-day state boundaries

Albers Equal-Area Projection

STRATEGIES FOR SUCCESS

INTERPRETING A SPECIAL-PURPOSE MAP
Special-purpose maps, as their name tells you, contain specific information. For example, a map that illustrates the growth of the canal system in America is a special-purpose map. Interpreting the information contained on a special-purpose map will help you to understand that aspect of history or geography.

How to Interpret a Special-Purpose Map
To interpret a special-purpose map, follow these guidelines.
1. **Use map basics.** Read the title, check the legend, and scale. These map parts will tell you the subject of the map and its extent.
2. **Note special symbols.** Special-purpose maps often use symbols to illustrate information.

Study the key to make sure you understand what the symbols on the map represent.
3. **Read the labels.** Identify each feature portrayed on the map.
4. **Study the map as a whole.** Note the overall pattern of the information. Is it concentrated in one area? Does it seem to be influenced by geographic factors?

Applying the Strategy
Study the map below. Note that it illustrates the railroad network in the United States in 1860. The paths of railroads are marked by red lines, and the main ones are labeled. What area of the country had the most railroad mileage? Why?

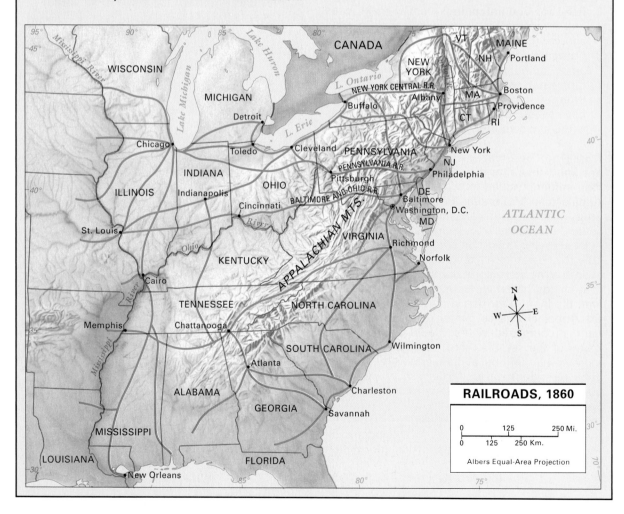

STRATEGIES FOR SUCCESS

USING PHOTOGRAPHS AS PRIMARY SOURCES

Photographs are important primary sources. Studying them for details can tell you much about a person, event, or time.

On this page are the photographs of the first three presidents of the United States to sit before the camera: John Quincy Adams, *upper right,* Andrew Jackson, *below,* and Martin Van Buren, *lower right.* It is hard today to believe that the camera lets us see so far into the past. In fact, we are able to view the actual images of all but 5 of the 41 presidents.

How to Use Photographs as Primary Sources

Follow these steps to use photographs as primary sources.

1. **Study the subject.** Identify the person, event or location in the photograph.
2. **Check for details.** Note the expression, action, or setting. Look closely at the style of dress and other details.
3. **Don't be misled.** Remember that many scenes are posed and exclude more than is included. Remember also that early photography took such a long time for the exposure that subjects appear unnaturally stiff.

Applying the Strategy

Study the photographs on this page. What do they tell you about these former presidents? About the early and mid-1800s?

Metropolitan Museum of Art

National Portrait Gallery

George Eastman House

STRATEGIES FOR SUCCESS

LEARNING FROM ART

Many books you study, as *The Story of America* does, contain reproductions of famous paintings and other artwork. Gathering information from these sources is a key strategy to understanding history. An engraving such as Currier & Ives' "Westward the Course of Empire Takes Its Way," shown below, can provide a great deal of historical information. This engraving, made by Fanny Palmer and James M. Ives in 1868, gives the artists' view of manifest destiny. More importantly, such a work of art can help shape the ideas of a nation. This Currier & Ives print has appeared in more history books than any other and greatly influenced the way Americans in the 1870s and 1880s viewed westward expansion.

How to Gather Information from Art

To effectively gather information from art, follow these steps.

1. **Determine the subject of the work.** Check its title or caption. Study the people, objects, and actions it depicts.
2. **Examine the details.** If it is a painting or drawing, study the background. Remember that *all* the visual evidence is important to understanding the historical event or period.
3. **Note the artist's point of view.** If possible, determine whether the events are portrayed favorably or unfavorably. Ask what impact the work might have on other viewers.
4. **Use the information carefully.** Remember that a work of art may be an artist's *interpretation* of an event. Try to determine how accurately it depicts the event before deciding how to use the information.

Applying the Strategy

James M. Ives and Nathaniel Currier were America's most popular makers of hand-colored prints (pictures from engravings). Carefully study their print below. The main title is "Across the Continent." Close study discloses a picture full of clues to the artists' optimistic view of the westward movement. Note the locomotive puffing on its endless tracks, hardworking men and women building their community, covered wagons heading for further frontiers, and the vast open spaces of yet-to-be-settled America. See if you can spot other historical details.

Museum of the City of New York

STRATEGIES FOR SUCCESS

COMPARING STATISTICS

Statistics are numerical facts. They are often organized into tables, charts, or graphs so they are easier to analyze. Comparing statistics from two or more sources will help you understand relationships among the statistics.

How to Compare Statistics

To effectively compare statistics, follow these guidelines.
1. **Identify the types of data being compared.** Read the titles, headings, labels, and footnotes of each source (chart, graph, or table.)
2. **Examine the data.** Note the specific statistics for each heading.
3. **Be sure you know what is being compared.** Check quantities and values. They may vary from column to column or source to source and may be misread if not noted carefully.
4. **Notice both similarities and differences.** Observe how the numbers are alike or how they differ.
5. **Look for relationships.** Note *trends*—if quantities seem to increase or decrease at the same time or rate. Make inferences and draw conclusions. Form hypotheses to explain the trends you discover. Consider cause and effect relationships.

Applying the Strategy

Study the bar graphs below. The bottom graph shows cotton production and the top graph measures the size of the slave population of the United States. Both contain statistics for the years 1820 to 1860. How do the statistics compare? Note that both graphs show a steady increase during the years they cover. How might the statistics for cotton production and the size of the slave population be related? Would increasing cotton production require more slaves? Would more slaves increase production? Are both possible?

The map below shows the major cotton-producing areas in 1839 and in 1859. Note that this area has increased. How is the information on this map related to the statistics on the graphs? What are some conclusions you can draw from the information shown on the map and charts on this page?

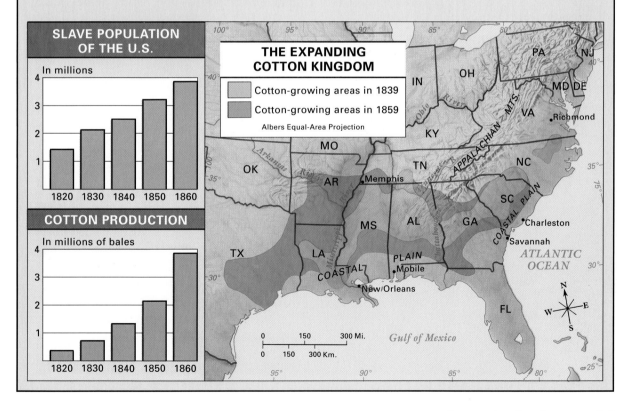

STRATEGIES FOR SUCCESS

UNDERSTANDING SEQUENCE

Many times history unfolds as a sequence of events. Social progress in the United States from the 1820s through the 1850s provides a good example. Recognizing sequence and relationships among the events will help you understand such periods in the nation's history.

How to Understand Sequence

To understand sequence, follow these guidelines.

1. **Check for dates.** The most obvious clues to a sequence of events are dates.
2. **Look for key words and phrases.** Note terms such as *then, gave rise to, next,* and *finally* that indicate a sequence of events.
3. **Identify relationships among the events.** Determine if one event leads directly to others, and if they in turn lead to still others.
4. **Notice the larger picture.** Remember events in one area might spur events in other areas.

Applying the Strategy

Study the list in the next column. It represents a sequential list of some of the key events in the early women's rights movement.

WOMEN AND REFORM

Plan for Improving Female Education published

Catherine and Mary Beecher open the Female Seminary in Connecticut

Sarah Grimké writes *Letters on the Equality of the Sexes and the Condition of Women*

Women banned from London antislavery conference

Women's Rights Convention in Seneca Falls, New York

Seneca Falls Declaration of Sentiments and Resolutions issued

Sara Josepha Hale becomes editor of *Godey's Lady Book*

Elizabeth Blackwell becomes first woman licensed to practice medicine (1850)

Antoinette Brown Blackwell is first woman to become a fully ordained minister

Note that educational opportunities for women were the first steps in the women's rights movement. Sarah Grimké's book and the exclusion of Lucretia Mott and Elizabeth Cady Stanton from the London antislavery conference led directly to the Seneca Falls Conference. The declaration of women's rights issued at Seneca Falls quickly led to reforms by several states in laws concerning women.

The Granger Collection

COMPARING MAPS

One of the most important ways to learn history through geography is by comparing maps. You have already been introduced to many of the strategies you need to compare maps. Review the strategies for reviewing map basics, interpreting physical maps, and comparing and contrasting ideas.

How to Compare Maps

To effectively compare maps, follow these guidelines.

1. **Select the maps to be compared carefully.** Make sure the areas covered, the dates of the information, and other important pieces of information provide a reliable picture.
2. **Note similarities and differences.** Examine the patterns and symbols closely.
3. **Apply critical thinking skills.** Make inferences, draw conclusions, and state generalizations about the evidence you find.

Applying the Strategy

The question of extending slavery into the western territories was hotly debated for more than half a century. Three times Congress acted to settle the matter. But it was not resolved by the Missouri Compromise (Compromise of 1820) or the Compromise of 1850. Four short years later Congress once again struggled with the problem before passing the Kansas-Nebraska Act of 1854.

Such a complex matter as the attempts to settle the slavery issue may be better understood by comparing maps of the compromises. Study the maps on this page. Note that they show the changing status of the territories as Congress passed each new compromise. How did the status of California change with the Compromise of 1850? How did the status of Nebraska change with the Kansas-Nebraska Act? What other details can you compare? Based on these maps, what generalizations can you state about the issue of extending slavery?

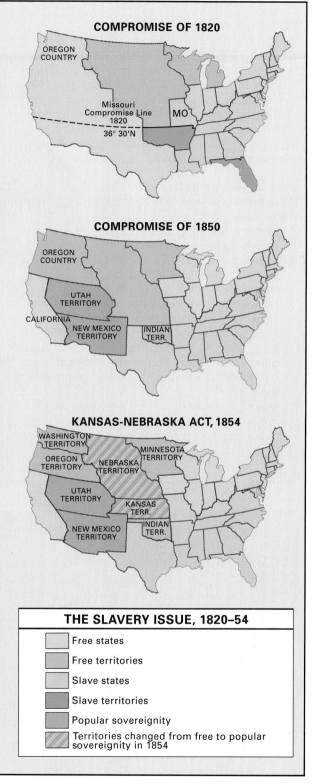

COMPROMISE OF 1820

COMPROMISE OF 1850

KANSAS-NEBRASKA ACT, 1854

THE SLAVERY ISSUE, 1820–54

- Free states
- Free territories
- Slave states
- Slave territories
- Popular sovereignty
- Territories changed from free to popular sovereignty in 1854

STRATEGIES FOR SUCCESS

READING A STATISTICAL CHART

As you learned in the strategy on page 671, statistics are often organized into chart form. An example is below. A chart is especially valuable for use in organizing several sets of numbers. Exact or round numbers may be used in any number of columns to show growth or change. The data shown on a chart is often related, helping you compare the numbers, recognize relationships, and see trends.

How to Read a Statistical Chart

To effectively read a statistical chart, follow these steps.

1. **Identify the type of data.** Read the chart's title. Note headings, subheadings, and labels.
2. **Examine the chart's components.** Study the specific statistics given under each heading. Read across rows and down columns.
3. **Relate numbers and values.** Note quantities. Often a chart will contain a note in parentheses that indicates if the data is to be read in thousands, millions, billions, tons, dollars, or other units. (Be sure to read any footnotes or other special notes at the bottom of the chart as well.)
4. **Use the information.** Ask "what do these statistics tell me?" Draw conclusions and form hypotheses. Compare and contrast the data to note trends and changes.

Applying the Strategy

Study the chart below. Note that it contains information about the Union and the Confederacy on the eve of war. Look at the left column. It lists nine categories of statistics on which you can compare the North and South. Reading across the row for each of these categories gives you both the total number and the percentage of the total for both sides. What was the population of the North? Of the South? As you can see from the chart, the North had more people, nearly three quarters of the total population of the United States.

The North also had more than 10 times the value of manufactured goods and produced more than 10 times the steel as the South. What do these two statistics mean in wartime? The North also had nearly three times the railroad mileage and bank assets as the South, and twice as many farms. Again, what might each of these figures mean on the eve of war? The South did have a small but significant advantage in the value of exports. How might this affect southern war strategy? Review all the statistics, and ask yourself what they meant to each side as the war erupted.

COMPARING THE NORTH AND THE SOUTH, 1860

	North		South	
	Total	%	Total	%
Land Area (square miles)	2,250,000	75.0	750,000	25.0
Population	21,800,000	71.3	8,800,000*	28.7
Farms	1,360,000	67.3	681,000	32.7
Factories	119,500	85.2	20,850	14.8
Value of Manufacturing	$1,730,000,000	91.5	$156,000,000	8.5
Iron Produced (long tons)	2,720,000	94.6	155,000	5.4
Railroad Mileage	21,500	71.0	8,500	28.7
Bank Assets	$345,900,000	72.0	$76,000,000	18.0
Value of Exports	$175,000,000	43.6	$226,000,000	56.4

*Southern population included 3.8 million slaves

Documents in American History

The Declaration of Independence (1776)

The Declaration of Independence puts into words the ideals of freedom. It has become the model for all who seek to protect fundamental human rights, human dignity, and above all democracy.

Adopted by the Continental Congress 15 months after the battles of Lexington and Concord, the Declaration listed colonial grievances against the British crown. It marked a complete break between the colonies and the mother country and represented a formal declaration of war.

THE DECLARATION OF INDEPENDENCE

The unanimous Declaration of the thirteen united States of America,
When in the Course of human events, it becomes necessary for one people to dissolve the political bands which have connected them with another, and to assume among the powers of the earth, the separate and equal station to which the Laws of Nature and of Nature's God entitle them, a decent respect to the opinions of mankind requires that they should declare the causes which impel them to the separation.—

We hold these truths to be self-evident, that all men are created equal, that they are endowed by their Creator with certain unalienable Rights, that among these are Life, Liberty, and the pursuit of Happiness.—

That to secure these rights, Governments are instituted among Men, deriving their just powers from the consent of the governed,—

That whenever any Form of Government becomes destructive of these ends, it is the Right of the People to alter or to abolish it, and to institute new Government, laying its foundation on such principles and organizing its powers in such form, as to them shall seem most likely to effect their Safety and Happiness. Prudence, indeed, will dictate that Governments long established should not be changed for light and transient causes; and accordingly all experience hath shown, that mankind are more disposed to suffer, while evils are sufferable, than to right themselves by abolishing the forms to which they are accustomed. But when a long train of abuses and usurpations, pursuing invariably the same Object evinces a design to reduce them under absolute

Despotism, it is their right, it is their duty, to throw off such Government, and to provide new Guards for their future security.—

Such has been the patient sufferance of these Colonies; and such is now the necessity which constrains them to alter their former Systems of Government. The history of the present King of Great Britain is a history of repeated injuries and usurpations, all having in direct object the establishment of an absolute Tyranny over these States. To prove this, let Facts be submitted to a candid world.—

He has refused his Assent to Laws, the most wholesome and necessary for the public good.—

He has forbidden his Governors to pass Laws of immediate and pressing importance, unless suspended in their operation till his Assent should be obtained; and when so suspended, he has utterly neglected to attend to them.—

He has refused to pass other Laws for the accommodation of large districts of people, unless those people would relinquish the right of Representation in the Legislature, a right inestimable to them and formidable to tyrants only.—

He has called together legislative bodies at places unusual, uncomfortable, and distant from the depository of their public Records, for the sole purpose of fatiguing them into compliance with his measures.—

He has dissolved Representative Houses repeatedly, for opposing with manly firmness his invasions on the rights of the people.—

He has refused for a long time, after such dissolutions, to cause others to be elected; whereby the Legislative powers, incapable of Annihilation, have returned to the People at large for their exercise; the State remaining in the meantime exposed to all the dangers of invasion from without, and convulsions within.—

He has endeavored to prevent the population of these States; for that purpose obstructing the Laws for Naturalization of Foreigners; refusing to pass others to encourage their migrations hither, and raising the conditions of new Appropriations of Lands.—

He has obstructed the Administration of Justice, by refusing his Assent to Laws for establishing Judiciary powers.—

He has made Judges dependent on his Will alone, for the tenure of their offices, and the amount and payment of their salaries.—

He has erected a multitude of New Offices, and sent hither swarms of Officers to harass our people, and eat out their substance.—

He has kept among us, in times of peace, Standing Armies without the Consent of our legislatures.—

He has affected to render the Military independent of and superior to the Civil power.—

He has combined with others to subject us to a jurisdiction foreign to our constitution, and unacknowledged by our laws; giving his Assent to their Acts of pretended Legislation:—

For quartering large bodies of armed troops among us:—

For protecting them, by a mock Trial, from punishment for any Murders which they should commit on the Inhabitants of these States:—

For cutting off our Trade with all parts of the world:—

For imposing Taxes on us without our Consent:—

For depriving us in many cases, of the benefits of Trial by Jury:—

For transporting us beyond Seas to be tried for pretended offences:—

For abolishing the free System of English Laws in a neighboring Province, establishing therein an Arbitrary government, and enlarging its Boundaries so as to render it at once an example and fit instrument for introducing the same absolute rule into these Colonies:—

For taking away our Charters, abolishing our most valuable Laws, and altering fundamentally the Forms of our Governments:—

For suspending our own Legislatures, and declaring themselves invested with power to legislate for us in all cases whatsoever.—

He has abdicated Government here, by declaring us out of his Protection and waging War against us.—

He has plundered our seas, ravaged our Coasts, burnt our towns, and destroyed the Lives of our people.—

He is at this time transporting large Armies of foreign Mercenaries to complete the works of death, desolation and tyranny, already begun with circumstances of Cruelty & perfidy scarcely paralleled in the most barbarous ages, and totally unworthy the Head of a civilized nation.—

He has constrained our fellow Citizens taken Captive on the high Seas to bear Arms against their Country, to become the executioners of their friends and Brethren, or to fall themselves by their Hands.—

He has excited domestic insurrections amongst us, and has endeavored to bring on the inhabitants of our frontiers, the merciless Indian Savages, whose known rule of warfare, is an undistinguished destruction of all ages, sexes and conditions.

In every stage of these Oppressions We have Petitioned for Redress in the most humble terms: Our repeated Petitions have been answered only by repeated injury. A Prince, whose character is thus marked by every act which may define a Tyrant, is unfit to be the ruler of a free people.

Nor have We been wanting in attentions to our British brethren. We have warned them from time to time of attempts by their legislature to extend an unwarrantable jurisdiction over us. We have reminded them of the circumstances of our emigration and settlement here. We have appealed to their native justice and magnanimity, and we have conjured them by the ties of our common kindred to disavow these usurpations, which would inevitably interrupt our connections and correspondence. They too have been deaf to the voice of justice and of consanguinity. We must, therefore, acquiesce in the necessity, which denounces our Separation, and hold them, as we hold the rest of mankind, Enemies in War, in Peace Friends.—

We, therefore, the Representatives of the united States of America, in General Congress, Assembled, appealing to the Supreme Judge of the world for the rectitude of our intentions, do, in the Name, and by Authority of the good People of these Colonies, solemnly publish and declare, That these United Colonies are, and of Right ought to be Free and Independent States; that they are Absolved from all Allegiance to the British Crown, and that all political connection between them and the State of Great Britain, is and ought to be totally dissolved; and that as Free and Independent States, they have full Power to levy War, conclude Peace, contract Alliances, establish Commerce, and to do all other Acts and Things which Independent States may of right do.—

And for the support of this Declaration, with a firm reliance on the protection of divine Providence, we mutually pledge to each other our Lives, our Fortunes and our sacred Honor.

John Hancock	*Benjamin Harrison*	*Lewis Morris*
Button Gwinnett	*Thomas Nelson, Jr.*	*Richard Stockton*
Lyman Hall	*Francis Lightfoot Lee*	*John Witherspoon*
George Walton	*Carter Braxton*	*Francis Hopkinson*
William Hooper	*Robert Morris*	*John Hart*
Joseph Hewes	*Benjamin Rush*	*Abraham Clark*
John Penn	*Benjamin Franklin*	*Josiah Bartlett*
Edward Rutledge	*John Morton*	*William Whipple*
Thomas Heyward, Jr.	*George Clymer*	*Samuel Adams*
Thomas Lynch, Jr.	*James Smith*	*John Adams*
Arthur Middleton	*George Taylor*	*Robert Treat Paine*
Samuel Chase	*James Wilson*	*Elbridge Gerry*
William Paca	*George Ross*	*Stephen Hopkins*
Thomas Stone	*Caesar Rodney*	*William Ellery*
Charles Carroll	*George Read*	*Roger Sherman*
of Carrollton	*Thomas McKean*	*Samuel Huntington*
George Wythe	*William Floyd*	*William Williams*
Richard Henry Lee	*Philip Livingston*	*Oliver Wolcott*
Thomas Jefferson	*Francis Lewis*	*Matthew Thornton*

The Constitution of the United States of America (1787)

The 55 delegates at the Constitutional Convention faced a difficult political problem: how can a group of states combine into a strong union without losing control over local affairs? Their answer was the United States Constitution, which called for a federal plan of government, separation of powers with checks and balances, and a procedure for orderly change to meet future circumstances.

A serious objection to the Constitution, however, was its lack of a "bill of rights." Many states ratified the document on the condition that such guarantees be added immediately after ratification. In December 1791, the first 10 amendments—the Bill of Rights—were ratified. Gradually over the years more amendments were added as political, economic, and social conditions changed.

Preamble

We the People of the United States, in Order to form a more perfect Union, establish Justice, insure domestic Tranquility, provide for the common defense, promote the general Welfare, and secure the Blessings of Liberty to ourselves and our Posterity, do ordain and establish this Constitution for the United States of America.

Article I

Section 1. All legislative Powers herein granted shall be vested in a Congress of the United States, which shall consist of a Senate and House of Representatives.

Section 2. The House of Representatives shall be composed of Members chosen every second Year by the People of the several States, and the Electors in each State shall have the Qualifications requisite for Electors of the most numerous Branch of the State Legislature.

No Person shall be a Representative who shall not have attained to the Age of twenty-five Years, and been seven Years a Citizen of the United States, and who shall not, when elected, be an inhabitant of that State in which he shall be chosen.

Representatives and direct Taxes shall be apportioned among the several States which may be included within this Union, according to their respective Numbers, which shall be determined by adding to the whole Number of free Persons, including those bound to Service for a Term of Years, and excluding Indians not taxed, three fifths of all other Persons. The actual Enumeration shall be made within three Years after the first Meeting of the Congress of the United States, and within every subsequent Term of ten Years, in such Manner as they shall by Law direct. The Number of Representatives shall not exceed one for every thirty Thousand, but each State shall have at Least one Representative; and until such enumeration shall be made, the State of New Hampshire shall be entitled to choose three; Massachusetts eight; Rhode Island and Providence Plantations one; Connecticut five; New York six; New Jersey four; Pennsylvania eight; Delaware one; Maryland six; Virginia ten; North Carolina five; South Carolina five; and Georgia three.

When vacancies happen in the Representation from any State, the Executive Authority thereof shall issue Writs of Election to fill such Vacancies.

The House of Representatives shall choose their Speaker and other Officers; and shall have the sole Power of Impeachment.

Section 3. The Senate of the United States shall be composed of two Senators from each State, chosen by the Legislature thereof, for six Years; and each Senator shall have one Vote.

Immediately after they shall be assembled in Consequence of the first Election, they shall be divided as equally as may be into three Classes. The Seats of the Senators of the first Class shall be vacated at the Expiration of the second Year, of the second Class at the Expiration of the fourth Year, and of the third Class at the Expiration of the sixth Year, so that one third may be chosen every second Year; and if Vacancies happen by Resignation, or otherwise, during the Recess of the Legislature of any State, the Executive thereof may make temporary Appointments until the next Meeting of the Legislature, which shall then fill such Vacancies.

No Person shall be a Senator who shall not have attained to the Age of thirty Years, and been nine Years a Citizen of the United States, and who shall not, when elected, be an Inhabitant of that State for which he shall be chosen.

The Vice President of the United States shall be President of the Senate, but shall have no Vote, unless they be equally divided.

The Senate shall choose their other Officers, and also a President pro tempore, in the Absence of the Vice President, or when he shall exercise the Office of President of the United States.

The Senate shall have the sole Power to try all Impeachments. When sitting for that Purpose, they shall be on Oath or Affirmation. When the President of the United States is tried, the Chief Justice shall preside: And no Person shall be convicted without the Concurrence of two thirds of the Members present.

Judgment in Cases of Impeachment shall not extend further than to removal from Office, and disqualification to hold and enjoy any Office of honor, Trust or Profit under the United States: but the Party convicted shall nevertheless be liable and subject to Indictment, Trial, Judgment and Punishment, according to Law.

Section 4. The Times, Places and Manner of holding Elections for Senators and Representatives, shall be prescribed in each State by the Legislature thereof; but the Congress may at any time by Law make or alter such Regulations, except as to the Places of choosing Senators.

The Congress shall assemble at least once in every Year, and such Meeting shall be on the first Monday in December, unless they shall by Law appoint a different Day.

Section 5. Each House shall be the Judge of the Elections, Returns and Qualifications of its own Members, and a Majority of each shall constitute a Quorum to do Business; but a smaller Number may adjourn from day to day, and may be authorized to compel the Attendance of absent Members, in such Manner, and under such Penalties as each House may provide.

Each House may determine the Rules of its Proceedings, punish its Members for disorderly Behavior, and, with the Concurrence of two thirds, expel a Member.

Each House shall keep a Journal of its Proceedings, and from time to time publish the same, excepting such Parts as may in their Judgment require Secrecy; and the Yeas and Nays of the Members of either House on any question shall, at the Desire of one fifth of those Present, be entered on the Journal.

Neither House, during the Session of Congress, shall, without the Consent of the other, adjourn for more than three days, nor to any other Place than that in which the two Houses shall be sitting.

Section 6. The Senators and Representatives shall receive a Compensation for their Services, to be ascertained by Law, and paid out of the Treasury of the United States. They shall in all Cases, except Treason, Felony and Breach of the Peace, be privileged from Arrest during their Attendance at the Session of their respective Houses, and in going to and returning from the same; and for any Speech or Debate in either House, they shall not be questioned in any other Place.

No Senator or Representative shall, during the Time for which he was elected, be appointed to any civil Office under the Authority of the United States, which shall have been created, or the Emoluments whereof shall have been increased during such time; and no Person holding any Office under the United States, shall be a Member of either House during his Continuance in Office.

Section 7. All Bills for raising Revenue shall originate in the House of Representatives; but the Senate may propose or concur with Amendments as on other Bills.

Every Bill which shall have passed the House of Representatives and the Senate, shall, before it become a Law, be presented to the President of the United States; If he approve he shall sign it, but if not he shall return it, with his Objections to that House in which it shall have originated, who shall enter the Objections at large on their Journal, and proceed to reconsider it. If after such Reconsideration two thirds of that House shall agree to pass the Bill, it shall be sent, together with the Objections, to the other House, by which it shall likewise be reconsidered, and if approved by two thirds of that House, it shall become a Law. But in all such Cases the Votes of both Houses shall be determined by Yeas and Nays, and the Names of the Persons voting for and against the Bill shall be entered on the Journal of each House respectively. If any Bill shall not be returned by the President within ten Days (Sundays excepted) after it shall have been presented to him, the Same shall be a Law, in like Manner as if he had signed it, unless the Congress by their Adjournment prevent its Return, in which Case it shall not be a Law.

Every Order, Resolution, or Vote to which the Concurrence of the Senate and House of Representatives may be necessary (except on a question of Adjournment) shall be presented to the President of the United States; and before the Same shall take Effect, shall be approved by him, or being disapproved by him, shall be repassed by two thirds of the Senate and House of Representatives, according to the Rules and Limitations prescribed in the Case of a Bill.

Section 8. The Congress shall have Power To lay and collect Taxes, Duties, Imposts and Excises, to pay the Debts and provide for the common Defense and general Welfare of the United States; but all Duties, Imposts and Excises shall be uniform throughout the United States;

To borrow Money on the credit of the United States;

To regulate Commerce with foreign Nations, and among the several States, and with the Indian Tribes;

To establish an uniform Rule of Naturalization, and uniform Laws on the subject of Bankruptcies throughout the United States;

To coin Money, regulate the Value thereof, and of foreign Coin, and fix the Standard of Weights and Measures;

To provide for the Punishment of counterfeiting the Securities and current Coin of the United States;

To establish Post Offices and post Roads;

To promote the Progress of Science and useful Arts, by securing for limited Times to Authors and Inventors the exclusive Right to their respective Writings and Discoveries;

To constitute Tribunals inferior to the supreme Court;

To define and punish Piracies and Felonies committed on the high Seas, and Offences against the Law of Nations;

To declare War, grant Letters of Marque and Reprisal, and make Rules concerning Captures on Land and Water;

To raise and support Armies, but no Appropriation of Money to that Use shall be for a longer Term than two Years;

To provide and maintain a Navy;

To make Rules for the Government and Regulation of the land and naval Forces;

To provide for calling forth the Militia to execute the Laws of the Union, suppress Insurrections and repel Invasions;

To provide for organizing, arming, and disciplining, the Militia, and for governing such Part of them as may be employed in the Service of the United States, reserving to the States respectively, the Appointment of the Officers, and the Authority of training the Militia according to the discipline prescribed by Congress.

To exercise exclusive Legislation in all Cases whatsoever, over such District (not exceeding ten Miles square) as may, by Cession of particular States, and the Acceptance of Congress, become the Seat of the Government of the United States, and to exercise like Authority over all Places purchased by the Consent of the Legislature of the State in which the Same shall be, for the Erection of Forts, Magazines, Arsenals, dock-Yards, and other needful Buildings;—And

To make all Laws which shall be necessary and proper for carrying into Execution the foregoing Powers, and all other Powers vested by this Constitution in the Government of the United States, or in any Department or Officer thereof.

Section 9. The Migration or Importation of such Persons as any of the States now existing shall think proper to admit, shall not be prohibited by the Congress prior to the Year one thousand eight hundred and eight, but a Tax or duty may be imposed on such Importation, not exceeding ten dollars for each Person.

The Privilege of the Writ of Habeas Corpus shall not be suspended, unless when in Cases of Rebellion or Invasion the public Safety may require it.

No Bill of Attainder or ex post facto Law shall be passed.

No Capitation, or other direct, Tax shall be laid, unless in Proportion to the Census or Enumeration herein before directed to be taken.

No Tax or Duty shall be laid on Articles exported from any State.

No Preference shall be given by any Regulation of Commerce or Revenue to the Ports of one State over those of another: nor shall Vessels bound to, or from, one State, be obliged to enter, clear, or pay Duties in another.

No Money shall be drawn from the Treasury, but in Consequence of Appropriations made by Law; and a regular Statement and Account of the Receipts and Expenditures of all public Money shall be published from time to time.

No Title of Nobility shall be granted by the United States: And no Person holding any Office of Profit or Trust under them, shall, without the Consent of the Congress, accept of any present, Emolument, Office, or Title, of any kind whatever, from any King, Prince, or foreign State.

Section 10. No State shall enter into any Treaty, Alliance, or Confederation; grant Letters of Marque and Reprisal; coin Money; emit Bills of Credit; make any Thing but gold and silver Coin a Tender in Payment of Debts; pass any Bill of Attainder, ex post facto Law, or law impairing the Obligation of Contracts, or grant any Title of Nobility.

No State shall, without the Consent of the Congress, lay any Imposts or Duties on Imports or Exports, except what may be absolutely necessary for executing its inspection Laws: and the net Produce of all Duties and Imposts, laid by any Senate on Imports or Exports, shall be for the Use of the Treasury of the United States; and all such Laws shall be subject to the Revision and Control of the Congress.

No State shall, without the Consent of Congress, lay any Duty of Tonnage, keep Troops, or Ships of War in time of Peace, enter into any Agreement or Compact with another State, or with a foreign Power, or engage in War, unless actually invaded, or in such imminent Danger as will not admit of delay.

Article II

Section 1. The executive Power shall be vested in a President of the United States of America. He shall hold his Office during the Term of four Years, and, together with the Vice President, chosen for the same Term, be elected, as follows.

Each State shall appoint, in such Manner as the Legislature thereof may direct, a Number of Electors, equal to the whole Number of Senators and Representatives to which the State may be entitled in the Congress: but no Senator or Representative, or Person holding an Office of Trust or Profit under the United States, shall be appointed an Elector.

The Electors shall meet in their respective States, and vote by Ballot for two Persons, of whom one at least shall not be an Inhabitant of the same State with themselves. And they shall make a List of all the Persons voted for, and of the Number of Votes for each; which List they shall sign and certify, and transmit sealed to the Seat of the Government of the United States, directed to the President of the Senate. The President of the Senate shall, in the Presence of the Senate and House of Representatives, open all the Certificates, and the Votes shall then be counted. The Person having the greatest Number of Votes shall be the President, if such Number be a Majority of the whole Number of Electors appointed; and if there be more than one who have such majority, and have an equal Number of Votes, then the House of Representatives shall immediately choose by Ballot one of them for President; and if no Person have a Majority, then from the five highest on the List the said House shall in like Manner choose the President. But in choosing the President, the Votes shall be taken by States, the Representation from each State having one Vote; A quorum for this Purpose shall consist of a Member or Members from two thirds of the States, and a Majority of all the States shall be necessary to a Choice. In every Case, after the Choice of the President, the Person having the greatest Number of Votes of the Electors shall be the Vice President. But if there should remain two or more who have equal Votes, the Senate shall choose from them by Ballot the Vice President.

The Congress may determine the Time of choosing the Electors, and the Day on which they shall give their Votes; which Day shall be the same throughout the United States.

No Person except a natural born Citizen, or a Citizen of the United States, at the time of the Adoption of this Constitution, shall be eligible to the Office of President; neither shall any Person be eligible to that Office who shall not have attained to the Age of thirty-five Years, and been fourteen Years a Resident within the United States.

In Case of the Removal of the President from Office, or of his Death, Resignation, or Inability to discharge the Powers and Duties of the said Office, the Same shall devolve on the Vice President, and the Congress may by Law provide for the Case of Removal, Death, Resignation or Inability, both of the President and Vice President, declaring what Officer shall then act as President, and such Officer shall act accordingly, until the Disability be removed, or a President shall be elected.

The President shall, at stated Times, receive for his Services, a Compensation, which shall neither be increased nor diminished during the

Period for which he shall have been elected, and he shall not receive within that Period any other Emolument from the United States, or any of them.

Before he enter on the Execution of his Office, he shall take the following Oath or Affirmation:—"I do solemnly swear (or affirm) that I will faithfully execute the Office of President of the United States, and will to the best of my Ability, preserve, protect and defend the Constitution of the United States."

Section 2. The President shall be Commander in Chief of the Army and Navy of the United States, and of the Militia of the several States, when called into the actual Service of the United States; he may require the Opinion, in writing, of the principal Officer in each of the executive Departments, upon any Subject relating to the Duties of their respective Offices, and he shall have Power to grant Reprieves and Pardons for Offenses against the United States, except in Cases of Impeachment.

He shall have Power, by and with the Advice and Consent of the Senate, to make Treaties, provided two thirds of the Senators present concur; and he shall nominate, and by and with the Advice and Consent of the Senate, shall appoint Ambassadors, other public Ministers and Consuls, Judges of the supreme Court, and all other Officers of the United States, whose Appointments are not herein otherwise provided for, and which shall be established by Law: but the Congress may by Law vest the Appointment of such inferior Officers, as they think proper, in the President alone, in the Courts of Law, or in the Heads of Departments.

The President shall have Power to fill up all Vacancies that may happen during the Recess of the Senate, by granting Commissions which shall expire at the End of their next Session.

Section 3. He shall from time to time give to the Congress Information of the State of the Union, and recommend to their Consideration such Measures as he shall judge necessary and expedient; he may, on extraordinary Occasions, convene both Houses, or either of them, and in Case of Disagreement between them, with Respect to the Time of Adjournment, he may adjourn them to such Time as he shall think proper; he shall receive Ambassadors and other public Ministers; he shall take Care that the Laws be faithfully executed, and shall Commission all the Officers of the United States.

Section 4. The President, Vice President and all civil Officers of the United States, shall be removed from Office on Impeachment for, and Conviction of, Treason, Bribery, or other high Crimes and Misdemeanors.

Article III

Section 1. The judicial Power of the United States, shall be vested in one supreme Court, and in such inferior Courts as the Congress may from time to time ordain and establish. The Judges, both of the supreme and inferior Courts, shall hold their Offices during good Behavior, and shall, at stated Times, receive for their Services, a Compensation, which shall not be diminished during their Continuance in Office.

Section 2. The judicial Power shall extend to all Cases, in Law and Equity, arising under this Constitution, the Laws of the United States, and Treaties made, or which shall be made, under their Authority;—to all Cases affecting Ambassadors, other public Ministers and Consuls;—to all Cases of admiralty and maritime Jurisdiction;—to Controversies to which the United States shall be a Party;—to Controversies between two or more States;—between a State and Citizens of another state;—between Citizens of different States;—between Citizens of the same State claiming Lands under Grants of different States, and between a State, or the Citizens thereof, and foreign States, Citizens or Subjects.

In all Cases affecting Ambassadors, other public Ministers and Consuls, and those in which a State shall be Party, the supreme Court shall have original Jurisdiction. In all the other Cases before mentioned, the supreme Court shall have appellate Jurisdiction, both as to Law and fact, with such Exceptions, and under such Regulations as the Congress shall make.

The Trial of all Crimes, except in Cases of Impeachment, shall be by Jury; and such Trial shall be held in the State where the said Crimes shall have been committed; but when not committed within any State, the Trial shall be at such Place or Places as the Congress may by Law have directed.

Section 3. Treason against the United States, shall consist only in levying War against them, or in adhering to their Enemies, giving them Aid and Comfort. No Person shall be convicted of Treason unless on the Testimony of two Witnesses to the same overt Act, or on Confession in open Court.

The Congress shall have Power to declare the Punishment of Treason, but no Attainder of Treason shall work Corruption of Blood, or Forfeiture except during the Life of the Person attainted.

Article IV

Section 1. Full Faith and Credit shall be given in each State to the public Acts, Records, and judicial Proceedings of every other State. And the Congress may by general Laws prescribe the Manner in which such Acts, Records and Proceedings shall be proved, and the Effect thereof.

Section 2. The Citizens of each State shall be entitled to all Privileges and Immunities of Citizens in the several States.

A Person charged in any State with Treason, Felony, or other Crime, who shall flee from Justice, and be found in another State, shall on Demand of the executive Authority of the State from which he fled, be delivered up, to be removed to the State having Jurisdiction of the Crime.

No Person held to Service of Labor in one State, under the Laws thereof, escaping into another, shall, in Consequence of any Law or Regulation therein, be discharged from such Service or Labor, but shall be delivered up on Claim of the Party to whom such Service or Labor may be due.

Section 3. New States may be admitted by the Congress into this Union; but no new State shall be formed or erected within the Jurisdiction of any other State; nor any State be formed by the Junction of two or more States, or Parts of States, without the Consent of the Legislatures of the States concerned as well as of the Congress.

The Congress shall have Power to dispose of and make all needful Rules and Regulations respecting the Territory or other Property belonging to the United States; and nothing in this Constitution shall be so construed as to Prejudice any Claims of the United States, or of any particular State.

Section 4. The United States shall guarantee to every State in this Union a Republican Form of Government, and shall protect each of them against Invasion; and on Application of the Legislature, or of the Executive (when the Legislature cannot be convened) against domestic Violence.

Article V

The Congress, whenever two thirds of both Houses shall deem it necessary, shall propose Amendments to this Constitution, or, on the Application of the Legislatures of two thirds of the several States, shall call a Convention for proposing Amendments, which, in either Case, shall be valid to all Intents and Purposes, as Part of this Constitution, when ratified by the Legislatures of three fourths of the several States, or by Conventions in three fourths thereof, as the one or the other Mode of Ratification may be proposed by the Congress; Provided that no Amendment which may be made prior to the Year One thousand eight hundred and eight shall in any Manner affect the first and fourth Clauses in the Ninth Section of the first Article; and that no State, without its Consent, shall be deprived of its equal Suffrage in the Senate.

Article VI

All Debts contracted and Engagements entered into, before the Adoption of this Constitution, shall be as valid against the United States under this Constitution, as under the Confederation.

This Constitution, and the Laws of the United States which shall be made in Pursuance thereof; and all Treaties made, or which shall be made, under the Authority of the United States, shall be the supreme Law of the Land; and the Judges in every State shall be bound thereby, any Thing in the Constitution or Laws of any State to the Contrary notwithstanding.

The Senators and Representatives before mentioned, and the Members of the several State Legislatures, and all executive and judicial Officers, both of the United States and of the several States, shall be bound by Oath or Affirmation, to support this Constitution; but no religious Test shall ever be required as a Qualification to any Office or public Trust under the United States.

Article VII

The Ratification of the Conventions of nine States, shall be sufficient for the Establishment of this Constitution between the States so ratifying the Same.

DONE in Convention by the Unanimous Consent of the States present the Seventeenth Day of September in the Year of our Lord one thousand seven hundred and Eighty seven and of the Independence of the United States of America the Twelfth. IN WITNESS whereof We have hereunto subscribed our Names.

George Washington—
President and deputy from Virginia

New Hampshire
John Langdon
Nicholas Gilman

Massachusetts
Nathaniel Gorham
Rufus King

Connecticut
William Samuel Johnson
Roger Sherman

New York
Alexander Hamilton

New Jersey
William Livingston
David Brearley
William Paterson
Jonathan Dayton

Pennsylvania
Benjamin Franklin
Thomas Mifflin
Robert Morris
George Clymer
Thomas FitzSimons
Jared Ingersoll
James Wilson
Gouverneur Morris

Delaware
George Read
Gunning Bedford, Jr.
John Dickinson
Richard Bassett
Jacob Broom

Maryland
James McHenry
Daniel of St. Thomas Jenifer
Daniel Carroll

Virginia
John Blair
James Madison, Jr.

North Carolina
William Blount
Richard Dobbs Spaight
Hugh Williamson

South Carolina
John Rutledge
Charles Cotesworth Pinckney
Charles Pinckney
Pierce Buttler

Georgia
William Few
Abraham Baldwin

Attest: *William Jackson,* Secretary

THE AMENDMENTS

ARTICLES in addition to, and Amendment of the Constitution of the United States of America, proposed by Congress, and ratified by the Legislatures of the several States, pursuant to the fifth Article of the original Constitution.

First Amendment

[The First through Tenth Amendments, now known as the Bill of Rights, were proposed on September 25, 1789, and declared in force on December 15, 1791.]

Congress shall make no law respecting an establishment of religion, or prohibiting the free exercise thereof; or abridging the freedom of speech, or of the press; or the right of the people peaceably to assemble, and to petition the Government for a redress of grievances.

Second Amendment

A well regulated Militia, being necessary to the security of a free State, the right of the people to keep and bear Arms, shall not be infringed.

Third Amendment

No Soldier shall, in time of peace, be quartered in any house, without the consent of the Owner, nor in time of war, but in a manner to be prescribed by law.

Fourth Amendment

The right of the people to be secure in their persons, houses, papers, and effects, against unreasonable searches and seizures, shall not be violated, and no Warrants shall issue, but upon probable cause, supported by Oath or affirmation, and particularly describing the place to be searched, and the persons or things to be seized.

Fifth Amendment

No person shall be held to answer for a capital, or otherwise infamous crime, unless on a presentment or indictment of a Grand Jury, except in cases arising in the land or naval forces, or in the Militia, when in actual service in time of War or public danger; nor shall any person be subject for the same offence to be twice put in jeopardy of life or limb; nor shall be compelled in any criminal case to be a witness against himself, nor be deprived of life, liberty, or property, without due process of law; nor shall private property be taken for public use, without just compensation.

Sixth Amendment

In all criminal prosecutions, the accused shall enjoy the right to a speedy and public trial, by an impartial jury of the State and district wherein the crime shall have been committed, which district shall have been previously ascertained by law, and to be informed of the nature and cause of the accusation; to be confronted with the witnesses against him; to have compulsory process for obtaining witnesses in his favor, and to have the Assistance of Counsel for his defense.

Seventh Amendment

In Suits at common law, where the value in controversy shall exceed twenty dollars, the right of trial by jury shall be preserved, and no fact tried by a jury shall be otherwise reexamined in any Court of the United States, than according to the rules of the common law.

Eighth Amendment

Excessive bail shall not be required, nor excessive fines imposed, nor cruel and unusual punishments inflicted.

Ninth Amendment

The enumeration in the Constitution, of certain rights, shall not be construed to deny or disparage others retained by the people.

Tenth Amendment

The powers not delegated to the United States by the Constitution, nor prohibited by it to the States, are reserved to the States respectively, or to the people.

Eleventh Amendment

[Proposed March 4, 1794; declared ratified January 8, 1798]

The Judicial power of the United States shall not be construed to extend to any suit in law or equity, commenced or prosecuted against one of the United States by Citizens of another State, or by Citizens or Subjects of any Foreign State.

Twelfth Amendment

[Proposed December 9, 1803; declared ratified September 25, 1804]

The Electors shall meet in their respective states and vote by ballot for President and Vice President, one of whom, at least, shall not be an inhabitant of the same state with themselves; they shall name in their ballots the person voted for as President, and in distinct ballots the person voted for as Vice President, and they shall make distinct lists of all persons voted for as President, and of all persons voted for as Vice President, and of the number of votes for each, which lists they shall sign and certify, and transmit sealed to the seat of the government of the United States, directed to the President of the Senate;—The President of the Senate shall, in the presence of the Senate and House of Representatives, open all the certificates and the votes shall then be counted;—The person having the greatest number of votes for President, shall be the President, if such number be a majority of the whole number of Electors appointed; and if no person have such majority, then from the persons having the highest numbers not exceeding three on the list of those voted for as President, the House of Representatives shall choose immediately, by ballot, the President. But in choosing the President, the votes shall be taken by states, the representation from each state having one vote; a quorum for this purpose shall consist of a member or members from two thirds of the states, and a majority of all the states shall be necessary to a choice. And if the House of Representatives shall not choose a President whenever the right of choice shall devolve upon them, before the fourth day of March next following, then the Vice President shall act as President, as in the case of the death or other constitutional disability of the President;—The person having the greatest number of votes as Vice President, shall be the Vice President, if such number be a majority of the whole number of Electors appointed, and if no person have a majority, then from the two highest numbers on the list, the Senate shall choose the Vice President; a quorum for the purpose shall consist of two thirds of the whole number of Senators, and a majority of the whole number shall be necessary to a choice. But no person constitutionally ineligible to the office of President shall be eligible to that of Vice President of the United States.

Thirteenth Amendment
[Proposed January 31, 1865; declared ratified December 18, 1865]
Section 1. Neither slavery nor involuntary servitude, except as a punishment for crime whereof the party shall have been duly convicted, shall exist within the United States, or any place subject to their jurisdiction.
Section 2. Congress shall have power to enforce this article by appropriate legislation.

Fourteenth Amendment
[Proposed June 13, 1866; declared ratified July 28, 1868]
Section 1. All persons born or naturalized in the United States, and subject to the jurisdiction thereof, are citizens of the United States and of the State wherein they reside. No State shall make or enforce any law which shall abridge the privileges or immunities of citizens of the United

States; nor shall any State deprive any person of life, liberty, or property, without due process of law; nor deny to any person within its jurisdiction the equal protection of the laws.

Section 2. Representatives shall be apportioned among the several States according to their respective numbers, counting the whole number of persons in each State, excluding Indians not taxed. But when the right to vote at any election for the choice of electors for President and Vice President of the United States, Representatives in Congress, the Executive and Judicial officers of a State, or the members of the Legislature thereof, is denied to any of the male inhabitants of such State, being twenty-one years of age, and citizens of the United States, or in any way abridged, except for participation in rebellion, or other crime, the basis of representation therein shall be reduced in the proportion which the number of such male citizens shall bear to the whole number of male citizens twenty-one years of age in such State.

Section 3. No person shall be a Senator or Representative in Congress, or elector of President and Vice President, or hold any office, civil or military, under the United States, or under any State, who, having previously taken an oath, as a member of Congress, or as an officer of the United States, or as a member of any State legislature, or as an executive or judicial officer of any State, to support the Constitution of the United States, shall have engaged in insurrection or rebellion against the same, or given aid or comfort to the enemies thereof. But Congress may by a vote of two thirds of each House, remove such disability.

Section 4. The validity of the public debt of the United States, authorized by law, including debts incurred for payment of pensions and bounties for services in suppressing insurrection or rebellion, shall not be questioned. But neither the United States nor any State shall assume or pay any debt or obligation incurred in aid of insurrection or rebellion against the United States, or any claim for the loss of emancipation of any slave; but all such debts, obligations and claims shall be held illegal and void.

Section 5. The Congress shall have power to enforce, by appropriate legislation, the provisions of this article.

Fifteenth Amendment
[Proposed February 26, 1869; declared ratified March 30, 1870]
Section 1. The right of citizens of the United States to vote shall not be denied or abridged by the United States or by any State on account of race, color, or previous condition of servitude.

Section 2. The Congress shall have power to enforce this article by appropriate legislation.

Sixteenth Amendment
[Proposed July 12, 1909; declared ratified February 25, 1913]
The Congress shall have power to lay and collect taxes on incomes,

from whatever source derived, without apportionment among the several States, and without regard to any census or apportionment among the several States, and without regard to any census or enumeration.

Seventeenth Amendment
[Proposed May 13, 1912; declared ratified May 31, 1913]

The Senate of the United States shall be composed of two Senators from each State, elected by the people thereof, for six years; and each Senator shall have one vote. The electors in each State shall have the qualifications requisite for electors of the most numerous branch of the State legislatures.

When vacancies happen in the representation of any State in the Senate, the executive authority of such State shall issue writs of election to fill such vacancies: *Provided,* That the legislature of any State may empower the executive thereof to make temporary appointments until the people fill the vacancies by election as the legislature may direct.

This amendment shall not be so construed as to affect the election or term of any Senator chosen before it becomes valid as part of the Constitution.

Eighteenth Amendment
[Proposed December 18, 1917; declared ratified January 29, 1919;
repealed by the Twenty-first Amendment December 5, 1933]

Section 1. After one year from the ratification of this article the manufacture, sale, or transportation of intoxicating liquors within, the importation thereof into, or the exportation thereof from the United States and all territory subject to the jurisdiction thereof for beverage purposes is hereby prohibited.

Section 2. The Congress and the several States shall have concurrent power to enforce this article by appropriate legislation.

Section 3. This article shall be inoperative unless it shall have been ratified as an amendment to the Constitution by the legislatures of the several States, as provided in the Constitution, within seven years from the date of the submission hereof to the States by the Congress.

Nineteenth Amendment
[Proposed June 4, 1919; declared ratified August 26, 1920]

The right of citizens of the United States to vote shall not be denied or abridged by the United States or by any State on account of sex.

Congress shall have power to enforce this article by appropriate legislation.

Twentieth Amendment
[Proposed March 2, 1932; declared ratified February 6, 1933]

Section 1. The terms of the President and Vice President shall end at noon on the 20th day of January, and the terms of Senators and Representatives at noon on the 3rd day of January, of the years in which such terms would have ended if this article had not been ratified; and the terms of their successors shall then begin.

Section 2. The Congress shall assemble at least once in every year, and such meeting shall begin at noon on the 3rd day of January, unless they shall by law appoint a different day.

Section 3. If, at the time fixed for the beginning of the term of the President, the President elect shall have died, the Vice President elect shall become President. If a President shall not have been chosen before the time fixed for the beginning of his term, or if the President elect shall have failed to qualify, then the Vice President elect shall act as President until a President shall have qualified; and the Congress may by law provide for the case wherein neither a President elect nor a Vice President elect shall have qualified, declaring who shall then act as President, or the manner in which one who is to act shall be selected, and such persons shall act accordingly until a President or Vice President shall have qualified.

Section 4. The Congress may by law provide for the case of the death of any of the persons from whom the House of Representatives may choose a President whenever the right of choice shall have devolved upon them, and for the case of the death of any of the persons from whom the Senate may choose a Vice President whenever the right of choice shall have devolved upon them.

Section 5. Sections 1 and 2 shall take effect on the 15th day of October following the ratification of this article.

Section 6. This article shall be inoperative unless it shall have been ratified as an amendment to the Constitution by the legislatures of three fourths of the several States within seven years from the date of its submission.

Twenty-first Amendment

[Proposed February 20, 1933; declared ratified December 5, 1933]

Section 1. The eighteenth article of amendment to the Constitution of the United States is hereby repealed.

Section 2. The transportation or importation into any State, Territory, or possession of the United States for delivery or use therein of intoxicating liquors, in violation of the laws thereof, is hereby prohibited.

Section 3. This article shall be inoperative unless it shall have been ratified as an amendment to the Constitution by conventions in the several States, as provided in the Constitution, within seven years from the date of the submission hereof to the States by the Congress.

Twenty-second Amendment

[Proposed March 24, 1947; declared ratified March 1, 1951]

Section 1. No person shall be elected to the office of the President more than twice, and no person who has held the office of President, or acted as President, for more than two years of a term to which some other person was elected President shall be elected to the office of the President more than once. But this Article shall not apply to any person holding the office of President when this Article was proposed by the Congress, and shall not prevent any person who may be holding the office of President, or acting as President, during the term within which this Article becomes operative from holding the office of President or acting as President during the remainder of such term.

Section 2. This article shall be inoperative unless it shall have been ratified as an amendment to the Constitution by the legislatures of three fourths of the several States within seven years from the date of its submission to the States by the Congress.

Twenty-third Amendment
[Proposed June 16, 1960; declared ratified April 3, 1961]

Section 1. The District constituting the seat of Government of the United States shall appoint in such manner as the Congress may direct:

A number of electors of President and Vice President equal to the whole number of Senators and Representatives in Congress to which the District would be entitled if it were a State, but in no event more than the least populous state; they shall be in addition to those appointed by the States, but they shall be considered, for the purposes of the election of President and Vice President, to be electors appointed by a State; and they shall meet in the District and perform such duties as provided by the twelfth article of amendment.

Section 2. The Congress shall have power to enforce this article by appropriate legislation.

Twenty-fourth Amendment
[Proposed August 27, 1962; declared ratified February 4, 1964]

Section 1. The right of citizens of the United States to vote in any primary or other election for President or Vice President, for electors for President or Vice President, or for Senator or Representative in Congress, shall not be denied or abridged by the United States or any State by reason of failure to pay any poll tax or other tax.

Section 2. The Congress shall have power to enforce this article by appropriate legislation.

Twenty-fifth Amendment
[Proposed July 6, 1965; declared ratified February 23, 1967]

Section 1. In case of removal of the President from office or of his death or resignation, the Vice President shall become President.

Section 2. Whenever there is a vacancy in the office of the Vice President, the President shall nominate a Vice President who shall take office upon confirmation by a majority vote of both Houses of Congress.

Section 3. Whenever the President transmits to the President pro tempore of the Senate and the Speaker of the House of Representatives his written declaration that he is unable to discharge the powers and duties of his office, and until he transmits to them a written declaration to the contrary, such powers and duties shall be discharged by the Vice President as Acting President.

Section 4. Whenever the Vice President and a majority of either the principal officers of the executive departments or of such other body as Congress may by law provide, transmit to the President pro tempore of the Senate and the Speaker of the House of Representatives their written declaration that the President is unable to discharge the powers and duties of his office, the Vice President shall immediately assume the powers and duties of the office as Acting President.

Thereafter, when the President transmits to the President pro tempore of the Senate and the Speaker of the House of Representatives his written declaration that no inability exists, he shall resume the powers and duties of his office unless the Vice President and a majority of either the principal officers of the executive department or of such other body as Congress may by law provide, transmit within four days to the President pro tempore of the Senate and the Speaker of the House of Representatives their written declaration that the President is unable to discharge the powers and duties of his office. Thereupon Congress shall decide the issue, assembling within forty-eight hours for that purpose if not in session. If the Congress, within twenty-one days after receipt of the latter written declaration, or, if Congress is not in session, within twenty-one days after Congress is required to assemble, determines by two-thirds vote of both Houses that the President is unable to discharge the powers and duties of his office, the Vice President shall continue to discharge the same as Acting President; otherwise, the President shall resume the powers and duties of his office.

Twenty-sixth Amendment
[Proposed March 23, 1971; declared ratified July 5, 1971]

Section 1. The right of citizens of the United States, who are eighteen years of age or older, to vote shall not be denied or abridged by the United States or by any State on account of age.

Section 2. The Congress shall have power to enforce this article by appropriate legislation.

From The Interstate Commerce Act (1887)

In 1886 the Supreme Court ruled that state legislatures had no power to regulate the prices shippers charged for moving goods from one state to another. Railroads were guilty of a number of unfair shipping practices, but after this decision states could do little to those railroads that crossed state lines. If anything was to be done, the federal government would have to act.

The Interstate Commerce Act, adopted by Congress in 1887, marked the first attempt by the federal government to regulate railroad rates. The law created the Interstate Commerce Commission, the first federal regulatory agency, a turning point in the history of relations between the government and business.

Be it enacted: . . . That the provisions of this act shall apply to any common carrier or common carriers engaged in the transportation of passengers or property wholly by railroad, or partly by railroad and partly by water when both are used, under a common control, management, or arrangement, for a continuous carriage or shipment, from one state or territory of the United States, or the District of Columbia, to any other state or territory of the United States, or the District of Columbia, or from any place in the United States to an adjacent foreign country, or from any place in the United States through a foreign country to any other place in the United States. . . .

The term "railroad" as used in this act shall include all bridges and ferries used or operated in connection with any railroad, and also all the road in use by any corporation operating a railroad, whether owned or operated under a contract, agreement, or lease; and the term "transportation" shall include all instrumentalities [vehicles] of shipment or carriage.

All charges made for any service rendered or to be rendered in the transportation of passengers or property as aforesaid, or in connection therewith, or for the receiving, delivering, storage, or handling of such property, shall be reasonable and just; and every unjust and unreasonable charge for such service is prohibited and declared to be unlawful.

Section 2. That if any common carrier subject to the provisions of this act shall, directly or indirectly, by any special rate, rebate, drawback, or other device, charge, demand, collect, or receive from any person or persons a greater or less compensation for any service rendered, or to be rendered, in the transportation of passengers or property, subject to the provisions of this act, than it charges, demands, collects, or receives from any other person or persons for doing for him or them a like and contemporaneous service [at the same time] in the transportation of a like kind of traffic under substantially similar circumstances and conditions, such common carrier shall be deemed [considered] guilty of unjust discrimination, which is hereby prohibited and declared to be unlawful.

Section 3. That it shall be unlawful for any common carrier subject to the provisions of this act to make or give any undue or unreasonable preference or advantage to any particular person, company, firm, corporation, or locality. . . .

Every common carrier subject to the provisions of this act shall, according to their respective powers, afford all reasonable, proper, and equal facilities for the interchange of traffic between their respective lines, and for the receiving, forwarding, and delivering of passengers and property to and from their several lines and those connecting therewith, and shall not discriminate in their rates [charge different customers different rates for the same service] and charges between such connecting lines; but this shall not be construed as requiring any such common carrier to give the use of its tracks or terminal facilities to another carrier engaged in like business.

Section 4. That it shall be unlawful for any common carrier subject to the provisions of this act to charge or receive any greater compensation in the aggregate for the transportation of passengers or of like kind of property, under substantially similar circumstances and conditions, for a shorter than for a longer distance over the same line, in the same direction, the shorter being included within the longer distance. . . .

Section 5. That it shall be unlawful for any common carrier subject to the provisions of this act to enter into any contract, agreement, or combination with any other common carrier or carriers for the pooling of freights of different and competing railroads, or to divide between them the aggregate or net [amount over and above expenses] proceeds of the earnings of such railroads, or any portion thereof; and in any case of an agreement for the pooling of freights as aforesaid, each day of its continuance shall be deemed a separate offense.

Section 11. That a Commission is hereby created and established to be known as the Interstate Commerce Commission, which shall be composed of five Commissioners, who shall be appointed by the President, by and with the advice and consent of the Senate. . . .

Section 12. That the Commission hereby created shall have authority to inquire into the management of the business of all common carriers subject to the provisions of this act. . . .

FROM The Sherman Antitrust Act (1890)

With the passage of the Sherman Antitrust Act of 1890, Congress for the first time undertook to make rules regulating the size and business policies of large corporations.

During the 1870s and the 1880s, a number of industries—oil, sugar refining, steel, among others—became concentrated in the hands of a small number of large companies. Then they were able to eliminate most of their competition and charge whatever prices they wished. The public complained bitterly about these near monopolies and demanded that the goverment break them up and restore "freedom of enterprise."

Congress responded with the Sherman Antitrust Act. Court decisions made the law difficult to enforce, but at least it established a precedent for later, more-effective legislation.

An act to protect trade and commerce against unlawful restraints and monopolies [exclusive controls]. . . .

Be it enacted:

Section 1. Every contract, combination in the form of trust or otherwise, or conspiracy, in restraint of trade or commerce among the several states, or with foreign nations, is hereby declared to be illegal. Every person who shall make any such contract or engage in any such combination or conspiracy, shall be deemed guilty of a misdemeanor, and, on conviction thereof, shall be punished by fine not exceeding five thousand dollars, or by imprisonment not exceeding one year, or by both said punishments . . . [at] the discretion of the Court.

Section 2. Every person who shall monopolize, or attempt to monopolize, or combine or conspire with any other person or persons, to monopolize any part of the trade or commerce among the several states, or with foreign nations, shall be deemed guilty of a misdemeanor, and, on conviction thereof, shall be punished by fine not exceeding five thousand dollars, or by imprisonment not exceeding one year, or by both said punishments . . . [at] the discretion of the Court.

Section 3. Every contract, combination in form of trust or otherwise, or conspiracy, in restraint of trade or commerce in any territory of the United States or of the District of Columbia, or in restraint of trade or commerce between any such territory and another, or between any such territory or territories and any state or states or the District of Columbia, or with foreign nations, or between the District of Columbia and any state or states or foreign nations, is hereby declared illegal. . . .

Section 4. The several circuit courts of the United States are hereby invested with jurisdiction [given the legal power] to prevent and restrain violations of this act; and it shall be the duty of the several district attorneys of the United States, in their respective districts, under the direction of the Attorney-General, to institute proceedings in equity to prevent and restrain such violations. . . .

Section 5. Whenever it shall appear to the court before which any proceeding under section four of this act may be pending, that the ends of justice require that other parties should be brought before the court, the court may cause them to be summoned, whether they reside in the district in which the court is held or not; and subpoenas [writs commanding a person to appear in court] to that end may be served in any district by the marshal thereof.

Section 6. Any property owned under any contract or by any combination, or pursuant to any conspiracy (and being the subject thereof) mentioned in section one of this act, and being in the course of transportation from one state to another, or to a foreign country, shall be forfeited to the United States, and may be seized and condemned by like proceedings as those provided by law for the forfeiture, seizure, and condemnation of property imported into the United States contrary to law.

Section 7. Any person who shall be injured in

his business or property by any other person or corporation by reason of anything forbidden or declared to be unlawful by this act may sue therefore in any circuit court of the United States in the district in which the defendant resides or is found, without respect to the amount in controversy, and shall recover threefold the damages by him sustained, and the costs of suit, including a reasonable attorney's fee.

FROM Theodore Roosevelt's "The New Nationalism" (1910)

In 1909, at the conclusion of his second term as president, Theodore Roosevelt accepted many invitations to deliver public addresses. In several of these speeches he advocated a program of political reforms that he called "The New Nationalism." These reforms would extend the powers of the federal government to stop unfair business practices and reduce the political influence of powerful industrialists. The following excerpt is from his speech at Osawatomie, Kansas, on August 31, 1910.

Every special interest is entitled to justice—full, fair, and complete. . . . But not one is entitled to a vote in Congress, to a voice on the bench, or to representation in any public office. The Constitution guarantees protection to property, and we must make that promise good. But it does not give the right of suffrage [the right to vote] to any corporation. . . .

There can be no effective control of corporations while their political activity remains. To put an end to it will be neither a short nor an easy task, but it can be done.

We must have complete and effective publicity of corporate affairs, so that the people may know beyond peradventure [doubt] whether the corporations obey the law and whether their management entitles them to the confidence of the public. It is necessary that laws should be passed to prohibit the use of corporate funds directly or indirectly for political purposes; it is still more necessary that such laws should be thoroughly enforced. Corporate expenditures for political purposes, and especially such expenditures by public service

corporations [public utilities], have supplied one of the principal sources of corruption in our political affairs. . . .

Combinations in industry are the result of an imperative [compulsory] economic law which cannot be repealed by political legislation. The effort of prohibiting all combination has substantially failed. The way out lies, not in attempting to prevent such combinations, but in completely controlling them in the interest of the public welfare. For that purpose the Federal Bureau of Corporations is an agency of first importance. Its powers, and, therefore, its efficiency, as well as that of the Interstate Commerce Commission, should be largely increased. We have a right to expect from the Bureau of Corporations and from the Interstate Commission a very high grade of public service. We should be as sure of the proper conduct of the interstate railways and the proper management of interestate business as we are now sure of the conduct and management of the national banks, and we should have as effective supervision in one case as in the other. . . .

The absence of effective state, and, especially, national, restraint upon unfair money-getting has tended to create a small class of enormously wealthy and economically powerful men, whose chief object is to hold and to increase their power. The prime need is to change the conditions which enable these men to accumulate power which it is not for the general welfare that they should hold or exercise. We grudge no man a fortune which represents his own power and sagacity [farsightedness], when exercised with entire regard to the welfare of his fellows. . . . We grudge no man a fortune in civil life if it is honorably obtained and well used. It is not even enough that it should have been gained without doing damage to the community. We should permit it to be gained only so long as the gaining represents benefit to the community. This, I know, implies a policy of a far more active governmental interference with social and economic conditions in this country than we have yet had, but I think we have got to face the fact that such an increase in governmental control is now necessary.

No man should receive a dollar unless that dollar has been fairly earned. Every dollar received should represent a dollar's worth of service rendered—not gambling in stocks, but service rendered. The really big fortune, the swollen fortune, by the mere fact of its size acquires qualities which differentiate it in kind as well as in degree from what is possessed by men of relatively small means. Therefore, I believe in a graduated income tax on big fortunes, and in another tax which is far more easily collected and far more effective—a graduated inheritance tax on big fortunes, properly safeguarded against evasion and increasing rapidly in amount with the size of the estate. . . .

I do not ask for overcentralization; but I do ask that we work in a spirit of broad and far-reaching nationalism when we work for what concerns our people as a whole. We are all Americans. Our common interests are as broad as the continent. I speak to you here in Kansas exactly as I would speak in New York or Georgia, for the most vital problems are those which affect us all alike. The national government belongs to the whole American people, and where the whole American people are interested, that interest can be guarded effectively only by the national government. The betterment which we seek must be accomplished, I believe, mainly through the national government.

The American people are right in demanding that New Nationalism, without which we cannot hope to deal with new problems. The New Nationalism puts the national need before sectional or personal advantage. It is impatient of the utter confusion that results from local legislatures attempting to treat national issues as local issues. It is still more impatient of the impotence which springs from overdivision of governmental powers, the impotence which makes it possible for local selfishness or for legal cunning, hired by wealthy special interests, to bring national activities to a deadlock. This New Nationalism regards the executive power as the steward of the public welfare. It demands of the judiciary that it shall be interested primarily in human welfare rather than in property, just as it demands that the representative body shall represent all the people. . . .

FROM Woodrow Wilson's War Message to Congress (1917)

After the First World War broke out in Europe in 1914, the United States managed to remain neutral for nearly three years. However, American ships on the high seas were stopped by the navies of the Allies, and German submarines sank many ships carrying American goods. In 1917 Germany sharply increased its submarine attacks. After a number of United States vessels had been torpedoed, President Wilson decided to ask Congress to declare war on Germany. On April 2, 1917, he delivered his "War Message" to Congress. Two days later, the Senate voted for war by a vote of 82 to 6. On April 6 the House did the same by a vote of 373 to 50.

I have called the Congress into extraordinary session because there are serious, very serious choices of policy to be made, and made immediately, which it was neither right nor constitutionally permissible that I should assume the responsibility of making.

On the third of February last I officially laid before you the extraordinary announcement of the Imperial German Government that on and after the first day of February it was its purpose to put aside all restraints of law or of humanity and use its submarines to sink every vessel that sought to approach either the ports of Great Britain and Ireland or the western coasts of Europe or any of the ports controlled by the enemies of Germany within the Mediterranean. . . . The new policy has swept every restriction aside. Vessels of every kind, whatever their flag, their character, their cargo, their destination, their errand, have been ruthlessly sent to the bottom without warning and without thought of help or mercy for those on board, the vessels of friendly neutrals along with those of belligerents [warring nations]. Even hospital ships and ships carrying relief to the sorely bereaved and stricken people of Belgium . . . have been sunk with the same reckless lack of compassion or of principle. . . . I am not now thinking of the loss of property involved. . . . Property can be paid for; the lives of the peaceful and innocent people cannot be. The present German submarine warfare against commerce is a warfare against mankind.

It is a war against all nations. American ships have been sunk, American lives taken, in ways which it has stirred us very deeply to learn of, but the ships and people of other neutral and friendly nations have been sunk and overwhelmed in the waters the same way. There has been no discrimination. The challenge is to all mankind. . . .

I advise that the Congress declare the recent course of the Imperial German Government to be in fact nothing less than war against the government and people of the United States; that it formally accept the status of belligerent which has been thrust upon it; and that it take immediate steps not only to put the country in a more thorough state of defense but also to exert all its power and employ all its resources to bring the government of the German Empire to terms and end the war.

What this will involve is clear. It will involve . . . the organization and mobilization of all the material resources of the country to supply materials of war and serve the incidental needs of the nation. . . . It will involve the immediate full equipment of the navy. . . . It will involve the immediate addition to the armed services of the United States . . . of at least five hundred thousand men, who should, in my opinion, be chosen upon the principle of universal liability [the obligation by law of all] to service. . . .

While we do these things, these deeply momentous things, let us be very clear, and make very clear to the world what our motives and our objects are. . . . Our object . . . is to vindicate the principles of peace and justice in the life of the world as against selfish and autocratic power [total control by a single ruler or ruling group]. . . . Neutrality is no longer feasible or desirable where the peace of the world is involved and the freedom of its peoples, and the menace to that peace and freedom lies on the existence of autocratic governments backed by organized force which is controlled wholly by their will, not by the will of the people. We have seen the last of neutrality in such circumstances. We are at the beginning of an age in which it will be insisted that the same standards of conduct shall be observed among nations and their governments that are observed among the individual citizens of civilized states. . . .

The world must be made safe for democracy. Its peace must be planted upon the tested foundations of political liberty. We have no selfish ends to serve. We desire no conquest, no domination. We seek no indemnities [securities from loss] for ourselves, no material compensation [repayment] for the sacrifices we shall freely make. We are but one of the champions of the rights of mankind. We shall be satisfied when those rights have been made as secure as the faith and the freedom of nations can make them. . . .

It is a distressing and oppressive duty, Gentlemen of the Congress, which I have performed in thus addressing you. There are, it may be, many months of fiery trial and sacrifice ahead of us. It is a fearful thing to lead this great peaceful people into war, into the most terrible and disastrous of all wars, civilization itself seeming to be in the balance. But the right is more precious than peace, and we shall fight for the things which we have always carried nearest our hearts—for democracy, for the right of those who submit to authority to have a voice in their own governments, for the rights and liberties of small nations, for the universal dominion of right by such a concert [mutual union] of free peoples as shall bring peace and safety to all nations and make the world itself at last free. To such a task we can dedicate our lives and our fortunes, everything that we are and everything that we have, with the pride of those who know that the day has come when America is privileged to spend her blood and her might for the principles that gave her birth and happiness and the peace which she has treasured. God helping her, she can do no other.

Woodrow Wilson's Fourteen Points (1918)

In his war message of April 2, 1917, President Wilson explained that the United States would be fighting to make the world "safe for democracy." However, the Allies in Europe had agreed among themselves in secret treaties to seize German and Austrian territory and otherwise punish the Central Powers if they succeeded in winning the war. Wilson felt that such a policy would only cause new wars. He was determined to secure "a just and stable peace."

On January 8, 1918, in a speech to Congress, Wilson described what he considered to be "the only possible program for world peace." There were 14 points in his plan. The 14th point, the heart of the program, called for creating "a general association of nations" that could provide "mutual guarantees of political independence and territorial integrity to great and small states alike."

Gentlemen of the Congress: . . .

We entered this war because violations of right had occurred which touched us to the quick and made the life of our own people impossible unless they were corrected and the world secured once and for all against their recurrence. What we demand in this war, therefore, is nothing peculiar to ourselves. It is that the world be made fit and safe to live in; and particularly that it be made safe for every peace-loving nation which, like our own, wishes to live its own life, determine its own institutions, be assured of justice and fair dealing by the other peoples of the world as against force and selfish aggression. All the peoples of the world are in effect partners in this interest, and for our own part we see very clearly that unless justice be done to others, it will not be done to us. The program of the world's peace, therefore, is our program; and that program, the only possible program, as we see it, is this:

I. Open covenants of peace, openly arrived at, after which there shall be no private international understandings of any kind but diplomacy shall proceed always frankly and in the public view.

II. Absolute freedom of navigation upon the seas, outside territorial waters, alike in peace and in war, except as the seas may be closed in whole or in part by international action for the enforcement of international covenants.

III. The removal, so far as possible, of all economic barriers and the establishment of an equality of trade conditions among all the nations consenting to the peace and associating themselves for its maintenance.

IV. Adequate guarantees given and taken that national armaments will be reduced to the lowest point consistent with domestic safety.

V. A free, open-minded, and absolutely impartial adjustment of all colonial claims, based upon a strict observance of the principle that in determining all such questions of sovereignty the interests of the populations concerned must have equal weight with the equitable claims of the government whose title is to be determined.

VI. The evacuation of all Russian territory and such a settlement of all questions affecting Russia as will secure the best and freest cooperation of the other nations of the world in obtaining for her an unhampered and unembarrassed [unhindered] opportunity for the independent determination of her own political development and national policy and assure her of a sincere welcome into the society of free nations under institutions of her own choosing; and, more than a welcome, assistance also of every kind that she may need and may herself desire. The treatment accorded Russia by her sister nations in the months to come will be the acid test of their good will, of their comprehension of her needs as distinguished from their own interests, and of their intelligent and unselfish sympathy.

VII. Belgium, the whole world will agree, must be evacuated and restored, without any attempt to limit the sovereignty which she enjoys in common with all other free nations. No other single act will serve as this will serve to restore confidence among the nations in the laws which they have themselves set and determined for the government of their relations with one another. Without this healing act the whole structure and validity of International law is forever impaired.

VIII. All French territory should be freed and the invaded portions restored, and the wrong done to France by Prussia in 1871 in the matter of Alsace-Lorraine, which has unsettled the peace of the world for nearly fifty years, should be righted, in order that peace may once more be made secure in the interest of all.

IX. A readjustment of the frontiers of Italy should be effected along clearly recognizable lines of nationality.

X. The peoples of Austria-Hungary, whose place among the nations we wish to see safeguarded and assured, should be accorded the freest opportunity of autonomous development.

XI. Rumania, Serbia, and Montenegro should be evacuated; occupied territories restored; Serbia accorded free and secure access to the sea; and the relations of the several Balkan states to one another determined by friendly counsel along historically established lines of allegiance and nationality; and international guarantees of the political and economic independence and territorial integrity of the several Balkan states should be entered into.

XII. The Turkish portions of the present Ottoman Empire should be assured a secure sovereignty, but the other nationalities which are now under Turkish rule should be assured an undoubted security of life and an absolutely unmolested opportunity of autonomous development, and the Dardanelles should be permanently opened as a free passage to the ships and commerce of all nations under international guarantees.

XIII. An independent Polish state should be erected which should include the territories inhabited by indisputably Polish populations, which should be assured a free and secure access to the sea, and whose political and economic independence and territorial integrity should be guaranteed by international covenant.

XIV. A general association of nations must be formed under specific covenants for the purpose of affording mutual guarantees of political independence and territorial integrity to great and small states alike.

In regard to these essential rectifications of wrong and assertions of right we feel ourselves to be intimate partners of all the governments and peoples associated together against the Imperialists. We cannot be separated in interest or divided in purpose. We stand together until the end.

For such arrangements and covenants we are willing to fight and to continue to fight until they are achieved; but only because we wish the right to prevail and desire a just and stable peace such as can be secured only by removing the chief provocations to war, which this program does not remove. . . .

We have spoken now, surely, in terms too concrete to admit . . . any further doubt or question. An evident principle runs through the whole program I have outlined. It is the principle of justice to all peoples and nationalities, and their right to live on equal terms of liberty and safety with one another, whether they be strong or weak. Unless this principle be made its foundation, no part of the structure of international justice can stand. The people of the United States could act upon no other principle; and to the vindication of this principle they are ready to devote their lives, their honor, and everything that they possess. The moral climax of this, the culminating and final war for human liberty, has come, and they are ready to put their own strength, their own highest purpose, their own integrity and devotion to the test.

FROM Franklin D. Roosevelt's First Inaugural Address (1933)

At noon on March 4, 1933, Franklin D. Roosevelt delivered his first inaugural address. The country had sunk into the worst depression in its history, and the future appeared grim. But Roosevelt, in a calm, confident voice, reassured Americans that their "great nation will endure as it has endured, will revive, and will prosper." It was a message of faith and hope and a promise of better days.

President Hoover, Mr. Chief Justice, my friends:

This is a day of national consecration, and I am certain that my fellow Americans expect that on my induction into the Presidency I will address them with a candor and a decision which the present situation of our nation impels.

This is pre-eminently the time to speak the truth, the whole truth, frankly and boldly. Nor need we shrink from honestly facing conditions in our country today. This great nation will endure as it has endured, will revive, and will prosper.

So, first of all, let me assert my firm belief that the only thing we have to fear is fear itself—nameless, unreasoning, unjustified terror which paralyzes needed efforts to convert retreat into advance.

In every dark hour of national life a leadership of frankness and vigor has met with that understanding and support of the people themselves which is essential to victory. I am convinced that you will again give that support to leadership in these critical days.

In such a spirit on my part and on yours we face our common difficulties. They concern, thank God, only materials things. Values have shrunken to fantastic levels; taxes have risen; our ability to pay has fallen; government of all kinds is faced by serious curtailment [reduction] of income; the means of exchange are frozen in the currents of trade; the withered leaves of industrial enterprise lie on every side; farmers find no markets for their produce; the savings of many years in thousands of families are gone.

More important, a host of unemployed citizens face the grim problem of existence, and an equally great number toil with little return. Only a foolish optimist can deny the dark realities of the moment.

Yet our distress comes from no failure of substance. We are stricken by no plague of locusts. Compared with the perils which our forefathers conquered because they believed and were not afraid, we have still much to be thankful for. Nature still offers her bounty and human efforts have multiplied it. Plenty is at our doorstep, but a generous use of it languishes in the very sight of the supply.

Primarily, this is because the rulers of the exchange of mankind's goods have failed through their own stubbornness and their own incompetence, have admitted their failure and abdicated [given up their position]. Practices of the unscrupulous [unprincipled] money-changers stand indicted in the court of public opinion, rejected by the hearts and minds of men.

True, they have tried, but their efforts have been cast in the pattern of an outworn tradition. Faced by failure of credit, they have proposed only the lending of more money.

Stripped of the lure of profit by which to induce our people to follow their false leadership, they have resorted to exhortations, pleading tearfully for restored confidence. They know only the rules of a generation of self-seekers.

They have no vision, and when there is no vision the people perish.

The money-changers have fled from their high seats in the temple of our civilization. We may now restore that temple to the ancient truths.

The measure of the restoration lies in the extent to which we apply social values more noble than mere monetary profit.

Happiness lies not in the mere possession of money; it lies in the joy of achievement, in the thrill of creative effort.

The joy and moral stimulation of work no longer must be forgotten in the mad chase of evanescent [tending to disappear like a vapor] profits. These dark days will be worth all they cost us if they teach us that our true destiny is not to be ministered unto but to minister to ourselves and to our fellow men.

Recognition of the falsity of material wealth as the standard of success goes hand in hand with the abandonment of the false belief that public office and high political position are to be valued only by the standards of pride of place and personal profit; and there must be an end to a conduct in banking and in business which too often has given to a sacred trust the likeness of callous and selfish wrongdoing.

Small wonder that confidence languishes, for it thrives only on honesty, on honor, on the sacredness of obligations, on faithful protection, on unselfish performance. Without them it cannot live.

Restoration calls, however, not for changes in ethics alone. This nation asks for action, and action now.

Our greatest primary task is to put people to work. This is no unsolvable problem if we face it wisely and courageously.

It can be accomplished in part by direct recruiting by the government itself, treating the task as we would treat the emergency of a war, but at the same time, through this employment, accomplishing greatly needed projects to stimulate and reorganize the use of our natural resources.

Hand in hand with this, we must frankly recognize the overbalance of population in our industrial centers and, by engaging on a national scale in a redistribution, endeavor to provide a better use of the land for those best fitted for the land.

The task can be helped by definite efforts to raise the values of agricultural products and with this the power to purchase the output of our cities.

It can be helped by preventing realistically the tragedy of the growing loss, through foreclosure, of our small houses and our farms.

It can be helped by insistence that the federal, state, and local governments act forthwith on the demand that their cost be drastically reduced.

It can be helped by the unifying of relief activities which today are often scattered, uneconomical and unequal. It can be helped by national planning for and supervision of all forms of transportaton and of communications and other utilities which have a definitely public character.

There are many ways in which it can be helped, but it can never be helped merely by talking about it. We must act, and act quickly.

Finally, in our progress toward a resumption of work we require two safeguards against a return of the evils of the old order; there must be a strict supervision of all banking and credits and investments; there must be an end to speculation with other people's money, and there must be provision for an adequate but sound currency.

These are the lines of attack. I shall presently urge upon a new Congress in special session detailed measures for their fulfillment, and I shall seek the immediate assistance of the several states.

From Franklin D. Roosevelt's Annual Message to Congress (1941)

Shortly after two o'clock on the afternoon of January 6, 1941, President Franklin D. Roosevelt entered the crowded House of Representatives to deliver his State of the Union message to Congress. The Congressional mood was gloomy. Although the United States had not yet become involved in the war which had been raging for 16 months on four continents, most of the legislators realized that American entry into the conflict was highly likely.

Roosevelt's mood was equally gloomy. He told Congress that the nation's security had been seriously threatened, and he appealed to all Americans to rededicate themselves to "the four essential human freedoms"—freedom of speech and expression, freedom of religion, freedom from want, and freedom from fear.

I address you, the members of the Seventy-seventh Congress, at a moment unprecedented in the history of the Union. I use the word "unprecedented," because at no previous time has American security been as seriously threatened from without as it is today. . . .

Every realist knows that the democratic way of life is at this moment being directly assailed [attacked] in every part of the world—assailed either by arms, or by secret spreading of poisonous propaganda by those who seek to destroy unity and promote discord in nations still at peace.

During sixteen months this assault has blotted out the whole pattern of democratic life in an appalling number of independent nations, great and small. The assailants are still on the march, threatening other nations, great and small.

Therefore, as your President, performing my constitutional duty to "give to the Congress information of the state of the Union," I find it necessary to report that the future and the safety of our country and of our democracy are overwhelmingly involved in events far beyond our borders.

Armed defense of democratic existence is now being gallantly waged in four continents. If that defense fails, all the population and all the resources of Europe, Asia, Africa, and Australia will be dominated by the conquerors. Let us remember that the total of those populations and their resources in those four continents greatly exceeds the sum total of the population of the resources of the whole of the Western Hemisphere many times over.

In times like these it is immature—and, incidentally, untrue—for anybody to brag that an unprepared America, singlehanded, and with one hand tied behind its back, can hold off the whole world.

No realistic American can expect from a dictator's peace international generosity, or return of true independence, or world disarmament, or freedom of expression, or freedom of religion—or even good business.

Such a peace would bring no security for us or for our neighbors. "Those who would give up essential liberty to purchase a little temporary safety deserve neither liberty nor safety." . . .

Just as our national policy in internal affairs has been based upon a decent respect for the rights and the dignity of all our fellow men within our gates, so our national policy in foreign affairs has been based on a decent respect for the rights and dignity of all nations, large and small. And the justice of morality must and will win in the end.

Our national policy is this:

First, by an impressive expression of the public will and without regard to partisanship, we are committed to all-inclusive national defense.

Second, by an impressive expression of the public will and without regard to partisanship, we are committed to full support of all those resolute peoples, everywhere, who are resisting aggression and are thereby keeping war away from our hemisphere. By this support, we express our determination that the democratic cause shall prevail; and we strengthen the defense and the security of our own nation.

Third, by an impressive expression of the public will and without regard to partisanship, we are committed to the proposition that principles of morality and considerations for our security will never permit us to acquiesce in [give in to] a peace dictated by aggressors and sponsored by appeasers [those who give in]. We know that enduring peace cannot be bought at the cost of other people's freedom. . . .

Let us say to the democracies: "We Americans are vitally concerned in your defense of freedom. We are putting forth our energies, our resources, and our organizing powers to give you the strength to regain and maintain a free world. We shall send you, in ever-increasing numbers, ships, planes, tanks, guns. This is our purpose and our pledge." . . .

The happiness of future generations of Americans may well depend upon how effective and how immediate we can make our aid felt. No one can tell the exact character of the emergency situations that we may be called upon to meet. The Nation's hands must not be tied when the Nation's life is in danger.

We must all prepare to make the sacrifices that the emergency—as serious as war itself—demands. Whatever stands in the way of speed and efficiency in defense preparations must give way to the national need. . . .

In the future days, which we seek to make secure, we look forward to a world founded upon four essential human freedoms.

The first is freedom of speech and expression—everywhere in the world.

The second is freedom of every person to worship God in his own way—everywhere in the world.

The third is freedom from want—which, translated into world terms, means economic understandings which will secure to every nation a healthy peacetime life for its inhabitants—everywhere in the world.

The fourth is freedom from fear—which, translated into world terms, means a world-wide reduction of armaments to such a point and in such a thorough fashion that no nation will be in a position to commit an act of physical aggression against any neighbor—anywhere in the world. . . .

This nation has placed its destiny in the hands and heads and hearts of its millions of free men and women; and its faith in freedom under the guidance of God. Freedom means the supremacy of human rights everywhere. Our support goes to those who struggle to gain those rights or keep them. Our strength is in our unity of purpose.

To that high concept there can be no end save victory.

The Atlantic Charter (1941)

On August 9, 1941, the British warship *Prince of Wales* anchored close to the United States cruiser *Augusta* in a bay off Newfoundland. Aboard the *Prince of Wales* was British Prime Minister Winston Churchill, while on the *Augusta* was President Franklin D. Roosevelt. The two leaders met to plan for even closer cooperation in the war against the Axis powers and to prepare a statement of principles to guide their conduct in the troubled years ahead. That statement soon came to be known as the Atlantic Charter.

The President of the United States of America and the Prime Minister, Mr. Churchill, representing His Majesty's Government in the United Kingdom, being met together, deem it right to make known certain common principles in the national policies of their respective countries on which they base their hopes for a better future for the world.

First, their countries seek no aggrandizement [growth], territorial or other.

Second, they desire to see no territorial changes that do not accord with the freely expressed wishes of the peoples concerned.

Third, they respect the right of all peoples to choose the form of government under which they will live; and they wish to see sovereign rights and self-government restored to those who have been forcibly deprived of them.

Fourth, they will endeavor, with due respect for their existing obligations, to further the enjoyment by all states, great or small, victor or vanquished, of access, on equal terms, to the trade and to the raw materials of the world which are needed for their economic prosperity.

Fifth, they desire to bring about the fullest collaboration between all nations in the economic field with object of securing, for all, improved labor standards, economic advancement, and social security.

Sixth, after the final destruction of the Nazi tyranny, they hope to see established a peace which will afford to all nations the means of dwelling in safety within their own boundaries, and which will afford assurance that all the men in all the lands may live out their lives in freedom from fear and want.

Seventh, such a peace should enable all men to traverse [cross] the high seas and oceans without hindrance.

Eighth, they believe that all of the nations of the world, for realistic as well as spiritual reasons, must come to the abandonment of the use of force. Since no future peace can be maintained if land, sea, or air armaments continue to be employed by nations which threaten, or may threaten, aggression outside of their frontiers, they believe, pending the establishment of a wider and permanent system of general security, that the disarmament of such nations is essential. They will likewise aid and encourage all other practicable measures which will lighten for peace-loving peoples the crushing burden of armaments.

FROM The Truman Doctrine (1947)

The United States responded to the threat of communist aggression after World War II with what was called the containment policy. The object was to contain, or restrict, Soviet territorial expansion and the spread of communism.

The policy was first applied to Greece and Turkey. In 1947 Greek communists, supported by the Soviet Union, were fighting to overthrow the Greek government. Turkey, along the southeastern border of the Soviet Union, was also threatened by communist groups. On March 12 President Harry S Truman announced his Truman Doctrine. He asked Congress for the authority to help Greece and Turkey. Congress promptly appropriated $400 million for economic and military assistance. Over the next 30 years the United States would spend many billions of dollars to carry out the objectives of the Truman Doctrine.

The gravity of the situation which confronts the world today necessitates my appearance before a joint session of the Congress.

The foreign policy and the national security of this country are involved.

One aspect of the present situation, which I wish to present to you at this time for your consideration and decision, concerns Greece and Turkey.

The United States has received from the Greek government an urgent appeal for financial and economic assistance. Preliminary reports from the American Economic Mission now in Greece and reports from the American Ambassador in Greece corroborate the statement of the Greek government that assistance is imperative if Greece is to survive as a free nation. . . .

The very existence of the Greek state is today threatened by the terrorist activities of several thousand armed men, led by Communists, who defy the government's authority at a number of points, particularly along the northern boundaries. . . .

Greece must have assistance if it is to become a self-supporting and self-respecting democracy. The United States must supply this assistance. We have already extended to Greece certain types of relief and economic aid, but these are inadequate. There is no other country to which democratic Greece can turn. No other nation is willing and able to provide the necessary support for a democratic Greek government. . . .

The future of Turkey as an independent and economically sound state is clearly no less important to the freedom-loving peoples of the world than the future of Greece. The circumstances in which Turkey finds itself today are considerably different from those of Greece. Turkey has been spared the disasters that have beset Greece. And during the war the United States and Great Britain furnished Turkey with material aid.

Nevertheless, Turkey now needs our support.

Since the war, Turkey has sought financial assistance from Great Britain and the United States for the purpose of affecting the modernization necessary for the maintenance of its national integrity.

That integrity is essential to the preservation of order in the Middle East. . . .

As in the case of Greece, if Turkey is to have the assistance it needs, the United States must supply it. We are the only country able to provide that help.

I am fully aware of the broad implications involved if the United States extends assistance to Greece and Turkey, and I shall discuss these implications with you at this time.

One of the primary objectives of the foreign policy of the United States is the creation of conditions in which we and other nations will be able to work out a way of life free from coercion. This was a fundamental issue in the war with Germany and Japan. Our victory was won over countries which sought to impose their will, and their way of life, upon other nations.

To ensure the peaceful development of nations, free from coercion [the use of force to dominate], the United States has taken a leading part in establishing the United Nations. The United Nations is designed to make possible lasting freedom and independence for all its members. We shall not realize our objectives, however, unless we are willing to help free peoples to maintain their free institutions and their national integrity against aggressive movements that seek to impose on the totalitarian regimes. This is no more than a frank recognition that totalitarian regimes imposed on free peoples, by direct or indirect aggression, undermine the foundations of international peace and hence the security of the United States.

The peoples of a number of countries of the world have recently had totalitarian regimes forced upon them against their will. The government of the United States has made frequent protests against coercion and intimidation in violation of the Yalta agreement, in Poland, Rumania, and Bulgaria. I must also state that in a number of other countries there have been similar developments.

At the present moment in world history nearly every nation must choose between alternative ways of life. The choice is too often not a free one.

One way of life is based upon the will of the majority, and is distinguished by free institutions, representative government, free elections, guarantees of individual liberty, freedom of speech and religion, and freedom from political oppression.

The second way of life is based upon the will of a minority forcibly imposed upon the majority. It relies upon terror and oppression, a controlled press and radio, fixed elections, and the suppression of personal freedoms.

I believe that it must be the policy of the United States to support free peoples who are resisting attempted subjugation by armed minorities or by outside pressures.

I believe that we must assist free peoples to work out their own destinies in their own way.

I believe that our help should be primarily through economic and financial aid which is essential to economic stability and orderly political processes.

The world is not static, and the status quo [the existing state of affairs] is not sacred. But we cannot allow changes in the status quo in violation of the charter of the United Nations by such methods as coercion, or by such subterfuges [deceptions] as political infiltration. In helping free and independent nations to maintain their freedom, the United States will be giving effect to the principles of the charter of the United Nations. . . .

The seeds of totalitarian regimes are nurtured by misery and want. They spread and grow in the evil soil of poverty and strife. They reach their full growth when the hope of a people for a better life has died.

We must keep that hope alive.

The free peoples of the world look to us for support in maintaining their freedoms.

If we falter in our leadership, we may endanger the peace of the world—and we shall surely endanger the welfare of our own Nation.

Great responsibilities have been placed upon us by the swift movement of events.

I am confident that the Congress will face these responsibilities squarely.

FROM George C. Marshall's Address at Harvard University (1947)

In June 1947 Secretary of State George C. Marshall made a speech at the graduation ceremonies at Harvard University. "I need not tell you, gentlemen," he began, "that the world situation is very serious." After reviewing the desperate situation in Europe, he offered a proposal designed to help the Europeans recover from the ravages of the most terrible war in history.

In 1948 Congress, working with European governments, adopted the European Recovery Plan, popularly known as the Marshall Plan. The secret of its success lay in the basic concept that American aid would be meaningful only to the extent that it helped Europeans mobilize their own efforts and creative energies.

In considering the requirements for the rehabilitation of Europe, the physical loss of life, the visible destruction of cities, factories, mines, and railroads was correctly estimated, but it has become obvious during recent months that this visible destruction was probably less serious than the dislocation of the entire fabric of European economy. For the past ten years conditions have been highly abnormal.

The feverish preparation for war and the more feverish maintenance of the war effort engulfed all aspects of national economies. Machinery has fallen into disrepair or is entirely obsolete. Under the arbitrary and destructive Nazi rule, virtually every possible enterprise was geared into the German war machine. Long-standing commercial ties, private institutions, banks, insurance companies, and shipping companies disappeared through loss of capital, absorption through nationalization [government takeover], or by simple destruction. . . .

The truth of the matter is that Europe's requirements for the next three or four years of foreign food and other essential products—principally from America—are so much greater than her present ability to pay that she must have substantial additional help, or face economic, social, and political deterioration of a very grave character.

The remedy lies in breaking the vicious circle and restoring the confidence of the European people in the economic future of their own countries and of Europe as a whole. The manufacturer and the farmer throughout wide areas must be able and willing to exchange their products for currencies, the continuing value of which is not open to question.

Aside from the demoralizing effect on the world at large and the possibilities of disturbances arising as a result of the desperation of the people concerned, the consequences to the economy of the United States should be apparent to all. It is logical that the United States should do whatever it is able to do to assist in the return of normal economic health in the world, without which there can be no political stability and no assured peace.

Our policy is directed not against any country or doctrine but against hunger, poverty, desperation, and chaos. Its purpose should be the revival of a working economy in the world so as to permit the emergence of political and social conditions in which free institutions can exist. Such assistance, I am convinced, must not be on a piecemeal basis as various crises develop. Any assistance that this Government may render in the future should provide a cure rather than a mere palliative [easing of symptoms].

Any government that is willing to assist in the task of recovery will find full co-operation, I am sure, on the part of the United States government. Any government which maneuvers to block the recovery of other countries cannot expect help from us. Furthermore, governments, political parties, or groups which seek to perpetuate human misery in order to profit therefrom, politically or otherwise, will encounter the opposition of the United States.

It is already evident that, before the United States Government can proceed much further in its effort to alleviate the situation and help start the European world on its way to recovery, there must be some agreement among the countries of Europe as to the requirements of the situation and the part those countries themselves will take in order to give proper effect to whatever action might be undertaken by this government. It would be neither fitting nor efficacious for this government to undertake to draw up unilaterally a program designed to place Europe on its feet economically. This is the business of the Europeans. The

initiative, I think, must come from Europe. The role of this country should consist of friendly aid in the drafting of a European program, and of later support of such a program so far as it may be practical for us to do so. The program should be a joint one, agreed to by a number, if not all European nations.

An essential part of any successful action on the part of the United States is an understanding on the part of the people of America of the character of the problem and the remedies to be applied. Political passion and prejudice should have no part. With foresight and a willingness on the part of our people to face up to the vast responsibility which history has clearly placed upon our country, the difficulties I have outlined can and will be overcome.

FROM A Declaration of Indian Purpose (1961)

From the day the first white settlers arrived in America, they began by hook or by crook to take over lands occupied by the native Americans, whom they called "Indians." As time passed, many bloody battles erupted. Treaties were made, then broken. By the late 1800s most of the Indians had been forced onto reservations. Many policy shifts followed. In 1924 all Indians were granted United States citizenship. Then in 1934 Congress passed the Indian Reorganization Act in an effort to revitalize Indian tribal life. Indians were encouraged to establish tribal governments and to return the lands their ancestors had obtained under the Dawes Act to tribal control. But the results of this change were disappointing. By the 1960s the Indians were demanding the return of much of the land they had lost, and they pursued these claims in courts. In June 1961 more than 400 Indians representing 90 tribes met in Chicago to draft an important policy statement called the "Declaration of Indian Purpose."

In the beginning the people of the New World, called Indians by accident of geography, were possessed of a continent and a way of life. In the course of many lifetimes, our people had adjusted to every climate and condition from the Arctic to the torrid zones. In their livelihood and family relationships, their ceremonial observances, they reflected the diversity of the physical world they occupied.

The conditions in which Indians live today reflect a world in which every basic aspect of life has been transformed. Even the physical world is no longer the controlling factor in determining where and under what conditions men may live. In region after region, Indian groups found their means of existence either totally destroyed or materially modified [greatly changed]. Newly introduced diseases swept away or reduced populations. These changes were followed by major shifts in the internal life of tribe and family.

The time came when the Indian people were no longer the masters of their situation. Their life ways survived subject to the will of a dominant sovereign power. This is said, not in a spirit of complaint; we understand that in the lives of all nations of people, there are times of plenty and times of famine. But we do speak out in a plea for understanding.

When we go before the American people, as we do in this Declaration, and ask for material assistance in developing our resources and developing our opportunities, we pose a moral problem which cannot be left unanswered. For the problem we raise affects the standing which our nation sustains before world opinion.

Our situation cannot be relieved by appropriated funds [funds set aside for a specific purpose] alone, though it is equally obvious that without capital investment and funded services, solutions will be delayed. Nor will the passage of time lessen the complexities which beset a people moving toward new meaning and purpose. The answers we seek are not commodities [goods] to be purchased, neither are they evolved automatically through the passing of time. . . .

When Indians speak of the continent they yielded, they are not referring only to the loss of some millions of acres in real estate. They have in mind that the land supported a universe of things they knew, valued, and loved.

With that continent gone, except for a few poor parcels they still retain, the basis of life is precariously held, but they mean to hold the scraps and parcels as earnestly as any small nation or ethnic group was ever determined to hold to identity and survival.

What we ask of America is not charity, not paternalism [treatment as from a father], even when benevolent. We ask only that the nature of our situation be recognized and made the basis of policy and action.

In short, the Indians ask for assistance, technical and financial, for the time needed, however long that may be, to regain in the America of the space age some measure of the adjustment they enjoyed as the original possessors of their native land.

Reverend Martin Luther King, Jr.: Letter from Birmingham Jail (1963)

The struggle of African Americans to secure equal rights was led by a Baptist minister, Martin Luther King, Jr., who urged his followers to resist discrimination with nonviolent direct action. In April 1963 King led a march in Birmingham, Alabama, to protest the city's segregation practices. The police reacted by turning police dogs and fire hoses on the marchers, and King and other leaders were arrested and thrown in jail. While in jail, King received a letter from a group of Alabama clergymen who accused him of being an "outside agitator." He responded to their accusations with this famous letter.

My Dear Fellow Clergymen:

While confined here in the Birmingham city jail, I came across your recent statement calling my present activities "unwise and untimely." Seldom do I pause to answer criticism of my work and ideas. If I sought to answer all the criticisms that cross my desk, my secretaries would have little time for anything other than such correspondence in the course of the day, and I would have no time for constructive work. But since I feel that you are men of genuine good will and that your criticisms are sincerely set forth, I want to try to answer your statement in what I hope will be patient and reasonable terms.

I think I should indicate why I am here in Birmingham, since you have been influenced by the view which argues against "outsiders coming in." I have the honor of serving as president of the Southern Christian Leadership Conference, an organization operating in every southern state, with headquarters in Atlanta, Georgia. We have some eighty-five affiliated organizations across the South, and one of them is the Alabama Christian Movement for Human Rights. Frequently we share staff, educational and financial resources with our affiliates. Several months ago the affiliate here in Birmingham asked us to be on call to engage in a nonviolent direct-action program if such were deemed necessary. We readily consented, and when the hour came we lived up to our promise. So I, along with several members of my staff, am here because I was invited here. I am here because I have organizational ties here.

But more basically, I am in Birmingham because injustice is here. Just as the prophets of the eighth century B.C. left their villages and carried their "thus saith the Lord" far beyond the boundaries of their home towns, and just as the Apostle Paul left his village of Tarsus and carried the gospel of Jesus Christ to the far corners of the Greco-Roman world, so am I compelled to carry the gospel of freedom beyond my own home town. Like Paul, I must constantly respond to the Macedonian call for aid. . . .

One of the basic points in your statement is that the action that I and my associates have taken in Birmingham is untimely. Some have asked: "Why didn't you give the new city administration time to act?" The only answer that I can give this query is that the new Birmingham administration must be prodded about as much as the outgoing one, before it will act. We are sadly mistaken if we feel that the election of Albert Boutwell as mayor will bring the millennium [biblical reference to the 1,000-year period of Christ's reign of peace and justice on earth] to Birmingham. While Mr. Boutwell is a much more gentle person than Mr. Connor, they are both segregationists, dedicated to maintenance of the status quo [the existing state of affairs]. I have hope that Mr. Boutwell will be reasonable enough to see the futility of massive resistance to desegregation. But he will not see this without pressure from devotees of civil rights. My friends, I must say to you that we have not made a single gain in civil rights without determined legal and nonviolent pressure. Lamentably, it is an historical fact that privileged groups seldom give up their privileges voluntarily. Individuals may see the moral light and voluntarily give up their unjust posture; but, as Reinhold Niebuhr [American clergyman and writer] has reminded us, groups tend to be more immoral than individuals.

We know through painful experience that freedom is never voluntarily given by the oppressor; it must be demanded by the oppressed. Frankly, I have yet to engage in a direct-action campaign that was "well timed" in the view of those who have not suffered unduly from the disease of segregation. For years now I have heard the word "Wait!" It rings in the ear of every Negro with piercing familiarity. This "Wait!" has almost always meant "Never." We must come to see, with one of our distinguished jurists, that "justice too long delayed is justice denied."

We have waited for more than 340 years for our constitutional and God-given rights. The nations of Asia and Africa are moving with jetlike speed toward gaining political independence, but we still creep at horse-and-buggy pace toward gaining a cup of coffee at a lunch counter. Perhaps it is easy for those who have never felt the stinging darts of segregation to say, "Wait." But when you have seen vicious mobs lynch your mothers and fathers at will and drown your sisters and brothers at whim; when you have seen hate-filled policemen curse, kick and even kill your black brothers and sisters; when you see the vast majority of your twenty million Negro brothers smothering in an airtight cage of poverty in the midst of an affluent society; when you suddenly find your tongue twisted and your speech stammering as you seek to explain to your six-year-old daughter why she can't go to the public amusement park that has just been advertised on television, and see tears welling up in her eyes when she is told that Funtown is closed to colored children, and see ominous clouds of inferiority beginning to form in her little mental sky, and see her beginning to distort her personality by developing an unconscious bitterness toward white people; when you have to concoct an answer for a five-year-old son who is asking: "Daddy, why do white people treat colored people so mean?"; when you take a cross-country drive and find it necessary to sleep night after night in the uncomfortable corners of your automobile because no motel will accept you; when you are humiliated day in and day out by nagging signs reading "white" and "colored"; when your first name becomes "nigger," your middle name becomes "boy" (however old you are) and your last name becomes "John," and your wife and mother are never given the respected title "Mrs."; when you are harried by day and haunted by night by the fact that you are a Negro, living constantly at tiptoe stance, never quite knowing what to expect next, and are plagued with inner fears and outer resentments; when you are forever fighting a degenerating sense of "nobodiness"—then you will understand why we find it difficult to wait. There comes a time when the cup of endurance runs over, and men are no longer willing to be plunged into the abyss of despair. I hope, sirs, you can understand our legitimate and unavoidable impatience.

You express a great deal of anxiety over our willingness to break laws. This is certainly a legitimate concern. Since we so diligently urge people to obey the Supreme Court's decision of 1954 outlawing segregation in the public schools, at first glance it may seem rather paradoxical [contradictory] for us consciously to break laws. One may well ask: "How can you advocate breaking some laws and obeying others?" The answer lies in the fact that there are two types of laws: just and unjust. I would be the first to advocate obeying just laws. One has not only a legal but a moral responsibility to obey just laws. Conversely, one has a moral responsibility to disobey unjust laws. I would agree with St. Augustine that "an unjust law is no law at all."

Now, what is the difference between the two? How does one determine whether a law is just or unjust? A just law is a man-made code that squares with the moral law or the law of God. An unjust law is a code that is out of harmony with the moral law. To put it in the terms of St. Thomas Aquinas: An unjust law is a human law that is not rooted in eternal law and natural law. Any law that uplifts human personality is just. Any law that degrades human personality is unjust. All segregation statutes are unjust because segregation distorts the soul and damages the personality. It gives the segregator a false sense of superiority and the segregated a false sense of inferiority. Segregation, to use the terminology of the Jewish philosopher Martin Buber, substitutes an "I-it" relationship for an "I-thou" relationship and ends up relegating persons to the status of things. Hence segregation is not only practically, economically and sociologically unsound, it is morally wrong and sinful. Paul Tillich [American clergyman and philosopher] has said that sin is separation. Is not segregation an . . . expression of man's tragic separation, his awful estrangement [distancing from others], his terrible sinfulness? Thus it is that I can urge men to obey the 1954 decision of the Supreme Court, for it is morally right; and I can urge them to disobey segregation ordinances, for they are morally wrong.

Let us consider a more concrete example of just and unjust laws. An unjust law is a code that a numerical or power majority group compels a minority group to obey but does not make binding on itself. This is *difference* made legal. By the same token, a just law is a code that a majority compels a minority to follow and that it is willing to follow itself. This is *sameness* made legal.

Let me give another explanation. A law is unjust if it is inflicted on a minority that, as a result of being denied the right to vote, had no part in enacting or devising the law. Who can say that the legislature of Alabama which set up that state's segregation laws was democratically elected? Throughout Alabama all sorts of devious methods are used to prevent·Negroes from becoming registered voters, and there are some countries in which, even though Negroes constitute a majority of the population, not a single Negro is registered. Can any law enacted under such circumstances be considered democratically structured?

Sometimes a law is just on its face and unjust in its application. For instance, I have been arrested on a charge of parading without a permit. Now, there is nothing wrong in having an ordinance which requires a permit for a parade. But such an ordinance becomes unjust when it is used to maintain segregation and to deny citizens the First-Amendment privilege of peaceful assembly and protest.

I hope you are able to see the distinction I am trying to point out. In no sense do I advocate evading or defying the law, as would the rabid [extreme] segregationist. That would lead to anarchy. One who breaks an unjust law must do so openly, lovingly, and with a willingness to accept the penalty. I submit that an individual who breaks a law that conscience tells him is unjust, and who willingly accepts the penalty of imprisonment in order to arouse the conscience of the community over its injustice, is in reality expressing the highest respect for the law.

Of course, there is nothing new about this kind of civil disobedience. It was evidenced sublimely in the refusal of Shadrach, Meschach and Abednego [three young Israelites who faced a fiery death rather than worship the gods of Babylon] to obey the laws of Nebuchadnezzar [the Babylonian king], on the ground that a higher moral law was at stake. It was practiced superbly by the early Christians, who were willing to face hungry lions and the excruciating pain of chopping blocks rather than submit to certain unjust laws of the Roman Empire. To a degree, academic freedom is a reality today because Socrates practiced civil disobedience. In our own nation, the Boston Tea Party represented a massive act of civil disobedience.

We should never forget that everything Adolf Hitler did in Germany was "legal" and everything the Hungarian freedom fighers did in Hungary was "illegal." It was "illegal" to aid and comfort a Jew in Hitler's Germany. Even so, I am sure that, had I lived in Germany at the time, I would have aided and comforted my Jewish brothers. If today, I lived in a Communist country where certain principles dear to the Christian faith are suppressed, I would openly advocate disobeying that country's antireligious laws.

FROM The Civil Rights Acts (1964–1968)

The Supreme Court's decision in *Brown v. the Board of Education of Topeka* in 1954 focused public attention on the problem of racial segregation. Protest by blacks and the violent reactions of whites pointed to the need for legislation in support of the principles set forth in the Fourteenth and Fifteenth Amendments. Beginning with the Civil Rights Act of 1957, Congress passed a steady stream of laws that clarified the meaning of equal rights.

Civil Rights Act of 1964

No person acting under order of law shall—in determining whether any individual is qualified under State law or laws to vote in any Federal election, apply any standard, practice, or procedure different from the standards, practices, or procedures applied under such law or laws to other individuals within the same county, parish, or similar political subdivision who have been found by State officials to be qualified to vote. . . .

All persons shall be entitled to the full and equal enjoyment of the goods, services, facilities, privileges, advantages, and accommodations of any place of public accommodation, as defined in this section, without discrimination or segregation on the ground of race, color, religion, or national origin. . . .

Whenever the Attorney General receives a complaint in writing [about discrimination in public education] . . . and the Attorney General believes the complaint is meritorious and certifies that the signer or signers of such complaint are unable, in his judgment, to initiate and maintain appropriate legal proceedings for relief and that the institution of an action will materially further the orderly achievement of desegregation in public education, the Attorney General is authorized, after giving notice of such complaint to the appropriate school board or college authority and after certifying that he is satisfied that such board or authority has had a reasonable time to adjust the conditions alleged in such complaint, to institute for or in the name of the United States a civil action in any appropriate district court of the United States against such parties and for such relief as may be appropriate. . . .

It shall be an unlawful employment practice for an employer—

to fail or refuse to hire or to discharge any individual, or otherwise to discriminate against any individual with respect to his compensation, terms, conditions, or privileges of employment, because of such individual's race, color, religion, sex, or national origin; or

to limit, segregate, or classify his employees in any way . . . because of such individual's race, color, religion, sex, or national origin. . . .

Voting Rights Act of 1965

To assure that the right of citizens of the United States to vote is not denied or abridged on account of race or color, no citizen shall be denied the right to vote in any Federal, State, or local election because of his failure to comply with any test or device in any State. . . .

The phrase "test or device" shall mean any requirement that a person as a prerequisite [condition in advance] for voting or registration for voting (1) demonstrate the ability to read, write, understand, or interpret any matter, (2) demonstrate any educational achievement of his knowledge of any particular subject, (3) possess good moral character, or (4) prove his qualifications by the voucher of registered voters or members of any other class. . . .

Documents in American History 713

No person who demonstrates that he has successfully completed the sixth primary grade in a public school in, or a private school accredited by, any State or territory, the District of Columbia, or the Commonwealth of Puerto Rico in which the predominant classroom language was other than English, shall be denied the right to vote in any Federal, State, or local election because of his inability to read, write, understand, or interpret any matter in the English language, except that in States in which State law provides that a different level of education is presumptive of literacy, he shall demonstrate that he has successfully completed an equivalent level of education. . . .

Whoever shall deprive or attempt to deprive any person of any right . . . shall be fined not more than $5,000, or imprisoned not more than five years, or both.

Fair Housing Act of 1968
It is the policy of the United States to provide, within constitutional limitations, for fair housing throughout the United States. . . .

It shall be unlawful—

To refuse to sell or rent after the making of a bona fide offer, or to refuse to negotiate for the sale or rental of, or otherwise make unavailable or deny, a dwelling to any person because of race, color, religion, or national origin.

To discriminate against any person in the terms, conditions, or privileges of sale or rental of a dwelling, or in the provision of services or facilities in connection therewith, because of race, color, religion, or national origin.

To make, print, or publish, or cause to be made, printed, or published any notice, statement, or advertisement, with respect to the sale or rental of a dwelling that indicates any preference, limitation, or discrimination based on race, color, religion, or national origin, or an intention to make any such preference, limitation, or discrimination.

To represent to any person because of race, color, religion, or national origin that any dwelling is not available for inspection, sale, or rental when such dwelling is in fact so available. . . .

Whenever the Attorney General has reasonable cause to believe that any person or group of persons is engaged in a pattern or practice of resistance to the full enjoyment of any of the rights granted by this title, or that any group of persons has been denied any of the rights granted by this title and such denial raises an issue of general public importance, he may bring a civil action in any appropriate United States district court. . . .

Equal Rights Amendment (1977)

The Equal Rights Amendment (ERA) drafted by Congress in 1972 outlawed discrimination "on account of sex." Many Americans supported the ERA, but others, women as well as men, did not. Opponents argued that the amendment was unnecessary and that by wiping out laws designed to protect women it would do more harm than good. They also claimed that the ERA would result in women being drafted into the armed forces in time of war. Nevertheless, by November 1977, 35 states had ratified the ERA. But 38 were needed, and that total was not achieved, even after Congress extended the deadline for ratification.

Section 1. Equality of rights under the law shall not be denied or abridged by the United States or by any State on account of sex.

Section 2. The Congress shall have the power to enforce, by appropriate legislation, the provisions of this article.

Section 3. This amendment shall take effect two years after the date of ratification.

FROM Ronald Reagan's State of the Union Address (1984)

In 1984, in his State of the Union message to Congress, President Ronald Reagan declared that America was now "standing tall." Under his leadership, he claimed, the nation's mood had become one of confidence and pride. Following are excerpts from Reagan's speech.

There is a renewed energy and optimism throughout the land. America is back—standing tall, looking to the '80's with courage, confidence, and hope. . . .

As we came to the decade of the '80's, we faced the worst crisis in our postwar history. The 70's were years of rising problems and falling confidence. There was a feeling government had grown beyond the consent of the governed. Families felt helpless in the face of mounting inflation and the indignity of taxes that reduced reward for hard work, thrift, and risk-taking. All this was overlaid by an every-growing web of rules and regulations.

On the international scene, we had an uncomfortable feeling that we had lost the respect of friend and foe. Some questioned whether we had the will to defend peace and freedom.

But America is too great for small dreams. There was a hunger in the land for a spiritual revival; if you will, a crusade for renewal. The American people said: Let us look to the future with confidence, both at home and abroad. Let us give freedom a chance.

But we know many of our fellow countrymen are still out of work, wondering what will come of their hopes and dreams. Can we love America and not reach out to tell them: You are not forgotten; we will not rest until each of you can reach as high as your God-given talents will take you.

The heart of America is strong, it's good, and true. The cynics were wrong—America never was a sick society. We're seeing rededication to bedrock values of faith, family, work, neighborhood, peace, and freedom—values that help bring us together as one people, from the youngest child to the most senior citizen. . . .

People everywhere hunger for peace and a better life. The tide of the future is a freedom tide, and our struggle for democracy cannot and will not be denied. This nation champions peace that enshrines liberty, democratic rights, and dignity for every individual. America's new strength, confidence, and purpose are carrying hope and opportunity far from our shores. A world economic recovery is under way. It began here. . . .

After all our struggles to restore America, to revive confidence in our country, hope for our future; after all our hard-won victories earned through the patience and courage of every citizen—we cannot, must not and will not turn back, we will finish our job. How could we do less? We are Americans. . . .

I've never felt more strongly that America's best days, and democracy's best days, lie ahead. We are a powerful force for good. With faith and courage, we can perform great deeds and take freedom's next step. And we will. We will carry on the traditions of a good and worthy people who have brought light where there was darkness, warmth where there was cold, medicine where there was disease, food where there was hunger, and peace where there was bloodshed.

Let us be sure that those who come after will say . . . that in our time we did everything that could be done: We finished the race, we kept them free, we kept the faith.

Glossary

This glossary contains the words you need to understand as you study American history. After each word there is a brief definition or explanation of the meaning of the word as it is used in *The Story of America*. The page number refers to the page on which the word first appears in the textbook.

Phonetic Respelling and Pronunciation Guide

Many of the key terms in this textbook have been respelled to help you pronounce them. The following Phonetic Respelling and Pronunciation Guide offers the simplest form of usage, and for this Glossary is adapted from *Webster's Ninth New Collegiate Dictionary, Webster's New Geographical Dictionary,* and *Webster's New Biographical Dictionary.* The letter combinations used in the respellings are explained below.

MARK	AS IN	RESPELLING	EXAMPLE
a	alphabet	a	*AL·fuh·bet
ā	Asia	ay	AY·zhuh
ä	cart, top	ah	KAHRT, TAHP
e	let, ten	e	LET, TEN
ē	even, leaf	ee	EE· vuhn, LEEF
i	it, tip, British	i	IT, TIP, BRIT·ish
ī	site, buy, Ohio	y	SYT, BY, oh·HY·oh
	iris	eye	EYE ·ris
k	card	k	KARD
ō	over, rainbow	oh	oh·vuhr, RAYN·boh
ů	book, wood	ooh	BOOHK, WOOHD
ò	all, orchid	aw	AWL, AWR·kid
òi	foil, coin	oy	FOYL, KOYN
aů	out	ow	OWT
ə	cup, butter	uh	KUHP, BUHT·uhr
ü	rule, food	oo	ROOL, FOOD
yü	few	yoo	FYOO
zh	vision	zh	VIZH·uhn

*A syllable printed in small capital letters receives heavier emphasis than the other syllable(s) in a word.

A

ABC Powers Argentina, Brazil, and Chile. **280**

Abilene, (AB·uh·leen) Kansas meeting place for western cattle ranchers and eastern buyers. **103**

abolitionist (ab·uh·LISH·uh·nist) Person who wanted to end slavery. **35**

absolute location Part of geographic theme of location, exactly where on earth a place is. **xxv**

absolute monarch Ruler who has complete control. **202**

accommodation Going along with the desires of others. **79**

ace Pilot in the Great War who shot down five or more enemy airplanes. **300**

acid rain Rain containing a high concentration of pollutants. **569**

affirmative action Government programs to encourage the hiring of women and minorities. **563**

Affluent (AF·loo·unt) **Society** Economist John Kenneth Galbraith's term to describe the wealthy U.S. after World War II. **494**

AFL-CIO Organization of labor unions formed when the American Federation of Labor and the Congress of Industrial Organizations merged in 1955. **496**

Age of Realism Literary and artistic movement characterized by works that portrayed life and people as they really were. **166**

Agricultural Adjustment Act (AAA) New Deal legislation passed in 1933 that aided farmers by paying them subsidies for land taken out of production, thus reducing crop surpluses and helping to raise prices for farm goods. **367**

air pollution Exhaust fumes and other pollutants that harm the earth's atmosphere. **343**

Alaskan Purchase Land deal by which the United States acquired Alaska from Russia for $7.2 million in 1867. **200**

Alien and Sedition (si·DISH·uhn) **Acts** Four 1798 laws aimed at foreigners and others in the U.S. who were supposedly undermining the government by helping France. **20**

alliance Agreement made among countries to support each other, especially in times of attack. **277**

Alliance for Progress President Kennedy's program to provide economic assistance for Latin American countries. **479**

Allies (AL·yz) Countries that fought together in World War I, including the U.S., Great Britain, Italy, and Russia; and those that fought together in World War II, including the U.S., Great Britain, France, and the Soviet Union. **277**

ambush Trap or surprise attack. **91**

amendment Change or addition to a bill or law such as to the Constitution. **19**

American Civil Liberties Union Organization created to protect and defend civil rights, especially of the disadvantaged. **198**

American expansionism Idea that all of North and South America and the Pacific islands should be under the control of the U.S. **198**

American Expeditionary (ek·spuh·DISH·uh·ner·ee) **Force** U.S. military forces that fought in Europe during the Great War. **293**

American Federation of Labor (AFL) National union of skilled workers founded in 1886. **141**

American Indian Movement (AIM) Organization founded in 1970 to work for fairer treatment of Native Americans. **515**

amnesty (AM·nuhs·tee) Official pardon for crimes committed against the government. **55**

Amnesty Act of 1872 Law that reversed the decision to bar former Confederate officials and soldiers from holding public office. **73**

anarchist (AN·uhr·kuhst) One who opposes all government. **227**

antibiotics Substances used to kill germs. **497**

anti-imperialist Person opposed to owning colonies. **222**

antitrust movement Organized effort to regulate business practices that restrained free trade. **136**

antiwar movement Campaign in the United States to end war, particularly the Vietnam War. **537**

Apache (uh·PAHCH·ee) Plains Indian group that lived in Texas and New Mexico. **83**

apartheid (uh·PAR·teyt) South African policy of separation of the races. **622**

Arab Oil Crisis Shortage of petroleum products in the United States in 1973 created by an Arab-controlled OPEC ban on the shipment of oil to countries that supported Israel. **544**

Arapaho (uh·RAP·uh·ho) Indian group that occupied the central region of the Great Plains. **83**

arbitration (ahr·buh·TRAY·shun) Hearing on and settlement of a dispute between two parties by a neutral third party. **205**

arbitration treaties Agreements between nations to try and settle differences and avoid war. **278**

archipelago (ahr·kuh·PEL·uh·go) Group of islands. **201**

armistice Truce, or agreement to stop fighting. **304**

Army-McCarthy Hearings Senator Joseph McCarthy's investigation of subversive activities in the army. **465**

Articles of Confederation Agreement in 1781 under which the 13 original colonies established an organization of states. **17**

article of impeachment Charge of wrongdoing against the president or other government official. **548**

assassination (uh·sas·uhn·AY·shuhn) Killing a public figure. **54**

assay Test or analyze for content. **99**

assembly Lawmaking body elected by the people. **9**

Atlanta Compromise Proposal by Booker T. Washington that blacks and whites both honor the separate-but-equal principle. **79**

Atlantic Charter Agreement between Great Britain and the U.S. to work for a world free of war, signed by Roosevelt and Churchill on August 14, 1941. **408**

atomic bomb Powerful explosive used by the United States to destroy two Japanese cities, ending World War II. **433**

Glossary 717

B

baby boom Tremendous increase in the U.S. birthrate from 1946 through the 1960s. **504**

balance of power Equal military and economic strength among nations. **277**

Bank Holiday Order by Franklin Roosevelt closing all banks for several days in 1933 while a program to protect the savings of the public was developed. **366**

barrio Neglected area of a city occupied by poor Hispanics. **560**

Bastogne (ba·STOHN) French town where Allied forces held back a German advance during World War II. **424**

Battle of the Argonne Forest World War I battle in 1918 in which American forces drove back German troops. **304**

Battle of the Atlantic Naval war waged between German submarines and the British navy and air force from 1941 to 1943. **407**

Battle of Britain Germany's attempt to break Britain's spirit and destroy its air force by massive bombings in 1940. **406**

Battle of the Bulge Major German counterattack in 1944 that created a bulge in the Allied line of advance in Europe during World War II. **424**

Battle of the Coral Sea World War II naval contest in 1942 in which heavy damage to the Japanese fleet stopped Japan's planned invasion of Australia. **426**

Battle of Kasserine (kas·uh·REEN) **Pass** World War II tank warfare in 1943 between Americans and Germans in North Africa. **421**

Battle of Leyte (LAYT·ee) **Gulf** World War II fight in 1944 in the Pacific in which the U.S. navy defeated the Japanese. **429**

Battle of the Little Big Horn Fight in 1876 between U.S. Cavalry led by Custer and Sioux warriors led by Crazy Horse in which Custer and his men were all killed. **92**

Battle of the Marne Great War conflict in 1914 in which French and British troops stopped German advance toward Paris. **282**

Battle of Midway Naval defeat of the Japanese in 1942 that gave the U.S. control of the central Pacific during World War II. **426**

Bay of Pigs Site in Cuba of a failed invasion in 1961 by exiles trained by the U.S. **478**

Berlin Capital of Germany that was divided into East and West Berlin after World War II. **425**

Berlin Airlift Rescue mission during the Cold War in which the U.S. flew supplies to West Berlin after the Soviets blocked roads. **451**

Berlin Wall Barrier built in 1961 to close off communist-controlled East Berlin from West Berlin. **479**

Bessemer (BES·uh·muhr) **converter** Invention by Henry Bessemer that made the mass production of steel possible. **121**

Bicentennial Nationwide celebration in 1976 of the 200th anniversary of the signing of the Declaration of Independence. **554**

Big Four Leaders of the Versailles Peace Conference after the Great War: British prime minister Lloyd George, French premier Clemenceau, Italian prime minister Orlando, and President Wilson. **308**

Big Red Scare Widespread fear of communism that swept the United States after World War I. **321**

big stick diplomacy In early 1900s, the threat of force in foreign relations, especially to enforce the Roosevelt Corollary; also called gunboat diplomacy. **237**

Big Three During World War II: British prime minister Churchill, U.S. president Roosevelt, and Soviet dictator Stalin. **442**

Bill of Rights Name given to the first ten amendments to the Constitution. **19**

Birmingham Alabama site of 1963 protest led by Reverend Martin Luther King, Jr., in which local police used dogs and fire hoses against demonstrators. **517**

Black Cabinet African American advisers during Franklin D. Roosevelt's New Deal. **383**

Black Codes Regulations passed by southern governments after Reconstruction to restrict the rights of African Americans. **56**

"black gold" Another name for oil. **124**

Black Muslim Member of the anti-white Nation of Islam religious sect. **521**

Black Panther party Organization of black militants begun in the 1960s. **521**

"Black Republican" Name given to the post-Civil War governments in the South. **65**

Black Tuesday Day the stock market crashed, October 29, 1929. **351**

blacklist List of workers in unions who were denied employment. **142**

Bland-Allison Act Law passed in 1878 that authorized the purchase and coinage of from $2 million to $4 million worth of silver each month. **179**

blue-collar worker Generally an industrial worker or one whose job involves manual labor. **498**

board of directors Group that makes the decisions for a corporation. **121**

Boland Amendment Law passed in 1984 that prohibited U.S. aid to foreign revolutionary groups. **580**

bonanza (buh·NAN·zuh) Rich deposit of ore. **99**

Bonus March March of Great War veterans on Washington in July 1932 to protest the government's decision to not pay in cash their compensation for their low pay as soldiers in the war. **361**

boom town Community that grows quickly, such as at a rich mining strike. **101**

boot hill Cemetery for cowboys who "died with their boots on." **107**

bootlegger Person who produces, sells, or transports liquor illegally, especially during Prohibition. **326**

border state State that held slaves but did not leave the Union during the Civil War. **44**

boss Leader of a city political machine. **159**

Boxer Rebellion Uprising in 1900 in China during which foreign property was destroyed and foreign missionaries and business people were held captive. **229**

boycott (BOY·kaht) Refusal to buy certain goods as a protest. **10**

Bozeman Trail Route across the Great Plains marked by John M. Bozeman. **90**

bracero (brah·SER·oh) Mexican farm laborer allowed to enter the United States temporarily. **418**

Brain Trust Advisers of Franklin Roosevelt who were mostly college professors. **373**

brand Mark burned on an animal's hide with a hot iron to show ownership. **105**

Brandeis (BRAN·dys) **brief** Argument by Louis D. Brandeis before the Supreme Court that long work hours injured the health of women and children; research for the brief was done by Florence Kelley and Josephine Goldmark. **255**

bread-and-butter issue Concern of labor such as higher wages, shorter hours, and better working conditions. **141**

breadbasket of America Name for the wheat-growing region of the Great Plains. **113**

breadline People waiting to be given free food during the Great Depression. **357**

brinksmanship Policy under President Eisenhower promoted by Secretary of State Dulles to risk all-out war to contain communism. **463**

Brooklyn Bridge Span between Brooklyn and Manhattan in New York City that, at the time of its completion in 1883, was the longest bridge in the world. **153**

Brown v. Board of Education of Topeka Landmark 1954 Supreme Court decision that schools must be integrated, overturning ''separate but equal'' ruling of *Plessy v. Ferguson.* **469**

buffalo soldier Nickname given to black soldiers by Indians during the late nineteenth century. **79**

Bull Moose party Nickname for the Progressive party when Theodore Roosevelt ran for president in 1912. **260**

business cycle Economic trends that move through periods of prosperity and recession. **355**

C

cable car Trolley car pulled up a steep hill by a moving cable. **152**

Cambodia (kam·BOH·dee·uh) Country bordering Vietnam where American troops were sent in 1970, causing widespread protest in the U.S; also called Kampuchea (kam·poo·CHEE·uh). **538**

Camelot (CAM·uh·laht) Legendary site of King Arthur's court, which was noted for its faith in human goodness; often applied to the years of the Kennedy administration. **481**

Camp David Accords Peace agreement between Israel's Premier Begin and Egypt's President Sadat initiated by President Carter in 1978. **573**

Canal Zone Strip of land leased to the U.S. by Panama that extends five miles on each side of the Panama Canal. **231**

capitalism Economic system in which individuals own and control the factors of production and in which government intervention is limited. **444**

Caribbean Basin Initiative U.S. program begun in 1982 to help Caribbean economies by promoting private enterprise and investment in the region. **618**

Carpetbagger Northerner who went to the South after the Civil War to profit financially from confused and unsettled conditions. **65**

cartographer Mapmaker. **635**

cash-and-carry policy Plan that allowed the United States to sell weapons to warring nations that paid cash and transported the goods in foreign ships. **403**

cattle baron Wealthy and powerful cattle rancher. **104**

cattle kingdom Grasslands that stretched from Texas to Canada and from the Rockies to eastern Kansas used to graze hundreds of thousands of cattle. **103**

cattle town Western town where cattle were bought and sold. **103**

Central American Common Market Agreement among several Central American countries reached in the 1970s to lower tariffs and promote other forms of economic cooperation. **613**

Central Intelligence Agency (CIA) U.S. government agency created in 1947 to gather and analyze political, economic, and military information about countries. **478**

Central Powers Alliance of Germany, Austria, and later Hungary, Turkey, and Bulgaria during the Great War. **277**

chain store Store with a number of outlets in different areas. **129**

Château-Thierry (sha·TOH ty·ree) French town where American and French forces stopped the German advance in 1918 in the Great War. **300**

checks and balances System of government in which each branch of government has power to limit the other branches so that no branch will become too powerful. **18**

Chernobyl (chuhr·NOH·buhl) Soviet nuclear power plant that exploded in 1986 and released massive amounts of radiation over a widespread area. **570**

Cheyenne (shy·AN) Indian group of the central Great Plains. **83**

Chicago Illinois city that is a major railway and meat-packing center. **103**

Chilean Crisis Tension in 1891-92 between Chile and the U.S. started by a fight in Valparaiso between U.S. sailors and Chileans. **204**

Chinese Exclusion Act Law passed in 1882 that barred Chinese laborers from entering the United States for 10 years. **149**

Chisholm Trail One main route over which Texans drove cattle to market. **103**

Chivington Massacre Slaughter of

Glossary 719

Cheyenne that provoked Indian attacks on settlers; also called the Sand Creek Massacre. **90**

citizenship Legal membership in a country or state; a citizen is granted rights by the country or state and in return has certain duties and obligations, such as obeying the law. **573**

Civil Rights Act of 1866 Law that made African Americans citizens of the United States. **57**

Civil Rights Act of 1875 Law that prohibited segregation of public places. **76**

Civil Rights Act of 1964 Law that made it easier and safer for blacks in the South to vote and that prohibited racial discrimination in public facilities. **491**

Civil Rights Cases Lawsuits concerning the constitutional rights of black Americans. **76**

Civil Rights Committee Group appointed by Truman in 1947 to recommend laws to protect the rights of African Americans. **455**

Civil Rights Movement Campaign in the 1960s to achieve equality for black Americans. **474**

Civil Service Commission Agency established in 1883 to design and administer examinations for certain government positions. **165**

civil service reform Effort to improve government service by adopting an employment system based on skill and merit rather than on political connections. **164**

Civil War Amendments Three constitutional amendments (13th, 14th, and 15th) guaranteeing civil rights to African Americans. **62**

Civil Works Authority New Deal agency created in 1933 to help the unemployed find jobs. **372**

Civilian Conservation Corps (CCC) New Deal agency that put some 3 million young men to work on conservation and rural improvement projects. **372**

Clayton Antitrust Act Law passed in 1914 that prohibited a person from serving as a director in more than one corporation and which exempted labor unions from anti-

trust laws. **264**

Clayton-Bulwer Treaty Agreement in 1850 between Great Britain and the U.S. that neither would take exclusive control of a canal between the Atlantic and Pacific. **230**

close state State neither strongly Republican nor strongly Democratic where either party might win in a national election. **158**

closed shop Business that hires only members of a labor union. **447**

Cold War Tensions between the U.S. and Soviet Union after World War II. **444**

collective bargaining Right of a labor union to bargain for all workers employed by a business. **142**

collective security World security guaranteed by an agreement among all nations to join in action against a nation that attacks any one of them. **401**

Comanche (kuh·MAN·chee) Plains Indians of Texas and New Mexico. **83**

Commodity Credit Corporation Organization created in 1938 that paid farmers money for surplus crops kept in storage, resulting in higher prices because there were fewer crops on the market. **386**

communications revolution More rapid, long-distance communication made possible by the telegraph and telephone. **125**

communism Economic system in which the government owns or controls almost all the means of production. **444**

Communist Revolution Rebellion in 1917 in Russia in which the Communist party took control. **298**

compass rose Type of directional indicator found on some maps. **634**

Compromise of 1877 Concessions made to settle the disputed election of 1876 by which Rutherford Hayes became president. **74**

computer Electronic machine that can store, retrieve, and process information rapidly. **501**

Comstock (KAHM·stahk) **Lode** Extremely rich silver deposit in Nevada. **99**

concentration System of separating and thereby controlling the Indian groups of the Great Plains by placing them on reservations. **86**

concentration camp Nazi prison where prisoners of war, especially the Jews, were held. **398**

Congress of Industrial Organizations (CIO) National labor union formed in 1935 to organize all the workers in mass-production industries. **387**

conscientious objector One who refuses to serve in the military because of moral or religious beliefs. **399**

consciousness-raising Increasing awareness, usually about a social or political issue. **514**

conservation Protection or preservation of natural resources from waste or loss. **xxv**

constitution Written plan of government that includes its laws and principles. **17**

Contadora Group Latin American nations that came out against President Reagan's Latin America policy in 1982. **618**

containment policy U.S. strategy in the 1950s aimed at limiting the spread of communism. **453**

continent One of seven large landmasses on the earth. **xxi**

Contras (KAWN·truhs) Nicaraguan fighters who received aid from the U.S. in their effort to overthrow the Sandinista government. **580**

convoy Fleet of ships accompanied or escorted by a protective force. **409**

"cooling-off" period Time that a union can be forced to delay a strike if that strike threatens the national interest. **447**

co-op (KOH·ahp) Group formed through the Farmers' Alliance in order to sell crops and to purchase goods at better prices for members. **180**

corporation Business owned by stockholders and run by a board of directors. **121**

Coxey's Army Band of unemployed workers who, led by Jacob Coxey, marched on Washington in

1894 to protest the plight of the unemployed. **184**

Crime of 1873 Name given by farmers and miners to the law that discontinued the minting of silver. **178**

crop-lien (KRAWP·leen) **system** Agreement in which supplies were lent to a farmer by merchants or landowners in exchange for portions of the crops. **70**

Cross of Gold speech William Jennings Bryan's stirring appeal for the free coinage of silver that got him the presidential nomination of both the Democratic party and the Populist party in 1896. **188**

Cuba Caribbean island with a communist government, about 90 miles south of Florida. **478**

Cuban Missile Crisis Tense confrontation in 1962 between the U.S. and the Soviet Union over the building of Soviet missile bases in Cuba. **480**

D

D-Day Beginning of the Allied invasion of France on June 6, 1944, to drive out Hitler's occupying army. **422**

Dawes Severalty (SEV·uh·ruhl·tee) **Act** Law passed in 1887 that divided reservations into quarter sections of land owned by individual Indian families. **98**

deficit (DEF·uh·suht) **spending** Paying out more public funds than are raised in taxes. **386**

deflation (de·FLAY·shun) Decline in prices caused by a decrease in money supply or spending. **163**

demand Amount of a product or service that the public is ready and able to buy. **355**

democracy Form of government in which power is vested in the people and exercised by them through free elections. **17**

department store Large store selling a variety of goods arranged in different sections. **129**

depression Stage of the economic cycle characterized by low economic activity and rising unemployment. **355**

détente (day·TAHNT) Reduction of tensions between two countries, particularly the United States and the Soviet Union. **540**

developing nation Poor country. **611**

development Suburban neighborhood in which a number of similar houses have been built; also describes economic progress. **506**

dictator (DIK·tayt·uhr) Ruler with absolute power. **397**

direct primary Preliminary election within a political party to choose candidates to run for public office. **251**

directional indicator Part of a map, such as a compass rose, that helps you determine directions. **634**

disarmament (dis·AHRM·uh·ment) Reduction or limitation in the number of weapons of war. **319**

division of labor Separation of the manufacturing steps into specialized tasks to speed and increase production. **123**

Dodge City Kansas cattle town famous as a rowdy entertainment center for cowboys. **107**

dogfight Air battle between fighter airplanes during World War I. **300**

dollar diplomacy U.S. policy in the early 1900s of investing money in Latin American countries in hopes that more stable governments would result. **237**

domino theory Idea that if a country fell to communism, the countries on its borders would also fall; key principle of U.S. foreign policy from the 1950s to the 1970s. **525**

dove Person opposed to war. **528**

"Drake's Folly" Nickname for the first oil well, drilled by E. L. Drake of Titusville, Pennsylvania in 1859. **124**

Dred Scott v. Sandford Supreme Court ruling in 1857 that Scott, a former slave who sued for his freedom, was still a slave despite living in a free state for a time. **42**

dropout Student who leaves school before graduating. **568**

drought Long period of dry weather that stunts crop growth. **111**

dry farming Technique used to raise crops in areas with little rainfall. **111**

dry states States that adopted prohibition. **326**

Dunkirk French town where German troops forced a major evacuation of Allied forces during World War II. **404**

duty Tariff or tax placed on foreign goods brought into a country. **10**

E

East Germany Country under communist control created when Germany was divided between Allied powers after World War II; reunited with West Germany in 1990; also called the German Democratic Republic. **465**

Eastern Front Combat zone in eastern Europe during the Great War. **282**

ecology Interrelationships of organisms and their environments. **xxv**

Economic Opportunity Act Law passed in 1964 that attacked poverty in the U.S. through programs such as Head Start, the Job Corps, and VISTA. **491**

Eighteenth Amendment Constitutional change in 1919 that prohibited the manufacture and sale of alcoholic beverages. **326**

El Caney (el·kuh·NAY) Site of major 1898 battle in Cuba during the Spanish-American War. **216**

electric light Invention by Edison that makes light by passing electricity through a fine wire housed in a bulb. **127**

electric trolley System of streetcars propelled along tracks by electric currents from overhead wires. **152**

Elementary and Secondary Education Act Law passed in 1965 that provided federal money to support school programs in low-income areas. **508**

elevation Height above sea level. **638**

Elk Hills Government-owned oil reserve in California. **344**

emancipation (i·man·suh·PAY·shun) Freedom. **17**

Emergency Quota Act Law passed in 1921 limiting by nationality the number of immigrants to the United States. **325**

entrepreneur (ahn·truh·pruh·NUHR) Person who develops a business. **130**

environment (in·VY·ruhn·muhnt) Everything in people's surroundings that affects them in any way; nature. **xxi**

Environmental Protection Agency (EPA) Department established in 1970 to monitor pollution and seek ways to reduce it. **570**

Equal Rights Amendment Failed constitutional amendment proposed in 1972 to guarantee equal rights for women. **565**

erosion Wearing down. **638**

escalation Increase in military involvement. **526**

Espionage Act Law passed in 1917 that made it a crime to help enemy countries or to interfere with military recruitment. **297**

ethnic neighborhood City community made up of immigrants from the same country. **145**

ever-normal granary System of storing grain in government granaries, rather than selling it, to help regulate prices and keep surpluses off the market. **386**

executive Person or branch of government responsible for enforcing or carrying out the laws. **17**

executive privilege Right to keep information about presidential matters secret. **547**

expatriate Person who leaves his or her native country permanently. **337**

expeditionary force Name given to American troops sent to foreign countries. **214**

F

factors of production Resources such as land and factories used to produce goods and services. **495**

Fair Deal President Harry Truman's proposals to extend New Deal programs. **446**

Fair Employment Practice Committee Commission created in 1941 to prevent job discrimination against racial and ethnic groups and women. **418**

Fair Labor Standards Act 1938 law that outlawed child labor and set a 40-hour work week. **387**

Farm Bloc Group of U.S. representatives from agricultural states who organized in 1921 to support the interests of farmers. **348**

Farmers Alliance Social organization that became a political force to represent farm interests. **180**

fascism (FASH·iz·uhm) Political movement that stresses nation and race, begun in Italy in the 1920s under Mussolini. **397**

federal deficit Shortage in federal income. **389**

Federal Deposit Insurance Corporation (FDIC) Federal agency created to protect savings deposits in banks. **366**

Federal Emergency Relief Administration Department created in 1933 to distribute money to agencies that helped the poor. **372**

Federal Highway Act Law passed in 1956 that provided federal funding for construction of interstate highways. **469**

Federal Republic of Germany Country formed by combining the zones of Germany controlled by Britain, France, and the U.S. after World War II; also called West Germany; reunited with East Germany in 1990. **451**

Federal Reserve Act Law passed in 1913 that created a national banking system of 12 Federal Reserve Banks. **264**

Federal Reserve Board Government agency that oversees the Federal Reserve system. **264**

Federal Securities Act Law passed in 1933 that regulated the way companies issue and sell stock. **369**

Federal Trade Commission Agency created in 1914 to help eliminate unfair business practices and to enforce antitrust laws. **264**

federalism Sharing of power by the national and state governments. **18**

Fifteenth Amendment Constitutional amendment that guarantees all citizens the right to vote. **62**

Fifty-Niner Nickname given to a prospector who went to Colorado in 1859 in search of gold. **90**

Final Solution Nazi term for program to eliminate the Jews and other "undesirables." **436**

fireside chat Informal presidential speech given by Franklin Roosevelt in the 1930s. **373**

fiscal (FIS·kuhl) **policy** Means of stimulating the economy through government spending and taxation. **503**

five themes of geography Basic concepts—location, place, relationships within places, movement, and region—considered by many geographers as key to the understanding of geography. **xxv**

Five-Power Naval Treaty Agreement in 1921 between the U.S., Great Britain, Japan, France, and Italy to a 10-year ban on the construction of warships. **319**

fixed cost Regular expense involved in running a business. **133**

flappers Young women whose bold actions and dress expressed a new spirit of freedom in the 1920s. **331**

Four Freedoms Freedom of speech and religion, freedom from want and fear, mentioned in 1941 Franklin Roosevelt speech. **407**

Fourteen Points Peace program outlined by President Wilson in 1918. **305**

Fourteenth Amendment Constitutional amendment that made blacks citizens of their states as well as of the U.S., guaranteed their civil rights, and gave them equal protection of the laws. **59**

franchise (FRAN·chyz) Right to do business granted by the government. **159**

free coinage Act of turning all available silver into coins. **180**

free enterprise Economic system in which there is limited government control over business. **137**

free soiler Person opposed to the

spread of slavery. **42**

Freedman's Bureau Organization run by the army to care for and protect southern blacks after the Civil War. **57**

freedmen Former slaves. **56**

frontier Edge of a settled region. **7**

Fugitive Slave Act 1850 law that made it a crime to assist escaping slaves and required northerners to help recapture them. **41**

fundamentalism Conservative religious beliefs. **328**

G

genocide Deliberate and planned destruction of a racial or cultural group. **437**

Gentlemen's Agreement Deal in 1907 in which Japan promised not to allow laborers to come to the United States. **265**

geography Study of the physical and cultural features of the earth. **xxi**

ghetto Section of a city where members of racial or ethnic groups live because of economic or social pressures. **322**

G.I. Bill of Rights Program established in 1944 which enabled veterans to obtain low-cost loans. **415**

Gilded Age Period between 1865 and 1900 that was marked by growth in industry and the availability of consumer goods but also by business corruption, greed, and materialism. **143**

glasnost (GLAS·nohst) Spirit of openness in the Soviet Union begun under Gorbachev. **582**

gold standard Monetary system that used only gold to mint coins and to back bank notes. **183**

Golden Age of Sports Period during the 1920s when radio, increased leisure time and money, and public relations efforts caused spectator sports to become very popular. **332**

Golden Rule Biblical principle of conduct that states: "Do unto others as you would have them

do unto you," followed by reform mayor Samuel M. Jones. **249**

Good Neighbor policy Shift in U.S. policy toward Latin America stated by President Franklin Roosevelt to treat those countries with mutual understanding and sympathetic appreciation of their points of view. **601**

grandfather clause Law that eliminated literacy tests and poll taxes for persons who had voted before 1867 and their descendants, meaning that only white men qualified to vote. **75**

"Great American Desert" Nickname given to the Great Plains by early explorers. **83**

Great Awakening Period in the 1700s of widespread religious fervor, a force for toleration in the colonies. **7**

Great Depression Economic crisis from 1929 to 1940. **355**

Great Plains Geographic region that extends from western Texas north to the Dakotas and into Canada and west to the foothills of the Rockies. **83**

Great Society Social and economic programs of President Lyndon Johnson. **492**

Great Stock Market Crash Disastrous fall in stock prices in 1929 that signaled the end of the prosperity of the 1920s. **351**

Great War Name given to World War I, which broke out in Europe in 1914. **269**

greenback Paper money that was not exchangeable for gold or silver coins. **162**

greenhouse effect Warming of the earth's surface caused by air pollution in the atmosphere. **569**

Guadalcanal (gwahd·uhl·ka·NAL) Pacific island that was the scene of heavy fighting during World War II. **428**

Guam (GWAHM) Pacific island that became U.S. territory after the Spanish-American War. **221**

guerrilla warfare Fighting by ambush and surprise raids, often behind enemy lines. **207**

gunboat diplomacy Name for the

policy of making a show of force to prevent both Latin American instability and European interference in events in the Western Hemisphere. **237**

H

Hanoi (ha·NOY) Capital of North Vietnam. **542**

hard money Gold or silver coins, or paper money that could be exchanged for gold or silver. **162**

Harlem Globetrotters Traveling basketball team of African Americans famous for their skill and fancy ball-handling. **334**

Harlem Renaissance (ren-uh-SAHNS) Period during the 1920s when New York City's Harlem neighborhood became an intellectual and cultural capital for African Americans. **332**

Hawaiian Islands Group of islands in the Pacific Ocean annexed by the United States in the 1890s; became a state in 1959. **201**

hawk Person who supports war. **528**

Hay-Bunau-Varilla Treaty Agreement with Panama in 1903 granting the U.S. a 10-mile canal zone through Panama. **232**

Haymarket bombing Incident during an 1886 Chicago strike in which a bomb exploded, turning public opinion against unions. **141**

Hay-Pauncefote (PAHNS-fooht) **Treaty** Agreement in 1901 between Great Britain and the U.S. giving the U.S. sole right to build and control a canal between the Atlantic and Pacific oceans. **230**

Head Start Program created in 1964 to give disadvantaged children a better start in school and life. **491**

Hepburn Act Law passed in 1906 giving the Interstate Commerce Commission the power to inspect the business records of railroad companies and to regulate rail rates. **257**

Highway Safety Act Law passed in 1966 that established safety standards for vehicles and roadways. **493**

hill Rounded bulge of land that rises at least 500 feet (152 meters) above the surrounding land. **638**

Hindenburg Line Line of trenches on the Western Front from which German forces launched attacks in the Great War. **304**

Hiroshima (hir·uh·SHEE·muh) Japanese city that was the site of the first atom-bombing by the U.S. in August 1945. **434**

Ho Chi Minh (ho·chee·MIN) **Trail** Path running from North Vietnam through Cambodia and Laos to South Vietnam, named after the leader of North Vietnam, that was used by the North Vietnamese as a supply trail during the Vietnam War. **538**

Holocaust (HO·luh·kawst) Hitler's program to exterminate the Jews. **436**

Home Owners' Loan Corporation (HOLC) Organization created in 1933 to help people meet house payments by refinancing home mortgages at lower rates. **369**

Homestead Strike Violent 1892 AFL strike in Homestead, Pennsylvania, during which steel workers and Pinkerton detectives were killed. **142**

"hot-line" Direct emergency telephone line set up in 1963 between Moscow and Washington, D.C., to reduce the risk of accidental war. **481**

Housing Act Law passed in 1961 that helped poor people pay their rent. **493**

Hull House Chicago settlement house founded in 1889 by social worker Jane Addams that became a model for others throughout the country. **151**

human right Privilege belonging to all human beings. **451**

Hundred Days First part of Franklin Roosevelt's first term during which Congress passed many New Deal programs. **366**

Hungary Eastern European nation in which revolts against communist control took place in 1956 and the 1980s. **465**

I

ideal community Settlement established far from other communities in which residents could live as they wished. **36**

Immigration Act of 1965 Law that changed admission quotas to the U.S. based on nationality. **492**

impeachment Formal charge of wrongdoing brought against an official of the federal government. **18**

imperialism Practice of establishing and controlling colonies. **199**

Inchon (IN·chawn) Korean port from which American forces launched a successful attack against the North Korean army during the Korean War. **460**

income tax Tax upon a person's earnings. **264**

Income Tax Act Law passed in 1986 that lowered income taxes, especially for the poor. **577**

Indian Rights Act Law passed in 1968 to protect the rights of American Indians. **515**

Industrial Revolution Change in production methods from human to machine power. **24**

industrial unions Organization of all the laborers involved in a particular industry. **387**

Industrial Workers of the World (IWW) Radical labor organization that wanted to put industry under the control of the workers. **297**

inflation Rise in prices resulting from an increase in the amount of money or a decrease in the amount of goods available for sale. **163**

inflation rate Amount of inflation, or the degree to which inflation affects the economy. **574**

initiative (in·ISH·uht·iv) Procedure by which voters propose a law to the legislature. **251**

inner city Usually an older, run-down and densely populated central section of a city. **567**

internationalism Policy of cooperation among nations. **319**

internationalists Those who support

political and economic involvement with other nations. **406**

internment (in·TUHRN·muhnt) **camps** Enclosed compounds in a barren section of the U.S. where Japanese Americans were held during World War II. **416**

interstate commerce Business deals between residents or companies in different states. **136**

Interstate Commerce Act Law passed in 1887 to regulate railroad freight rates and business practices and which set up a commission to oversee railroads. **136**

Interstate System Network of superhighways begun in 1956 under President Eisenhower. **469**

Iran Country in the Middle East where 53 Americans were held hostage during the Carter administration and which fought a long war with Iraq. **574**

Iraq Country in the Middle East that invaded Kuwait in 1990, starting a war that involved the U.S. **628**

Iron Curtain Term Winston Churchill used to describe the barrier of censorship and secrecy between communist countries and the rest of the Western world. **448**

Irreconcilables Group of senators who refused to approve the Versailles Peace Treaty under any condition. **313**

island hopping Military strategy used in World War II by the Allies in the Pacific, where important islands were seized while other islands were bypassed. **428**

isolationism (y·suh·LAY·shuh·niz·uhm) Policy that stresses national self-sufficiency and freedom from foreign alliances. **197**

Israel Country in the Middle East formed in 1948 for Jewish people. **466**

isthmus Narrow strip of land connecting two larger segments of land. **230**

Iwo Jima (EEH·woh JEE·muh) Small Pacific island captured by the Americans in World War II after heavy fighting with the Japanese. **429**

J

Jackson State Mississippi university where two students were killed in 1970 by state police during a protest of the Vietnam War. **538**

jazz Music created by African American musicians in New Orleans in the late 1800s that became popular during the 1920s. **330**

Jazz Age Nickname for the 1920s. **331**

Jim Crow law Any law that promoted segregation; named for black-faced characters in 19th-century song-and-dance acts. **76**

Job Corps Great Society program to train poor, unskilled workers. **491**

joint-stock company Group of investors formed to outfit colonial expeditions in the early 1600s. **4**

judiciary Branch of government that includes the courts. **17**

junta (HOON·tah) In this case, committee established in the U.S. by Cuban revolutionaries to gather support in the late 1890s. **209**

K

kamikaze (kom·i·KAH·zee) Japanese pilots who committed suicide with honor by crashing their planes into enemy targets. **430**

Kent State Northern Ohio university where four students were killed by national guard troops in 1970 during a protest against the Vietnam War. **538**

kickbacks Illegal practice of receiving back part of the money paid for a job. **159**

Knights of Labor Union of skilled and unskilled workers founded in 1869. **140**

Korean War Conflict in 1950-52 between North and South Korea in which South Korea was supported by UN troops, mainly from the U.S. **461**

Ku Klux Klan (koo·kluhks·KLAN) Secret organization that has terrorized African Americans as well as Roman Catholics, Jews, and other groups. **72**

L

landform Shape on the earth's surface such as a mountain. **638**

latitude Imaginary lines that are parallel to the equator and are used to measure distance north or south of it. **xxv**

League of Nations International organization established in 1920 to seek world peace; dissolved in 1946 when many of the League's functions were taken over by the United Nations. **306**

leftist Person or policy advocating reform or overthrow of existing institutions. **610**

legend Part of a map that explains the meanings of the symbols and colors used on the map; also called the key. **634**

legislature Elected body given the responsibility of making laws. **17**

Lend-Lease Act Law passed in 1941 that allowed for the sale or lease of war supplies to any country whose defense was important to the security of the U.S. **407**

liberal Open-minded; supportive of change. **389**

lien (leen) Claim on property as security for a debt. **70**

limited liability One advantage of corporations; investors risk only the amount of money they have invested. **121**

literacy test Proof of a person's ability to read and write as a requirement for voting. **75**

Little Rock Arkansas capital where U.S. soldiers were sent in 1957 to escort black students to a high school in enforcement of a court desegregation order. **472**

lobbyist Person representing a special interest group who tries to influence legislators. **251**

locator map Map that shows the location of the area of the main map in relation to other areas. **635**

lock Canal chamber where ships are raised or lowered from one water level to another. **232**

lockout Refusal by an employer to allow employees to come to work unless they agree to the employer's terms. **142**

Lodge Reservations Changes to the Versailles Peace Treaty that were supported by Senator Henry Cabot Lodge. **313**

long drive Two-month journey that brought cattle from Texas to the railroads. **103**

Long Night Period of racial segregation after the Civil War. **75**

longitude Imaginary lines drawn from pole to pole that crisscross the parallels and are used to measure distance east or west of the prime meridian. **xxv**

Lusitania British passenger ship sunk by German U-boats in May 1915 during the Great War; 128 Americans were among the more than 1,200 people who died. **286**

M

McCarran Internal Security Act 1950 law that required communists to register with the government and made it illegal for communists to work for the government. **461**

McCarthyism Use of American suspicion of communists in the 1950s by Senator Joseph McCarthy to gain power by presenting charges of communist infiltration in the state department. **459**

McKinley Tariff Act passed in 1890 that lifted the tariff on raw sugar imports, causing Hawaii's sugar industry to suffer. **202**

machine guns Automatic weapons that fire a rapid, continuous stream of bullets. **300**

mandate Wishes of the people expressed to a candidate as an authorization to follow campaign proposals; also a territory or colony under the management of the League of Nations. **172**

Manhattan Project Code name for the top-secret plan to develop the atomic bomb. **433**

manifest destiny Belief in the 1840s that the obvious future role of the U.S. was to conquer the West and to extend the nation's boundaries to the Pacific. **32**

Manila (mah·NIL·ah) **Bay** Site in the Philippines of Commodore Dewey's 1898 victory over the Spanish fleet in the first battle of the Spanish-American War. **212**

map projection Technique used by mapmakers to show the spherical earth on a flat map. **635**

Marbury v. Madison Legal case that established the power of the Supreme Court to declare an act of Congress unconstitutional. **21**

March on Washington 1963 civil rights demonstration in Washington, D.C., where Martin Luther King, Jr., delivered his famous "I Have a Dream" speech. **517**

market Economic term for the selling and buying of goods and services. **348**

Marshall Plan United States program for the economic recovery of Europe after World War II. **450**

mass production Manufacture, usually by machinery, of goods in large quantities. **124**

massive retaliation (ri·tal·ee·AY·shun) U.S. policy under Eisenhower that threatened to respond to Soviet aggression with nuclear weapons. **463**

matériel (mah·TEER·ee·el) Equipment and supplies used by a military force. **291**

mediate (MEE·dee·ayt) To attempt, as an impartial party, to help settle a dispute between two parties. **280**

Medicare Great Society program that provides health insurance for people over 65. **492**

megalopolis Continuous, heavily populated urban area connecting a number of cities. **xxiv**

melting pot Idea that immigrants of various racial and cultural backgrounds eventually become adapted to mainstream American ways. **265**

mercantilism Economic policy in which a country controls the imports and exports of its colonies. **10**

merchants of death Nickname given to companies that profit from the manufacture of weapons; first used during World War I. **400**

merit system Policy adopted by the U.S. Civil Service to base government appointments and promotions on ability rather than political connections. **164**

Mesabi (muh·SAH·bee) **Range** Region in Minnesota where rich deposits of iron ore were found in the 1890s. **122**

Mexican Revolution Rebellion beginning in 1910 that ended the dictatorship of Porfírio Díaz and led to a constitutional government begun in 1917. **280**

Midway Islands Islands northwest of the Hawaiian islands that were occupied by the U.S. navy in 1867; site of an important U.S. naval victory in World War II. **198**

mild reservationists Republican senators who would accept the Treaty of Versailles with only a few minor changes. **313**

military dictatorship Control of a country by the leaders of the military. **280**

minimum wage Least pay a worker can receive by law. **255**

Missouri Compromise Act passed in 1820 that allowed Missouri to become a slave state and Maine a free state and attempted to settle the question of slavery's spread by allowing it only in territories south of 36°30′ N. **33**

Model A Ford car made after the Model T that introduced different colors and body styles. **340**

Model T First mass-produced car that made automobile transportation affordable for many Americans; introduced by Henry Ford in 1908. **340**

Moderate Republican who during Reconstruction believed in "malice toward none;" also a person who avoids extreme political views. **55**

monetary (MAHN·uh·ter·ee) **policy** Plan that dictates the size of the money supply; also method of regulating business activity by raising or lowering interest rates on loans. **162**

monopoly (muh·NAHP·uh·lee) Exclusive control of a product or service that results in fixed prices and elimination of competition. **133**

Monroe Doctrine Important statement of foreign policy that said that the United States would not tolerate European interference in the Western Hemisphere. **23**

Montevideo Pact Statement made at a 1933 meeting between the U.S. and Latin American nations that states that the U.S. would limit its right to intervene in Latin American affairs. **602**

Montgomery Bus Boycott 1955 protest by African Americans against segregation of city buses in Montgomery, Alabama. **475**

mountain Landform that rises to a height of over 2,000 feet (610 meters); also climate in which elevation causes temperature and precipitation variations. **638**

movement Geographic theme that describes the continuous spread or advance of people, goods, and ideas. **xxvi**

moving assembly line Method of mass production used by Henry Ford in which each worker or team performed one task as the product moved past them. **340**

muckraker (MUHK·rayk·uhr) Reporter who exposed corruption in the early 1900s. **245**

municipal socialism Plan that transferred private ownership of utilities to city governments. **252**

N

Nagasaki (nah·gah·SAH·kee) Japanese city that was the site of the second atom-bombing by the U.S. in 1945. **435**

National Aeronautics (ar·oh·NAH·tiks) **and Space Administration** (NASA) Government agency responsible for space programs. **504**

National Association for the Advancement of Colored People (NAACP) Civil rights organization formed in 1909. **268**

National Farm Workers Association Labor union of Mexican-born farm workers founded by migrant leader César Chávez. **558**

National Grange (GRAYNJ) Farmers' organization that became politically active during the 1870s. **175**

National Industrial Recovery Act (NIRA) New Deal law that allowed industry to set fair codes of competition, guaranteed the right of workers to join unions, and set minimum wage rates. **366**

National Labor Relations Board (NLRB) Board created by the Wagner Labor Relations Act to settle union disputes and guarantee fair union elections. **378**

National Organization for Women (NOW) Association founded by Betty Friedan and others in 1966 to promote equal rights and opportunities for women. **514**

National Origins Act Law passed in 1924 that severely restricted immigration from certain countries to the United States. **325**

National Recovery Administration (NRA) Group organized in 1933 to supervise the industrial codes created under the National Industrial Recovery Act. **366**

National War Labor Board Board created during World War II to stabilize wages and settle labor disputes. **415**

National Youth Administration New Deal agency that helped college students find employment. **376**

nationalism Patriotic feelings for one's country. **277**

nationalize Put under government ownership. **602**

native son Political candidate from a key state who is nominated in hopes of carrying that state in a national election. **158**

natural landscape Vegetation, wildlife, climate, and soil of an area; also called the physical setting. **638**

natural resources Riches of nature, such as vegetation, wildlife, minerals, water, and soil. **xxiv**

Nazis (NAHT·seez) Members of the National Socialist party, which controlled Germany from 1933 to 1945 under Adolf Hitler. **397**

neutrality Policy of avoiding permanent ties with other nations. **279**

neutrality acts Laws passed in the 1930s to prevent United States involvement in another war. **400**

New Deal Franklin Roosevelt's program to revive the country from the Great Depression. **365**

New Freedom Woodrow Wilson's progressive program proposed in 1912. **262**

New Frontier John F. Kennedy's social and economic program of the early 1960s. **476**

New Immigration Wave of immigration between 1880 and the 1920s that brought millions of people from eastern and southern Europe to America. **146**

New Nationalism Theodore Roosevelt's progressive platform in 1912. **260**

Nez Perce (NEZ·puhrs) Indian group routed out of western Idaho and eventually moved to reservations in Oklahoma. **94**

Niagara (ny·AG·ruh) **Movement** Effort begun in 1905 by prominent African American leaders to fight racial segregation. **268**

Nineteenth Amendment Constitutional amendment in 1920 that gave women the right to vote. **318**

no man's land Devastated area between the trenches on the Western Front during the Great War. **283**

nonviolent direct action Method proposed by Martin Luther King, Jr., for protesting without violence against discrimination. **516**

nonviolent resistance Showing opposition to something without the use of violence. **475**

Normandy Northern French province that was the site of the D-Day invasion during World War II. **422**

North Atlantic Treaty Organization (NATO) Agreement made in 1949 to stand firm against Soviet military threats, made between the U.S., Great Britain, France, and eight other nations. **453**

North Korea Korea north of the 38th parallel and allied with the Soviet Union since World War II. **459**

Northern Securities Case Antitrust lawsuit in which the Supreme Court dissolved the combination of three major railroads. **256**

nuclear energy Energy released by controlled nuclear reactions, developed in the twentieth century as an alternative energy source to fossil fuels. **496**

O

oil refining Removing the impurities from crude oil. **124**

Okinawa (ohk·i·NAH·wa) Japanese island captured by American forces in World War II after heavy losses on both sides. **430**

Open Door U.S. policy first stated in 1899 that called for equal trade rights for all nations with an independent China. **320**

Open Door Note Note sent to other nations in 1899 by Secretary of State John Hay requesting them to accept the Open Door policy. **228**

open range Government-owned grazing land used by ranchers to feed their herds. **103**

Operation Overlord British and American invasion of France that began the Allied conquest of Europe during World War II. **422**

Operation Sail Procession of decorated ships in New York Harbor in honor of the American Bicentennial. **555**

Operation Torch Allied occupation of French North Africa led by General Eisenhower during World War II. **421**

Organization of American States (OAS) Regional agency within the UN established in 1948 with membership open to countries in the Western Hemisphere for promoting peace, democracy, and economic development. **604**

Organization of Petroleum Exporting

Countries (OPEC) Oil cartel founded in 1960 that includes Venezuela, Saudi Arabia, Iran, Kuwait, and Iraq. **544**

overhead Fixed costs. **133**

override Constitutional power of Congress to overrule a presidential veto by a two-thirds vote. **58**

P

Pacific Railway Act Law passed in 1862 authorizing construction of a railroad from Nebraska to the Pacific Coast. **87**

pacifist Person who is against violence and war. **399**

Palmer raids Raids on radical groups ordered by Attorney General A. Mitchell Palmer during the Big Red Scare after World War I. **321**

Pan-American Conference 1889 meeting with representatives of Latin American countries sponsored by the U.S. with the hopes of bringing the nations of the Western Hemisphere closer together. **204**

partnership Business organization of two or more people who share the profits and losses. **121**

patronage Awarding of government positions by officeholders to their political supporters. **165**

Pawnee (paw·NEE) Indian group that occupied western Nebraska. **83**

Peace Corps Program established by President Kennedy that sent trained American volunteers to needy countries. **479**

peace movement Efforts made by organized groups to promote peace among nations. **278**

peace without victory Topic of a speech by President Wilson calling for the Allies and Central Powers to end the war. **289**

Pearl Harbor Port in the Hawaiian Islands where American navy ships were destroyed in a surprise Japanese attack in 1941. **410**

Pendleton Act (1883) Law that created a Civil Service Commission to administer exams for those seeking government jobs. **165**

People's party Third party formed in 1892 that represented the interests of farmers and labor unions; also called the Populist party. **181**

perestroika (per·uh·STROY·kuh) Plan initiated by Premier Gorbachev to improve and broaden the Soviet economy. **582**

Permanent Joint Board on Defense U.S.-Canadian committee formed in 1939 to coordinate the defense of northern North America. **593**

Philippine Islands South Pacific islands that became a battleground for Japanese and U.S. forces during World War II. **426**

phonograph Machine invented by Thomas Edison that reproduced sound from tracings made on a cylinder or disk. **127**

physical setting Natural landscape of an area; the landforms, vegetation, climate, and soil. **638**

place Geographic theme relating to the physical features of a location. **xxvi**

plain Nearly flat or gently rolling land. **638**

Plains Indians Members of Indian groups that lived on the grasslands between the Rocky Mountains and the Mississippi River. **83**

plateau Relatively flat land that rises sharply from the surrounding landscape to 2,000 feet (610 meters) or more on at least one side. **638**

Platt Amendment Amendment to 1901 treaty giving Cuba its independence that allowed the U.S. to keep naval bases in Cuba and limited the Cuban government's power to accumulate debts and make treaties. **596**

Plessy v. Ferguson Supreme Court case concerning civil rights that legalized the "separate but equal" principle. **76**

poison gas Chemical weapon first used by the Germans during World War I. **298**

polio vaccine (vak·SEEN) Inoculation developed by Dr. Jonas Salk that protected people from the polio virus. **497**

political machine Big-city organization run by bosses who won elections by controlling poor and immigrant voters. **158**

poll tax Fee charged for voting. **75**

pollution Harmful substances that affect the quality of the environment. **568**

pool Agreement between businesses to charge the same rates and share available markets. **133**

popular sovereignty (SAHV uh ruhn tee) System that allowed settlers in each territory to decide whether they would have slavery. **33**

popular vote Vote of the people. **30**

Populist party Third party formed in 1892 that represented the interests of farmers and labor unions, also called the People's party. **181**

postwar reaction Response to the horrors of the Great War felt by many young people characterized by xenophobia, disillusionment, and, for some, a return to fundamental values. **320**

poverty line Level of income below which one is classified as poor. **515**

primary elections Process for selecting candidates to run for public office. **251**

Progressive Movement Period in the early 1900s marked by social reforms and a general feeling of hope and optimism. **241**

Progressive party Third party formed to support Theodore Roosevelt in 1912; and party formed in 1948 to support Henry A. Wallace's bid for the presidency against Truman. **260**

progressives People who sought to improve American society. **241**

prohibition Act of forbidding the manufacture, transportation, and sale of alcoholic beverages; national movement that culminated in passage of the Eighteenth Amendment. **36**

Promontory Utah city where the Union Pacific and Central Pacific railroads met to complete the first American transcontinental railroad. **88**

propaganda Information or ideas

spread in order to gain public support for a cause or to damage an opposing cause. **296**

prosperity Term for a time of high economic production and low unemployment. **355**

protective tariff Tax on imports to increase their cost, helping American manufacturers compete. **24**

public housing project Housing development for low-income families that is made affordable by public funds. **507**

public works Roads, bridges, and other structures that are built for public use at public cost. **359**

Puerto Rico (pohrt·uh·REE·koh) Island east of Cuba and southeast of Florida ceded to the United States after the Spanish-American War; now a self-governing commonwealth of the U.S. **216**

Pullman Strike Major railway work stoppage in 1894 begun by workers of the Pullman Palace Car Company that resulted in a violent clash with federal troops. **185**

puppet government Government whose actions are dictated or controlled by another nation. **443**

Pure Food and Drug Act Law passed in 1906 that provided for the inspection of food and drugs and the supervision of slaughterhouses. **257**

Q

quadruplex (kwah·DROO·plehx) **telegraph** Thomas Edison's first major invention, a machine that could send four messages over one wire at the same time. **127**

quarantine (KWAHR·un·teen) Policy of isolating aggressor nations in the 1930s. **401**

R

Radical Republican who during Reconstruction was determined to protect the newly freed slaves and punish the Confederates; also a

person who favors sudden or extreme changes. **55**

railroad barons Men who financed and profited from railroads. **120**

range right Claim in dry areas to the water of a stream that allowed control of the lands around it. **103**

range war Battle in the 1880s between sheep and cattle ranchers for control of grasslands. **108**

rebate (REE·bayt) Kickback, or money returned; an illegal incentive to preferred shippers by the railroads in the 1870s. **133**

recall Process of removing an official from office by public vote. **251**

reciprocity (re·suh·PRAH·suh·tee) Mutual exchange of privileges. **592**

reconcentrado (ree·kawn·sen·TRAH·doh) Concentration camp in Cuba in the 1890s. **209**

Reconstruction Process after the Civil War of bringing the southern states back into the Union. **57**

Reconstruction Act Measure passed in 1867 that ordered a military occupation of the South and ordered southerners to give African Americans constitutional rights. **60**

recovery Part of the New Deal plan to boost the economy; also, an upswing in the economy. **355**

Red Power Term used in the 1960s to rally support for the Indian rights movement. **514**

referendum (ref·uh·REN·duhm) Legal procedure by which the people can revoke a law passed by the legislature. **251**

reform Part of the New Deal plan aimed at preventing another depression. **366**

regime (ruh·zheem) Form of government. **526**

region Geographic theme in which areas of the earth are identified by common features. **xxvi**

regulatory (REG·yuh·luh·tohr·ee) **agency** Government department that supervises business operations. **136**

relationships within places Geographic theme that describes all

interactions within an environment. **xxvi**

relative location Part of geographic theme of location: where a place is in relation to other places. **xxv**

relief Aim of Roosevelt's New Deal to relieve the poverty of many Americans following the depression; also, shading used on maps to show the existence of mountains and valleys. **365**

reparations (rep·ah·RAY·shunz) Money paid by defeated nations as payment for wrongs, damages, or injuries suffered by other nations during a war. **308**

repeal To reject or revoke a law. **327**

Republic of Panama Country formed in 1903 after Panamanians revolted, with U.S. support, against the Republic of Colombia. **231**

reservations Limiting conditions or specific objections. **316**

restraint of trade Interference with the free flow of goods or with fair competition. **256**

right of way Strip of land granted by the government, as land granted to railroad companies laying down tracks. **87**

right wing Person or policy that seeks to preserve the status quo, or established institutions. **617**

Rome-Berlin-Tokyo Axis Alliance formed by Italy, Germany, and Japan during World War II. **410**

Roosevelt Corollary Policy that extended the Monroe Doctrine and said that the United States had the right to force countries in the Western Hemisphere to pay their debts in order to prevent European interference. **236**

Rough Rider Member of Theodore Roosevelt's regiment sent to Cuba during the Spanish-American War. **214**

round up Bringing together of cattle scattered over the open range. **105**

runaway inflation Uncontrollable rise in prices due to a large amount of money in circulation and a shortage of goods. **178**

rural Outside the city. **xxiv**

Rural Electrification Administration New Deal agency that helped bring electricity to remote areas. **375**

S

Saigon (sy·GON) Former capital of South Vietnam, renamed Ho Chi Minh City in 1975. **531**

St. Lawrence Seaway Waterway created by deepening the St. Lawrence River from the Atlantic Ocean to the Great Lakes. **469**

Saint-Mihiel salient (san·mee·YEL sayl·yahnt) Point on the Western Front where U.S. forces defeated the Germans in World War I. **304**

San Francisco Conference Meeting held in 1945 to draft the United Nations Charter. **440**

San Juan (san·WAHN) **Hill** Site in Cuba of a key victory in 1898 by Roosevelt's Rough Riders during Spanish-American War. **216**

sanction Penalty for violating a treaty. **309**

Sandinistas (san-duh·NEES·tuhs) Rebels in Nicaragua who led the overthrow of dictator Somoza and then set up a government friendly to the Soviets. **576**

Santiago (sant·ee·AHG·oh) Cuban seaport captured by American forces during the Spanish-American War. **215**

satellite nation Country that is politically or economically controlled by a larger, stronger country. **451**

Saturday Night Massacre Resignations and discharges, in one evening, of top officials in the Justice Department who refused to aid President Nixon in the Watergate cover-up. **547**

Scalawag (SKAL·i·wag) Southern white in the Republican party during Reconstruction. **65**

scale Part of a map that tells how to relate the distance shown on the map with distance on earth. **634**

secession (si·SESH·uhn) Withdrawal from an association or group. **43**

Second New Deal Reforms introduced by President Roosevelt in 1935 after many of his original New Deal reforms were declared unconstitutional. **378**

Second Open Door Note Second half of U.S. Open Door policy that declared opposition to foreign occupation of China. **229**

Second World War Conflict provoked in 1939 by Germany's invasion of Poland, which caused England and France to declare war on Germany; the United States became involved after the bombing of Pearl Harbor. **397**

sectional conflict Disagreements between the Northeast, South, and West. **30**

Sedition Act Law passed in 1918 that made it illegal to oppose the government and its policies. **297**

segregation Separation of people on the basis of racial, religious, or social differences. **59**

Selective Service Act Law passed in 1917 that provided for the draft of men into military service for World War I. **293**

self-determination Principle that all people should be able to decide for themselves which nation they belong to. **306**

separate but equal Argument that supported the legality of segregation when races were separated in supposedly equal public schools or other facilities. **78**

settlement house Community center in an urban neighborhood. **151**

Seventeenth Amendment Constitutional amendment that provided for the election of senators by popular vote. **251**

"Seward's Folly" Nickname Americans gave the purchase of Alaska in 1867 by Secretary of State William Seward. **201**

sharecropping System in which landowners provided laborers with farm supplies in exchange for a portion of their crops. **68**

Sherman Antitrust Act Law enacted in 1890 to prevent monopolies by banning trusts and other business combinations that restricted competition. **136**

Sherman Silver Purchase Act Law passed in 1890 that increased the amount of silver bought to 4.5 million ounces a month. **179**

shopping center Stores and other businesses grouped together and sharing one parking lot. **506**

shopping mall Large enclosed building that houses a number of stores and businesses. **507**

shuttle diplomacy Negotiations carried out by a diplomat who travels back and forth between countries; used most often to describe Henry Kissinger's role in seeking peace in the Middle East in the 1970s. **544**

Sicily (SIH·suh·lee) Italian island in the Mediterranean taken by Allies prior to the occupation of Italy during World War II. **421**

sick industry Business such as coal or textiles that did not prosper during the 1920s. **348**

Sioux (SOO) Plains Indians who occupied the Dakotas; also called the Dakota. **83**

sit-in Form of protest where a group sits down in a public place and refuses to leave. **475**

sitting on the fence Term for not taking a strong stand on a political issue. **161**

Six Days' War Conflict in 1967 between Egypt and Israel quickly won by Israel. **544**

Sixteenth Amendment Constitutional amendment that gave Congress the power to levy an income tax. **264**

skyscraper Very tall building. **128**

smelt To melt away impurities in ore to obtain metal. **122**

smog Term for air pollution produced by smoke and chemical fumes; coined by combining "smoke" and "fog". **568**

Social Gospel Idea preached by urban religious progressives that it was a person's moral obligation to help those less fortunate. **243**

Social Security Act Law passed in 1935 that created a system to provide old-age insurance and unemployment compensation. **379**

socialist Person who believes in public ownership and operation of all means of production and distribution of goods. **252**

sod house Home made of chunks of grassy soil built by the pioneers of the Great Plains. **110**

Solid South Term applied to the southern states that as a group supported the Democratic party after the Civil War. **157**

soup kitchen Place where food was served to the needy during the Great Depression. **357**

South Korea Korea south of the 38th parallel and backed by U.S. support since World War II. **459**

Spanish-American War Conflict between Spain and the United States in 1898 over Cuban independence. **212**

specialization (spesh·i·luh·ZAY·shun) Concentration on the manufacture of a particular product; division of labor in which each person does one specific part of the whole process. **138**

special-purpose map Map that illustrates a specific category of information. **638**

spheres of influence Area controlled in large part by a more powerful country, such as parts of China in the 19th century dominated by European nations. **228**

spoils system Practice by an elected party of rewarding party supporters with appointments to government offices. **30**

stagflation Term coined by combining "*stag*nation" and "*in*flation" that means a combination of inflation and a sluggish economy. **554**

stalemate (STAYL·mayt) Deadlock in which neither opposing side can act effectively or gain victory. **283**

standard of living Average quantity and quality of goods, services, and comforts available. **494**

Standard Oil Company Business founded in 1870 and built into a monopoly by John D. Rockefeller. **134**

states' rights Doctrine that holds that the states, not the federal government, have the ultimate power. **31**

States' Rights party Political party formed by southern Democrats (Dixiecrats) in 1948. **455**

Statue of Liberty Statue of the Goddess of Liberty in New York Harbor that was given to the United States by France. **143**

stock certificate Document that shows ownership of stock in a corporation. **121**

stockholder Person who buys shares in a corporation. **121**

Strategic (struh·TEE·jik) **Arms Limitation Treaty** (SALT) Agreement between the U.S. and the Soviet Union to limit nuclear weapons. **540**

strategic defense initiative Complex, computerized antimissile system, called "Star Wars" by some, that President Reagan urged Congress to support with large sums of money. **582**

strike Refusal of employees to work until their demands are met. **140**

strong reservationists Republican senators who would not support the Treaty of Versailles unless it underwent major changes. **313**

subsidy (SUB·suh·dee) Money provided by the government for programs that benefit the public. **348**

suburb Residential area located near a city. **342**

Suez Canal International waterway in the Middle East invaded by British, French, and Israeli troops in 1956 but held by Egypt. **466**

summit meeting Conference between the heads of governments to settle political issues. **467**

Sun Belt Warm weather states in the South and Southwest where population is increasing. **504**

supply Quantity of a product or service offered for sale at a certain time or price. **348**

supply-side economics Policy followed by President Reagan that lowered tax rates for the wealthy in order to increase investment in business, which would thereby increase tax revenues. **576**

Supreme Court Reform Plan President Roosevelt's unsuccessful plan to add New Deal supporters to the Supreme Court. **385**

suspension bridge Roadway held up by chains or cables anchored on either side. **128**

Sussex pledge Promise made by the Germans during World War I not to sink passenger or merchant ships. **287**

sweatshop Factory in which workers toil in bad working conditions for low pay. **139**

synthetic Artificial substance. **347**

synthetic textile Cloth made from artificial substances. **497**

T

Taft-Hartley Act Law passed in 1947 to regulate labor union activities and outlaw unfair practices by unions as well as employers. **447**

Tammany (TAM·uh·nee) **Hall** Political machine run by New York City Democrats. **158**

tanks Heavily armed vehicles that move on metal belts, first used during World War I. **298**

Teapot Dome Government oil reserve in Wyoming that was the subject of a scandal involving the illegal leasing of federal lands during the Harding administration. **344**

telegraph Machine invented by Samuel F. B. Morse in 1837 that transmitted messages as electrical signals sent over wire. **125**

telephone Instrument invented by Alexander Graham Bell in 1876 that sends speech over distances by turning sound into electrical current. **125**

television Process of transmitting pictures and sound in electrical waves. **499**

Teller Amendment Congressional resolution adopted on the eve of the Spanish-American War stating that the United States would not take control of Cuba. **212**

temperance (TEM·puh·ruhns) Movement to restrict the drinking of alcoholic beverages. **36**

Tennessee Valley Authority (TVA) Federal agency established in 1933 to develop the waterpower and other resources of Tennessee River valley. **368**

Tenure (TEN·yuhr) **of Office Act** Law passed in 1867 that prohibited the president from removing appointed officials without the consent of Congress. **60**

Tet offensive Major attack in 1968 on South Vietnamese cities by the North Vietnamese. **531**

Texas longhorn Type of cattle with low, wide horns that once grazed freely in Texas. **103**

third party Political group organized to compete against the two major political parties, usually in a national election. **172**

Thirteenth Amendment Constitutional amendment that abolished slavery. **56**

Three Mile Island Nuclear power plant in Pennsylvania that was the site of an accident in 1979. **570**

title Part of a map that tells you what the map is about. **634**

Tonkin Gulf Resolution Authority granted by Congress to President Lyndon Johnson in 1964 to approve and support in advance the use of U.S. forces in Vietnam. **525**

total war Strategy that calls for the destruction of the resources of an enemy's civilian population as well as its army. **47**

totalitarian (toh·tal·uh·TER·ee·uhn) Type of government in which the state has absolute control over all citizens and no opposition to the government is allowed. **397**

tourism Traveling or sight-seeing for pleasure. **341**

Trade Agreements Act Law passed by Congress in 1934 that lowered or eliminated tariffs on many Latin American imports. **602**

transcontinental railroad Railway that extends across North America from coast to coast. **88**

transistor Miniature electronic device used to control and increase an electronic current. **497**

trench warfare Fighting during World War I that took place in trenches that ran across northern France. **283**

Triangle Fire New York factory fire that killed 140 women and prompted the passing of factory inspection laws. **253**

Tripartite Pact Mutual defense treaty signed by Germany, Italy, and Japan during World War II. **410**

Truman Doctrine U.S. policy to give financial and military aid to nations so they could resist communist rule. **450**

trust Group of corporations formed by a legal agreement and organized especially for the purpose of reducing competition. **134**

trust buster Person who wants to dissolve an established trust. **256**

Tuskegee (tuhs·KEE·gee) **Airmen** Much-decorated group of African American pilots in World War II (the 332nd Fighter Group—the "Red-Tailed Black Eagles") trained in segregated quarters in Alabama. **417**

Tuskegee Institute School for African Americans located in Alabama and founded by Booker T. Washington. **79**

Twenty-fifth Amendment Constitutional amendment that states that if the president is removed from office, the vice president shall become president and that a vacancy in the vice president's office shall be filled by presidential appointment. **547**

Twenty-first Amendment Constitutional amendment that ended prohibition by repealing the Eighteenth Amendment. **327**

Twenty-second Amendment Constitutional amendment that states that no one can hold the office of president for more than two terms. **447**

Twenty-sixth Amendment Constitutional amendment that gave 18- to 20-year-olds the right to vote. **572**

U

U-2 Affair Incident in 1960 when an American spy plane was shot down over the Soviet Union. **467**

U-boats German submarines or "undersea ships" used during World War II. **284**

ultimatum (uhl·tuh·MAYT·uhm) Final offer or demand. **212**

Underwood Tariff Act passed in 1913 that created an income tax and reduced tariffs on imports where American goods controlled the market. **264**

United Farm Workers Organizing Committee Labor union for migrant farm workers. **558**

United Nations International organization of nations formed in 1945 to promote world peace; replaced the League of Nations. **440**

urban Of cities and towns. **xxiv**

urban decay Decline in a city area caused in part by a population shift to the suburbs. **568**

Urban League Organization founded in 1910 to work for equal rights for African Americans. **383**

urbanization Growth of cities. **24**

V

V-E Day Allied victory in World War II when Germany surrendered on May 8, 1945. **425**

V-J Day Allied victory in World War II when Japan signed the surrender terms on September 2, 1945. **435**

vaqueros (vah·KAH·rohs) Spanish cowhands who invented most of the cowhand's tools. **105**

Venezuela Boundary Dispute Disagreement between Great Britain and Venezuela over boundary between British Guiana and Venezuela that was settled by United States arbitration in 1899. **206**

Verdun Site of one of the longest battles of World War I. **300**

Versailles (vuhr·SY) **Peace Treaty** Agreement ending World War I that placed the blame for the war on Germany and also created the League of Nations. **309**

veto Presidential power to reject bills passed by Congress. **57**

Viet Cong Procommunist South Vietnamese guerrilla soldiers. **525**

Vietnam Southeast Asian country

where United States and South Vietnamese forces fought a war against the communist North Vietnamese and the Viet Cong. **465**

Vietnamization Policy of building up the South Vietnamese army so that American troops could be withdrawn. **537**

vigilance committee Group of volunteers organized to keep watch over a town. **102**

vigilante Volunteer crime fighter; member of a vigilance committee. **102**

Virginia City Famous Nevada mining boom town. **101**

Volstead Act Law passed in 1919 to enforce prohibition. **326**

Volunteers in Service to America (VISTA) Organization similar to the overseas Peace Corps that operates domestically. **491**

voter participation rate Percentage of eligible voters who vote. **572**

Voting Rights Act Law passed in 1965 that greatly increased the number of African American voters by putting an end to literacy tests and other practices used to keep African Americans from registering. **520**

W

wage and price controls Economic controls set by the government during World War II. **446**

wage and price freeze Controls imposed for 90 days by President Nixon in 1971 to regulate the economy. **536**

Wagner Labor Relations Act Law passed in 1935 that gave labor unions the right to organize and bargain collectively. **378**

War Industries Board Group that reorganized American industry to support the war effort during World War I. **291**

warlords Military leaders who control the government of an area or

country, as in Japan in the 1930s and 1940s. **397**

Warren Court Supreme Court under the leadership of liberal Chief Justice Earl Warren from 1953 to 1968 that passed important civil rights legislation. **469**

Warsaw Pact Twenty-year mutual defense agreement signed in response to NATO by most of the communist countries of Eastern Europe. **453**

Washita (WAHSH·uh·taw) Site in present-day Oklahoma where Arapaho and Cheyenne groups were defeated by American troops in 1868. **90**

Watergate Affair Government scandal that began in 1972 and led to the resignation of President Nixon in 1974. **545**

watershed Important turning point in history. **55**

welfare state Situation in which the government assumes a large measure of responsibility for the social well-being of the people. **261**

Western Front World War I combat zone between the Allied states of Belgium, France, and Italy and the Central Powers of Germany and Austria-Hungary. **282**

white backlash Negative attitude among whites regarding black power movement in the 1960s. **521**

white-collar worker Generally a professional whose job does not involve manual labor. **498**

wildcatter Name given to oil prospectors in the 1860s. **124**

Wisconsin Idea Program of progressive reforms by Governor Robert M. La Follette of Wisconsin in the early 1900s. **250**

withholding system System of paying income taxes in which the employer withholds part of an employee's wages owed as taxes to the government. **415**

Wobblies Nickname for the Industrial Workers of the World. **297**

wolf packs Groups of German U-

boats that attacked convoys in the Atlantic during World War II. **407**

Women's Liberation Movement Campaign of political action and demonstrations begun in the late 1960s aimed at attaining equal rights for women. **513**

Works Progress Administration (WPA) New Deal agency that found useful work for millions of unemployed people. **375**

world market International demand for goods and services. **70**

Wounded Knee Site in South Dakota where Sioux Indian families were massacred by United States troops in 1890; also site of 1973 Indian protest. **97**

X

xenophobia Fear of foreigners or strangers. **325**

Y

Yalta Conference Meeting in 1945 at Yalta on the Crimean peninsula between Churchill, Stalin and Roosevelt to plan the defeat and occupation of Germany and German-occupied territories. **442**

Yalu (YOL·oo) **River** River that marks the border between China and North Korea. **461**

yellow-dog contract Agreement signed by an employee that the employee will not join a union. **142**

Z

Zimmermann Note Secret document that showed that Germany was trying to make an alliance with Mexico in 1917, prompting the U.S. to declare war on Germany. **290**

INDEX

Page numbers in *italics* that have a *p* written before them refer to pictures or photographs; *c,* to charts, graphs, tables, or diagrams; and *m,* to maps.

Index 739

rice, 8
Richardson, Elliot L., 547
Richmond, Battle of, 47
Richmond, Va., 152
Rickenbacker, "Eddie," 300
Riegal, Robert E., 93
Riis, Jacob, 151, 247-48, *p248*
Rio Grande, *m646-47*
Rio Treaty, 604
riots, 320, 520-21
rivers, 25. *See also* names of specific rivers
roads, 24-25, 341, *p342*
Roaring Twenties, 330-39
Robeson, Paul, 459
Robinson, Jackie, 510
Robinson, Sallie J., 76
robots, 501-02
Rochester, N.Y., 139
Rockefeller, John D., 130, 133-34, *p134,* 135-36, 247
Rockefeller, Nelson, 553
rockets, 414
Rockne, Knute, 333-34
Rocky Mountains, 83, 107, *m646-47*
Roe v. Wade, 578
Roebling, John A., 153
Roebling, Washington, 153
Rölvaag, O. E., 108
Roman Catholics. *See* Catholics
Rome-Berlin-Tokyo Axis, 410
Romero, Oscar, 617
Rommel, Erwin, 421, *p421*
Roosevelt, Eleanor, 384, *p384*
Roosevelt, Franklin Delano: advisors of, 373, 383; African Americans and, 382-83, 418; Atlantic Charter and, 408-09, *p409;* atomic bomb and, 433; criticisms of, 377-78, *p377;* death of, 425; election of 1940, 406-07; election of 1944, 424; end of New Deal, 384-87, *p385;* family of, 384; fireside chats of, 373; first inaugural address of, 364-65; Hundred Days, 365-72; Latin American policy of, 601-03, *p601;* Lend-Lease Act, 407; neutrality acts and, 400-01, 403; New Deal, 365-73, 375-89; personality of, 363-64, 373, 375; polio of, 363, 384, 497; political career of, 363, 364, *p364;* and powers of the presidency, 389; Second New Deal, 378-79, *p379;* significance of New Deal, 387-89; Supreme Court and, 384-85; totalitarian states and,

401; United Nations and, 440-41; as vice presidential candidate, 318, *p318,* 363; World War II and, 405, 407-09, *p409,* 410, 412, 419; Yalta Conference and, 442-43, *p443*
Roosevelt, Theodore: African Americans and, 267; biography of, 213-14, 226-27; Canada and, 591; election of 1912, 260, 261, 262-63; family of, 318, 384; on the Great War, 288; Latin American policy of, 596-97, *p596, p597;* muckrakers and, 245; New Nationalism of, 260-61, 264; Panama Canal and, 231-37, *p597;* personality of, 258; presidency of, 227, 230-37, *p235, p236,* 240, 256-59, 291; as rancher, 108; Spanish-American War and, 212, 213-16; vice presidential campaign of, *p225,* 226
Roosevelt Corollary, 236-37, 596-97, *p596,* 600
Ross, Betsy, 470
Rough Riders, 214, *p214, p215,* 216
Ruef, Abraham, 249
Rumania, *m453, m642-43*
Rural Electrification Administration, 375
Russia, 200, 276, 277, *m278,* 282, *m282,* 298, 320. *See also* Soviet Union
Rustin, Bayard, 521
Ruth, Babe, 334, *p334,* 336, 350

S

Sacco, Nicola, 325, *p325*
Sadat, Anwar, 573, *p573*
Saigon, *m527,* 531. *See also* Ho Chi Minh City
St. Lawrence River, *m646-47*
St. Lawrence Seaway, 469, 593
St. Louis, Mo., *c148,* 296, *p342*
Saint-Mihiel salient, *m301,* 304
Salisbury, Lord, 205-06
SALT. *See* Strategic Arms Limitation Treaty
San Francisco, Calif., 143, *m144,* 249, 273
San Francisco Conference, 440-41
San Jacinto, Battle of, 32
San Juan Hill, Battle of, *p214, p215,* 216, *m216*
Sandburg, Carl, 249-50, 393

Sandinistas, 576, 580, 603, 613
Sandino, Augusto César, 600, *p600,* 613
Santa Anna, Antonio López de, 32, *p32*
Santiago, Battle of, 216, *m216*
Saperstein, Abe, 334
satellite nations, of Soviet Union, 451, *m453,* 459, 465, 582, 624, 625-27, *p625*
Saturday Night Massacre, 547
Scalawags, 65
Scalia, Antonin, 578
Scandinavian Americans, 143
Schechter v. U.S. 377
Schenck v. United States, 298
schools. *See* education; private schools; public schools; universities and colleges
Schurz, Carl, 224
Schwieger, Walter, 287
science and technology, 3, 328-29, 496-502, 580, *c656*
Scopes, John T., 329
Scopes Trial, 328-29
Scott, Dred, 42, *p42*
Scott, Emmett J., 294
Scott, Winfield, 33
Sears, Roebuck, 129
Seattle, Wash., 201, 320
secession, 43
Second New Deal, 378-79, *p379*
Second Open Door Note, 229
Second World War. *See* World War II
Sedition Act (1918), 297
segregation, 59, 75-79, 247, 382, 417-18, 455, 469, 472-75. *See also* Birmingham Bus Boycott; *Brown v. Board of Education of Topeka;* Jim Crow laws; Martin Luther King, Jr.; prejudice and discrimination
Selective Service Act, 293, 294. *See also* draft
self-determination, 306, 309
Senate, U.S., 18, 19, 251-52
separate-but-equal principle (*Plessy v. Ferguson,* 1896), 76-79, 469
Serbia, 276, 277, *m278,* 282, *m282*
Serviceman's Readjustment Act, 415
settlement houses, 151, 243
Seward, William H., 200
Seward's Folly (Alaska), 201
Seymour, Horatio, 62
Shafter, William R., 216

Index 749

Index 753

Picture credits

Acknowledgments

Saturday Evening Post Company: From ''Death in the Ia Drang Valley'' by Jack P. Smith from *The Saturday Evening Post*, January 28, 1967, 240th year, no. 2. Copyright © 1967 by The Curtis Publishing Company.

Charles Scribner's Sons, an imprint of Macmillan Publishing Company: From *The Great Gatsby* by F. Scott Fitzgerald. Copyright 1925 by Charles Scribner's Sons; copyright renewed 1953 by Frances Scott Fitzgerald Lanahan. From *A Farewell to Arms* by Ernest Hemingway. Copyright 1929 by Charles Scribner's Sons; copyright renewed © 1957 by Ernest Hemingway.

Simon & Schuster, Inc.: From ''The Montgomery Bus Boycott'' from *Parting the Waters* by Taylor Branch. Copyright © 1989 by Taylor Branch. Excerpts from *A Government as Good as Its People* by Jimmy Carter. Copyright © 1977 by The Carter Foundation for Governmental Affairs, Inc. From ''Sun City—1983'' from *Cities on a Hill* by Frances FitzGerald. Copyright © 1981, 1983, 1986 by Frances FitzGerald. From *The Making of the Atomic Bomb* by Richard Rhodes. Copyright © 1986 by Richard Rhodes.

State Historical Society of Wisconsin: Adapted from ''Documents: The Letters of Eldon J. Canright'' from ''Some War-Time Letters'' from *The Wisconsin Magazine of History*, vol. V, 1921-1922. Copyright 1921 by The State Historical Society of Wisconsin.

Summit Books, a division of Simon & Schuster, Inc.: From *The Fords: An American Epic* by Peter Collier and David Horowitz. Copyright © 1987 by Peter Collins and David Horowitz.

Time, Inc.: From ''Lessons for a Lost War'' from *Time*, April 15, 1985. Copyright © 1985 by Time, Inc. From ''Hospital Number 1, As Told to Annalee Jacoby'' from *History in the Writing* by the Foreign Correspondents of Time, Life & Fortune, selected and edited by Gordon Carroll. Copyright 1945 by Time, Inc. ''For President Kennedy: An Epilogue'' by Theodore H. White from *Life*, vol. 55, no. 23, December 6, 1963. Copyright © 1963 by Time, Inc.

University of Nebraska Press: From *Black Elk Speaks: Being the Life Story of a Holy Man of the Oglala Sioux*, as told through John G. Neihardt (Flaming Rainbow). Copyright 1932, 1959, 1972 by John G. Neihardt; copyright © 1961 by the John G. Neihardt Trust; copyright © 1979 by the University of Nebraska Press.

The University of North Carolina Press: Adapted from *Down & Out in the Great Depression: Letters from the ''Forgotten Man''*, edited by Robert S. McElvaine. Copyright © 1983 by The University of North Carolina Press.

University of Oklahoma Press: From *The Mining Frontier: Contemporary Accounts from the American West in the Nineteenth Century*, collected and edited by Martin Lewis. Copyright © 1967 by the University of Oklahoma Press.

Viking Penguin Inc., a division of Penguin Books USA: ''American Bores Common, Ex Div.'' from *Christopher Columbus and Other Patriotic Verses* by Franklin P. Adams. Copyright 1931 by Franklin P. Adams. From *Henderson The Rain King* by Saul Bellow. Copyright © 1958, 1959 by Saul Bellow. From ''Italy'' from *Once There Was a War* by John Steinbeck. Copyright © 1943, 1958 by John Steinbeck. From *Eyes on the Prize: America's Civil Right Years, 1954-1965* by Juan Williams, with the Eyes on the Prize Production Team. Copyright © 1987 by Blackside, Inc.

A. P. Watt Limited: From *The Outline of History: Being a Plain History of Life and Mankind* by H. G. Wells. Copyright 1920, 1931, 1940 by H. G. Wells; copyright 1949 by Doubleday & Company, Inc.

Wylie, Aitken & Stone, Inc.: From ''The Truce with Irrationality—I'' from *A Turn in the South* by V. S. Naipaul. Copyright © 1989 by V. S. Naipaul.